The Best Just Got Better

Welcome to the exciting new 9th edition of

Criminalistics: An Introduction to Forensic Science.

The best-selling and single most respected textbook in forensic science **just got better.**

The next several pages will guide you through all the new features and let you **experience the excitement** of this significant revision. *Criminalistics* has always set the standard of **excellence.** Once you turn the page, you too will agree: the best just got better!

New Look

New Look

New!
4-Color Presentation!

We live in a visual world, and the functional use of full color will better convey forensic science to today's students.

New!
Exciting Full-Color Photos

Over 150 full-color photos have been added to this edition, effectively bringing the world of forensic science to life.

The following is the textbook spread shown in the illustration:

Figure 4-8 Diagram of a sodium chloride crystal. Sodium is represented by the darker spheres, chlorine by the lighter spheres.

Figure 4-9 Representation of the dispersion of light by a glass prism.

Like density, the refractive index is an intensive physical property of matter and characterizes a substance. However, any procedure used to determine a substance's refractive index must be performed under carefully controlled temperature and lighting conditions, because the refractive index of a substance varies with its temperature and the wavelength of light passing through it. Nearly all tabulated refractive indices are determined at a standard wavelength, usually 589.3 nanometers; this is the predominant wavelength emitted by sodium light and is commonly known as the sodium D light.

When a transparent solid is immersed in a liquid with a similar refractive index, light is not refracted as it passes from the liquid into the solid. For this reason, the eye cannot distinguish the liquid–solid boundary, and the solid seems to disappear from view. This observation, as we will see, offers the forensic scientist a simple method for comparing the refractive indices of transparent solids.

Normally, we expect a solid or a liquid to exhibit only one refractive index value for each wavelength of light; however, many crystalline solids have two refractive indices whose values depend in part on the direction in which the light enters the crystal with respect to the crystal axis. Crystalline solids have definite geometric forms because of the orderly arrangement of the fundamental particle of a solid, the atom. In any type of crystal, the relative locations and distances between its atoms are repetitive throughout the solid. Figure 4-8 shows the crystalline structure of sodium chloride, or ordinary table salt. Sodium chloride is an example of a cubic crystal in which each sodium atom is surrounded by six chloride atoms and each chloride atom by six sodium atoms, except at the crystal surface. Not all solids are crystalline in nature; some, such as glass, have their atoms arranged randomly throughout the solid; these materials are known as amorphous solids.

Most crystals, excluding those that have cubic configurations, refract a beam of light into two different light-ray components. This phenomenon, known as double refraction, can be observed by studying the behavior of the crystal calcite. When the calcite is laid on a printed page, the observer sees not one but two images of each word covered. The two light rays that give rise to the double image are refracted at different angles, and each has a different refractive index value. The indices of refraction for calcite are 1.486 and 1.658, and subtracting the two values yields a difference of 0.172;

this difference is known as birefringence. Thus, the optical properties of crystals provide points of identification that help characterize them.

Many of us have held a glass prism up toward the sunlight and watched it transform light into the colors of the rainbow. This observation demonstrates that visible "white light" is not homogeneous but is actually composed of many different colors. The process of separating light into its component colors is called dispersion. The ability of a prism to disperse light into its component colors is explained by the property of refraction. Each color component of light, on passing through the glass, is slowed to a speed slightly different from those of the others, causing each component to bend at a different angle as it emerges from the prism. As shown in Figure 4-9, the component colors of visible light extend from red to violet. We will learn in Chapter 5 that each color actually corresponds to a different range of wavelengths of light. Dispersion thus separates light into its component wavelengths and demonstrates that glass has a slightly different index of refraction for each wavelength of light passing through it.

Now that we have investigated various physical properties of objects, we are ready to apply such properties to the characterization of two substances—glass and soil—that commonly must be examined by the criminalist.

Comparing Glass Fragments

Glass that is broken and shattered into fragments and minute particles during the commission of a crime can be used to place a suspect at the crime scene. For example, chips of broken glass from a window may lodge in a suspect's shoes or garments during a burglary, or particles of headlight glass found at the scene of a hit-and-run accident may offer clues that can confirm the identity of a suspect vehicle. All of these possibilities require the comparison of glass fragments found on the suspect, whether a person or vehicle, with the shattered glass remaining at the crime scene.

Glass is a hard, brittle, amorphous substance composed of sand (silicon oxides) mixed with various metal oxides. When sand is mixed with other metal oxides, melted at high temperatures, and then cooled to a rigid condition without crystallization, the product is glass. Soda (sodium carbonate) is normally added to the sand to lower its melting point and make it easier to work with. Another necessary ingredient is lime (calcium oxide), needed to prevent the "soda lime" glass from dissolving in water. The forensic scientist is often asked to analyze soda-lime glass, which is used

Crystalline Solid
A solid in which the constituent atoms have a regular arrangement.

Atom
The smallest unit of an element; not divisible by ordinary chemical means. Atoms are made up of electrons, protons, and neutrons plus other subatomic particles.

Amorphous Solid
A solid in which the constituent atoms or molecules are arranged in random or disordered positions. There is no regular order in amorphous solids.

Birefringence
A difference in the two indices of refraction exhibited by most crystalline materials.

Dispersion
The separation of light into its component wavelengths.

New! Chapter Openers

A stunning new visual element starts off each chapter, bringing to life the topic that will be covered in that chapter.

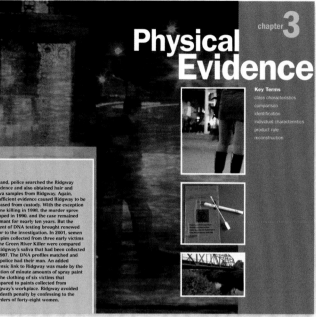

New! Dimensional Illustrations

The full-color art program helps students better understand key forensics information.

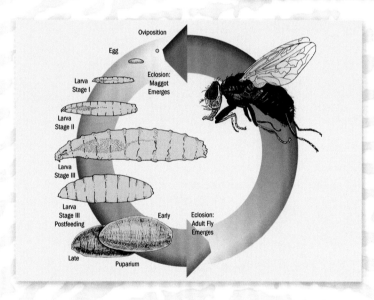

New! Open & Accessible Design

This is the most accessible edition. Every detail has been carefully thought out, even the new font and added open space.

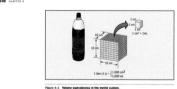

New Learning Tools

New!
Engaging Chapter Openers

Each chapter begins with a gripping forensics case, showing students how that chapter relates to the real world of forensics.

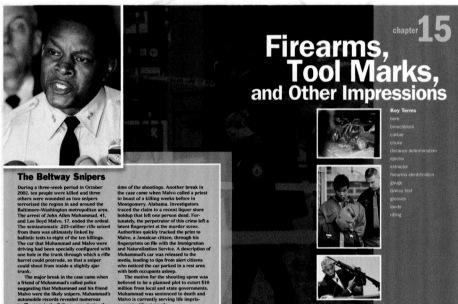

chapter 15

Firearms, Tool Marks, and Other Impressions

Key Terms
bore
breechblock
caliber
choke
distance determination
ejector
extractor
firearms identification
gauge
Greiss test
grooves
lands
rifling

The Beltway Snipers

During a three-week period in October 2002, ten people were killed and three others were wounded as two snipers terrorized the region in and around the Baltimore–Washington metropolitan area. The arrest of John Allen Muhammad, 41, and Lee Boyd Malvo, 17, ended the ordeal. The semiautomatic .223-caliber rifle seized from them was ultimately linked by ballistic tests to eight of the ten killings. The car that Muhammad and Malvo were driving had been specially configured with one hole in the trunk through which a rifle barrel could protrude, so that a sniper could shoot from inside a slightly ajar trunk.

The major break in the case came when a friend of Muhammad's called police suggesting that Muhammad and his friend Malvo were the likely snipers. Muhammad's automobile records revealed numerous traffic stops in the Beltway area during the time of the shootings. Another break in the case came when Malvo called a priest to boast of a killing weeks before in Montgomery, Alabama. Investigators traced the claim to a recent liquor store holdup that left one person dead. Fortunately, the perpetrator of this crime left a latent fingerprint at the murder scene. Authorities quickly tracked the print to Malvo, a Jamaican citizen, through his fingerprints on file with the Immigration and Naturalization Service. A description of Muhammad's car was released to the media, leading to tips from alert citizens who noticed the car parked in a rest area with both occupants asleep.

The motive for the shooting spree was believed to be a planned plot to extort $10 million from local and state governments. Muhammad was sentenced to death and Malvo is currently serving life imprisonment without parole.

WebExtra 2.2
Patricia Cornwell's Challenge
www.prenhall.com/Saferstein

New! Web Links

With a click of the mouse, the power of the Web will effectively bring forensic principles to life.

Forensics at Work
The Crash of TWA Flight 800 *(continued)*

FBI agents and New York State Police guard the reconstruction of TWA Flight 800.
Source: Mark Lennihan, AP Wide World Photos

materials—to carpet fibers and upholstery and plastics, and it can be trapped in the surface material through all sorts of means. And certainly water washes away some kinds of residues."

But the July 17 explosion of Flight 800, which killed all 230 people on board, remains a puzzle in many pieces. As Mr. Ronay and others point out, the airplane may or may not have been brought down by a bomb. And if a bomb was the cause, the explosive material could have been one of several kinds. And depending on the kind of explosive, ocean water could either wash away the chemical residue or have little effect.

Dr. Jesse L. Beauchamp, a chemistry professor at the California Institute of Technology in Pasadena, said: "It goes without saying that any traces of explosives that were present on wreckage would likely be partially removed—not entirely removed—by continued exposure to saltwater. But it depends on the type of explosives."

Mr. Ronay, who helped coordinate the bureau's successful investigation into the fatal explosion of Pan Am Flight 103 over Lockerbie, Scotland, in 1988, expressed confidence in the F.B.I. laboratory's sophisticated equipment and in Tom Thurman, his successor as chief of the explosives unit and the case agent in the Lockerbie investigation.

Mr. Thurman and his team of forensic specialists have been examining the recovered airplane debris at a hangar in Calverton, L.I. In general they are concentrating on two avenues of inquiry: finding any explosive's chemical residue, and searching for pockmarks, tearing and other signs found on items that were

continued

New! "Forensics at Work" Boxes

These descriptions of forensics applications provide students with examples from real-world forensic science.

Forensic Brief

Bill Cosby and his son Ennis Cosby. *Courtesy of George Kalinsky, People/In Style Syndication*

The murder of Ennis Cosby, son of entertainer Bill Cosby, at first appeared unsolvable. It was a random act. When his car tire went flat, he pulled off the road and called a friend on his cellular phone to ask for assistance. Shortly thereafter, an assailant demanded money and, when Cosby didn't respond quickly enough, shot him once in the temple. Acting on a tip from a friend of the assailant, police investigators later found a .38 revolver wrapped in a blue cap miles from the crime scene. Mikail Markhasev was arrested and charged with murder. At trial, the district attorney introduced firearms evidence to show that the recovered gun had fired the bullet aimed at Cosby. However, a single hair also recovered from the hat dramatically linked Markhasev to the crime. Los Angeles Police Department forensic analyst Harry Klann identified six DNA markers from the follicular tissue adhering to the hair root that matched Markhasev's DNA. This particular DNA profile is found in one out of 15,500 members of the general population. Upon hearing all the evidence, the jury deliberated and convicted Markhasev of murder.

New! "Forensic Brief" Boxes

Linked to the chapter material, these boxes provide students with quick and pertinent facts about forensics cases.

Updated Case Studies

End-of-Chapter in-depth cases that explore the world of forensic science.

Learning Objectives

After studying this chapter you should be able to:

- Review the common types of physical evidence encountered at crime scenes
- Explain the difference between the identification and comparison of physical evidence
- Define and contrast individual and class characteristics of physical evidence
- Appreciate the value of class evidence as it relates to a criminal investigation
- List and explain the function of national databases available to forensic scientists
- Explain the purpose physical evidence plays in reconstructing the events surrounding the commission of a crime

New! Learning Objectives

This new feature provides students with a better concept of what will be covered in the chapter.

Crystalline Solid
A solid in which the constituent atoms have a regular arrangement.

Atom
The smallest unit of an element; not divisible by ordinary chemical means. Atoms are made up of electrons, protons, and neutrons plus other subatomic particles.

Amorphous Solid
A solid in which the constituent atoms or molecules are arranged in random or disordered positions. There is no regular order in amorphous solids.

Updated Key Terms

Forensic-specific vocabulary is explained in the margins.

New!

A Full Chapter on Computer Forensics

More than ever before, computers are playing an increasingly significant role in criminal activity. This new chapter will show students how forensic evidence is collected using computers.

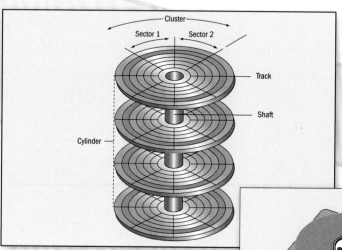

There are, however, sound forensic practices that apply to all these devices. The most logical place to start to examine these practices is with the most common form of electronic data: the personal computer.

From Input to Output: How Does the Computer Work?

Hardware versus Software

Before we get into the nuts and bolts of computers, we must establish the important distinction between hardware and software. Hardware comprises the physical components of the computer: the computer chassis, monitor, keyboard, mouse, hard disk drive, random-access memory (RAM), and central processing unit (CPU), and so on (see Figure 17–1). The list is much more extensive, but generally speaking, if it is a computer component or peripheral that you can see, feel, and touch, it is hardware.

Software, conversely, is a set of instructions compiled into a program that performs a particular task. Software consists of programs and applications that carry out a set of instructions on the hardware. Operating systems (Windows, Mac OS, Linux, Unix), word-processing programs (Microsoft Word, WordPerfect), web-browsing applications (Internet Explorer, Netscape Navigator, Firefox), and accounting applications (Quicken, QuickBooks, Microsoft Money) are all examples of software. It is important

Hardware
The physical components of a computer: case, keyboard, monitor, motherboard, RAM, HDD, mouse, and so on. Generally speaking, if it is a computer component you can touch, it is hardware.

Software
A set of instructions compiled into a program that performs a particular task. Software consists of programs and applications that carry out a set of instructions on the hardware.

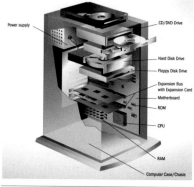

Figure 17–1 Cutaway diagram of a personal computer showing the tangible hardware components of a computer system. *Courtesy Tim Downs*

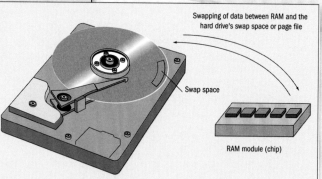

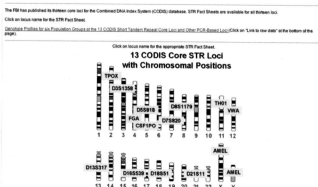

New! WebExtras

Essential information, interactive activities, and in-depth information are just a click away. Selected by the author, WebExtras introduce incredible information, further enhancing this new edition.

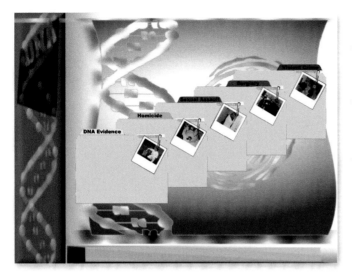

New! DNA CD-ROM Packaged with Every Book

Now every text is packaged with two CD-ROMs from the U.S. Department of Justice: "What Every Law Enforcement Officer Should Know About DNA Evidence," Beginning and Advanced Modules. These CDs bring students to various mock crime scenes, and teach them the proper procedures, including recognition and proper collection of physical evidence.

562 CHAPTER 18

Table 18-2 Forensic Science Web Sites*

- *American Academy of Forensic Sciences*—professional society dedicated to the application of science to the law and committed to the promotion of education in the forensic sciences.
- *American Board of Forensic Entomology*—provides information about the field's history, case studies, and professional status.
- *American Board of Forensic Toxicology Inc.*—working to establish and revise as necessary standards of qualification for those who practice forensic toxicology.
- *American College of Forensic Examiners (ACFE)*—dedicated to members of the forensic community. Also provides links to help people find expert witnesses in the forensic field.
- *American Society of Crime Laboratory Directors (ASCLD)*—nonprofit professional society devoted to the improvement of crime laboratory operations through sound management practices.
- *American Society of Questioned Document Examiners*—online references, technical notes on handwriting identification, and other areas of professional interest to the forensic document analyst.
- *ASCLD: Laboratory Accreditation Board*—offers the general public and users of laboratory services a means of identifying those laboratories which have demonstrated that they meet established standards.
- *Association for Crime Scene Reconstruction (ACSR)*—members are law enforcement investigators, forensic experts, and educators.
- *Association of Firearm and Tool Mark Examiners*—defines standards and ethics for individual workers in the field of firearms and toolmark examination.
- *California Association of Criminalists*—membership is offered to those who are presently employed as laboratory scientists and are professionally engaged in one or more fields directly related to the forensic sciences.
- *Canadian Society of Forensic Science*—includes journal abstracts, history, and meeting information.
- *European Association for Forensic Entomology*—created in May 2002 in Rosny sous Bois, France, to promote forensic entomology in Europe.
- *Forensic Science Service*
- *Forensic Science Society*—provides information on careers, conferences, and publications.
- *International Association for Identification*—professional association for those engaged in forensic identification, investigation, and scientific examination.
- *International Association of Bloodstain Pattern Analysis*—organization of forensic experts promoting education, establishing training standards, and encouraging research in the field of bloodstain pattern analysis.
- *International Association of Forensic Toxicologists*
- *International Organisation on Electronic Evidence (IOCE)*—formed to develop international principles for the procedures relating to digital evidence.
- *National Resources DNA Profiling and Forensic Centre*—dedicated to supporting forensic science laboratories to achieve the highest possible quality of operations.
- *Natural Resources DNA Profiling and Forensic Centre*—undertakes research on natural populations of animals and plants for the purpose of providing information to managers charged with conserving biodiversity and ensuring the sustainable use of Canada's biological resources.
- *Society of Forensic Toxicologists*

*Web sites are hypertexted at http://dir.yahoo.com/Science/Forensics/Organizations/?o=a.

Forensic Science and the Internet **569**

Furthermore, many programs such as America Online Instant Messenger, Yahoo Messenger, and mIRC (Internet Relay Chat) create files regarding the rooms or channels a user chatted in or the screen names with which a user sent instant messages. Each application needs to be researched and the computer forensic examination guided by an understanding of how it functions.

Hacking

Unauthorized computer intrusion, more commonly referred to as hacking, is the concern of every computer administrator. Hackers penetrate computer systems for a number of reasons. Sometimes the motive is corporate espionage; other times it is merely for bragging rights within the hacker community. Most commonly, though, a rogue or disgruntled employee with some knowledge of the computer network is looking to cause damage. Whatever the motivation, corporate America frequently turns to law enforcement to investigate and prosecute these cases.

Generally speaking, when investigating an unauthorized computer intrusion, investigators concentrate their efforts in three locations: *log files, volatile memory,* and *network traffic.* Logs and anomalies typically document the IP address of the computer that made the connection. Logs can be located in several locations on computer network. Most servers on the Internet track connections made to them through the use of logs. Additionally the router (the device responsible for directing data) may contain log files detailing connections. Similarly, devices known as firewalls may contain log files listing computers that were allowed access to the network or an individual system. Firewalls are devices (taking the form of either hardware or software) that permit only requested traffic to enter a computer system (or, more appropriately, a network). In other words, if a user didn't send out a request for Internet traffic from a specific system, the firewall should blocks its entry. If the log files captured the IP address of the intruder, then revealing the user behind the IP is the same process as for e-mail. Investigating a computer intrusion, however, does get a bit more complicated than this.

Frequently, in cases of unlawful access to a computer network, the perpetrator attempts to cover the tracks of his or her IP address. In these instances, advanced investigative techniques might be necessary to discover the hacker's true identity. When an intrusion is in progress, the investigator may have to capture volatile data (data in RAM). The data in RAM at the time of an intrusion may provide valuable clues into the identity of the intruder, or at the very least his or her method of attack. As in the case of the instant message or chat conversation, the data in RAM needs to be acquired. Another standard tactic for investigating intrusion cases is to document all programs installed and running on a system, in order to discover malicious software installed by the perpetrator to facilitate entry. The investigator uses specialized software to document running processes, registry entries, open ports, and any installed files.

Additionally, the investigator may want to capture live network traffic as part of the evidence collection and investigation process. Traffic that travels the network does so in the form of data packets. In addition to data, these packets also contain source and destination IP addresses. If the attack requires two-way communication, as in the case of a hacker stealing

WebExtra 18.8
Follow the trail of an e-mail as it travels through the Internet
www.prenhall.com/Saferstein

Hacking
Has various meanings, but is frequently used as a slang term for an unauthorized computer or network intrusion.

Firewall
Hardware or software designed to protect intrusions into an Internet network.

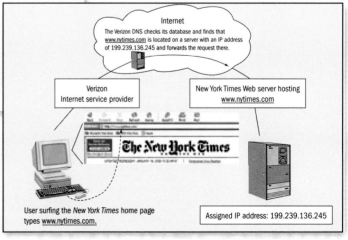

Updated and Expanded Chapter on Forensic Science on the Internet

Almost every computer is connected to the Internet. This chapter explains the role the Web plays in forensic science.

CRIMINALISTICS

AN INTRODUCTION TO FORENSIC SCIENCE

NINTH EDITION

RICHARD SAFERSTEIN, Ph.D.

Forensic Science Consultant, Mt. Laurel, New Jersey
Lecturer, Widener University School of Law

PEARSON
Prentice
Hall

Pearson Education International

Editor-in-Chief: Vernon R. Anthony
Executive Editor: Frank Mortimer, Jr.
Assistant Editor: Mayda Bosco
Marketing Manager: Adam Kloza
Editorial Assistant: Jillian Allison
Production Editor: Linda Zuk
Production Liaison: Barbara Marttine Cappuccio
Director of Manufacturing and Production: Bruce Johnson
Managing Editor: Mary Carnis
Manufacturing Manager: Ilene Sanford
Manufacturing Buyer: Cathleen Petersen
Senior Design Coordinator: Mary Siener
Interior Design: Pronk and Associates
Cover Designer: Jonathan Boylan
Cover Images: DNA strand, Chad Baker, Getty Images; Footprints, Alan Polansky: Broken glass: K. Hackenberg/zefa/Corbis; Fiber, Graeme Montgomery, Getty Images.
Director, Image Resource Center: Melinda Patelli
Manager, Rights and Permissions: Zina Arabia
Manager, Visual Research: Beth Brenzel
Manager, Cover Visual Research & Permissions: Karen Sanatar
Image Permission Coordinator: Richard Rodrigues
Photo Researcher: Melinda Alexander
Media Editor: John J. Jordan
Manager of Media Production: Amy Peltier
Media Production Project Manager: Lisa Rinaldi
Formatting: Carlisle Publishing Services
Printing and Binding: R.R. Donnelley & Sons, Willard, Ohio
Cover Printer: Lehigh Press

10 9 8 7 6 5 4 3 2
ISBN 0-13-224397-0

To the Memory of Fran and Michael

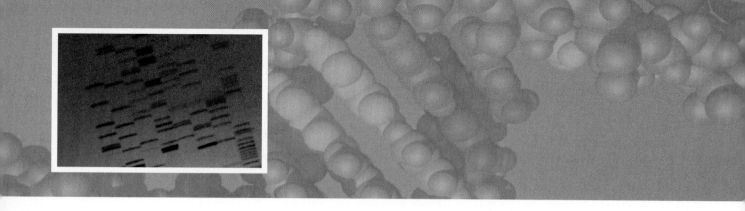

Criminalistics Now Accompanied by DNA Evidence CD-ROMs

A feature of this edition of *Criminalistics* is two CD-ROMs. One of the difficulties that instructors of forensic science have encountered in the past was how to bring the student reader to the crime scene. The recognition and proper collection of physical evidence at the crime scene is an integral part of forensic science. Yet because of the elaborate classroom preparation required, the task of enabling the student to experience a mock crime scene is not feasible for most instructors. The U.S. Department of Justice has helped to rectify this problem by creating a series of virtual crime scenes. In the words of the National Criminal Justice Reference Service:

"The two CD-ROMs present training modules that provide students with interactive training on the basic information about the identification, preservation, and collection of DNA evidence at a crime scene.

"The tutorial module presents best practices based on the work of the Crime Scene Investigation Working Group of the National Commission on the Future of DNA Evidence. The Commission was established by the Attorney General to achieve maximum usefulness of DNA evidence in the criminal justice system. The module presents background information regarding DNA evidence and its use. It also presents interactive scenarios in which the first responding officer, investigating officer and/or evidence technician make choices regarding the handling of crime scenes and evidence collection related to homicide, sexual assault, burglary, and violent crime. The training modules also include tests that last 20–30 minutes, a glossary, and 15 references."

Contents

Chapter 10

Forensic Toxicology 278

Chapter 11

Forensic Aspects of Arson and Explosion Investigations 310

Chapter 12

Forensic Serology 344

Chapter 13

DNA: The Indispensable Forensic Science Tool 380

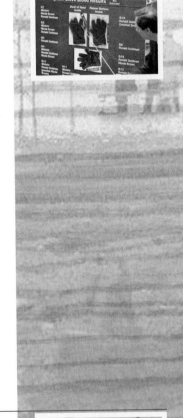

Chapter 14

Fingerprints 426

Chapter 15

Firearms, Tool Marks, and Other Impressions   458

Chapter 16

Document and Voice Examination   496

APPENDIXES

Preface

The ninth edition of *Criminalistics* has a new look. Wider margins along with color photographs and figures have been incorporated into the book's design. A new chapter on computer forensics has been added. What has not changed is the basic aim of the book: to make the subject of forensic science comprehensible to a wide variety of readers who are or plan to be aligned with the forensic science profession, as well as to those who are curious about the subject's underpinnings. Many readers of this book have been drawn to the subject by the assortment of television shows that are based on it. Story lines depicting the crime-solving abilities of forensic scientists have excited the imagination of the general public. Perhaps we can attribute our obsession with forensic science to the yearnings of a society bent on apprehending criminals but desirous of a system of justice that ensures the correctness of its verdicts. The level of sophistication that forensic science has brought to criminal investigations is awesome. But one cannot lose sight of the fact that, once one puts aside all the drama of a forensic science case, what remains is an academic subject emphasizing logic and technology. It is to this end that the ninth edition of *Criminalistics* is dedicated.

Criminalistics strives to make the technology of the modern crime laboratory clear and comprehensible to the nonscientist. The nature of physical evidence is defined, and the limitations that technology and current knowledge impose on its individualization and characterization are examined. By combining case stories with applicable technology, *Criminalistics* endeavors to capture the pulse and fervor of forensic science investigations.

One of the constants of forensic science is how frequently its applications become front-page news. Whether the story is of sniper shootings or the tragic consequences of the terrorist attacks of September 11, 2001, forensic science is at the forefront of the public response. The horror of the terrorist attacks exemplified the critical role DNA has come to play in identifying victims of mass disaster. In this new century, the science of DNA profiling has altered the complexion of criminal investigation. DNA collected from saliva on a cup or from dandruff or sweat on a hat exemplifies the emergence of nontraditional forms of evidence collection at crime scenes. The criminal justice system is creating vast DNA data banks designed to snare the criminal who is unaware of the consequence of leaving the minutest quantity of biological material behind at a crime scene.

During the highly publicized O. J. Simpson criminal and civil trials, forensic scientists systematically placed Simpson at the crime scene through DNA analyses, hair and fiber comparisons, and footwear impressions. As millions of Americans watched the case unfold, they, in a sense, became students of forensic science. Intense media coverage of the crime-scene search and investigation, as well as the ramifications of findings of physical evidence at the crime scene, all became the subject of study, commentary, and conjecture.

For those of us who have taught forensic science in the classroom, it comes as no surprise that forensic science can grab and hold the attention of those who otherwise would have no interest in any area of science. The O. J. Simpson case amply demonstrates how intertwined criminal investigation has become with forensic science. Through nine editions, *Criminalistics* has striven to depict the role of the forensic scientist in the criminal justice system. The current edition builds on the content of its predecessors and updates the reader on the latest technologies available to crime laboratory personnel.

Like all facets of modern life, forensic science has been touched by the computer and the Internet. This new edition introduces the reader to basic computer technologies and concepts relied on during the forensic investigation of crimes. Retrieval of computerized information thought to be lost or erased is explored, as is the investigation of hacking incidents. Exploration of web sites particularly relevant to forensic science and criminal investigation is emphasized.

A major portion of the text centers on discussions of the common items of physical evidence encountered at crime scenes. These chapters include descriptions of forensic analysis, as well as updated techniques for the proper collection and preservation of evidence at crime scenes. Particular attention is paid to the meaning and role of probability in interpreting the evidential significance of scientifically evaluated evidence.

The implications of DNA profiling are important enough to warrant their inclusion in a separate chapter in *Criminalistics*. The topic of DNA is described in a manner that is comprehensible and relevant to readers who lack a scientific background. The discussion defines DNA and explains its central role in controlling the body's chemistry. Finally, the chapter explains the process of DNA typing and illustrates its application to criminal investigations through the presentation of actual case histories.

The content of *Criminalistics* is a reflection of the author's experience both as an active forensic scientist and as an instructor of forensic science at the college level. No prior knowledge of scientific principles or techniques is assumed of the reader. The areas of chemistry and biology relating to the analysis of physical evidence are presented with a minimum of scientific terminology and equations. The discussion involving chemistry and biology is limited to a minimum core of facts and principles that will make the subject matter comprehensible and meaningful to the nonscientist. Although it is not the intent of this book to make scientists or forensic experts of readers, it will certainly be gratifying if the book motivates some students to seek further scientific knowledge and perhaps direct their education toward a career in forensic science.

Although *Criminalistics* is an outgrowth of a one-semester course offered as part of a criminal justice program at many New Jersey colleges, its subject matter is not limited to the college student. Optimum utilization of crime laboratory services requires that criminal investigators have a knowledge of the techniques and capabilities of the laboratory that extends beyond any summary that may be gleaned from departmental brochures dealing with the collection and packaging of physical evidence. Only by combining a knowledge of the principles and techniques of forensic science with logic and common sense will the investigator gain comprehensive insight into the meaning and significance of physical evidence and its role in criminal investigations. Forensic science begins at the crime scene. If the investigator cannot recognize, collect, and package evidence properly, no amount of equipment or expertise will salvage the situation.

Likewise, there is a dire need to bridge the "communication gap" among lawyers, judges, and the forensic scientist. An intelligent evaluation of the scientist's data and any subsequent testimony again depends on familiarity with the underlying principles of forensic science. Too many practitioners of the law profess ignorance of the subject or attempt to gain a superficial understanding of its meaning and significance only minutes before meeting the expert witness. It is hoped that the book will provide a painless route to comprehending the nature of the science.

In order to merge theory with practice, a number of actual forensic case histories are included in the text. The intent is for these illustrations to move forensic science from the domain of the abstract into the real world of criminal investigation.

Acknowledgments

I am most appreciative of the contribution that Detective Sergeant Andrew (Drew) Donofrio of New Jersey's Bergen County Prosecutor's Office made to this new edition of *Criminalistics*. I was fortunate to find in Drew a contributor who not only possesses extraordinary skill, knowledge, and hands-on experience with computer forensics, but was able to combine those attributes with sophisticated communication skills.

Sarah A. Skorupsky-Borg, MSFS, invested an extraordinary amount of time and effort in preparing an accompanying supplement to this edition: *Basic Laboratory Exercises for Forensic Science*. Her skills and tenacity in carrying out this task are acknowledged and greatly appreciated.

Many people provided assistance and advice in the preparation of this book. Many faculty members, colleagues, and friends have read and commented on various portions of the text. Particular thanks go to the following people for their critical reading and discussions of the manuscript: Norman Demeter, John Lintott, Charles Midkiff, Raymond Murray, and Richard Tidey. In addition, I would like to acknowledge the contributions of Jeffrey C. Kercheval, Robert Thompson, Roger Ely, Jose R. Almirall, Darlene Brezinski, Michael Malone, and Ray Feldherr.

The following reviewers provided insightful reviews and suggestions on this new edition: Professor John Kavanagh, Scottsdale Community College, Scottsdale, AZ; Professor Suzanne Montiel, Nash Community College, Rocky Mount, NC; Professor Walter F. Rowe; George Washington University; Wasington, D.C.; Professor David Tate, Purdue University, West Lafayette, IN; and Professor Sue Salem, Washburn University, Topeka, KS.

The assistance of Pamela Cook and Gonul Turhan, whose research efforts are an integral part of this text, was invaluable. I am also appreciative of the time and talent given by Peggy Cole; development editor Mayda Bosco; and production editor Linda Zuk.

I am grateful to the law enforcement agencies, government agencies, private individuals, and equipment manufacturers cited in the text for contributing their photographs and illustrations. Finally, I particularly wish to express my appreciation to Major E. R. Leibe (retired) and Major V. P. O'Donoghue (retired) for their encouragement and support.

Any author of a textbook must be prepared to contribute countless hours to the task, often at the expense of family obligations. My efforts would have fallen well short of completion without the patience and encouragement of my wife Gail. Her typing and critical readings of the manuscript, as well as her strength of character under circumstances that were less than ideal, will always be remembered.

Richard Saferstein, Ph.D.

About the Author

Richard Saferstein, Ph.D., retired in 1991 after serving twenty-one years as the Chief Forensic Scientist of the New Jersey State Police Laboratory, one of the largest crime laboratories in the United States. He currently acts as a consultant for attorneys and the media in the area of forensic science. During the O. J. Simpson criminal trial, Dr. Saferstein provided extensive commentary on forensic aspects of the case for the *Rivera Live* show, the E! television network, ABC radio, and various radio talk shows. Dr. Saferstein holds degrees from the City College of New York and earned his doctorate degree in chemistry in 1970 from the City University of New York. From 1972 to 1991, he taught an introductory forensic science course in the criminal justice programs at the College of New Jersey and Ocean County College. These teaching experiences played an influential role in Dr. Saferstein's authorship in 1977 of the widely used introductory textbook *Criminalistics: An Introduction to Forensic Science,* currently in this ninth edition. Saferstein's basic philosophy in writing *Criminalistics* is to make forensic science understandable and meaningful to the nonscience reader, while giving the reader an appreciation for the scientific principles that underlie the subject.

Dr. Saferstein currently teaches a course on the role of the expert witness in the courtroom at the law school of Widener University in Wilmington, Delaware. He has authored or co-authored more than forty-two technical papers covering a variety of forensic topics. Dr. Saferstein has co-authored *Lab Manual for Criminalistics* (Prentice Hall, 2004). He has also edited the widely used professional reference books *Forensic Science Handbook,* Volume 1, 2nd edition (Prentice Hall, 2002), *Forensic Science Handbook,* Volume 2, 2nd edition (Prentice Hall, 2005), and *Forensic Science Handbook,* Volume 3 (Prentice Hall, 1993). Dr. Saferstein is a member of the American Chemical Society, the American Academy of Forensic Sciences, the Forensic Science Society of England, the Canadian Society of Forensic Scientists, the International Association for Identification, the Mid-Atlantic Association of Forensic Scientists, the Northeastern Association of Forensic Scientists, the Northwestern Association of Forensic Scientists, and the Society of Forensic Toxicologists.

In 2006, Dr. Saferstein received the American Academy of Forensic Sciences Paul L. Kirk award for distinguished service and contributions to the field of criminalistics.

CRIMINALISTICS

Ted Bundy, Serial Killer

The name Ted Bundy is synonymous with the term *serial killer*. This handsome, gregarious, and worldly onetime law student is believed to be responsible for forty murders between 1964 and 1978. His reign of terror stretched from the Pacific Northwest down into California and into Utah, Idaho, and Colorado, finally ending in Florida. His victims were typically young women, usually murdered with a blunt instrument or by strangulation and sexually assaulted before and after death. First convicted in Utah in 1976 on a charge of kidnapping, Bundy managed to escape after his extradition to Colorado on a murder charge. Ultimately, Bundy found his way to the Tallahassee area of Florida. There he unleashed mayhem killing two women at a Florida State University sorority house and then murdering a 12-year-old girl three weeks later. Fortunately, future victims were spared when Bundy was arrested while driving a stolen vehicle. As police investigated the sorority murders, they noted that one victim, who had been beaten over the head with a log, raped, and strangled, also had bite marks on her left buttock and breast.

Supremely confident that he could beat the sorority murder charges, the arrogant Bundy insisted on acting as his own attorney. His unfounded optimism was shattered in the courtroom when a forensic odontologist matched the bite mark on the victim's buttock to Bundy's front teeth. Bundy was ultimately executed in 1989.

chapter 1

Introduction

Key Terms

algor mortis

autopsy

expert witness

livor mortis

Locard's exchange principle

rigor mortis

Learning Objectives

After studying this chapter you should be able to:

- Define and distinguish forensic science and criminalistics

- Recognize the major contributors to the development of forensic science

- Account for the rapid growth of forensic laboratories in the past forty years

- Describe the services of a typical comprehensive crime laboratory in the criminal justice system

- Compare and contrast the *Frye* and *Daubert* decisions relating to the admissibility of scientific evidence in the courtroom

- Explain the role and responsibilities of the expert witness

- Understand what specialized forensic services, aside from the crime laboratory, are generally available to law enforcement personnel

Definition and Scope of Forensic Science

Forensic science in its broadest definition is the application of science to law. As our society has grown more complex, it has become more dependent on rules of law to regulate the activities of its members. Forensic science applies the knowledge and technology of science to the definition and enforcement of such laws.

Each year, as government finds it increasingly necessary to regulate the activities that most intimately influence our daily lives, science merges more closely with civil and criminal law. Consider, for example, the laws and agencies that regulate the quality of our food, the nature and potency of drugs, the extent of automobile emissions, the kind of fuel oil we burn, the purity of our drinking water, and the pesticides we use on our crops and plants. It would be difficult to conceive of any food and drug regulation or environmental protection act that could be effectively monitored and enforced without the assistance of scientific technology and the skill of the scientific community.

Laws are continually being broadened and revised to counter the alarming increase in crime rates. In response to public concern, law enforcement agencies have expanded their patrol and investigative functions, hoping to stem the rising tide of crime. At the same time they are looking more to the scientific community for advice and technical support for their efforts. Can the technology that put astronauts on the moon, split the atom, and eradicated most dreaded diseases be enlisted in this critical battle? Unfortunately, science cannot offer final and authoritative solutions to problems that stem from a maze of social and psychological factors. However, as the contents of this book will attest, science does occupy an important and unique role in the criminal justice system—a role that relates to the scientist's ability to supply accurate and objective information that reflects the events that have occurred at a crime. It will also become apparent to the reader that a good deal of work remains to be done if the full potential of science as applied to criminal investigations is to be realized.

Considering the vast array of civil and criminal laws that regulate society, forensic science, in its broadest sense, has become so comprehensive a subject as to make a meaningful introductory textbook treatment of its role and techniques most difficult, if not overwhelming. For this reason, we must find practical limits that narrow the scope of the subject. Fortunately, common usage provides us with such a limited definition: **Forensic science is the application of science to the criminal and civil laws that are enforced by police agencies in a criminal justice system.**

Even within this limited definition, we will restrict our discussion in this book to only the areas of chemistry, biology, physics, geology, and computer technology, which are useful for determining the evidential value of crime-scene and related evidence, omitting any references to medicine and law. Forensic pathology, psychology, anthropology, and odontology encompass important and relevant areas of knowledge and practice in law enforcement, each being an integral part of the total forensic science service that is provided to any up-to-date criminal justice system. However, except for a brief discussion at the end of this chapter, these subjects go beyond the intended range of this book, and the reader is referred elsewhere for discussions of their applications and techniques.[1] Instead, we will attempt to focus on the services of what has popularly become known as the crime laboratory, where the principles and techniques of the physical and natural sciences are practiced and applied to the analysis of crime-scene evidence.

For many, the term *criminalistics* seems more descriptive than *forensic science* for describing the services of a crime laboratory. The two terms will be used interchangeably in this text. Regardless of title—criminalist or forensic scientist—the trend of events has made the scientist in the crime laboratory an active participant in the criminal justice system.

History and Development of Forensic Science

Forensic science owes its origins first to the individuals who developed the principles and techniques needed to identify or compare physical evidence, and second to those who recognized the need to merge these principles into a coherent discipline that could be practically applied to a criminal justice system.

Today, many believe that Sir Arthur Conan Doyle had a considerable influence on popularizing scientific crime-detection methods through his fictional character Sherlock Holmes, who first applied the newly developing principles of serology (see Chapter 12), fingerprinting, firearms identification, and questioned-document examination long before their value was first recognized and accepted by real-life criminal investigators. Holmes's feats excited the imagination of an emerging generation of forensic scientists and criminal investigators. Even in the first Sherlock Holmes novel, *A Study in Scarlet*, published in 1887, we find examples of Doyle's uncanny ability to describe scientific methods of detection years before they were actually discovered and implemented.

---

[1] Two excellent references are André A. Moenssens, Fred E. Inbau, James Starrs, and Carol E. Henderson, *Scientific Evidence in Civil and Criminal Cases,* 4th ed. (Mineola, N.Y.: Foundation Press, 1995); and Werner U. Spitz, ed., *Medicolegal Investigation of Death,* 3rd ed. (Springfield, Ill.: Charles C. Thomas, 1993).

For instance, here Holmes probes and recognizes the potential usefulness of forensic serology to criminal investigation:

> "I've found it. I've found it," he shouted to my companion, running towards us with a test tube in his hand. "I have found a reagent which is precipitated by hemoglobin and by nothing else. . . . Why, man, it is the most practical medico-legal discovery for years. Don't you see that it gives us an infallible test for blood stains? . . . The old guaiacum test was very clumsy and uncertain. So is the microscopic examination for blood corpuscles. The latter is valueless if the stains are a few hours old. Now, this appears to act as well whether the blood is old or new. Had this test been invented, there are hundreds of men now walking the earth who would long ago have paid the penalty of their crimes. . . . Criminal cases are continually hinging upon that one point. A man is suspected of a crime months perhaps after it has been committed. His linen or clothes are examined and brownish stains discovered upon them. Are they blood stains, or rust stains, or fruit stains, or what are they? That is a question which has puzzled many an expert, and why? Because there was no reliable test. Now we have the Sherlock Holmes test, and there will no longer be any difficulty."

Many people can be cited for their specific contributions to the field of forensic science. The following is just a brief list of those who made the earliest contributions to formulating the disciplines that now constitute forensic science.

Mathieu Orfila (1787–1853). Orfila is considered the father of forensic toxicology. A native of Spain, he ultimately became a renowned teacher of medicine in France. In 1814, Orfila published the first scientific treatise on the detection of poisons and their effects on animals. This treatise established forensic toxicology as a legitimate scientific endeavor.

Alphonse Bertillon (1853–1914). Bertillon devised the first scientific system of personal identification. In 1879, Bertillon began to develop the science of *anthropometry* (see Chapter 14), a systematic procedure of taking a series of body measurements as a means of distinguishing one individual from another. See Figure 1–1. For nearly two decades, this system was considered the most accurate method of personal identification. Although anthropometry was eventually replaced by fingerprinting in the early 1900s, Bertillon's early efforts have earned him the distinction of being known as the father of criminal identification.

Francis Galton (1822–1911). Galton undertook the first definitive study of fingerprints and developed a methodology of classifying them for filing. In 1892, he published a book titled *Finger Prints,* which contained the first statistical proof supporting the uniqueness of his method of personal identification. His work went on to describe the basic principles that form the present system of identification by fingerprints.

Leone Lattes (1887–1954). In 1901, Dr. Karl Landsteiner discovered that blood can be grouped into different categories. These blood groups or types are now recognized as A, B, AB, and O. The possibility that blood grouping could be a useful characteristic for the identification of an individual intrigued Dr. Lattes, a professor at the Institute of Forensic Medicine

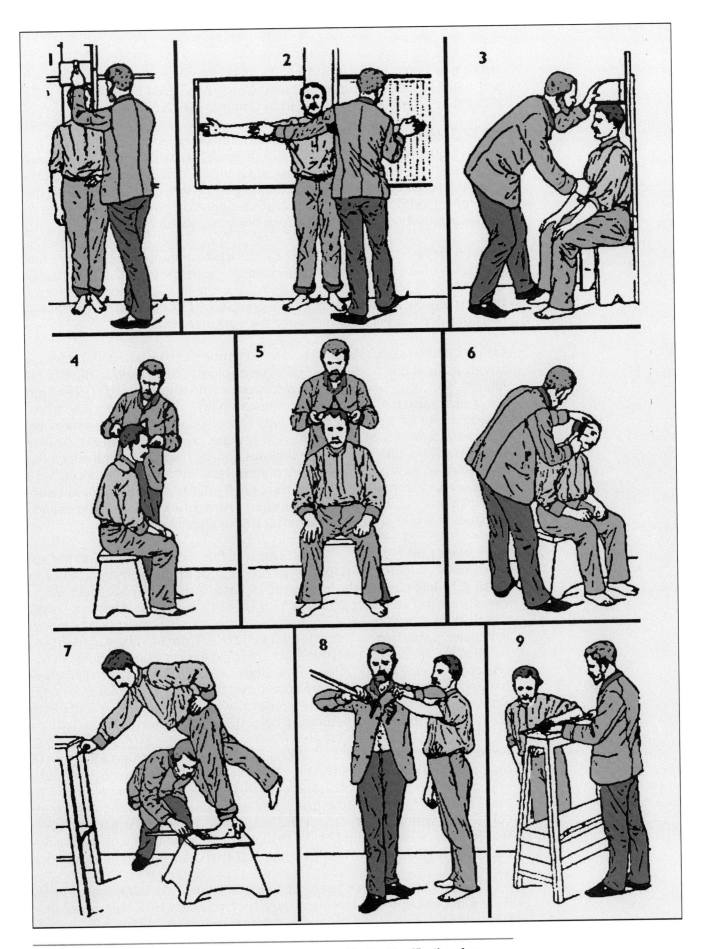

Figure 1–1   Bertillon's system of bodily measurements as used for the identification of an individual. *Courtesy Sirchie Finger Print Laboratories, Inc., Youngsville, N.C., www.sirchie.com*

at the University of Turin in Italy. In 1915, he devised a relatively simple procedure for determining the blood group of a dried bloodstain, a technique that he immediately applied to criminal investigations.

Calvin Goddard (1891–1955). To determine whether a particular gun has fired a bullet requires a comparison of the bullet with one that has been test-fired from the suspect's weapon. Goddard, a U.S. Army colonel, refined the techniques of such an examination by using the comparison microscope. Goddard's expertise established the comparison microscope as the indispensable tool of the modern firearms examiner.

Albert S. Osborn (1858–1946). Osborn's development of the fundamental principles of document examination was responsible for the acceptance of documents as scientific evidence by the courts. In 1910, Osborn authored the first significant text in this field, *Questioned Documents*. This book is still considered a primary reference for document examiners.

Walter C. McCrone (1916–2002). Dr. McCrone's career paralleled startling advances in sophisticated analytical technology. Nevertheless, during his lifetime McCrone became the world's preeminent microscopist. Through his books, journal publications, and research institute, McCrone was a tireless advocate for applying microscopy to analytical problems, particularly forensic science cases. McCrone's exceptional communication skills made him a much-sought-after instructor, and he was responsible for educating thousands of forensic scientists throughout the world in the application of microscopic techniques. Dr. McCrone used microscopy, often in conjunction with other analytical methodologies, to examine evidence in thousands of criminal and civil cases throughout a long and illustrious career.

Hans Gross (1847–1915). Gross wrote the first treatise describing the application of scientific disciplines to the field of criminal investigation in 1893. A public prosecutor and judge in Graz, Austria, Gross spent many years studying and developing principles of criminal investigation. In his classic book *Handbuch für Untersuchungsrichter als System der Kriminalistik* (later published in English under the title *Criminal Investigation*), he detailed the assistance that investigators could expect from the fields of microscopy, chemistry, physics, mineralogy, zoology, botany, anthropometry, and fingerprinting. He later introduced the forensic journal *Archiv für Kriminal Anthropologie und Kriminalistik*, which still serves as a medium for reporting improved methods of scientific crime detection.

Edmond Locard (1877–1966). Although Gross was a strong advocate of the use of the scientific method in criminal investigation, he did not make any specific technical contributions to this philosophy. Locard, a Frenchman, demonstrated how the principles enunciated by Gross could be incorporated within a workable crime laboratory. Locard's formal education was in both medicine and law. In 1910, he persuaded the Lyons police department to give him two attic rooms and two assistants to start a police laboratory.

During Locard's first years of work, the only available instruments were a microscope and a rudimentary spectrometer. However, his enthusiasm quickly overcame the technical and monetary deficiencies he encountered. From these modest beginnings, Locard's research and accomplishments became known throughout the world by forensic scientists and criminal investigators. Eventually he became the founder and director of the Institute of Criminalistics at the University of Lyons; this quickly developed into a leading international center for study and research in forensic science.

Locard believed that when a person comes in contact with an object or person, a cross-transfer of materials occurs (**Locard's exchange principle**). Locard maintained that every criminal can be connected to a crime by dust particles carried from the crime scene. This concept was reinforced by a series of successful and well-publicized investigations. In one case, presented with counterfeit coins and the names of three suspects, Locard urged the police to bring the suspects' clothing to his laboratory. On careful examination, he located small metallic particles in all the garments. Chemical analysis revealed that the particles and coins were composed of exactly the same metallic elements. Confronted with this evidence, the suspects were arrested and soon confessed to the crime. After World War I, Locard's successes served as an impetus for the formation of police laboratories in Vienna, Berlin, Sweden, Finland, and Holland.

The most ambitious commitment to forensic science occurred in the United States. In 1932, the Federal Bureau of Investigation (FBI), under the directorship of J. Edgar Hoover, organized a national laboratory that offered forensic services to all law enforcement agencies in the country. During its formative stages, agents consulted extensively with business executives, manufacturers, and scientists whose knowledge and experience were useful in guiding the new facility through its infancy. The FBI Laboratory is now the world's largest forensic laboratory, performing more than one million examinations every year. Its accomplishments have earned it worldwide recognition, and its structure and organization have served as a model for forensic laboratories formed at the state and local levels in the United States as well as in other countries. Furthermore, the opening of the FBI's Forensic Science Research and Training Center in 1981 gave the United States, for the first time, a facility dedicated to conducting research to develop new and reliable scientific methods that can be applied to forensic science. This facility is also used to train crime laboratory personnel in the latest forensic science techniques and methods.

The oldest forensic laboratory in the United States is that of the Los Angeles Police Department, created in 1923 by August Vollmer, a police chief from Berkeley, California. In the 1930s, Vollmer headed the first U.S. university institute for criminology and criminalistics at the University of California at Berkeley. However, this institute lacked any official status in the university until 1948, when a school of criminology was formed. The famous criminalist Paul Kirk (see Figure 1–2) was selected to head its criminalistics department. Many graduates of this school have gone on to help develop forensic laboratories in other parts of the state and country.

California has numerous federal, state, county, and city crime laboratories, many of which operate independently. However, in 1972 the California Department of Justice embarked on an ambitious plan to create a network of state-operated crime laboratories. As a result, California has created a model system of integrated forensic laboratories consisting of regional and satellite facilities. An informal exchange of information and expertise is facilitated among California's criminalist community through a regional professional society, the California Association of Criminalists. This organization was the forerunner of a number of regional organizations that have developed throughout the United States to foster cooperation among the nation's growing community of criminalists.

Locard's Exchange Principle

Whenever two objects come into contact with one another, there is exchange of materials between them.

Figure 1–2 Paul Leland Kirk, 1902—1970. *Courtesy Blackstone-Shelburne, N.Y.*

In contrast to the American system of independent local laboratories, Great Britain has developed a national system of regional laboratories under the direction of the government's Home Office. England and Wales are serviced by six regional laboratories, including the Metropolitan Police Laboratory (established in 1935), which services London. In the early 1990s, the British Home Office reorganized the country's forensic laboratories into the Forensic Science Service and instituted a system in which police agencies are charged a fee for services rendered by the laboratory. The fees are based on "products," or a set of examinations that are packaged together and designed to be suitable for particular types of physical evidence. The fee-for-service concept has encouraged the creation of a number of private laboratories that provide services to both police and criminal defense attorneys. One such laboratory, Forensic Alliance, has two facilities employing more than one hundred forensic scientists.

Organization of a Crime Laboratory

The development of crime laboratories in the United States has been characterized by rapid growth accompanied by a lack of national and regional planning and coordination. At present, approximately 350 public crime laboratories operate at various levels of government—federal, state, county, and municipal—more than three times the number of crime laboratories operating in 1966.

The size and diversity of crime laboratories make it impossible to select any one model that can best describe a typical crime laboratory. Although most of these facilities function as part of a police department, others operate under the direction of the prosecutor's or district attorney's office; some work with the laboratories of the medical examiner or coroner. Far fewer are affiliated with universities or exist as independent agencies in government. Laboratory staff sizes range from one person to more than a hundred, and their services may be diverse or specialized, depending on the responsibilities of the agency that houses the laboratory.

Crime laboratories have mostly been organized by agencies that either foresaw their potential application to criminal investigation or were pressed by the increasing demands of casework. Several reasons explain the unparalleled growth of crime laboratories during the past thirty-five years. Supreme Court decisions in the 1960s were responsible for greater police emphasis on securing scientifically evaluated evidence. The requirement to advise criminal suspects of their constitutional rights and their right of immediate access to counsel has all but eliminated confessions as a routine investigative tool. Successful prosecution of criminal cases requires a thorough and professional police investigation, frequently incorporating the skills of forensic science experts. Modern technology has provided forensic scientists with many new skills and techniques to meet the challenges accompanying their increased participation in the criminal justice system.

Coinciding with changing judicial requirements has been the staggering increase in crime rates in the United States over the past forty years. This factor alone would probably have accounted for the increased use of crime laboratory services by police agencies, but only a small percentage of police investigations generate evidence requiring scientific examination. There is, however, one important exception to this observation: drug-related arrests. All illicit-drug seizures must be sent to a forensic laboratory for confirmatory chemical analysis before the case can be adjudicated. Since the mid-1960s, drug abuse has accelerated to nearly uncontrollable levels and has resulted in crime laboratories being inundated with drug specimens.

A more recent impetus leading to the growth and maturation of crime laboratories has been the advent of DNA profiling. Since the early 1990s, this technology has progressed to the point at which traces of blood; semen stains; hair; and saliva residues left behind on stamps, cups, bite marks, and so on have made possible the individualization or near-individualization of biological evidence. To meet the demands of DNA technology, crime labs have expanded staff and in many cases modernized their physical plants. While drug cases still far outnumber DNA cases, the labor-intensive demands and sophisticated technology requirements of the latter have affected the structure of the forensic laboratory as has no other technology in the past fifty years. Likewise, DNA profiling has become the dominant factor in explaining how the general public perceives the workings and capabilities of the modern crime laboratory. In coming years an estimated ten thousand forensic scientists will be added to the rolls of both public and private forensic laboratories to process crime-scene evidence for DNA and to acquire DNA profiles, as mandated by state laws, from the hundreds of thousands of individuals convicted of crimes. This will more than double the number of scientists employed by forensic laboratories in the United States. These DNA profiles are continually added to state and national DNA data banks, which have proven to be invaluable investigative resources for law enforcement. The United States has a substantial backlog of samples requiring DNA analysis. Approximately 200,000 to 300,000 convicted-offender samples and more than 540,000 evidentiary samples, for which no suspect has been located, currently remain to be analyzed nationwide.

Historically, a federal system of government, combined with a desire to retain local control, has produced a variety of independent laboratories in the United States, precluding the creation of a national system. Crime laboratories to a large extent mirror the fragmented law enforcement structure that exists on the national, state, and local levels. The federal government has no single law enforcement or investigative agency with unlimited jurisdiction. Four major federal crime laboratories have been created to help

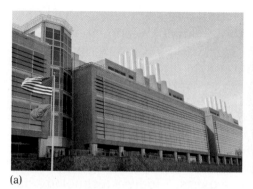

(a)   (b)

Figure 1–3   (a) Exterior and (b) interior views of the FBI crime laboratory in Quantico, Virginia.
Courtesy AP Wide World Photos

investigate and enforce criminal laws that extend beyond the jurisdictional boundaries of state and local forces. The FBI (Department of Justice) maintains the largest crime laboratory in the world. An ultramodern facility housing the FBI's forensic science services is located in Quantico, Virginia (see Figure 1–3). Its expertise and technology support its broad investigative powers. The Drug Enforcement Administration laboratories (Department of Justice) analyze drugs seized in violation of federal laws regulating the production, sale, and transportation of drugs. The laboratories of the Bureau of Alcohol, Tobacco, Firearms and Explosives (Department of Justice) analyze alcoholic beverages and documents relating to alcohol and firearm excise tax law enforcement and examine weapons, explosive devices, and related evidence to enforce the Gun Control Act of 1968 and the Organized Crime Control Act of 1970. The U.S. Postal Inspection Service maintains laboratories concerned with criminal investigations relating to the postal service. Each of these federal facilities will offer its expertise to any local agency that requests assistance in relevant investigative matters.

Most state governments maintain a crime laboratory to service state and local law enforcement agencies that do not have ready access to a laboratory. Some states, such as Alabama, California, Illinois, Michigan, New Jersey, Texas, Washington, Oregon, Virginia, and Florida, have developed a comprehensive statewide system of regional or satellite laboratories. These operate under the direction of a central facility and provide forensic services to most areas of the state. The concept of a regional laboratory operating as part of a statewide system has increased the accessibility of many local law enforcement agencies to a crime laboratory, while minimizing duplication of services and ensuring maximum interlaboratory cooperation through the sharing of expertise and equipment.

Local laboratories provide services to county and municipal agencies. Generally, these facilities operate independently of the state crime laboratory and are financed directly by local government. However, as costs have risen, some counties have combined resources and created multicounty laboratories to service their jurisdictions. Many of the larger cities in the United States maintain their own crime laboratories, usually under the direction of the local police department. Frequently, high population and high crime rates combine to make a municipal facility, such as that of New York City, the largest crime laboratory in the state.

Like the United States, most countries in the world have created and now maintain forensic facilities. The British regional laboratory system has already been discussed. In Canada, forensic services are provided by three government-funded institutes: (1) six Royal Canadian Mounted Police regional laboratories, (2) the Centre of Forensic Sciences in Toronto, and (3) the Institute of Legal Medicine and Police Science in Montreal. Altogether, more than a hundred countries throughout the world have at least one laboratory facility offering services in the field of forensic science.

Services of the Crime Laboratory

Bearing in mind the independent development of crime laboratories in the United States, the wide variation in total services offered in different communities is not surprising. There are many reasons for this, including (1) variations in local laws, (2) the different capabilities and functions of the organization to which a laboratory is attached, and (3) budgetary and staffing limitations.

In recent years, many local crime laboratories have been created solely to process drug specimens. Often these facilities were staffed with few personnel and operated under limited budgets. Although many have expanded their forensic services, some still primarily perform drug analyses. However, even among crime laboratories providing services beyond drug identification, the diversity and quality of services rendered varies significantly. For the purposes of this text, I have taken the liberty of arbitrarily designating the following units as those that should constitute a "full-service" crime laboratory.

Basic Services Provided by Full-Service Crime Laboratories

Physical Science Unit. The physical science unit applies principles and techniques of chemistry, physics, and geology to the identification and comparison of crime-scene evidence. It is staffed by criminalists who have the expertise to use chemical tests and modern analytical instrumentation to examine items as diverse as drugs, glass, paint, explosives, and soil. In a laboratory that has a staff large enough to permit specialization, the responsibilities of this unit may be further subdivided into drug identification, soil and mineral analyses, and examination of a variety of trace physical evidence.

Biology Unit. The biology unit is staffed with biologists and biochemists who identify and perform DNA profiling on dried bloodstains and other body fluids, compare hairs and fibers, and identify and compare botanical materials such as wood and plants.

Firearms Unit. The firearms unit examines firearms, discharged bullets, cartridge cases, shotgun shells, and ammunition of all types. Garments and other objects are also examined to detect firearms discharge residues and to approximate the distance from a target at which a weapon was fired. The basic principles of firearms examination are also applied here to the comparison of marks made by tools.

Document Examination Unit. The document examination unit studies the handwriting and typewriting on questioned documents to ascertain authenticity and/or source. Related responsibilities include analyzing paper and ink and examining indented writings (the term usually applied to the partially visible depressions appearing on a sheet of paper underneath the one on which the visible writing appears), obliterations, erasures, and burned or charred documents.

Photography Unit. A complete photographic laboratory examines and records physical evidence. Its procedures may require the use of highly specialized photographic techniques, such as digital imaging, infrared, ultraviolet, and X-ray photography, to make invisible information visible to the naked eye. This unit also prepares photographic exhibits for courtroom presentation.

Optional Services Provided by Full-Service Crime Laboratories

Toxicology Unit. The toxicology group examines body fluids and organs to determine the presence or absence of drugs and poisons. Frequently, such functions are shared with or may be the sole responsibility of a separate laboratory facility placed under the direction of the medical examiner's or coroner's office.

In most jurisdictions, field instruments such as the Intoxilyzer are used to determine the alcoholic consumption of individuals. Often the toxicology section also trains operators and maintains and services these instruments.

Latent Fingerprint Unit. The latent fingerprint unit processes and examines evidence for latent fingerprints when they are submitted in conjunction with other laboratory examinations.

Polygraph Unit. The polygraph, or lie detector, has come to be recognized as an essential tool of the criminal investigator rather than the forensic scientist. However, during the formative years of polygraph technology, many police agencies incorporated this unit into the laboratory's administrative structure, where it sometimes remains today. In any case, its functions are handled by people trained in the techniques of criminal investigation and interrogation.

Voiceprint Analysis Unit. In cases involving telephoned threats or tape-recorded messages, investigators may require the skills of the voiceprint analysis unit to tie the voice to a particular suspect. To this end, a good deal of casework has been performed with the sound spectrograph, an instrument that transforms speech into a visual display called a *voiceprint*. The validity of this technique as a means of personal identification rests on the premise that the sound patterns produced in speech are unique to the individual and that the voiceprint displays this uniqueness.

Crime-Scene Investigation Unit. The concept of incorporating crime-scene evidence collection into the total forensic science service is slowly gaining recognition in the United States. This unit dispatches specially trained personnel (civilian and/or police) to the crime scene to collect and preserve physical evidence that will later be processed at the crime laboratory.

Whatever the organizational structure of a forensic science laboratory may be, specialization must not impede the overall coordination of services demanded by today's criminal investigator. Laboratory administrators need to keep open the lines of communication between analysts (civilian and uniform), crime-scene investigators, and police personnel. Inevitably, forensic investigations require the skills of many individuals. One notoriously high-profile investigation illustrates this process—the search to uncover the source of the anthrax letters mailed shortly after September 11, 2001. Figure 1–4 shows one of the letters and illustrates the multitude of skills required in the investigation—skills possessed by forensic chemists and biologists, fingerprint examiners, and forensic document examiners.

WebExtra 1.1

Take a Virtual Tour of a Forensic Laboratory
www.prenhall.com/Saferstein

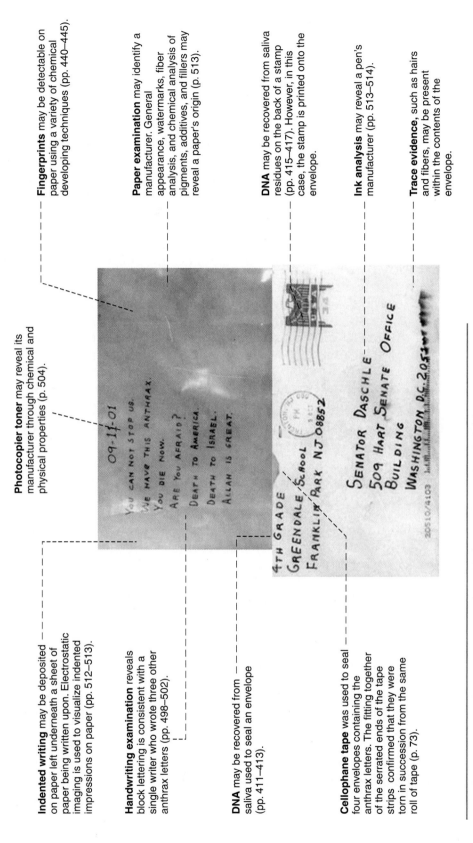

Fingerprints may be detectable on paper using a variety of chemical developing techniques (pp. 440–445).

Paper examination may identify a manufacturer. General appearance, watermarks, fiber analysis, and chemical analysis of pigments, additives, and fillers may reveal a paper's origin (p. 513).

DNA may be recovered from saliva residues on the back of a stamp (pp. 415–417). However, in this case, the stamp is printed onto the envelope.

Ink analysis may reveal a pen's manufacturer (pp. 513–514).

Trace evidence, such as hairs and fibers, may be present within the contents of the envelope.

Photocopier toner may reveal its manufacturer through chemical and physical properties (p. 504).

Indented writing may be deposited on paper left underneath a sheet of paper being written upon. Electrostatic imaging is used to visualize indented impressions on paper (pp. 512–513).

Handwriting examination reveals block lettering is consistent with a single writer who wrote three other anthrax letters (pp. 498–502).

DNA may be recovered from saliva used to seal an envelope (pp. 411–413).

Cellophane tape was used to seal four envelopes containing the anthrax letters. The fitting together of the serrated ends of the tape strips confirmed that they were torn in succession from the same roll of tape (p. 73).

Figure 1–4   An envelope containing anthrax spores along with an anonymous letter was sent to the office of Senator Tom Daschle shortly after the terrorist attacks of September 11, 2001. A variety of forensic skills were used to examine the envelope and letter. Also, bar codes placed on the front and back of the envelope by mail-sorting machines contain address information and information about where the envelope was first processed. *Courtesy Getty Images, Inc.*

Functions of the Forensic Scientist

Analysis of Physical Evidence

First and foremost the forensic scientist must be skilled in applying the principles and techniques of the physical and natural sciences to the analysis of the many types of evidence that may be recovered during a criminal investigation. However, the scientist must also be aware of the demands and constraints imposed by the judicial system. The procedures and techniques used in the laboratory must not only rest on a firm scientific foundation but also satisfy the criteria of admissibility that have been established by the courts.

In rejecting the scientific validity of the lie detector (polygraph), the District of Columbia Circuit Court in 1923 set forth what has since become a standard guideline for determining the judicial admissibility of scientific examinations. In *Frye* v. *United States*,[2] the court stated the following:

> Just when a scientific principle or discovery crosses the line between the experimental and demonstrable stages is difficult to define. Somewhere in this twilight zone the evidential force of the principle must be recognized, and while the courts will go a long way in admitting expert testimony deduced from a well-recognized scientific principle or discovery, the thing from which the deduction is made must be sufficiently established to have gained general acceptance in the particular field in which it belongs.

To meet the *Frye* standard, the court must decide whether the questioned procedure, technique, or principle is "generally accepted" by a meaningful segment of the relevant scientific community. In practice, this approach required the proponent of a scientific test to present to the court a collection of experts who could testify that the scientific issue before the court is generally accepted by the relevant members of the scientific community. Furthermore, in determining whether a novel technique meets criteria associated with "general acceptance," courts have frequently taken note of books and papers written on the subject, as well as prior judicial decisions relating to the reliability and general acceptance of the technique. In recent years this approach has engendered a great deal of debate as to whether it is sufficiently flexible to deal with new and novel scientific issues that may not have gained widespread support within the scientific community.

As an alternative to the *Frye* standard, some courts came to believe that the Federal Rules of Evidence espoused a more flexible standard that did not rely on general acceptance as an absolute prerequisite for admitting scientific evidence. Part of the Federal Rules of Evidence governs the admissibility of all evidence, including expert testimony, in federal courts, and many states have adopted codes similar to those of the Federal Rules. Specifically, Rule 702 of the Federal Rules of Evidence deals with the admissibility of expert testimony:

> If scientific, technical, or other specialized knowledge will assist the trier of fact to understand the evidence or to determine a fact in issue, a witness qualified as an expert by knowledge, skill, experience, training, or education, may testify thereto in the form of an

---

[2] 293 Fed. 1013 (D.C. Cir. 1923).

opinion or otherwise, if (1) the testimony is based upon sufficient facts or data, (2) the testimony is the product of reliable principles and methods, and (3) the witness has applied the principles and methods reliably to the facts of the case.

In a landmark ruling in the 1993 case of *Daubert* v. *Merrell Dow Pharmaceuticals, Inc.,*[3] the U.S. Supreme Court asserted that "general acceptance," or the *Frye* standard, is not an absolute prerequisite to the admissibility of scientific evidence under the Federal Rules of Evidence. According to the Court, the Rules of Evidence—especially Rule 702—assign to the trial judge the task of ensuring that an expert's testimony rests on a reliable foundation and is relevant to the case. Although this ruling applies only to federal courts, many state courts are expected to use this decision as a guideline in setting standards for the admissibility of scientific evidence.

What the Court advocates in *Daubert* is that trial judges assume the ultimate responsibility for acting as a "gatekeeper" in judging the admissibility and reliability of scientific evidence presented in their courts. The Court offered some guidelines as to how a judge can gauge the veracity of scientific evidence, emphasizing that the inquiry should be flexible. Suggested areas of inquiry include the following:

1. Whether the scientific technique or theory can be (and has been) tested

2. Whether the technique or theory has been subject to peer review and publication

3. The technique's potential rate of error

4. Existence and maintenance of standards controlling the technique's operation

5. Whether the scientific theory or method has attracted widespread acceptance within a relevant scientific community

Some legal practitioners have expressed concern that abandoning *Frye*'s general-acceptance test will result in the introduction of absurd and irrational pseudoscientific claims in the courtroom. The Supreme Court rejected these concerns:

> In this regard the respondent seems to us to be overly pessimistic about the capabilities of the jury and of the adversary system generally. Vigorous cross-examination, presentation of contrary evidence, and careful instruction on the burden of proof are the traditional and appropriate means of attacking shaky but admissible evidence.

In a 1999 decision, *Kumho Tire Co., Ltd.* v. *Carmichael,*[4] the Court unanimously ruled that the "gatekeeping" role of the trial judge applied not only to scientific testimony, but to all expert testimony:

> We conclude that *Daubert*'s general holding—setting forth the trial judge's general "gatekeeping" obligation—applies not only to testimony based on "scientific" knowledge, but also to testimony based on "technical" and "other specialized" knowledge. . . . We also conclude that a trial court may consider one or more of the

---

[3] 509 U.S. 579 (1993).
[4] 526 U.S. 137 (1999).

more specific factors that *Daubert* mentioned when doing so will help determine that testimony's reliability. But, as the Court stated in *Daubert,* the test of reliability is "flexible," and *Daubert's* list of specific factors neither necessarily nor exclusively applies to all experts in every case.

A leading case that exemplifies the type of flexibility and wide discretion that the *Daubert* ruling, twenty-five years later, apparently gives trial judges in matters of scientific inquiry is *Coppolino* v. *State.*[5] Here a medical examiner testified to his finding that the victim had died of an overdose of a drug known as succinylcholine chloride. This drug had never before been detected in the human body. The medical examiner's findings were dependent on a toxicological report that identified an abnormally high concentration of succinic acid, a breakdown product of the drug, in the victim's body. The defense argued that this test for the presence of succinylcholine chloride was new and the absence of corroborative experimental data by other scientists meant that it had not yet gained general acceptance in the toxicology profession. The court, in rejecting this argument, recognized the necessity for devising new scientific tests to solve the special problems that are continually arising in the forensic laboratory. It emphasized, however, that although these tests may be new and unique, they are admissible only if they are based on scientifically valid principles and techniques: "The tests by which the medical examiner sought to determine whether death was caused by succinylcholine chloride were novel and devised specifically for this case. This does not render the evidence inadmissible. Society need not tolerate homicide until there develops a body of medical literature about some particular lethal agent."

Provision of Expert Testimony

Because their work product may ultimately be a factor in determining a person's guilt or innocence, forensic scientists may be required to testify with respect to their methods and conclusions at a trial or hearing. Trial courts have broad discretion in accepting an individual as an expert witness on any particular subject. Generally, if a witness can establish to the satisfaction of a trial judge that he or she possesses a particular skill or has knowledge in a trade or profession that will aid the court in determining the truth of the matter at issue, that individual will be accepted as an expert witness. Depending on the subject area in question, the court will usually consider knowledge acquired through experience, training, education, or a combination sufficient grounds for qualification as an expert witness.

In court, the qualifying questions that counsel asks the expert are often directed toward demonstrating the witness's ability and competence pertaining to the matter at hand. Competency may be established by having him or her cite educational degrees, participation in special courses, membership in professional societies, and any professional articles or books published. Also important is the number of years of occupational experience the witness has in areas related to the matter before the court.

Unfortunately, few schools confer degrees in forensic science. Most chemists, biologists, geologists, and physicists prepare themselves for careers in forensic science by combining training under an experienced examiner with independent study. Of course, formal education provides the

Expert Witness
An individual whom the court determines to possess knowledge relevant to the trial that is not expected of the average layperson.

---

[5] 223 So. 2d 68 (Fla. Dist. Ct. App. 1968), *app. dismissed,* 234 So. 2d 120 (Fla. 1969), *cert. denied,* 399 U.S. 927 (1970).

scientist with a firm foundation for learning and understanding the principles and techniques of forensic science. Nevertheless, for the most part, courts must rely on training and years of experience as a measurement of the knowledge and ability of the expert.

Before the judge rules on the witness's qualifications, the opposing attorney is given the opportunity to cross-examine the witness and to point out weaknesses in his or her background and knowledge. Most courts are very reluctant to disqualify an individual as an expert even when presented with someone whose background is only remotely associated with the issue at hand. The question of what credentials are suitable for qualification as an expert is ambiguous and highly subjective and one that the courts wisely try to avoid. However, the weight that a judge or jury assigns to "expert" testimony in subsequent deliberations is quite another matter. Undoubtedly, education and experience have considerable bearing on the value assigned to the expert's opinions. Just as important may be the witness's demeanor and ability to explain scientific data and conclusions clearly, concisely, and logically to a judge and jury composed of nonscientists. The problem of sorting out the strengths and weaknesses of expert testimony falls to prosecution and defense counsel, who must endeavor to prepare themselves adequately for this undertaking.

The ordinary or lay witness must give testimony on events or observations that arise from personal knowledge. This testimony must be factual and, with few exceptions, cannot contain the personal opinions of the witness. On the other hand, the expert witness is called on to evaluate evidence when the court lacks the expertise to do so. This expert then expresses an opinion as to the significance of the findings. The views expressed are accepted only as representing the expert's opinion and may later be accepted or ignored in jury deliberations.

It must be recognized that the expert cannot render any view with absolute certainty. At best, he or she may only be able to offer an opinion that is based on a reasonable scientific certainty derived from training and experience. Obviously, the expert is expected to defend vigorously the techniques and conclusions of the analysis, but at the same time must not be reluctant to discuss impartially any findings that could minimize the significance of the analysis. The forensic scientist should not be an advocate of one party's cause, but only an advocate of truth. An adversary system of justice must give the prosecutor and defense ample opportunity to offer expert opinions and to argue the merits of such testimony. Ultimately, the duty of the judge or jury is to weigh the pros and cons of all the information presented in deciding guilt or innocence.

WebExtra 1.2

Watch a Forensic Expert Witness Testify—I
www.prenhall.com/Saferstein

WebExtra 1.3

Watch a Forensic Expert Witness Testify—II
www.prenhall.com/Saferstein

Furnishing Training in the Proper Recognition, Collection, and Preservation of Physical Evidence

The competence of a laboratory staff and the sophistication of its analytical equipment have little or no value if relevant evidence cannot be properly recognized, collected, and preserved at the site of a crime. For this reason, the forensic staff must have responsibilities that will influence the conduct of the crime-scene investigation.

The most direct and effective response to this problem has been to dispatch specially trained evidence-collection technicians to the crime scene. A growing number of crime laboratories and the police agencies they service keep trained "evidence technicians" on 24-hour call to help criminal investigators retrieve evidence. These technicians are trained by the laboratory staff to recognize and gather pertinent physical evidence at the crime scene. They are administratively assigned to the laboratory to facilitate their continued exposure to forensic techniques and procedures. They have at their disposal all the proper tools and supplies for proper collection and packaging of evidence for future scientific examination.

Unfortunately, many police forces have still not adopted this approach. Often a patrol officer or detective is charged with collecting the evidence. His or her effectiveness in this role depends on the extent of his or her training and working relationship with the laboratory. For maximum use of the skills of the crime laboratory, training of the crime-scene investigator must go beyond superficial classroom lectures to involve extensive personal contact with the forensic scientist. Each must become aware of the other's problems, techniques, and limitations.

The training of police officers in evidence collection and their familiarization with the capabilities of a crime laboratory should not be restricted to a select group of personnel on the force. Every officer engaged in fieldwork, whether it be traffic, patrol, investigation, or juvenile control, often must process evidence for laboratory examination. Obviously, it would be a difficult and time-consuming operation to give everyone the in-depth training and attention that a qualified criminal investigator requires. However, familiarity with crime laboratory services and capabilities can be facilitated through periodic lectures, laboratory tours, and dissemination of manuals prepared by the laboratory staff that outline proper methods for collecting and submitting physical evidence to the laboratory. Examples of such manuals are shown in Figure 1–5.

A brief outline describing the proper collection and packaging of common types of physical evidence is found in Appendix I. The procedures and information summarized in this appendix are discussed in greater detail in forthcoming chapters.

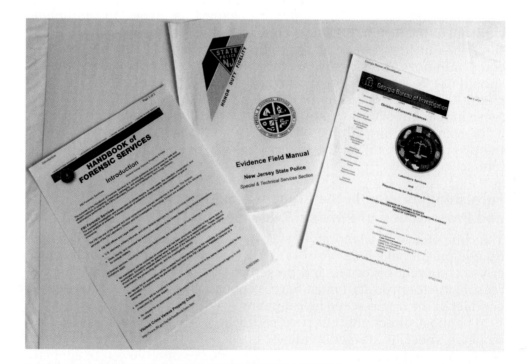

Figure 1–5 **Representative evidence-collection guides prepared by various police agencies.**

Other Forensic Science Services

Even though this textbook is devoted to describing the services normally provided by a crime laboratory, the field of forensic science is by no means limited to the areas covered in this book. A number of specialized forensic science services outside the crime laboratory are routinely available to law enforcement personnel. These services are important aids to a criminal investigation and require the involvement of individuals who have highly specialized skills.

Forensic Pathology. This field involves the investigation of sudden, unnatural, unexplained, or violent deaths. Typically, forensic pathologists, in their role as medical examiners or coroners, must answer several basic questions: Who is the victim? What injuries are present? When did the injuries occur? Why and how were the injuries produced? The primary role of the medical examiner is to determine the cause of death. If a cause cannot be found through observation, an autopsy is normally performed to establish the cause of death. The manner in which death occurred is classified into five categories: natural, homicide, suicide, accident, or undetermined, based on the circumstances surrounding the incident.

After a human body expires, it goes through several stages of decomposition. A medical examiner participating in a criminal investigation can often estimate the time of death by evaluating the stage of decomposition in which the victim was found. Immediately following death, the muscles relax and then become rigid. This condition, rigor mortis, manifests itself within the first twenty-four hours and disappears within thirty-six hours. Another condition occurring in the early stages of decomposition is livor mortis. When the human heart stops pumping, the blood begins to settle in the parts of the body closest to the ground. The skin will appear dark blue or purple in these areas. The onset of this condition begins immediately and continues for up to twelve hours after death. The skin will not appear discolored in areas where the body is restricted by either clothing or an object pressing against the body. This information can be useful in determining if the victim's position was changed after death occurred.

Other physical and chemical changes within the body are also helpful in approximating the time of death. Algor mortis is the process by which the body temperature continually cools after death until it reaches the ambient or room temperature. The rate of heat loss is influenced by factors such as the location and size of the body, the victim's clothing, and weather conditions. Because of such factors, this method can only estimate the approximate time period since death. As a general rule, beginning about an hour after death, the body will lose heat at a rate of approximately 1–1.5°F per hour until the body reaches the environmental temperature.

Another approach helpful for estimating the time of death is determining potassium levels in the ocular fluid (vitreous humor). After death, cells within the inner surface of the eyeball release potassium into the ocular fluid. By analyzing the amount of potassium present at various intervals after death, the forensic pathologist can determine the rate at which potassium is released into the vitreous humor and use it to approximate the time of death. During the autopsy, other factors may indicate the time period in which death occurred. For example, the amount of food in the stomach can help estimate when a person's last meal was eaten. This information can be valuable when investigating a death.

Autopsy
The medical dissection and examination of a body in order to determine the cause of death.

Rigor Mortis
The medical condition that occurs after death and results in the stiffening of muscle mass. The rigidly of the body normally occurs within 24 hours of death and disappears within 36 hours.

Livor Mortis
The medical condition that occurs after death and results in the settling of blood in areas of the body closest to the ground.

Algor Mortis
Postmortem changes that cause a body to lose heat.

Frequently, medical examiners must perform autopsies if a death is deemed suspicious or unexplained. The cause of death may not always be what it seems at first glance. For example, a decedent with a gunshot wound and a gun in his hand may appear to have committed suicide. However, an autopsy may reveal that the victim actually died of suffocation and the gunshot wound occurred after death to cover up the commission of a crime.

Forensic Anthropology. Forensic anthropology is concerned primarily with the identification and examination of human skeletal remains. Skeletal bones are remarkably durable and undergo an extremely slow breakdown process that lasts decades or centuries. Because of their resistance to rapid decomposition, skeletal remains can provide a multitude of individual characteristics. An examination of bones may reveal their sex, approximate age, race, and skeletal injury. See Figure 1–6. For example, a female's bone structure will differ from a male's, especially within the pelvic area because of a woman's childbearing capabilities. This area of expertise is not limited just to identification, however. A forensic anthropologist may also be of assistance in creating facial reconstructions to help identify skeletal remains. With the help of this technique, a composite of the victim can be drawn and advertised in an attempt to identify the victim. Forensic anthropologists are also helpful in identifying victims of a mass disaster such as a plane crash. When such a tragedy occurs, forensic anthropologists can help identify victims through the collection of bone fragments.

Forensic Entomology. The study of insects and their relation to a criminal investigation is known as forensic entomology. Such a practice is commonly used to estimate the time of death when the circumstances surrounding the crime are unknown. After decomposition begins, insects

WebExtra 1.4

See How an Autopsy Is Done
www.prenhall.com/Saferstein

WebExtra 1.5

Explore Forensic Anthropology
www.prenhall.com/Saferstein

Figure 1–6   Crime-scene site showing a pelvis partly buried in sand and a femur lying across a pistol. *Courtesy Paul Sledzik.*

such as blowflies are the first to infest the body. Their eggs are laid in the human remains and ultimately hatch into maggots or fly larvae (see Figure 1–7), which consume human organs and tissues. Forensic entomologists can identify the specific insects present in the body and approximate how long a body has been left exposed by examining the stage of development of the fly larvae. These determinations are not always straightforward, however. The time required for stage development is affected by environmental influences such as geographical location, climate, and weather conditions. For example, cold temperatures hinder the development of fly eggs into adult flies. The forensic entomologist must consider these conditions when estimating the postmortem interval. Knowledge of insects, their life cycles, and their habits make entomological evidence an invaluable tool for an investigation. See Figure 1–8.

Forensic Psychiatry. Forensic psychiatry is a specialized area in which the relationship between human behavior and legal proceedings is examined. Forensic psychiatrists are retained for both civil and criminal litigations. For civil cases, forensic psychiatrists normally determine whether people are competent to make decisions about preparing wills, settling property, or refusing medical treatment. For criminal cases, they evaluate behavioral disorders and determine whether people are competent to stand trial. Forensic psychiatrists also examine behavioral patterns of criminals as an aid in developing a suspect's behavioral profile.

Forensic Odontology. Practitioners of forensic odontology help identify victims when the body is left in an unrecognizable state. Teeth are composed of enamel, the hardest substance in the body. Because of enamel's resilience, the teeth outlast tissues and organs as decomposition begins. The characteristics of teeth, their alignment, and the overall structure of the mouth provide individual evidence for identifying a specific person. With the use of dental records such as X-rays and dental casts or even a photograph of the

Figure 1–7 **A scanning electron micrograph of 2-hour-old blowfly maggots.** *Courtesy Dr. Jeremy Burgess, Photo Researchers, Inc.*

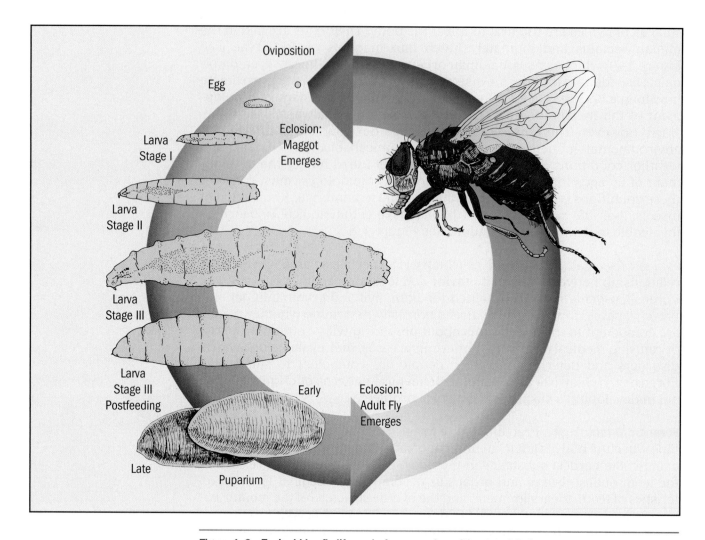

Figure 1–8 **Typical blowfly life cycle from egg deposition to adult fly emergence. This cycle is representative of any one of the nearly ninety species of blowflies in North America.** *Courtesy E. P. Catts, Ph.D., deceased, and Neal H. Haskell, Ph.D., forensic entomology consultant www.forensic-entomology.com*

WebExtra 1.6

Explore Forensic Dentistry
www.prenhall.com/Saferstein

person's smile, a set of dental remains can be compared to a suspected victim. Another application of forensic odontology to criminal investigations is bite mark analysis. At times in assault cases, bite marks are left on the victim. A forensic odontologist can compare the marks left on a victim and the tooth structure of the suspect. See Figure 1–9.

Forensic Engineering. Forensic engineers are concerned with failure analysis, accident reconstruction, and causes and origins of fires or explosions. Forensic engineers answer questions such as these: How did an accident or structural failure occur? Were the parties involved responsible? If so, how were they responsible? Accident scenes are examined, photographs are reviewed, and any mechanical objects involved are inspected.

Forensic Computer and Digital Analysis. Forensic computer science is a new and fast-growing field that involves the identification, collection, preservation, and examination of information derived from computers and other digital devices, such as cell phones. Law enforcement aspects of this

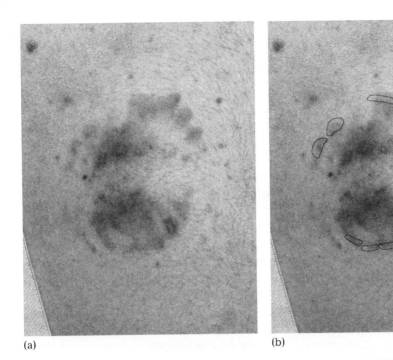

(a)   (b)

Figure 1–9   (a) Bite mark on victim's body. (b) Comparison to suspect's teeth. *Courtesy David Sweet, DMD, Ph.D., DABFO BOLD Forensic Laboratory, Vancouver, BC Canada*

work normally involve the recovery of deleted or overwritten data from a computer's hard drive and the tracking of hacking activities within a compromised system. This field of forensic computer analysis will be addressed in detail in Chapters 17 and 18.

Chapter Summary

In its broadest definition, forensic science is the application of science to criminal and civil laws. This book emphasizes the application of science to the criminal and civil laws that are enforced by police agencies in a criminal justice system. Forensic science owes its origins to individuals such as Bertillon, Galton, Lattes, Goddard, Osborn, and Locard, who developed the principles and techniques needed to identify or compare physical evidence.

The development of crime laboratories in the United States has been characterized by rapid growth accompanied by a lack of national and regional planning and coordination. At present, approximately 350 public crime laboratories operate at various levels of government—federal, state, county, and municipal.

The technical support provided by crime laboratories can be assigned to five basic services. The physical science unit uses the principles of chemistry, physics, and geology to identify and compare physical evidence. The biology unit uses knowledge of biological sciences to investigate blood samples, body fluids, hair, and fiber samples. The firearms unit investigates discharged bullets, cartridge cases, shotgun shells, and ammunition. The document examination unit performs handwriting analysis and other questioned-document examination. Finally, the photography unit uses specialized photographic techniques to record and examine physical evidence. Some crime laboratories offer the optional services of toxicology, fingerprint analysis, polygraph administration, voiceprint analysis, and crime-scene investigation and evidence collection.

A forensic scientist must be skilled in applying the principles and techniques of the physical and natural sciences to the analysis of the many types of evidence that may be recovered during a criminal investigation. A forensic scientist may also provide expert court testimony. An expert witness is called on to evaluate evidence based on specialized training and experience and to express an opinion as to the significance of the findings. Also, forensic scientists participate in training law enforcement personnel in proper recognition, collection, and preservation of physical evidence.

The *Frye* v. *United States* decision set guidelines for determining the admissibility of scientific evidence into the courtroom. To meet the *Frye* standard, the evidence in question must be "generally accepted" by the scientific community. However, in the 1993 case of *Daubert* v. *Merrell Dow Pharmaceuticals, Inc.,* the U.S. Supreme Court asserted that the *Frye* standard is not an absolute prerequisite to the admissibility of scientific evidence. Trial judges were said to be ultimately responsible as "gatekeepers" for the admissibility and validity of scientific evidence presented in their courts.

A number of special forensic science services are available to the law enforcement community to augment the services of the crime laboratory. These services include forensic pathology, forensic anthropology, forensic entomology, forensic psychiatry, forensic odontology, forensic engineering, and forensic computer and digital analysis.

Review Questions

1. The application of science to law describes _____.
2. The fictional exploits of _____ excited the imagination of an emerging generation of forensic scientists and criminal investigators.
3. A system of personal identification using a series of body measurements was first devised by _____.
4. _____ is responsible for developing the first statistical study proving the uniqueness of fingerprints.
5. The Italian scientist _____ devised the first workable procedure for typing dried bloodstains.
6. The comparison microscope became an indispensable tool of firearms examination through the efforts of _____.
7. Early efforts at applying scientific principles to document examination are associated with _____.
8. The application of science to criminal investigation was advocated by the Austrian magistrate _____.
9. One of the first functional crime laboratories was formed in Lyons, France, under the direction of _____.
10. The transfer of evidence expected to occur when two objects come in contact with one another was a concept first advocated by the forensic scientist _____.
11. The first forensic laboratory in the United States was created in 1923 by the _____ Police Department.

12. The state of _____ is an excellent example of a geographical area in the United States that has created a system of integrated regional and satellite laboratories.

13. In contrast to the United States, Britain's crime laboratory system is characterized by a national system of _____ laboratories.

14. The increasing demand for _____ analyses has been the single most important factor in the recent expansion of crime laboratory services in the United States.

15. Four important federal agencies offering forensic services are _____, _____, _____, and _____.

16. A decentralized system of crime laboratories currently exists in the United States under the auspices of various governmental agencies at the _____, _____, _____, and _____ levels of government.

17. The application of chemistry, physics, and geology to the identification and comparison of crime-scene evidence is the function of the _____ unit of a crime laboratory.

18. The examination of blood, hairs, fibers, and botanical materials is conducted in the _____ unit of a crime laboratory.

19. The examination of bullets, cartridge cases, shotgun shells, and ammunition of all types is the responsibility of the _____ unit.

20. The examination of body fluids and organs for drugs and poisons is a function of the _____ unit.

21. The _____ unit dispatches trained personnel to the scene of a crime to retrieve evidence for laboratory examination.

22. The "general acceptance" principle, which serves as a criterion for the judicial admissibility of scientific evidence, was set forth in the case of _____.

23. In the case of _____, the Supreme Court ruled that in assessing the admissibility of new and unique scientific tests the trial judge did not have to rely solely on the concept of "general acceptance."

24. True or False: The U.S. Supreme Court decision in *Kumho Tire Co., Ltd.* v. *Carmichael* restricted the "gatekeeping" role of a trial judge only to scientific testimony. _____

25. A Florida case that exemplifies the flexibility and wide discretion that the trial judge has in matters of scientific inquiry is _____.

26. A(n) _____ is a person who can demonstrate a particular skill or has knowledge in a trade or profession that will help the court determine the truth of the matter at issue.

27. True or False: The expert witness's courtroom demeanor may play an important role in deciding what weight the court will assign to his or her testimony. _____

28. True or False: The testimony of an expert witness incorporates his or her personal opinion relating to a matter he or she has either studied or examined. _____

29. The ability of the investigator to recognize and collect crime-scene evidence properly depends on the amount of _____ received from the crime laboratory.

30. When _____ sets in after death, the skin appears dark blue or purple in the areas closest to the ground.

31. True or False: One method for approximating the time of death is to determine body temperature. _____

Further References

Berg, Stanton O., "Sherlock Holmes: Father of Scientific Crime Detection," *Journal of Criminal Law, Criminology and Police Science* 61, no. 3 (1970): 446–52.

Cohen, Stanley A., "The Role of the Forensic Expert in a Criminal Trial," *Canadian Society of Forensic Science Journal* 12 (1979): 75.

Doyle, Sir Arthur Conan, *The Complete Sherlock Holmes,* Vol. 1. New York: Doubleday, 1956.

Gallop, A. M. C., "Forensic Science Coming of Age," *Science & Justice,* 43 (2003): 55.

James, S. H., and Nordby, J. J., eds., *Forensic Science—An Introduction to Scientific and Investigative Techniques,* 2nd ed. Boca Raton, Fla.: Taylor & Francis, 2005.

Kagan, J. D., "On Being a Good Expert Witness in a Criminal Case," *Journal of Forensic Sciences* 23 (1978): 190.

Lucas, D. M., "North of 49–The Development of Forensic Science in Canada," *Science & Justice* 37 (1997): 47.

Midkiff, C. R., "More Mountebanks," in R. Saferstein, ed., *Forensic Science Handbook,* vol. 2, 2nd ed. Upper Saddle River, N.J.: Prentice Hall, 2005.

Sapir, Gil I., "Legal Aspects of Forensic Science," in R. Saferstein, ed., *Forensic Science Handbook,* vol. l, 2nd ed. Upper Saddle River, N.J.: Prentice Hall, 2002.

Starrs, James E., "Mountebanks among Forensic Scientists," in R. Saferstein, ed., *Forensic Science Handbook,* vol. 2, 2nd ed. Upper Saddle River, N.J.: Prentice Hall, 2005.

Case Study
Detection of Curare in the Jascalevich Murder Trial

Dr. Mario E. Jascalevich and his wife Nora display the "V for Victory" sign at their attorney's office in Hackensack, NJ. *Courtesy AP Wide World Photos*

The case of *State* v. *Jascalevich* that follows preceded the *Daubert* ruling by fifteen years. Nevertheless, it is interesting to note that the trial judge, after listening to both sides in his "gatekeeping" role, admitted into testimony what in 1978 were rather novel scientific test procedures for the drug curare. The case offers an excellent example of the legal and scientific issues involved in assessing the admissibility and value of scientific evidence in the courtroom. Dr. Jascalevich was accused of murdering a number of his patients by administering lethal doses of curare. The issue of whether the curare was detected and identified in the exhumed bodies of the alleged murder victims was central to proving the state's case against the defendant. What ensued at the trial was a

classic illustration of conflicting expert testimony on both sides of a scientific issue. Ultimately, it was the jury's task to weigh the data and arguments presented by both sides and to reach a verdict.

The murder trial of Dr. Mario E. Jascalevich was one of the most complicated criminal proceedings ever tried in an American courtroom. The 34-week trial before a Superior Court judge in New Jersey resulted in a not-guilty verdict for the Englewood Cliffs, N.J., surgeon. The questions concerning analytical chemistry raised in the trial will continue to be discussed in years to come.

Not since the controversial trial of Dr. Carl Coppolino—convicted in a Florida courtroom in 1967 of murdering his wife with succinylcholine chloride—have so many forensic experts of national and international stature labored so long over the scientific questions at issue in the case:

> What happens to human tissue embalmed and interred for a decade?
>
> Assuming lethal doses of a drug such as curare were given to hospital patients, would the drug have changed chemically or have been destroyed entirely over a 10-year period?
>
> Assuming again that the drug had been injected, what analytical techniques could be employed to trace submicrogram amounts of it?
>
> Could components of embalming fluids or bacteria in the earth react chemically, forming substances giving a false positive reading in the analytical procedures used?

Forensic scientists first grappled with these questions during the latter part of 1966. Two of Jascalevich's colleagues at Riverdell Hospital in Oradell, N.J.— Dr. Stanley Harris, a surgeon, and Dr. Allan Lans, an osteopathic physician—

Lawrence H. Hall
Star-Ledger, Newark, New Jersey

Roland H. Hirsch
Chemistry Department, Seton Hall University
South Orange, New Jersey

suspected him of murdering their patients with curare. There were no eyewitnesses to the alleged murders, but Drs. Harris and Lans discovered 18 vials of curare in Jascalevich's surgical locker after breaking into it.

They took their suspicions to the Bergen County Prosecutor's office in November 1966, and a brief but unpublicized investigation was launched. Items taken from the surgeon's locker, including the vials of curare and syringes, were sent for analysis at the New York City Medical Examiner's office.

In the interim, Jascalevich told authorities he used the muscle-relaxant drug in animal experiments at the Seton Hall Medical College. The surgeon presented the prosecutor his medical research papers and other documentation to support his contention. In addition, he reviewed the medical charts of the alleged murder victims and told the prosecutor there was no need for the operations the patients received. Malpractice and misdiagnosis were the causes of the deaths, Jascalevich stated at that time.

Dr. Milton Helpern, chief of the New York City Medical Examiner's office, and his staff in early 1967 concluded their testing on the items taken from Jascalevich's locker. Dog hair and animal blood were detected on the vials of curare and syringes.

The prosecutor's office terminated its investigation and stated there were more reasons to look into allegations of malpractice than murder at the small osteopathic hospital.

In January 1976 a series of articles about a "Doctor X" suspected of murdering patients at Riverdell Hospital appeared in the *New York Times,* and the Bergen County Prosecutor's office reopened its case.

A month prior to the case being officially reopened, however, New York Deputy Medical Examiner Dr. Michael Baden

supplied an affidavit to the Superior Court in Bergen County stating that at least a score of patients who died at Riverdell in 1966 succumbed from other reasons than those stated on death certificates.

In his affidavit in support of exhumation of the patients' remains, Dr. Baden stated,

> It is my professional opinion that the majority of these cases reviewed are not explainable on the basis of natural causes and are consistent with having been caused by a respiratory depressant.
>
> [The deputy medical examiner continued] I am aware that because unexplainable respiratory arrests have been involved in many of these deaths, the possibility of poisoning by a curare-like substance (specifically *d*-tubocurarine) was considered and investigated at the time of the initial inquiry in 1966.
>
> The ability to identify *d*-tubocurarine, often referred to as curare, in human tissue was limited at the time of the initial investigation.
>
> It is my professional opinion that recent technological advances now permit the detection of very minute amounts of d-tubocurarine in tissues removed from dead bodies. This is because d-tubocurarine is a chemically stable compound that can exist unaltered for many years.
>
> Therefore, the aforementioned new techniques to detect curare-like compounds can be applied to tissues removed from bodies that have been interred for long periods of time.

A Superior Court judge signed the order in January 1976, granting the prosecutor's office the right to exhume the bodies of Nancy Savino, 4; Emma Arzt, 70; Frank Biggs, 59; Margaret Henderson, 27; and Carl Rohrbeck, 73.

All these patients entered Riverdell Hospital between December 1965 and September 1966 for routine surgical procedures and succumbed days afterward.

In mid-January 1976 the body of the Savino child was exhumed from a gravesite in Bergen County and taken to the medical examiner's office in New York City.

There, Dr. Baden, in the presence of New Jersey State Medical Examiner Dr. Edwin Albano and others, began performing the almost 4-hour examination of the child's body, which was said to be well preserved.

Assisting Dr. Baden in the analytical studies carried out on the tissues were Dr. Leo Dal Cortivo, chief toxicologist for Suffolk County, N.Y., and Dr. Richard J. Coumbis, chief toxicologist for the New Jersey Medical Examiner's office. The defense experts, headed by former Westchester County (N.Y.) Medical Examiner Dr. Henry Siegel, were not permitted to be present at the reautopsies.

The state began its work. In March, a week before the grand jury met, a newspaper article declared that curare had been detected in the Savino child. However, in his grand jury testimony weeks later, Dr. Baden stated his experts could not be certain if curare could be detected: "We have to look and see whether or not we can develop adequate procedures."

On May 18, 1976, Dr. Jascalevich was indicted for five murders.

A little more than a year later, the state's forensic experts began using radioimmunoassay (RIA) and high-performance liquid chromatography (HPLC) on the tissue specimens. In the fall of 1977, the defense received from Drs. Baden and Dal Cortivo samples of tissues and embalming fluids of the alleged murder victims.

For the remainder of the year, both the defense and the state experts worked to develop analytical procedures to settle the question of detection of curare in human tissue.

In addition, there were numerous pretrial hearings at which time the defense, headed by Jersey City attorney Raymond Brown, requested medical slides, reports, and patient charts relating to the alleged murder victims, as well as the methodologies used in treating the specimens.

On February 28, 1978, a panel of 18 jurors was chosen for what was to become the second longest criminal trial in the nation's history. At the outset, the defense wanted a hearing to ascertain the validity of the scientific procedures employed by the state to reportedly detect curare.

The defense contended that RIA and HPLC were relatively new procedures and could not be used to detect curare in human tissue. RIA, for example, could only be used to detect drugs in blood and body fluids, according to defense experts.

The defense motion for a hearing outside of the presence of the jury was denied by Superior Court Judge William J. Arnold, who maintained the motion could be made later in the trial when the evidence obtained by the analytical techniques would actually be scheduled for presentation to the jury.

The trial got underway with testimony by osteopathic physicians, nurses, and other hospital personnel employed by Riverdell during the time the alleged murders were committed. The physicians told Assistant Prosecutor Sybil Moses that in each instance the patient had been recovering from surgery when he succumbed.

However, on cross-examination, the physicians admitted they had misdiagnosed their patients' conditions and that there was inferior postoperative care. For example, in the case of the Savino child, the defense experts held that the little girl died of acute diffuse peritonitis—the source of her abdominal pain when she was brought into Riverdell after having been diagnosed as having acute appendicitis.

After the prosecution completed presentation of the medical aspects of its case, the defense renewed its request for a special hearing on the admissibility of the evidence obtained by radioimmuno-assay, liquid chromatography, and other analytical techniques. This request came as Dr. Baden took the witness stand to explain why he had recommended reautopsy of the bodies. The prosecution was opposed to a hearing:

> The techniques used by the State are not new toxicological methodologies, but are standard methods, used widely throughout the field. These methodologies include radioimmuno-assay and high-pressure liquid chromatography. . . .
> Since the methodologies used to detect the curare are widely accepted in the scientific community, there is no necessity for the Court to conduct a hearing as to their reliability.

Nevertheless, Judge Arnold ruled that a hearing should be held. Arguments began, in the absence of the jury, on June 10. Both sides presented statements by their technical experts and affidavits from other scientists regarding the validity of the analytical methods. The prosecution cited various cases in support of its position:

> Practically every new scientific discovery had its detractors and unbelievers, but neither unanimity of opinion nor universal infallibility is required for judicial acceptance of generally recognized matters [State v. Johnson, 42 N.J. 146, 171 (1964)].
> The law, in its efforts to enforce justice by demonstrating a fact in issue, will allow evidence of those scientific processes, which are the work of educated and skillful men in their various departments and apply them to the demonstration of a fact, leaving the weight and effect to be given to the effort and its results entirely to the consideration of the jury [State v. Cerciello, 86 N.J.L. 309, 314 (E&A 1914)].

The prosecution stated, "Federal courts have held that newness or lack of absolute certainty in a test does not require its inadmissibility." In one case involving neutron-activation analysis, a federal appellate court held in part:

> Every useful new development must have its first day in court. And court records are full of the conflicting opinions of doctors, engineers, and accountants to name just a few of the legions of expert witnesses [United States v. Stifel, 433 F. 2d. 431, 437, 438 (6th Cir. 1970)].

The prosecution noted,

> The Florida Appellate Court in Coppolino v. State . . . held that not only established techniques but methods developed specifically for that case could be used to detect a previously undetectable drug in the body of the decedent. . . .
> The tests by which the medical examiner sought to determine whether death was caused by succinylcholine chloride were novel and devised specifically for this case. This does not render the evidence inadmissible. Society need not tolerate homicide until there develops a body of medical knowledge about some particular lethal agent. The expert witnesses were examined and cross-examined at great length and the jury could either believe or doubt the prosecution's testimony as it chose [Coppolino v. State, 223 So. 2d. 75 (Fla. App. 1968)].

Finally, the prosecution noted the following holding of the New Jersey Superior Court Appellate Division:

> The general rule in New Jersey regarding the admissibility of scientific test results is that, if the equipment or the methodology used is proven to have a high degree of scientific reliability, and if the test is performed or administered by qualified persons, the results will be admissible at trial

[State *v.* Chatman, *101 N.J.L.S. index 307, 308 (App. Div. 1973)*].

The defense contended that

The methodologies of thin layer chromatography (TLC), high pressure liquid chromatography, ultraviolet spectrophotometry, and radio-immunoassay which have been utilized by the State do not meet the required level of acceptance under the circumstances of the tissues in this case. . . . Since there have never been any attempts to demonstrate the presence of *d*-tubocurarine in embalmed, buried tissue . . . the State cannot even assert that the techniques it wishes to utilize to demonstrate this have been generally accepted.

The defense presented affidavits from a variety of forensic scientists, from which we present one example:

It should be noted that even though the newer analytical methods and some of the sophisticated equipment are extremely sensitive for drug detection, the sensitivity of some method is not a criterion of its specificity. Sensitivity is the minimum amount of an unknown substance below which a test gives a negative result. Specificity is the ability of a test to establish the individual characteristics and/or configuration of a particular substance by differentiating it from all other substances, especially in a biologic mixture.

Currently, the reported analytical methods, which include ultraviolet absorption spectrophotometry, thin layer chromatography and radioimmunoassay, alone or in conjunction, lack such a degree of specificity with any degree of scientific certainty required to support the opinion that they identified the isolated material as *d*-tubocurarine in embalmed, decomposed and skeletonizing tissues that have been

in the ground for ten years under varying climatic conditions [Abraham Stolman, Chief Toxicologist, State of Connecticut Department of Health].

On June 20 the judge ruled that the analytical evidence was admissible. He stated,

All I'm saying is under the law the evidence is admissible. I'm not going to comment on the value or trust-worthiness of the witnesses [who testified]. The ultimate decision must be made by the jury.

Following this decision, the jury began listening to the scientific evidence, with the State's and the defense's witnesses in the process explaining such points as: What is curare, and specifically *d*-tubocurarine? What is radioimmunoassay? What is an antibody, and how is the antibody for *d*-tubocurarine created? What is high-pressure liquid chromatography?

Dr. Richard Coumbis testified about his finding tubocurarine in tissues from four of the five patients: "can only state there is presumptive evidence" that curare was discovered in the fifth patient. Under cross-examination by defense attorney Raymond Brown, Coumbis maintained that the RIA and HPLC procedures were valid methods of detecting curare because "on the basis of my personal experience, I did not find any other substance interfering with curare."

The toxicologist admitted that the counting efficiencies of the instruments he used to get the RIA displacement values varied from day to day and were subject to error. Brown disagreed with the displacement figures Coumbis arrived at, and wanted to know whether there was a "cut-off point" whereby he arrived at the conclusion that curare was or was not present in tissues. The RIA results ranged from as low as 77 counts all the way up to 700. Somewhere within that range, Brown argued, was a point at which Coumbis arrived at the decision that the drug was detected or not. Where, he asked, was that point? The toxicologist responded by saying that the higher the figure, the more likely curare was present. He said in many instances, however, he had to use his discretion to determine the cut-off point.

Dr. David Beggs of Hewlett-Packard then testified that he found curare in the Savino lung and liver samples using mass spectrometry. He said the Biggs and Arzt samples contained possible traces of curare; however, he could not be scientifically certain of this. He stated that mass spectrometry "is not an absolute test" for curare, but "just indicated that it is probably there." He did carry out a solvent blank as a means of eliminating false positives. He held under cross-examination that the electron impact technique used by him resulted in a spectrum with 12 major peaks and that 10 were sufficient for "fingerprint" identification of curare.

Dr. Sidney Spector of the Roche Institute testified about how he had developed the antibody for d-tubocurarine and applied it in RIA analysis of body fluids such as urine and blood. He had not himself run any tests for curare in human tissue samples and stated, "If there were curare in tissues, there is the possibility it could be detected." He said that the State's RIA experiments were "inadequate" in relying on aqueous solutions of curare to develop a standard curve. He held that the RIA procedure could give an indication that curare was present, but that the finding would only be presumptive evidence and not sufficient to say that the muscle-relaxant drug was positively present. He made the same point about HPLC and said that even if the two techniques were used together, there still would only be presumptive proof that the drug was present.

Dr. Leo Dal Cortivo then took the witness stand and testified that he had found curare in tissue remains of three of the patients using HPLC. He also had measured curare in vials found in the defendant's locker at Riverdell Hospital in 1966, which the defense contended had been used in animal experiments conducted by Jascalevich at the College of Medicine in Jersey City. It was necessary to use RIA for the detection of curare in the HPLC eluates. The samples were prepared for LC analysis by an extraction procedure which Dal Cortivo stated gave a 75 percent recovery. He rejected the contention that the extraction and LC method might have allowed positive results because of an interfering substance.

The prosecution then completed its case. At this point Judge Arnold dismissed two counts of murder and stated that the prosecution had not presented scientific evidence for the presence of curare in the bodies of Emma Arzt and Margaret Henderson. The defense then began presentation of its case with testimony about the medical aspects.

In September, attention returned to the analytical data. Drs. Frederick Rieders and Bo Holmstedt testified about the experiments they carried out on the samples provided by the prosecution. The major question they addressed was that of the long-term stability of curare under the conditions to which the bodies were subjected between 1966 and 1976.

Dr. Rieders maintained that, in his opinion, the RIA was not specific enough and "could only raise suspicions that something is there but it might not be there." The only procedure he found specific enough to be confident of identification of curare was mass spectrometry, using the entire spectrum, not just selected ion monitoring. In critical analyses, a four-step extraction procedure was used to isolate d-tubocurarine from the samples . . . .

Rieders tested for the stability of curare and found that both embalming fluids and tissue juices (from the patients) had destructive effects on this compound. He added curare to these liquids and could detect it by TLC initially, but after a few days could find no trace of it or other nitrogenous bases. These liquids altered curare chemically to the point where it was no longer recognizable as such. He concluded that the rapid rate of decomposition meant that to detect curare in the specimens in 1976 would have required huge, medically impossible amounts to have been present in 1966.

Rieders tested the samples for curare and found it only in the liver specimen of Nancy Savino. He stated that mass spectrometry indicated that the curare in this sample was highly pure and could not have been present in the ground for 10 years. Furthermore, if curare was present in the liver, it should also have been found in the child's muscle tissue. That it was not detected in the latter specimen was a "tremendous inconsistency."

Dr. Bo Holmstedt then stated that curare could not survive in embalmed bodies for

10 years, especially because of the effects of bacteria and repeated fluctuations in temperature of the bodies. He reviewed experiments which showed that curare, upon injection, shows levels of the same order of magnitude in liver and muscle tissues. After 10 minutes, "40 percent of the drug is to be found in the muscle and 3 percent in the liver."

On October 14 the defense rested its case. On October 23, after both sides had presented summations of their cases, Judge Arnold gave his charge to the jury. The next day, October 24, 1978—seven and a half months after the trial had begun—the jury received the case. After just over 2 hours of deliberations, the jury returned a unanimous verdict of not guilty on all three remaining counts of murder. Two years and five months after the indictments against him had been returned, Dr. Mario Jascalevich was free.

Mr. Ramsey,

Listen carefully! We [are a]
group of individuals that [represent]
a small foreign faction. We [do]
respect your bussiness but not [the]
country that it serves. At [this time]
[w]e have your daughter [in our possession.]
She is safe and [unharmed and if]
you want her to see [1997, you must]
[follow] our instructi[ons to the let-]
ter.
[Yo]u will withdraw $118[,000 from]
[yo]ur account. $100,000 [will be]
[in $100] bills and the remain[ing $18,000]
in $20 bills. Make [sure that]
[y]ou bring an adequate [size attache.]

JonBenet Ramsey: Who Did It?

Patsy Ramsey awoke just after five a.m. on December 26, 1996, and walked downstairs to her kitchen. At the foot of the staircase, she found a two-and-a-half-page note saying that her 6-year-old daughter, JonBenet, had been kidnapped. The note contained a ransom demand of $118,000. Patsy and John Ramsey were in the upper crust of Boulder, Colorado, society. In the span of five short years, John had built his computer company into a billion-dollar corporation. When the police arrived to investigate, it was quite apparent to all that JonBenet was missing. In retrospect, some serious mistakes were made in securing the crime scene—the Ramsey household. Initially, the police conducted a cursory search of the house, but failed to find JonBenet. The house was not sealed off; in fact, four friends along with the Ramsey pastor were let into the home and allowed to move about at will. John was permitted to leave the premises unattended for one and a half hours. One hour after his return, John and two of his friends searched the house again. This time John went down into the basement, where he discovered JonBenet's body. He removed a white blanket from JonBenet and carried her upstairs, placing the body on the living room floor.

The murder of JonBenet Ramsey remains as baffling a mystery today as it was on its first day. Ample physical evidence exists to support the theory that the crime was committed by an outsider, and also that JonBenet was murdered by someone who resided in the Ramsey household. Perhaps better care at securing and processing the crime scene could have resolved some of the crime's outstanding questions.

The
Crime Scene

chapter 2

Key Terms

buccal swab

chain of custody

finished sketch

physical evidence

rough sketch

standard/reference sample

substrate control

Learning Objectives

After studying this chapter you should be able to:

- Define physical evidence

- Discuss the responsibilities of the first police officer who arrives at a crime scene

- Explain the steps to be taken to thoroughly record the crime scene

- Describe proper procedures for conducting a systematic search of a crime scene for physical evidence

- Describe proper techniques for packaging common types of physical evidence

- Define and understand the concept of chain of custody

- Relate what steps are typically required to maintain appropriate health and safety standards at the crime scene

- Understand the implications of the *Mincey* and *Tyler* cases

Processing the Crime Scene

Physical Evidence
Any object that can establish that a crime has been committed or can link a crime and its victim or its perpetrator.

As automobiles run on gasoline, crime laboratories "run" on physical evidence. Physical evidence encompasses any and all objects that can establish that a crime has been committed or can link a crime and its victim or its perpetrator. But if physical evidence is to be used effectively to aid the investigator, its presence first must be recognized at the crime scene. If all the natural and commercial objects within a reasonable distance of a crime were gathered so that the scientist could uncover significant clues from them, the deluge of material would quickly immobilize the laboratory facility. Physical evidence can achieve its optimum value in criminal investigations only when its collection is performed with a selectivity governed by the collector's thorough knowledge of the crime laboratory's techniques, capabilities, and limitations.

Forthcoming chapters will be devoted to discussions of methods and techniques available to forensic scientists for the evaluation of physical evidence. Although current technology has given the crime laboratory capabilities far exceeding those of past decades, these advances are no excuse for complacency on the part of criminal investigators. Crime laboratories do not solve crimes; only a thorough and competent investigation conducted by professional police officers will enhance the chances for a successful criminal investigation. Forensic science is, and will continue to be, an important element of the total investigative process, but it is only one aspect of an endeavor that must be a team effort. The investigator who believes the crime laboratory to be a panacea for laxity or ineptness is in for a rude awakening.

Forensic science begins at the crime scene. If the investigator cannot recognize physical evidence or cannot properly preserve it for laboratory examination, no amount of sophisticated laboratory instrumentation or technical expertise can salvage the situation. The know-how for conducting a proper crime-scene search for physical evidence is not beyond the grasp of any police department, regardless of its size. With proper training, police agencies can ensure competent performance at crime scenes. In many jurisdictions, police agencies have delegated this task to a specialized team of technicians. However, the techniques of crime-scene investigation are not difficult to master and certainly lie within the bounds of comprehension of the average police officer.

Not all crime scenes require retrieval of physical evidence, and limited resources and personnel have forced many police agencies to restrict their efforts in this area to crimes of a more serious nature. Once the commitment is made to completely process a crime site for physical evidence, however, certain fundamental practices must be followed.

Secure and Isolate the Crime Scene

The first officer arriving on the scene of a crime is responsible for preserving and protecting the area as much as possible. Of course, first priority should be given to obtaining medical assistance for individuals in need of it and to arresting the perpetrator. However, as soon as possible, extensive efforts must be made to exclude all unauthorized personnel from the scene. As additional officers arrive, measures are immediately initiated to isolate the area. See Figure 2–1. Ropes or barricades along with strategic positioning of guards will prevent unauthorized access to the area.

Sometimes the exclusion of unauthorized personnel proves more difficult than expected. Violent crimes are especially susceptible to attention from higher-level police officials and members of the press, as well as by emotionally charged neighbors and curiosity seekers. Every individual who enters the scene is a potential destroyer of physical evidence, even if it is by unintentional carelessness. If proper control is to be exercised over the crime scene, the officer charged with the responsibility for protecting it must have the authority to exclude everyone, including fellow police officers not directly involved in processing the site or in conducting the investigation. Seasoned criminal investigators are always prepared to relate horror stories about crime scenes where physical evidence was rendered totally valueless by hordes of people who, for one reason or another, trampled through the site. Securing and isolating the crime scene are critical steps in an investigation, the accomplishment of which is the mark of a trained and professional crime-scene investigative team.

Figure 2–1   The first investigators to arrive must secure the crime scene and establish the crime-scene perimeter. *Courtesy Sirchie Finger Print Laboratories, Inc., Youngsville, N.C., www.sirchie.com*

Once the scene has been secured, a lead investigator starts evaluating the area. First, he or she determines the boundaries of the scene, and then establishes the perpetrator's path of entry and exit. Logic dictates that obvious items of crime-scene evidence will first come to the attention of the crime-scene investigator. These items must be documented and photographed. The investigator then proceeds with an initial walk-through of the scene to gain an overview of the situation and develop a strategy for systematically examining and documenting the entire crime scene.

Record the Scene

Investigators have only a limited amount of time to work a crime site in its untouched state. The opportunity to permanently record the scene in its original state must not be lost. Such records not only will prove useful during the subsequent investigation but are also required for presentation at a trial in order to document the condition of the crime site and to delineate the location of physical evidence. Photography, sketches, and notes are the three methods for crime-scene recording (see Figure 2–2). Ideally all three should be employed; however, personnel and monetary limitations often prohibit the use of photography at every crime site. Under these circumstances, departmental guidelines will establish priorities for deploying photographic resources. However, there is no reason not to make sketches and notes at the crime scene.

Photography.   The most important prerequisite for photographing a crime scene is for it to be unaltered. Unless injured people are involved, objects must not be moved until they have been photographed from all necessary angles. If objects are removed, positions changed, or items added, the photographs may not be admissible as evidence at a trial, and their intended

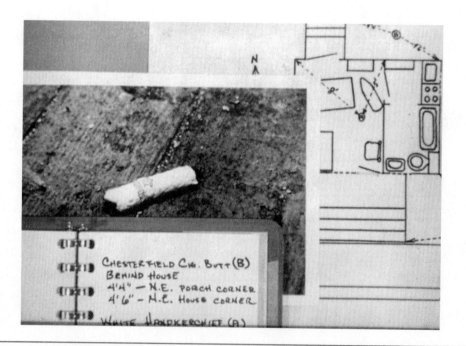

Figure 2–2   **The finding of an evidential cigarette butt at the crime scene requires photographing it, making a sketch showing its relation to the crime scene, and recording the find in field notes.** *Courtesy Police Science Services, Niles, Ill.*

value will be lost. If evidence has been moved or removed prior to photography, the fact should be noted in the report, but the evidence should not be reintroduced into the scene in order to take photographs.

Each crime scene should be photographed as completely as possible. This means that the crime scene should include the area in which the crime actually took place and all adjacent areas where important acts occurred immediately before or after the commission of the crime. Overview photographs of the entire scene and surrounding area, including points of exit and entry, must be taken from various angles. If the crime took place indoors, the entire room should be photographed to show each wall area. Rooms adjacent to the actual crime site must be similarly photographed. If the crime scene includes a body, photographs must be taken to show the body's position and location relative to the entire scene. Close-up photos depicting injuries and weapons lying near the body are also necessary. After the body is removed from the scene, the surface beneath the body should be photographed.

As items of physical evidence are discovered, they are photographed to show their position and location relative to the entire scene. After these overviews are taken, close-ups should be taken to record the details of the object itself. When the size of an item is of significance, a ruler or other measuring scale may be inserted near the object and included in the photograph as a point of reference. The digital revolution promises to bring enhanced photographic capabilities to the crime scene. For example, individual images of the crime scene captured with a digital camera can be stitched together electronically to reveal a near three-dimensional panoramic view of the crime scene (see Figure 2–3). With the aid of a computer, any area of the scene captured digitally can be enhanced and examined in fine detail.

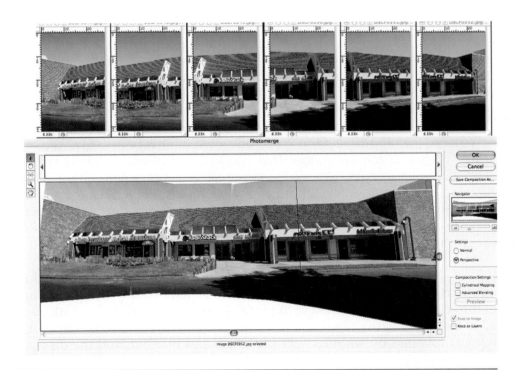

Figure 2–3 Individual images (top) are shown before being electronically stitched together into a single panoramic image (bottom). Individual photographs should be taken with about a 30 percent overlap. *Courtesy Imaging Forensics, Fountain Valley, Calif., www.imagingforensics.com*

The use of videotape at crime scenes is becoming increasingly popular because the cost of this equipment is decreasing. The same principles used in crime-scene photographs apply to videotaping. As with conventional photography, videotaping should include the entire scene and the immediate surrounding area. Long shots as well as close-ups should be taken in a slow and systematic manner. Furthermore, it is desirable to have one crime-scene investigator narrate the events and scenes being taped while another does the actual shooting.

While videotaping can capture the sounds and scenes of the crime site with relative ease, the technique cannot at this time be used in place of still photography. The still photograph remains unsurpassed in the definition of detail it provides to the human eye.

Sketches. Once photographs have been taken, the crime-scene investigator sketches the scene. The investigator may have neither the skill nor the time to make a polished sketch of the scene. However, this is not required during the early phase of the investigation. What is necessary is a rough sketch containing an accurate depiction of the dimensions of the scene and showing the location of all objects having a bearing on the case.

A rough sketch is illustrated in Figure 2–4. It shows all recovered items of physical evidence, as well as other important features of the crime scene. Objects are located in the sketch by distance measurements from two fixed points, such as the walls of a room. It is important that distances shown on the sketch be accurate and not the result of a guess or estimate. For this reason, all measurements are made with a tape measure. The simplest way to designate an item in a sketch is to assign it a number or letter. A legend or list placed below the sketch then correlates the letter to the item's description. The sketch should also show a compass heading designating north.

Unlike the rough sketch, the finished sketch in Figure 2–5 is constructed with care and concern for aesthetic appearance. When the finished sketch is completed, it must reflect information contained within the rough sketch in order to be admissible evidence in a courtroom. Computer-aided drafting (CAD) has become the norm to reconstruct crime scenes from rough sketches. The software, ranging from simple, low-cost programs to complex, expensive programs, contains predrawn intersections and roadways or buildings and rooms onto which information can be entered (see Figure 2–6). A generous symbol library provides the operator with a variety of images that can be used to add intricate details such as blood spatters to a crime-scene sketch. Equipped with a zoom function, computerized sketching can focus on a specific area for a more detailed picture. CAD programs allow the operator to select scale size so that the ultimate product can be produced in a size suitable for courtroom presentation.

Notes. Note taking must be a constant activity throughout the processing of the crime scene. These notes must include a detailed written description of the scene with the location of items of physical evidence recovered. They must also identify the time an item of physical evidence was discovered, by whom, how and by whom it was packaged and marked, and the disposition of the item after it was collected. The note taker has to keep in mind that this written record may be the only source of information for refreshing one's memory months, perhaps years, after a crime has been processed. The notes must be sufficiently detailed to anticipate this need.

WebExtra 2.1

Making a Photographic Record of the Crime Scene
www.prenhall.com/Saferstein

Rough Sketch
A draft representation of all essential information and measurements at a crime scene. This sketch is drawn at the crime scene.

Finished Sketch
A precise rendering of the crime scene, usually drawn to scale.

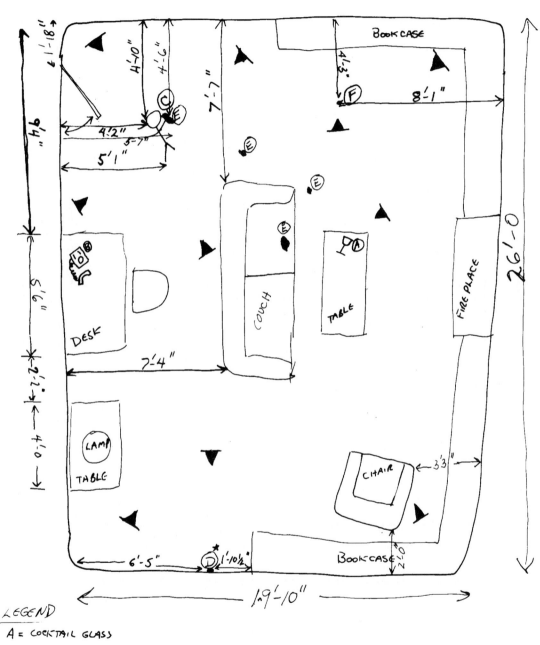

CASE 10-789-96
301 N. CENTRE ST.
OCT. 6, 1996   11:40 PM
HOMICIDE

VICTIM: LESTER W. BROWN
INVESTIGATOR: SGT. L.A. DUFFY
ASS'T BY: PTLM. R.W. HICKS

LEGEND

A = COCKTAIL GLASS
B = TELEPHONE
C = VICTIM
D = BULLET HOLE
E = BLOOD STAINS
F = SHELL CASING
▲ = CAMERA LOCATIONS

D 3'-4¾" FROM FLOOR

¼" = 1 FOOT

Figure 2–4   Rough-sketch diagram of a crime scene. *Courtesy Sirchie Finger Print Laboratories, Inc., Youngsville, N.C., www.sirchie.com*

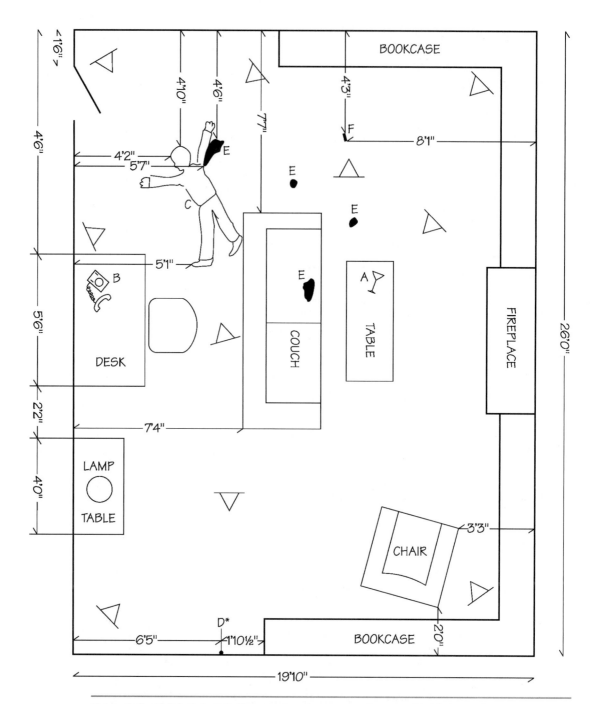

Figure 2–5 **Finished-sketch diagram of a crime scene.** *Courtesy Sirchie Finger Print Laboratories, Inc., Youngsville, N.C., www.sirchie.com*

Tape-recording notes at a scene can be advantageous—detailed notes can be taped much faster than they can be written. Another method of recording notes is to narrate a videotape of the crime scene. This has the advantage of combining note taking with photography. However, at some point the tape must be transcribed into a written document.

Conduct a Systematic Search for Evidence

The search for physical evidence at a crime scene must be thorough and systematic. For a factual, unbiased reconstruction of the crime, the investigator, relying on his or her training and experience, must not overlook

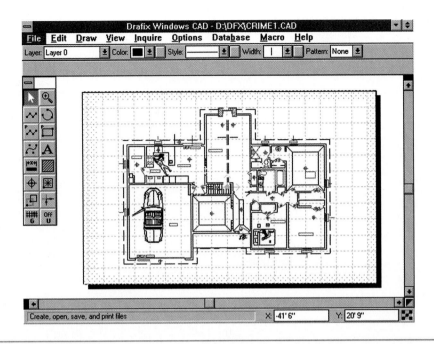

Figure 2–6   Construction of a crime-scene diagram with the aid of a computer-aided drafting program. *Courtesy Sirchie Finger Print Laboratories, Inc., Youngsville, N.C., www.sirchie.com*

any pertinent evidence. Even when suspects are immediately seized and the motives and circumstances of the crime are readily apparent, a thorough search for physical evidence must be conducted at once. Failure in this, even though it may seem unnecessary, can lead to accusations of negligence or charges that the investigative agency knowingly "covered up" evidence that would be detrimental to its case.

Assigning those responsible for searching a crime scene is a function of the investigator in charge. Except in major crimes, or when the evidence is very complex, it is usually not necessary to have the assistance of a forensic scientist at the crime scene; his or her role appropriately begins with the submission of evidence to the crime laboratory. As has already been observed, some police agencies have trained field evidence technicians to search for physical evidence at the crime scene. They have the equipment and skill to photograph the scene and examine it for the presence of fingerprints, footprints, tool marks, or any other type of evidence that may be relevant to the crime.

How one conducts a crime-scene search will depend on the locale and size of the area, as well as on the actions of the suspect(s) and victim(s) at the scene. When possible, one person should supervise and coordinate the collection of evidence. Without proper control, the search may be conducted in an atmosphere of confusion with needless duplication of effort. Evidence collectors may subdivide the scene into segments and search each segment individually, or the search may start at some outer point and gradually move toward the center of the scene in a circular fashion (see Figure 2–7). The areas searched must include all probable points of entry and exit used by the criminals.

What to search for will be determined by the particular circumstances of the crime. Obviously, the skill of crime-scene investigators at recognizing evidence and searching relevant locations is paramount to successful processing of the crime scene. While training will impart general

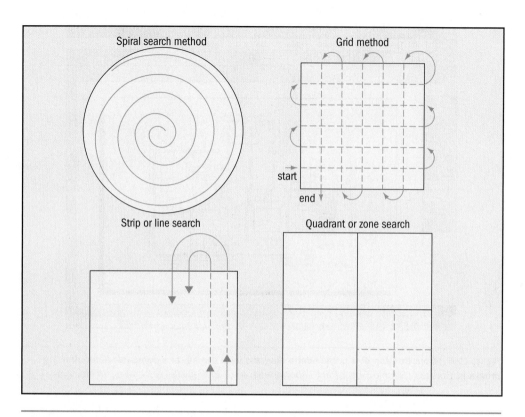

Figure 2–7   Several typical examples of crime-scene search patterns. The pattern selected normally depends on the size and locale of the scene and the number of collectors participating in the search.

knowledge for conducting a proper crime-scene investigation, ultimately the investigator must rely on the experience gained from numerous investigations to formulate a successful strategy for recovering relevant physical evidence at crime scenes. For example, in the case of homicide, the search will center on the weapon and any type of evidence left as a result of contact between the victim and the assailant. The cross-transfer of evidence, such as hairs, fibers, and blood, between individuals involved in the crime is particularly useful for linking suspects to the crime site and for corroborating events that transpired during the commission of the crime. During the investigation of a burglary, efforts will be made to locate tool marks at the point of entry. In most crimes, a thorough and systematic search for latent fingerprints is required.

Vehicle searches must be carefully planned and systematically carried out. The nature of the case determines how detailed the search must be. In hit-and-run cases, the outside and undercarriage of the car must be examined with care. Particular attention is paid to looking for any evidence resulting from a cross-transfer of evidence between the car and the victim—this includes blood, tissue, hair, fibers, and fabric impressions. Traces of paint or broken glass may be located on the victim. In cases of homicide, burglary, kidnapping, and so on, all areas of the vehicle, inside and outside, are searched with equal care for physical evidence.

Physical evidence can be anything from massive objects to microscopic traces. Often, many items of evidence are obvious in their presence, but others may be detected only through examination in the crime laboratory. For example, minute traces of blood may be discovered on garments only after a thorough search in the laboratory, or the presence

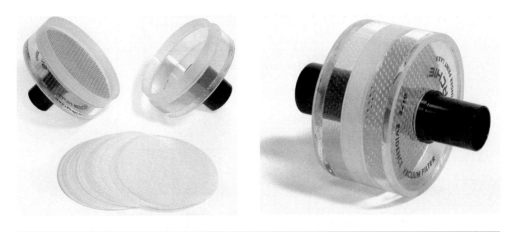

Figure 2–8 Vacuum sweeper attachment, constructed of clear plastic in two pieces that are joined by a threaded joint. A metal screen is mounted in one half to support a filter paper to collect debris. The unit attaches to the hose of the vacuum sweeper. After a designated area of the crime scene is vacuumed, the filter paper is removed and retained for laboratory examination. *Courtesy Sirchie Finger Print Laboratories, Inc., Youngsville, N.C., www.sirchie.com*

of hairs and fibers may be revealed in vacuum sweepings or on garments only after close laboratory scrutiny. For this reason, it is important to collect possible carriers of trace evidence in addition to more discernible items. Hence, it may be necessary to take custody of all clothing worn by the participants in a crime. Each clothing item should be handled carefully and wrapped separately to avoid loss of trace materials. Critical areas of the crime scene should be vacuumed and the sweepings submitted to the laboratory for analysis. The sweepings from different areas must be collected and packaged separately. A portable vacuum cleaner equipped with a special filter attachment is suitable for this purpose (see Figure 2–8). Additionally, fingernail scrapings from individuals who were in contact with other individuals may contain minute fragments of evidence capable of linking the assailant and victim. The undersurface of each nail is best scraped with a dull object such as a toothpick to avoid cutting the skin. These scrapings will be subjected to microscopic examination in the laboratory.

The search for physical evidence must extend beyond the crime scene to the autopsy room of a deceased victim. Here, the medical examiner or coroner carefully examines the victim to establish a cause and manner of death. Tissues and organs are routinely retained for pathological and toxicological examination. At the same time, arrangements must be made between the examiner and investigator to secure a variety of items that may be obtainable from the body for laboratory examination. The following are to be collected and sent to the forensic laboratory:

1. Victim's clothing

2. Fingernail scrapings

3. Head and pubic hairs

4. Blood (for DNA typing purposes)

5. Vaginal, anal, and oral swabs (in sex-related crimes)

6. Recovered bullets from the body

7. Hand swabs from shooting victims (for gunshot residue analysis)

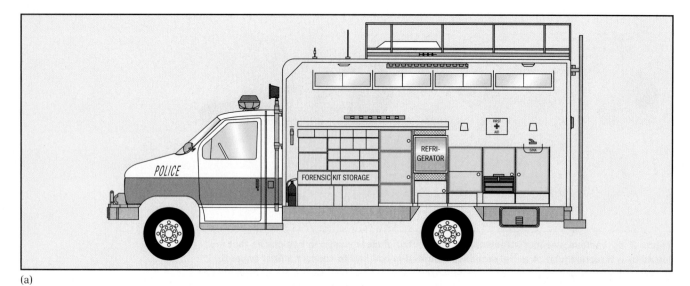

(a)

(b)

Figure 2–9   Inside view of a mobile crime-scene van: (a) driver's side and (b) passenger's side.
Courtesy Sirchie Finger Print Laboratories, Inc., Youngsville, N.C., www.sirchie.com

Once the body is buried, efforts at obtaining these items may prove difficult or futile. Furthermore, a lengthy time delay in obtaining many of these items will diminish or destroy their forensic value.

In recent years, many police departments have gone to the expense of purchasing and equipping "mobile crime laboratories" (see Figure 2–9) for their evidence technicians. However, the term *mobile crime laboratory* is a misnomer. These vehicles carry the necessary supplies to protect the crime scene; photograph, collect, and package physical evidence; and perform latent print development. They are not designed to carry out the functions of a chemical laboratory. *Crime-scene search vehicle* would be a more appropriate but perhaps less dramatic name for such a vehicle.

Collect and Package Physical Evidence

Physical evidence must be handled and processed in a way that prevents any change from taking place between the time it is removed from the crime scene and the time it is received by the crime laboratory. Changes can arise through contamination, breakage, evaporation, accidental scratching or bending, or loss through improper or careless packaging.

The integrity of evidence is best maintained when the item is kept in its original condition as found at the crime site. Whenever possible, evidence should be submitted to the laboratory intact. Blood, hairs, fibers, soil particles, and other types of trace evidence should not normally be removed from garments, weapons, or other articles that bear them. Instead, the entire object is to be sent to the laboratory for processing. Of course, if evidence is adhering to an object in a precarious manner, good judgment dictates removing and packaging the item. If evidence is found adhering to large structures, such as a door, wall, or floor, common sense must be used; remove the specimen with a forceps or other appropriate tool. In the case of a bloodstain, one has the option of either scraping the stain off the surface, transferring the stain to a moistened swab, or cutting out the area of the object bearing the stain.

Each different item or similar items collected at different locations must be placed in a separate container. Packaging evidence separately prevents damage through contact and prevents cross-contamination.

The well-prepared evidence collector arrives at a crime scene with a large assortment of packaging materials and tools, ready to encounter any type of situation. Forceps and similar tools may have to be used to pick up small items. Unbreakable plastic pill bottles with pressure lids are excellent containers for hairs, glass, fibers, and various other kinds of small or trace evidence. Alternatively, manila envelopes, screw-cap glass vials, or cardboard pillboxes are adequate containers for most trace evidence encountered at crime sites. Ordinary mailing envelopes should not be used as evidence containers because powders and fine particles will leak out of their corners. Small amounts of trace evidence can also be conveniently packaged in a carefully folded paper, using what is known as a "druggist fold." This consists of folding one end of the paper over one-third, then folding the other end (one-third) over that, and repeating the process from the other two sides. After the paper is folded in this manner, the outside two edges are tucked into each other to produce a closed container that keeps the specimen from falling out.

Although manila envelopes, pillboxes, and sealable plastic bags, as shown in Figure 2–10, are good universal containers for most trace evidence, two frequent finds at crime scenes warrant special attention. If bloodstained materials are stored in airtight containers, the accumulation of moisture may encourage the growth of mold, which can destroy the evidential value of blood. In these instances, wrapping paper, manila envelopes, or paper bags are recommended packaging materials (see Figure 2–11). As a matter of routine, all items of clothing are to be air-dried and placed individually in separate paper bags to ensure constant circulation of air through them. This will prevent the formation of mold and mildew. On the other hand, charred debris recovered from the scene of a suspicious fire must be sealed in an airtight container to prevent the evaporation of volatile petroleum residues. New paint cans or tightly sealed jars are recommended in such situations.

A detailed description of the proper collection and packaging of various types of physical evidence will be discussed in forthcoming chapters; additionally, most of this information is summarized in the evidence guide found in Appendix I.

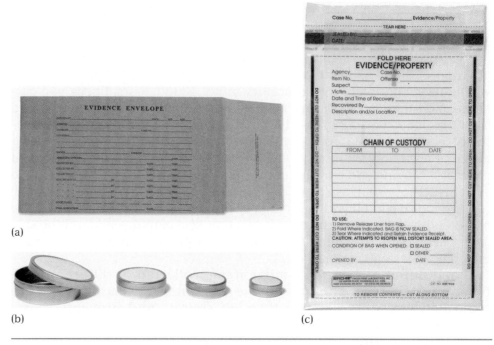

(a)

(b)

(c)

Figure 2–10   (a) Manila evidence envelope, (b) metal pillboxes, (c) sealable plastic evidence bag. *Courtesy Sirchie Finger Print Laboratories, Inc., Youngsville, N.C., www.sirchie.com*

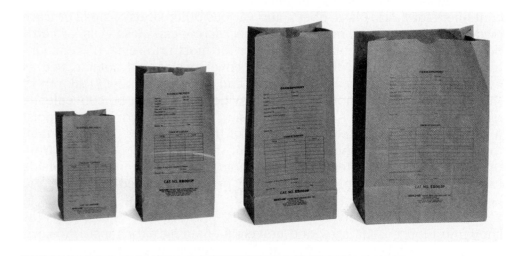

Figure 2–11   Paper bags are recommended evidence containers for objects suspected of containing blood and semen stains. Each object should be packaged in a separate bag. *Courtesy Sirchie Finger Print Laboratories, Inc., Youngsville, N.C., www.sirchie.com*

Maintain the Chain of Custody

Chain of Custody

A list of all people who came into possession of an item of evidence.

Continuity of possession, or the **chain of custody**, must be established whenever evidence is presented in court as an exhibit. Adherence to standard procedures in recording the location of evidence, marking it for identification, and properly completing evidence submission forms for laboratory analysis are the best guarantee that the evidence will withstand inquiries of what happened to it from the time of its finding to its presentation in court. This means that every person who handled or examined the evidence must be accounted for. Failure to substantiate the evidence's chain of custody may lead to serious questions regarding the authenticity and integrity of the evidence and examinations of it.

All items of physical evidence should be carefully packaged and marked upon their retrieval at crime sites. This should be done with the utmost care to avoid destroying their evidential value or restricting the number and kind of examinations to which they may be subjected by the criminalist. If at all possible, the evidence itself should be marked for identification. Normally, the collector's initials and the date of collection are inscribed directly on the article. However, if the evidence collector is unsure of the necessity of marking the item itself, or has doubts as to where to mark it, it is best to omit this step. When appropriate, the evidence is to be tagged for identification. Once an evidence container is selected for the evidence, whether a box, bag, vial, or can, it also must be marked for identification. A minimum record would show the collector's initials, location of the evidence, and date of collection. If the evidence is turned over to another individual for care or delivery to the laboratory, this transfer must be recorded in notes and other appropriate forms. In fact, every individual who possesses the evidence must maintain a written record of its acquisition and disposition. Frequently, all of the individuals involved in the collection and transportation of the evidence may be requested to testify in court. Thus, to avoid confusion and to retain complete control of the evidence at all times, the chain of custody should be kept to a minimum.

Obtain Standard/Reference Samples

The examination of evidence, whether soil, blood, glass, hair, fibers, and so on, often requires comparison with a known **standard/reference sample**. Although most investigators have little difficulty recognizing and collecting relevant crime-scene evidence, few seem aware of the necessity and importance of providing the crime lab with a thorough sampling of standard/reference materials. Such materials may be obtained from the victim, a suspect, or other known sources. For instance, investigation of a hit-and-run incident might require the removal of standard/reference paint from a suspect vehicle. This will permit its comparison to paint recovered at the scene. Similarly, hair found at the crime scene will be of optimum value only when compared to standard/reference hairs removed from the suspect and victim. Likewise, bloodstained evidence must be accompanied by a whole-blood or **buccal swab** standard/reference sample obtained from all relevant crime-scene participants. The quality and quantity of standard/reference specimens often determine the evidential value of crime-scene evidence, and these standard/reference specimens must be treated with equal care.

Some types of evidence must also be accompanied by the collection of **substrate controls**. These are materials adjacent or close to areas where physical evidence has been deposited. For example, substrate controls are normally collected at arson scenes. If an investigator suspects that a particular surface has been exposed to gasoline or some other accelerant, the investigator should also collect a piece of the same surface material that is believed *not* to have been exposed to the accelerant. At the laboratory, the substrate control is tested to ensure that the surface on which the accelerant was deposited does not interfere with testing procedures. Another common example of a substrate control is a material on which a bloodstain has been deposited. Unstained areas close to the stain may be sampled for the purpose of determining whether this material will have an impact on the interpretation of laboratory results.

Standard/Reference Sample
Physical evidence whose origin is known, such as blood or hair from a suspect, that can be compared to crime-scene evidence.

Buccal Swab
A swab of the inner portion of the cheek; cheek cells are usually collected to determine the DNA profile of an individual.

Substrate Control
Uncontaminated surface material close to an area where physical evidence has been deposited. This sample is to be used to ensure that the surface on which a sample has been deposited does not interfere with laboratory tests.

Thorough collection and proper packaging of standard/reference specimens and substrate controls are the mark of a skilled investigator.

Submit Evidence to the Laboratory

Evidence is usually submitted to the laboratory either by personal delivery or by mail shipment. The method of transmittal is determined by the distance the submitting agency must travel to the laboratory and the urgency of the case. If the evidence is delivered personally, the deliverer should be familiar with the case, to facilitate any discussions between laboratory personnel and the deliverer concerning specific aspects of the case.

If desired, most evidence can be conveniently shipped by mail. However, postal regulations restrict the shipment of certain chemicals and live ammunition and prohibit the mailing of explosives. In such situations, the laboratory must be consulted to determine the disposition of these substances. Care must also be exercised in the packaging of evidence in order to prevent breakage or other accidental destruction while it is in transit to the laboratory.

Most laboratories require that an evidence submission form accompany all evidence submitted. One such form is shown in Figure 2–12. This form must be properly completed. Its information will enable the laboratory analyst to make an intelligent and complete examination of the evidence. Particular attention should be paid to providing the laboratory with a brief description of the case history. This information will allow the examiner to analyze the specimens in a logical sequence and make the proper comparisons, and it will also facilitate the search for trace quantities of evidence.

The particular kind of examination requested for each type of evidence is to be delineated. However, the analyst will not be bound to adhere strictly to the specific tests requested by the investigator. As the examination proceeds, new evidence may be uncovered, and as a result the complexity of the case may change. Furthermore, the analyst may find the initial requests incomplete or not totally relevant to the case. Finally, a list of items submitted for examination must be included on the evidence submission form. Each item is to be packaged separately and assigned a number or letter, which should be listed in an orderly and logical sequence on the form.

Ensure Crime-Scene Safety

The increasing spread of AIDS and hepatitis B has sensitized the law enforcement community to the potential health hazards at crime scenes. Law enforcement officers have an extremely small chance of contracting AIDS or hepatitis at the crime scene. Both diseases are normally transmitted by the exchange of body fluids, such as blood, semen, and vaginal and cervical secretions; intravenous drug needles and syringes; and transfusion of infected blood products. However, the presence of blood and semen at crime scenes presents the investigator with biological specimens of unknown origin; the investigator has no way of gauging what health hazards they may contain. Therefore, caution and protection must be used at all times.

Fortunately, inoculation can easily prevent hepatitis B infection in most people. Furthermore, the federal Occupational Safety and Health Administration (OSHA) requires that law enforcement agencies offer hepatitis B vaccinations to all officers who may have contact with body fluids while on the job, at no expense to the officer.

CRIME:					COUNTY OF:			
Homicide; Aggravated Sexual Assault					Mercer			

VICTIM:	Age	Sex	Race	SUSPECT:	Age	Sex	Race
Jane Doe (v)	25	F	C	John Doe(s)	30	M	C

SUBMITTING AGENCY: (Address)
Trenton P.D. Central Evidence 225 N. Clinton Avenue, Trenton, N.J. 08609

FORWARD REPLIES TO:	(Name)	(Address)	Telephone Number:
Capt. John Smith, Chief of Detectives	Same as above		609 555-5555

INVESTIGATED BY:	DELIVERED BY: (Signature of Person Delivering Evidence)
Detective John Jones	

BRIEF HISTORY OF CASE: (Include Date and Location, if Applicable)
On March 1st, 2001 the victim was found dead in her bedroom. Victim was partially clothed and autopsy revealed that victim was stabbed numerous times and medical examiner stated that there was evidence of sexual assault. Victim was last seen drinking with suspect at a local tavern. Suspect was arrested and item # 23, a folding knife, was found in his pocket.

* Note* Suspect is HIV+

EXAMINATION REQUESTED ON SPECIMENS LISTED BELOW:

Examine items 2, 5, 8-11, 13-15, 18 and 19 for seminal material and compare to controls #'s 12 and 26. Examine #1, 2, 4, 7,13, 14, 15, 18, 20, 21, 22 and 23 for trace evidence transfer. Examine #3 for saliva from suspect. Examine #6 for skin, blood and trace evidence. Examine #'s 20-23 for transfer blood evidence and compare to control #'s 12 and 26.

Item #	* Code	LIST OF SPECIMENS *SOURCE OF EVIDENCE CODE (V-Victim, S-Suspect, SC-Scene)
1	V	Debris collection
2	V	Clothing, white panties
3	V	Dried Secretions/bite marks
4	V	Head Hair Combings
5	V	Oral Specimens
6	V	Fingernail Specimens
7	V	Pubic Hair Combings
8	V	External Genital Specimen
9	V	Vaginal Specimens
10	V	Cervical Specimens

Right margin (LABORATORY USE ONLY): DRUG ☐ TRACE ☐ BIO/CHEM ☐ TOX ☐ ABC ☐ EQUINE ☐ BALLISTICS ☐

FOR ADDITIONAL INFORMATION USE FORM 631A AND ATTACH   Page 1 of 2 pages

Figure 2–12 An example of a properly completed evidence submission form. *Courtesy New Jersey State Police*

The International Association for Identification Safety Committee has proposed the following guidelines to protect investigators at crime scenes containing potentially infectious materials:

1. Forensic and crime-scene personnel may encounter potentially infectious materials, such as in the case of a homicide, in which blood or body fluids may be localized to the area of the body or dispersed throughout the crime scene. At such scenes, it is recommended that personnel wear a minimum of latex gloves (double gloved) and protec-

tive (Tyvek-type) shoe covers. In cases of large contamination areas, liquid repellent coveralls (Tyvek or Kleengard suits) are recommended along with the gloves and shoe covers.

2. The use of a particle mask/respirator, goggles, or face shield is recommended in addition to the protective items listed in item 1 when potentially infectious dust or mist may be encountered at the crime scene. This includes the collection of dried bloodstains by scraping; the collection, folding, and preservation of garments that may be contaminated with blood or body fluids, especially if they are in a dried state; and the application of aerosol chemicals to bloodstains or prints for their detection and/or enhancement.

3. When processing and collecting evidence at a crime scene, personnel should be alert to sharp objects, knives, hypodermic syringes, razor blades, and similar items. In the event that such sharp objects are encountered and must be recovered as evidence, the items should be placed in an appropriate container and properly labeled. When conventional latent-print powder techniques are used in or around areas contaminated with blood, a specific brush should be designated so that it can be subsequently decontaminated or appropriately disposed of after processing is complete. If latents are developed in or around blood-contaminated areas, they should be photographed, or lifted and placed in a sealed plastic bag. The sealed bag then should be affixed with an appropriate biohazard label.

   Evidence collected for transport should be packaged to maintain its integrity and to prevent contamination of personnel or personal items. Evidence contaminated with wet blood should first be placed in a paper bag and then temporarily stored in a red biohazard plastic bag for immediate transport to an appropriate drying facility.

4. When potentially infectious materials are present at a crime scene, personnel should maintain a red biohazard plastic bag for the disposal of contaminated gloves, clothing, masks, pencils, wrapping paper, and so on. On departure from the scene, the biohazard bag must be taped shut and transported to an approved biohazardous waste pickup site.

5. Note taking should be done while wearing uncontaminated gloves to avoid contamination of pens, pencils, notebook, paper, and so on. Pens or markers used to mark and package contaminated evidence should be designated for proper disposal in a red biohazard bag before investigators leave the crime scene.

6. If individual protective equipment becomes soiled or torn, it must be removed immediately. Personnel must then disinfect/decontaminate the potentially contaminated body areas using a recommended solution, such as a 10 percent bleach solution, or an antimicrobial soap or towelette. After cleansing, the area must be covered with clean, replacement protective equipment. On departure from the scene, this procedure should be repeated on any body area where contamination could have occurred.

7. Eating, drinking, smoking, and application of makeup are prohibited at the immediate crime scene.

8. All nondisposable items, such as lab coats, towels, and personal clothing, that may be contaminated with potentially infectious material

should be placed in a yellow plastic bag labeled "Infectious Linen" and laundered, at the expense of the employer, by a qualified laundry service. Personal clothing that may have been contaminated should never be taken home for cleaning.

Legal Considerations at the Crime Scene

In police work, there is perhaps no experience more exasperating or demoralizing than to watch valuable evidence excluded from use against the accused because of legal considerations. This situation most often arises from what is deemed an "unreasonable" search and seizure of evidence. Therefore, the removal of any evidence from a person or from the scene of a crime must be done in conformity with Fourth Amendment privileges: "The right of the people to be secure in their persons, houses, papers, and effects, against unreasonable searches and seizure, shall not be violated, and no warrants shall issue, but upon probable cause, supported by oath or affirmation, and particularly describing the place to be searched, and the persons or things to be seized."

Since the 1960s, the Supreme Court has been particularly concerned with defining the circumstances under which the police can search for evidence in the absence of a court-approved search warrant. A number of allowances have been made to justify a warrantless search: (1) the existence of emergency circumstances, (2) the need to prevent the immediate loss or destruction of evidence, (3) a search of a person and property within the immediate control of the person provided it is made incident to a lawful arrest, and (4) a search made by consent of the parties involved. In cases other than these, police must be particularly cautious about processing a crime scene without a search warrant. In 1978, the Supreme Court addressed this very issue and in so doing set forth guidelines for investigators to follow in determining the propriety of conducting a warrantless search at a crime scene. Significantly, the two cases decided on this issue related to homicide and arson crime scenes, both of which are normally subjected to the most intensive forms of physical evidence searches by police.

In the case of *Mincey* v. *Arizona,*[1] the Court dealt with the legality of a four-day search at a homicide scene. The case involved a police raid on the home of Rufus Mincey, who had been suspected of dealing drugs. Under the pretext of buying drugs, an undercover police officer forced entry into Mincey's apartment and was killed in a scuffle that ensued. Without a search warrant, the police spent four days searching the apartment, recovering, among other things, bullets, drugs, and drug paraphernalia. These items were subsequently introduced as evidence at the trial. Mincey was convicted and on appeal contended that the evidence gathered from his apartment, without a warrant and without his consent, was illegally seized. The Court unanimously upheld Mincey's position, stating:

> We do not question the right of the police to respond to emergency situations. Numerous state and federal cases have recognized that the Fourth Amendment does not bar police officers from making warrantless entries and searches when they reasonably believe that a person within is in need of immediate aid. Similarly, when the po-

---

[1] 437 U.S. 385 (1978).

lice come upon the scene of a homicide they may make a prompt warrantless search of the area to see if there are other victims or if a killer is still on the premises. . . . Except for the fact that the offense under investigation was a homicide, there were no exigent circumstances in this case. . . . There was no indication that evidence would be lost, destroyed or removed during the time required to obtain a search warrant. Indeed, the police guard at the apartment minimized that possibility. And there is no suggestion that a search warrant could not easily and conveniently have been obtained. We decline to hold that the seriousness of the offense under investigation itself creates exigent circumstances of the kind that under the Fourth Amendment justify a warrantless search.

In *Michigan* v. *Tyler*,[2] a business establishment leased by Loren Tyler and a business partner was destroyed by fire. The fire was finally extinguished in the early hours of the morning; however, hampered by smoke, steam, and darkness, fire officials and police were prevented from thoroughly examining the scene for evidence of arson. The building was then left unattended until eight a.m. of that day, when officials returned and began an inspection of the burned premises. During the morning search, assorted items of evidence were recovered and removed from the building. On three other occasions—four days, seven days, and twenty-five days after the fire—investigators reentered the premises and removed additional items of evidence. Each of these searches was made without a warrant or without consent, and the evidence seized was used to convict Tyler and his partner of conspiracy to burn real property and related offenses. The Supreme Court upheld the reversal of the conviction, holding the initial morning search to be proper but contending that evidence obtained from subsequent reentries to the scene was inadmissible: "We hold that an entry to fight a fire requires no warrant, and that once in the building, officials may remain there for a reasonable time to investigate the cause of a blaze. Thereafter, additional entries to investigate the cause of the fire must be made pursuant to the warrant procedures."

The message from the Supreme Court is clear: When time and circumstances permit, obtain a search warrant before investigating and retrieving physical evidence at the crime scene.

WebExtra 2.2

Patricia Cornwell's Challenge
www.prenhall.com/Saferstein

Chapter Summary

Physical evidence includes any and all objects that can establish that a crime has been committed or can link a crime and its victim or its perpetrator. Forensic science begins at the crime scene. Here, investigators must recognize and properly preserve evidence for laboratory examination. The first officer to arrive is responsible for securing the crime scene. Once the scene is secured, relevant investigators record the crime scene by using photographs, sketches, and notes. Before processing the crime scene for physical evidence, the investigator should make a preliminary examination of the scene as it was left by the perpetrator. The search for physical evidence at a crime scene must be thorough and systematic. The search pattern selected normally depends on the size and locale of the scene and the number of collectors participating in the search.

---

[2] 436 U.S. 499 (1978).

Physical evidence can be anything from massive objects to microscopic traces. Often, many items of evidence are clearly visible but others may be detected only through examination at the crime laboratory. For this reason, it is important to collect possible carriers of trace evidence, such as clothing, vacuum sweepings, and fingernail scrapings, in addition to more discernible items. Each different item or similar items collected at different locations must be placed in a separate container. Packaging evidence separately prevents damage through contact and prevents cross-contamination.

During the collection of evidence, the chain of custody, a record for denoting the location of the evidence, must be maintained. In addition, proper standard/reference samples, such as hairs, blood, and fibers, must be collected at the crime scene and from appropriate subjects for comparison in the laboratory. The removal of any evidence from a person or from the scene of a crime must be done in accordance with appropriate search and seizure protocols.

Review Questions

1. The term _____ encompasses all objects that can establish whether a crime has been committed or can link a crime and its victim or its perpetrator.

2. True or False: Scientific evaluation of crime-scene evidence can usually overcome the results of a poorly conducted criminal investigation. _____

3. True or False: The techniques of physical evidence collection require a highly skilled individual who must specialize in this area of investigation. _____

4. All unauthorized personnel must be _____ from crime scenes.

5. Three methods for recording the crime scene are _____, _____, and _____.

6. The most important prerequisite for photographing a crime scene is to have it in a(n) _____ condition.

7. Photographs of physical evidence must include overviews as well as _____ to record the details of objects.

8. An investigator need only draw a(n) _____ sketch at the crime scene to show its dimensions and pertinent objects.

9. A detailed search of the crime scene for physical evidence must be conducted in a(n) _____ manner.

10. Besides the more obvious items of physical evidence, possible _____ of trace evidence must be collected for detailed examination in the laboratory.

11. In cooperation with the medical examiner or coroner, evidence retrieved from a deceased victim to be submitted to the crime laboratory should include _____, _____, _____, _____, _____, _____, and _____.

12. Whenever possible, trace evidence (is, is not) to be removed from the object that bears it.

13. Each item collected at the crime scene must be placed in a(n) _____ container.

14. True or False: An ordinary mailing envelope is considered a good general-purpose evidence container. _____

15. An airtight container (is, is not) recommended packaging material for blood-stained garments.

16. As a matter of routine, all items of clothing are to be _____ before packaging.

17. True or False: Charred debris recovered from the scene of an arson is best placed in a porous container. _____

18. The possibility of future legal proceedings requires that a(n) _____ be established with respect to the possession and location of physical evidence.

19. Most physical evidence collected at the crime site will require the accompanying submission of _____ material for comparison purposes.

20. In the case of *Mincey* v. *Arizona,* the Supreme Court restricted the practice of conducting a(n) _____ search at a homicide scene.

21. In the case of *Michigan* v. *Tyler,* the Supreme Court dealt with search and seizure procedures at a(n) _____ scene.

Further References

Geberth, Vernon J., *Practical Homicide Investigation: Tactics, Procedures, and Forensic Techniques,* 4th ed. Boca Raton, Fla.: Taylor & Francis, 2006.

Nickell, J., and J. F. Fischer, *Crime Scene: Methods of Forensic Detection.* Lexington: University Press of Kentucky, 1999.

Ogle, R. R., Jr., *Crime Scene Investigation and Reconstruction.* Upper Saddle River, N.J.: Prentice Hall, 2004.

Osterburg, James W., and Richard H. Ward, *Criminal Investigation—A Method for Reconstructing the Past,* 3rd ed. Cincinnati, Ohio: Anderson, 2000.

Case Study
The Enrique Camarena Case: A Forensic Nightmare

On February 7, 1985, U.S. Drug Enforcement Agency (DEA) Special Agent (SA) Enrique Camarena was abducted near the U.S. Consulate in Guadalajara, Mexico. A short time later, Capt. Alfredo Zavala, a DEA source, was also abducted from a car near the Guadalajara Airport. These two abductions would trigger a series of events leading to one of the largest investigations ever conducted by the DEA and would result in one of the most extensive cases ever received by the FBI Laboratory.

Throughout this lengthy investigation, unusual forensic problems arose that required unusual solutions. Eventually, numerous suspects were arrested, both in the United States and Mexico, which culminated in an 8-week trial held in U.S. District Court in Los Angeles, CA.

The Abduction

On February 7, 1985, SA Camarena left the DEA Resident Office to meet his wife for lunch. On this day, a witness observed a man being forced into the rear seat of a light-colored compact car in front of the Camelot Restaurant and provided descriptions of several of the assailants. After some initial reluctance, Primer Comandante Pavon-Reyes of the Mexican Federal Judicial Police (MFJP) was put in charge of the investigation, and Mexican investigators were assigned to the case. Two known drug traffickers, Rafael Caro-Quintero and Ernesto Fonseca, were quickly developed as suspects. A short time later at the Guadalajara Airport, as Caro-Quintero and his men attempted to flee by private jet, a confrontation developed between Caro-Quintero's men,

the MFJP, and DEA agents. After some discussion, Caro-Quintero and his men were permitted to board and leave. It was later learned that a 6-figure bribe had been paid to Pavon-Reyes to allow this departure.

The Investigation

During February 1985, searches of several residences and ranches throughout Mexico proved fruitless, despite the efforts of the DEA task force assigned to investigate this matter and the tremendous pressure being applied by the U.S. Government to accelerate the investigation. High-level U.S. government officials, as well as their Mexican counterparts, were becoming directly involved in the case. It is believed that because of this "heat," the Mexican drug traffickers and certain Mexican law

Michael P. Malone
Special Agent, Laboratory Division
Federal Bureau of Investigation,
Washington, D.C.

Undated photo of Enrique Camarena. *Courtesy AP Wide World Photos*

**Reprinted from *FBI Law Enforcement Bulletin*,
September 1989.**

enforcement officials fabricated a plan. According to the plan, the MFJP would receive an anonymous letter indicating that SA Camarena and Captain Zavala were being held at the Bravo drug gang's ranch in La Angostura, Michoacan, approximately 60 miles southeast of Guadalajara. The MFJP was supposed to raid the ranch, eliminate the drug gang, and eventually discover the bodies of SA Camarena and Captain Zavala buried on the ranch. The DEA would then be notified and the case would be closed. Thus, the Bravo gang would provide an easy scapegoat.

During early March, MFJP officers raided the Bravo ranch before the DEA Agents arrived. In the resulting shootout, all of the gang members, as well as one MFJP officer, were killed. However, due to a mix-up, the bodies of SA Camarena and Captain Zavala were not buried on the Bravo ranch in time to be discovered as planned. The individuals paid to do this job simply left them by the side of a road near the ranch. It was later learned that certain Mexican law enforcement officials were paid a large sum of money to formulate and carry out this plan in order to obstruct and prematurely conclude the investigation.

Shortly after this shootout, a passerby found two partially decomposed bodies, wrapped in plastic bags, along a road near the Bravo ranch. The bodies were removed and transported to a local morgue where they were autopsied. The DEA was then advised of the discovery of the bodies and their subsequent removal to another morgue in Guadalajara, where a second autopsy was performed.

On March 7, 1985, the FBI dispatched a forensic team to Guadalajara. They immediately proceeded to the morgue to identify the bodies and to process any evidence which might be present. After much bureaucratic delay from the local officials, they were finally allowed to proceed. The bodies were identified only

as cadavers number 1 and number 2. It was apparent that each body had been autopsied and that both were in an advanced state of decomposition. Cadaver number 1 was quickly identified by the fingerprint expert as that of SA Camarena. Mexican officials would not allow the second body to be identified at this time; however, it was later identified through dental records as Captain Zavala.

The FBI forensic team requested permission to process the clothing, cordage, and burial sheet found with the bodies but the request was denied. However, they were allowed to cut small, "known" samples from these items and obtain hair samples from both bodies. Soil samples were also removed from the bodies and the clothing items.

A forensic pathologist from the Armed Forces Institute of Pathology was allowed to examine the body of SA Camarena. He concluded that SA Camarena's death was caused by blunt-force injuries. In addition, SA Camarena had a hole in his skull caused by a rod-like instrument. SA Camarena's body was then released to the American officials and immediately flown to the United States.

The next day, both FBI and DEA personnel proceeded to the Bravo ranch where the bodies were initially found. Because this site had been a completely uncontrolled crime scene, contaminated by both police personnel and onlookers, only a limited crime-scene search was conducted. It was immediately noted that there was no grave site in the area and that the color of the soil where the bodies had been deposited differed from the soil that had been removed from the bodies. Therefore, "known" soil samples from the drop site were taken to compare with soil removed from the victims. It was also noted that there were no significant body fluids at the "burial" site. This led the forensic team to conclude that the bodies had been buried elsewhere, exhumed, and transported to this site.

The MFJP officials were later confronted with the evidence that the bodies had been relocated to the Michoacan area. This was one of the factors which led to a new, unilateral MFJP investigation. As a result, several suspects, including State Judicial Police Officers, were arrested and interrogated concerning the kidnapping of SA Camarena. Primer Comandante Pavon-Reyes was fired, and arrest warrants were issued for a number of international drug traffickers, including Rafael Caro-Quintero and Ernesto Fonseca.

In late March 1985, DEA agents located a black Mercury Gran Marquis which they believed was used in the kidnapping or transportation of SA Camarena. The vehicle had been stored in a garage in Guadalajara, and a brick wall had been constructed at the entrance to conceal it. The vehicle was traced to a Ford dealership owned by Caro-Quintero. Under the watchful eye of the MFJP at the Guadalajara Airport, the FBI forensic team processed the vehicle for any hair, fiber, blood, and/or fingerprint evidence it might contain.

During April 1985, the MFJP informed the DEA that they believed they had located the residence where SA Camarena and Captain Zavala had been held. The FBI forensic team was immediately dispatched to Guadalajara; however, they were not allowed to proceed to the residence, located at 881 Lope De Vega, until an MFJP forensic team had processed the residence and had removed all of the obvious evidence. The DEA was also informed that since the abduction of SA Camarena, all of the interior walls had been painted, the entire residence had recently been cleaned, and that a group of MFJP officers were presently occupying, and thereby contaminating, the residence.

On the first day after the arrival of the FBI forensic team, they surveyed and began a crime scene search of the residence and surrounding grounds. The residence consists of a large, two-story structure with a swimming pool, covered patio, aviary, and tennis court surrounded by a common wall. The most logical place to hold a prisoner at this location would be in the small outbuilding located to the rear of the main residence. This outbuilding, designated as the "guest house," consisted of a small room, carpeted by a beige rug, with an adjoining bathroom. The entire room and bathroom were processed for hairs, fibers, and latent fingerprints. The single door into this room was made of steel and reinforced by iron bars. It was ultimately determined by means of testimony and forensic evidence that several individuals interrogated and tortured SA Camarena in this room. In addition, a locked bedroom, located on the second floor of the main house, was also processed, and the bed linens were removed from a single bed. Known carpet samples were taken from every room in the residence.

A beige VW Atlantic, which fit the general description of the smaller vehicle noted by the person who witnessed SA Camarena's abduction, was parked under a carport at the rear of the residence. The VW Atlantic was also processed for hairs, fibers, and fingerprints.

On the second day, a thorough grounds search was conducted. As FBI forensic team members were walking around the tennis court, they caught a glimpse of something blue in one of the drains. Upon closer inspection, it appeared to be a folded license plate, at the bottom of the drain. However, a heavy iron grate covered the drain and prevented the plate's immediate retrieval.

When one of the FBI agents returned to the main house to ask the MFJP officers for a crowbar, they became extremely curious and followed the agent as he returned, empty handed, to the tennis court. By this time, a second agent had managed to remove the grate by using a heavy-wire coat hanger. The license plate was retrieved, unfolded, and photographed.

The MFJP officers, all of whom were now at the tennis court, became upset at this discovery, and one of them immediately contacted his superior at MFJP headquarters, who ordered them to secure the license plate until the Assistant Primer Comandante arrived on the scene. After his arrival approximately 20 minutes later, he seized the license plate and would not allow the Americans to conduct any further searches.

However, by this time, five very large plastic bags of evidence had been recovered and were placed in the rear of a DEA truck. The evidence was quickly transported to the DEA vault in the U.S. Consulate.

After negotiations between the United States and Mexico, the MFJP did allow a second, final search of the residence. On June 24, 1985, a forensic team returned and processed the four remaining rooms on the first floor of the main house.

By this point in the investigation, an associate of Rafael Caro-Quintero had been arrested and interrogated by the MFJP. He stated that the bodies of two Americans, Albert Radelat and John Walker, who had been abducted and killed by Mexican drug traffickers, were buried on the south side of La Primavera Park, a large, primitive park west of Guadalajara. The bodies of Radelat and Walker were located and recovered. Soil samples taken from the surface of an area near their graves were similar in most respects to the soil recovered earlier from the bodies of SA Camarena and Captain Zavala.

In September 1985, DEA personnel went to La Primavera Park and sampled an area approximately 2 feet below the surface near the same site. This sample matched the soil samples from SA Camarena and Captain Zavala almost grain for grain, indicating that this site was almost certainly their burial site before they were relocated to the Bravo ranch.

Later that fall, after further negotiations between the U.S. and the Mexican

governments, permission was finally granted for an FBI forensic team to process the evidence seized by the MFJP forensic team from 881 Lope De Vega the previous April. The evidence consisted of small samples the MFJP had taken of SA Camarena's burial sheet, a piece of rope used to bind SA Camarena, a portion of a pillowcase removed from bedroom number 3, a piece of unsoiled rope removed from the covered patio, and a laboratory report prepared by the MFJP Crime Laboratory. The remainder of the evidence had been destroyed for "health reasons."

In January 1986, a drug trafficker named Rene Verdugo, who was considered to be a high-ranking member of the Caro-Quintero gang, was apprehended and taken to San Diego, where he was arrested by the DEA. He was then transported to Washington, D.C., where hair samples were taken. He refused to testify before a federal grand jury investigating the Camarena case. Later that year, DEA personnel obtained hair samples in Mexico City from Sergio Espino-Verdin, a former federal comandante, who is believed to have been SA Camarena's primary interrogator during his ordeal at 881 Lope De Vega.

The Trial

In July 1988, the main trial of the murder, interrogation, and abduction of SA Camarena began in U.S. District Court in Los Angeles, CA. The forensic evidence presented in this trial identified 881 Lope De Vega as the site where SA Camarena had been held. [See Figure 1.] The evidence also strongly associated two Mexican citizens, Rene Verdugo and Sergio Espino-Verdin, with the "guest house" at 881 Lope De Vega. Several types of forensic evidence were used to associate SA Camarena with 881 Lope De Vega: forcibly removed head hairs, found in the "guest house" and bedroom number 4, in the VW Atlantic and in the Mercury Gran Marquis, and two types of polyester rug fibers, a dark, rose-colored fiber and a light-colored fiber. [See

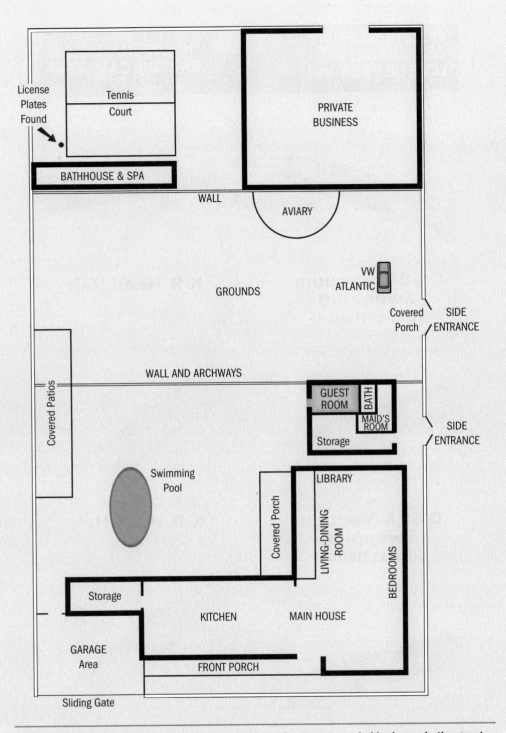

License Plates Found

Tennis Court

PRIVATE BUSINESS

BATHHOUSE & SPA

WALL

AVIARY

VW ATLANTIC

GROUNDS

Covered Porch

SIDE ENTRANCE

WALL AND ARCHWAYS

Covered Patios

GUEST ROOM

BATH

MAID'S ROOM

Storage

SIDE ENTRANCE

Swimming Pool

LIBRARY

Covered Porch

LIVING-DINING ROOM

BEDROOMS

Storage

KITCHEN

MAIN HOUSE

GARAGE Area

FRONT PORCH

Sliding Gate

Figure 1   Diagram of the 881 Lope De Vega grounds. Camarena was held prisoner in the guest house.

Figures 2 and 3.] Fabric evidence was also presented, which demonstrated the similarities of color, composition, construction, and design between SA Camarena's burial sheet and the two pillowcases recovered from bedrooms number 3 and 5.

Based on this evidence associating SA Camarena and 881 Lope De Vega, the FBI Laboratory examiner was able to testify that SA Camarena was at this residence, as well as in the VW Atlantic and the Mercury Gran Marquis, and that he had been in a position such that his head hairs

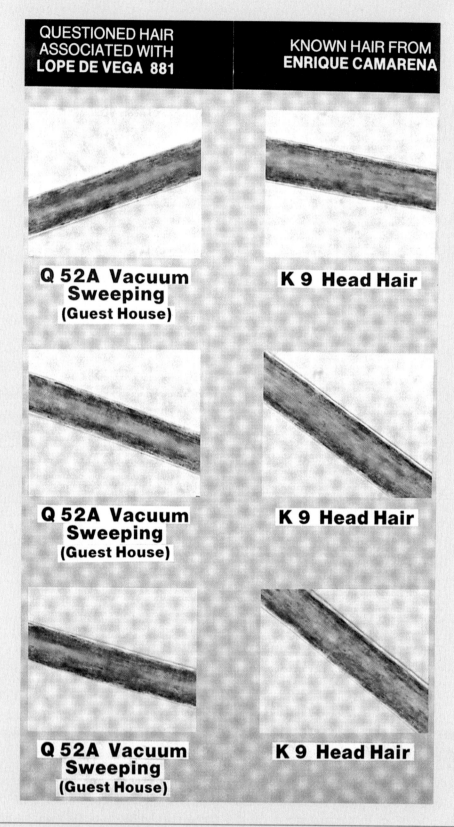

Figure 2 Trial chart showing hair comparisons between known Camarena hairs and hairs recovered from 881 Lope De Vega.

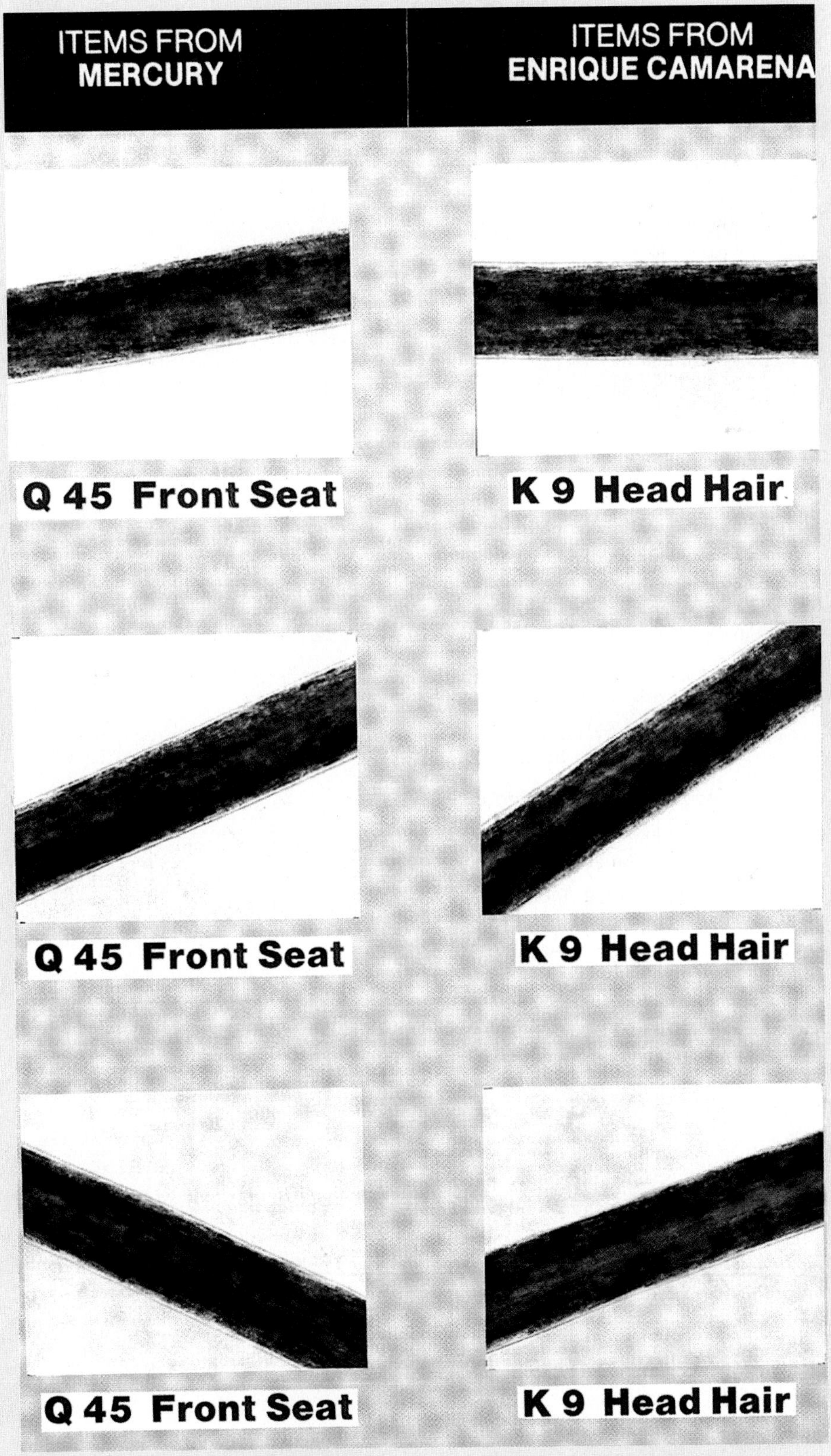

ITEMS FROM MERCURY

ITEMS FROM ENRIQUE CAMARENA

Q 45 Front Seat

K 9 Head Hair

Q 45 Front Seat

K 9 Head Hair

Q 45 Front Seat

K 9 Head Hair

Figure 3 **Trial chart showing hair comparisons between known Camarena hairs and hairs recovered from the Mercury Gran Marquis.**

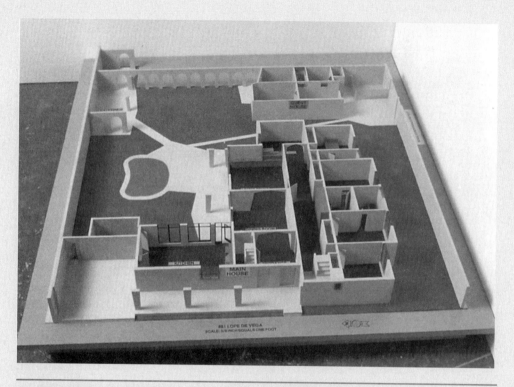

Figure 4   A model of 881 Lope De Vega prepared as a trial exhibit.

were forcibly removed. Captain Alfredo Zavala was also found to be associated with the "guest house" at 881 Lope De Vega. Light-colored nylon rug fibers, found on samples of his clothing taken at the second autopsy, matched the fibers from the "guest house" carpet.

A detailed model of the residence at 881 Lope De Vega was prepared by the Special Projects Section of the FBI Laboratory for the trial. [See Figure 4.] Over 20 trial charts were also prepared to explain the various types of forensic evidence. These charts proved invaluable in clarifying the complicated techniques and characteristics used in the examination of the hair, fiber, fabric, and cordage evidence. [See Figure 5.]

Conclusion

The forensic pitfalls and problems in this case (i.e., destruction of evidence, contamination of crime scenes) were eventually resolved. In some cases, certain routine procedures had to be ignored or unconventional methods employed. However, in many instances, detailed trial testimony overcame the limitations of certain evidence, and eventually, almost all of the evidence introduced at the trial made a tremendous impact on the outcome of this proceeding. After an 8-week trial, conducted under tight security and involving hundreds of witnesses, all of the defendants were found guilty, convicted on all counts, and are currently serving lengthy sentences.

CATEGORIES OF FORENSIC EVIDENCE
IN CAMARENA CASE

	TYPE OF EVIDENCE					
LOCATION	*Hair*	*Carpet Fibers*	*Fabric Match*	*Cordage Match*	*Tape Match*	*Misc.*
Mercury	**Camarena Head Hair**					Blood on Floor Mat
VW Atlantic	**Camarena Head Hair**					Blood on Tissue
Guest House	**Camarena Head Hair**	Zavala Clothes Nylon				
Bedroom #3		Camarena Blindfold Polyester	Pillow Case Camarena Burial Sheet			
Bedroom #4	**Camarena Head Hair**	Camarena Blindfold & Burial Sheet Polyester				
Bedroom #5			Pillow Case Camarena Burial Sheet			
Tennis Court						License Plate VW/Merc.
Camarena Burial Sheet	**Camarena Head Hair**	Bedroom #4 Polyester	Pillow Case Bedrooms #3 and #5			Soil La Primavera
Source — Blindfold/ Rope	**Camarena Head Hair**	Bedrooms #3 and #4 Polyester			Camarena Blindfold Tape	
Camarena Burial Cordage				Burial Rope from Covered Patio		
Zavala Clothing	**Zavala Head Hair**	Guest House Nylon				Soil La Primavera

Figure 5 Trial chart used to show the association of Camarena and Zavala with various locations.

The Green River Killer

This case takes its name from the Green River, which flows through Washington State and empties into Puget Sound in Seattle. In 1982, within six months the bodies of five females were discovered in or near the river. The majority of the victims were known prostitutes who were strangled and apparently raped. As police focused their attention on an area known as Sea-Tac Strip, a haven for prostitutes, girls mysteriously disappeared with increasing frequency. By the end of 1986, the body count in the Seattle region rose to forty, all of whom were believed to have been murdered by the Green River Killer. As the investigation pressed on into 1987, the police renewed their interest in one suspect, Gary Ridgway, a local truck painter. Ridgway had been known to frequent the Sea-Tac Strip. Interestingly, in 1984 Ridgway had actually passed a lie detector test. Now with a search warrant in hand, police searched the Ridgway residence and also obtained hair and saliva samples from Ridgway. Again, insufficient evidence caused Ridgway to be released from custody. With the exception of one killing in 1998, the murder spree stopped in 1990, and the case remained dormant for nearly ten years. But the advent of DNA testing brought renewed vigor to the investigation. In 2001, semen samples collected from three early victims of the Green River Killer were compared to Ridgway's saliva that had been collected in 1987. The DNA profiles matched and the police had their man. An added forensic link to Ridgway was made by the location of minute amounts of spray paint on the clothing of six victims that compared to paints collected from Ridgway's workplace. Ridgway avoided the death penalty by confessing to the murders of forty-eight women.

chapter 3

Physical Evidence

Key Terms

class characteristics

comparison

identification

individual characteristics

product rule

reconstruction

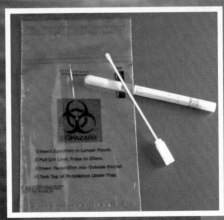

Learning Objectives

After studying this chapter you should be able to:

- Review the common types of physical evidence encountered at crime scenes

- Explain the difference between the identification and comparison of physical evidence

- Define and contrast individual and class characteristics of physical evidence

- Appreciate the value of class evidence as it relates to a criminal investigation

- List and explain the function of national databases available to forensic scientists

- Explain the purpose physical evidence plays in reconstructing the events surrounding the commission of a crime

It would be impossible to list all the objects that could conceivably be of importance to a crime; every crime scene obviously has to be treated on an individual basis, having its own peculiar history, circumstances, and problems. It is practical, however, to list items whose scientific examination is likely to yield significant results in ascertaining the nature and circumstances of a crime. The investigator who is thoroughly familiar with the recognition, collection, and analysis of these items, as well as with laboratory procedures and capabilities, can make logical decisions when the uncommon and unexpected are encountered at the crime scene. Just as important, a qualified evidence collector cannot rely on collection procedures memorized from a pamphlet but must be able to make innovative, on-the-spot decisions at the crime scene.

Common Types of Physical Evidence

1. *Blood, semen, and saliva.* All suspected blood, semen, or saliva—liquid or dried, animal or human—present in a form to suggest a relation to the offense or people involved in a crime. This category includes blood or semen dried onto fabrics or other objects, as well as cigarette butts that may contain saliva residues. These substances are subjected to serological and biochemical analysis to determine identity and possible origin.

2. *Documents.* Any handwriting and typewriting submitted so that authenticity or source can be determined. Related items include paper, ink, indented writings, obliterations, and burned or charred documents.

3. *Drugs.* Any substance seized in violation of laws regulating the sale, manufacture, distribution, and use of drugs.

4. *Explosives.* Any device containing an explosive charge, as well as all objects removed from the scene of an explosion that are suspected to contain the residues of an explosive.

5. *Fibers.* Any natural or synthetic fiber whose transfer may be useful in establishing a relationship between objects and/or people.

6. *Fingerprints.* All prints of this nature, latent and visible.

7. *Firearms and ammunition.* Any firearm, as well as discharged or intact ammunition, suspected of being involved in a criminal offense.

8. *Glass.* Any glass particle or fragment that may have been transferred to a person or object involved in a crime. Windowpanes containing holes made by a bullet or other projectile are included in this category.

9. *Hair.* Any animal or human hair present that could link a person with a crime.

10. *Impressions.* Tire markings, shoe prints, depressions in soft soils, and all other forms of tracks. Glove and other fabric impressions, as well as bite marks in skin or foodstuffs, are also included.

11. *Organs and physiological fluids.* Body organs and fluids are submitted for toxicology to detect possible existence of drugs and poisons. This category includes blood to be analyzed for the presence of alcohol and other drugs.

12. *Paint.* Any paint, liquid or dried, that may have been transferred from the surface of one object to another during the commission of a crime. A common example is the transfer of paint from one vehicle to another during an automobile collision.

13. *Petroleum products.* Any petroleum product removed from a suspect or recovered from a crime scene. The most common examples are gasoline residues removed from the scene of an arson, or grease and oil stains whose presence may suggest involvement in a crime.

14. *Plastic bags.* A disposable polyethylene bag such as a garbage bag may be evidential in a homicide or drug case. Examinations are conducted to associate a bag with a similar bag in the possession of a suspect.

15. *Plastic, rubber, and other polymers.* Remnants of these manufactured materials recovered at crime scenes may be linked to objects recovered in the possession of a suspect perpetrator.

16. *Powder residues.* Any item suspected of containing firearm discharge residues.

17. *Serial numbers.* This category includes all stolen property submitted to the laboratory for the restoration of erased identification numbers.

18. *Soil and minerals.* All items containing soil or minerals that could link a person or object to a particular location. Common examples are soil imbedded in shoes and safe insulation found on garments.

19. *Tool marks.* This category includes any object suspected of containing the impression of another object that served as a tool in a crime. For example, a screwdriver or crowbar could produce tool marks by being impressed into or scraped along a surface of a wall.

20. *Vehicle lights.* Examination of vehicle headlights and taillights is normally conducted to determine whether a light was on or off at the time of impact.

21. *Wood and other vegetative matter.* Any fragments of wood, sawdust, shavings, or vegetative matter discovered on clothing, shoes, or tools that could link a person or object to a crime location.

The Significance of Physical Evidence

The examination of physical evidence by a forensic scientist is usually undertaken for identification or comparison.

Identification

Identification has as its purpose the determination of the physical or chemical identity of a substance with as near absolute certainty as existing analytical techniques will permit. For example, the crime laboratory is frequently asked to identify the chemical composition of an illicit-drug preparation that may contain heroin, cocaine, barbiturates, and so on. It may be asked to identify gasoline in residues recovered from the debris of a fire, or it may have to identify the nature of explosive residues—for example, dynamite or TNT. Also, the identification of blood, semen, hair, or wood would, as a matter of routine, include a determination for species origin. For example, did an evidential bloodstain originate from a human as opposed to a dog or cat? Each of these requests requires the analysis and ultimate identification of a specific physical or chemical substance to the exclusion of all other possible substances.

The process of identification first requires the adoption of testing procedures that give characteristic results for specific standard materials. Once these test results have been established, they may be permanently recorded and used repeatedly to prove the identity of suspect materials. For example, to ascertain that a particular suspect powder is heroin, the test results on the powder must be identical to those that have been previously obtained from a known heroin sample. Second, identification requires that the number and type of tests needed to identify a substance be sufficient to exclude all other substances. This means that the examiner must devise a specific analytical scheme that will eliminate all but one substance from consideration. Hence, if the examiner concludes that a white powder contains heroin, the test results must have been comprehensive enough to have excluded all other drugs—or, for that matter, all other substances—from consideration.

Simple rules cannot be devised for defining what constitutes a thorough and foolproof analytical scheme. Each type of evidence obviously requires different tests, and each test has a different degree of specificity. Thus, one substance could conceivably be identified by one test, whereas another may require a combination of five or six different tests to arrive at an identification. In a science in which the practitioner has little or no control over the quality and quantity of the specimens received, a standard series of tests cannot encompass all possible problems and pitfalls. So the forensic scientist must determine at what point the analysis can be concluded and the criteria for positive identification satisfied; for this, he or she must rely on knowledge gained through education and experience. Ultimately, the conclusion will have to be substantiated beyond any reasonable doubt in a court of law.

Comparison

A comparison analysis subjects a suspect specimen and a standard/reference specimen to the same tests and examinations for the ultimate purpose of determining whether they have a common origin. For example, the forensic scientist may place a suspect at a particular location by noting the similarities of a hair found at the crime scene to hairs re-

Identification

The process of determining a substance's physical or chemical identity. Drug analysis, species determination, and explosive residue analysis are typical examples of this undertaking in a forensic setting.

Comparison

The process of ascertaining whether two or more objects have a common origin.

moved from a suspect's head. Or a paint chip found on a hit-and-run victim's garment may be compared with paint removed from a vehicle suspected of being involved in the incident. The forensic comparison is actually a two-step procedure. First, combinations of select properties are chosen from the suspect and the standard/reference specimen for comparison. The question of which and how many properties are selected obviously depends on the type of materials being examined. (This subject will receive a good deal of discussion in forthcoming chapters.) The overriding consideration must be the ultimate evidential value of the conclusion. This brings us to the second objective. Once the examination has been completed, the forensic scientist must draw a conclusion about the origins of the specimens. Do they or do they not come from the same source? Certainly if one or more of the properties selected for comparison do not agree, the analyst will not hesitate to conclude that the specimens are not the same and hence could not have originated from the same source. Suppose, on the other hand, that all the properties do compare and the specimens, as far as the examiner can determine, are indistinguishable. Does it logically follow that they come from the same source? Not necessarily so.

To comprehend the evidential value of a comparison, one must appreciate the role that probability has in ascertaining the origins of two or more specimens. Simply defined, *probability* is the frequency of occurrence of an event. If a coin is flipped one hundred times, in theory we can expect heads to come up fifty times. Hence, the probability of the event (heads) occurring is 50 in 100. In other words, probability defines the odds at which a certain event will occur.

Individual Characteristics.   Evidence that can be associated with a common source with an extremely high degree of probability is said to possess individual characteristics. Examples of this are the ridge characteristics of fingerprints, random striation markings on bullets or tool marks, irregular and random wear patterns in tire or footwear impressions, handwriting characteristics, irregular edges of broken objects that can be fitted together like a jigsaw puzzle (see Figure 3–1), or sequentially made plastic bags that can be matched by striation marks running across the bags (see Figure 3–2). In all of these cases, it is not possible to state with mathematical exactness the probability that specimens are of common origin; it can only be concluded that this probability is so high as to defy mathematical calculations or human comprehension. Furthermore, the conclusion of common origin must be substantiated by the practical experience of the examiner. For example, the French scientist Victor Balthazard has mathematically determined that the probability of two individuals having the same fingerprints is one out of 1×10^{60}, or 1 followed by sixty zeros. This probability is so small as to exclude the possibility of any two individuals having the same fingerprints. This contention is also supported by the experience of fingerprint examiners who, after classifying millions of prints over the past hundred years, have never found any two to be exactly alike.

Individual Characteristics
Properties of evidence that can be attributed to a common source with an extremely high degree of certainty.

Class Characteristics.   One disappointment awaiting the investigator unfamiliar with the limitations of forensic science is the frequent inability of the laboratory to relate physical evidence to a common origin with a high degree of certainty. Evidence is said to possess class characteristics when it can be associated only with a group and never with a single source. Here again, probability is a determining factor. For example, if we compare two one-layer automobile paint chips of a similar color, their chance of originat-

Class Characteristics
Properties of evidence that can be associated only with a group and never with a single source.

Figure 3–1 The body of a woman was found with evidence of beating about the head and a stablike wound in the neck. Her husband was charged with the murder. The pathologist found a knife blade tip in the wound in the neck. The knife blade tip was compared with the broken blade of a penknife found in the trousers pocket of the accused. Note that in addition to the fit of the indentations on the edges, the scratch marks running across the blade tip correspond in detail to those on the broken blade. *Courtesy Centre of Forensic Sciences, Toronto, Canada*

Figure 3–2 The bound body of a young woman was recovered from a river. Her head was covered with a black polyethylene trash bag (shown on the right). Among the items recovered from one of several suspects was a black polyethylene trash bag (shown on the left). A side-by-side comparison of the two bags' extrusion marks and pigment bands showed them to be consecutively manufactured. This information allowed investigators to focus their attention on one suspect, who ultimately was convicted of the homicide. *Courtesy George W. Neighbor, New Jersey State Police*

ing from the same car is not nearly as great as when we compare two paint chips having seven similar layers of paint, not all of which were part of the car's original color. The former will have class characteristics and could only be associated at best with one car model (which may number in the thousands), whereas the latter may be judged to have individual characteristics and to have a high probability of originating from one specific car.

Blood offers another good example of evidence that can have class characteristics. For example, suppose that two blood specimens are compared and both are found to be of human origin, type A. The frequency of occurrence in the population of type A blood is 26 percent—hardly offering a basis for establishing the common origin of the stains. However, if other blood factors are also determined and are found to compare, the probability that the two blood samples originated from a common source increases. Thus, if one uses a series of blood factors that occur independently of each other, one can apply the product rule to calculate the overall frequency of occurrence of the blood in a population.

Product Rule
Multiplying together the frequencies of independently occurring genetic markers to obtain an overall frequency of occurrence for a genetic profile.

For example, in the O. J. Simpson case, a bloodstain located at the crime scene was found to contain a number of factors that compared to O. J.'s blood:

Blood Factors	Frequency
A	26%
EsD	85%
PGM 2+2−	2%

The product of all the frequencies shown in the table determines the probability that any one individual possesses such a combination of blood factors. In this instance, applying the product rule, $0.25 \times 0.85 \times 0.02$ equals 0.0044. or 0.44 percent, or 1 in 200 people who would be expected to have this particular combination of blood factors. These bloodstain factors did not match either of the two victims, Nicole Brown Simpson or Ronald Goldman, thus eliminating them as possible sources of the blood. Although the forensic scientist has still not individualized the bloodstains to one person—in this case, O. J. Simpson—data have been provided that will permit investigators and the courts to better assess the evidential value of the crime-scene stain. As we will learn in Chapter 13, the product rule is used to determine the frequency of occurrence of DNA profiles typically determined from blood and other biological materials. Importantly, modern DNA technology provides enough factors to allow an analyst to individualize blood, semen, and other biological materials to a single person.

One of the current weaknesses of forensic science is the inability of the examiner to assign exact or even approximate probability values to the comparison of most class physical evidence. For example, what is the probability that a nylon fiber originated from a particular sweater, or that a hair came from a particular person's head, or that a paint chip came from a car suspected to have been involved in a hit-and-run accident? Very few statistical data are available from which to derive this information, and in a society that is increasingly dependent on mass-produced products, the gathering of such data is becoming an increasingly elusive goal. One of the primary endeavors of forensic scientists must be to create and update statistical databases for evaluating the significance of class physical evidence. Of course, when such information—for example, the population frequency of blood factors—is available, it is used; but for the most part, the forensic scientist must rely on personal experience when called on to interpret the significance of class physical evidence.

People who are unfamiliar with the realities of modern criminalistics are often disappointed to learn that most items of physical evidence retrieved at crime scenes cannot be linked definitively to a single person or object. Although investigators always try to uncover physical evidence with individual characteristics—such as fingerprints, tool marks, and bullets—the chances of finding class physical evidence are far greater. To deny or belittle the value of such evidence is to reject the potential role that criminalistics can play in a criminal investigation. In practice, criminal cases are fashioned for the courtroom around a collection of diverse elements, each pointing to the guilt or involvement of a party in a criminal act. Often, most of the evidence gathered is subjective in nature, prone to human error and bias. The believability of eyewitness accounts, confessions, and informant testimony can all be disputed, maligned, and subjected to severe attack and skepticism in the courtroom. Under these circumstances, errors in human judgment are often magnified to detract from the credibility of the witness.

The value of class physical evidence lies in its ability to corroborate events with data in a manner that is, as nearly as possible, free of human error and bias. It is the thread that binds together other investigative findings that are more dependent on human judgments and, therefore, more prone to human failings. The fact that scientists have not yet learned to individualize many kinds of physical evidence means that criminal investigators should not abdicate or falter in their pursuit of all investigative leads. However, the ability of scientists to achieve a high degree of success in evaluating class physical evidence means that criminal investigators can pursue their work with a much greater chance of success.

Admittedly, in most situations, trying to define the significance of an item of class evidence in exact mathematical terms is a difficult if not impossible goal. While class evidence is by its very nature not unique, our common experience tells us that meaningful items of physical evidence, such as those listed on pages 70–71, are extremely diverse in our environment. Select, for example, a colored fiber from an article of clothing and try to locate the exact same color on the clothing of random individuals you meet, or select a car color and try to match it to other automobiles you see on local streets. Furthermore, keep in mind that a forensic comparison actually goes beyond a mere color comparison and involves examining and comparing a variety of chemical and/or physical properties. The point is that the chances are low of encountering two indistinguishable items of physical evidence at a crime scene that actually originated from different sources. Obviously, given these circumstances, only those objects that exhibit a significant amount of diversity in our environment are deemed appropriate for classification as physical evidence.

In the same way, when one is dealing with more than one type of class evidence, their collective presence may lead to an extremely high certainty that they originated from the same source. As the number of different objects linking an individual to a crime increases, the probability of involvement increases dramatically. A classic example of this situation can be found in the evidence presented at the trial of Wayne Williams (see the case reading at the end of this chapter). Wayne Williams was charged with the murders of two individuals in the Atlanta, Georgia, metropolitan area; he was also linked to the murders of ten other boys or young men. An essential element of the state's case involved the association of Williams with the victims through a variety of fiber evidence. Actually, twenty-eight different types of fibers linked Williams to the murder victims, evidence that the forensic examiner characterized as "overwhelming."

In further evaluating the contribution of physical evidence, one cannot overlook one important reality in the courtroom: The weight or significance accorded physical evidence is a determination left entirely to the trier of fact, usually a jury of laypeople. Given the high esteem in which scientists are generally held by society and the infallible image created for forensic science by books and television, it is not hard to understand why scientifically evaluated evidence often takes on an aura of special reliability and trustworthiness in the courtroom. Often physical evidence, whether individual or class, is accorded great weight during jury deliberations and becomes a primary factor in reinforcing or overcoming lingering doubts about guilt or innocence. In fact, a number of jurists have already cautioned against giving carte blanche approval to admitting scientific testimony without first giving due consideration to its relevancy in a case. Given the potential weight of scientific evidence, failure to take proper safeguards may unfairly prejudice a case against the accused.

Physical evidence may also exclude or exonerate a person from suspicion. For instance, if type A blood is linked to the suspect, all individuals who have type B, AB, or O blood can be eliminated from consideration. Because it is not possible to assess at the crime scene what value, if any, the scientist will find in the evidence collected, or what significance such findings will ultimately have to a jury, it is imperative that a thorough collection and scientific evaluation of physical evidence become a routine part of all criminal investigations.

Just when an item of physical evidence crosses the line that distinguishes class from individual is a difficult question to answer and is often the source of heated debate and honest disagreement among forensic scientists. How many striations are necessary to individualize a mark to a single tool and no other? How many color layers individualize a paint chip to a single car? How many ridge characteristics individualize a fingerprint, and how many handwriting characteristics tie a person to a signature? These questions defy simple answers. The task of the forensic scientist is to find as many characteristics as possible to compare one substance with another. The significance attached to the findings is decided by the quality and composition of the evidence, the case history, and the examiner's experience. Ultimately, the conclusion can range from mere speculation to near certainty.

There are practical limits to the properties and characteristics the forensic scientist can select for comparison. Carried to the extreme, no two things in this world are alike in every detail. Modern analytical techniques have become so sophisticated and sensitive that the criminalist must be careful to define the limits of natural variation among materials when interpreting the data gathered from a comparative analysis. For example, we will learn in the next chapter that two properties, density and refractive index, are best suited for comparing two pieces of glass. But the latest techniques that have been developed to measure these properties are so sensitive that they can even distinguish glass originating from a single pane of glass. Certainly this goes beyond the desires of a criminalist trying to determine only whether two glass particles originated from the same window. Similarly, if the surface of a paint chip is magnified 1,600 times with a powerful scanning electron microscope, it is apparent that the fine details that are revealed could not be duplicated in any other paint chip. Under these circumstances, no two paint chips, even those coming from the same surface, could ever compare in the true sense of the word. Therefore, practicality dictates that such examinations be conducted at a less revealing, but more meaningful, magnification (see Figure 3–3).

Distinguishing evidential variations from natural variations is not always an easy task. Learning how to use the microscope and all the other modern instruments in a crime laboratory properly is one thing; gaining the

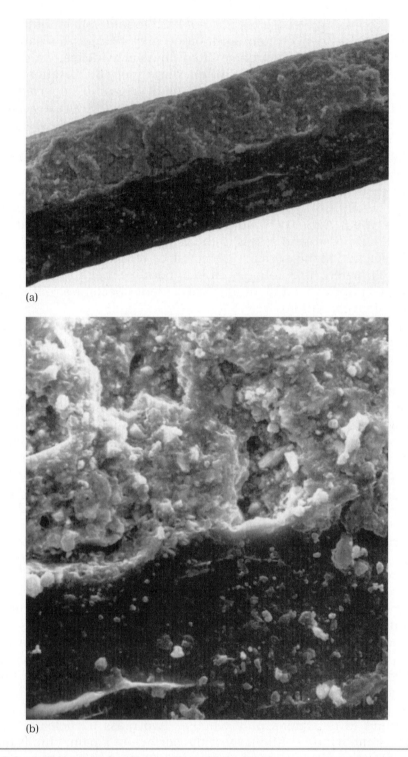

(a)

(b)

Figure 3–3 **(a) Two-layer paint chip magnified 244 times with a scanning electron microscope. (b) The same paint chip viewed at a magnification of 1,600 times.** *Courtesy Jeff Albright*

proficiency needed to interpret the observations and data is another. As new crime laboratories are created and others expand to meet the requirements of the law enforcement community, many individuals are starting new careers in forensic science. They must be cautioned that merely reading relevant textbooks and journals is no substitute for experience in this most practical of sciences.

Forensic Databases

In a criminal investigation, the ultimate contribution a criminalist can make is to link a suspect to a crime through comparative analyses. This comparison defines the unique role of the criminalist in a criminal investigation. Of course, a one-on-one comparison requires a suspect. Little or nothing of evidential value can be accomplished if crime-scene investigators acquire fingerprints, hairs, fibers, paint, blood, and semen without the ability to link these items to a suspect. In this respect, computer technology has dramatically altered the role of the crime laboratory in the investigative process. No longer is the crime laboratory a passive bystander waiting for investigators to uncover clues about who may have committed a crime. Today, the crime laboratory is on the forefront of the investigation seeking to identify perpetrators. This dramatic reversal of the role of forensic science in criminal investigation has come about through the creation of computerized databases that not only link all fifty states, but tie together police agencies throughout the world.

The premier model of all forensic database systems is the *Integrated Automated Fingerprint Identification System* (IAFIS), a national fingerprint and criminal history system maintained by the FBI. IAFIS first became operational in 1999. IAFIS contains fingerprints and access to corresponding criminal history information for nearly 50 million subjects (or 500 million fingerprint images), which are submitted voluntarily to the FBI by state, local, and federal law enforcement agencies. In the United States each state has its own *Automated Fingerprint Identification System* (AFIS), which is linked to the FBI's IAFIS. A crime-scene fingerprint or latent fingerprint is a dramatic find for the criminal investigator. Once the quality of the print has been deemed suitable for the IAFIS search, the latent-print examiner creates a digital image of the print with either a digital camera or a scanner. Next, the examiner, with the aid of a coder, marks points on the print to guide the computerized search. The print is then

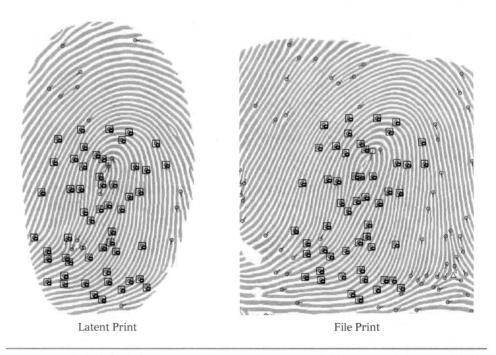

Latent Print   File Print

Figure 3–4 The computerized search of a fingerprint database first requires that selected ridge characteristics be designated by a coder. The positions of these ridge characteristics serve as a basis for comparing the latent print against file fingerprints. *Courtesy Sirchie Finger Print Laboratories, Inc., Youngsville, N.C., www.sirchie.com*

electronically submitted to IAFIS and within minutes the search is completed against all fingerprint images in IAFIS and the examiner may receive a list of potential candidates and their corresponding fingerprints for comparison and verification (see Figure 3–4).

Many countries throughout the world have created *National Automated Fingerprint Identification Systems* that are comparable to the FBI's model. For example, a computerized fingerprint database containing nearly nine million ten-print records connects the Home Office and forty-three police forces throughout England and Wales.

Forensic Brief

In 1975, police found Gerald Wallace's body on his living room couch. He had been savagely beaten, his hands bound with an electric cord. Detectives searched his ransacked house, cataloging every piece of evidence they could find. None of it led to the murderer. They had no witnesses. Sixteen years after the fact, a lone fingerprint, lifted from a cigarette pack found in Wallace's house and kept for sixteen years in the police files, was entered into the Pennsylvania State Police AFIS database. Within minutes, it hit a match. That print, police say, gave investigators the identity of a man who had been at the house the night of the murder. Police talked to him. He led them to other witnesses, who led them to the man police ultimately charged with the murder of Gerald Wallace.

In 1998, the FBI's *Combined DNA Index System* (CODIS) became fully operational. CODIS enables federal, state, and local crime laboratories to electronically exchange and compare DNA profiles, thereby linking crimes to each other and to convicted offenders. All fifty states have enacted legislation to establish a data bank containing DNA profiles of individuals convicted of felony sexual offenses (and other crimes, depending on each state's statute). CODIS creates investigative leads from two indexes: the *forensic* and *offender* indexes. The forensic index currently contains about 110,000 DNA profiles from unsolved crime-scene evidence. Based on a match, police in multiple jurisdictions can identify serial crimes, allowing coordination of investigations and sharing of leads developed independently. The offender index contains the profiles of nearly three million convicted or arrested individuals. (Unfortunately, hundreds of thousands of samples are backlogged, still awaiting DNA analysis and entry into the offender index.) Law enforcement agencies search this index against DNA profiles recovered from biological evidence found at unsolved crime scenes. This approach has proven to be tremendously successful in identifying perpetrators because most crimes involving biological evidence are committed by repeat offenders.

Several countries throughout the world have initiated national DNA data banks. The United Kingdom's *National DNA Database*, established in 1995, was the world's first national database. Currently it holds about three million profiles, and DNA can be taken for entry into the database from anyone arrested for an offense likely to involve a prison term. In a typical month, matches are found linking suspects to 26 murders; 57 rapes and other sexual offenses; and 3,000 motor vehicle, property, and drug crimes.

Forensic Brief

Fort Collins, Colorado, and Philadelphia, Pennsylvania, are separated by nearly 1,800 miles, but in 2001 they were tragically linked though DNA. Troy Graves left the Philadelphia area in 1999, joined the Air Force, and settled down with his wife in Colorado. A frenzied string of eight sexual assaults around the Colorado University campus set off a manhunt that ultimately resulted in the arrest of Graves. However, his DNA profile inextricably identified him as Philadelphia's notorious "Center City rapist." This assailant attacked four women in 1997 and brutally murdered Shannon Schieber, a Wharton School graduate student, in 1998. His last known attack in Philadelphia was the rape of an 18-year-old student in August 1999, shortly before he left the city. In 2002 Graves was returned to Philadelphia, where he was sentenced to life in prison without parole.

The *National Integrated Ballistics Information Network* (NIBIN), maintained by the Bureau of Alcohol, Tobacco, Firearms and Explosives, allows firearms analysts to acquire, digitize, and compare markings made by a firearm on bullets and cartridge casings recovered from crime scenes. The NIBIN program currently has 236 sites that are electronically joined to sixteen multistate regions. The heart of NIBIN is the *Integrated Ballistic Identification System* (IBIS), comprising a microscope and a computer unit that can capture an image of a bullet or cartridge casing. The images are then forwarded to a regional server, where they are stored and correlated against other images in the regional database. IBIS does not positively match bullets or casings fired from the same weapon; this must be done by a firearms examiner. IBIS does, however, facilitate the work of the firearms examiner by producing a short list of candidates for the examiner to manually compare. Nearly 900,000 pieces of crime scene evidence have been entered in NIBIN and more than 10,000 "hits" have been recorded, many of them yielding investigative information not obtainable by other means.

Forensic Brief

After a series of armed robberies in which suspects fired shots, the sheriff's office of Broward County, Florida, entered the cartridge casings from the crime scenes into NIBIN. Through NIBIN, four of the armed robberies were linked to the same 40-caliber handgun. A short time later, sheriff's deputies noticed suspicious activity around a local business. When they attempted to interview the suspects, the suspects fled in a vehicle. During the chase, the suspects attempted to dispose of a handgun; deputies recovered the gun after making the arrests. The gun was test-fired and the resulting evidence entered into NIBIN, which indicated a possible link between this handgun and the four previous armed robberies. Firearms examiners confirmed the link through examination of the original evidence. The suspects were arrested and charged with four prior armed robbery offenses.

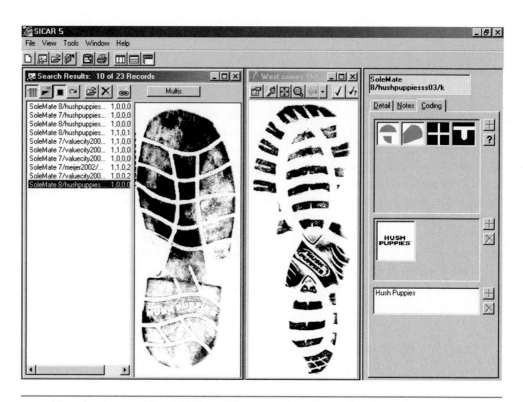

Figure 3–5 **The crime-scene footwear print on the right is being searched against eight thousand sole patterns to determine its make and model.** *Courtesy Foster & Freeman Limited, Worcestershire, U.K., www.fosterfreeman.co.uk*

The *International Forensic Automotive Paint Data Query* (PDQ) database contains chemical and color information pertaining to original automotive paints. This database, developed and maintained by the Forensic Laboratory Services of the Royal Canadian Mounted Police (RCMP), contains information about make, model, year, and assembly plant on more than 13,000 vehicles with a library of more than 50,000 layers of paint. Contributors to the PDQ include the RCMP and forensic laboratories in Ontario and Quebec, as well as forty U.S. forensic laboratories and police agencies in twenty-one other countries. Accredited users of PDQ are required to submit sixty new automotive paint samples per year for addition to the database. The PDQ database has found it's greatest utility in the investigation of hit-and-runs by providing police with possible make, model, and year information to aid in the search for the unknown vehicle.

The previously described databases are maintained and controlled by government agencies. There is one exception: a commercially available computer retrieval system for comparing and identifying crime-scene shoe prints known as *SICAR* (shoeprint image capture and retrieval).[1] SICAR's pattern-coding system enables an analyst to create a simple description of a shoe print by assigning codes to individual pattern features (see Figure 3–5). Shoe print images can be entered into SICAR by either a scanner or a digital camera. This product has a comprehensive shoe sole database that includes more than three hundred manufacturers of shoes with more than eight thousand different sole patterns, providing investigators with a means for linking a crime-scene footwear impression to a particular shoe manufacturer.

---

[1] Foster & Freeman Limited, *http://www.fosterfreeman.co.uk*.

Crime Scene Reconstruction

Previous discussions of identification and comparison have stressed laboratory work routinely performed by forensic scientists. However, there is another dimension to the role of forensic scientists in a criminal investigation: working as a team to reconstruct events before, during, and after the commission of a crime. Reconstructing the circumstances of a crime scene entails a collaborative effort that includes experienced law enforcement personnel, medical examiners, and criminalists. All of the professionals contribute a unique perspective to develop the crime-scene reconstruction. Was more than one person involved? How was the victim killed? Were actions taken to cover up what actually took place? To answer these questions, everyone involved with the investigation must pay careful attention and apply logical thinking.

The physical evidence left behind at a crime scene plays a crucial role in reconstructing the events that took place surrounding the crime. Although the evidence alone does not describe everything that happened, it can support or contradict accounts given by witnesses and/or suspects. Information obtained from physical evidence can also generate leads and confirm the reconstruction of a crime to a jury. The collection and documentation of physical evidence is the foundation of a reconstruction. **Reconstruction supports a likely sequence of events by observing and evaluating physical evidence and statements made by witnesses and those involved with the incident.**

Law enforcement personnel must take the proper actions to enhance all aspects of the crime-scene search so as to optimize the crime-scene reconstruction. First, and most important, is securing and protecting the crime scene. Protecting the scene is a continuous endeavor from the beginning to the end of the search. Evidence that can be invaluable to reconstructing the crime can be unknowingly altered or destroyed by people trampling through the scene, rendering the evidence useless. The issue of possible contamination of evidence will certainly be attacked during the litigation process and could make the difference between a guilty and not-guilty verdict.

Before processing the crime scene for physical evidence, the investigator should make a preliminary examination of the scene as it was left by the perpetrator. Each crime scene presents its own set of circumstances. The investigator's experience and the presence or absence of physical evidence become critical factors in reconstructing a crime. The investigator captures the nature of the scene as a whole by performing an initial walk-through of the crime scene and contemplating the events that took place. Using the physical evidence available to the naked eye, he or she can hypothesize about what occurred, where it occurred, and when it occurred. During the walk-through, the investigator's task is to document observations and formulate how the scene should ultimately be processed. As the collection of physical evidence begins, any and all observations should be recorded through photographs, sketches, and notes. By carefully collecting physical evidence and thoroughly documenting the crime scene, the investigator can begin to unravel the sequence of events that took place during the commission of the crime.

Often reconstruction requires the involvement of a medical examiner or a criminalist. The positioning of the victim in a crime scene can often reveal pertinent information for the investigation. Trained medical examiners can examine the victim at a crime scene and determine whether the body has been moved after death by evaluating the livor distribution

Reconstruction
The method used to support a likely sequence of events by observing and evaluating physical evidence and statements made by those involved with the incident.

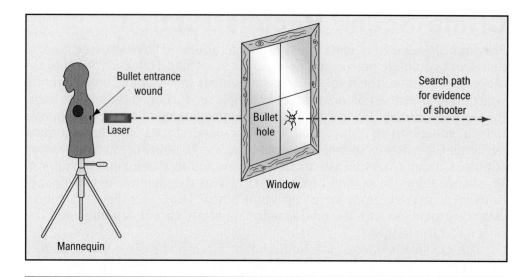

Figure 3–6 A laser beam is used to determine the search area for the position of a shooter who has fired a bullet through a window and wounded a victim. The bullet path is determined by lining up the victim's bullet wound with the bullet hole present in the glass pane.

within the body (see p. 21). For example, if livor has developed in areas other than those closest to the ground, the medical examiner can reason that the victim was probably moved after death. Likewise, the examiner can determine whether the victim was clothed subsequent to death, because livor will not develop in areas of the body that are restricted by clothing. A criminalist or trained crime-scene investigator can also bring special skills to the reconstruction of events that occurred during the commission of a crime. For example, a criminalist using a laser beam to plot the approximate bullet path in trajectory analysis can help determine the probable position of the shooter relative to that of the victim (see Figure 3–6). Other skills that a criminalist may employ during a crime-scene reconstruction analysis include blood spatter analysis (see pp. 359–364), determining the direction of impact of projectiles penetrating glass objects (see pp. 116–118), locating gunshot residues deposited on the victim's clothing for the purpose of estimating the distance of a shooter from a target (see pp. 471–474), and searching for primer residues deposited on the hands of a suspect shooter (see pp. 475–478).

Reconstruction is a team effort that involves putting together many different pieces of a puzzle (see Figure 3–7). The right connections must be made among all the parts involved so as to portray the relationship among the victim, the suspect, and the crime scene. If successful, reconstruction can play a vital role in helping a jury arrive at an appropriate verdict.

Chapter Summary

The examination of physical evidence by a forensic scientist is usually undertaken for identification or comparison purposes. The object of identification is to determine the physical or chemical identity with as near absolute certainty as existing analytical techniques will permit. Identification first requires the adoption of testing procedures that give characteristic results for specific standard materials. Once this is done, the examiner uses an appropriate number of tests to identify a substance and exclude all

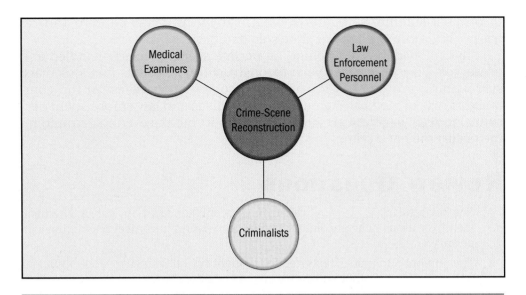

Figure 3–7 Crime-scene reconstruction relies on the combined efforts of medical examiners, criminalists, and law enforcement personnel to recover physical evidence and to sort out the events surrounding the occurrence of a crime.

other substances from consideration. The identification process is normally used in crime laboratories to identify drugs, explosives, and petroleum products. Also, the identification of evidence such as blood, semen, or hair is routinely undertaken in a crime laboratory. Normally, these identifications would include a determination for species origin (such as human blood or rabbit hair).

A comparative analysis has the important role of determining whether a suspect specimen and a standard/reference specimen have a common origin. Both the standard/reference and the suspect specimen are subject to the same tests. Evidence that can be associated with a common source with an extremely high degree of probability is said to possess individual characteristics. Evidence associated only with a group is said to have class characteristics. Nevertheless, the high diversity of class evidence in our environment makes their comparison significant in the context of a criminal investigation. As the number of different objects linking an individual to a crime scene increases, so does the likelihood of that individual's involvement with the crime. Importantly, a person may be exonerated or excluded from suspicion if physical evidence collected at a crime scene is found to be different from standard/reference samples collected from that subject.

A dramatic enhancement of the role of forensic science in criminal investigation has come about through the creation of computerized databases. The Integrated Automated Fingerprint Identification System (IAFIS), a national fingerprint and criminal history system, is maintained by the FBI. The FBI's Combined DNA Index System (CODIS) enables federal, state, and local crime laboratories to electronically exchange and compare DNA profiles, thereby linking crimes to each other and to convicted offenders. The National Integrated Ballistics Information Network (NIBIN), maintained by the Bureau of Alcohol, Tobacco, Firearms and Explosives, allows firearms analysts to acquire, digitize, and compare markings made by a firearm on bullets and cartridge casings recovered from crime scenes. The International Forensic Automotive Paint Data Query (PDQ) database contains chemical and color information pertaining to original automotive paints. SICAR (shoeprint image capture and retrieval) has a comprehensive shoe sole database.

Physical evidence left behind at a crime scene, properly handled and preserved, plays a crucial role in reconstructing the events that took place surrounding the crime. Crime-scene reconstruction relies on the combined efforts of medical examiners, criminalists, and law enforcement personnel to recover physical evidence and to sort out the events surrounding the occurrence of a crime.

Review Questions

1. The process of _____ determines a substance's physical or chemical identity with as near absolute certainty as existing analytical techniques will permit.

2. The number and type of tests needed to identify a substance must be sufficient to _____ all other substances from consideration.

3. A(n) _____ analysis subjects a suspect and a standard/reference specimen to the same tests and examination for the ultimate purpose of determining whether they have a common origin.

4. _____ is the frequency of occurrence of an event.

5. Evidence that can be traced to a common source with an extremely high degree of probability is said to possess _____ characteristics.

6. Evidence associated with a group and not to a single source is said to possess _____ characteristics.

7. True or False: One of the major deficiencies of forensic science is the inability of the examiner to assign exact or approximate probability values to the comparison of most class physical evidence. _____

8. The value of class physical evidence lies in its ability to _____ events with data in a manner that is, as nearly as possible, free of human error and bias.

9. The _____ accorded physical evidence during a trial is left entirely to the trier of fact.

10. True or False: Physical evidence cannot be used to exclude or exonerate a person from suspicion of committing a crime. _____

11. True or False: The distinction between individual and class evidence is always easy to make. _____

12. Modern analytical techniques have become so sensitive that the forensic examiner must be aware of the _____ among materials when interpreting the significance of comparative data.

13. True or False: A fingerprint can be positively identified through the IAFIS database. _____

14. A database applicable to DNA profiling is _____.

15. True or False: A crime can accurately be reconstructed solely on the presence or absence of physical evidence. _____

Further References

Houck, M. M., and J. A. Siegel. *Fundamentals of Forensic Science.* Burlington, MA: Elsevier Academic Press, 2006.

Kirk, Paul L., in John I. Thornton, ed., *Crime Investigation,* 2nd ed. New York: Wiley, 1974.

Osterburg, James W., "The Evaluation of Physical Evidence in Criminalistics: Subjective or Objective Process?" *Journal of Criminal Law, Criminology and Police Science* 60 (1969): 97.

Case Study
Fiber Evidence and the Wayne Williams Trial

On February 26, 1982, a Fulton County, Ga., Superior Court jury returned a verdict of "guilty as charged" on two counts of murder brought against Wayne Bertram Williams by a Fulton County grand jury in July 1981. Williams had been on trial since December 28, 1981, for the asphyxial murders of Nathaniel Cater and Jimmy Payne in April and May of 1981. During the 8-week trial, evidence linking Williams to those murders and to the murders of 10 other boys or young men was introduced.

An essential part of this case, presented by the Fulton County District Attorney's Office, involved the association of fibrous debris removed from the bodies of 12 murder victims with objects from the everyday environment of Williams.

Fiber evidence has often been an important part of criminal cases, but the Williams trial differed from other cases in several respects. Fiber evidence has not played a significant role in any case involving a large number of murder victims. The victims whose deaths were charged to Williams were 2 of 30 black children and black young men who were reported missing or who had died under suspicious circumstances in the Atlanta area over a 22-month period beginning in July 1979. During the trial, fiber evidence was used to associate Williams with 12 of those victims.

Fiber evidence is often used to corroborate other evidence in a case—it is used to support other testimony presented at a trial. This was not the situation in the Williams trial. Other evidence and other aspects of the trial were important but

were used to support and complement the fiber evidence, not the usual order of things. The "hair and fiber matches" between Williams's environment and 11 of the 12 murder victims discussed at the trial were so significant that, in the author's opinion, these victims were positively linked to both the residence and automobiles that were a major part of the world of Wayne Williams.

Another difference between this case and most other cases was the extremely large amount of publicity surrounding both the investigation of the missing and murdered children and the arrest and subsequent trial of Williams. Few other murder trials have received the attention that the Williams case received. . . .

It is often difficult to get an accurate picture from press reports of the physical evidence introduced at a trial and the significance of that evidence. This article will also set forth in some detail the fiber evidence that linked Williams to the murder victims.

By discussing only the fiber evidence introduced at the trial, many other aspects of the case against Williams are being neglected. Additional evidence dealing with Williams's motivations—his character and behavior, his association with several of the victims by eyewitness accounts, and his link to a victim recovered from a river in Atlanta—[were] also essential to the case. . . .

Development of Williams as a Murder Suspect

Before Wayne Williams became a suspect in the Nathaniel Cater murder case, the Georgia State Crime Laboratory located a number of yellowish-green nylon fibers and some violet acetate fibers on the bodies and clothing of the murder victims whose

Harold A. Deadman
Special Agent, Microscopic Analysis Unit, Laboratory Division Federal Bureau of Investigation, Washington, D.C.
Reprinted in part from *FBI Law Enforcement Bulletin,* March and May 1984.

Reprinted in part from FBI Law Enforcement Bulletin, March and May 1984.

Wayne Williams is shown talking to police outside his home. *Courtesy Corbis Bettmann*

bodies had been recovered during the period of July 1979 to May 1981. The names of those victims were included on the list of missing and murdered children that was compiled by the Atlanta Task Force (a large group of investigators from law enforcement agencies in the Atlanta area). The yellowish-green nylon fibers were generally similar to each other in appearance and properties and were considered to have originated from a single source. This was also true of the violet acetate fibers. Although there were many other similarities that would link these murders together, the fiber linkage was notable since the possibility existed that a source of these fibers might be located in the future.

Initially, the major concern with these yellowish-green nylon fibers was determining what type of object could have been their source. This information could provide avenues of investigative activity. The fibers were very coarse and had a lobed cross-sectional appearance, tending to indicate that they originated from a carpet or a rug. The lobed cross-

sectional shape of these fibers, however, was unique, and initially, the manufacturer of these fibers could not be determined. Photomicrographs of the fibers were prepared for display to contacts within the textile industry. On one occasion, these photomicrographs were distributed among several chemists attending a meeting at the research facilities of a large fiber producer. The chemists concurred that the yellowish-green nylon fiber was very unusual in cross-sectional shape and was consistent with being a carpet fiber, but again, the manufacturer of this fiber could not be determined. Contacts with other textile producers and textile chemists likewise did not result in an identification of the manufacturer.

In February 1981, an Atlanta newspaper article publicized that several different fiber types had been found on two murder victims. Following the publication of this article, bodies recovered from rivers in the Atlanta metropolitan area were either nude or clothed only in undershorts. It appeared possible that the victims were being disposed of in this undressed state and in rivers in order to eliminate fibers from being found on their bodies.[2]

On May 22, 1981, a four-man surveillance team of personnel from the Atlanta Police Department and the Atlanta Office of the FBI was situated under and at both ends of the James Jackson Parkway Bridge over the Chattahoochee River in northwest Atlanta. Around 2 a.m., a loud splash alerted the surveillance team to the presence of an automobile being driven slowly off the bridge. The driver was stopped and identified as Wayne Bertram Williams.

Two days after Williams's presence on the bridge, the nude body of Nathaniel Cater was pulled from the Chattahoochee River, approximately 1 mile downstream from the James Jackson Parkway Bridge. A yellowish-green nylon carpet-type fiber, similar to the nylon fibers discussed above, was recovered from the head hair of Nathaniel Cater. When details of Williams's reason for being on the bridge at 2 a.m. could not be confirmed, search warrants for Williams's home and automobile were obtained and were served on the afternoon of June 3, 1981. During the late evening hours of the same day, the initial associations of fibers from Cater and other murder victims were made with a green carpet in the home of Williams. Associations with a bedspread from Williams's bed and with [Williams's] family dog were also made at that time.

An apparent source of the yellowish-green nylon fibers had been found. It now became important to completely characterize these fibers in order to verify the associations and determine the strength of the associations resulting from the fiber matches. Because of the unusual cross-sectional appearance of the nylon fiber and the difficulty in determining the

manufacturer, it was believed that this was a relatively rare fiber type, and therefore, would not be present in large amounts (or in a large number of carpets).

[Williams's] Carpet

Shortly after Williams was developed as a suspect, it was determined the yellowish-green nylon fibers were manufactured by the Wellman Corporation. The next step was to ascertain, if possible, how much carpet like Williams's bedroom carpet had been sold in the Atlanta area—carpet composed of the Wellman fiber and dyed with the same dye formulation as [Williams's] carpet. Names of Wellman Corporation customers who had purchased this fiber type, technical information about the fiber, and data concerning when and how much of this fiber type had been manufactured were obtained.

It was confirmed that the Wellman Corporation had, in fact, manufactured the fiber in Williams's carpet and that no other fiber manufacturer was known to have made a fiber with a similar cross section. It was also determined that fibers having this cross-sectional shape were manufactured and sold during the years 1967 through 1974. Prior to 1967, this company manufactured only a round cross section; after 1974, the unusual trilobal cross section seen in Williams's carpet was modified to a more regular trilobal cross-sectional shape. A list of sales of that fiber type during the period 1967 through 1974 was compiled. . . .

Through numerous contacts with yarn spinners and carpet manufacturers, it was determined that the West Point Pepperell Corporation of Dalton, Ga., had manufactured a line of carpet called "Luxaire," which was constructed in the same manner as [Williams's] carpet. One

---

[2] Prior to the publication of the February 11, 1981, newspaper article, one victim from the task force list, who was fully clothed, had been recovered from a river in the Atlanta area. In the 2½-month period after publication, the nude or nearly nude bodies of 7 of the 9 victims added to the task force list were recovered from rivers in the Atlanta area.

of the colors offered in the "Luxaire" line was called "English Olive," and this color was the same as that of [Williams's] carpet (both visually and by the use of discriminating chemical and instrumental tests).

It was learned that the West Point Pepperell Corporation had manufactured the "Luxaire" line for a five-year period from December 1970 through 1975; however, it had only purchased Wellman 181B fiber for this line during 1970 and 1971. In December 1971, the West Point Pepperell Corporation changed the fiber composition of the "Luxaire" line to a different nylon fiber, one that was dissimilar to the Wellman 181B fiber in appearance. Accordingly, "Luxaire" carpet, like [Williams's] carpet, was only manufactured for a 1-year period. This change of carpet fiber after only 1 year in production was yet another factor that made [Williams's] carpet unusual.

It is interesting to speculate on the course the investigation would have taken if the James Jackson Parkway Bridge had not been covered by the surveillance team. The identification of the manufacturer of the nylon fibers showing up on the bodies could still have occurred and the same list of purchasers of the Wellman fiber could have been obtained. The same contacts with the yarn and carpet manufacturers could have been made; however, there would not have been an actual carpet sample to display. It is believed that eventually the carpet manufacturer could have been determined. With a sample of carpet supplied by West Point Pepperell—which they had retained in their files for over 10 years—it would have been possible to conduct a house-by-house search of the Atlanta area in an attempt to find a similar carpet. Whether this very difficult task would have been attempted, of course, will never be known. A search of that type, however, would have accurately answered an important question that was discussed at the trial—the question of how many other homes in the Atlanta area had a carpet like [Williams's] carpet. An estimation, to be discussed later, based on sales records provided by the West Point Pepperell Corporation indicated that there was a very low chance (1/7792) of finding a carpet like Williams's carpet by randomly selecting occupied residences in the Atlanta area.

Only the West Point Pepperell Corporation was found to have manufactured a carpet exactly like [Williams's] carpet. Even though several manufacturers had gone out of business and could not be located, it was believed that, considering the many variables that exist in the manufacture of carpet and the probable uniqueness of each carpet manufacturer's dye formulations, it would be extremely unlikely for two unrelated companies to construct a carpet or dye the carpet fibers in exactly the same way. A large number of other green fibers, visually similar in color to Williams's carpet, were examined. None was found to be consistent with fibers from [Williams's] carpet.

Probability Determinations

To convey the unusual nature of [Williams's] residential carpet, an attempt was made to develop a numerical probability—something never before done in connection with textile materials used as evidence in a criminal trial.[3] The following information was gathered from the West Point Pepperell Corporation:

1. West Point Pepperell reported purchases of Wellman 181B fiber for the "Luxaire" line during a 1-year period. The Wellman 181B fiber was used to manufacture "Luxaire" carpet from December 1970 until December 1971, at which time a new fiber type replaced that Wellman fiber.

---

[3] J. Mitchell and D. Holland, "An Unusual Case of Identification of Transferred Fibers," *Journal of the Forensic Science Society,* vol. 19, 1979, p. 23. This article describes a case in which carpet fibers transferred to a murder victim's body in England were traced back to the carpet manufacturer and finally to an automobile owned by the person who eventually confessed to the murder.

2. In 1971, West Point Pepperell sold 5,710 square yards of English Olive "Luxaire" and "Dreamer" carpet to Region C (10 southeastern states which include Georgia). "Dreamer" was a line of carpet similar to "Luxaire" but contained a less dense pile. In order to account for the carpet manufactured during 1971, but sold after that time, all of the "Luxaire" English Olive carpet sold during 1972 to Region C (10,687 square yards) was added to the 1971 sales. Therefore, it was estimated that a total of 16,397 square yards of carpet containing the Wellman 181B fiber and dyed English Olive in color was sold by the West Point Pepperell Corporation to retailers in 10 southeastern states during 1971 and 1972. (In 1979, existing residential carpeted floor space in the United States was estimated at 6.7 billion square yards.)[4]

3. By assuming that this carpet was installed in one room, averaging 12 feet by 15 feet in size, per house, and also assuming that the total sales of carpet were divided equally among the 10 southeastern states, then approximately 82 rooms with this carpet could be found in the state of Georgia.

4. Information from the Atlanta Regional Commission showed that there were 638,995 occupied housing units in the Atlanta metropolitan area in November 1981.[5] Using this figure, the chance of randomly selecting an occupied housing unit in metropolitan Atlanta and finding a house with a room having carpet like Williams's carpet was determined to be 1 chance in 7,792—a very low chance.

To the degree that the assumptions used in calculating the above probability number are reasonable, we can be confident in arriving at a valid probability number. . . .

The probability figures illustrate clearly that [Williams's] carpet is, in fact, very uncommon. To enhance the figures even further, it is important to emphasize that these figures are based on the assumption that none of the carpet of concern had been discarded during the past 11 years. In fact, carpet of this type, often used in commercial settings, such as apartment houses, would probably have had a normal life span of only 4 or 5 years. . . .[6]

The Williams Trial

To any experienced forensic fiber examiner, the fiber evidence linking Williams to the murder victims was overwhelming. But regardless of the apparent validity of the fiber findings, it was during the trial that its true weight would be determined. Unless it could be conveyed meaningfully to a jury, its effect would be lost. Because of this, considerable time was spent determining what should be done to convey the full significance of the fiber evidence. Juries are not usually composed of individuals with a scientific background, and therefore, it was necessary to "educate" the jury in what procedures were followed and the significance of the fiber results. In the Williams case, over 40 charts with over 350 photographs were prepared to

---

[4] This information was taken from a study by E. I. du Pont de Nemours & Co. concerned with the existing residential floor space with carpet in the United States. This study was reported in a marketing survey conducted by the Marketing Corporation of America, Westport, Conn.

[5] Information regarding the number of housing units in the Atlanta metropolitan area was obtained from a report provided by the Atlanta Regional Commission. The report, dated November 11, 1981, contained population and housing counts for counties, super districts, and census tracts in the Atlanta metropolitan area.

[6] Information about carpet similar to Williams's carpet was developed through contacts with carpet manufacturers and carpet salesmen in Georgia. It was determined that this type carpet was often installed in commercial settings, such as apartments, and in those settings, had an average life span of 4 to 5 years.

illustrate exactly what the crime laboratory examiners had observed. . . .

Representatives of the textile fiber industry, including technical representatives from the Wellman and West Point Pepperell Corporations, were involved in educating the jury regarding textile fibers in general and helped lay the foundation for the conclusions of the forensic fiber examiners. The jury also was told about fiber analysis in the crime laboratory.

The trial, as it developed, can be divided into two parts. Initially, testimony was given concerning the murders of Nathaniel Cater and Jimmy Ray Payne, the two victims included in the indictment drawn against Williams in July 1981. Testimony was then given concerning Williams's association with 10 other murder victims.

The fiber matches made between fibers in Williams's environment and fibers from victims Payne and Cater were discussed. The items from Williams's environment that were linked to either or both of the victims are shown in the center of the chart. (See Figure 1.) Not only is Payne linked to Williams's environment by seven items and Cater linked by six items, but both of the victims are linked strongly to each other based on the fiber matches and circumstances surrounding their deaths.

In discussing the significance or strength of an association based on textile fibers, it was emphasized that the more uncommon the fibers, the stronger the association. None of the fiber types from the items in Williams's environment shown in the center of Figure 1 is by definition a "common" fiber type. Several of the fiber types would be termed "uncommon."

One of the fibers linking the body of Jimmy Ray Payne to the carpet in the 1970 station wagon driven by Williams was a small rayon fiber fragment recovered from Payne's shorts. Data were obtained from the station wagon's manufacturer concerning which automobile models produced prior to 1973 contained carpet made of this fiber type. These data were coupled with additional information from Georgia concerning the number of these models registered in the Atlanta metropolitan area during 1981. This allowed a calculation to be made relating to the probability of randomly selecting an automobile having carpet like that in the 1970 Chevrolet station wagon from the 2,373,512 cars registered in the Atlanta

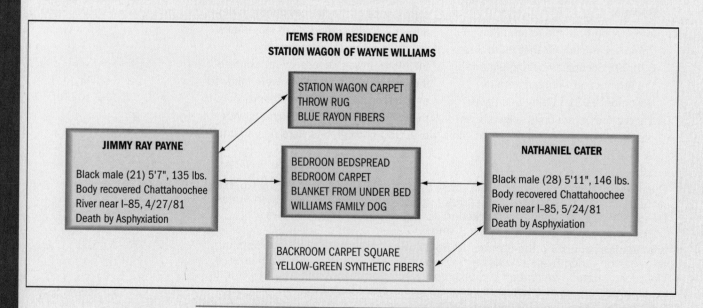

ITEMS FROM RESIDENCE AND STATION WAGON OF WAYNE WILLIAMS

STATION WAGON CARPET
THROW RUG
BLUE RAYON FIBERS

JIMMY RAY PAYNE

Black male (21) 5'7", 135 lbs.
Body recovered Chattahoochee
River near I-85, 4/27/81
Death by Asphyxiation

BEDROON BEDSPREAD
BEDROOM CARPET
BLANKET FROM UNDER BED
WILLIAMS FAMILY DOG

NATHANIEL CATER

Black male (28) 5'11", 146 lbs.
Body recovered Chattahoochee
River near I-85, 5/24/81
Death by Asphyxiation

BACKROOM CARPET SQUARE
YELLOW-GREEN SYNTHETIC FIBERS

Figure 1 **Items from residence and station wagon of Wayne Williams that were found on Jimmy Ray Payne and Nathaniel Cater.**

metropolitan area. This probability is 1 chance in 3,828, a very low probability representing a significant association.

Another factor to consider when assessing the significance of fiber evidence is the increased strength of the association when multiple fiber matches become the basis of the association. This is true if different fiber types from more than one object are found and each fiber type either links two people together or links an individual with a particular environment. As the number of different objects increases, the strength of an association increases dramatically. That is, the chance of randomly finding several particular fiber types in a certain location is much smaller than the chance of finding one particular fiber type.

The following example can be used to illustrate the significance of multiple fiber matches linking two items together. If one were to throw a single die one time, the chance or probability of throwing a particular number would be one chance in six. The probability of throwing a second die and getting that same number also would be one chance in six. However, the probability of getting 2 of the same numbers on 2 dice thrown simultaneously is only 1 in every 36 double throws—a much smaller chance than with either of the single throws. This number is a result of the product rule of probability theory. That is, the probability of the joint occurrence of a number of mutually independent events equals the product of the individual probabilities of each of the events (in this example—$\frac{1}{6} \times \frac{1}{6} = \frac{1}{36}$). Since numerous fiber types are in existence, the chance of finding one particular fiber type, other than a common type, in a specific randomly selected

location is small. The chance then of finding several fiber types together in a specific location is the product of several small probabilities, resulting in an extremely small chance. . . .

However, no attempt was made to use the product rule and multiply the individual probability numbers together to get an approximation of the probability of finding carpets like Williams's residential carpet and Williams's automobile carpet in the same household. The probability numbers were used only to show that the individual fiber types involved in these associations were very uncommon. . . .[7]

In addition to the two probability numbers already discussed (bedroom and station wagon carpets), each of the other fiber types linking Williams to both Cater and Payne has a probability of being found in a particular location. The chance of finding all of the fiber types indicated on the chart [Figure 1] in one location (seven types on Payne's body and six types on Cater's body) would be extremely small. Although an actual probability number for those findings could not be determined, it is believed that the multiple fiber associations shown on this chart are proof that Williams is linked to the bodies of these two victims, even though each fiber match by itself does not show a positive association with Williams's environment.

Studies have been conducted in England that show that transferred fibers are usually lost rapidly as people go about their daily routine.[8] Therefore, the foreign fibers present on a person are most often from recent surroundings. The fibrous debris found on a murder victim reflects the body's more recent surroundings,

---

[7] Joseph L. Peterson, ed., *Forensic Science* (New York: AMS Press, 1975), pp. 181–225. This collection of articles, dealing with various aspects of forensic science, contains five papers concerned with using statistics to interpret the meaning of physical evidence. It is a good discussion of probability theory and reviews cases where probability theory has been used in trial situations.

[8] C. A. Pounds and K. W. Smalldon, "The Transfer of Fibers between Clothing Materials During Simulated Contacts and Their Persistence During Wear," *Journal of the Forensic Science Society,* vol. 15, 1975, pp. 29–37.

especially important if the body was moved after the killing. Accordingly, the victims' bodies in this particular case are not only associated with Williams but are apparently associated with Williams shortly before or after their deaths. It was also pointed out during the trial that the locations of the fibers—on Payne's shorts and in Cater's head hairs and pubic hairs—were not those where one would expect to find fibrous debris transferred from an automobile or a house to victims who had been fully clothed.

Although from these findings it would appear that the victims were in the residence of Williams, there was one other location that contained many of the same fibers as those in the composition of various objects in his residence—Williams's station wagon. The environment of a family automobile might be expected to reflect, to some extent, fibers from objects located within the residence. This was true of the 1970 station wagon. With one exception, all of the fiber types removed from Payne and Cater, consistent with originating from items shown in the center of Figure 1, were present in debris removed by vacuuming the station wagon. The automobile would be the most logical source of the foreign fibers found on both Payne and Cater if they were associated with Williams shortly before or after their deaths. It should also be pointed out that two objects, the bedspread and the blanket, were portable and could have at one time been present inside the station wagon.

Both Payne and Cater were recovered from the Chattahoochee River. Their bodies had been in the water for several days. Some of the fibers found on these victims were like fibers in the compositions of the bedroom carpet and bedspread except for color intensity. They appeared to have been bleached. By subjecting various known fibers to small amounts of Chattahoochee River water for different periods of time, it was found that

bleaching did occur. This was especially true with the carpet and bedspread fibers from Williams's bedroom.

Two crime laboratory examiners testified during the closing stages of the first part of the trial about Williams's association with Payne and Cater. They concluded that it was highly unlikely that any environment other than that present in Wayne Williams's house and car could have resulted in the combination of fibers and hairs found on the victims and that it would be virtually impossible to have matched so many fibers found on Cater and Payne to items in Williams's house and car unless the victims were in contact with or in some way associated with the environment of Wayne Williams.

After testimony was presented concerning the Payne and Cater cases, the Fulton County District Attorney's Office asked the court to be allowed to introduce evidence in the cases of 10 other victims whose murders were similar in many respects. Georgia law allows evidence of another crime to be introduced ". . . if some logical connection can be shown between the two from which it can be said that proof of the one tends to establish the other as relevant to some fact other than general bad character."[9] There need be no conviction for the other crime in order for details about that crime to be admissible.

It was ruled that evidence concerning other murders could be introduced in an attempt to prove a "pattern or scheme" of killing that included the two murders with which Williams was charged. The additional evidence in these cases was to be used to help the jury ". . . decide whether Williams had committed the two murders with which he is charged."[10]

There were similarities between these additional victims and Payne and Cater. (See Figure 2.) Although some differences can also be seen on this chart, the prosecution considered these differences

---

[9] *Encyclopedia of Georgia Law,* vol. 11A (The Harrison Company, 1979), p. 70.

VICTIM'S NAME	DATE VICTIM MISSING	DAYS MISSING	BODY RECOVERY AREA	CAUSE OF DEATH	AGE	WEIGHT	HEIGHT
EVANS	7/25/79	3	WOODED AREA S.W. ATLANTA	PROBABLE ASPHYXIATION/ STRANGULATION	13	87 LBS.	5'4"
MIDDLEBROOKS	5/18/80	1	NEAR STREET S.E. ATLANTA	BLUNT TRAUMA TO HEAD	14	88 LBS.	4'10"
STEPHENS	10/9/80	1	NEAR STREET S.E. ATLANTA	ASPHYXIATION	10	120 LBS.	5'0"
GETER	1/3/81	33	WOODED AREA FULTON COUNTY	MANUAL STRANGULATION	14	130 LBS.	5'4"
PUE	1/22/81	1	NEAR HIGHWAY ROCKDALE CO.	LIGATURE STRANGULATION	15	105 LBS.	5'5"
BALTAZAR	2/6/81	7	NEAR HIGHWAY DEKALB CO.	LIGATURE STRANGULATION	12	125 LBS.	5'4"
BELL	3/2/81	31	SOUTH RIVER DEKALB CO.	ASPHYXIATION	16	100 LBS.	5'2"
ROGERS	3/30/81	10	NEAR STREET N.W. ATLANTA	ASPHYXIATION/ STRANGULATION	20	110 LBS.	5'3"
PORTER	4/10/81	1	NEAR STREET S.W. ATLANTA	STABBING	28	123 LBS.	5'7"
PAYNE	4/22/81	5	CHATTAHOOCHEE RIVER FULTON COUNTY	ASPHYXIATION	21	135 LBS.	5'7"
BARRETT	5/11/81	1	NEAR STREET DEKALB CO.	LIGATURE STRANGULATION (3 PUNCTURE WOUNDS)	17	125 LBS.	5'4"
CATER	5/21/81	3	CHATTAHOOCHEE RIVER FULTON COUNTY	ASPHYXIATION/ STRANGULATION	28	146 LBS.	5'11"

Figure 2   Chart used during the trial to show similarities between Payne and Cater and 10 other murder victims.

to fit within the "pattern of killing" of which Payne and Cater were a part. The most important similarities between these additional victims were the fiber matches that linked 9 of the 10 victims to Williams's environment. The fiber findings discussed during the trial and used to associate Williams to the 12 victims were illustrated during the trial. (See Figure 3.)

The 12 victims were listed in chronological order based on the dates their bodies were recovered. The time period covered by this chart, approximately 22 months, is from July 1979 until May 1981. During that time period, the Williams family had access to a large number of automobiles, including a number of rental cars. Three of these automobiles are listed at the top of Figure 3. If one or more of the cars was in the possession of the Williams family at the time a victim was found to be missing, the space under that car(s) and after the particular victim's name is shaded.

Four objects (including the dog) from Williams's residence are listed horizontally across the top of Figure 3, along with objects from three of his automobiles. An "X" on the chart indicates an apparent transfer of textile fibers from the listed object to a victim. Other objects from Williams's environment which were linked to various victims by an apparent fiber transfer are listed on the right side of the chart. Fiber types from objects (never actually located) that were matched to fiber types from one or more victims are also listed either at the top or on the right side of the chart. Fourteen specific objects

10 *The Atlanta Constitution,* "Williams Jury Told of Other Slayings," Sec. 1-A, 1/26/82, p. 25.

NAME OF VICTIM	VIOLET-GREEN BEDSPREAD WILLIAMS' BEDROOM	GREEN CARPET WILLIAMS' BEDROOM	DOG HAIRS WILLIAMS' DOG	YELLOW BLANKET WILLIAMS' BEDROOM	BLUE RAYON FIBERS, DEBRIS FROM WILLIAMS' HOME	TRUNK LINER 1978 PLYMOUTH	CARPET 1979 FORD	CARPET 1970 CHEVROLET	ADDITIONAL ITEMS FROM WILLIAMS' HOME, AUTOMOBILES OR PERSON
Alfred Evans	X	X	X			X			
Eric Middlebrooks	X		X				X		YELLOW NYLON — FORD TRUNK LINER
Charles Stephens	X	X	X		X				YELLOW NYLON; WHITE POLYESTER / BACKROOM CARPET; FORD TRUNK LINER
Lubie Geter	X	X	X					X	KITCHEN CARPET
Terry Pue	X	X	X						WHITE POLYESTER / BACKROOM CARPET
Patrick Baltazar	X	X	X	X				X	YELLOW NYLON; WHITE POLYESTER; HEAD HAIR / GLOVE; JACKET; PIGMENTED POLYPROPYLENE
Joseph Bell	X				X				
Larry Rogers	X	X	X	X				X	YELLOW NYLON / PORCH BEDSPREAD
John Porter	X	X	X	X	X			X	PORCH BEDSPREAD
Jimmy Payne	X	X	X	X	X			X	BLUE THROW RUG
William Barrett	X	X	X	X	X			X	GLOVE
Nathaniel Cater	X	X	X	X					BACKROOM CARPET; YELLOW-GREEN SYNTHETIC

Figure 3 Fiber findings discussed during the trial and used to associate Williams with the 12 victims.

and five fiber types (probably from five other objects) listed on this chart are linked to one or more of the victims. More than 28 different fiber types, along with the dog hairs, were used to link up to 19 objects from Williams's environment to 1 or more of the victims. Of the more than 28 fiber types from Williams's environment, 14 of these originated from a rug or carpet.

The combination of more than 28 different fiber types would not be considered so significant if they were primarily common fiber types. In fact, there is only 1 light green cotton fiber of the 28 that might be considered common. This cotton fiber was blended with acetate fibers in Williams's bedspread. Light green cotton fibers removed from many victims were not considered or compared unless they were physically intermingled with violet acetate fibers which were consistent with originating from the bedspread. It should be noted that a combination of cotton and acetate fibers blended together in a single textile material, as in the bedspread, is in itself uncommon. . . .

The previous discussion concerning the significance of multiple fiber matches can be applied to the associations made in the cases of all the victims except Bell, but especially to the association of Patrick Baltazar to Williams's environment. Fibers and animal hairs consistent with having originated from 10 sources were removed from Baltazar's body. These 10 sources include the uncommon bedroom carpet and station wagon carpet. In addition to the fiber (and animal hair) linkage, two head hairs of Negroid origin were removed from Baltazar's body that were consistent with originating from the scalp area of Williams.

Head hair matches were also very significant in linking Williams to Baltazar's body. In the opinion of the author, the association based upon the hair and fiber analyses is a positive association.

Another important aspect of the fiber linkage between Williams and these victims is the correspondence between the fiber findings and the time periods during which Williams had access to the three automobiles listed on the chart. Nine victims are linked to automobiles used by the Williams family. When Williams did not have access to a particular car, no fibers were recovered that were consistent with having originated from that automobile. Trunk liner fibers of the type used in the trunks of many late-model Ford Motor Company automobiles were also recovered from the bodies of two victims.

One final point should be made concerning Williams's bedroom and station wagon carpets where probability numbers had been determined. Fibers consistent with having originated from both of these "unusual" carpets were recovered from Payne's body. Of the 9 victims who were killed during the time period when Williams had access to the 1970 station wagon, fibers consistent with having originated from both the station wagon carpet and the bedroom carpet were recovered from 6 of these victims.

The apparent bleaching of several fibers removed from the bodies of Payne and Cater was consistent with having been caused by river water. Several fibers similar to those from Payne and Cater were removed from many of the victims whose bodies were recovered on land. Consistent with the bleaching argument, none of the fibers from the victims found on land showed any apparent bleaching. The finding of many of the same fiber types on the remaining victims, who were recovered from many different locations, refutes the possibility that Payne's and Cater's bodies picked up foreign fibers from the river.

The fact that many of the victims were involved with so many of the same fiber types, all of which linked the victims to Williams's environment, is the basis for arguing conclusively against these fibers originating from a source other than Williams's environment.

It is hoped that this article has provided valuable insight concerning the use of fiber evidence in a criminal trial, has provided answers to questions from those in the law enforcement community about textile fiber evidence in general, and has presented convincing arguments to establish Wayne Williams's association with the bodies of the murder victims.

Murder and the Horse Chestnut Tree

Roger Severs was the son of a wealthy English couple, Eileen and Derek Severs. The elder Serverses were reported missing in 1983. Police investigators were greeted at the Severs home by Roger, who at first explained that his parents had decided to spend some time in London. Suspicion of foul play quickly arose when investigators located traces of blood in the residence. More blood was found in Derek's car and signs of blood spatter were on the garage door. Curiously, a number of green fibers were located throughout the house, as well as in the trunk of Derek's car. A thorough geological examination of soil and vegetation caked onto Severs' car wheel rims seemed to indicate that the car had been in a location at the edge of a wooded area. Closer examination of the debris also revealed the presence of horse chestnut pollen. Horse chestnut is an exceptionally rare tree in the region of the Severs residence. Using land maps, a geologist was able to locate possible areas where horse chestnut pollen might be found. In one of the locations, investigators found a shallow grave that contained the bludgeoned bodies of the elder Severses. Not surprisingly, they were wrapped in a green blanket. A jury rejected Roger's defense of diminished capacity and found him guilty of murder.

chapter 4

Physical Properties: Glass and Soil

Key Terms

amorphous solid

atom

Becke line

birefringence

Celsius scale

chemical property

concentric fracture

crystalline solid

density

density-gradient tube

dispersion

Fahrenheit scale

intensive property

laminated glass

mass

mineral

physical property

radial fracture

refraction

refractive index

tempered glass

weight

Learning Objectives

After studying this chapter you should be able to:

- Define and distinguish the physical and chemical properties of matter

- Understand how to use the basic units of the metric system

- Define and understand the properties of density and refractive index

- Understand and explain the dispersion of light through a prism

- List and explain forensic methods for comparing glass fragments

- Understand how to examine glass fractures to determine the direction of impact for a projectile

- List the important forensic properties of soil

- Describe the proper collection of glass and soil evidence

Physical Property
Describes the behavior of a substance without having to alter the substance's composition through a chemical reaction.

Chemical Property
Describes the behavior of a substance when it reacts or combines with another substance.

The forensic scientist must constantly determine the properties that impart distinguishing characteristics to matter, giving it a unique identity. The continuing search for distinctive properties ends only when the scientist has completely individualized a substance to one correct source. Properties are the identifying characteristics of substances. In this and succeeding chapters, we will examine properties that are most useful for characterizing soil, glass, and other physical evidence. However, before we begin, we can simplify our understanding of the nature of properties by classifying them into two broad categories: physical and chemical.

Physical properties **describe a substance without reference to any other substance.** For example, weight, volume, color, boiling point, and melting point are typical physical properties that can be measured for a particular substance without altering the material's composition through a chemical reaction; they are associated only with the physical existence of that substance. A chemical property **describes the behavior of a substance when it reacts or combines with another substance.** For example, when wood burns, it chemically combines with oxygen in the air to form new substances; this transformation describes a chemical property of wood. In the crime laboratory, a routine procedure for determining the presence of heroin in a suspect specimen is to react it with a chemical reagent known as the Marquis reagent, which turns purple in the presence of heroin. This color transformation becomes a chemical property of heroin and provides a convenient test for its identification.

Which physical and chemical properties the forensic scientist ultimately chooses to observe and measure depends on the type of material that is being examined. Logic requires, however, that if the property can be assigned a numerical value, it must relate to a standard system of measurement accepted throughout the scientific community.

The Metric System

Although scientists, including forensic scientists, throughout the world have been using the metric system of measurement for more than a century, the United States still uses the cumbersome "English system" to express length in inches, feet, or yards; weight in ounces or pounds; and volume in pints or quarts. The inherent difficulty of this system is that no simple numerical relationship exists between the various units of measurement. For example, to convert inches to feet one must know that 1 foot is equal to 12 inches; conversion of ounces to pounds requires the knowledge that 16 ounces is equivalent to 1 pound. In 1791, the French Academy of Science devised the simple system of measurement known as the metric system. This system uses a simple decimal relationship so that a unit of length, volume, or mass can be converted into a subunit by simply multiplying or dividing by a multiple of 10—for example, 10, 100, or 1,000.

Even though the United States has not yet adopted the metric system, its system of currency is decimal and, hence, is analogous to the metric system. The basic unit of currency is the dollar. A dollar is divided into 10 equal units called dimes, and each dime is further divided into 10 equal units of cents.

The metric system has basic units of measurement for length, mass, and volume: the meter, gram, and liter, respectively. These three basic units can be converted into subunits that are decimal multiples of the basic unit by simply attaching a prefix to the unit name. The following are common prefixes and their equivalent decimal value:

Prefix	Equivalent Value
deci-	1/10 or 0.1
centi-	1/100 or 0.01
milli-	1/1000 or 0.001
micro-	1/100,000 or 0.000001
nano-	1/1,000,000,000 or 0.000000001
kilo-	1,000
mega-	1,000,000

Hence, 1/10 or 0.1 gram (g) is the same as a decigram (dg), 1/100 or 0.01 meter is equal to a centimeter (cm), and 1/1,000 liter is a milliliter (mL). A metric conversion is carried out simply by moving the decimal point to the right or left and inserting the proper prefix to show the direction and number of places that the decimal point has been moved. For example, if the weight of a powder is 0.0165 gram, it may be more convenient to multiply this value by 100 and express it as 1.65 centigrams or by 1,000 to show it as its equivalent value of 16.5 milligrams. Similarly, an object that weighs 264,450 grams may be expressed as 264.45 kilograms simply by dividing it by 1,000. It is important to remember that in any of these conversions, the value of the measurement has not changed; 0.0165 gram is still equivalent to 1.65 centigrams, just as one dollar is still equal to 100 cents. We have simply adjusted the position of the decimal and shown the extent of the adjustment with a prefix.

One interesting aspect of the metric system is that volume can be defined in terms of length. A liter by definition is the volume of a cube with sides of length 10 centimeters. One liter is therefore equivalent to a volume of 10 cm × 10 cm × 10 cm, or 1,000 cubic centimeters (cc). Thus, 1/1,000 liter or 1 milliliter (mL) is equal to 1 cubic centimeter (cc) (see Figure 4–1). Scientists commonly use the subunits mL and cc interchangeably to express volume.

At times, it may be necessary to convert units from the metric system into the English system, or vice versa (see Figure 4–2). To accomplish this,

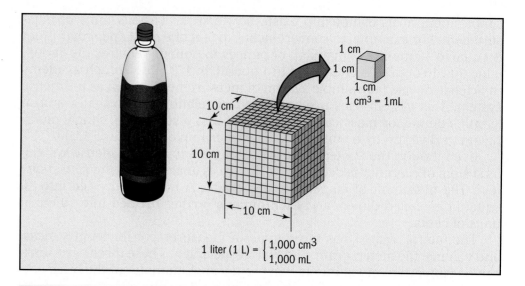

Figure 4–1   Volume equivalencies in the metric system.

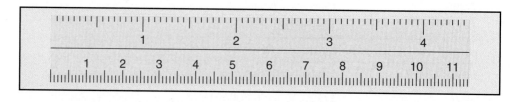

Figure 4–2   Comparison of the metric and English systems of length measurement; 2.54 centimeters = 1 inch.

we must consult references that list English units and their metric equivalents. Some of the more useful equivalents follow:

1 inch = 2.54 centimeters
1 meter = 39.37 inches
1 pound = 453.6 grams
1 liter = 1.06 quarts
1 kilogram = 2.2 pounds

The general mathematical procedures for converting from one system to another can be illustrated by converting 12 inches into centimeters. To change inches into centimeters, we need to know that there are 2.54 centimeters per inch. Hence, if we multiply 12 inches by 2.54 centimeters per inch (12 in. × 2.54 cm/in.), the unit of inches will cancel out, leaving the product 30.48 cm. Similarly, applying the conversion of grams to pounds, 227 grams is equivalent to 227 g × 1 lb/453.6 g or 0.5 lb.

Physical Properties

Temperature

Determining the physical properties of any material often requires measuring its temperature. For instance, the temperatures at which a substance melts or boils are readily determinable characteristics that will help identify it. Temperature is a measure of heat intensity, or the amount of heat in a substance. Temperature is usually measured by causing a thermometer to come into contact with a substance. The familiar mercury-in-glass thermometer functions because mercury expands more than glass when heated and contracts more than glass when cooled. Thus, the length of the mercury column in the glass tube provides a measure of the surrounding environment's temperature. The construction of a temperature scale requires two reference points and a choice of units. The reference points most conveniently chosen are the freezing point and boiling point of water. The two most common temperature scales used are the Fahrenheit and Celsius (formerly called *centigrade*) scales.

The Fahrenheit scale is based on the assignment of the value 32°F to the freezing point of water and 212°F to its boiling point. The difference between the two points is evenly divided into 180 units. Thus, a degree Fahrenheit is 1/180 of the temperature change between the freezing point and boiling point of water. The Celsius scale is derived by assigning the freezing point of water a value of 0°C and its boiling point a value of 100°C. A degree Celsius is thus 1/100 of the temperature change between the two reference points. Scientists in most countries use the Celsius scale to measure temperature. A comparison of the two scales is shown in Figure 4–3.

Fahrenheit Scale
The temperature scale using the melting point of ice as 32° and the boiling point of water as 212°, with 180 equal divisions or degrees between.

Celsius Scale
The temperature scale using the melting point of ice as 0° and the boiling point of water as 100°, with 100 equal divisions or degrees between.

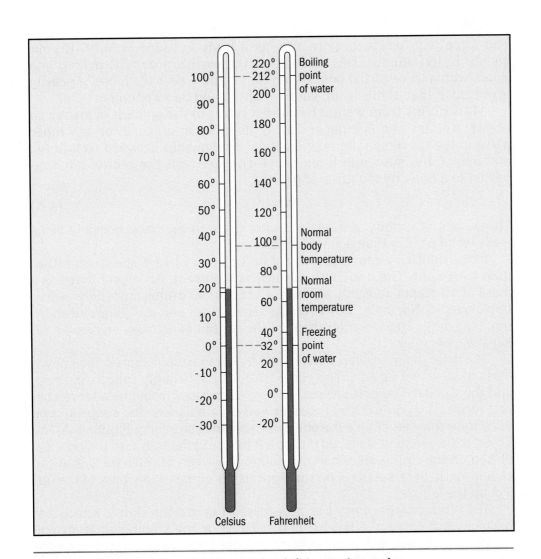

Figure 4–3 Comparison of the Celsius and Fahrenheit temperature scales.

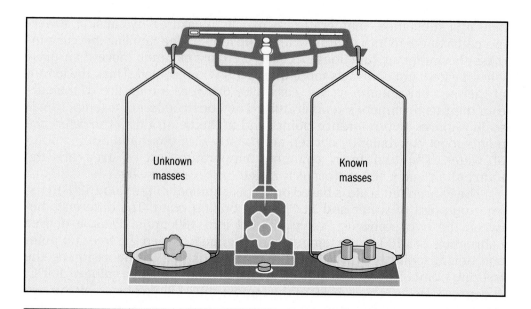

Figure 4–4   The measurement of mass.

Weight and Mass

Weight
A property of matter that depends on both the mass of a substance and the effects of gravity on that mass.

Mass
A constant property of matter that reflects the amount of material present.

The force with which gravity attracts a body is called weight. If your weight is 180 pounds, this means that the earth's gravity is pulling you down with a force of 180 pounds; on the moon, where the force of gravity is one-sixth that of the earth, your weight would be 30 pounds.

Mass differs from weight because it refers to the amount of matter an object contains and is independent of its location on earth or any other place in the universe. The mathematical relationship between weight (w) and mass (m) is shown in Equation (4–1), where g is the acceleration imparted to a body by the force of gravity.

$$W = mg \qquad\qquad (4–1)$$

The weight of a body is directly proportional to its mass; hence, a large mass weighs more than a small mass.

In the metric system, the mass of an object is always specified, rather than its weight. The basic unit of mass is the gram. An object that has a mass of 40 grams on earth will have a mass of 40 grams anywhere else in this universe. Normally, however, the terms *mass* and *weight* are used interchangeably, and we often speak of the weight of an object when we really mean its mass.

The mass of an object is determined by comparing it against the known mass of standard objects. The comparison is confusingly called *weighing,* and the standard objects are called *weights* (*masses* would be a more correct term). The comparison is performed on a balance. The simplest type of balance for weighing is the equal-arm balance shown in Figure 4–4. The object to be weighed is placed on the left pan, and the standard weights are placed on the right pan; when the pointer between the two pans is at the center mark, the total mass on the right pan is equal to the mass of the object on the left pan.

The modern laboratory has progressed beyond the simple equal-arm balance, and either the top-loading balance or the single-pan analytical balance (see Figure 4–5) is now likely to be used. The choice depends on the accuracy required and the amount of material being weighed. Each works on the same counterbalancing principle as the simple equal-arm balance.

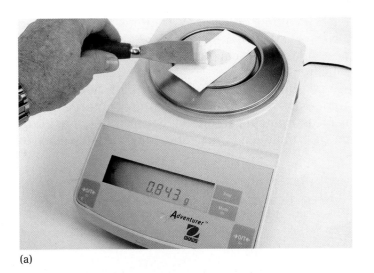

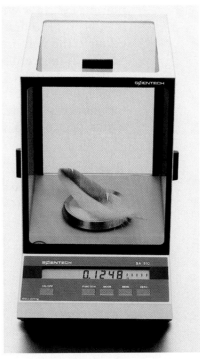

(a)

(b)

Figure 4–5   (a) Top-loading balance. (b) Single-pan analytical balance. *(a) Courtesy Sirchie Finger Print Laboratories, Inc., Youngsville, N.C., www.sirchie.com; (b) Courtesy Scientech, Inc., Boulder, Colo., www.scientech-inc.com*

Earlier versions of the single-pan balance had a second pan, the one on which the standard weights were placed. This pan was hidden from view within the balance's housing. Once the object whose weight was to be determined was placed on the visible pan, the operator selected the proper standard weights (also contained within the housing) by manually turning a set of knobs located on the front side of the balance. At the point of balance, the weights selected were automatically recorded on optical readout scales. Modern single-pan balances rely on an electromagnetic field to generate a current to balance the force pressing down on the pan from the sample being weighed. When the scale is properly calibrated, the amount of current needed to keep the pan balanced is used to determine the weight of the sample. The strength of the current is converted to a digitized signal for a readout. The top-loading balance can accurately weigh an object to the nearest 1 milligram or 0.001 gram; the analytical balance is even more accurate, weighing to the nearest tenth of a milligram or 0.0001 gram.

Density

A most important physical property of matter with respect to the analysis of certain kinds of physical evidence is density. **Density is defined as mass per unit volume** [see Equation (4–2)].

$$\text{Density} = \frac{\text{mass}}{\text{volume}} \qquad (4\text{–}2)$$

Density is an intensive property of matter—that is, it is the same regardless of the size of a substance; thus, it is a characteristic property of a substance and can be used as an aid in identification. Solids tend to be more dense than liquids, and liquids more dense than gases. The densities of some common substances are shown in Table 4–1.

A simple procedure for determining the density of a solid is illustrated in Figure 4–6. First, the solid is weighed on a balance against known standard gram weights to determine its mass. The solid's volume is then determined from the volume of water it displaces. This is easily measured by

Density
A physical property of matter that is equivalent to the mass per unit volume of a substance.

Intensive Property
A property that is not dependent on the size of an object.

filling a cylinder with a known volume of water (V_1), adding the object, and measuring the new water level (V_2). The difference $V_2 - V_1$ in milliliters is equal to the volume of the solid. Density can now be calculated from Equation (4–2) in grams per milliliter.

The volumes of gases and liquids vary considerably with temperature; hence, when determining density, it is important to control and record the temperature at which the measurements are made. For example, 1 gram of water occupies a volume of 1 milliliter at 4°C and thus has a density of

Table 4–1	Densities of Select Materials (at 20°C unless otherwise stated)
Substance	**Density (g/mL)**
Solids	
Silver	10.5
Lead	11.5
Iron	7.8
Aluminum	2.7
Window glass	2.47–2.54
Ice (0°C)	0.92
Liquids	
Mercury	13.6
Benzene	0.88
Ethyl alcohol	0.79
Gasoline	0.69
Water at 4°C	1.00
Water	0.998
Gases	
Air (0°C)	0.0013
Chlorine (0°C)	0.0032
Oxygen (0°C)	0.0014
Carbon dioxide (0°C)	0.0020

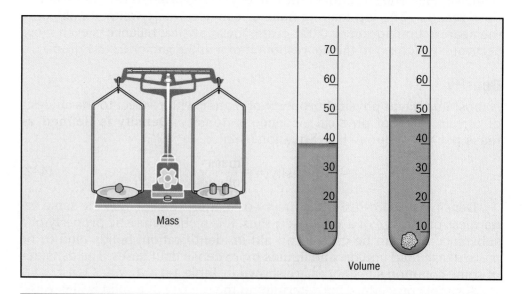

Mass

Volume

Figure 4–6 A simple procedure for determining the density of a solid is to first weigh it and then measure its volume by noting the volume of water it displaces.

1.0 g/mL. However, as the temperature of water increases, its volume expands. Therefore, at 20°C (room temperature) one gram of water occupies a volume of 1.002 mL and will have a density of 0.998 g/mL.

The observation that a solid object either sinks, floats, or remains suspended when immersed in a liquid can be accounted for by the property of density. For instance, if the density of a solid is greater than that of the liquid in which it is immersed, the object sinks; if the solid's density is less than that of the liquid, it floats; and when the solid and liquid have equal densities, the solid remains suspended in the liquid. As we will shortly see, these observations provide a convenient technique for comparing the densities of solid objects.

Refractive Index

Light, as we will learn in the next chapter, can have the property of a wave. Light waves travel in air at a constant velocity of nearly 300 million meters per second until they penetrate another medium, such as glass or water, at which point they are suddenly slowed, causing the rays to bend. The bending of a light wave because of a change in velocity is called refraction.

Refraction
The bending of a light wave as it passes from one medium to another.

The phenomenon of refraction is apparent when we view an object that is immersed in a transparent medium; because we are accustomed to thinking that light travels in a straight line, we often forget to take refraction into account. For instance, suppose a ball is observed at the bottom of a pool of water; the light rays reflected from the ball travel through the water and into the air to reach the eye. As the rays leave the water and enter the air, their velocity suddenly increases, causing them to be refracted. However, because of our assumption that light travels in a straight line, our eyes deceive us and make us think we see an object lying at a higher point than is actually the case. This phenomenon is illustrated in Figure 4–7.

The ratio of the velocity of light in a vacuum to that in any medium determines the refractive index of that medium and is expressed as follows:

Refractive Index
The ratio of the speed of light in a vacuum to its speed in a given substance.

$$\text{Refractive index} = \frac{\text{velocity of light in vacuum}}{\text{velocity of light in medium}} \quad (4\text{–}3)$$

For example, at 25°C the refractive index of water is 1.333. This means that light travels 1.333 times as fast in a vacuum as it does in water at this temperature.

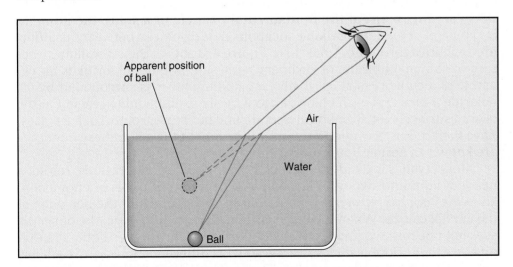

Figure 4–7   Light is refracted when it travels obliquely from one medium to another.

Figure 4–8   Diagram of a sodium chloride crystal. Sodium is represented by the darker spheres, chlorine by the lighter spheres.

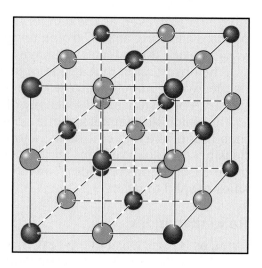

Like density, the refractive index is an intensive physical property of matter and characterizes a substance. However, any procedure used to determine a substance's refractive index must be performed under carefully controlled temperature and lighting conditions, because the refractive index of a substance varies with its temperature and the wavelength of light passing through it. Nearly all tabulated refractive indices are determined at a standard wavelength, usually 589.3 nanometers; this is the predominant wavelength emitted by sodium light and is commonly known as the sodium D light.

When a transparent solid is immersed in a liquid with a similar refractive index, light is not refracted as it passes from the liquid into the solid. For this reason, the eye cannot distinguish the liquid–solid boundary, and the solid seems to disappear from view. This observation, as we will see, offers the forensic scientist a simple method for comparing the refractive indices of transparent solids.

Normally, we expect a solid or a liquid to exhibit only one refractive index value for each wavelength of light; however, many crystalline solids have two refractive indices whose values depend in part on the direction in which the light enters the crystal with respect to the crystal axis. Crystalline solids **have definite geometric forms because of the orderly arrangement of the fundamental particle of a solid, the** atom. In any type of crystal, the relative locations and distances between its atoms are repetitive throughout the solid. Figure 4–8 shows the crystalline structure of sodium chloride, or ordinary table salt. Sodium chloride is an example of a cubic crystal in which each sodium atom is surrounded by six chloride atoms and each chloride atom by six sodium atoms, except at the crystal surface. Not all solids are crystalline in nature; some, such as glass, have their atoms arranged randomly throughout the solid; these materials are known as amorphous solids.

Most crystals, excluding those that have cubic configurations, refract a beam of light into two different light-ray components. This phenomenon, known as *double refraction,* can be observed by studying the behavior of the crystal calcite. When the calcite is laid on a printed page, the observer sees not one but two images of each word covered. The two light rays that give rise to the double image are refracted at different angles, and each has a different refractive index value. The indices of refraction for calcite are 1.486 and 1.658, and subtracting the two values yields a difference of 0.172;

Crystalline Solid
A solid in which the constituent atoms have a regular arrangement.

Atom
The smallest unit of an element; not divisible by ordinary chemical means. Atoms are made up of electrons, protons, and neutrons plus other subatomic particles.

Amorphous Solid
A solid in which the constituent atoms or molecules are arranged in random or disordered positions. There is no regular order in amorphous solids.

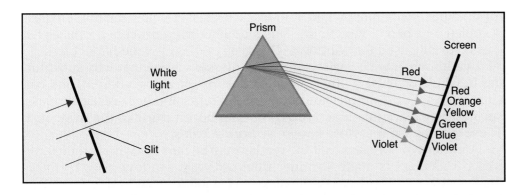

Figure 4–9   Representation of the dispersion of light by a glass prism.

this difference is known as birefringence. Thus, the optical properties of crystals provide points of identification that help characterize them.

 Many of us have held a glass prism up toward the sunlight and watched it transform light into the colors of the rainbow. This observation demonstrates that visible "white light" is not homogeneous but is actually composed of many different colors. The process of separating light into its component colors is called dispersion. The ability of a prism to disperse light into its component colors is explained by the property of refraction. Each color component of light, on passing through the glass, is slowed to a speed slightly different from those of the others, causing each component to bend at a different angle as it emerges from the prism. As shown in Figure 4–9, the component colors of visible light extend from red to violet. We will learn in Chapter 5 that each color actually corresponds to a different range of wavelengths of light. Dispersion thus separates light into its component wavelengths and demonstrates that glass has a slightly different index of refraction for each wavelength of light passing through it.

 Now that we have investigated various physical properties of objects, we are ready to apply such properties to the characterization of two substances—glass and soil—that commonly must be examined by the criminalist.

Birefringence
A difference in the two indices of refraction exhibited by most crystalline materials.

Dispersion
The separation of light into its component wavelengths.

Comparing Glass Fragments

Glass that is broken and shattered into fragments and minute particles during the commission of a crime can be used to place a suspect at the crime scene. For example, chips of broken glass from a window may lodge in a suspect's shoes or garments during a burglary, or particles of headlight glass found at the scene of a hit-and-run accident may offer clues that can confirm the identity of a suspect vehicle. All of these possibilities require the comparison of glass fragments found on the suspect, whether a person or vehicle, with the shattered glass remaining at the crime scene.

 Glass is a hard, brittle, amorphous substance composed of sand (silicon oxides) mixed with various metal oxides. When sand is mixed with other metal oxides, melted at high temperatures, and then cooled to a rigid condition without crystallization, the product is glass. Soda (sodium carbonate) is normally added to the sand to lower its melting point and make it easier to work with. Another necessary ingredient is lime (calcium oxide), needed to prevent the "soda lime" glass from dissolving in water. The forensic scientist is often asked to analyze soda-lime glass, which is used for manufacturing most window and bottle glass. Usually the molten glass is cooled on a bed of molten tin. This manufacturing process produces flat glass typically used for windows. This type of glass is called *float glass*.

In addition, a wide variety of special glasses can be made by substituting in whole or in part other metal oxides for the silica, sodium, and calcium oxides. For example, automobile headlights and heat-resistant glass, such as Pyrex, are manufactured by adding boron oxide to the oxide mix. These glasses are therefore known as *borosilicates*.

Another type of glass that the reader may be familiar with is tempered glass. This glass is made stronger than ordinary window glass by introducing stress through rapid heating and cooling of the glass surfaces. When tempered glass breaks, it does not shatter but rather fragments or "dices" into small squares with little splintering. Because of this safety feature, tempered glass is used in the side and rear windows of automobiles made in the United States, as well as in the windshields of some foreign-made cars. The windshields of all cars manufactured in the United States are constructed from laminated glass. This glass derives its strength by sandwiching one layer of plastic between two pieces of ordinary window glass.

For the forensic scientist, comparing glass consists of finding and measuring the properties that will associate one glass fragment with another while minimizing or eliminating the possible existence of other sources. Needless to say, considering the prevalence of glass in our society, it is easy to appreciate the magnitude of this analytical problem. Obviously, glass possesses its greatest evidential value when it can be individualized to one source. Such a determination, however, can be made only when the suspect and crime-scene fragments are assembled and physically fitted together. Comparisons of this type require piecing together irregular edges of broken glass as well as matching all irregularities and striations on the broken surfaces (see Figure 4–10). The possibility that two pieces of glass originating from different sources will fit together exactly is so unlikely as to exclude all other sources from practical consideration.

Unfortunately, most glass evidence is either too fragmentary or too minute to permit a comparison of this type. In such instances, the search for individual properties has proven fruitless. For example, the general

Tempered Glass
Glass that is strengthened by introducing stress through rapid heating and cooling of the glass surfaces.

Laminated Glass
Two sheets of ordinary glass bonded together with a plastic film.

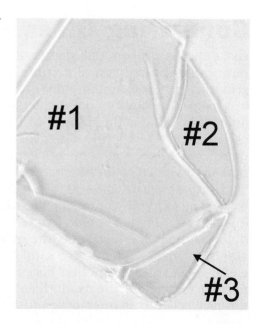

Figure 4–10 Match of broken glass. Note the physical fit of the edges. *Courtesy Sirchie Finger Print Laboratories, Inc., Youngsville, N.C., www.sirchie.com*

chemical composition of various window glasses within the capability of current analytical methods has so far been found relatively uniform among various manufacturers and thus offers no basis for individualization. However, trace elements present in glass have been shown to be useful for narrowing the origin of a glass specimen. **The physical properties of density and refractive index are most widely used for characterizing glass particles.** However, these properties are class characteristics, which cannot provide the sole criteria for individualizing glass to a common source. They do, however, give the analyst sufficient data to evaluate the significance of a glass comparison, and the absence of comparable density and refractive index values will certainly exclude glass fragments that originate from different sources.

Recall that a solid particle will either float, sink, or remain suspended in a liquid, depending on its density relative to the liquid. This knowledge gives the criminalist a rather precise and rapid method for comparing densities of glass. In a method known as *flotation,* a standard/reference glass particle is immersed in a liquid; a mixture of bromoform and bromobenzene may be used. The composition of the liquid is carefully adjusted by the addition of small amounts of bromoform or bromobenzene until the glass chip remains suspended in the liquid medium. At this point, the standard/reference glass and liquid each have the same density. Glass chips of approximately the same size and shape as the standard/reference are now added to the liquid for comparison. If both the unknown and the standard/reference particles remain suspended in the liquid, their densities are equal to each other and to that of the liquid.[1] Particles of different densities either sink or float, depending on whether they are more or less dense than the liquid.

The density of a single sheet of window glass is not completely homogeneous throughout. It has a range of values that can differ by as much as 0.0003 g/mL. Therefore, in order to distinguish between the normal internal density variations of a single sheet of glass and those of glasses of different origins, it is advisable to let the comparative density approach but not exceed a sensitivity value of 0.0003 g/mL. The flotation method meets this requirement and can adequately distinguish glass particles that differ in density by 0.001 g/mL.

Once glass has been distinguished by a density determination, different origins are immediately concluded. Comparable density results, however, require the added comparison of refractive indices. This determination is best accomplished by the *immersion method.* For this, glass particles are immersed in a liquid medium whose refractive index is adjusted until it equals that of the glass particles. At this point, known as the *match point,* the observer notes the disappearance of the Becke line and minimum contrast between the glass and liquid medium. The Becke line is a bright halo that is observed near the border of a particle that is immersed in a liquid of a different refractive index. This halo disappears when the medium and fragment have similar refractive indices.

The refractive index of an immersion fluid is best adjusted by changing the temperature of the liquid. Temperature control is, of course, critical to

Becke Line
A bright halo that is observed near the border of a particle immersed in a liquid of a different refractive index.

---

[1] As an added step, the analyst can determine the exact numerical density value of the particles of glass by transferring the liquid to a density meter, which will electrically measure and calculate the liquid's density. See A. P. Beveridge and C. Semen, "Glass Density Measurement Using a Calculating Digital Density Meter," *Canadian Society of Forensic Science Journal* 12 (1979): 113.

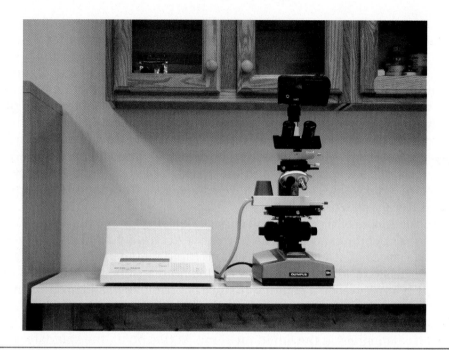

Figure 4–11   Hot-stage microscope. *Courtesy Chris Palenik, Ph.D., Microtrace, Elgin, IL.,* www.microtracescientific.com

the success of the procedure. One approach to this procedure is to heat the liquid in a special apparatus known as a *hot stage*. The glass is immersed in a boiling liquid, usually a silicone oil, and heated at the rate of 0.2°C per minute until the match point is reached. Increasing the temperature of the liquid has a negligible effect on the refractive index of glass, while the liquid's index decreases at the rate of approximately 0.0004 per degree Celsius. The hot stage, as shown in Figure 4–11, is designed to be used in conjunction with a microscope, through which the examiner can observe the disappearance of the Becke line on minute glass particles that are illuminated with sodium D light or other wavelengths of light. If all the glass fragments examined have similar match points, it can be concluded that they have comparable refractive indices (see Figure 4–12). Furthermore, the examiner can determine the refractive index value of the immersion fluid as it changes with temperature. With this information, the exact numerical value of the glass refractive index can be calculated at the match point temperature.[2]

An automated approach for measuring the refractive index of glass fragments by temperature control using the immersion method with a hot stage is with the instrument known as GRIM 3 (Glass Refractive Index Measurement) (see Figure 4–13). The GRIM 3 is a personal computer/video system designed to automate the measurements of the match temperature and refractive index for glass fragments. This instrument uses a video camera to view the glass fragments as they are being heated. As the immersion oil is heated or cooled, the contrast of the video image is measured continually until a minimum, the match point, is detected (see Figure 4–14). The match point temperature is then converted to a refractive index using stored calibration data.

---

[2] A. R. Cassista and P. M. L. Sandercock, "Precision of Glass Refractive Index Measurements: Temperature Variation and Double Variation Methods, and the Value of Dispersion," *Canadian Society of Forensic Science Journal* 27 (1994): 203.

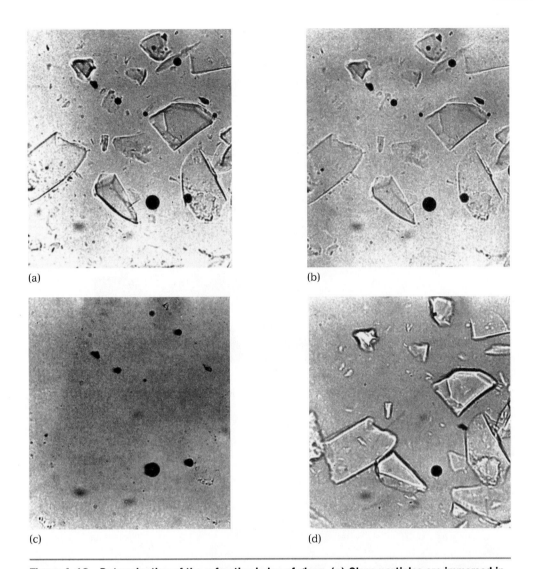

(a)

(b)

(c)

(d)

Figure 4–12 Determination of the refractive index of glass. (a) Glass particles are immersed in a liquid of a much higher refractive index at a temperature of 77°C. (b) At 87°C the liquid still has a higher refractive index than the glass. (c) The refractive index of the liquid is closest to that of the glass at 97°C, as shown by the disappearance of the glass and the Becke lines. (d) At the higher temperature of 117°C, the liquid has a much lower index than the glass, and the glass is plainly visible. *Courtesy Walter C. McCrone*

As with density, glass fragments removed from a single sheet of plate glass may not have a uniform refractive index value; instead, their values may vary by as much as 0.0002. Hence, for comparison purposes, the difference in refractive index between a standard/reference and questioned glass must exceed this value. This allows the examiner to differentiate between the normal internal variations present in a sheet of glass and those present in glasses that originated from completely different sources.

A significant difference in either density or refractive index proves that the glasses examined do not have a common origin. But what if two pieces of glass exhibit comparable densities and comparable refractive indices? How certain can one be that they did, indeed, come from the same source? After all, there are untold millions of windows and other glass objects in this world. To provide a reasonable answer to this question, the FBI Laboratory has collected density and refractive index values from glass submitted to it for examination. What has emerged is a data bank correlating

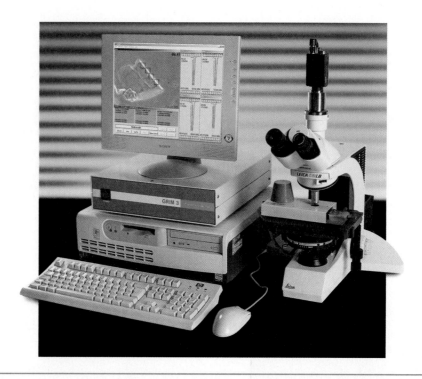

Figure 4–13   An automated system for glass fragment identification. *Courtesy Foster & Freeman Limited, Worcestershire, U.K., www.fosterfreeman.co.uk*

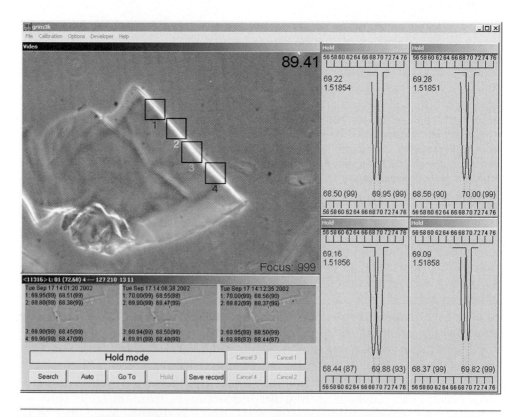

Figure 4–14   GRIM 3 identifies the refraction match point by monitoring a video image of four different areas of the glass fragment immersed in an oil. As the immersion oil is heated or cooled, the contrast of the image is measured continuously until a minimum, the match point, is detected. *Courtesy Foster & Freeman Limited, Worcestershire, U.K., www.fosterfreeman.co.uk*

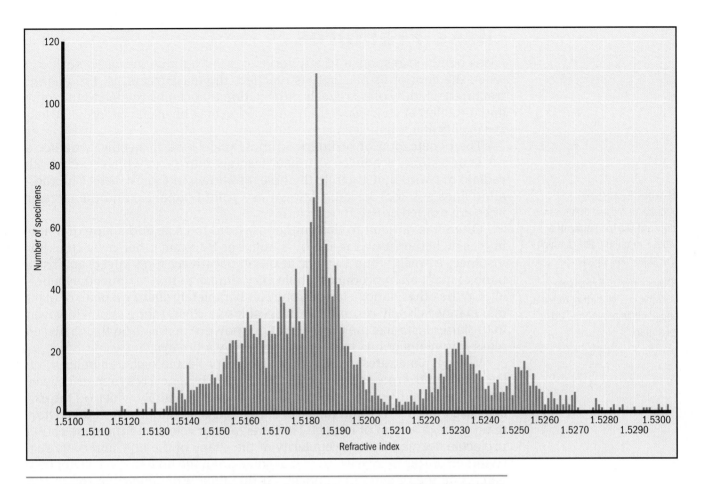

Figure 4–15   Frequency of occurrence of refractive index values (measured with sodium D light) for approximately two thousand flat glass specimens received by the FBI Laboratory. *Courtesy FBI Laboratory, Washington, D.C.*

these values to their frequency of occurrence in the glass population of the United States. This collection is available to all forensic laboratories in the United States.

Once a criminalist has completed a comparison of glass fragments, he or she can correlate their density and refractive index values to their frequency of occurrence and assess probability that the fragments came from the same source. Figure 4–15 shows the distribution of refractive index values (measured with sodium D light) for approximately two thousand glasses analyzed by the FBI. The wide distribution of values clearly demonstrates that the refractive index is a highly distinctive property of glass and is thus useful for defining its frequency of occurrence and hence its evidential value. For example, a glass fragment with a refractive index value of 1.5290 is found in approximately only 1 out of 2,000 specimens, while glass with a value of 1.5180 occurs approximately in 22 glasses out of 2,000.

The distinction between tempered and nontempered glass particles can be made by slowly heating and then cooling the glass (a process known as *annealing*). The change in the refractive index value for tempered glass upon annealing is significantly greater when compared to nontempered glass and thus serves as a point of distinction.[3]

---

[3] G. Edmondstone, "The Identification of Heat Strengthened Glass in Windshields," *Canadian Society of Forensic Science Journal* 30 (1997): 181.

Glass Fractures

Glass bends in response to any force exerted on any one of its surfaces; when the limit of its elasticity is reached, the glass fractures. Frequently, fractured window glass reveals information that can be related to the force and direction of an impact; such knowledge may be useful for reconstructing events at a crime-scene investigation.

The penetration of ordinary window glass by a projectile, whether a bullet or a stone, produces a familiar fracture pattern in which cracks both radiate outward and encircle the hole, as shown in Figure 4–16. The radiating lines are appropriately known as radial fractures, and the circular lines are termed concentric fractures.

Often it is difficult to determine just from the size and shape of a hole in glass whether it was made by a bullet or by some other projectile. For instance, a small stone thrown at a comparatively high speed against a pane of glass often produces a hole very similar to that produced by a bullet. On the other hand, a large stone can completely shatter a pane of glass in a manner closely resembling the result of a close-range shot. However, in the latter instance, the presence of gunpowder deposits on the shattered glass fragments points to damage caused by a firearm.

When it penetrates glass, a high-velocity projectile such as a bullet often leaves a round, crater-shaped hole surrounded by a nearly symmetrical pattern of radial and concentric cracks. The hole is inevitably wider on the exit side (see Figure 4–17), and hence examining it is an important step in determining the direction of impact. However, as the velocity of the penetrating projectile decreases, the irregularity of the shape of the hole and of its surrounding cracks increases, so that at some point the hole shape will not help determine the direction of impact. At this time, examining the radial and concentric fracture lines may help determine the direction of impact.

When a force pushes on one side of a pane of glass, the elasticity of the glass permits it to bend in the direction of the force applied. Once the elastic limit is exceeded, the glass begins to crack. As shown in Figure 4–18, the first fractures form on the surface opposite that of the penetrating force and develop into radial lines. The continued motion of the force places tension on the front surface of the glass, resulting in the formation of concentric cracks. An examination of the edges of the radial and concentric cracks frequently reveals stress markings *(Wallner lines)* whose shape can be related to the side on which the window first cracked.

Radial Fracture
A crack in a glass that extends outward like the spoke of a wheel from the point at which the glass was struck.

Concentric Fracture
A crack in a glass that forms a rough circle around the point of impact.

Figure 4–16 Radial and concentric fracture lines in a sheet of glass. *Courtesy Sirchie Finger Print Laboratories, Inc., Youngsville, N.C., www.sirchie.com*

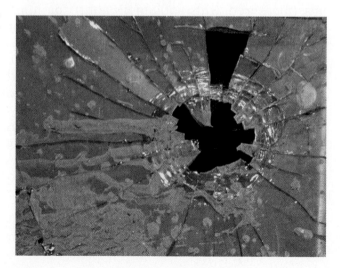

Stress marks, shown in Figure 4–19, are shaped like arches that are perpendicular to one glass surface and curved nearly parallel to the opposite surface. The importance of stress marks stems from the observation that the perpendicular edge always faces the surface on which the crack originated. Thus, in examining the stress marks on the edge of a radial crack near the point of impact, the perpendicular end is always found opposite the side from which the force of impact was applied. For a concentric fracture, the perpendicular end always faces the surface on which the force originated. A convenient way for remembering these observations is the 3R rule—**Radial cracks form a Right angle on the Reverse side of the force.** These facts enable the examiner to determine the side on which a window was broken.

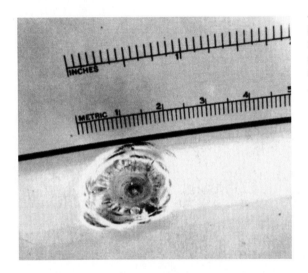

Figure 4–17   Crater-shaped hole made by a pellet passing through glass. The upper surface is the exit side of the projectile. *Courtesy New Jersey State Police*

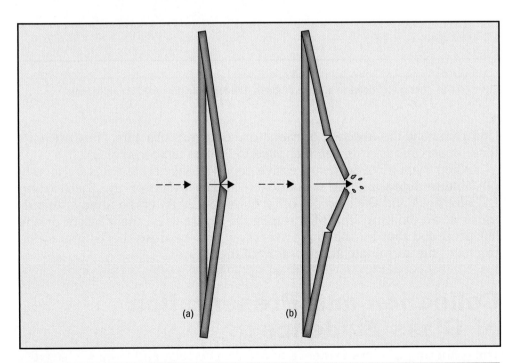

(a)   (b)

Figure 4–18   Production of radial and concentric fractures in glass. (a) Radial cracks are formed first, commencing on the side of the glass opposite to the destructive force. (b) Concentric cracks occur afterward, starting on the same side as the force.

Figure 4–19   Stress marks on the edge of a radial glass fracture. Arrow indicates direction of force. *Courtesy New Jersey State Police*

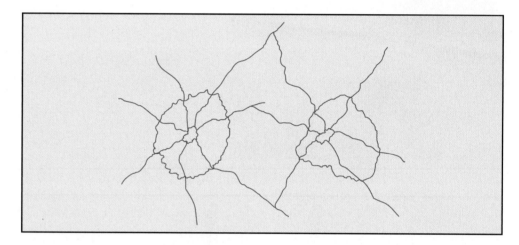

Figure 4–20   Two bullet holes in a piece of glass. The left hole preceded the right hole.

Unfortunately, the absence of radial or concentric fracture lines prevents these observations from being applied to broken tempered glass.

When there have been successive penetrations of glass, it is frequently possible to determine the sequence of impact by observing the existing fracture lines and their points of termination. **A fracture always terminates at an existing line of fracture.** In Figure 4–20, the fracture on the left preceded that on the right; we know this because the latter's radial fracture lines terminate at the cracks of the former.

Collection and Preservation of Glass Evidence

The gathering of glass evidence at the crime scene and from the suspect must be thorough if the examiner is to have any chance to individualize the fragments to a common source. If even the remotest possibility exists that fragments may be pieced together, every effort must be made to collect all

Figure 4–21 **Presence of black tungsten oxide on the upper filament indicates that the filament was on when it was exposed to air. The lower filament was off, but its surface was coated with a yellow/white tungsten oxide, which was vaporized from the upper ("on") filament and condensed onto the lower filament.** *Courtesy New Jersey State Police*

the glass found. For example, evidence collection at hit-and-run scenes must include all the broken parts of the headlight and reflector lenses. This evidence may ultimately prove invaluable in placing a suspect vehicle at the accident scene by matching the fragments with glass remaining in the headlight or reflector shell of the suspect vehicle. In addition, examining the headlight's filaments may reveal whether an automobile's headlights were on or off before the impact (see Figure 4–21).

When an individual fit is improbable, the evidence collector must submit all glass evidence found in the possession of the suspect along with a sample of broken glass remaining at the crime scene. This standard/reference glass should always be taken from any remaining glass in the window or door frames, as close as possible to the point of breakage. About one square inch of sample is usually adequate for this purpose. The glass fragments should be packaged in solid containers to avoid further breakage. If the suspect's shoes and/or clothing are to be examined for the presence of glass fragments, they should be individually wrapped in paper and transmitted to the laboratory. The field investigator should avoid removing such evidence from garments unless absolutely necessary for its preservation.

When a determination of the direction of impact is desired, all broken glass must be recovered and submitted for analysis. Wherever possible, the exterior and interior surfaces of the glass must be indicated. When this is not immediately apparent, the presence of dirt, paint, grease, or putty may indicate the exterior surface of the glass.

Forensic Characteristics of Soil

There are many definitions for the term *soil*; however, for forensic purposes, soil may be thought of as any disintegrated surface material, natural or artificial, that lies on or near the earth's surface. Therefore, the forensic examination of soil not only is concerned with the analysis of naturally occurring rocks, minerals, vegetation, and animal matter—it also encompasses the detection of such manufactured objects as glass, paint chips, asphalt, brick fragments, and cinders, whose presence may impart soil with characteristics that will make it unique to a particular location. When this material is collected accidentally or deliberately in a manner that will associate it with a crime under investigation, it becomes valuable physical evidence.[4]

The value of soil as evidence rests with its prevalence at crime scenes and its transferability between the scene and the criminal. Thus, soil or dried mud found adhering to a suspect's clothing or shoes, or to an automobile, when compared to soil samples collected at the crime site, may provide associative evidence that can link a suspect or object to the crime scene. As with most types of physical evidence, forensic soil analysis is comparative in nature; soil found in the possession of the suspect must be carefully collected to be compared to soil samplings from the crime scene and the surrounding vicinity. However, one should not rule out the value of soil even if the site of the crime has not been ascertained. For instance, small amounts of soil may be found on a person or object far from the actual site of a crime. A geologist who knows the local geology may be able to use geological maps to direct police to the general vicinity where the soil was originally picked up and the crime committed.

Most soils can be differentiated and distinguished by their gross appearance. A side-by-side visual comparison of the color and texture of soil specimens is easy to perform and provides a sensitive property for distinguishing soils that originate from different locations. Soil is darker when it is wet; therefore, color comparisons must always be made when all the samples are dried under identical laboratory conditions. It is estimated that there are nearly 1,100 distinguishable soil colors; hence, the comparison of color offers a logical first step in a forensic soil comparison.

Low-power microscopic examination of soil reveals the presence of plant and animal materials as well as of artificial debris. Further high-power microscopic examination will help characterize minerals and rocks present in earth materials. Although this approach to forensic soil identification requires the expertise of an investigator trained in geology, it can provide the most varied and significant points of comparison between soil samples. Only by carefully examining and comparing the minerals and rocks naturally present in soil can one take advantage of the large number of variations between soils and thus add to the evidential value of a positive comparison.[5] A mineral is a naturally occurring crystal, and like any other crystal, its physical properties—for example, color, geometric shape, density, and refractive index or birefringence—are most useful for identification. More than 2,200 minerals exist; however, most are so rare that forensic geologists usually encounter only about twenty of the more common ones. Rocks are composed of a combination of minerals and therefore

Mineral
A naturally occurring crystalline solid.

---

[4] E. P. Junger, "Assessing the Unique Characteristics of Close-Proximity Soil Samples: Just How Useful Is Soil Evidence?" *Journal of Forensic Sciences* 41 (1996): 27.

[5] W. J. Graves, "A Mineralogical Soil Classification Technique for the Forensic Scientist," *Journal of Forensic Sciences* 24 (1979): 323; M. J. McVicar and W. J. Graves, "The Forensic Comparison of Soil by Automated Scanning Electron Microscopy," *Canadian Society of Forensic Science Journal* 30 (1997): 241.

exist in thousands of varieties on the earth's surface. Their identification is usually made by characterizing their mineral content and grain size.

Considering the vast variety of minerals and rocks and the possible presence of artificial debris in soil, the forensic geologist is presented with many points of comparison between two or more specimens. The number of comparative points and their frequency of occurrence must all be considered before similarity between specimens can be concluded and the probability of common origin judged.

Rocks and minerals not only are present in earth materials but also are used to manufacture a wide variety of industrial and commercial products. For example, the tools and garments of an individual suspected of breaking into a safe often contain traces of safe insulation. Safe insulation may be made from a wide combination of mineral mixtures that can provide significant points of identification. Similarly, building materials, such as brick, plaster, and concrete blocks, are combinations of minerals and rocks that can easily be recognized and compared microscopically to similar minerals found on a breaking-and-entering suspect.

Some forensic laboratories currently rely on the density-gradient tube technique to compare soil specimens. Typically, glass tubes 6 to 10 millimeters in diameter and from 25 to 40 centimeters in length are filled with layers of two liquids mixed in varying proportions so that each layer has a different density value. For example, tetrabromoethane (density 2.96 g/mL) and ethanol (density 0.789 g/mL) may be mixed so that each successive layer has a lower density than the preceding one, from the bottom to the top of the tube. The simplest gradient tube may have from six to ten layers, in which the bottom layer is pure tetrabromoethane and the top layer is pure ethanol, with corresponding variations of concentration in the layers between these two extremes. When soil is added to the density-gradient tube, its particles sink to the portion of the tube that has a density of equal value; the particles remain suspended in the liquid at this point. In this way, a density distribution pattern of soil particles can be obtained and compared to other specimens treated in a similar manner (see Figure 4–22).

Density-Gradient Tube
A glass tube filled from bottom to top with liquids of successively lighter densities; used to determine the density distribution of soil.

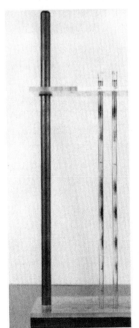

Figure 4–22   A soil comparison by density-gradient tubes. *Courtesy Philadelphia Police Department Laboratory*

Many crime laboratories use this procedure to compare soil evidence. However, there is evidence that this test is far from definitive, because many soils collected from different locations yield similar density distribution patterns.[6] At best, the density-gradient test is useful for comparing soils when it is used in combination with other tests.

The ultimate forensic value of soil evidence depends on its variation at the crime scene. If, for example, soil is indistinguishable for miles surrounding the location of a crime according to the methods used in the examination, it will have limited value in associating soil found on the suspect with that particular site. Significant conclusions relating the suspect to a particular crime-scene location through a soil comparison may be made when variations in soil composition occur every 10 to 100 yards from the crime site. However, even when such variations do exist, the forensic geologist usually cannot individualize soil to any one location unless an unusual combination of rare minerals, rocks, or artificial debris can be located. No statistically valid forensic studies have examined the variability of soil evidence. A pilot study recently conducted in southern Ontario, Canada, seems to indicate that soil in that part of Canada shows extensive diversity; it found that the probability is smaller than 1 in 50 of finding two soils that are indistinguishable in both color and mineral properties but that originate in two different locations separated by a distance on the order of 1,000 feet. Based on these preliminary results, similar diversity may be expected in the northern United States, Canada, northern Europe, and eastern Europe. However, such probability values can only generally indicate the variation of soil within these geographical areas. Each crime scene must be evaluated separately to establish its own soil variation probabilities.

Collection and Preservation of Soil Evidence

Establishing soil variation at the crime scene must be given primary consideration when the evidence collector gathers soil specimens. For this reason, standard/reference soils are to be collected at various intervals within a 100-yard radius of the crime scene, as well as at the site of the crime, for comparison to the questioned soil. Additionally, soil specimens should also be collected at all possible alibi locations that the suspect may claim. It is important that the specimens be representative of the soil that was removed by the suspect. In most cases, only the top layer of soil is picked up during the commission of a crime. Thus, standard/reference specimens must be removed from the surface without digging too deeply into the unrepresentative subsurface layers. A quantity of soil equal to approximately a tablespoon or two is all the laboratory needs for a thorough comparative analysis. All specimens collected should be packaged in individual containers, such as plastic vials. Each vial should be marked to indicate the location at which the sampling was made.

Soil found on a suspect must be carefully preserved for analysis. If it is found adhering to an object, as in the case of soil on a shoe, the investigator must not remove it. Instead, each object should be individually wrapped in paper, with the soil intact, and transmitted to the laboratory.

---

[6] K. Chaperlin and P. S. Howarth, "Soil Comparison by the Density Gradient Method—A Review and Evaluation," *Forensic Science International* 23 (1983): 161–77.

Similarly, no effort should be made to remove loose soil adhering to garments; these items should be carefully and individually wrapped in paper bags and sent to the laboratory for analysis. Care must be taken that all particles that may accidentally fall off the garment during transportation will remain within the paper bag.

When a lump of soil is found, it should be collected and preserved intact. For example, an automobile tends to collect and build up layers of soil under the fenders, body, and so on. The impact of an automobile with another object may jar some of this soil loose. Once the suspect car has been apprehended, a comparison of the soil left at the scene with soil remaining on the automobile may help establish that the car was present at the accident scene. In these situations, separate samples are collected from under all the fender and frame areas of the vehicle; care is taken to remove the soil in lump form in order to preserve the order in which the soil adhered to the car. Undoubtedly, during the normal use of an automobile, soil will be picked up from numerous locations over a period of months and years. This layering effect may impart soil with greater variation, and hence greater evidential value, than that which is normally associated with loose soil.

The prevalence of glass and soil in our environment makes them common types of physical evidence at crime scenes. Their proper collection and preservation by the criminal investigator will help ensure that a proper scientific examination can support investigative conclusions placing a suspect or object at the crime scene. Equally important is that glass and soil, like other types of physical evidence, when properly collected and examined may exonerate the innocent from involvement in a crime.

Chapter Summary

The forensic scientist must constantly determine the properties that impart distinguishing characteristics to matter, giving it a unique identity. Physical properties such as weight, volume, color, boiling point, and melting point describe a substance without reference to any other substance. A chemical property describes the behavior of a substance when it reacts or combines with another substance. Scientists throughout the world use the metric system of measurement. The metric system has basic units of measurement for length, mass, and volume: the meter, gram, and liter, respectively. Temperature is a measure of heat intensity, or the amount of heat in a substance. In science, the most commonly used temperature scale is the Celsius scale. This scale is derived by assigning the freezing point of water a value of 0°C and its boiling point a value of 100°C.

To compare glass fragments, a forensic scientist evaluates two important physical properties: density and refractive index. Density is defined as the mass per unit volume. Refractive index is the ratio of the velocity of light in a vacuum to that in the medium under examination. Crystalline solids have definite geometric forms because of the orderly arrangement of their atoms. These solids refract a beam of light in two different light-ray components. This results in double refraction. Birefringence is the numerical difference between these two refractive indices. Not all solids are crystalline in nature. For example, glass has a random arrangement of atoms to form an amorphous or noncrystalline solid.

The flotation and immersion methods are best used to determine a glass fragment's density and refractive index, respectively. In the flotation method, a glass particle is immersed in a liquid. The density of the liquid is carefully adjusted by the addition of small amounts of an appropriate liquid until the glass chip remains suspended in the liquid medium. At this point, the glass will have the same density as the liquid medium and can be compared to other relevant pieces of glass. The immersion method involves immersing a glass particle in a liquid medium whose refractive index is varied until it is equal to that of the glass particle. At this point, known as the match point, minimum contrast between liquid and particle is observed.

By analyzing the radial and concentric fracture patterns in glass, the forensic scientist can determine the direction of impact. This can be accomplished by applying the 3R Rule: *R*adial cracks form a *R*ight angle on the *R*everse side of the force.

The value of soil as evidence rests with its prevalence at crime scenes and its transferability between the scene and the criminal. Most soils can be differentiated by their gross appearance. A side-by-side visual comparison of the color and texture of soil specimens is easy to perform and provides a sensitive property for distinguishing soils that originate from different locations. In many forensic laboratories, forensic geologists characterize and compare the mineral content of soils. Some crime laboratories use density-gradient tubes to compare soils. These tubes are typically filled with layers of liquids that have different density values.

Review Questions

1. A(n) _____ property describes the behavior of a substance without reference to any other substance.

2. A(n) _____ property describes the behavior of a substance when it reacts or combines with another substance.

3. The _____ system of measurement was devised by the French Academy of Science in 1791.

4. The basic units of measurement for length, mass, and volume in the metric system are the _____, _____, and _____, respectively.

5. A centigram is equivalent to _____ gram(s).

6. A milliliter is equivalent to _____ liter(s).

7. 0.2 gram is equivalent to _____ milligram(s).

8. One cubic centimeter (cc) is equivalent to one _____.

9. True or False: One meter is slightly longer than a yard. _____

10. The equivalent of 1 pound in grams is _____.

11. True or False: A liter is slightly larger than a quart. _____

12. _____ is a measure of a substance's heat intensity.

13. There are _____ degrees Fahrenheit between the freezing and boiling points of water.

14. There are _____ degrees Celsius between the freezing and boiling points of water.

15. The amount of matter an object contains determines its _____.

16. The simplest type of balance for weighing is the _____.

17. Mass per unit volume defines the property of _____.

18. If an object is immersed in a liquid of greater density, it will (sink, float).

19. The bending of a light wave because of a change in velocity is called _____.

20. The physical property of _____ is determined by the ratio of the velocity of light in a vacuum to light's velocity in a substance.

21. True or False: Solids having an orderly arrangement of their constituent atoms are crystalline. _____

22. Solids that have their atoms randomly arranged are said to be _____.

23. The crystal calcite has two indices of refraction. The difference between these two values is known as _____.

24. The process of separating light into its component colors or frequencies is known as _____.

25. A hard, brittle, amorphous substance composed mainly of silicon oxides is _____.

26. Glass that can be physically pieced together has _____ characteristics.

27. The two most useful physical properties of glass for forensic comparisons are _____ and _____.

28. Comparing the relative densities of glass fragments is readily accomplished by a method known as _____.

29. When glass is immersed in a liquid of similar refractive index, its _____ disappears and minimum contrast between the glass and liquid is observed.

30. The exact numerical density and refractive indices of glass can be correlated to _____ in order to assess the evidential value of the comparison.

31. The fracture lines radiating outward from a crack in glass are known as _____ fractures.

32. A crater-shaped hole in glass is (narrower, wider) on the side where the projectile entered the glass.

33. True or False: It is easy to determine from the size and shape of a hole in glass whether it was made by a bullet or some other projectile. _____

34. True or False: Stress marks on the edge of a radial crack are always perpendicular to the edge of the surface on which the impact force originated. _____

35. A fracture line (will, will not) terminate at an existing line fracture.

36. True or False: Most soils have indistinguishable color and texture. _____

37. Naturally occurring crystals commonly found in soils are _____.

38. A comparison of the density of soil particles is readily accomplished through the use of _____ tubes.

39. True or False: The ultimate value of soil as evidence depends on its variation at the crime scene. _____

Further References

Caddy, B., ed., *Forensic Examination of Glass and Paint.* New York: Taylor & Francis, 2001.

Demmelmeyer, H., and J. Adam, "Forensic Investigation of Soil and Vegetable Materials," *Forensic Science Review* 7 (1995): 119–42.

Koons, R. D., J. Buscaglia, M. Bottrell, and E. T. Miller, "Forensic Glass Comparisons," in R. Saferstein, ed., *Forensic Science Handbook* vol. 1, 2nd ed. Upper Saddle River, N.J.: Prentice Hall, 2002.

Murray, R. C. *Evidence from the Earth: Forensic Geology and Criminal Investigation.* Missoula, Mont.: Mountain Press, 2004.

Murray, R. C., and L. P. Solebello, "Forensic Examination of Soil," in R. Saferstein, ed., *Forensic Science Handbook* vol. 1, 2nd ed. Upper Saddle River, N.J.: Prentice Hall, 2002.

Thornton, J. I., "Interpretation of Physical Aspects of Glass Evidence," in B. Caddy, ed., *Forensic Examination of Glass and Paint.* New York: Taylor & Francis, 2001.

Death by Tylenol

In 1982, two firefighters from a Chicago suburb were casually discussing four bizarre deaths that had recently taken place in a neighboring area. As they discussed the circumstances of the deaths, they realized that each of the victims had taken Tylenol. Their suspicions were immediately reported to police investigators. Tragically, before the general public could be alerted, three more victims died after taking poison-laced Tylenol capsules. Seven individuals, all in the Chicago area, were the first victims to die from what has become known as *product tampering*. A forensic chemical analysis of Tylenol capsules recovered from the victims' residences showed that the capsules were filled with potassium cyanide in a quantity ten thousand times what was needed to kill an average person. It was quickly determined that the cyanide was not introduced into the bottles at the factory. Instead, the perpetrator methodically emptied each of twenty to thirty capsules and then refilled them with potassium cyanide. The tampered capsules were rebottled, carefully repackaged, and placed on the shelves of six different stores. The case of the Tylenol murders remains unsolved, and the $100,000 reward offered by Tylenol's manufacturer remains unclaimed.

chapter 5

Organic Analysis

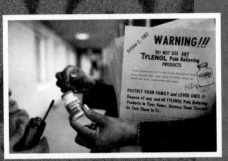

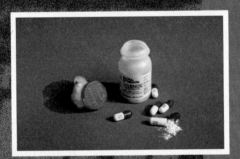

Key Terms

chromatography

compound

electromagnetic spectrum

electrophoresis

element

enzyme

fluoresce

frequency

gas (vapor)

infrared

inorganic

ion

laser

liquid

matter

monochromatic light

monochromator

organic

periodic table

phase

photon

physical state

proteins

pyrolysis

solid

spectrophotometry

sublimation

ultraviolet

visible light

wavelength

X-ray

Learning Objectives

After studying this chapter you should be able to:

- Define and distinguish elements and compounds

- Contrast the differences between a solid, liquid, and gas

- Define and distinguish organic and inorganic compounds

- Understand the difference between qualitative and quantitative analysis

- Describe and explain the process of chromatography

- List and describe the parts of a gas chromatograph

- Explain the difference between thin-layer chromatography, gas chromatography, and electrophoresis

- Understand the differences between the wave and particle theories of light

- Describe the electromagnetic spectrum

- Name the parts of a simple absorption spectrophotometer

- Describe the utility of ultraviolet and infrared spectroscopy for the identification of organic compounds

- Describe the concept and utility of mass spectrometry for identification analysis

In the previous chapter, some physical properties were described and used to characterize glass and soil evidence. Before we can apply other physical properties, as well as chemical properties, to the identification and comparison of evidence, we need to gain an insight into the composition of matter. Beginning with knowledge of the fundamental building block of all substances—the element—it will be convenient for us to classify all evidence as either organic or inorganic. The procedures used to measure the properties associated with each class are distinctly different and merit separate chapters for their description. In later chapters, we will continually return to these procedures as we discuss the examination of the various kinds of physical evidence. This chapter will be devoted, in large part, to reviewing a variety of techniques and instruments that have become the indispensable tools of the forensic scientist for examining organic evidence.

Matter
All things of substance. Matter is composed of atoms or molecules.

Element
A fundamental particle of matter. An element cannot be broken down into simpler substances by chemical means.

Periodic Table
A chart of elements arranged in a systematic fashion. Vertical rows are called groups or families; horizontal rows are called series. Elements in a given row have similar properties.

Elements and Compounds

Matter is anything that has mass and occupies space. As we examine the world that surrounds us and consider the countless variety of materials that we encounter, we must consider one of humankind's most remarkable accomplishments the discovery of the concept of the atom to explain the composition of all matter. This search had its earliest contribution from the ancient Greek philosophers, who suggested air, water, fire, and earth as matter's fundamental building blocks. It culminated with the development of the atomic theory and the discovery of matter's simplest identity, the **element**.

An element is the simplest substance known and provides the building block from which all matter is composed. At present, 118 elements have been identified (see Table 5–1); of these, 89 occur naturally on the earth, and the remainder have been created in the laboratory. In Figure 5–1, all the elements are listed by name and symbol in a form that has become known as the **periodic table**. This table is most useful to chemists because it systematically arranges elements with similar chemical properties in the same vertical row or group.

Table 5–1 List of Elements with Their Symbols and Atomic Masses

Element	Symbol	Atomic Mass[a] (amu)	Element	Symbol	Atomic Mass[a] (amu)
Actinum	Ac	(227)	Lanthanum	La	138.9055
Aluminum	Al	26.9815	Lawrencium	Lr	(257)
Americium	Am	(243)	Lead	Pb	207.2
Antimony	Sb	121.75	Lithium	Li	6.941
Argon	Ar	39.948	Lutetium	Lu	174.97
Arsenic	As	74.9216	Magnesium	Mg	24.305
Astatine	At	(210)	Manganese	Mn	54.9380
Barium	Ba	137.34	Meitnerium	Mt	(266)
Berkelium	Bk	(247)	Mendelevium	Md	(256)
Beryllium	Be	9.01218	Mercury	Hg	200.59
Bismuth	Bi	208.9806	Molybdenum	Mo	95.94
Bohrium	Bh	(262)	Neodymium	Nd	144.24
Boron	B	10.81	Neon	Ne	20.179
Bromine	Br	79.904	Neptunium	Np	237.0482
Cadmium	Cd	112.40	Nickel	Ni	58.71
Calcium	Ca	40.08	Niobium	Nb	92.9064
Californium	Cf	(251)	Nitrogen	N	14.0067
Carbon	C	12.011	Nobelium	No	(254)
Cerium	Ce	140.12	Osmium	Os	190.2
Cesium	Cs	132.9055	Oxygen	O	15.9994
Chlorine	Cl	35.453	Palladium	Pd	106.4
Chromium	Cr	51.996	Phosphorus	P	30.9738
Cobalt	Co	58.9332	Platinum	Pt	195.09
Copper	Cu	63.546	Plutonium	Pu	(244)
Curium	Cm	(247)	Polonium	Po	(209)
Darmstadtium	Ds	(271)	Potassium	K	39.102
Dubnium	Db	(260)	Praseodymium	Pr	140.9077
Dysprosium	Dy	162.50	Promethium	Pm	(145)
Einsteinium	Es	(254)	Protactinium	Pa	231.0359
Erbium	Er	167.26	Radium	Ra	226.0254
Europium	Eu	151.96	Radon	Rn	(222)
Fermium	Fm	(253)	Rhenium	Re	186.2
Fluorine	F	18.9984	Rhodium	Rh	102.9055
Francium	Fr	(223)	Roentgenium	Rg	(272)
Gadolinium	Gd	157.25	Rubidium	Rb	85.4678
Gallium	Ga	69.72	Ruthenium	Ru	101.07
Germanium	Ge	72.59	Rutherfordium	Rf	(257)
Gold	Au	196.9665	Samarium	Sm	105.4
Hafnium	Hf	178.49	Scandium	Sc	44.9559
Hassium	Hs	(265)	Seaborgium	Sg	(263)
Helium	He	4.00260	Selenium	Se	78.96
Holmium	Ho	164.9303	Silicon	Si	28.086
Hydrogen	H	1.0080	Silver	Ag	107.868
Indium	In	114.82	Sodium	Na	22.9898
Iodine	I	126.9045	Strontium	Sr	87.62
Iridium	Ir	192.22	Sulfur	S	32.06
Iron	Fe	55.847	Tantalum	Ta	180.9479
Krypton	Kr	83.80	Technetium	Tc	98.9062

continued

Table 5–1 Continued

Element	Symbol	Atomic Mass[a] (amu)	Element	Symbol	Atomic Mass[a] (amu)
Tellurium	Te	127.60	Ununpentium	Uup	(288)
Terbium	Tb	158.9254	Ununhexium	Uuh	(292)
Thallium	Tl	204.37	Ununseptium	Uus	(?)
Thorium	Th	232.0381	Ununoctium	Uuo	(?)
Thulium	Tm	168.9342	Uranium	U	238.029
Tin	Sn	118.69	Vanadium	V	50.9414
Titanium	Ti	47.90	Xenon	Xe	131.3
Tungsten	W	183.85	Ytterbium	Yb	173.04
Ununbium	Uub	(285)	Yttrium	Y	88.9059
Ununtrium	Uut	(284)	Zinc	Zn	65.57
Ununquadium	Uuq	(289)	Zirconium	Zr	91.22

[a]Based on the assigned relative atomic mass of C = exactly 12; parentheses denote the mass number of the isotope with the longest half-life.

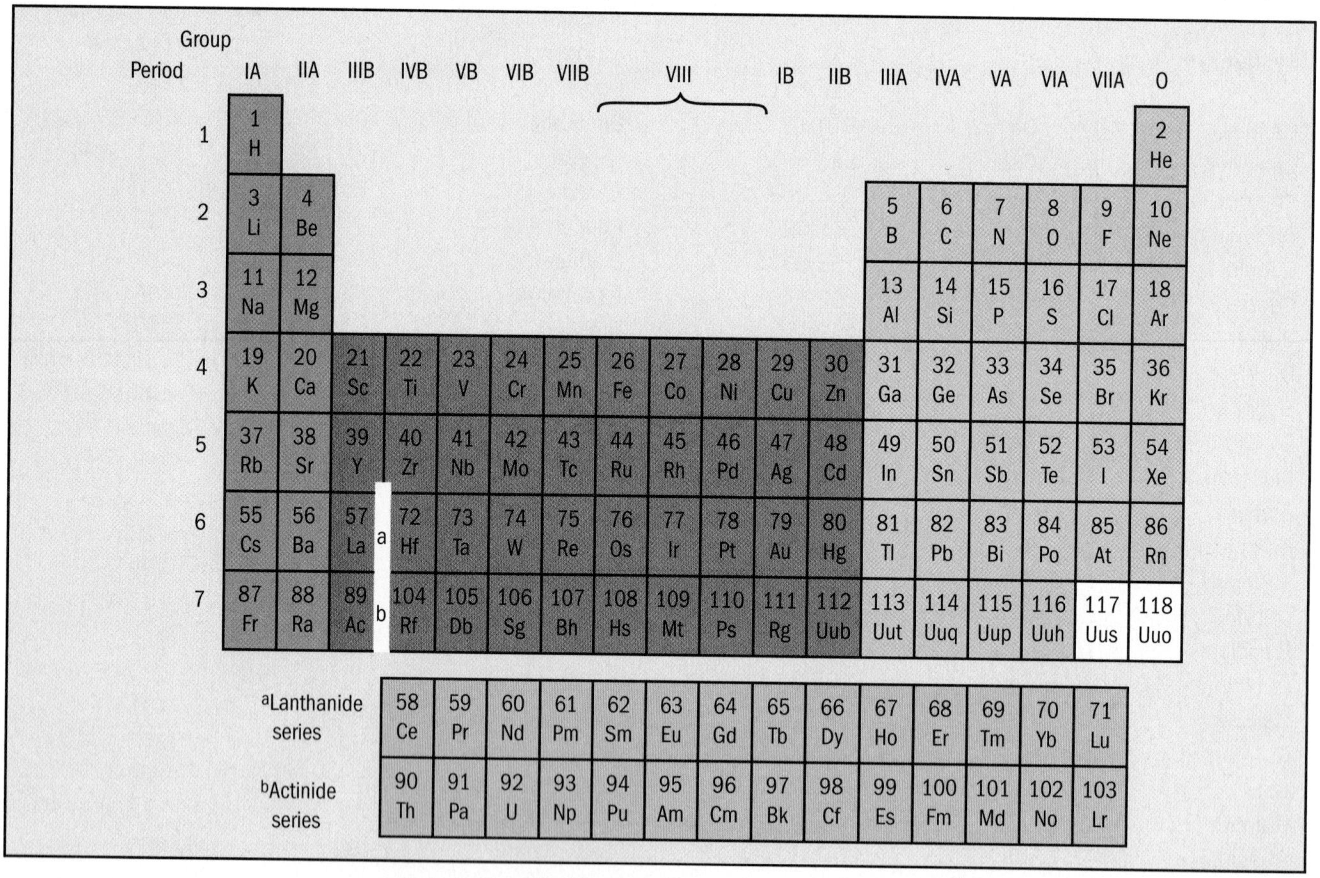

Figure 5–1   The periodic table.

For convenience, chemists have chosen letter symbols to represent the elements. Many of these symbols come from the first letter of the element's English name—for example, carbon (C), hydrogen (H), and oxygen (O). Others are two-letter abbreviations of the English name—for example, calcium (Ca) and zinc (Zn). Some symbols are derived from the first letters of

Latin or Greek names. Thus, the symbol for silver, Ag, comes from the Latin name *argentum;* copper, Cu, from the Latin *cuprum;* and helium, He, from the Greek name *helios.*

The smallest particle of an element that can exist and still retain its identity as that element is the atom. When we write the symbol C we mean one atom of carbon; the chemical symbol for carbon dioxide, CO_2, signifies one atom of carbon combined with two atoms of oxygen. When two or more elements are combined to form a substance, as with carbon dioxide, a new substance is created, different in its physical and chemical properties from its elemental components. This new material is called a compound. Compounds contain at least two elements. Considering that there are eighty-nine natural elements, it is easy to imagine the large number of possible elemental combinations that may form compounds. Not surprisingly, more than 16 million known compounds have already been identified.

Just as the atom is the basic particle of an element, the molecule is the smallest unit of a compound. Thus, a molecule of carbon dioxide is represented by the symbol CO_2, and a molecule of table salt is symbolized by NaCl, representing the combination of one atom of the element sodium (Na) with one atom of the element chlorine (Cl).

As we look around us and view the materials that make up the earth, it becomes an awesome task even to attempt to estimate the number of different kinds of matter that exist. A much more logical approach is to classify matter according to the physical form it takes. These forms are called physical states. There are three such states: solid, liquid, and gas (vapor). A solid is rigid and therefore has a definite shape and volume. A liquid also occupies a specific volume, but its fluidity causes it to take the shape of the container in which it is residing. A gas has neither a definite shape nor volume, and it will completely fill any container into which it is placed.

Substances can change from one state to another. For example, as water is heated, it is converted from a liquid form into a vapor. At a high enough temperature (100°C), water boils and rapidly changes into steam. Similarly, at 0°C, water solidifies or freezes into ice. Under certain conditions, some solids can be converted directly into a gaseous state. For instance, a piece of dry ice (solid carbon dioxide) left standing at room temperature quickly forms carbon dioxide vapor and disappears. This change of state from a solid to a gas is called sublimation.

In each of these examples, no new chemical species are formed; matter is simply being changed from one physical state to another. Water, whether in the form of liquid, ice, or steam, remains chemically H_2O. Simply, what has been altered are the attractive forces between the water molecules. In a solid, these forces are very strong, and the molecules are held closely together in a rigid state. In a liquid, the attractive forces are not as strong, and the molecules have more mobility. Finally, in the vapor state, appreciable attractive forces no longer exist among the molecules; thus, they may move in any direction at will.

Chemists are forever combining different substances, no matter whether they are in the solid, liquid, or gaseous states, hoping to create new and useful products. Our everyday observations should make it apparent that not all attempts at mixing matter can be productive. For instance, oil spills demonstrate that oil and water do not mix. **Whenever substances can be distinguished by a visible boundary, different phases are said to exist.** Thus, oil floating on water is an example of a

Compound
A pure substance composed of two or more elements.

Physical State
A condition or stage in the form of matter; a solid, liquid, or gas.

Solid
A state of matter in which the molecules are held closely together in a rigid state.

Liquid
A state of matter in which molecules are in contact with one another but are not rigidly held in place.

Gas (Vapor)
A state of matter in which the attractive forces between molecules are small enough to permit them to move with complete freedom.

Sublimation
A physical change from the solid state directly into the gaseous state.

Phase
A uniform body of matter; different phases are separated by definite visible boundaries.

two-phase system. The oil and water each constitute a separate liquid phase, clearly distinct from each other. Similarly, when sugar is first added to water, it does not dissolve, and two distinctly different phases exist: the solid sugar and the liquid water. However, after stirring, all the sugar dissolves, leaving just one liquid phase.

Selecting an Analytical Technique

Now that the basic components of matter have been defined, proper selection of analytical techniques that enable the forensic scientist to identify or compare matter can best be understood by categorizing all substances into one of two broad groups: organics and inorganics.

Organic substances contain carbon, commonly in combination with hydrogen, oxygen, nitrogen, chlorine, phosphorus, or other elements. Inorganic substances encompass all other known chemical substances. Each of these two broad groups has distinctive and characteristic properties. Thus, once the analyst has determined whether a material is organic or inorganic, the properties to be measured and the choice of analytical techniques to be used are generally the same for all materials in each group.

Another consideration in selecting an analytical technique is the need for either a *qualitative* or a *quantitative* determination. The former relates just to the identity of the material, whereas the latter refers to the percentage combination of the components of a mixture. Hence, a qualitative identification of a powder may reveal the presence of heroin and quinine, whereas a quantitative analysis may conclude the presence of 10 percent heroin and 90 percent quinine. Obviously, a qualitative identification must precede any attempt at quantitation, for little value is served by attempting to quantitate a material without first determining its identity. Essentially, a qualitative analysis of a material requires the determination of numerous properties using a variety of analytical techniques. On the other hand, a quantitative measurement is usually accomplished by the precise measurement of a single property of the material.

Most evidence received by crime laboratories requires identification of organic compounds. These compounds may include substances such as commonly abused drugs (such as alcohol, marijuana, heroin, amphetamines, and barbiturates), synthetic fibers, petroleum products, paint binders, and high-order explosives. As we have already observed, organic compounds are composed of a combination of a relatively small number of elements that must include carbon; fortunately, the nature of the forces or bonds between these elements is such that the resultant compounds can readily be characterized by their absorption of light. The study of the absorption of light by chemical substances, known as spectrophotometry, is a basic tool for the characterization and identification of organic materials. Although spectrophotometry is most applicable to organic analysis, its optimal use requires that a material be in a relatively pure state. Because the purity of physical evidence is almost always beyond the control of the criminalist, this criterion often is not met. For this reason, the analytical technique of chromatography is widely applied for the analysis of physical evidence. **Chromatography is a means of separating and tentatively identifying the components of a mixture.** We will discuss both techniques in this chapter.

Organic
Describes a substance composed of carbon and often smaller amounts of hydrogen, oxygen, nitrogen, chlorine, phosphorus, or other elements.

Inorganic
Describes a chemical compound not based on carbon.

Spectrophotometry
An analytical method for identifying a substance by its selective absorption of different wavelengths of light.

Chromatography
Any of several analytical techniques for separating organic mixtures into their components by attraction to a stationary phase while being propelled by a moving phase.

Chromatography

Theory of Chromatography

Chromatography as a technique for purifying substances is particularly useful for analyzing the multicomponent specimens that are frequently received in the crime laboratory. For example, illicit drugs sold on the street are not manufactured to meet government labeling standards; instead, they may be diluted with practically any material at the disposal of the drug dealer to increase the quantity of product available to prospective customers. Hence, the task of identifying an illicit-drug preparation would be arduous without the aid of chromatographic methods to first separate the mixture into its components.

The theory of chromatography is based on the observation that chemical substances tend to partially escape into the surrounding environment when dissolved in a liquid or when absorbed on a solid surface. This is best illustrated by a gas dissolved in a beaker of water kept at a constant temperature. It will be convenient for us to characterize the water in the beaker as the liquid phase and the air above it as the gas phase. If the beaker is covered with a bell jar, as shown in Figure 5–2, some of the gas molecules (represented by the green balls) escape from the water into the surrounding enclosed air. The molecules that remain are said to be in the liquid phase; the molecules that have escaped into the air are said to be in the gas phase. As the gas molecules escape into the surrounding air, they accumulate above the water; here, random motion carries some of them back into the water. Eventually, a point is reached at which the number of molecules leaving the water is equal to the number returning. At this time, the liquid and gas phases are in *equilibrium*. If the temperature of the water is increased, the equilibrium state readjusts itself to a point at which more gas molecules move into the gas phase.

This behavior was first observed in 1803 by a British chemist, William Henry. His explanation of this phenomenon, known appropriately as Henry's law, may be stated as follows: *When a volatile chemical compound is dissolved in a liquid and is brought to equilibrium with air, there is a fixed ratio between the concentration of the volatile compound in air and its concentration in the liquid, and this ratio remains constant for a given temperature.*

The distribution or partitioning of a gas between the liquid and gas phases is determined by the solubility of the gas in the liquid. The higher its

Figure 5–2 Evaporation of a liquid.

solubility, the greater the tendency of the gas molecules to remain in the liquid phase. If two different gases are simultaneously dissolved in the same liquid, each will reach a state of equilibrium with the surrounding air independently of the other. For example, as shown in Figure 5–3, gas A (green balls) and gas B (blue balls) are both dissolved in water. At equilibrium, gas A has a greater number of molecules dissolved in the water than does gas B. This is so because gas A is more soluble in water than gas B.

Now return to the concept of chromatography. In Figures 5–2 and 5–3, both phases—liquid and gas—were kept stationary; that is, they were not moving. During a chromatographic process, this is not the case; instead, one phase is always made to move continuously in one direction over a stationary or fixed phase. For example, in Figure 5–3, showing the two gases represented by blue and green balls dissolved in water, chromatography will occur only when the air is forced to move continuously in one direction over the water. Because gas B has a greater percentage of its molecules in the moving gas phase than does gas A, its molecules will travel over the liquid at a faster pace than those of gas A. Eventually, when the moving phase has advanced a reasonable distance, gas B will become entirely separated from gas A and the chromatographic process will be complete. This process is illustrated in Figure 5–4.

Simply, we can think of chromatography as being analogous to a race between chemical compounds. At the starting line, all the partici-

Figure 5–3 At equilibrium, there are more gas A molecules (green balls) than gas B molecules (blue balls) in the liquid phase.

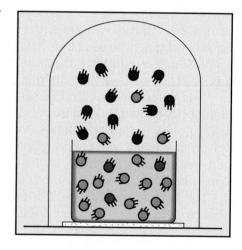

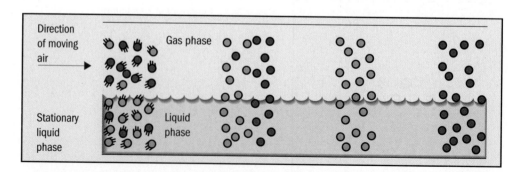

Figure 5–4 In this illustration of chromatography, the molecules represented by the blue balls have a greater affinity for the upper phase and hence will be pushed along at a faster rate by the moving air. Eventually, the two sets of molecules will separate from each other, completing the chromatographic process.

pating substances are mixed together; however, as the race progresses, materials that prefer the moving phase slowly pull ahead of those that prefer to remain in the stationary phase. Finally, at the end of the race, all the participants are separated, each crossing the finish line at different times.

The different types of chromatographic systems are as varied as the number of stationary and moving-phase combinations that can be devised. However, three chromatographic processes—gas chromatography, high-performance liquid chromatography, and thin-layer chromatography—are most applicable for solving many analytical problems in the crime laboratory.

Gas Chromatography (GC)

Gas chromatography (GC) separates mixtures on the basis of their distribution between a stationary liquid phase and a moving gas phase. This technique is widely used because of its ability to resolve a highly complex mixture into its components, usually within minutes.

In gas chromatography, the moving phase is actually a gas called the *carrier gas*, which flows through a column constructed of stainless steel or glass. The stationary phase is a thin film of liquid within the column. Two types of columns are used: the *packed column* and the *capillary column*. With the packed column, the stationary phase is a thin film of liquid that is fixed onto small granular particles packed into the column. This column is usually constructed of stainless steel or glass and is 2 to 6 meters in length and about 3 millimeters in diameter. Capillary columns are composed of glass and are much longer than packed columns—15 to 60 meters in length. These types of columns are very narrow, ranging from 0.25 to 0.75 millimeter in diameter. Capillary columns can be made narrower than packed columns because their stationary liquid phase is actually coated as a very thin film directly onto the column's inner wall. In any case, as the carrier gas flows through the packed or capillary column, it carries with it the components of a mixture that have been injected into the column. Components with a greater affinity for the moving gas phase travel through the column more quickly than those with a greater affinity for the stationary liquid phase. Eventually, after the mixture has traversed the length of the column, it emerges separated into its components.

A simplified scheme of the gas chromatograph is shown in Figure 5–5. The operation of the instrument can be summed up briefly as follows: A gas stream, the so-called carrier gas, is fed into the column at a constant rate. The carrier gas is chemically inert and is generally nitrogen or helium. The sample under investigation is injected as a liquid into a heated injection port with a syringe, where it is immediately vaporized and swept into the column by the carrier gas. The column itself is heated in an oven in order to keep the sample in a vapor state as it travels through the column. In the column, the components of the sample travel in the direction of the carrier gas flow at speeds that are determined by their distribution between the stationary and moving phases. If the analyst has selected the proper liquid phase and has made the column long enough, the components of the sample will be completely separated as they emerge from the column.

As each component emerges from the column, it enters a detector. One type of detector uses a flame to ionize the emerging chemical substance, thus generating an electrical signal. The signal is recorded onto a strip-chart recorder as a function of time. This written record of the sep-

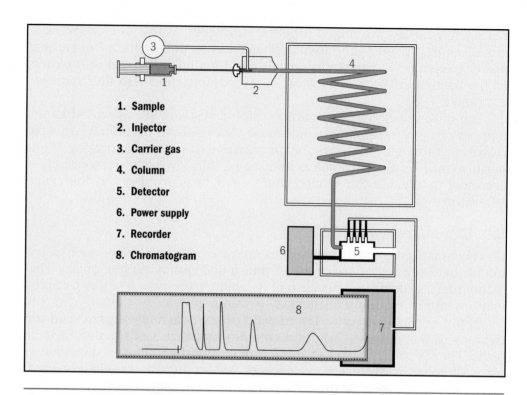

1. Sample
2. Injector
3. Carrier gas
4. Column
5. Detector
6. Power supply
7. Recorder
8. Chromatogram

Figure 5–5 **Basic gas chromatography. Gas chromatography permits rapid separation of complex mixtures into individual compounds and allows identification and quantitative determination of each compound. As shown, a sample is introduced by a syringe (1) into a heated injection chamber (2). A constant stream of nitrogen gas (3) flows through the injector, carrying the sample into the column (4), which contains a thin film of liquid. The sample is separated in the column, and the carrier gas and separated components emerge from the column and enter the detector (5). Signals developed by the detector activate the recorder (7), which makes a permanent record of the separation by tracing a series of peaks on the chromatograph (8). The time of elution identifies the component present, and the peak area identifies the concentration.** *Courtesy Varian Inc., Palo Alto, Calif.*

aration is called a *chromatogram*. A gas chromatogram is a plot of the recorder response (vertical axis) versus time (horizontal axis). A typical chromatogram shows a series of peaks, each peak corresponding to one component of the mixture. The time required for a component to emerge from the column from the time of its injection into the column is known as the *retention time,* which is a useful identifying characteristic of a material. Figure 5–6(a) shows the chromatogram of two barbiturates; each barbiturate has tentatively been identified by comparing its retention time to those of known barbiturates, shown in Figure 5–6 (b). (See Appendix III for chromatographic conditions.) However, because other substances may have comparable retention times under similar chromatographic conditions, gas chromatography cannot be considered an absolute means of identification. Conclusions derived from this technique must be confirmed by other testing procedures.

An added advantage of gas chromatography is that it is extremely sensitive and can yield quantitative results. The amount of substance passing through the GC detector is proportional to the peak area recorded; therefore, by chromatographing a known concentration of a material and comparing it to the unknown, the amount of the sample may be determined by

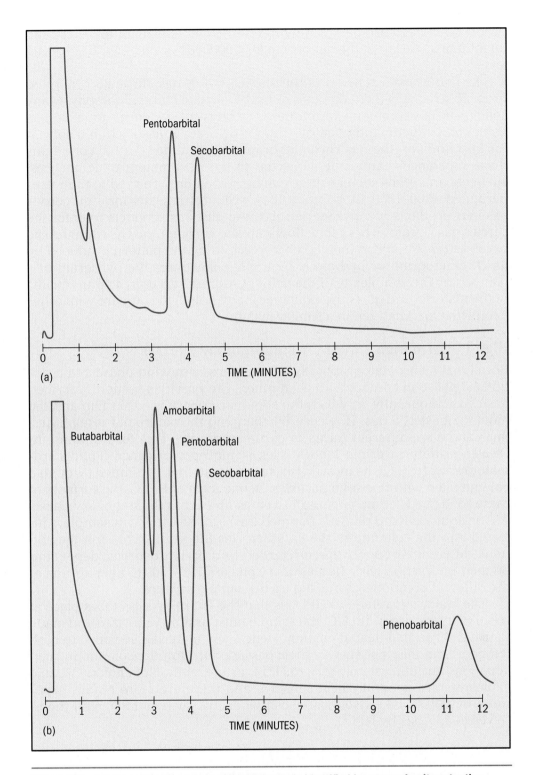

Figure 5–6 **(a) An unknown mixture of barbiturates is identified by comparing its retention times to (b), a known mixture of barbiturates.** *Courtesy Varian Inc., Palo Alto, Calif.*

Pyrolysis
The decomposition of organic matter by heat.

WebExtra 5.1

Watch the Gas Chromatograph at Work
www.prenhall.com/Saferstein

proportion. Gas chromatography has sufficient sensitivity to detect and quantitate materials at the nanogram (0.000000001 gram or 1×10^{-29} gram) level.[1]

An important extension of the application of gas chromatography to forensic science is the technique of pyrolysis *gas chromatography.* Many solid materials commonly encountered as physical evidence—for example, paint chips, fibers, and plastics—cannot be readily dissolved in a solvent for injection into the gas chromatograph. Thus, under normal conditions these substances cannot be subjected to gas chromatographic analysis. However, materials such as these can be heated or pyrolyzed to high temperatures (500–1000°C) so that they will decompose into numerous gaseous products. Pyrolyzers permit these gaseous products to enter the carrier gas stream, where they flow into and through the GC column. The pyrolyzed material can then be characterized by the pattern produced by its chromatogram or *pyrogram.* Figure 5–7 illustrates the pyrogram of a paint chip. The complexity of the paint pyrogram serves as a "fingerprint" of the material and gives the examiner many points to compare with other paints that are analyzed in a similar fashion.

High-Performance Liquid Chromatography (HPLC)

Recall that a chromatographic system requires a moving phase and a stationary phase in contact with each other. The previous section described gas chromatography, in which the stationary phase is a thin film and the moving phase is a gas. However, by changing the nature of these phases, one can create different forms of chromatography. One form finding increasing utility in crime laboratories is high-performance liquid chromatography (HPLC). Its moving phase is a liquid that is pumped through a column filled with fine solid particles. In one form of HPLC, the surfaces of these solid particles are chemically treated and act as the stationary phase. As the liquid moving phase is pumped through the column, a sample is injected into the column. As the liquid carries the sample through the column, different components are retarded to different degrees, depending on their interaction with the stationary phase. This leads to a separation of the different components making up the sample mixture.

The major advantage of HPLC is that the entire process takes place at room temperature. With GC, the sample must first be vaporized and made to travel through a heated column. Hence, any materials sensitive to high temperatures may not survive their passage through the column. In such situations, the analyst may turn to HPLC as the method of choice. Organic explosives are generally heat sensitive and therefore more readily separated by HPLC. Likewise, heat-sensitive drugs, such as LSD, lend themselves to analysis by HPLC.

Thin-Layer Chromatography (TLC)

The technique of thin-layer chromatography (TLC) uses a solid stationary phase and a moving liquid phase to separate the constituents of a mixture. A thin-layer plate is prepared by coating a glass plate with a thin film of a

---

[1] Powers of 10 are quite useful and simple for handling large or small numbers. The exponent expresses the number of places the decimal point must be moved. If the exponent is positive, the decimal point is moved to the right; if it is negative, the decimal point is moved to the left. Thus, to express 1×10^{-9} as a number, the decimal point is simply moved nine places to the left of 1.

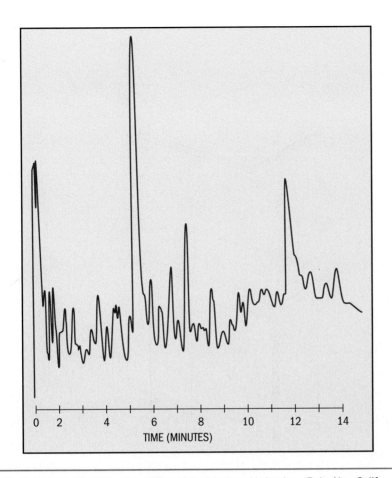

Figure 5–7 Pyrogram of a GM automobile paint. *Courtesy Varian Inc., Palo Alto, Calif.*

granular material, usually silica gel or aluminum oxide. This granular material serves as the solid stationary phase and is usually held in place on the plate with a binding agent such as plaster of Paris. If the sample to be analyzed is a solid, it must first be dissolved in a suitable solvent and a few microliters of the solution spotted with a capillary tube onto the granular surface near the lower edge of the plate. A liquid sample may be applied directly to the plate in the same manner. The plate is then placed upright into a closed chamber that contains a selected liquid, with care that the liquid does not touch the sample spot.

The liquid slowly rises up the plate by capillary action. This rising liquid is the moving phase in thin-layer chromatography. As the liquid moves past the sample spot, the components of the sample become distributed between the stationary solid phase and the moving liquid phase. The components with the greatest affinity for the moving phase travel up the plate faster than those that have greater affinity for the stationary phase. When the liquid front has moved a sufficient distance (usually 10 cm), the development is complete, and the plate is removed from the chamber and dried (see Figure 5–8). An example of the chromatographic separation of ink is shown in Figure 5–9.

Because most compounds are colorless, no separation will be noticed after development unless the materials are *visualized*. To accomplish this, the plates are placed under ultraviolet light, revealing select materials that fluoresce as bright spots on a dark background. When a fluorescent dye has been incorporated into the solid phase, nonfluorescent substances appear as dark spots against a fluorescent background when exposed to the

Fluoresce
To emit visible light when exposed to light of a shorter wavelength—that is, ultraviolet light.

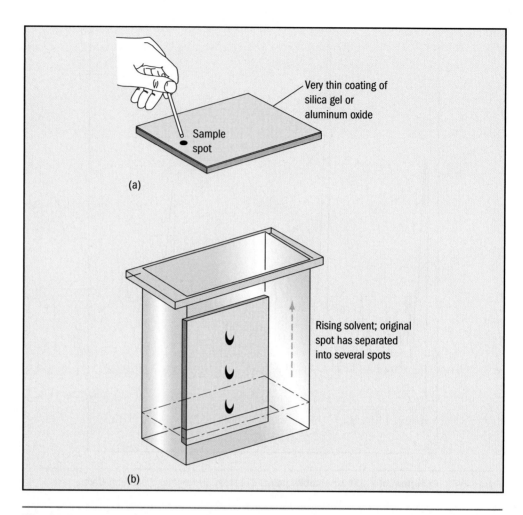

Figure 5–8 **(a) In thin-layer chromatography, a liquid sample is spotted onto the granular surface of a gel-coated plate. (b) The plate is placed into a closed chamber that contains a liquid. As the liquid rises up the plate, the components of the sample distribute themselves between the coating and the moving liquid. The mixture is separated, with substances with a greater affinity for the moving liquid traveling up the plate at a faster speed.**

Figure 5–9 **(a) The liquid phase begins to move up the stationary phase. (b) Liquid moves past the ink spot carrying the ink components up the stationary phase. (c) The moving liquid has separated the ink into its several components.** *Courtesy Fundamental Photographs, NYC*

ultraviolet light. In a second method of visualization, the plate is sprayed with a chemical reagent that reacts with the separated substances and causes them to form colored spots. Figure 5–10 shows the chromatogram of a marijuana extract that has been separated into its components by TLC and visualized by having been sprayed with a chemical reagent.

Once the components of a sample have been separated, their identification must follow. For this, the questioned sample must be developed alongside an authentic or standard sample on the same TLC plate. If both the standard and the unknown travel the same distance up the plate from their origins, they can tentatively be identified as being the same. For example, suppose a sample suspected of containing heroin and quinine is chromatographed alongside known heroin and quinine standards, as shown in Figure 5–11. The identity of the suspect material is confirmed by comparing the migration distances of the heroin and quinine standards against those of the components of the unknown material. If the distances are the same, a tentative identification can be made. However, such an identification cannot be considered definitive, for numerous other substances can migrate the same distance up the plate when chromatographed under similar conditions. Thus, thin-layer chromatography alone cannot provide an absolute identification; it must be used in conjunction with other testing procedures to prove absolute identity.

The distance a spot has traveled up a thin-layer plate can be assigned a numerical value known as the R_f value. This value is defined as the distance traveled by the component divided by the distance traveled by the moving liquid phase. For example, in Figure 5–11 the moving phase traveled 10

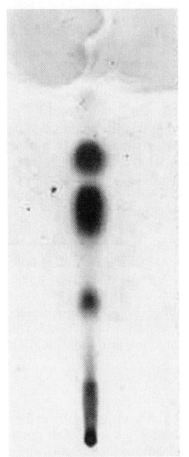

Figure 5–10 Thin-layer chromatogram of a marijuana extract. *Courtesy Sirchie Finger Print Laboratories, Inc., Youngsville, N.C., www.sirchie.com*

Figure 5–11 Chromatograms of known heroin (1) and quinine (2) standards alongside suspect sample (3).

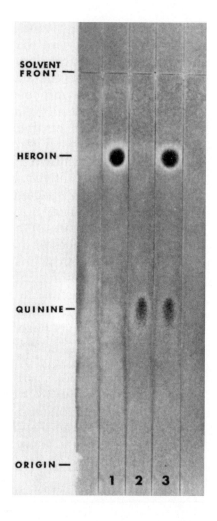

centimeters up the plate before the plate was removed from the tank. After visualization, the heroin spot moved 8 centimeters, which has an R_f value of 0.8; the quinine migrated 4 centimeters, for an R_f value of 0.4.

Thousands of possible combinations of liquid and solid phases can be chosen in thin-layer chromatography. Fortunately, years of research have produced much published data relating to the proper selection of TLC conditions for separating and identifying specific classes of substances—for example, drugs, dyes, and petroleum products. These references, along with the experience of the analyst, will aid in the proper selection of TLC conditions for specific problems.

Thin-layer chromatography is a powerful tool for solving many of the analytical problems presented to the forensic scientist. The method is both rapid and sensitive; moreover, less than 100 micrograms of suspect material are required for the analysis. In addition, the equipment necessary for TLC work has minimal cost and space requirements. Importantly, numerous samples can be analyzed simultaneously on one thin-layer plate. The principal application of this technique is in the detection and identification of components in complex mixtures.

Electrophoresis

Electrophoresis is somewhat related to thin-layer chromatography in that it separates materials according to their migration rates on a stationary solid phase. However, it does not use a moving liquid phase to move the

---

WebExtra 5.2

Watch Animated Depictions of Thin-Layer Chromatography and Gas Chromatography
www.prenhall.com/Saferstein

Electrophoresis
A technique for separating molecules through migration on a support medium while under the influence of an electrical potential.

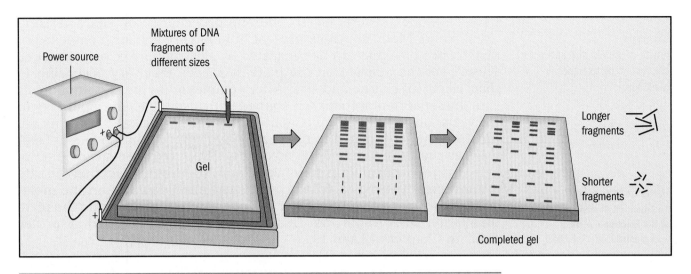

Figure 5–12 Electrophoresis separates mixtures of DNA by forcing them to migrate across a gel-coated plate under the influence of an electrical potential. Due to variations in size, DNA fragments move across the plate at different speeds.

Figure 5–13 DNA fragments separated by gel electrophoresis are visualized under a UV light.
Courtesy Cytographics, Visuals Unlimited

material; instead, an electrical potential is placed across the stationary medium. The nature of this medium can vary; most forensic applications call for a starch or agar gel coated onto a glass plate. Under these conditions, only substances that possess an electrical charge migrate across the stationary phase (see Figure 5–12). The technique is particularly useful for separating and identifying complex biochemical mixtures. In forensic science, electrophoresis finds its most successful application in the characterization of **proteins** and DNA in dried blood (see Figure 5–13).

Because many substances in blood carry an electrical charge, they can be separated and identified by electrophoresis. Forensic serologists

Proteins
Polymers of amino acids that play basic roles in the structures and functions of living things.

Enzyme
A type of protein that acts as a catalyst for certain specific reactions.

WebExtra 5.3
An Animated Demonstration of Gel Electrophoresis
www.prenhall.com/Saferstein

Visible Light
Colored light ranging from red to violet in the electromagnetic spectrum.

Wavelength
The distance between crests of adjacent waves.

Frequency
The number of waves that pass a given point per second.

have developed several electrophoretic procedures for characterizing dried blood. Many enzymes present in blood are actually composed of distinct proteins that can be separated by electrophoresis on starch gel. These proteins migrate on the plate at speeds that vary according to their electrical charge and size. After completion of the electrophoresis run, the separated proteins are stained with a suitable developing agent for visual observation. In this manner, characteristic band patterns are obtained that are related to the enzyme type present in the blood. Likewise, as shown in Figure 5–12, mixtures of DNA fragments can be separated by gel electrophoresis by taking advantage of the fact that the rate of movement of DNA across a gel-coated plate depends on the molecule's size. Smaller DNA fragments move at a faster rate along the plate than larger DNA fragments. This technique will be discussed in further detail in Chapters 12 and 13.

Spectrophotometry
Theory of Light

We have already seen that when white light passes through a glass prism, it is dispersed into a continuous spectrum of colors. This phenomenon demonstrates that white light is not homogeneous but is actually composed of a range of colors that extends from red through violet. Similarly, the observation that a substance has a color is also consistent with this description of white light. For example, when light passes through a red glass, the glass absorbs all the component colors of light except red, which passes through or is transmitted by the glass. Likewise, one can determine the color of an opaque object by observing its ability to absorb some of the component colors of light while reflecting others back to the eye. Color is thus a visual indication that objects absorb certain portions of visible light and transmit or reflect others. Scientists have long recognized this phenomenon and have learned to characterize different chemical substances by the type and quantity of light they absorb.

To understand why materials absorb light, one must first comprehend the nature of light. Two simple models explain light's behavior. **The first model describes light as a continuous wave; the second depicts it as a stream of discrete energy particles.** Together, these two very different descriptions explain all of the observed properties of light, but by itself, no one model can explain all the facets of the behavior of light.

The wave concept depicts light as having an up-and-down motion of a continuous wave, as shown in Figure 5–14. Several terms are used to describe such a wave. The distance between two consecutive crests (or one trough to the next trough) is called the wavelength; the Greek letter *lambda* (λ) is used as its symbol, and the unit of nanometers is frequently used to express its value. The number of crests (or troughs) passing any one given point in a unit of time is defined as the frequency of the wave. Frequency is normally designated by the letter *f* and is expressed in cycles per second (cps). The speed of light in a vacuum is a universal constant at 300 million meters per second and is designated by the symbol *c*. Frequency and wavelength are inversely proportional to one another, as shown by the relationship expressed in Equation (5–1):

$$F = c/\lambda \qquad (5\text{–}1)$$

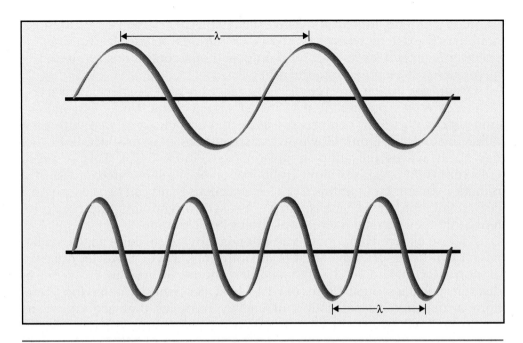

Figure 5–14   The frequency of the lower wave is twice that of the upper wave.

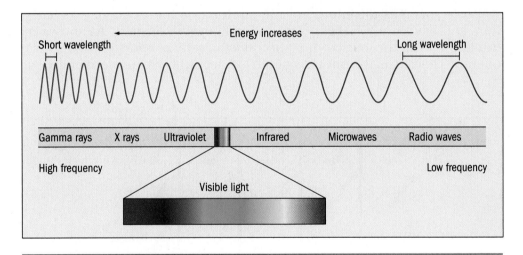

Figure 5–15   The electromagnetic spectrum.

Actually, visible light is only a small part of a large family of radiation waves known as the electromagnetic spectrum. All electromagnetic waves travel at the speed of light (*c*) and are distinguishable from one another only by their different wavelengths or frequencies. (Figure 5–15 illustrates the various types of electromagnetic waves in order of decreasing frequency.) Hence, the only property that distinguishes X-rays from radio waves is the different frequencies the two types of waves possess. Similarly, the range of colors that make up the visible spectrum can be correlated with frequency. For instance, the lowest frequencies of visible light are red; waves with a lower frequency fall into the invisible infrared (IR) region. The highest frequencies of visible light are violet; waves with a higher

Electromagnetic Spectrum
The entire range of radiation energy from the most energetic cosmic rays to the least energetic radio waves.

X-ray
A high-energy, short-wavelength form of electromagnetic radiation.

frequency extend into the invisible ultraviolet (UV) region. No definite boundaries exist between any colors or regions of the electromagnetic spectrum; instead, each region is composed of a continuous range of frequencies, each blending into the other.

Ordinarily, light in any region of the electromagnetic spectrum is a collection of waves possessing a range of wavelengths. Under normal circumstances, this light comprises waves that are all out of step with each other (incoherent light). However, scientists can now produce light that has all its waves pulsating in unison (see Figure 5–16). This is called **coherent light** or a laser (*l*ight *a*mplification by the *s*timulated *e*mission of *r*adiation) beam. Light in this form is very intense and can be focused on a very small area. Laser beams can be focused to pinpoints that are so intense that they can zap microscopic holes in a diamond.

As long as electromagnetic radiation is moving through space, its behavior can be described as that of a continuous wave; however, once radiation is absorbed by a substance, the model of light as a stream of discrete particles must be invoked to best describe its behavior. Here, light is depicted as consisting of energy particles that are known as **photons**. Each photon has a definite amount of energy associated with its behavior. This energy is related to the frequency of light, as shown by Equation (5–2):

$$E = hf \qquad\qquad (5\text{–}2)$$

where E specifies the energy of the photon, f is the frequency of radiation, and h is a universal constant called Planck's constant. As shown by Equation (5–2), the energy of a photon is directly proportional to its frequency. Therefore, the photons of ultraviolet light will be more energetic

Laser
An acronym for light amplification by stimulated emission of radiation; light that has all its waves pulsating in unison.

Photon
A small packet of electromagnetic radiation energy. Each photon contains a unit of energy equal to the product of Planck's constant and the frequency of radiation: $E = hf$.

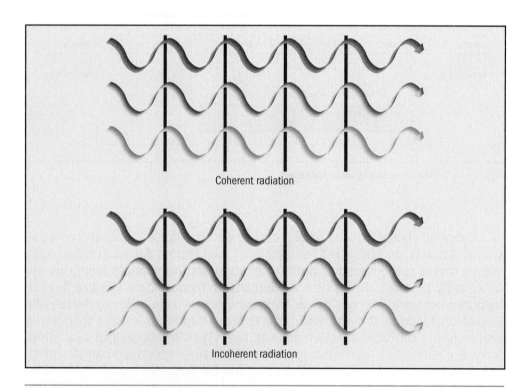

Figure 5–16   Coherent and incoherent radiation.

than the photons of visible or infrared light, and exposure to the more energetic photons of X-rays presents more danger to human health than exposure to the photons of radio waves.

Absorption of Electromagnetic Radiation

Just as a substance can absorb visible light to produce color, many of the invisible radiations of the electromagnetic spectrum are likewise absorbed. This absorption phenomenon is the basis for spectrophotometry, an important analytical technique in chemical identification. Spectrophotometry measures the quantity of radiation that a particular material absorbs as a function of wavelength or frequency.

We have already observed in the description of color that an object does not absorb all the visible light it is exposed to; instead, it selectively absorbs some frequencies and reflects or transmits others. Similarly, the absorption of other types of electromagnetic radiation by chemical substances is also selective. These key questions must be asked: Why does a particular substance absorb only at certain frequencies and not at others? And are these frequencies predictable? The answers are not simple. Scientists find it difficult to predict with certainty all the frequencies at which any one substance will absorb in a particular region of the electromagnetic spectrum. What is known, however, is that a chemical substance absorbs photons of radiation with a frequency that corresponds to an energy requirement of the substance, as defined by Equation (5–2). Different materials have different energy requirements and therefore absorb at different frequencies. Most important to the analyst is that these absorbed frequencies are measurable and can be used to characterize a material.

The selective absorption of a substance is measured by an instrument called a *spectrophotometer,* which produces a graph or *absorption spectrum* that depicts the absorption of light as a function of wavelength or frequency. The absorption of ultraviolet (UV), visible, and infrared (IR) radiation is particularly applicable for obtaining qualitative data pertaining to the identification of organic substances.

Absorption at a single wavelength or frequency of light is not 100 percent complete—some radiation is transmitted or reflected by the material. Just how much radiation a substance absorbs is defined by a fundamental relationship known as Beer's law, shown in Equation (5–3):

$$A = kc \qquad\qquad (5\text{–}3)$$

Here, A symbolizes the absorption or the quantity of light taken up at a single frequency, c is the concentration of the absorbing material, and k is a proportionality constant. This relationship shows that the quantity of light absorbed at any frequency is directly proportional to the concentration of the absorbing species; the more material you have, the more radiation it will absorb. By defining the relationship between absorbance and concentration, Beer's law permits spectrophotometry to be used as a technique for quantification.

The Spectrophotometer

The spectrophotometer measures and records the absorption spectrum of a chemical substance. The basic components of a simple spectrophotometer are the same regardless of whether it is designed to measure the

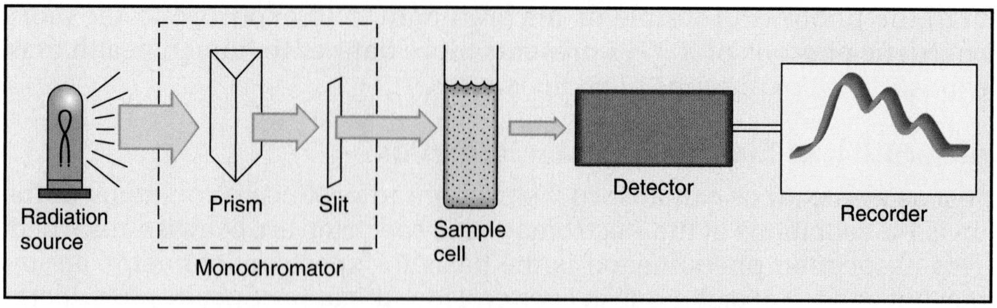

Figure 5–17   Parts of a simple spectrophotometer.

absorption of UV, visible, or IR radiation. These components are illustrated in Figure 5–17. They include (1) a radiation source, (2) a monochromator or frequency selector, (3) a sample holder, (4) a detector to convert electromagnetic radiation into an electrical signal, and (5) a recorder to produce a record of the signal.

The choice of source will vary with the type of radiation desired. For visible radiation, an ordinary tungsten bulb provides a convenient source of radiation. In the UV region, a hydrogen or deuterium discharge lamp is normally used, and a heated molded rod containing a mixture of rare-earth oxides is a good source of IR light.

The function of the monochromator is to select a single wavelength or frequency of light from the source—monochromatic light. Some inexpensive spectrophotometers pass the light through colored glass filters to remove all radiation from the beam except for a desired range of wavelengths. More precise spectrophotometers use a prism or diffraction grating to disperse radiation into its component wavelengths or frequencies.[2] The desired wavelength is obtained when the dispersed radiation is focused onto a narrow slit that permits only selected wavelengths to pass through.

Most laboratory infrared spectrophotometers use Fourier transform analysis to measure the wavelengths of light at which a material will absorb in the infrared spectrum. This approach does not use any dispersive elements that select single wavelengths or frequencies of light emitted from a source; instead, the heart of a *Fourier transform infrared* (FT-IR) *spectrometer* is the Michelson interferometer. The interferometer uses a beam-splitting prism and two mirrors, one movable and one stationary, to direct light toward a sample. As the wavelengths pass through the sample and reach a detector, they are all measured simultaneously. A mathematical operation, the Fourier transform method, is used to decode the measured signals and record the wavelength data. These Fourier calculations are rapidly carried out by a computer. In a matter of seconds, a computer-operated FT-IR instrument can produce an infrared absorption pattern compatible to one generated by a prism instrument.

Monochromator
A device for isolating individual wavelengths or frequencies of light.

Monochromatic Light
Light having a single wavelength or frequency.

---

[2] A diffraction grating is made by scratching thousands of parallel lines on a transparent surface such as glass. As light passes through the narrow spacings between the lines, it spreads out and produces a spectrum similar to that formed by a prism.

Sample preparation varies with the type of radiation being studied. Absorption spectra in the UV and visible regions are usually obtained from samples that have been dissolved in an appropriate solvent. Because the cells holding the solution must be transparent to the light being measured, glass cells are used in the visible region and quartz cells in the ultraviolet region. Practically all substances absorb in some region of the IR spectrum, so sampling techniques must be modified to measure absorption in this spectral region; special cells made out of sodium chloride or potassium bromide are commonly used because they will not absorb light over a wide range of the IR portion of the electromagnetic spectrum.

The detector measures the quantity of radiation that passes through the sample by converting it to an electrical signal. UV and visible spectrophotometers employ photoelectric tube detectors. A signal is generated when the photons strike the tube surface to produce a current that is directly proportional to the intensity of the light transmitted through the sample. When this signal is compared to the intensity of light that is transmitted to the detector in the absence of an absorbing material, the absorbance of a substance can be determined at each wavelength or frequency of light selected. The signal from the detection system is then fed into a recorder, which plots absorbance as a function of wavelength or frequency. Modern spectrophotometers are designed to trace an entire absorption spectrum automatically.

WebExtra 5.4
See How a
Spectrophotometer Works
www.prenhall.com/Saferstein

Ultraviolet, Visible, and Infrared Spectrophotometry

Ultraviolet and visible spectrophotometry measure the absorbance of UV and visible light as a function of wavelength or frequency. For example, the UV absorption spectrum of heroin shows a maximum absorption band at a wavelength of 278 nanometers (see Figure 5–18). This

Ultraviolet
Invisible long frequencies of light beyond violet in the visible spectrum.

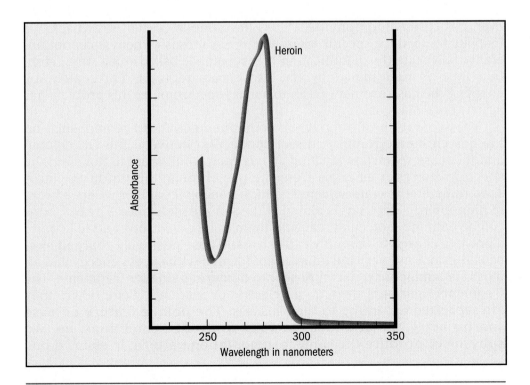

Figure 5–18 The ultraviolet spectrum of heroin.

shows that the simplicity of a UV spectrum facilitates its use as a tool for determining a material's probable identity. For instance, a white powder may have a UV spectrum comparable to heroin and therefore may be tentatively identified as such. (Fortunately, sugar and starch, common diluents of heroin, do not absorb UV light.) However, this technique will not provide a definitive result; other drugs or materials may have a UV absorption spectrum similar to that of heroin. But this lack of specificity does not diminish the value of the technique, for the analyst has quickly eliminated thousands of other possible drugs from consideration and can now proceed to conduct other confirmatory tests, such as thin-layer or gas chromatography, to complete the identification.

In contrast to the simplicity of a UV spectrum, absorption in the infrared region provides a far more complex pattern. Figure 5–19 depicts the IR spectra of heroin and secobarbital. Here, the absorption bands are so numerous that each spectrum can provide enough characteristics to identify a substance specifically. **Different materials always have distinctively different infrared spectra; each IR spectrum is therefore equivalent to a "fingerprint" of that substance and no other.** This technique is one of the few tests available to the forensic scientist that can be considered specific in itself for identification. The IR spectra of thousands of organic compounds have been collected, indexed, and cataloged to serve as invaluable references for identifying organic substances.

Infrared
Invisible short frequencies of light before red in the visible spectrum.

Mass Spectrometry

A previous section discussed the operation of the gas chromatograph. This instrument is one of the most important tools in a crime laboratory. Its ability to separate the components of a complex mixture is unsurpassed. However, gas chromatography (GC) does have one important drawback—its inability to produce specific identification. A forensic chemist cannot unequivocally state the identification of a substance based solely on a retention time as determined by the gas chromatograph. Fortunately, by coupling the gas chromatograph to a mass spectrometer this problem has largely been overcome.

The separation of a mixture's components is first accomplished on the gas chromatograph. A direct connection between the GC column and the mass spectrometer then allows each component to flow into the spectrometer as it emerges from the gas chromatograph. In the mass spectrometer, the material enters a high-vacuum chamber where a beam of high-energy electrons is aimed at the sample molecules. The electrons collide with the molecules, causing them to lose electrons and to acquire a positive charge (commonly called ions). These positively charged molecules or ions are very unstable or are formed with excess energy and almost instantaneously decompose into numerous smaller fragments. The fragments then pass through an electric or magnetic field, where they are separated according to their masses. **The unique feature of mass spectrometry is that under carefully controlled conditions, no two substances produce the same fragmentation pattern.** In essence, one

Ion
An atom or molecule bearing a positive or negative charge.

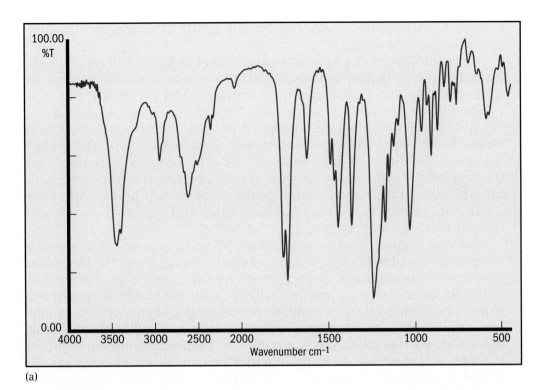

(a)

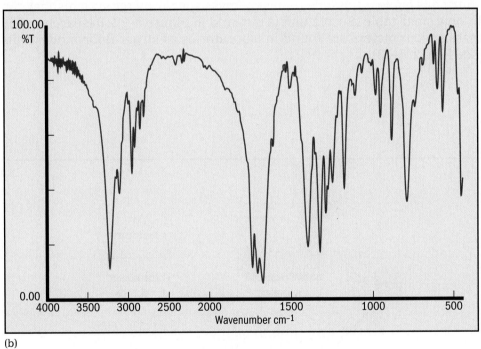

(b)

Figure 5–19   (a) Infrared spectrum of heroin. (b) Infrared spectrum of secobarbital.

can think of this pattern as a "fingerprint" of the substance being examined (see Figure 5–20).

The technique thus provides a specific means for identifying a chemical structure. It is also sensitive to minute concentrations. At present, mass spectrometry finds its widest application in the identification of drugs; however, further research is expected to yield significant applications for identifying other types of physical evidence. Figure 5–21 illustrates the mass spectra of heroin and cocaine; each line represents a fragment of a different mass (actually the ratio of mass to charge), and the line height reflects the relative abundance of each fragment. Note how different the fragmentation patterns of heroin and cocaine are. Each mass spectrum is unique to each drug and therefore serves as a specific test for identifying it.

The combination of the gas chromatograph and mass spectrometer is further enhanced when a computer is added to the system. The integrated gas chromatograph/mass spectrometer/computer system provides the ultimate in speed, accuracy, and sensitivity. With the ability to record and store in its memory several hundred mass spectra, such a system can detect and identify substances present in only one-millionth-of-a-gram quantities. Furthermore, the computer can be programmed to compare an unknown spectrum against a comprehensive library of mass spectra stored in its memory. The advent of personal computers and microcircuitry has made it possible to design mass spectrometer systems that can fit on a small table. Such a unit is pictured in Figure 5–22. Research-grade mass spectrometers are found in laboratories as larger floor-model units (see Figure 5–23).

WebExtra 5.5

Watch the Gas Chromatograph/Mass Spectrometer at Work
www.prenhall.com/Saferstein

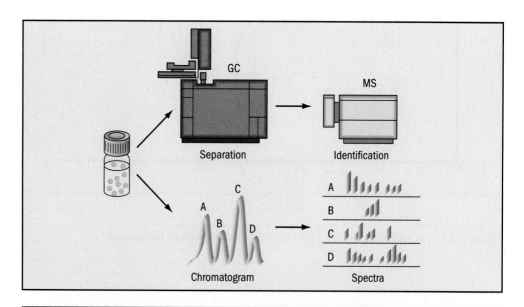

Figure 5–20 How GC/MS works. Left to right, the sample is separated into its components by the gas chromatograph, and then the components are ionized and identified by characteristic fragmentation patterns of the spectra produced by the mass spectrometer. *Courtesy Agilent Technologies, Inc., Palo Alto, Calif.*

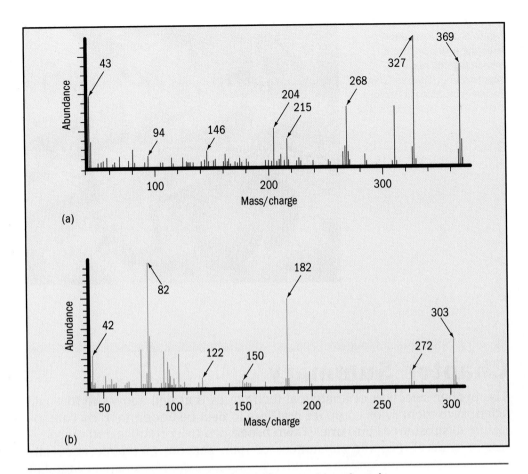

(a)

(b)

Figure 5–21 (a) Mass spectrum of heroin. (b) Mass spectrum of cocaine.

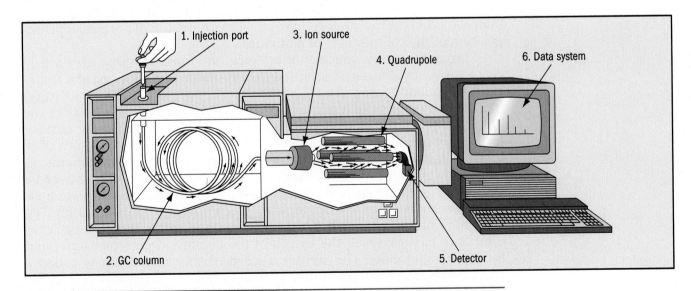

Figure 5–22 A tabletop mass spectrometer. (1) The sample is injected into a heated inlet port, and a carrier gas sweeps it into the column. (2) The GC column separates the mixture into its components. (3) In the ion source, a filament wire emits electrons that strike the sample molecules, causing them to fragment as they leave the GC column. (4) The quadrupole, consisting of four rods, separates the fragments according to their mass. (5) The detector counts the fragments passing through the quadrupole. The signal is small and must be amplified. (6) The data system is responsible for total control of the entire GC/MS system. It detects and measures the abundance of each fragment and displays the mass spectrum. *Courtesy Agilent Technologies, Inc., Palo Alto, Calif.*

Figure 5–23 A scientist injecting a sample into a research-grade mass spectrometer. *Courtesy Geoff Tompkinson/Science Photo Library, Photo Researchers, Inc.*

Chapter Summary

The proper selection of analytical techniques that will allow the forensic scientist to identify or compare matter can best be understood by categorizing all substances into one of two broad groups: organics and inorganics. In general, organic substances contain carbon. Inorganic materials encompass all other known chemical substances. Another consideration in selecting an analytical technique is the need for either a qualitative or a quantitative determination. The former relates just to the identity of the material, whereas the latter requires the determination of the percent composition of the components of a mixture.

Chromatography, spectrophotometry, and mass spectrometry are all readily used by a forensic scientist to identify or compare organic materials. Chromatography is a means of separating and tentatively identifying the components of a mixture. Spectrophotometry is the study of the absorption of light by chemical substances. Mass spectrometry characterizes organic molecules by observing their fragmentation pattern after their collision with a beam of high-energy electrons. Gas chromatography (GC) separates mixtures on the basis of their distribution between a stationary liquid phase and a mobile gas phase. In GC, the moving phase is actually a gas called the carrier gas, which flows through a column. The stationary phase is a thin film of liquid contained within the column. After a mixture has traversed the length of the column, it emerges separated into its components. The written record of this separation is called a chromatogram. A direct connection between the GC column and the mass spectrometer allows each component to flow into the mass spectrometer as it emerges from the GC. Fragmentation of each component by high-energy electrons produces a "fingerprint" pattern of the substance being examined.

Other forms of chromatography applicable to forensic science are high-performance liquid chromatography (HPLC) and thin-layer chromatography (TLC). HPLC separates compounds using a stationary phase and a mobile liquid phase and is used with temperature-sensitive compounds. TLC uses a solid stationary phase, usually coated onto a glass plate, and a mobile liquid phase to separate the components of the mixture. A technique analogous to TLC is electrophoresis, in which materials are forced to move across a gel-coated plate under the influence of an electrical potential. In this manner, substances such as proteins and DNA can be separated and characterized.

Most forensic laboratories use ultraviolet (UV) and infrared (IR) spectrophotometers to characterize chemical compounds. In contrast to the simplicity of a UV spectrum, absorption in the infrared region provides a far more complex pattern. Different materials always have distinctively different infrared spectra; each IR spectrum is therefore equivalent to a "fingerprint" of that substance.

Review Questions

1. Anything that has mass and occupies space is defined as _____.
2. The basic building blocks of all substances are the _____.
3. The number of elements known today is _____.
4. An arrangement of elements by similar chemical properties is accomplished in the _____ table.
5. A(n) _____ is the smallest particle of an element that can exist.
6. Substances composed of two or more elements are called _____.
7. A(n) _____ is the smallest unit of a compound formed by the union of two or more atoms.
8. The physical state that retains a definite shape and volume is a(n) _____.
9. A gas (has, has no) definite shape or volume.
10. During the process of _____, solids go directly to the gaseous state, bypassing the liquid state.
11. The attraction forces between the molecules of a liquid are (more, less) than those in a solid.
12. Different _____ are separated by definite visible boundaries.
13. Carbon-containing substances are classified as _____.
14. _____ substances encompass all non-carbon-containing materials.
15. A(n) _____ analysis describes the identity of a material, and a(n) _____ analysis relates to a determination of the quantity of a substance.
16. The study of the absorption of light by chemical substances is known as _____.
17. A mixture's components can be separated by the technique of _____.
18. True or False: Henry's law describes the distribution of a volatile chemical compound between its liquid and gas phases. _____
19. The (higher, lower) the solubility of a gas in a liquid, the greater its tendency to remain dissolved in that liquid.
20. True or False: In order for chromatography to occur, one phase must move continuously in one direction over a stationary phase. _____
21. A technique that separates mixtures on the basis of their distribution between a stationary liquid phase and a moving gas phase is _____.
22. The time required for a substance to travel through the gas chromatographic column is a useful identifying characteristic known as _____.

23. Solid materials that are not readily dissolved in solvents for injection into the gas chromatograph can be _____ into numerous gaseous products prior to entering the gas chromatograph.

24. A major advantage of high-performance liquid chromatography is that the entire process takes place at _____ temperature.

25. A technique that uses a moving liquid phase and a stationary solid phase to separate mixtures is _____.

26. Because most chemical compounds are colorless, the final step of the thin-layer development usually requires that they be _____ by spraying with a chemical reagent.

27. The distance a spot has traveled up a thin-layer plate can be assigned a numerical value known as the _____ value.

28. True or False: Thin-layer chromatography yields the positive identification of a material. _____

29. The migration of materials along a stationary phase under the influence of an electrical potential describes the technique of _____.

30. True or False: Color is a usual indication that substances selectively absorb light. _____

31. The distance between two successive identical points on a wave is known as _____.

32. True or False: Frequency and wavelength are directly proportional to one another. _____

33. Light, X-rays, and radio waves are all members of the _____ spectrum.

34. Red light is (higher, lower) in frequency than violet light.

35. Light that has all its waves pulsating in unison is called a(n) _____.

36. One model of light depicts it as consisting of energy particles known as _____.

37. True or False: The energy of a light particle (photon) is directly proportional to its frequency. _____

38. Red light is (more, less) energetic than violet light.

39. The selective absorption of electromagnetic radiation by materials (can, cannot) be used as an aid for identification.

40. The amount of radiation a substance will absorb is directly proportional to its concentration as defined by _____ law.

41. The _____ is the instrument used to measure and record the absorption spectrum of a chemical substance.

42. The function of the _____ is to select a single frequency of light emanating from the spectrophotometer's source.

43. An (ultraviolet, infrared) absorption spectrum provides a unique "fingerprint" of a chemical substance.

44. The technique of _____ exposes molecules to a beam of high-energy electrons in order to fragment them.

45. True or False: A mass spectrum is normally considered a specific means for identifying a chemical substance. _____

Further References

Northrop, David, "Forensic Applications of High-Performance Liquid Chromatography and Capillary Electrophoresis," in R. Saferstein, ed., *Forensic Science Handbook,* vol. 1, 2nd ed. Upper Saddle River, N.J.: Prentice Hall, 2002.

Saferstein, Richard, "Forensic Applications of Mass Spectrometry," in R. Saferstein, ed., *Forensic Science Handbook,* vol. 1, 2nd ed. Upper Saddle River, N.J.: Prentice Hall, 2002.

Stafford, David T., "Forensic Capillary Gas Chromatography," in R. Saferstein, ed., *Forensic Science Handbook,* vol. 2, 2nd ed. Upper Saddle River, N.J.: Prentice Hall, 2005.

Suzuki, Edward M., "Forensic Applications of Infrared Spectroscopy," in R. Saferstein, ed., *Forensic Science Handbook,* Vol. 3. Upper Saddle River, N.J.: Prentice Hall, 1993.

What Killed Napoleon?

Napoleon I, emperor of France, was sent into exile on the remote island of St. Helena by the British after his defeat at the Battle of Waterloo. St. Helena was hot, unsanitary, and rampant with disease. There, in 1815, Napoleon was confined to a large reconstructed agricultural building known as Longwood House. Boredom and unhealthy living conditions gradually took their toll on Napoleon's mental and physical state. He began suffering from severe abdominal pains and experienced swelling of the ankles and general weakness of his limbs. From the fall of 1820, Napoleon's health began to deteriorate at a rapid rate until death arrived on May 5, 1821. An autopsy concluded the cause of death to be stomach cancer.

It was inevitable that dying under British control, as Napoleon did, would bring with it numerous conspiratorial theories to account for his death. One of the more fascinating inquiries was conducted by a Swedish dentist, Sven Forshufvud, who systematically correlated the clinical symptoms of Napoleon's last days to those of arsenic poisoning. For Forshufvud, the key to unlocking the cause of Napoleon's death rested with Napoleon's hair. Forshufvud arranged to have Napoleon's hair measured for arsenic content by neutron activation analysis and found it consistent with arsenic poisoning over a lengthy period of time. Nevertheless, the cause of Napoleon's demise is still a matter for debate and speculation. Other Napoleon hairs have been examined and found to be low in arsenic content. Some question whether Napoleon even had clinical symptoms associated with arsenic poisoning. In truth, forensic science may never be able to answer the question—what killed Napoleon?

chapter 6

Inorganic Analysis

Key Terms

alpha ray

atomic mass

atomic number

beta ray

continuous spectrum

electron

electron orbital

emission spectrum

excited state

gamma ray

isotope

line spectrum

neutron

nucleus

proton

radioactivity

X-ray diffraction

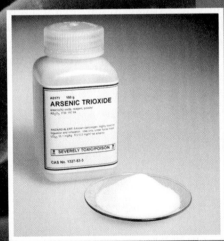

Learning Objectives

After studying this chapter you should be able to:

- Describe the usefulness of trace elements for forensic comparison of various types of physical evidence

- Distinguish continuous and line emission spectra

- Understand the parts of a simple emission spectrograph

- List the parts of a simple atomic absorption spectrophotometer

- Define and distinguish protons, neutrons, and electrons

- Define and distinguish atomic number and atomic mass number

- Appreciate the phenomenon of how an atom absorbs and releases energy in the form of light

- Explain the concept of an isotope

- Understand how elements can be made radioactive

- Describe why an X-ray diffraction pattern is useful for chemical identification

In the previous chapter, analytical techniques were described for characterizing a class of matter known as organics. Generally, these materials contain carbon. Although organic substances constitute a substantial portion of the physical evidence submitted to crime laboratories, carbon does not appear among the earth's most abundant elements. Surprisingly about three-quarters of the weight of the earth's crust is composed of only two elements—oxygen and silicon. In fact, only ten elements make up approximately 99 percent of the earth's crust (see Table 6–1). The remaining elements may almost be considered impurities, although exceedingly important ones. Carbon, the element that is a constituent of most chemical compounds, constitutes less than 0.1 percent of the earth's crust.

Considering these facts, it is certainly reasonable that non-carbon-containing substances—that is, inorganics—are encountered as physical evidence at crime scenes. One only has to consider the prevalence of metallic materials, such as iron, steel, copper, and aluminum, in our society to understand the possibilities of finding tools, coins, weapons, and metal scrapings at crime scenes.

Table 6–1 Elemental Abundances as Percentages in the Earth's Crust	
Element	Percentage by Weight
Oxygen	47.3
Silicon	27.7
Aluminum	7.9
Iron	4.5
Calcium	3.5
Sodium	2.5
Potassium	2.5
Magnesium	2.2
Titanium	0.5
Hydrogen	0.2
Other elements	1.2

Less well known, but perhaps almost as significant to the criminalist, is the use of inorganic chemicals as pigments in paints and dyes, the incorporation of inorganics into explosive formulations, and the prevalence of inorganic poisons such as mercury, lead, and arsenic.

To appreciate fully the role of inorganic analysis in forensic science, we must first examine its application to the basic objectives of the crime laboratory—identification and comparison of physical evidence. Identification of inorganic evidence is exemplified by a typical request to examine an explosive formulation suspected of containing potassium chlorate, or perhaps to examine a poisonous powder thought to be arsenic. In each case, the forensic scientist must perform tests that will ultimately determine the specific chemical identity of the suspect materials to the exclusion of all others. Only after completing the tests and finding their results identical to previously recorded tests for a known potassium chlorate or a known arsenic can the forensic scientist draw a valid conclusion about the chemical identity of the evidence.

However, comparing two or more objects in order to ascertain their common origin presents a different problem. For example, a criminalist may be asked to determine whether a piece of brass pipe found in the possession of a suspect compares to a broken pipe found at the crime scene. The condition of the two pipes might not allow for comparison by physically fitting together any broken edges. Under these circumstances, the only alternative will be to attempt a comparison through chemical analysis. It is not enough for the analyst to conclude that the pipes are alike because they are brass (an alloy of copper and zinc). After all, hundreds of thousands of brass pipes exist, a situation that is hardly conducive to proving that these two particular pipes were at one time a single unit. The examiner must go a step further to try to distinguish these pipes from all others. Although this may not be possible, a comparison of the pipes' trace elements—that is, elements present in small quantities—will provide a meaningful criterion for at least increasing the probability that the two pipes originated from the same source.

Considering that most of our raw materials originate from the earth's crust, it is not surprising that they are rarely obtained in pure form; instead, they include numerous elemental impurities that usually have to be eliminated through industrial processing. However, in most cases it is not economically feasible to completely exclude all such minor impurities, especially when their presence will have no effect on the appearance or performance of the final product. For this reason, many manufactured products, and even most natural materials, contain small quantities of elements present in concentrations of less than 1 percent. For the criminalist, the presence of *trace elements* is particularly useful because they provide "invisible" markers that may establish the source of a material or at least provide additional points for comparison. Table 6–2 illustrates how two types of brass alloys can readily be distinguished by their elemental composition. Similarly, the comparison of trace elements present in paint or other types of metallic specimens may provide particularly meaningful data with respect to source or origin. Forensic investigators have examined the evidential value of trace elements present in soil, fibers, and glass, as well as in all types of metallic objects. One example of this application occurred with the examination of the bullet and bullet fragments recovered after the assassination of President Kennedy.

Table 6–2 Elemental Analysis of Brass Alloys

Element	High-Tensile Brass (percentage)	Manganese Brass (percentage)
Copper	57.0	58.6
Aluminum	2.8	1.7
Zinc	35.0	33.8
Manganese	2.13	1.06
Iron	1.32	0.90
Nickel	0.48	1.02
Tin	0.64	1.70
Lead	0.17	0.72
Silicon	0.08	Nil

Source: R. L. Williams, "An Evaluation of the SEM with X-Ray Microanalyzer Accessory for Forensic Work," in O. Johari and I. Corvin, eds., *Scanning Electron Microscopy/1971*, (Chicago: IIT Research Institute, 1971), p. 541.

Evidence in the Assassination of President Kennedy

Ever since President Kennedy was killed in 1963, questions have lingered about whether Lee Harvey Oswald was part of a conspiracy to assassinate the president or, as the Warren Commission concluded, a lone assassin. In arriving at their conclusions, the Warren Commission reconstructed the crime as follows: Oswald fired three shots from behind the president while positioned in the Texas School Book Depository building. The president was struck by two bullets, with one bullet totally missing the president's limousine. One bullet hit the president in the back, exited his throat, and then went on to strike Governor Connally, who was sitting in a jump seat in front of the president. The bullet hit Connally first in his back, then exited his chest, struck his right wrist, and temporarily lodged in his left thigh. This bullet was later found in the governor's stretcher at the hospital. A second bullet in the skull fatally wounded the president.

In a room at the Texas School Book Depository, a 6.5-mm Mannlicher-Carcano military rifle was found with Oswald's palm print on it. Also found were three spent 6.5-mm Western Cartridge Co./ Mannlicher-Carcano (WCC/MC) cartridge cases. Oswald, an employee of the depository, had been seen there that morning and also a few minutes after the assassination, disappearing soon thereafter. He was apprehended a few miles from the depository nearly two hours after the shooting.

Critics of the Warren Commission have long argued that evidence exists that would prove Oswald did not act alone. Eyewitness accounts and acoustical data interpreted by some experts have been used to advocate the contention that someone else fired at the president from a region in front of the limousine (the so-called grassy knoll). Furthermore, it is argued that the Warren Commission's reconstruction of the crime relied on the assumption that only one bullet caused both the president's throat wound and Connally's back wound. Critics contend that such damage would have deformed and mutilated a bullet. Instead, the recovered bullet showed some flattening, no deformity, and only about 1 percent weight loss.

President John F. Kennedy, Governor John Connally of Texas, and Mrs. Jacqueline Kennedy ride through Dallas moments before the assassination. *Courtesy Corbis/Bettmann*

In 1977, at the request of the U.S. House of Representatives Select Committee on Assassinations, the bullet taken from Connally's stretcher along with bullet fragments recovered from the car and various wound areas were examined for trace element levels.

Lead alloys used for the manufacture of bullets contain an assortment of trace elements. For example, antimony is often added to lead as a hardening agent; copper, bismuth, and silver are other trace elements commonly found in bullet lead. In this case, the bullet and bullet fragments were compared for their antimony and silver content. Previous studies had amply demonstrated that the levels of these two elements are particularly important for characterizing WCC/MC bullets. Bullet lead from this type of ammunition ranges in antimony concentration from 20 to 1,200 parts per million (ppm) and 5 to 15 ppm in silver content.

As can be seen in Table 6–3, the samples designated Q1 and Q9 (the Connally stretcher bullet and fragments from Connally's wrist, respectively) are indistinguishable from one another in antimony and silver content. The samples Q2; Q4, 5; and Q14 (Q4, 5 being fragments from Kennedy's brain, and Q2 and Q14 being fragments recovered from two different areas in the car) also are indistinguishable in antimony and silver content but are different from Q1 and Q9.

The conclusions derived from studying these results are as follows:

1. There is evidence of only two bullets—one composed of 815 ppm antimony and 9.3 ppm silver, the other composed of 622 ppm antimony and 8.1 ppm silver.

2. Both bullets have a composition highly consistent with WCC/MC bullet lead, although other sources cannot entirely be ruled out.

Table 6–3 Antimony and Silver Concentrations in the Kennedy Assassination Bullets

	Silver (parts per million)[a]	Antimony (parts per million)	Sample Sample Description
Q1	8.8 ± 0.5	833 ± 9	Connally stretcher bullet
Q9	9.8 ± 0.5	797 ± 7	Fragments from Connally's wrist
Q2	8.1 ± 0.6	602 ± 4	Large fragment from car
Q4, 5	7.9 ± 0.3	621 ± 4	Fragments from Kennedy's brain
Q14	8.2 ± 0.4	642 ± 6	Small fragments found in car

[a]One part per million equals 0.0001 percent.

Source: Reprinted with permission from V. P. Guinn, "JFK Assassination: Bullet Analyses," *Analytical Chemistry*, 51 (1979), 484 A. Copyright 1979, American Chemical Society.

3. The bullet found in the Connally stretcher also damaged Connally's wrist. The absence of bullet fragments from the back wounds of Kennedy and Connally prevented any effort at linking these wounds to the stretcher bullet.

None of these conclusions can totally verify the Warren Commission's reconstruction of the assassination, but the results are at least consistent with the commission's findings.

The analyses on the Kennedy assassination bullets were performed by neutron activation analysis. The remainder of this chapter describes this and other techniques currently used to examine inorganic physical evidence.

The Emission Spectrum of Elements

We have already observed that organic molecules can readily be characterized by their selective absorption of ultraviolet, visible, or infrared radiation. Equally significant to the analytical chemist is the knowledge that elements also selectively absorb and emit light. These observations form the basis of two important analytical techniques designed to determine the elemental composition of materials—*emission spectroscopy* and *atomic absorption spectrophotometry*.

The statement that elements emit light should not come as a total surprise, for one need only observe the common tungsten incandescent lightbulb or the glow of a neon light to confirm this observation. When the light emitted from a bulb or from any other light source is passed through a prism, it is separated into its component colors or frequencies. The resulting display of colors is called an emission spectrum.

When sunlight or the light from an incandescent bulb is passed through a prism, we have already observed that a range of rainbow colors is produced. This emission spectrum is called a continuous spectrum because all the colors merge or blend into one another to form a continuous band. However, not all light sources produce such a spectrum. For example, if the light from a sodium lamp, a mercury arc lamp, or a neon light were passed through a prism, the resultant spectrum would consist not of a continuous band but of several individual colored lines separated by dark spaces. Here, each line represents a definite wavelength or frequency of

Emission Spectrum
Light emitted from a source and separated into its component colors or frequencies.

Continuous Spectrum
A type of emission spectrum showing a continuous band of colors all blending into one another.

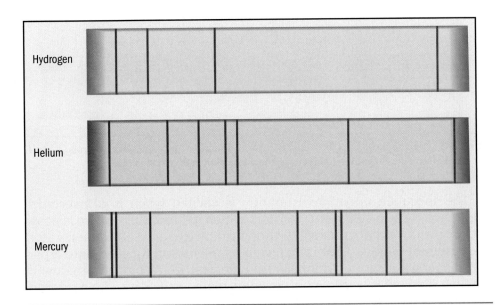

Figure 6–1   Some characteristic emission spectra.

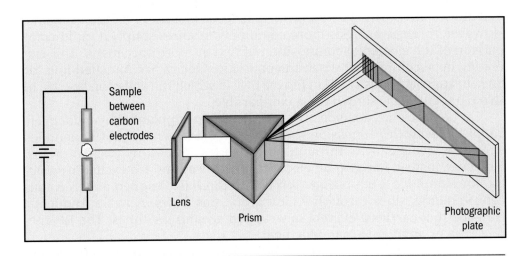

Figure 6–2   Parts of a simple emission spectrograph.

light that is separate and distinct from all others present in the spectrum. This type of spectrum is called a line spectrum. Figure 6–1 shows the line spectra of three elements.

Heated matter in a solid or liquid state produces a continuous spectrum that is not very indicative of its composition. However, if this same matter is vaporized and "excited" by exposure to high temperature, each element present emits light composed of select frequencies that are characteristic of the element. This spectrum is in essence a "fingerprint" of an element and offers a practical method of identification. Sodium vapor, for example, always shows the same line spectrum, which differs from the spectrum of all other elements.

An *emission spectrograph* is an instrument used to obtain and record the line spectra of elements. Essentially, this instrument requires a means for vaporizing and exciting the atoms of elements so that they emit light, a means for separating this light into its component frequencies, and a means of recording the resultant spectrum. A simple emission spectrograph is depicted in Figure 6–2.

Line Spectrum
A type of emission spectrum showing a series of lines separated by black areas. Each line represents a definite wavelength or frequency.

Figure 6–3   A comparison of paint chips 1 and 2 by emission spectrographic analysis. A line-for-line comparison shows that the paints have the same elemental composition.

The specimen under investigation is excited when it is inserted between two carbon electrodes through which a direct current arc is passed. The arc produces enough heat to vaporize and excite the specimen's atoms. The resultant emitted light is collected by a lens and focused onto a prism that disperses it into component frequencies. The separated frequencies are then directed toward a photographic plate, where they are recorded as line images. Normally, a specimen consists of numerous elements; hence, the typical emission spectrum contains many lines. Each element present in the spectrum can be identified when it is compared to a standard chart that shows the position of the principal spectral lines of all the elements. However, forensic analysis more commonly requires simply a rapid comparison of the elemental composition of two or more specimens. This can readily be accomplished when the emission spectra are matched line for line, an approach illustrated in Figure 6–3, in which the emission spectra of two paint chips are shown to be comparable.

Carbon arc emission spectrometry has been supplanted by *inductively coupled plasma (ICP) emission spectrometry*. Like the former, ICP identifies and measures elements through light energy emitted by excited atoms. However, instead of using an electrical arc, the atoms are excited by placing the sample in a hot plasma torch. The torch is designed as three concentric quartz tubes through which argon gas flows. A radio frequency (RF) coil that carries a current is wrapped around the tubes. The RF current creates an intense magnetic field.

The process begins when a high-voltage spark is applied to the argon gas flowing through the torch. This strips some electrons from their argon atoms. These electrons are then caught and accelerated in the magnetic field such that they collide with other argon atoms, stripping off still more electrons. The collision of electrons and argon atoms continues in a chain reaction, breaking down the gas into argon atoms, argon ions, and electrons and forming an *inductively coupled plasma discharge*. The discharge is sustained by RF energy that is continuously transferred to it from the coil. The plasma discharge acts like a very intense continuous flame generating extremely high temperatures in the range of 7,000–10,000°C. The sample, in the form of an aerosol, is then introduced into the hot plasma, where it collides with the energetic argon electrons generating charged particles (ions) that emit light of characteristic wavelengths corresponding to the identity of the elements present (see Figure 6–4).

Two areas of forensic casework in which ICP has been applied are the identification and characterization of mutilated bullets[1] and glass frag-

---

[1] R. D. Koons and J. Buscaglia, "Forensic Significance of Bullet Lead Compositions." *Journal of Forensic Sciences* 50 (2005): 341; C. A. Peters. "The Basis for Compositional Bullet Lead Comparisons," *Forensic Science Communications* 4 (2002), *http://www.fbi.gov/hq/lab/fsc/backissu/july2002/peters.htm.*

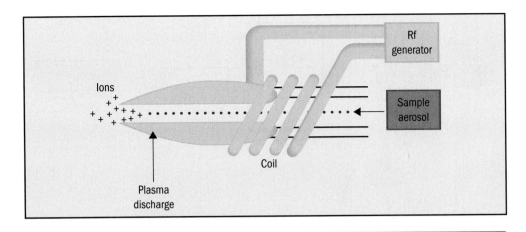

Figure 6–4   The creation of charged particles in the torch of an ICP discharge.

ments.[2] Mutilated bullets often are not suitable for traditional microscopic comparisons against an exemplar test-fired bullet. In such situations, ICP has been used to obtain an elemental profile of the questioned bullet fragment for comparison against an unfired bullet generally found in the possession of the suspect. For a number of years forensic scientists have taken advantage of significant compositional differences among lead sources for the manufacture of lead-based bullets. Compositional differences in the trace elements that constitute lead bullets are typically reflected in the copper, arsenic, silver, antimony, bismuth, cadmium, and tin profiles of lead bullets. When two or more bullets have comparable elemental compositions, evidence of their similarity may be offered in a court of law. In this respect, the comparison of lead bullets faces the same quandary as most common types of class physical evidence—how can a forensic analyst explain to a jury that such a finding has meaningful consequences to a criminal inquiry without being able to provide statistical or probability data to support such a contention? Furthermore, the creation of meaningful databases to statistically define the significance of bullets compared by their elemental profiles is currently an unrealistic undertaking. Nevertheless, the significant diversity of bullet lead compositions in our population, like other class evidence such as fibers, hairs, paint, plastics, and glass, makes their chance occurrence at a crime scene and subsequent link to a defendant a highly unlikely event. However, care must be taken to avoid giving the trier of fact the impression that elemental profiles constitute a definitive match. Given the millions of bullets produced each year, one cannot conclusively rule out the possibility of a coincidental match with a non-case-related bullet.

Atomic Absorption Spectrophotometer

When an atom is vaporized, it absorbs many of the same frequencies of light that it emits in an excited state. The selective absorption of light by atoms is the basis for a technique known as *atomic absorption spectrophotometry*. A simple atomic absorption spectrophotometer is illustrated in Figure 6–5.

---

[2] S. Montero, A. L. Hobbs, T. A. French, and J. Almirall, "Elemental Analysis of Glass Fragments by ICP-MS as Evidence of Association: Analysis of a Case," *Journal of Forensic Sciences* 48 (2003): 1101.

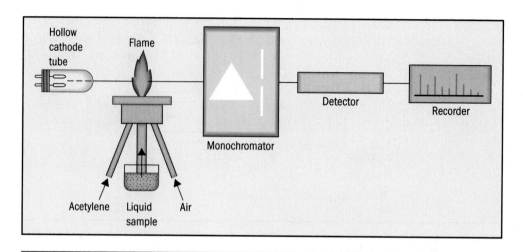

Figure 6–5   Parts of a simple flame atomic absorption spectrophotometer.

In atomic absorption spectrophotometry, the specimen is heated to a temperature that is hot enough to vaporize its atoms while leaving a substantial number of atoms in an unexcited state. Normally, the specimen is inserted into an air-acetylene flame to achieve this temperature. The vaporized atoms are then exposed to radiation emitted from a light source. The technique achieves great specificity by using as its radiation source a discharge tube made of the same element being analyzed in the specimen. When the discharge lamp is turned on, it emits only the frequencies of light that are present in the emission spectrum of the element. Likewise, the sample absorbs these frequencies only when it contains the same element. Therefore, to determine the presence of antimony in a specimen, the atomic absorption spectrophotometer must be fitted with a discharge lamp that is constructed of antimony. Under these conditions, the sample will absorb light only when it contains antimony.

Once the radiation has passed through the sample, a monochromator, consisting of a prism or a diffraction grating and a slit, isolates the desired radiation frequency and transmits it to a detector. The detector converts the light into an electrical signal, the intensity of which is recorded on a strip-chart recorder.

The absorption of light by the element of interest is the phenomenon that is being measured in atomic absorption spectrophotometry. The concentration of the absorbing element is directly proportional to the quantity of the light absorbed. The higher the concentration of the element, the more light is absorbed. For this reason, atomic absorption spectroscopy is most useful for accurately determining an element's concentration in a sample. Furthermore, the technique is sufficiently sensitive to find wide application in detecting and quantitating elements that are present at trace levels. However, the technique does have one drawback in that the analyst can determine only one element at a time, each time having to select the proper lamp to match the element under investigation.

Although atomic absorption spectrophotometry has been used for chemical analysis since 1955, it has not yet found wide application for solving forensic problems. However, a modification in the design of the instrument promises to change this situation. By substituting a heated graphite furnace or a heated strip of metal (tantalum) for the flame, analysts have achieved a more efficient means of atomic volatilization and as a result have substantially increased the sensitivity of the technique. Many elements can now be detected at levels that approach one-trillionth of a gram.

The high sensitivity of "flameless" atomic absorption now equals or surpasses that of most known analytical procedures. Considering the relative simplicity and low cost of the technique, atomic absorption spectrophotometry has become an attractive method for detecting and measuring the smallest levels of trace elements present in physical evidence.

The Origin of Emission and Absorption Spectra

Any proposed theory that attempts to explain the origin of emission and absorption spectra must relate to the fundamental structure of the element— the atom. Scientists now know that the atom is composed of even more elementary particles that are collectively known as *subatomic particles*. The most important subatomic particles are the proton, electron, and neutron. The masses of the proton and neutron are each about 1,837 times the mass of an electron. The proton has a positive electrical charge; the electron has a negative charge equal in magnitude to that of the proton; and the neutron is a neutral particle having neither a positive nor a negative charge. The properties of the proton, neutron, and electron are summarized in the following table:

Proton
A positively charged particle that is one of the basic structures in the nucleus of an atom.

Electron
A negatively charged particle that is one of the fundamental structural units of the atom.

Neutron
A particle with no electrical charge that is one of the basic structures in the nucleus of an atom.

Particle	Symbol	Relative Mass	Electrical Charge
Proton	P	1	+1
Neutron	n	1	0
Electron	e	1/1837	−1

A popular descriptive model of the atom, and the one that will be adopted for the purpose of this discussion, pictures an atom as consisting of electrons orbiting around a central nucleus—an image that is analogous to our solar system, in which the planets revolve around the sun.[3] The nucleus of the atom is composed of positively charged protons and neutrons that have no charge. Because the atom has no net electrical charge, the number of protons must always be equal to the number of negatively charged electrons in orbit around the nucleus.

Nucleus
The core of an atom containing the protons and neutrons.

With this knowledge, we can now begin to describe the atomic structure of the elements; for example, hydrogen has a nucleus consisting of one proton and no neutrons, and it has one orbiting electron. Helium has a nucleus comprising two protons and two neutrons, with two electrons in orbit around the nucleus (see Figure 6–6).

The behavior and properties that distinguish one element from another must be related to the differences in the atomic structure of each element. One such distinction is that each element possesses a different number of protons. This number is called the atomic number of the element. As we look back at the periodic table illustrated in Figure 5–1, we see that the elements are numbered consecutively. Those numbers represent the atomic

Atomic Number
The number of protons in the nucleus of an atom. Each element has its own unique atomic number.

---

[3] Actually, the electrons are moving so rapidly around the nucleus as to best be visualized as being in the form of an electron cloud spread out over the surface of the atom.

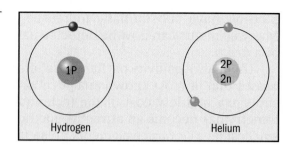

Figure 6–6 The atomic structures of hydrogen and helium.

number or number of protons associated with each element. **An element is therefore a collection of atoms that all have the same number of protons.** Thus, each atom of hydrogen has one and only one proton, each atom of helium has 2 protons, each atom of silver has 47 protons, and each atom of lead has 82 protons in its nucleus.

To explain the origin of atomic spectra, our attention must now focus on the electron orbitals of the atom. As electrons move around the nucleus, they are confined to a path from which they cannot stray. This orbital path is associated with a definite amount of energy and is therefore called an *energy level*. Each element has its own set of characteristic energy levels at varying distances from the nucleus. Some levels are occupied by electrons; others are empty.

An atom is in its most stable state when all of its electrons are positioned in their lowest possible energy orbitals in the atom. When an atom absorbs energy, such as heat or light, its electrons are pushed into higher-energy orbitals. In this condition, the atom is in an excited state. However, because energy levels have fixed values, only a definite amount of energy can be absorbed in moving an electron from one level to another. This is a most important observation, for it means that atoms absorb only a definite value of energy, and all other energy values will be excluded. In atomic absorption spectrophotometry, a photon of light interacts with an electron, causing it to jump into a higher orbital, as shown in Figure 6–7(a). A specific frequency of light is required to cause this transition, and its energy must correspond to the exact energy difference between the two orbitals involved in the transition. This energy difference is expressed by the relationship $E = hf$, where E represents the energy difference between the two orbitals, f is the frequency of absorbed light, and h is a universal constant called Planck's constant. Any energy value that is more or less than this difference will not produce the transition. Hence, an element is selective in the frequency of light it will absorb, and this selectivity is determined by the electron energy levels each element possesses.

In the same manner, if atoms are exposed to intense heat, enough energy is generated to push electrons into unoccupied higher-energy orbitals. Normally, the electron does not remain in this excited state for

Electron Orbital

The path of electrons as they move around the nuclei of atoms; each orbital is associated with a particular electronic energy level.

Excited State

The state in which an atom absorbs energy and an electron moves from a lower to a higher energy level.

Figure 6–7 (a) The absorption of light by an atom, causing an electron to jump into a higher orbital. (b) The emission of light by an atom, caused by an electron falling back to a lower orbital.

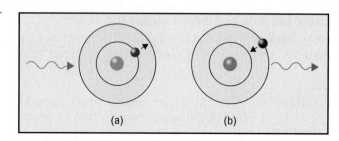

(a)   (b)

long, and it quickly falls back to its original energy level. As the electron falls back, it releases energy. An emission spectrum testifies to the fact that this energy loss comes about in the form of light emission [see Figure 6–7(b)]. The frequency of light emitted is again determined by the relationship $E = hf$, where E is the energy difference between the upper and lower energy levels and f is the frequency of emitted light. Because each element has its own characteristic set of energy levels, each emits a unique set of frequency values. The emission spectrum thus provides a "picture" of the energy levels that surround the nucleus of each element.

Thus, we see that as far as atoms are concerned, energy is a two-way street. Energy can be put into the atom at the same time that energy is given off; what goes in must come out. The chemist can study the atom using either approach. Atomic absorption spectrophotometry carefully measures the value and amount of light energy going into the atom; emission spectroscopy collects and measures the various light energies given off. The result is the same: atoms are identified by the existence of characteristic energy levels.

Neutron Activation Analysis

Once scientists realized that it was possible to change the number of subatomic particles in the atom's nucleus, the unleashing of a new source of energy—nuclear energy—was inevitable. This energy has proven so awesome in its power that the survival of civilization will depend on our ability to refrain from using its destructive forces. Of course, this threat does not obscure the fact that controlled nuclear energy promises to be a source of power capable of relieving our dependency on the earth's dwindling reserves of fossil fuels. For the chemist, nuclear chemistry provides a new tool for identifying and quantitating the elements.

Until now, our discussion of subatomic particles has been limited to the proton and electron. However, to understand the principles of nuclear chemistry, we must look at the other important subatomic particle, the neutron. Although the atoms of a single element must have the same number of protons, nothing prevents them from having different numbers of neutrons. The total number of protons and neutrons in a nucleus is known as the **atomic mass** number. Atoms with the same number of protons but differing solely in the number of neutrons are called **isotopes**. For example, hydrogen consists of three isotopes; besides ordinary hydrogen, which has one proton and no neutrons, two other isotopes exist, deuterium and tritium. Deuterium (or heavy hydrogen) also has one proton but contains one neutron as well. Tritium has one proton and two neutrons in its nucleus. The atomic structures of these isotopes are shown in Figure 6–8. Therefore, all the isotopes of hydrogen have an atomic number of 1 but differ in their atomic mass numbers. Hydrogen has an atomic mass number of 1, deuterium a mass of 2, and tritium a mass of 3. Ordinary hydrogen makes up 99.98 percent of all the hydrogen atoms found in nature.

Like hydrogen, most elements are known to have two or more isotopes. Tin, for example, has ten isotopes. Many of these isotopes are quite stable, and for all intents and purposes, the isotopes of any one element have indistinguishable properties. Others, however, are not as stable and decompose with time by a process known as *radioactive decay*. **Radioactivity** is the emission of radiation that accompanies the spontaneous disintegration

Atomic Mass Number
The sum of the number of protons and neutrons in the nucleus of an atom.

Isotope
An atom differing from another atom of the same element in the number of neutrons in its nucleus.

Radioactivity
The particle and/or gamma-ray radiation emitted by the unstable nucleus of some isotopes.

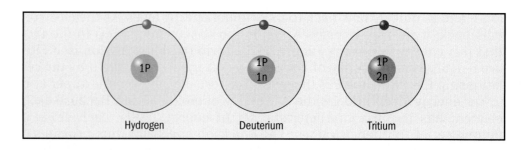

Figure 6–8   Isotopes of hydrogen.

Alpha Ray

A type of radiation emitted by a radioactive element. The radiation is composed of helium atoms minus their orbiting electrons.

Beta Ray

A type of radiation emitted by a radioactive element. The radiation consists of electrons.

Gamma Ray

A high-energy form of electromagnetic radiation emitted by a radioactive element.

of unstable nuclei. Radioactivity is actually composed of three types of radiation: alpha rays, beta rays, and gamma rays.

Alpha rays are positively charged particles, each with a mass approximately four times that of a hydrogen atom. These particles are helium atoms stripped of their orbiting electrons. Beta rays are actually electrons, and gamma rays are electromagnetic radiations similar to X-rays but of a higher frequency and energy (refer to the electromagnetic spectrum in Figure 5–15) . Fortunately, most naturally occurring isotopes are not radioactive, and those that are—radium, uranium, and thorium—are found in such small quantities in the earth's crust that their radioactivity presents no hazard to human survival.

The existence of isotopes would be of little importance to the forensic chemist were it not for the fact that scientists have mastered the techniques for synthesizing radioactive isotopes. If the only distinction between isotopes of an element is the number of neutrons each possesses, is it not reasonable to assume that when atoms are bombarded with neutrons, some neutrons will be captured to make new isotopes? This is exactly what happens in a nuclear reactor. A nuclear reactor is simply a source of neutrons that can be used to bombard the atoms of a specimen, thereby creating radioactive isotopes. When the nucleus of an atom captures a neutron, a new isotope with one additional neutron is formed. In this state, the nuclei are said to be activated, and many immediately begin to decompose by emitting radioactivity.

To identify the activated isotope, it is necessary to measure the energy of the gamma rays emitted as radioactivity. The gamma rays of each element can be associated with a characteristic energy value. Furthermore, once the element has been identified, its concentration can be measured by the intensity of its gamma-ray radiation; intensity is directly proportional to the concentration of the element in a specimen. The technique of bombarding specimens with neutrons and measuring the resultant gamma-ray radioactivity is known as *neutron activation analysis*. The process is depicted in Figure 6–9.

The major advantage of neutron activation analysis is that it provides a nondestructive method for identifying and quantitating trace elements. A median detection sensitivity of one-billionth of a gram (one nanogram) makes neutron activation analysis one of the most sensitive methods available for the quantitative detection of many elements. Further, neutron activation can simultaneously analyze twenty to thirty elements. A major drawback to the technique is its expense and regulatory requirements. Only a handful of crime laboratories worldwide have access to a nuclear reactor; in addition, sophisticated analyzers are needed to detect and discriminate gamma-ray emissions.

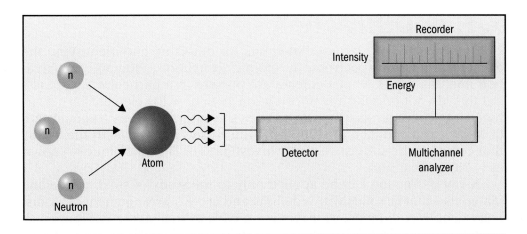

Figure 6–9   The neutron activation process requires the capture of a neutron by the nucleus of an atom. The new atom is now radioactive and emits gamma rays. A detector permits identification of the radioactive atoms present by measuring the energies and intensities of the gamma rays emitted.

Table 6–4 Concentration of Trace Elements in Copper Wire				
	Selenium	Gold	Antimony	Silver
Control Wire				
A$_1$	2.4	0.047	0.16	12.7
A$_2$	3.5	0.064	0.27	17.2
A$_3$	2.6	0.050	0.20	13.3
A$_4$	1.9	0.034	0.21	12.6
Suspect Wire				
B	2.3	0.042	0.15	13.0

Note: Average concentration measured in parts per million.

Source: R. K. H. Chan, "Identification of Single-Stranded Copper Wires by Nondestructive Neutron Activation Analysis," *Journal of Forensic Sciences,* **17 (1972), 93. Reprinted by permission of the American Society for Testing and Materials, copyright 1972.**

As far as forensic analysis is concerned, neutron activation has been used to characterize trace elements present in metals, drugs, paint, soil, gunpowder residues, and hair. A typical illustration of its application occurred during the investigation of a theft of copper telegraphic wires in Canada. Four lengths of copper wire (A$_1$, A$_2$, A$_3$, A$_4$) found at the scene of the theft were compared by neutron activation with a length of copper wire (B) seized at a scrap yard and suspected of being stolen. All were bare, single-strand wire with the same general physical appearance and a diameter of 0.28 centimeter. Prior experiments had revealed that significant variations could be expected in the concentration levels of the trace elements selenium, gold, antimony, and silver for wires originating from different sources. A comparison of these elements present in the wire involved in the theft was undertaken. After exposing the wires to neutrons in a nuclear reactor, neutron activation analysis revealed a match between A$_1$ and B that was well within experimental error (see Table 6–4). The findings suggested a common origin of the control and suspect wires.

X-Ray Diffraction

Until now, we have discussed methods for detecting and identifying the elements. Emission spectroscopy, atomic absorption, and neutron activation analysis tell us what elements are present in a particular substance, but they do not provide any information as to how the elements are combined into compounds. One way to elicit this information is to aim a beam of X-rays at a crystal and study how the X-rays interact with the atoms that compose the substance under investigation. This technique is known as X-ray diffraction.

X-ray diffraction
An analytical technique for identifying crystalline materials.

X-ray diffraction can be applied only to the study of solid, crystalline materials—that is, solids with a definite and orderly arrangement of atoms. For example, sodium chloride (common table salt), pictured in Figure 4–8, is crystalline. Fortunately, many substances, including 95 percent of all inorganic compounds, are crystalline and thus identifiable by X-ray diffraction analysis. The atoms in a crystal can be thought of as being composed of a series of parallel planes. As the X-rays penetrate the crystal, a portion of the beam is reflected by each of the atomic planes. As the reflected beams leave the crystal's planes, they combine with one another to form a series of light and dark bands known as a *diffraction pattern*. Every compound produces a unique diffraction pattern, thus giving analysts a means for "fingerprinting" compounds.

A diagram depicting the X-ray diffraction process is illustrated in Figure 6–10. Diffraction patterns for potassium nitrate and potassium chlorate, two common constituents of homemade explosives, are shown in Figure 6–11. Comparing a questioned specimen with a known X-ray pattern is a rapid and specific way to prove chemical identity.

One drawback to X-ray diffraction is its lack of sensitivity. The technique is suitable for identifying the major constituents of a mixture, but it often fails to detect the presence of substances constituting less than 5 percent of a mixture. For this reason, the forensic chemist must use more sensitive techniques—emission spectroscopy, atomic absorption, and neutron activation analysis—to identify trace elements that may be present.

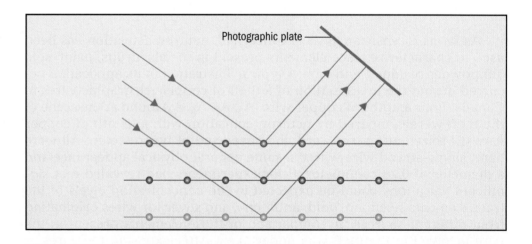

Photographic plate

Figure 6–10 **A beam of X-rays being reflected off the atomic planes of a crystal. The diffraction patterns that form are recorded on photographic film. These patterns are unique for each crystalline substance.**

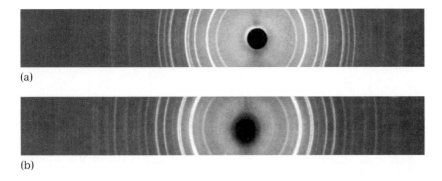

(a)

(b)

Figure 6–11   X-ray diffraction patterns for (a) potassium nitrate and (b) potassium chlorate.

Chapter Summary

Inorganic substances are encountered by forensic scientists as tools, explosives, poisons, and metal scrapings as well as trace components in paints and dyes. Many manufactured products and even most natural materials contain small quantities of elements in concentrations of less than 1 percent. For the criminalist, the presence of these trace elements is particularly useful, because they provide "invisible" markers that may establish the source of a material or at least provide additional points for comparison.

Emission spectroscopy, inductively coupled plasma, and atomic absorption spectrophotometry are three techniques available to forensic scientists for determining the elemental composition of materials. An emission spectrograph vaporizes and heats samples to a high temperature so that the atoms present in the material achieve an "excited" state. Under these circumstances, the excited atoms emit light. If the light is separated into its components, one observes a line spectrum. Each element present in the spectrum can be identified by its characteristic line frequencies. In inductively coupled plasma, the sample, in the form of an aerosol, is introduced into a hot plasma, creating charged particles that emit light of characteristic wavelengths corresponding to the identity of the elements present.

In atomic absorption spectrophotometry, the specimen is heated to a temperature that is hot enough to vaporize its atoms while leaving a substantial number of atoms in an unexcited state. The vaporized atoms are then exposed to radiation emitted from a light source specific for a particular element. If the element is present in the material under investigation, a portion of the light is absorbed by the substance. In this manner, many elements can be detected at levels that approach one-trillionth of a gram. Neutron activation analysis measures the gamma-ray frequencies of specimens that have been bombarded with neutrons. This method provides a highly sensitive and nondestructive analysis for simultaneously identifying and quantitating twenty to thirty trace elements. Because this technique requires access to a nuclear reactor, however, it has limited value to forensic analysis.

X-ray diffraction is used to study solid, crystalline materials. As the X-rays penetrate the crystal, a portion of the beam is reflected by each atomic plane. As the reflected beams leave the crystal's planes, they combine with one another to form a series of light and dark bands known as a diffraction pattern. Every compound produces a unique diffraction pattern, thus giving analysts a means for "fingerprinting" inorganic compounds.

Review Questions

1. The elements _____ and _____ make up 75 percent of the weight of the earth's crust.

2. Only _____ elements make up about 99 percent of the weight of the earth's crust.

3. The presence of _____ elements in materials provides useful "invisible" markers when comparing physical evidence.

4. The knowledge that elements selectively _____ and _____ light provides the basis for important analytical techniques designed to detect the presence of elements in materials.

5. A(n) _____ is a display of colors or frequencies emitted from a light source.

6. True or False: A continuous spectrum consists of a blending of colors. _____

7. A(n) _____ spectrum shows distinct frequencies or wavelengths of light.

8. A line spectrum of an element (is, is not) characteristic of the element.

9. True or False: Matter in a solid or liquid state produces an emission spectrum that is characteristic of its composition. _____

10. The _____ is an instrument used to obtain and record the line spectrum of elements.

11. Excitation of a specimen can be accomplished when it is inserted between two _____ electrodes.

12. The selective absorption of light by atoms is the basis for a technique known as _____.

13. The composition of the discharge lamp (does, does not) have to be taken into consideration when performing an analysis by atomic absorption for a particular element.

14. True or False: One advantage of atomic absorption analysis is that it can simultaneously detect twenty to thirty elements. _____

15. Three important subatomic particles of the atom are the _____, _____, and _____.

16. The proton and electron (are, are not) of approximately equal mass.

17. A proton imparts the nucleus of an atom with a _____ charge.

18. The number of protons (is, is not) always equal to the number of electrons in orbit around the nucleus of an atom.

19. Each atom of the same element always has the same number of _____ in its nucleus.

20. The number of protons in the nucleus of an atom is called the _____.

21. True or False: Each element has its own characteristic set of energy levels. _____

22. True or False: To move an electron from one energy level to the next requires a definite amount of energy. _____

23. As an electron falls from a higher to a lower energy level, it emits _____.

24. The total number of protons and neutrons present in a nucleus is known as the _____.

25. Atoms differing only in the number of neutrons present in their nuclei are called _____.

26. True or False: Deuterium has the greatest number of protons of all the isotopes of hydrogen. _____

27. Radioactivity is composed of the following emissions: _____, _____, and _____.

28. Beta rays are identical to _____.

29. Electromagnetic waves similar to X-rays but of a higher energy are _____.

30. A nuclear reactor is a source of _____.

31. The technique of bombarding specimens with neutrons and measuring the resultant gamma ray emissions is known as _____.

32. As X-rays are reflected off a material's surface, they form a series of light and dark bands known as a(n) _____.

33. X-ray diffraction patterns are obtained from (crystalline, amorphous) substances.

Further References

Forensic Analysis. Weighing Bullet Lead Evidence. Washington D.C.: National Academies Press, 2004.

Guinn, V. P., "The Elemental Comparison of Bullet-Lead Evidence Specimens," in S. M. Gerber, ed., *Chemistry and Crime.* Washington, D.C.: American Chemical Society, 1983.

Houck, Max M., ed., *Mute Witness-Trace Evidence Analysis.* Burlington, Mass.: Elsevier Academic Press, 2001.

Houck, Max M., ed., *Trace Evidence Analysis—More Cases in Mute Witnesses.* Burlington, Mass.: Elsevier Academic Press, 2004.

Settle, F. A., ed., *Handbook of Instrumental Techniques for Analytical Chemistry.* Upper Saddle River, N.J.: Prentice Hall, 1998.

The Lindbergh Baby Case

On the evening of March 1, 1932, a kidnapper crept up his homemade ladder and stole the baby of Charles and Anne Lindbergh directly from the second-floor nursery of their house in Hopewell, New Jersey. The only evidence of his coming was a ransom note, the ladder, a chisel, and the tragic absence of the infant. A couple of months later, though the $50,000 ransom had been paid, the baby turned up dead in the woods a mile away. There was no additional sign of the killer. Fortunately, when finally studied by wood technologist Arthur Koehler, the abandoned ladder yielded some important investigative clues (see case study on page 198).

By studying the types of wood used and the cutter marks on the wood, Koehler ascertained where the materials might have come from and what specific equipment was used to create them. Koehler traced the wood from a South Carolina mill to a lumberyard in the Bronx, New York. Unfortunately the trail went cold, as the lumberyard did not keep sales records of purchases. The break in the case came in 1934, when Bruno Richard Hauptmann paid for gasoline with a bill that matched a serial number on the ransom money. Koehler showed that microscopic markings on the wood were made by a tool in Hauptmann's possession. Ultimately, handwriting analysis of the ransom note clearly showed it to be written by Hauptmann.

The Microscope

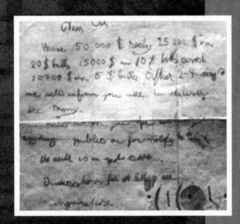

Learning Objectives

After studying this chapter you should be able to:

- List and understand the parts of the compound microscope

- Define magnification, field of view, working distance, and depth of focus

- Contrast the comparison and compound microscopes

- Understand the theory and utility of the stereoscopic microscope

- Appreciate how a polarizing microscope is designed to characterize polarized light

- Appreciate how a microspectrophotometer can be used to examine trace physical evidence

- Compare and contrast the image formation mechanism of a light microscope to that of a scanning electron microscope

- Outline some forensic applications of the scanning electron microscope

Virtual Image
An image that cannot be seen directly. It can be seen only by a viewer looking through a lens.

Real Image
An image formed by the actual convergence of light rays on a screen.

A microscope is an optical instrument that uses a lens or a combination of lenses to magnify and resolve the fine details of an object. The earliest methods for examining physical evidence in crime laboratories relied almost solely on the microscope to study the structure and composition of matter. Even the advent of modern analytical instrumentation and techniques has done little to diminish the usefulness of the microscope for forensic analysis. If anything, the development of the powerful scanning electron microscope promises to add a new dimension to forensic science heretofore unattainable within the limits of the ordinary light microscope.

The earliest and simplest microscope was the single lens commonly referred to as a *magnifying glass*. The handheld magnifying glass makes things appear larger than they are because of the way light rays are refracted, or bent, in passing from the air into the glass and back into the air. The magnified image is observed by looking through the lens, as shown in Figure 7–1. Such an image is known as a virtual image; it can be seen only by looking through a lens and cannot be viewed directly. This is distinguished from a real image, which can be seen directly, like the image that is projected onto a motion picture screen.

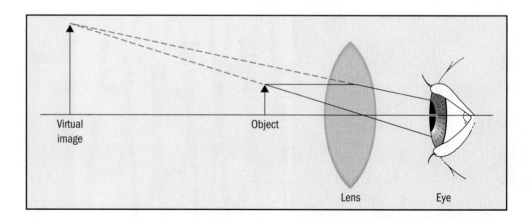

Figure 7–1 The passage of light through a lens, showing how magnification is obtained.

The ordinary magnifying glass can achieve a magnification of about 5 to 10 times. Higher magnifying power is obtainable only with a *compound microscope,* constructed of two lenses mounted at each end of a hollow tube. The object to be magnified is placed under the lower lens, called the objective lens, and the magnified image is viewed through the upper lens, known as the eyepiece lens. As shown in Figure 7–2, the objective lens forms a real, inverted, magnified image of the object. The eyepiece, acting just like a simple magnifying glass, further magnifies this image into a virtual image, which is what is seen by the eye. The combined magnifying power of both lenses can produce an image magnified up to 1,500 times.

The optical principles of the compound microscope are incorporated into the basic design of different types of light microscopes. The microscopes most applicable for examining forensic specimens are as follows:

1. The compound microscope

2. The comparison microscope

3. The stereoscopic microscope

4. The polarizing microscope

5. The microspectrophotometer

After describing these five microscopes, we will talk about a completely different approach to microscopy, the scanning electron microscope (SEM). This instrument focuses a beam of electrons, instead of visible light, onto the specimen to produce a magnified image. The principle and design of this microscope permit magnifying powers as high as 100,000 times.

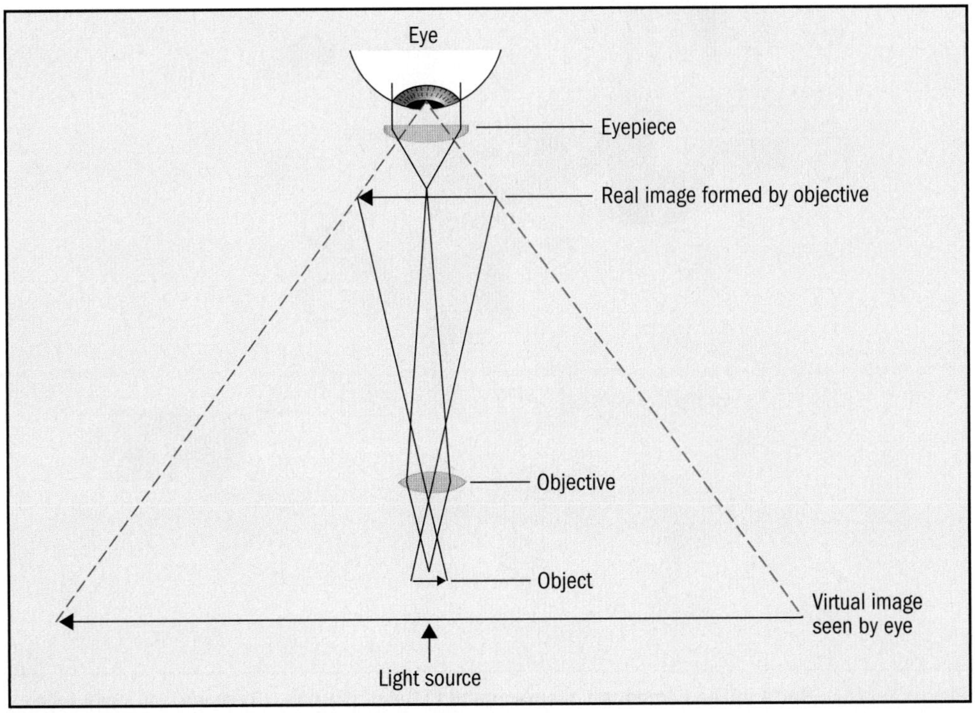

Objective Lens
The lower lens of a microscope, which is positioned directly over the specimen.

Eyepiece Lens
The lens of a microscope into which the viewer looks; same as the ocular lens.

Figure 7–2 **The principle of the compound microscope. The passage of light through two lenses forms the virtual image of the object seen by the eye.**

The Compound Microscope

The parts of the compound microscope are illustrated in Figure 7–3(a). Basically, this microscope consists of a mechanical system, which supports the microscope, and an optical system. The optical system illuminates the object under investigation and passes the light through a series of lenses to form an image of the specimen on the retina of the eye. The optical path of light through a compound microscope is shown in Figure 7–3(b).

The mechanical system is composed of six parts:

Base (1).   The support on which the instrument rests.

Arm (2).   A C-shaped upright structure, hinged to the base, that supports the microscope and acts as a handle for carrying.

Stage (3).   The horizontal plate on which the specimens are placed for study. The specimens are normally mounted on glass slides that are held firmly in place on the stage by spring clips.

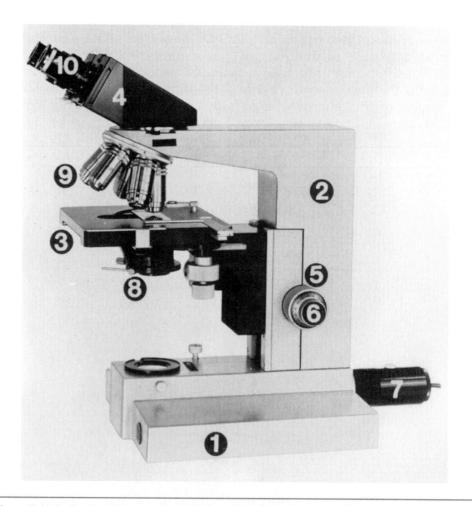

Figure 7–3(a)   Parts of the compound microscope: (1) base, (2) arm, (3) stage, (4) body tube, (5) coarse adjust, (6) fine adjust, (7) illuminator, (8) condenser, (9) objective lens, and (10) eyepiece lens. *Courtesy Leica Microsystems, Buffalo, N.Y., www.leica-microsystems.com*

Body tube (4). A cylindrical hollow tube on which the objective and eyepiece lenses are mounted at opposite ends. This tube merely serves as a corridor through which light passes from one lens to another.

Coarse adjustment (5). This knob focuses the microscope lenses on the specimen by raising and lowering the body tube.

Fine adjustment (6). The movements effected by this knob are similar to those of the coarse adjustment but are of a much smaller magnitude.

The optical system is made up of four parts:

Illuminator (7). Most modern microscopes use artificial light supplied by a lightbulb to illuminate the specimen being examined. If the specimen is transparent, the light is directed up toward and through the specimen stage from an illuminator built into the base of the microscope. This is known as transmitted illumination. When the object is opaque—that is, not transparent—the light source must be placed above the specimen so that it can reflect off the specimen's surface and into the lens system of the microscope. This type of illumination is known as vertical or reflected illumination.

Condenser (8). The condenser collects light rays from the base illuminator and concentrates them on the specimen. The simplest condenser is known as the *Abbé condenser*. It consists of two lenses held together in a metal mount. The condenser also includes an iris diaphragm that can be opened or closed to control the amount of light passing into the condenser.

Transmitted Illumination
Light that passes up from the condenser and through the specimen.

Vertical or Reflected Illumination
Illumination of a specimen from above; in microscopy it is used to examine opaque specimens.

Condenser
The lens system under the microscope stage that focuses light onto the specimen.

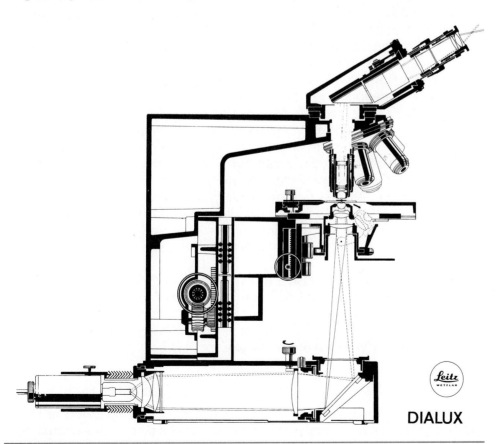

DIALUX

Figure 7–3(b) Optics of the compound microscope. *Courtesy Leica Microsystems, Buffalo, N.Y., www.leica-microsystems.com*

Parfocal

Describes a microscope such that when an image is focused with one objective in position, the other objective can be rotated into place and the field will remain in focus.

Monocular

Describes a microscope with one eyepiece.

Binocular

Describes a microscope with two eyepieces.

Field of View

The area of the specimen that can be seen after it is magnified.

Depth of Focus

The thickness of a specimen that is entirely in focus under a microscope.

WebExtra 7.1

Explore the Concept of Magnification with a Compound Microscope
www.prenhall.com/Saferstein

WebExtra 7.2

Scan a Sample under the Compound Microscope
www.prenhall.com/Saferstein

WebExtra 7.3

Observe the Concept of Depth of Focus
www.prenhall.com/Saferstein

Objective lens (9). This is the lens positioned closest to the specimen. To facilitate changing from one objective lens to another, several objectives are mounted on a revolving nosepiece or turret located above the specimen. Most microscopes are parfocal, meaning that when the microscope is focused with one objective in position, the other objective can be rotated into place by revolving the nosepiece while the specimen remains very nearly in correct focus.

Eyepiece or ocular lens (10). This is the lens closest to the eye. A microscope with only one eyepiece is monocular; one constructed with two eyepieces (one for each eye) is binocular.

Each microscope lens is inscribed with a number signifying its magnifying power. The image viewed by the microscopist will have a total magnification equal to the product of the magnifying power of the objective and eyepiece lenses. For example, an eyepiece lens with a magnification of 10 times (10×) used in combination with an objective lens of 10 times has a total magnification power of 100 times (100×). Most forensic work requires a 10× eyepiece in combination with either a 4×, 10×, 20×, or 45× objective. The respective magnifications will be 40×, 100×, 200×, and 450×.

In addition, each objective lens is inscribed with its numerical aperture (N.A.). The ability of an objective lens to resolve details into separate images instead of one blurred image is directly proportional to the numerical aperture value of the objective lens. For example, an objective lens of N.A. 1.30 can separate details at half the distance of a lens with an N.A. of 0.65. The maximum useful magnification of a compound microscope is approximately 1,000 times the N.A. of the objective being used. This magnification is sufficient to permit the eye to see all the detail that can be resolved. Any effort to increase the total magnification beyond this figure will yield no additional detail and is referred to as *empty magnification.*

Although a new student of the microscope may be tempted to immediately choose the highest magnifying power available to view a specimen, the experienced microscopist weighs a number of important factors before choosing a magnifying power. A first consideration must be the size of the specimen area, or the field of view, that the examiner wishes to study. As magnifying power increases, the field of view decreases. Thus, it is best to first select a low magnification in which a good general overall view of the specimen is seen and to switch later to a higher power in which a smaller portion of the specimen can be viewed in more detail.

The depth of focus is also a function of magnifying power. After a focus has been achieved on a specimen, the depth of focus defines the thickness of that specimen. Areas above and below this region will be blurred and can be viewed only when the focus is readjusted. Depth of focus decreases as magnifying power increases.

The Comparison Microscope

Forensic microscopy often requires a side-by-side comparison of specimens. This kind of examination can best be performed with a comparison microscope, such as the one pictured in Figure 7–4. Basically, the comparison microscope is two compound microscopes combined into one unit.

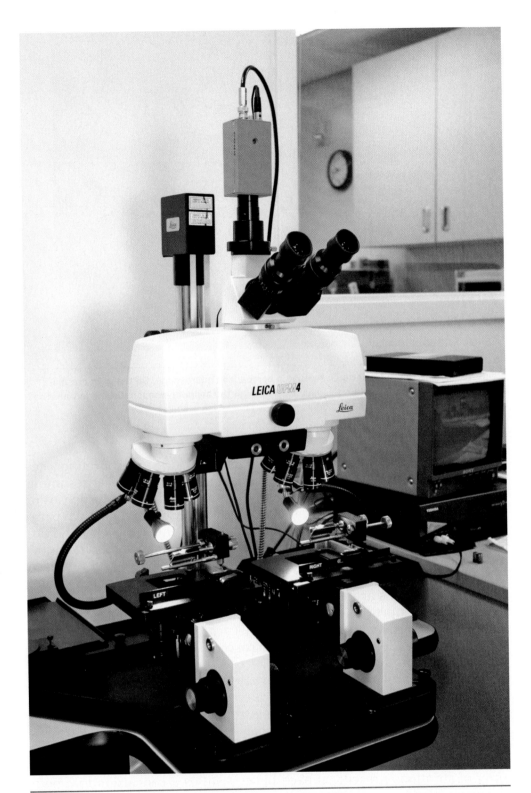

Figure 7–4   The comparison microscope—two independent objective lenses joined together by an optical bridge. *Courtesy Leica Microsystems*

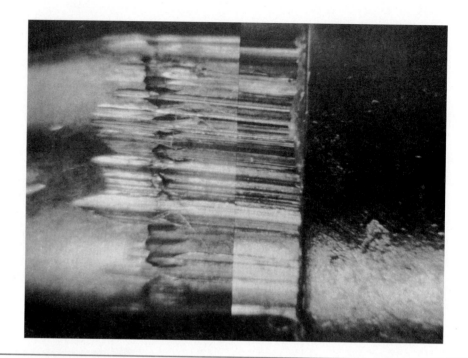

Figure 7–5 Photomicrograph taken through a comparison microscope. On the right are the striation markings on the test-fired bullet, fired through the suspect weapon. On the left are the markings of the crime-scene bullet. *Courtesy Getty Images Inc.—Hulton Archive*

The unique feature of its design is that it uses a bridge incorporating a series of mirrors and lenses to join two independent objective lenses into a single binocular unit. When a viewer looks through the eyepiece lenses of the comparison microscope, a circular field, equally divided into two parts by a fine line, is observed. The specimen mounted under the left-hand objective is seen in the left half of the field, and the specimen under the right-hand objective is observed in the right half of the field. It is important to closely match the optical characteristics of the objective lenses to ensure that both specimens are seen at equal magnification and with minimal but identical lens distortions. Comparison microscopes designed to compare bullets, cartridges, and other opaque objects are equipped with vertical or reflected illumination. Comparison microscopes used to compare hairs or fibers use transmitted illumination.

Figure 7–5 shows the striation markings on two bullets that have been placed under the objective lenses of a comparison microscope. Modern firearms examination began with the introduction of the comparison microscope, with its ability to give the firearms examiner a side-by-side magnified view of bullets. Bullets that are fired through the same rifle barrel display comparable rifling markings on their surfaces. Matching the majority of striations present on each bullet justifies a conclusion that both bullets traveled through the same barrel.

WebExtra 7.4

Practice Matching Bullets with the Aid of a 3-D Interactive Illustration
www.prenhall.com/Saferstein

The Stereoscopic Microscope

The details that characterize the structures of many types of physical evidence do not always require examination under very high magnifications. For such specimens, the stereoscopic microscope has proven quite

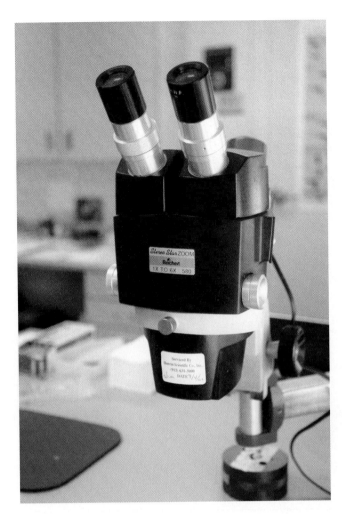

Figure 7–6 A stereoscopic microscope. *Courtesy of Mikael Karlsson, Arresting Images*

adequate, providing magnifying powers from 10× to 125×. This microscope has the advantage of presenting a distinctive three-dimensional image of an object. Also, whereas the image formed by the compound microscope is inverted and reversed (upside-down and backward), the stereoscopic microscope is more convenient because of the prisms in its light path that permit the formation of a right-side-up image. The stereoscopic microscope, shown in Figure 7–6, is actually two monocular compound microscopes properly spaced and aligned to present a three-dimensional image of a specimen to the viewer, who looks through both eyepiece lenses. The light path of a stereoscopic microscope is shown in Figure 7–7.

The stereoscopic microscope is undoubtedly the most frequently used and versatile microscope found in the crime laboratory. Its wide field of view and great depth of focus make it an ideal instrument for locating trace evidence in debris, garments, weapons, or tools. Furthermore, its potentially large *working distance* (the distance between the objective lens and the specimen) makes it quite applicable for the microscopic examination of big, bulky items. When fitted with vertical illumination, the stereoscopic microscope becomes the primary tool for characterizing physical evidence as diverse as paint, soil, gunpowder residues, and marijuana.

WebExtra 7.5

Explore the Stereoscopic Microscope

www.prenhall.com/Saferstein

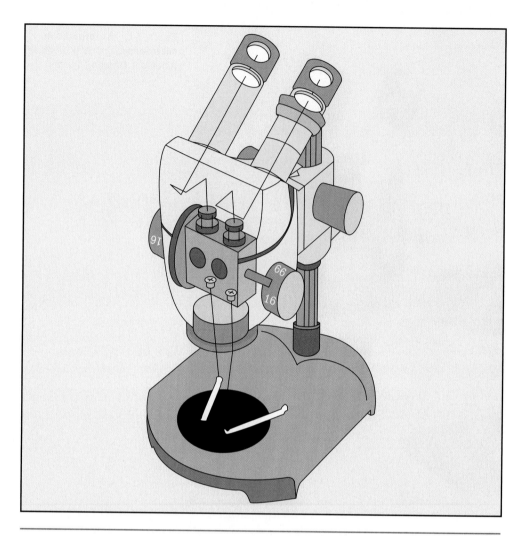

Figure 7–7 Schematic diagram of a stereoscopic microscope. This microscope is actually two separate monocular microscopes, each with its own set of lenses except for the lowest objective lens, which is common to both microscopes.

The Polarizing Microscope

Recall from Chapter 5 that light's wavelike motion in space can be invoked to explain many facets of its behavior. The waves that compose a beam of light can be pictured as vibrating in all directions perpendicular to the direction in which the light is traveling. However, when a beam of light passes through certain types of specially fabricated crystalline substances, it emerges vibrating in only one plane. Light that is confined to a single plane of vibration is said to be plane-polarized. The device that polarizes light in this manner is called a polarizer. A common example of this phenomenon is the passage of sunlight through polarized sunglasses. By transmitting light vibrating in the vertical plane only, these sunglasses eliminate or reduce light glare. Most glare consists of partially polarized light that has been reflected off horizontal surfaces and thus is vibrating in a horizontal plane.

Because polarized light appears no different to the eye from ordinary light, special means must be devised for detecting it. This is accomplished simply by placing a second polarizing crystal, called an *analyzer*, in the path of the polarized beam. As shown in Figure 7–8, if the polarizer and analyzer are aligned parallel to each other, the polarized light passes through and is seen by the eye. If, on the other hand, the polarizer and analyzer are

Plane-Polarized Light
Light confined to a single plane of vibration.

Polarizer
A device that permits the passage of light waves vibrating in only one plane.

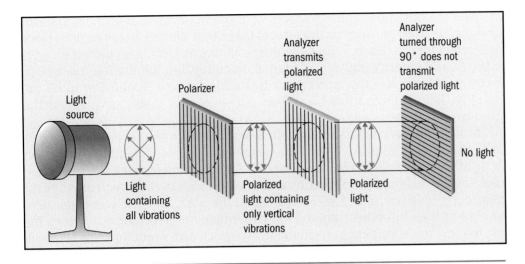

Figure 7–8   Polarization of light.

set perpendicular to one another, or are "crossed," no light penetrates, and the result is total darkness or *extinction*.

In this manner, a compound or stereoscopic microscope can be outfitted with a polarizer and analyzer to allow the viewer to detect polarized light. Such a microscope is known as a *polarizing microscope*. Essentially, the polarizer is placed between the light source and the sample stage to polarize the light before it passes through the specimen. The polarized light penetrating the specimen must then pass through an analyzer before it reaches the eyepiece and finally the eye. Normally, the polarizer and analyzer are "crossed" so that when no specimen is in place, the field appears dark. However, introducing a specimen that polarizes light reorients the polarized light, allowing it to pass through the analyzer. This result produces vivid colors and intensity contrasts that make the specimen readily distinguishable.

The most obvious and important applications of this microscope relate to studying materials that polarize light. For example, as we learned in Chapter 4 (see pp. 108–109), many crystalline substances are birefringent; that is, they split a beam of light into two light-ray components of different refractive index values. What makes this observation particularly relevant to our discussion of the polarizing microscope is that the light beams are polarized at right angles to each other. Thus, polarizing microscopy has found wide application for the examination of birefringent minerals present in soil. By using the immersion method (see pp. 111–112) and selecting the proper immersion liquids, a refractive index corresponding to each plane of polarized light can be determined. Thus, when a mineral is viewed under polarized light in a liquid that matches one of its refractive indices, the Becke line will no longer be visible. This information, plus observations on crystal color, form, and so on, makes it possible for the microscopist to identify the mineral. Similarly, criminalists use the fact that many synthetic fibers are birefringent to characterize them with a polarizing microscope.

WebExtra 7.6

Explore the Polarizing Microscope–I
www.prenhall.com/Saferstein

WebExtra 7.7

Explore the Polarizing Microscope–II
www.prenhall.com/Saferstein

The Microspectrophotometer

From a practical point of view, few instruments in a crime laboratory can match the versatility of the microscope. The microscope's magnifying power is indispensable for finding minute traces of physical evidence. Many items of physical evidence can be characterized by a microscopic examination of their morphological features. Likewise, the microscope can

Microspectrophotometer
An instrument that links a microscope to a spectrophotometer.

be used to study how light interacts with the material under investigation, or it can be used to observe the effects that other chemical substances have on such evidence. Each of these features allows an examiner to better characterize and identify physical evidence. Recently, linking the microscope to a computerized spectrophotometer has added a new dimension to its capability. This combination has given rise to a new instrument called the microspectrophotometer.

In many respects, this is an ideal marriage from the forensic scientist's viewpoint. In Chapter 5, we saw how a chemist can use selective absorption of light by materials to characterize them. In particular, light in the ultraviolet, visible, and infrared regions of the electromagnetic spectrum is most helpful for this purpose. Unfortunately, in the past, forensic chemists were unable to take full advantage of the capabilities of spectrophotometry for examining trace evidence, because most spectrophotometers are not well suited for examining the very small particles frequently encountered as evidence. However, with the development of the microspectrophotometer, a forensic analyst can now view a particle under a microscope while a beam of light is directed at the particle in order to obtain its absorption spectrum. Depending on the type of light employed, an examiner can acquire either a visible or an IR spectral pattern of the substance being viewed under the microscope. The obvious advantage of this approach is to provide the forensic scientist with added information that will characterize trace quantities of evidence. A microspectrophotometer designed to measure the uptake of visible light by materials is shown in Figure 7–9.

Visual comparison of color is usually one of the first steps in examining paint, fiber, and ink evidence. Such comparisons are easily obtained using a comparison microscope. Now, with the use of the microspectrophotome-

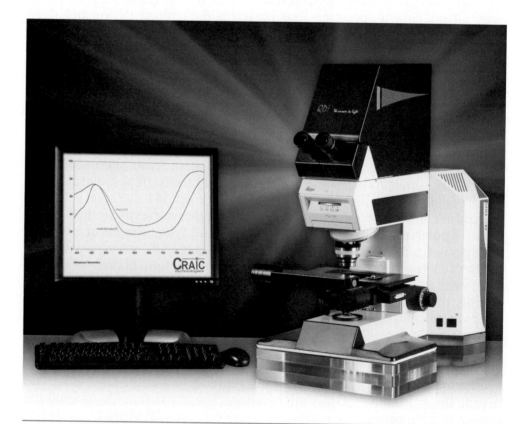

Figure 7–9   A visible-light microspectrophotometer. *Courtesy Craig Technologies Inc., Altadena, Calif., www.microspectra.com*

ter, not only can the color of materials be compared visually but, at the same time, an absorption spectrum can be plotted for each item under examination to display the exact wavelengths at which it absorbs in the visible-light spectrum. Occasionally colors that appear similar by visual examination show significant differences in their absorption spectra. An example of this approach is shown in Figure 7–10, in which the microspectrophotometer is

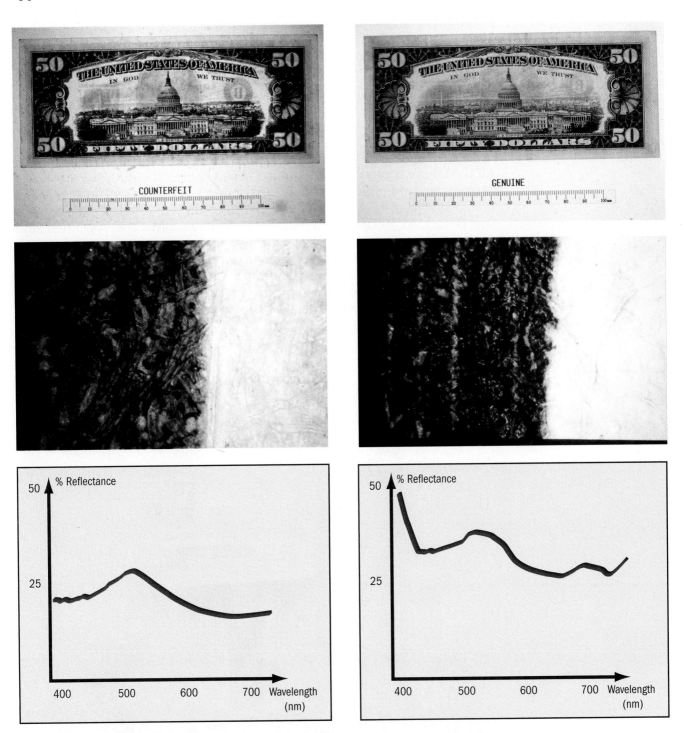

Figure 7–10 Two $50 bills are shown at top; one is genuine and the other is counterfeit. Below each bill is a microphotograph of an inked line present on each bill. Each line was examined under a visible-light microspectrophotometer. As shown, the visible absorption spectrum of each line is readily differentiated, thus allowing the examiner to distinguish a counterfeit bill from genuine currency. *Courtesy Peter W. Pfefferli, forensic scientist, Lausanne, Switzerland*

used to distinguish counterfeit and authentic currency by comparing the spectral patterns of inked lines on currency.

Another emerging technique in forensic science is the use of the infrared microspectrophotometer to examine fibers and paints. The "fingerprint" IR spectrum (see p. 150) is unique for each chemical substance. Therefore, obtaining such a spectrum from either a fiber or a paint chip allows the analyst to better identify and compare the type of chemicals from which these materials are manufactured. With a microspectrophotometer, a forensic analyst can view a substance through the microscope and at the same time have the instrument plot the infrared absorption spectrum for that material.

The Scanning Electron Microscope (SEM)

All the microscopes described thus far use light coming off the specimen to produce a magnified image. The scanning electron microscope is, however, a special case in the family of microscopes (see Figure 7–11). The image is formed by aiming a beam of electrons onto the specimen and studying electron emissions on a closed TV circuit. The beam of electrons is emitted from a hot tungsten filament and is focused by electromagnets onto the surface of the specimen. This primary electron beam causes the emission of electrons, known as secondary electrons, from the elements that make up the upper layers of the specimen. Also, 20 to 30 percent of the

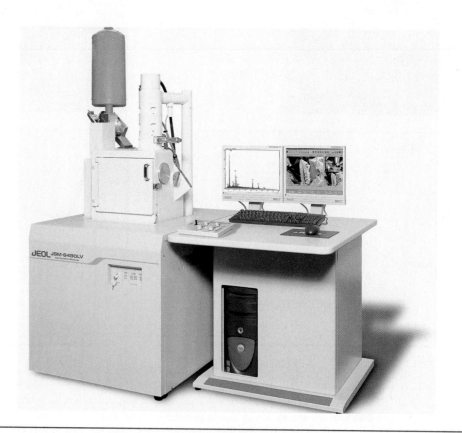

Figure 7–11 A scanning electron microscope. *Courtesy Jeol USA Inc., Peabody, Mass., www.jeolusa.com*

primary electrons rebound off the surface. These electrons are known as *backscattered electrons*. The emitted electrons (both secondary and backscattered) are collected and the amplified signal is displayed on a cathode-ray or TV tube. By scanning the primary electron beam across the specimen's surface in synchronization with the cathode-ray tube, it is possible to convert the emitted electrons into an image of the specimen for display on the cathode-ray tube.

The major attractions of the SEM image are its high magnification, high resolution, and great depth of focus. In its usual mode, the SEM has a magnification that ranges from 10× to 100,000×. Its depth of focus is some 300 times better than optical systems at similar magnifications, and the resultant picture is almost stereoscopic in appearance. Its great depth of field and magnification are exemplified by the magnification of cystolithic hair on the marijuana leaf, as shown in Figure 7–12. An SEM image of a vehicle's headlight filaments may reveal whether the headlights were on or off at the time of a collision (see Figures 7–13 and 7–14).

Another facet of scanning electron microscopy has been the use of X-ray production to determine the elemental composition of a specimen. X-rays are generated when the electron beam of the scanning electron microscope strikes a target. When the SEM is coupled to an X-ray analyzer, the emitted X-rays can be sorted according to their energy values and used to build up a picture of the elemental distribution in the specimen. Because each element emits X-rays of characteristic energy values, the X-ray analyzer can identify the elements present in a specimen.

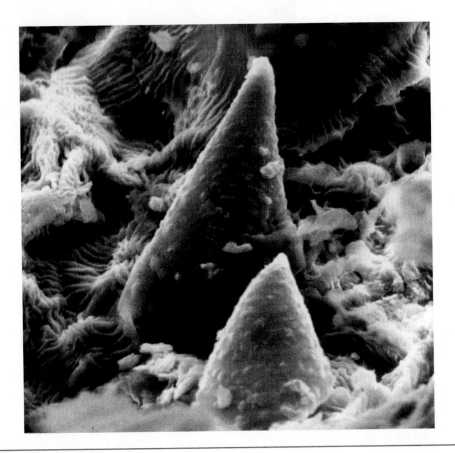

Figure 7–12   The cystolithic hairs of the marijuana leaf, as viewed with a scanning electron microscope (800×). *Courtesy Jeff Albright*

Figure 7–13 The melted ends of a hot filament break indicate that the headlights were on when an accident occurred. *Courtesy Jeol USA Inc., Peabody, Mass., www.jeolusa.com*

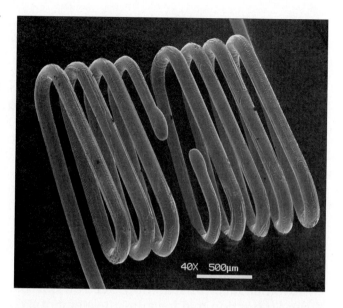

Figure 7–14 The sharp ends of a cold filament break indicate that the headlights were off when an accident occurred. *Courtesy Jeol USA Inc., Peabody, Mass., www.jeolusa.com*

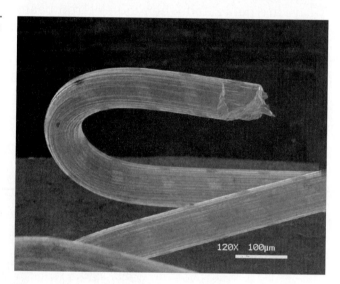

Furthermore, the element's concentration can be determined by measuring the intensity of the X-ray emission.

One application of scanning electron microscopy has been to determine whether a suspect has recently fired a gun. In this case, an attempt is made to remove any gunshot particles that remain on a shooter's hands by lifting them off with a piece of adhesive tape. The tape is then examined under the SEM for the presence of particles that may have originated from the bullet primer. These particles can be characterized by their size, shape, and elemental composition. As shown in Figure 7–15, when the sample of gunshot residue is exposed to a beam of electrons from the scanning electron microscope, X-rays are emitted. These X-rays are passed into a detector, where they are converted into electrical signals. These signals are sorted and displayed according to the energies of the emitted X-rays. Through the use of this technique, the elements lead, antimony, and barium, frequently found in most primers, can be rapidly detected and identified.

WebExtra 7.8

Explore the Scanning Electron Microscope

www.prenhall.com/Saferstein

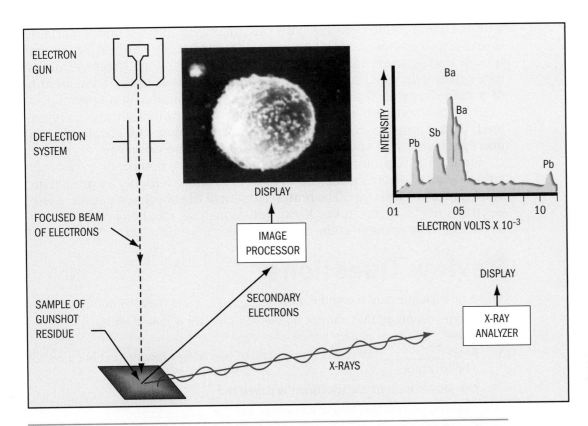

Figure 7–15 A schematic diagram of a scanning electron microscope displaying the image of a gunshot residue particle. Simultaneously, an X-ray analyzer detects and displays X-ray emissions from the elements lead (Pb), antimony (Sb), and barium (Ba) present in the particle. *Courtesy Aerospace Corp., El Segundo, Calif.*

Chapter Summary

A microscope is an optical instrument that uses a lens or a combination of lenses to magnify and resolve the fine details of an object. Various types of microscopes are used to analyze forensic specimens. In the basic compound microscope, the object to be magnified is placed under the lower lens, called the objective lens, and the magnified image is viewed through the upper lens, known as the eyepiece lens. Forensic microscopy often requires side-by-side comparison of specimens. The comparison microscope consists of two independent objective lenses joined together by an optical bridge to a common eyepiece lens. When a viewer looks through the eyepiece lens of the comparison microscope, the objects under investigation are observed side-by-side in a circular field that is equally divided into two parts. Modern firearms examination began with the introduction of the comparison microscope, with its ability to give the firearms examiner a side-by-side magnified view of bullets. The stereoscopic microscope is actually two monocular compound microscopes properly spaced and aligned to present a three-dimensional image of a specimen to the viewer, who looks through both eyepiece lenses. Its large working distance makes it quite applicable for the microscopic examination of big, bulky items.

Light that is confined to a single plane of vibration is said to be plane-polarized. The examination of the interaction of plane-polarized light with matter is made possible with the polarizing microscope. Polarizing microscopy has found wide applications for the study of birefringent materials, that is, materials that have a double refraction. These refractive index data help identify minerals present in a soil sample or the identity of a manufactured fiber. The microspectrophotometer is a spectrophotometer coupled with a light microscope. The examiner studying a specimen under a microscope can simultaneously obtain the visible absorption spectrum or IR spectrum of the material being observed.

Finally, the scanning electron microscope (SEM) bombards a specimen with a beam of electrons instead of light to produce a highly magnified image from 10× to 100,000×. The bombardment of the specimen's surface with electrons normally produces X-ray emissions that can be used to characterize elements present in the material under investigation.

Review Questions

1. A microscope uses a combination of _____ to magnify an image.
2. A type of image that cannot be viewed directly is called a(n) _____ image.
3. A(n) _____ microscope consists of two lenses mounted at each end of a hollow tube.
4. The lens closest to the specimen is called the _____.
5. The lens nearest the viewer's eye is called the _____.
6. The image seen through a compound microscope is (virtual, real).
7. True or False: The coarse and fine adjustments are part of the microscope's mechanical system. _____
8. A transparent specimen is viewed through a microscope using _____ light.
9. An opaque object requires _____ illumination for viewing with a microscope.
10. A(n) _____ collects light rays from the base illuminator and concentrates them on the specimen.
11. A microscope that remains in focus regardless of which objective lens is rotated into place is _____.
12. A microscope with only one eyepiece is _____; one with two eyepieces is _____.
13. Each microscope lens is inscribed with a number signifying its _____.
14. An eyepiece lens of 10× used in combination with an objective lens of 20× has a total magnification power of _____.
15. The ability of an objective lens to resolve details into separate images is directly proportional to its _____.
16. The size of the specimen area in view is known as the _____.
17. As magnification increases, the field of view (increases, decreases).
18. The thickness of a specimen in view is known as the _____.
19. The depth of focus (increases, decreases) with increasing magnification.
20. A side-by-side view of two specimens is best obtained with the _____ microscope.
21. True or False: A bridge is used to join two independent objective lenses into a single binocular unit to form a comparison microscope. _____
22. Two monocular compound microscopes properly spaced and aligned describe the _____ microscope.

23. True or False: The stereoscopic microscope is the least frequently used microscope in a typical crime laboratory. _____

24. The stereoscopic microscope offers a large _____ between the objective lens and the specimen.

25. Light confined to a single plane of vibration is said to be _____.

26. If a polarizer and analyzer are placed (perpendicular, parallel) to each other, no light penetrates.

27. The _____ microscope allows a viewer to detect polarized light.

28. Crystals that are _____ produce two planes of polarized light, each perpendicular to the other.

29. By using the _____, one can view a particle under a microscope while a beam of light is directed at the particle in order to obtain its absorption spectrum.

30. The _____ microscope focuses a beam of electrons on a specimen to produce an image.

31. When a beam of electrons strikes a specimen, _____ are emitted whose energies correspond to elements present in the specimen.

Further References

Bartick, E. G., and M. W. Tungol, "Infrared Microscopy and Its Forensic Applications," in R. Saferstein, ed., *Forensic Science Handbook*, vol. 3. Upper Saddle River, N.J.: Prentice Hall, 1993.

"Basic Concepts in Optical Microscopy," http://micro.magnet.fsu.edu/primer/anatomy/anatomy.html.

De Forest, Peter R., "Foundations of Forensic Microscopy," in R. Saferstein, ed., *Forensic Science Handbook*, vol. 1, 2nd ed. Upper Saddle River, N.J.: Prentice Hall, 2002.

Eyring, Michael B., "Visible Microscopical Spectrophotometry in the Forensic Sciences," in R. Saferstein, ed., *Forensic Science Handbook*, vol. 1, 2nd ed. Upper Saddle River, N.J.: Prentice Hall, 2002.

Palenik, S., and C. Palenik, "Microscopy and Microchemistry of Physical Evidence," in R. Saferstein, ed., *Forensic Science Handbook*, vol. 2, 2nd ed. Upper Saddle River, N.J.: Prentice Hall, 2005.

Petraco, N., and T. Kubic, *Basic Concepts in Optical Microscopy for Criminalists, Chemists, and Conservators*. Boca Raton, Fla.: Taylor & Francis, 2004.

Stoney, D. A., and P. M. Dougherty, "The Microscope in Forensic Science," in S. M. Gerber and R. Saferstein, eds., *More Chemistry and Crime*. Washington, D.C.: American Chemical Society, 1997.

Case Study
Microscopic Trace Evidence—The Overlooked Clue
Arthur Koehler—Wood Detective

Skip Palenik
Walter C. McCrone Associates Inc.

. . . Arthur Koehler . . . wood technologist and chief of the division of silvicultural relations at the U.S. Forest Products Laboratory in Madison, Wisconsin, . . . was born on June 4, 1885, in Mishicot, Wisconsin. His father was a carpenter and young Koehler grew up on a farm with a love of both wood and fine tools. This love naturally led him into forestry and he received a B.S. degree in the subject from the University of Michigan in 1911. . . . Upon graduation he went to work for the U.S. Forest Service in Washington, D.C., and three years later obtained a post at the U.S. Forest Products Laboratory where he served in various capacities until his retirement.

Although his primary responsibilities lay in wood identification and the correlation of microscopic wood structure and end use, Koehler also began to build a reputation as a wood detective after his success in obtaining evidence from wood fragments which were submitted to the laboratory in several cases of local importance. . . . The case which thrust Koehler into the limelight of international publicity, however, was the Lindbergh kidnapping case in which he, by the most painstaking work, traced the kidnap ladder back to the lumberyard from which its constituent parts had been purchased.

Sometime between the hours of 8 and 10 p.m. on the night of March 1, 1932, a kidnapper climbed into the nursery of the newly completed home of Charles and Anne Lindbergh in Hopewell, New Jersey, and abducted their infant son. The only clues left behind were a few indistinct

muddy footprints, a ransom note in the nursery, a homemade ladder and a chisel found a short distance from the house. Scarcely two months later, on May 12, the dead body of the child was found, half buried in the woods, about a mile from the Lindbergh home. One of the most intensive manhunts in U.S. history ensued, but failed to uncover any trace of the kidnapper or the ransom money which had been paid.[1]

Shortly after the news of the kidnapping broke in the press Koehler wrote a letter to Colonel Lindbergh offering his services to help with the investigation of the ladder. He never received a reply (which was not surprising considering the flood of mail which arrived at the Lindbergh home in the weeks following the kidnapping). He was not entirely surprised though when his boss, Carlyle P. Winslow, placed before him some slivers of the ladder with the request that the wood be accurately identified.[2] This Koehler did, noting in his report the presence of golden brown, white and black wool fibers which he speculated might be from clothing worn by the kidnapper. That was the last he heard about the ladder for almost a year. During this time it was carried around the country (carefully wrapped in a wool blanket) to various experts including specialists at the National Bureau of Standards.[3]

---

[1] Waller, George. *Kidnap: The Story of the Lindbergh Case.* Dial Press, New York, 1961.

[2] Koehler, Arthur. "Who Made That Ladder?" as told to Boyden Sparkes. *The Saturday Evening Post,* 297, p. 10, April 20, 1935.

[3] Saylor, Charles Proffer. "Optical Microscopy as Used in Unorthodox Ways," *SPIE,* 104, Multi-disciplinary Microscopy, 31–33, 1977.

However, after a year of investigation the authorities were no closer to arresting a suspect than they were the day after the crime.

It was almost a year after the kidnapping when Koehler was asked by the head of the U.S. Forest Service, Major Robert Y. Stuart, to travel to Trenton to give the ladder an in-depth examination. Discussions between Colonel Norman Schwarzkopf, who headed the New Jersey State Police (and the kidnap investigation), and Major Stuart had convinced Colonel Schwarzkopf that the ladder might still yield clues about its maker if Koehler were given a chance to examine it thoroughly. Schwarzkopf wasn't too certain about Koehler's ability ("Wasn't he the one who identified the blanket fibers on the wood we sent him?" he asked) but felt he had nothing to lose.

For the first time, Koehler saw the ladder (Figure 1). He was immediately struck by the fact that, although it was cleverly contrived, it was shamefully constructed. Instead of rungs it had cleats, which had been carelessly mortised with a dull chisel. A dull hand plane had been used needlessly in some places and a handsaw had been drawn carelessly across some of the boards.

Alone for four days, Koehler studied the ladder in the police training school in Wilburtha. He then returned to the Forest Products Laboratory with the ladder and closed himself up in a private laboratory with the best optical equipment available.[4] He began by completely dissecting the ladder into its component parts. Each piece was numbered. The cleats were labeled 1 (bottom) through 11 (top). The rails were numbered starting from 12 (bottom left) to 17 (right-hand top). . . . Each mark was noted and indexed. After probing with microscopes,

Figure 1   The ladder used in the kidnapping of the Lindbergh baby. *© CORBIS. All rights reserved.*

calipers and a variety of lighting and photographic techniques, the ladder slowly began to give up its secrets.

The sheer number of observations, facts and deductions about the origin of the ladder (and its producer) made by Koehler are truly staggering. We are concerned here only with those facts and observations which (1) allowed the parts to be traced and (2) described the carpenter and the previous environment of the ladder. The results were presented not as the subject of a single report but of daily letters to the director of the laboratory. As certain aspects were revealed they were pursued until the object

---

[4] Koehler, Arthur. *The Saturday Evening Post*, 297, p. 84, April 20, 1935.

could be traced no further. The most pertinent observations and deductions are listed and described below.

1. Microscopical examination showed four types of wood were used (Table 1). North Carolina pine is a trade name for wood from the southern yellow pine group which grows in commercial stands in the Southern U.S. along the Gulf of Mexico and along the Eastern Seaboard up into New Jersey and southern New York.[5] Douglas fir and ponderosa pine grow in the Western U.S. and birch is found throughout the country.[6]

2. Rails 12 and 13 showed faint marks which gave information about the planer in the mill where the wood was

dressed. . . . Figure 2 shows the operation of a mill planer in diagrammatic form. Defects in the cutters allowed the number of knives in the cutters to be determined by counting cutter marks between defect marks. Eight cutter heads dressed the wide surface and six heads the edges. . . .

The lumber went through the planer at a rate of 0.93 inches per complete revolution of the top and bottom cutter heads and 0.86 inches per revolution of the cutter heads that dressed the edges. This was determined by the distance of identical cuts made by a defective knife on each surface. . . .[7] Using the fact that the cutters in mill planers are usually driven at 3600 revolutions per minute it was possible to calculate the speed at which the wood passed into the planer as 258 feet per minute for the edge and 279 feet per minute for the board surfaces. The difference in the speed of the horizontal and vertical heads indicated that the planer was belt driven.

3. Rail 16 had four nail holes made by old fashioned square cut 8-penny nails. The holes had no connection with the construction of the ladder and therefore indicated prior use. The nail holes were clean and free from rust indicating inside use. This was confirmed by the general appearance of the rail which, although sapwood, showed no sign of exposure to the weather for any length of time since it was bright and unchecked. Therefore,

Table 1 Woods Used in Kidnap Ladder

Cleats

1–10	**Ponderosa pine** 1 × 6-inch boards ripped lengthwise into strips 2¾ inches wide to make cleats.
11	**Douglas fir** Grain matched bottom of rail 15.

Side Rails

12, 13—	**North Carolina pine.** Second growth. Cut from one board originally 14 feet long. Dressed to 3¾ inches in width. Both dressed on same planer.
14, 15—	**Douglas fir** Dressed on two different planers.
16—	**North Carolina pine** Narrowed from a wider board as indicated by handsaw and hand-planer marks on edges.
17—	**Douglas fir** Dressed on different planers than 14 and 15.

Dowel Pins

	Birch

[5] Isenberg, Irving. *Pulpwoods of the United States and Canada.* Institute of Paper Chemistry, Appleton, Wisc., pp. 19–22, 1951.

[6] Christensen, Donna. *Wood Technology and the Lindbergh Kidnap Case.* Report, May 1971.

[7] Koehler, Arthur. "Techniques Used in Tracing the Lindbergh Kidnapping Ladder," *Am. J. Police Science,* 27, 5 (1937).

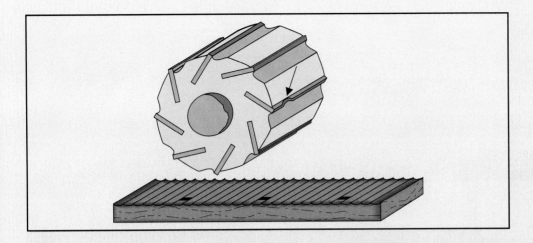

Figure 2 Detail of a cutter head illustrating how a defect allowed the number of knives to be determined.

it must have been nailed down indoors. Since it was low-grade lumber it would not have been used for finish purposes, but for rough construction. The spacing of the nails at 16 and 32 inches was considered significant and the suggestion was made that the rail came from the interior of a barn, garage or attic.

After an initial, futile attempt to trace the birch dowels, Koehler set out to try and trace the North Carolina rails (numbers 12 and 13). Although North Carolina pine grew in a large region it would not be profitable to ship it far, and since the ladder had turned up in New Jersey he felt certain that it had been milled somewhere in the Atlantic States. Using the Southern Lumberman's Directory, a list of 1598 planing mills from Alabama to New York was compiled. A confidential letter from Colonel Schwarzkopf and a two-page description written by Koehler were sent off to all of the mills on the list.

Of all the letters sent, only 25 mills reported having planers which matched the specifications outlined in the letter. Two were immediately excluded since they didn't dress lumber of the requisite size. Samples of 1- × 4-inch wood were requested from each of the remaining 23 mills. A sample received from the M. G.

and J. J. Dorn mill of McCormick, South Carolina, showed exactly the marks Koehler was looking for.

A visit to the mill showed that the particular spacing was due to a pulley which had been purchased in September of 1929. The records of the mill showed that forty-six carloads of 1×4 had been shipped north of the Potomac River in the time between the purchases of the pulley and the kidnapping. . . . After personally visiting the final destination of each of the shipments, Koehler and Detective Bornmann finally arrived at a Bronx firm, the National Lumber and Millwork Company. Although the entire shipment had long before been sold, the foreman remembered that some storage bins had been built from some of the wood. The wood matched that from the ladder perfectly (Figures 3 and 4). Examination of wood from shipments before and after the Bronx carload showed that the belt on the planer had been changed and the knife sharpened. This meant that this shipment was the only one from which the two particular rails from the attic could have come. Whoever built the ladder had purchased part of the wood here!

Koehler was unprepared for the foreman's answer to his request to see the sales

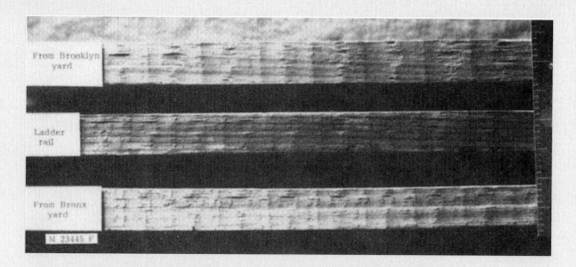

Figure 3   Comparison of knife marks from mill planer on edges of 1- × 4-inch pine from two shipments from the Dorn mill and a ladder rail.

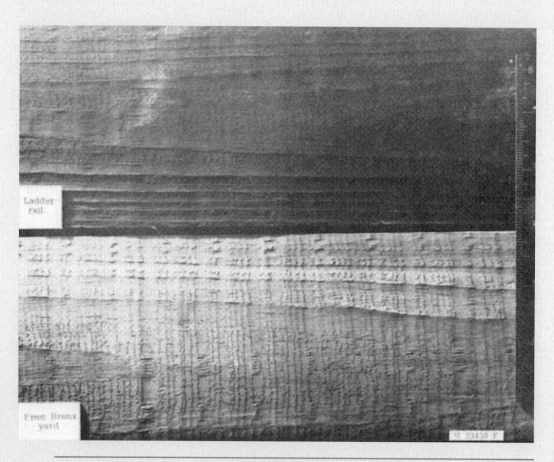

Figure 4   Comparison of knife marks on upper surface of ladder rail and North Carolina pine board located in shipment to the National Lumber and Millwork Company.

records. They had none. They had started selling cash and carry sometime before the Dorn shipment arrived and had no records. Although he had failed to come up with the carpenter's name, the authorities at least now knew the region where the kidnapper lived and bought his wood for the ladder.

Koehler went back to his laboratory and, undaunted, started tracing the Douglas fir rails. At the time a suspect was arrested, he had succeeded in tracing one of the boards to a mill in Bend, Oregon, and another to Spokane, Washington. With the arrest of Richard Hauptmann on September 19, 1934, . . . his role in the case changed from an investigative to a comparative one. In Hauptmann's garage a variety of tools were found whose markings could be compared with those from the ladder. Comparative micrographs of marks made with Hauptmann's plane and plane marks on the ladder showed that his plane was used to plane the cleats (Figure 5). Finally, one of the investigators searching the attic of the suspect's home found that a board had been sawed out of the floor (Figure 6).

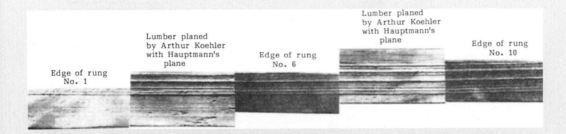

Figure 5 **Comparison of defect marks in Hauptmann's hand-plane with marks on cleats (runs) from the ladder.**

Figure 6 **Rail 16 fitted into its original position in Hauptmann's attic.**

Koehler's examination showed that the nail holes in the floor joists and the ladder rail (No. 16) aligned perfectly. A detailed analysis of the grain and wood itself showed that rail 16 and the section of board remaining in the attic were originally all one piece (Figure 7 and Figure 8).

Richard Bruno Hauptmann was convicted and sentenced to death in a sensational trial. Although, in retrospect, there may have been many errors and a good deal of prejudice in the trial itself, the professionalism and objectiveness of Arthur Koehler still stand as an example of science at its best in the service of the law. . . .

Figure 7 Composite photograph by Koehler showing comparison of end grain (growth rings) in board from attic and rail 16.

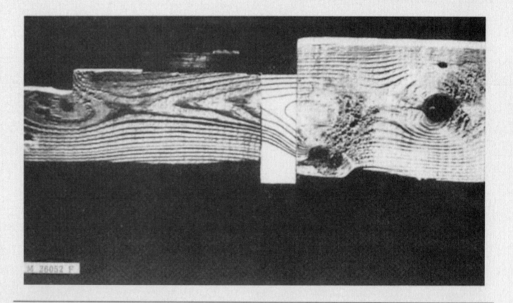

Figure 8 Construction by Koehler showing probable grain pattern of missing piece between attic board and rail 16.

Acknowledgment

The author gratefully acknowledges the invaluable assistance of Dr. Regis Miller and Donna Christensen of the Forest Products Laboratory in Madison, Wisconsin, for making available documents and photographs which were necessary to this article. Additional thanks are due Jame Gerakaris of McCrone Associates for preparing the drawings of the ladder and mill planer.

Jeffrey MacDonald: Fatal Vision

The grisly murder scene that confronted police on February 17, 1970, is one that cannot be wiped from memory. Summoned to the Fort Bragg residence of Captain Jeffrey MacDonald, a physician, police found the bludgeoned body of MacDonald's wife. She had been repeatedly knifed and her face was smashed to a pulp. MacDonald's two children, ages 2 and 5, had been brutally and repeatedly knifed and battered to death. Suspicion quickly fell on MacDonald. To the eyes of investigators, the murder scene had a staged appearance. MacDonald described a frantic effort to subdue four intruders who had slashed at him with an ice pick. However, the confrontation left MacDonald with minor wounds and no apparent defense wounds on his arms. MacDonald then described how he had covered his slashed wife with his blue pajama top. Interestingly, when the body was removed blue threads were observed under the body. In fact, blue threads matching the

pajama top turned up throughout the house—nineteen in one child's bedroom, including one beneath her fingernail, and two in the other child's bedroom. Eighty-one blue fibers were recovered from the master bedroom, and two were located on a bloodstained piece of wood outside the house. Later forensic examination showed that the forty-eight ice pick holes in the pajama top were smooth and cylindrical, a sign that the top was stationary when it was slashed. Also, folding the pajama top demonstrated that the forty-eight holes actually could have been made by twenty-one thrusts of an ice pick. This coincided with the number of wounds that MacDonald's wife sustained. As described in the book *Fatal Vision*, which chronicled the murder investigation, when MacDonald was confronted with adulterous conduct, he replied, "You guys are more thorough than I thought." MacDonald is currently serving three consecutive life sentences.

chapter 8

Hairs, Fibers, and Paint

Key Terms

anagen phase

catagen phase

cortex

cuticle

follicular tag

macromolecule

manufactured fibers

medulla

mitochondrial DNA

molecule

monomer

natural fibers

nuclear DNA

polymer

telogen phase

The trace evidence transferred between individuals and objects during the commission of a crime, if recovered, often corroborates other evidence developed during the course of an investigation. Although in most cases physical evidence cannot by itself positively identify a suspect, laboratory examination may narrow the origin of such evidence to a group that includes the suspect. Using many of the instruments and techniques described in the previous three chapters, the crime laboratory has developed a variety of procedures for comparing and tracing the origins of physical evidence. This and the forthcoming chapters discuss how to apply these techniques to the analysis of the types of physical evidence most often encountered at crime scenes. We begin with a discussion of hairs, fibers, and paint.

Morphology of Hair

Hair is encountered as physical evidence in a wide variety of crimes. However, any review of the forensic aspects of hair examination must start with the observation that it is not yet possible to individualize a human hair to any single head or body through its morphology. Over the years, criminalists have tried to isolate the physical and chemical properties of hair that could serve as individual characteristics of identity. Partial success has finally been achieved by isolating and characterizing the DNA present in hair. The importance of hair as physical evidence cannot be underemphasized. Its removal from the body often denotes physical contact between a victim and perpetrator and hence a crime of a serious or violent nature. When hair is properly collected at the crime scene and submitted to the laboratory along with enough standard/reference samples, it can provide strong corroborative evidence for placing an individual at a crime site.

The first step in the forensic examination of hair logically starts with its color and structure, or morphology, and, if warranted, progresses to the more detailed DNA extraction, isolation, and characterization.

Hair is an appendage of the skin that grows out of an organ known as the *hair follicle*. The length of a hair extends from its root or bulb embed-

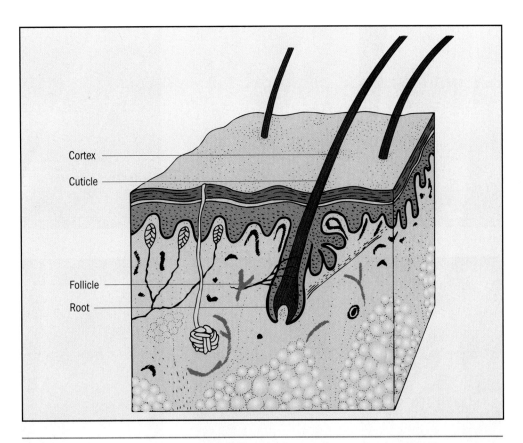

Cortex

Cuticle

Follicle

Root

Figure 8–1   Cross section of skin showing hair growing out of a tubelike structure called the follicle.

ded in the follicle, continues into the shaft, and terminates at the tip end. The shaft, which is composed of three layers—the cuticle, cortex, and medulla—is subjected to the most intense examination by the forensic scientist (see Figure 8–1).

Cuticle.   Two features that make hair a good subject for establishing individual identity are its resistance to chemical decomposition and its ability to retain structural features over a long period of time. Much of this resistance and stability is attributed to the cuticle or outside covering of the hair. The cuticle is formed by overlapping scales that always point toward the tip end of each hair. The scales form from specialized cells that have hardened *(keratinized)* and flattened in progressing from the follicle. The scales of most animal hair can best be described as looking like shingles on a roof. Although the scale pattern is not a useful characteristic for individualizing human hair, the variety of patterns formed by animal hair makes it an important feature for species identification. Figure 8–2 shows the scale patterns of some animal hairs and of a human hair as viewed by the scanning electron microscope. Another method of studying the scale pattern of hair is to make a cast of its surface. This is done by embedding the hair in a soft medium, such as clear nail polish or softened vinyl. When the medium has hardened, the hair is removed, leaving a clear, distinct impression of the hair's cuticle, ideal for examination with a compound microscope.

Cuticle
The scale structure covering the exterior of the hair.

Cortex
The main body of the hair shaft.

Medulla
A cellular column running through the center of the hair.

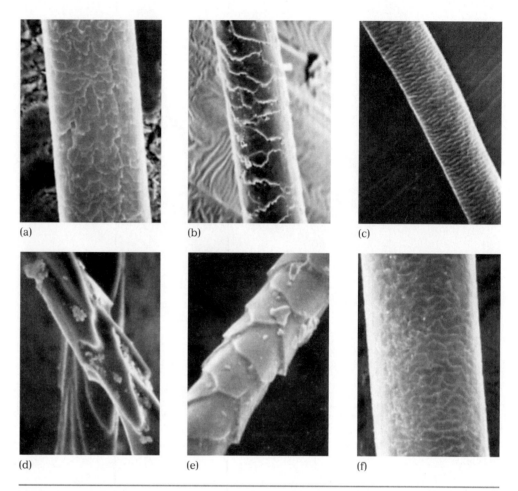

Figure 8–2   Scale patterns of various types of hair. (a) Human head hair (600×), (b) dog (1250×), (c) deer (120×), (d) rabbit (300×), (e) cat (2000×), and (f) horse (450×). *Courtesy International Scientific Instruments, Mountain View, Calif., and New Jersey State Police*

Cortex.   Contained within the protective layer of the cuticle is the cortex. The cortex is actually made up of spindle-shaped cortical cells aligned in a regular array, parallel to the length of the hair. The cortex derives its major forensic importance from the fact that it is embedded with the pigment granules that give hair its color. The color, shape, and distribution of these granules provide important points of comparison among the hairs of different individuals.

The structural features of the cortex are examined microscopically after the hair has been mounted in a liquid medium with a refractive index close to that of the hair. Under these conditions, the amount of light reflected off the hair's surface is minimized, and the amount of light penetrating the hair is optimized.

Medulla.   The medulla is a collection of cells that looks like a central canal running through a hair. In many animals, this canal is a predominant feature, occupying more than half of the hair's diameter. The *medullary index* measures the diameter of the medulla relative to the diameter of the hair shaft and is normally expressed as a fraction. For humans, the index is generally less than one-third; for most other animals, the index is one-half or greater.

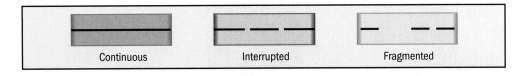

Continuous   Interrupted   Fragmented

Figure 8–3 Medulla patterns.

The presence and appearance of the medulla vary from individual to individual and even among the hairs of a given individual. Not all hairs have medullae, and when they do exist, the degree of medullation can vary. In this respect, medullae may be classified as being continuous, interrupted, fragmented, or absent (see Figure 8–3). Human head hairs generally exhibit no medullae or have fragmented ones; they rarely show continuous medullation. One noted exception is the Mongoloid race, whose members usually have head hairs with continuous medullae. Also, most animals have medullae that are either continuous or interrupted.

Another interesting feature of the medulla is its shape. Humans, as well as many animals, have medullae that give a nearly cylindrical appearance. Other animals exhibit medullae that have a patterned shape. For example, the medulla of a cat can best be described as resembling a string of pearls, whereas members of the deer family show a medullary structure consisting of spherical cells occupying the entire hair shaft. Figure 8–4 illustrates medullary sizes and forms for a number of common animal hairs and a human head hair.

A searchable database on CD-ROM of the thirty-five most common animal hairs encountered in forensic casework is commercially available.[1] This database allows an examiner to rapidly search for animal hairs based on scale patterns and/or medulla type using a PC. A typical screen presentation arising from such a data search is shown in Figure 8–5.

Root. The root and other surrounding cells within the hair follicle provide the tools necessary to produce hair and continue its growth. Human head hair grows in three developmental stages, and the shape and size of the hair root is determined by the growth phase in which the hair happens to be. The three phases of hair growth are the anagen, catagen, and telogen phases. In the anagen phase, which may last up to six years, the root is attached to the follicle for continued growth, giving the root bulb a flame-shaped appearance [Figure 8–6(a)]. When pulled from the root, some hairs in the anagen phase have a follicular tag. With the advent of DNA analysis, this follicular tag is important for individualizing hair. Hair continues to grow, but at a decreasing rate, during the catagen phase, which can last anywhere from two to three weeks. In the catagen phase, roots typically take on an elongated appearance [Figure 8–6(b)] as the root bulb shrinks and is pushed out of the hair follicle. Once hair growth ends, the telogen phase begins and the root takes on a club-shaped appearance [Figure 8–6(c)]. Over two to six months, the hair is pushed out of the follicle, causing the hair to be naturally shed.

WebExtra 8.1
Test Your Skills as a Forensic Hair Examiner
www.prenhall.com/Saferstein

Anagen Phase
The initial growth phase during which the hair follicle actively produces hair.

Catagen Phase
A transition stage between the anagen and telogen phases of hair growth.

Telogen Phase
The final growth phase in which hair naturally falls out of the skin.

Follicular Tag
A translucent piece of tissue surrounding the hair's shaft near the root. It contains the richest source of DNA associated with hair.

Figure 8–4   Medulla patterns for various types of hair. (a) Human head hair (400×), (b) dog (400×), (c) deer (500×), (d) rabbit (450×), (e) cat (400×), and (f) mouse (500×).

Identification and Comparison of Hair

Most often the prime purpose for examining hair evidence in a crime laboratory is to establish whether the hair is human or animal in origin or to determine whether human hair retrieved at a crime scene compares with hair from a particular individual. Although animal hair can normally be distinguished from human hair with little difficulty, human hair comparisons must be undertaken with extreme caution and with an awareness of hair's tendency to exhibit variable morphological characteristics, not only from one person to another but also within a single individual.

A careful microscopic examination of hair reveals morphological features that can distinguish human hair from animal hair. The hair of various

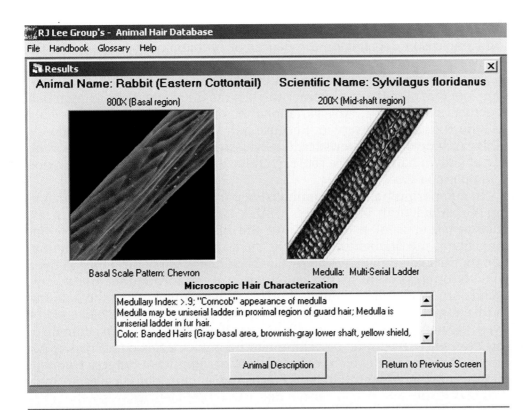

Figure 8–5   **Information on rabbit hair contained within the *Forensic Animal Hair Atlas*.** *Courtesy RJ Lee Group, Inc. Monroeville, Pa.*

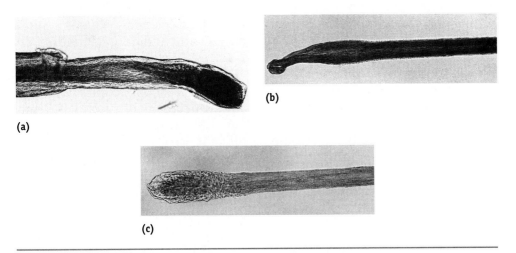

Figure 8–6   **Hair roots in the (a) anagen phase, (b) catagen phase, and (c) telogen phase (100×).** *Courtesy Charles A. Linch*

animals also differs enough in structure that the examiner can often identify the species. Before reaching such a conclusion, however, the examiner must have access to a comprehensive collection of reference standards and the accumulated experience of hundreds of prior hair examinations. Scale structure, medullary index, and medullary shape are particularly important in hair identification.

The most common request when hair is used as forensic evidence is to determine whether hair recovered at the crime scene compares to hair removed from a suspect. In most cases, such a comparison relates to hair obtained from the scalp or pubic area. Ultimately, the evidential value of the comparison depends on the degree of probability with which the examiner can associate the hair in question with a particular individual.

In making a hair comparison, a comparison microscope is an invaluable tool that allows the examiner to view the questioned and known hair together, side by side. Any variations in the microscopic characteristics will thus be readily observed. Because hair from any part of the body exhibits a range of characteristics, it is necessary to have an adequate number of known hairs that are representative of all its features when making a comparison.

In comparing hair, the criminalist is particularly interested in matching the color, length, and diameter. Other important features are the presence or absence of a medulla and the distribution, shape, and color intensity of the pigment granules in the cortex. A microscopic examination may also distinguish dyed or bleached hair from natural hair. A dyed color is often present in the cuticle as well as throughout the cortex. Bleaching, on the other hand, tends to remove pigment from the hair and to give it a yellowish tint. If hair has grown since it was last bleached or dyed, the natural-end portion will be quite distinct in color. An estimate of the time since dyeing or bleaching can be made because *hair grows approximately one centimeter per month*. Other significant but less frequent features may be observed in hair. For example, morphological abnormalities may be present due to certain diseases or deficiencies. Also, the presence of fungal and nit infections can further link a hair specimen to a particular individual.

While microscopic comparison of hairs has long been accepted as an appropriate approach for including and excluding questioned hairs against standard/reference hairs, many forensic scientists have long recognized that this approach is very subjective and is highly dependent on the skills and integrity of the analyst, as well as the hair morphology being examined. However, until the advent of DNA analysis, the forensic science community had no choice but to rely on the microscope to carry out hair comparisons. Any lingering doubts about the necessity of augmenting microscopic hair examinations with DNA analysis evaporated with the publication of an FBI study describing significant error rates associated with microscopic comparison of hairs.[2] Hair evidence submitted to the FBI for DNA analysis between 1996 and 2000 was examined both microscopically and by DNA analysis. Approximately 11 percent of the hairs (9 out of 80) in which FBI hair examiners found a positive microscopic match between questioned and standard/reference hairs were found to be nonmatches when they were later subjected to DNA analysis. The course of events is clear; microscopic hair comparisons must be regarded by police and courts as presumptive in nature and all positive microscopic hair comparisons must be confirmed by DNA determinations.

A number of questions may be asked to further ascertain the present status of forensic hair examinations.

Can the Body Area from Which a Hair Originated Be Determined? Normally, it is easy to determine the body area from which a hair came. For example, scalp hairs generally show little diameter variation and have a more

---

[2] M. M. Houk and B. Budowle, "Correlation of Microscopic and Mitochondrial DNA Hair Comparisons," *Journal of Forensic Sciences* 47 (2002): 964.

Forensics at Work
The Central Park Jogger Case Revisited

Battery Park at night. *Courtesy of Hans Deumling, Getty Images Inc. Image Bank*

On April 19, 1989, a young lady left her apartment around nine p.m. to jog in New York's Central Park. Nearly five hours later, she was found comatose lying in a puddle of mud in the park. She had been raped, her skull was fractured, and she had lost 75 percent of her blood. When the woman recovered, she had no memory of what happened to her. The brutality of the crime sent shock waves through the city and seemed to fuel a national perception that crime was running rampant and unchecked through the streets of New York.

Already in custody at the station house of the Central Park Precinct was a group of 14- and 15-year-old boys who had been rounded up leaving the park earlier in the night by police who suspected that they had been involved in a series of random attacks.

Over the next two days, four of the teenagers gave videotape statements, which they later recanted, admitting to participating in the attack. Ultimately, five of the teenagers were charged with the crime. Interestingly, none of the semen collected from the victim could be linked to any of the defendants. However, according to the testimony of a forensic analyst, two head hairs collected from the clothing of one of the defendants microscopically compared to those of the victim, and a third hair collected from the same defendant's T-shirt microscopically compared to the victim's pubic hair. Besides these three hairs, a fourth hair was found microscopically similar to the victim's. This hair was recovered from the clothing of Steven Lopez, who was originally charged with rape but not prosecuted for the crime. Hairs were the only pieces of physical evidence offered by the district attorney to directly link any of the teenagers to the crime. The hairs were cited by the district attorney as a way for the jury to know that the videotaped confessions of the teenagers were reliable. The five defendants were convicted and ultimately served from nine to thirteen years.

Matias Reyes was arrested in August 1989, more than three months after the jogger attack. He pleaded guilty to murdering a pregnant woman, raping three others, and committing a robbery. He was sentenced to thirty-three years to life. In January 2002, Reyes confessed to the Central Park attack. Follow-up tests revealed that Reyes's DNA compared to semen recovered from the jogger's body and her sock. Other DNA tests showed that the hairs offered into evidence at the original trial did not come from the victim, and so could not be used to link the teenagers to the crime as the district attorney had argued.

After an eleven-month reinvestigation of the original charges, a New York State Supreme Court judge dismissed all the convictions against the five teenage suspects in the Central Park jogger case.

uniform distribution of pigment color when compared to other body hairs. Pubic hairs are short and curly, with wide variations in shaft diameter, and usually have continuous medullae. Beard hairs are coarse, are normally triangular in cross section, and have blunt tips acquired from cutting or shaving.

Can the Racial Origin of Hair Be Determined? In many instances, the examiner can distinguish hair originating from members of different races; this is especially true of Caucasian and Negroid head hair. Negroid hairs are normally kinky, containing dense, unevenly distributed pigments. Caucasian hairs are usually straight or wavy, with very fine to coarse pigments that are more evenly distributed when compared to Negroid hair. Sometimes a cross-sectional examination of hair may aid in the identification of race. Cross-sections of hair from Caucasians are oval to round in shape, whereas cross-sections of Negroid hair are flat to oval in shape. However, all of these observations are general in nature, with many possible exceptions. The criminalist must approach the determination of race from hair with caution and a good deal of experience.

Can the Age and Sex of an Individual Be Determined from a Hair Sample? The age of an individual cannot be learned from a hair examination with any degree of certainty except with infant hair. Infant hairs are fine, are short in length, have fine pigment, and are rudimentary in character. Although the presence of dye or bleach on the hair may offer some clue to sex, present hairstyles make these characteristics less valuable than they were in the past. The recovery of nuclear DNA either from tissue adhering to hair or from the root structure of the hair will allow a determination of whether the hair originated from a male or female (see p. 401).

Is It Possible to Determine Whether Hair Was Forcibly Removed from the Body? A microscopic examination of the hair root may establish whether the hair fell out or was pulled out of the skin. A hair root with follicular tissue (root sheath cells) adhering to it, as shown in Figure 8–7, indicates a hair that has been pulled out either by a person or by brushing or combing. Hair naturally falling off the body has a bulbous-shaped root free of any adhering tissue. However, the absence of sheath cells cannot always be relied on for correctly judging whether hair has been forcibly pulled

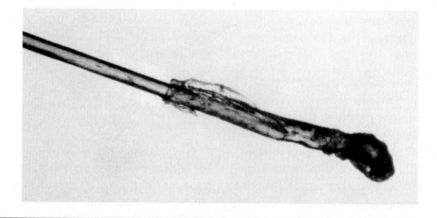

Figure 8–7 **Forcibly removed head hair, with follicular tissue attached.** *Courtesy New Jersey State Police*

from the body. In some cases the root of a hair is devoid of any adhering tissue even when it has been pulled from the body. Apparently, an important consideration is how quickly the hair is pulled out of the head. Hairs pulled quickly from the head are much more likely to have sheath cells compared to hairs that have been removed slowly from the scalp.[3]

Are Efforts Being Made to Individualize Human Hair?   As we will learn in Chapter 13, forensic scientists are routinely isolating and characterizing individual variations in DNA. Forensic hair examiners can link human hair to a particular individual by characterizing the nuclear DNA in the hair root or in follicular tissue adhering to the root (see Figure 8–7). Recall that the follicular tag is the richest source of DNA associated with hair. In the absence of follicular tissue, an examiner must extract DNA from the hair root. The growth phase of hair (see p. 211) is a useful predictor of the likelihood of successfully typing DNA in human hair.[4] Examiners have a higher rate of success in extracting DNA from hair roots in the anagen phase or from anagen-phase hairs entering the catagen phase of growth. Telogen-phase hairs have an inadequate amount of DNA for successfully typing. Because most hairs are naturally shed and are expected to be in the telogen stage, these observations do not portend well for hairs collected at crime scenes. However, some crime scenes are populated with forcibly removed hairs that are expected to be rich sources for nuclear DNA.

When a questioned hair does not have adhering tissue or a root structure amenable to the isolation of nuclear DNA, there is an alternative—mitochondrial DNA. Unlike the nuclear DNA described earlier, which is located in the nuclei of practically every cell in our body, mitochondrial DNA is found in cellular material outside the nucleus. Interestingly, unlike nuclear DNA, which is passed down to us from both parents, mitochondrial DNA is transmitted only from mother to child. Importantly, many more copies of mitochondrial DNA are located in our cells as compared to nuclear DNA. For this reason, the success rate of finding and typing mitochondrial DNA is much greater from samples, such as hair, that have limited quantities of nuclear DNA. Hairs 1–2 centimeters long can be subjected to mitochondrial analysis with extremely high odds of success. This subject is discussed in greater detail in Chapter 13.

Can DNA Individualize a Human Hair?   In some cases, the answer is yes. As we will learn in Chapter 13, nuclear DNA produces frequency of occurrences as low as one in billions or trillions. On the other hand, mitochondrial DNA cannot individualize human hair, but its diversity within the human population often permits exclusion of a significant portion of a population as potential contributors of a hair sample. Ideally, the combination of a positive microscopic comparison and an association through nuclear or mitochondrial DNA analysis provides a strong and meaningful link between a questioned hair and standard/reference hairs. However, a word of caution: mitochondrial DNA cannot distinguish microscopically similar hairs from different individuals who are maternally related.

Nuclear DNA
DNA present within the nucleus of a cell. This form of DNA is inherited from both parents.

Mitochondrial DNA
DNA present in small structures (mitochondria) outside the nucleus of a cell. Mitochondria supply energy to the cell. This form of DNA is inherited maternally (from the mother).

---

[3] L. A. King, R. Wigmore, and J. M. Twibell, "The Morphology and Occurrence of Human Hair Sheath Cells," *Journal of the Forensic Science Society* 22 (1982): 267.

[4] C. A. Linch et al., "Evaluation of the Human Hair Root for DNA Typing Subsequent to Microscopic Comparison," *Journal of Forensic Sciences* 43 (1998): 305.

Collection and Preservation of Hair Evidence

When questioned hairs are submitted to a forensic laboratory for examination, they must always be accompanied by an adequate number of standard/ reference samples from the victim of the crime and from individuals suspected of having deposited hair at the crime scene. We have learned that hair from different parts of the body varies significantly in its physical characteristics. Likewise, hair from any one area of the body can also have a wide range of characteristics. For this reason, the questioned and standard/reference hairs must come from the same area of the body; one cannot, for instance, compare head hair to pubic hair. It is also important that the collection of standard/reference hair be carried out in a way to ensure a representative sampling of hair from any one area of the body.

Forensic Brief

Bill Cosby and his son Ennis Cosby. *Courtesy of George Kalinsky, People/In Style Syndication*

The murder of Ennis Cosby, son of entertainer Bill Cosby, at first appeared unsolvable. It was a random act. When his car tire went flat, he pulled off the road and called a friend on his cellular phone to ask for assistance. Shortly thereafter, an assailant demanded money and, when Cosby didn't respond quickly enough, shot him once in the temple. Acting on a tip from a friend of the assailant, police investigators later found a .38 revolver wrapped in a blue cap miles from the crime scene. Mikail Markhasev was arrested and charged with murder. At trial, the district attorney introduced firearms evidence to show that the recovered gun had fired the bullet aimed at Cosby. However, a single hair also recovered from the hat dramatically linked Markhasev to the crime. Los Angeles Police Department forensic analyst Harry Klann identified six DNA markers from the follicular tissue adhering to the hair root that matched Markhasev's DNA. This particular DNA profile is found in one out of 15,500 members of the general population. Upon hearing all the evidence, the jury deliberated and convicted Markhasev of murder.

Forensic hair comparisons generally involve either head hair or pubic hair. Collecting fifty full-length hairs from all areas of the scalp normally ensures a representative sampling of head hair. Likewise, a minimum collection of twenty-four full-length pubic hairs should cover the range of characteristics present in this type of hair. In rape cases, care must first be taken to comb the pubic area with a clean comb to remove all loose foreign hair present before the victim is sampled for standard/reference hair. The comb should then be packaged in a separate envelope.

Because a hair may show variation in color and other morphological features over its entire length, the entire hair length is collected. This requirement is best accomplished by either pulling the hair out of the skin or clipping it at the skin line. During an autopsy, hair samples are collected from a victim of suspicious death as a matter of routine. Because the autopsy may occur early in an investigation, the need for hair standard/reference samples may not always be apparent. However, one should never rule out the possible involvement of hair evidence in subsequent investigative findings. Failure to make this simple collection at an opportune time may result in complicated legal problems at a later date.

Types of Fibers

Just as hair left at a crime scene can serve as identification, the same logic can reasonably be extended to the fibers that compose our fabrics and garments. Fibers may become important evidence in incidents that involve personal contact—such as homicide, assault, or sexual offenses—in which cross-transfers may occur between the clothing of suspect and victim. Similarly, the force of impact between a hit-and-run victim and a vehicle often leaves fibers, threads, or even whole pieces of clothing adhering to parts of the vehicle. Fibers may also become fixed in screens or glass broken in the course of a breaking-and-entering attempt.

Regardless of where and under what conditions fibers are recovered, their ultimate value as forensic evidence depends on the criminalist's ability to narrow their origin to a limited number of sources or even to a single source. Unfortunately, mass production of garments and fabrics has limited the value of fiber evidence in this respect, and only under the most unusual circumstances does the recovery of fibers at a crime scene provide individual identification with a high degree of certainty.

For centuries, humans depended on natural sources derived from plants and animals for textile fibers. Early in the twentieth century, the first manufactured fiber—rayon—became a practical reality, followed in the 1920s by the introduction of cellulose acetate. Since the late 1930s, scientists have produced dozens of new fibers. In fact, the development of fibers, fabrics, finishes, and other textile-processing techniques has made greater advances since 1900 than in the five thousand years of recorded history before the twentieth century. Today, such varied items as clothing, carpeting, drapes, wigs, and even artificial turf attest to the predominant role that manufactured fibers have come to play in our culture and environment.

For the purpose of discussing the forensic examination of fibers, it is convenient to classify them into two broad groups: *natural* and *manufactured*.

Natural Fibers

Natural fibers are wholly derived from animal or plant sources. Animal fibers comprise the majority of the natural fibers encountered in crime laboratory examinations. These include hair coverings from such animals as sheep (wool), goats (mohair, cashmere), camels, llamas, alpacas, and vicuñas; fur fibers include those obtained from animals such as mink, rabbit, beaver, and muskrat.

Forensic examination of animal fibers uses the same procedures discussed in the previous section for the forensic examination of animal hairs. Identification and comparison of such fibers relies solely on a microscopic

Natural Fibers
Fibers derived entirely from animal or plant sources.

Figure 8–8   Photomicrograph of cotton fiber (450×).

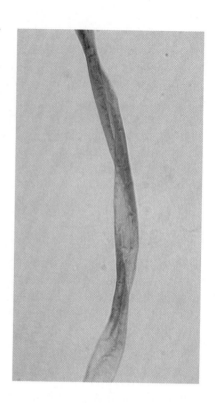

examination of color and morphological characteristics. Again, a sufficient number of standard/reference specimens must be examined to establish the range of fiber characteristics that comprise the suspect fabric.

By far the most prevalent plant fiber is cotton. The wide use of undyed white cotton fibers in clothing and other fabrics has made its evidential value almost meaningless, although the presence of dyed cotton in a combination of colors has, in some cases, enhanced its evidential significance. The microscopic view of cotton fiber shown in Figure 8–8 reveals its most distinguishing feature—a ribbonlike shape with twists at irregular intervals.

Manufactured Fibers

Manufactured Fibers
Fibers derived from either natural or synthetic polymers; the fibers are typically made by forcing the polymeric material through the holes of a spinneret.

Beginning with the introduction of rayon in 1911 and the development of nylon in 1939, manufactured fibers have increasingly replaced natural fibers in garments and fabrics. Today, such fibers are marketed under hundreds of different trade names. To reduce consumer confusion, the U.S. Federal Trade Commission has approved "generic" or family names for the grouping of all manufactured fibers. Many of these generic classes are produced by several manufacturers and are sold under a confusing variety of trade names. For example, in the United States, polyesters are marketed under names that include Dacron, Fortrel, and Kodel. In England, polyesters are called Terylene. Table 8–1 lists major generic fibers, along with common trade names and their characteristics and applications.

The first machine-made fibers were manufactured from raw materials derived from cotton or wood pulp. These materials are processed, and pure cellulose is extracted from them. Depending on the type of fiber desired, the cellulose may be chemically treated and dissolved in an appropriate solvent before it is forced through the small holes of a spinning jet or spinneret to produce the fiber. Fibers manufactured from natural raw materials in this manner are classified as *regenerated fibers* and commonly include rayon, acetate, and triacetate, all of which are produced from regenerated cellulose.

Table 8–1 Major Generic Fibers

Major Generic Fiber	Characteristics	Major Domestic and Industrial Uses
ACETATE	<ul><li>Luxurious feel and appearance</li><li>Wide range of colors and lusters</li><li>Excellent drapability and softness</li><li>Relatively fast-drying</li><li>Shrink-, moth-, and mildew-resistant</li></ul>	**Apparel:** Blouses, dresses, foundation garments, lingerie, linings, shirts, slacks, sportswear **Fabrics:** Brocade, crepe, double knits, faille, knitted jerseys, lace, satin, taffeta, tricot **Home Furnishings:** Draperies, upholstery **Other:** Cigarette filters, fiberfill for pillows, quilted products
ACRYLIC	<ul><li>Soft and warm</li><li>Wool-like</li><li>Retains shape</li><li>Resilient</li><li>Quick-drying</li><li>Resistant to moths, sunlight, oil, and chemicals</li></ul>	**Apparel:** Dresses, infant wear, knitted garments, skiwear, socks, sportswear, sweaters **Fabrics:** Fleece and pile fabrics, face fabrics in bonded fabrics, simulated furs, jerseys **Home Furnishings** Blankets. carpets, draperies, upholstery **Other:** Auto tops, awnings, hand-knitting and craft yarns, industrial and geotextile fabrics
ARAMID	<ul><li>Does not melt</li><li>Highly flame-resistant</li><li>Great strength</li><li>Great resistance to stretch</li><li>Maintains shape and form at high temperatures</li></ul>	Hot-gas filtration fabrics, protective clothing, military helmets, protective vests, structural composites for aircraft and boats, sailcloth, tires, ropes and cables, mechanical rubber goods, marine and sporting goods
BICOMPONENT	<ul><li>Thermal bonding</li><li>Self-bulking</li><li>Very fine fibers</li><li>Unique cross-sections</li><li>The functionality of special polymers or additives at reduced cost</li></ul>	Uniform distribution of adhesive; fiber remains a part of structure and adds integrity; customized sheath materials to bond various materials; wide range of bonding temperatures; cleaner, environmentally friendly (*no effluent*); recyclable; lamination / molding / densification of composites
LYOCELL	<ul><li>Soft, strong, absorbent</li><li>Good dyeability</li><li>Fibrillates during wet processing to produce special textures</li></ul>	Dresses, slacks, and coats
MELAMINE	<ul><li>White and dyeable</li><li>Flame resistance and low thermal conductivity</li><li>High-heat dimensional stability</li><li>Processable on standard textile equipment</li></ul>	**Fire-Blocking Fabrics:** Aircraft seating, fire blockers for upholstered furniture in high-risk occupancies (e.g., to meet California TB 133 requirements) **Protective Clothing:** Firefighters' turnout gear, insulating thermal liners, knit hoods, molten metal splash apparel, heat-resistant gloves **Filter Media:** High-capacity, high-efficiency, high-temperature baghouse air filters
MODACRYLIC	<ul><li>Soft</li><li>Resilient</li><li>Abrasion- and flame-resistant</li><li>Quick-drying</li><li>Resists acids and alkalies</li><li>Retains shape</li></ul>	**Apparel:** Deep-pile coats, trims, linings, simulated fur, wigs, and hairpieces **Fabrics:** Fleece fabrics, industrial fabrics, knit-pile fabric backings, nonwoven fabrics **Home Furnishings:** Awnings, blankets, carpets, flame-resistant draperies and curtains, scatter rugs **Other:** Filters, paint rollers, stuffed toys

continued

Table 8–1 Major Generic Fibers *(continued)*

Major Generic Fiber	Characteristics	Major Domestic and Industrial Uses
NYLON	• Exceptionally strong • Supple • Abrasion-resistant • Lustrous • Easy to wash • Resists damage from oil and many chemicals • Resilient • Low in moisture absorbency	*Apparel:* Blouses, dresses, foundation garments, hosiery, lingerie and underwear, raincoats, ski and snow apparel, suits, windbreakers *Home Furnishings:* Bedspreads, carpets, draperies, curtains, upholstery *Other:* Air hoses, conveyor and seat belts, parachutes, racket strings, ropes and nets, sleeping bags, tarpaulins, tents, thread, tire cord, geotextiles
OLEFIN	• Unique wicking properties that make it very comfortable • Abrasion-resistant • Quick-drying • Resistant to deterioration from chemicals, mildew, perspiration, rot, and weather • Sensitive to heat • Soil resistant • Strong; very lightweight • Excellent colorfastness	*Apparel:* Pantyhose, underwear, knitted sports shirts, men's half-hose, men's knitted sportswear, sweaters *Home Furnishings:* Carpet and carpet backing, slipcovers, upholstery *Other:* Dye nets, filter fabrics, laundry and sandbags, geotextiles, automotive interiors, cordage, doll hair, industrial sewing thread
POLYESTER	• Strong • Resistant to stretching and shrinking • Resistant to most chemicals • Quick-drying • Crisp and resilient when wet or dry • Wrinkle- and abrasion-resistant • Retains heat-set pleats and creases • Easy to wash	*Apparel:* Blouses, shirts, career apparel, children's wear, dresses, half-hose, insulated garments, ties, lingerie and underwear, permanent press garments, slacks, suits *Home Furnishings:* Carpets, curtains, draperies, sheets and pillowcases *Other:* Fiberfill for various products, fire hose, power belting, ropes and nets, tire cord, sail, V-belts
PBI	• Extremely flame resistant • Outstanding comfort factor combined with thermal and chemical stability properties • Will not burn or melt • Low shrinkage when exposed to flame	Suitable for high-performance protective apparel such as firefighters' turnout coats, astronaut space suits, and applications in which fire resistance is important
RAYON	• Highly absorbent • Soft and comfortable • Easy to dye • Versatile • Good drapability	*Apparel:* Blouses, coats, dresses, jackets, lingerie, linings, millinery. rainwear, slacks, sports shirts, sportswear, suits, ties, work clothes *Home Furnishings:* Bedspreads, blankets, carpets, curtains, draperies, sheets, slipcovers, tablecloths, upholstery *Other:* Industrial products, medical-surgical products, nonwoven products, tire cord
SPANDEX	• Can be stretched 500 percent without breaking • Can be stretched repeatedly and recover original length • Lightweight • Stronger and more durable than rubber • Resistant to body oils	*Articles* (in which stretch is desired): Athletic apparel, bathing suits, delicate laces, foundation garments, golf jackets, ski pants, slacks, support and surgical hose

Source: American Fiber Manufacturers Assoc. Inc., Washington, D.C., http://www.fibersource.com/f-tutor/q-guide.htm.

Most of the fibers currently manufactured are produced solely from synthetic chemicals and are therefore classified as *synthetic fibers*. These include nylons, polyesters, and acrylics. The creation of synthetic fibers became a reality only when scientists developed a method of synthesizing long-chained molecules called polymers.

In 1930, chemists discovered an unusual characteristic of one of the polymers under investigation. When a glass rod in contact with viscous material in a beaker was slowly pulled away, the substance adhered to the rod and formed a fine filament that hardened as soon as it entered the cool air. Furthermore, the cold filaments could be stretched several times their extended length to produce a flexible, strong, and attractive fiber. The first synthetic fiber was improved and then marketed as nylon. Since then, fiber chemists have successfully synthesized new polymers and have developed more efficient methods for manufacturing them. These efforts have produced a multitude of synthetic fibers.

Polymers

The polymer is the basic chemical substance of all synthetic fibers. Indeed, an almost unbelievable array of household, industrial, and recreational products is manufactured from polymers; these include plastics, paints, adhesives, and synthetic rubber. Polymers exist in countless forms and varieties and with the proper treatment can be made to assume different chemical and physical properties.

As we have already observed, chemical substances are composed from basic structural units called molecules. The molecules of most materials are composed of just a few atoms; for example, water, H_2O, has 2 atoms of hydrogen and 1 atom of oxygen. The heroin molecule, $C_{21}H_{23}O_5N$, contains 21 atoms of carbon, 23 atoms of hydrogen, 5 atoms of oxygen, and 1 atom of nitrogen. Polymers, on the other hand, are formed by linking a large number of molecules, so that it is not unusual for a polymer to contain thousands or even millions of atoms. This is why polymers are often referred to as macromolecules, or "big" molecules.

Simply, a polymer can be pictured as resembling a long, repeating chain, with each link representing the basic structure of the polymer (see Figure 8–9). The repeating molecular units in the polymer, called monomers, are joined end to end, so that thousands are linked to form a long chain. What makes polymer chemistry so fascinating is the countless possibilities for linking different molecules. By simply varying the chemical structure of the basic molecules, or monomers, and by devising numerous ways to weave them together, chemists have created polymers that exhibit different properties. This versatility enables polymer chemists to synthesize glues, plastics, paints, and fibers.

Polymer
A substance composed of a large number of atoms. These atoms are usually arranged in repeating units or monomers.

Molecule
Two or more atoms held together by chemical bonds.

Macromolecule
A molecule with a high molecular mass.

Monomer
The basic unit of structure from which a polymer is constructed.

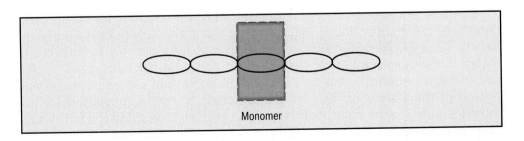

Monomer

Figure 8–9 The chain-link model of a segment of a polymer molecule. The actual molecule may contain as many as several million monomer units or links.

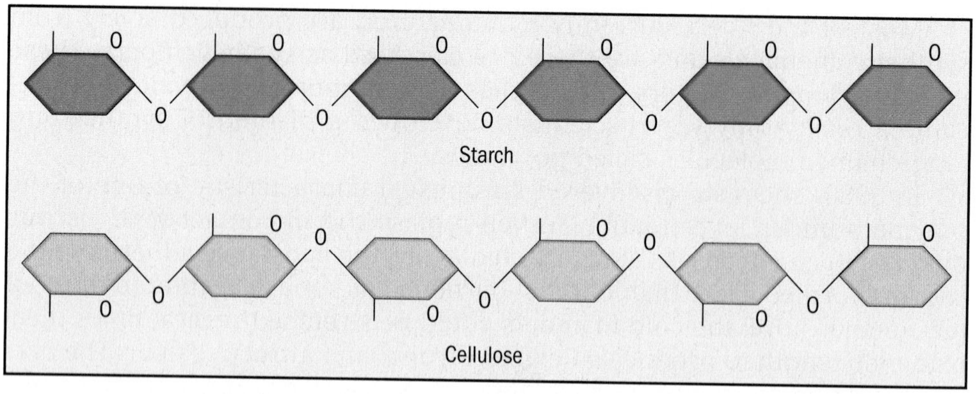

Figure 8–10   Starch and cellulose are natural carbohydrate polymers consisting of a large number of repeating units or monomers.

It would be a mistake to give the impression that all polymers are synthesized in the chemical laboratory. Indeed, this is far from true, for nature has produced polymers that humans have not yet been able to copy. For example, the proteins that form the basic structure of animal hairs, as well as of all living matter, are polymers, composed of thousands of amino acids linked in a highly organized arrangement and sequence. Similarly, cellulose, the basic ingredient of wood and cotton, and starch are both natural polymers built by the combination of several thousand carbohydrate monomers, as shown in Figure 8–10. Hence, the synthesis of manufactured fibers merely represents an extension of chemical principles that nature has successfully used to produce hair and vegetable fibers.

Identification and Comparison of Manufactured Fibers

The evidential value of fibers lies in the criminalist's ability to trace their origin. Obviously, if the examiner is presented with fabrics that can be exactly fitted together at their torn edges, it is a virtual certainty that the fabrics were of common origin. Such a fit is demonstrated in Figure 8–11 for a piece of fabric that was removed from a vehicle suspected of involvement in a hit-and-run fatality. The exact fit with the remains of the victim's trousers resulted in the direct implication of the car's driver in the incident.

However, more often the criminalist obtains a limited number of fibers for identification and comparison. Generally, in these situations, the possibilities for obtaining a physical match are nonexistent, and the examiner must resort to a side-by-side comparison of the standard/reference and crime-scene fibers.

The first and most important step in the examination is a microscopic comparison for color and diameter using a comparison microscope. Unless these two characteristics agree, there is little reason to suspect a match. Other morphological features that could be present to aid in the comparison are lengthwise striations on the surface of some fibers and the pitting of the fiber's surface with delustering particles (usually titanium dioxide) added in the manufacturing process to reduce shine (Figure 8–12). The cross-sectional shape of a fiber may also help characterize the fiber.[5]

---

[5] S. Palenik and C. Fitzsimons, "Fiber Cross-Sections: Part I," *Microscope* 38 (1990): 187.

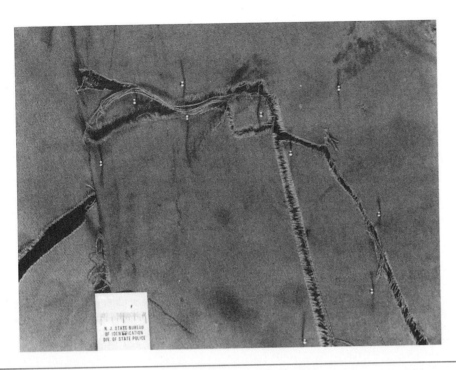

Figure 8–11 **A piece of fabric found on a suspect hit-and-run vehicle inserted into the torn trousers of the victim.** *Courtesy New Jersey State Police*

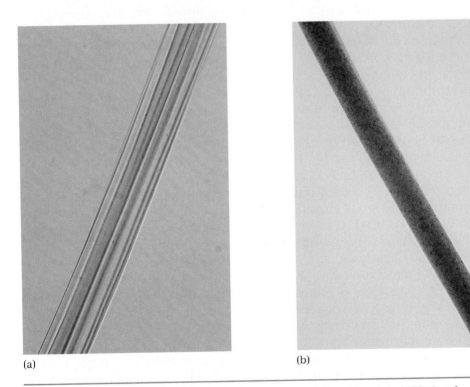

(a)   (b)

Figure 8–12 **Photomicrographs of synthetic fibers: (a) cellulose triacetate (450×) and (b) olefin fiber embedded with titanium dioxide particles (450×).**

In the Wayne Williams case (see Chapter 3), unusually shaped yellow-green fibers discovered on a number of the murder victims were ultimately linked to a carpet in the Williams home. This fiber was a key element in proving Williams's guilt. A photomicrograph of this unusually shaped fiber is shown in Figure 8–13.

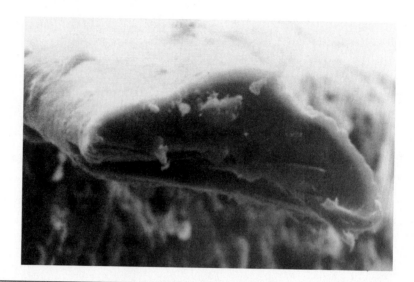

Figure 8–13 **A scanning electron photomicrograph of the cross-section of a nylon fiber removed from a sheet used to transport the body of a murder victim. The fiber, associated with a carpet in Wayne Williams's home, was manufactured in 1971 in relatively small quantities.** *Courtesy Federal Bureau of Investigation, Washington, D.C.*

Although two fibers may seem to have the same color when viewed under the microscope, compositional differences may actually exist in the dyes that were applied to them during their manufacture. In fact, most textile fibers are impregnated with a mixture of dyes selected to obtain a desired shade or color. The significance of a fiber comparison is enhanced when the forensic examiner can show that the questioned and standard/reference fibers have the same dye composition. The visible-light microspectrophotometer (pp. 189–192) is a convenient way for analysts to compare the colors of fibers through spectral patterns. This technique is not limited by sample size—a fiber as small as one millimeter or less in length can be examined by this type of microscope. The examination is nondestructive and is carried out on fibers simply mounted on a microscope slide. A more detailed analysis of the fiber's dye composition can be obtained through a chromatographic separation of the dye constituents. To accomplish this, small strands of fibers are compared for dye content by first extracting the dye off each fiber with a suitable solvent and then spotting the dye solution onto a thin-layer chromatography plate. The dye components of the questioned and standard/reference fibers are separated on the thin-layer plate and compared side by side for similarity.[6]

Once this phase of the analysis is complete, and before any conclusion can be reached that two or more fibers compare, they must be shown to have the same chemical composition. In this respect, tests are performed to confirm that all of the fibers involved belong to the same broad generic class. Additionally, the comparison will be substantially enhanced if it can be demonstrated that all of the fibers belong to the same subclassification within their generic class. For example, at least four different types of nylon are available in commercial and consumer markets, including nylon 6, nylon 6–10, nylon 11, and nylon 6–6. Although all types of nylon have many

---

[6] D. K. Laing et al., "The Standardisation of Thin-Layer Chromatographic Systems for Comparisons of Fibre Dyes," *Journal of the Forensic Science Society* 30 (1990): 299.

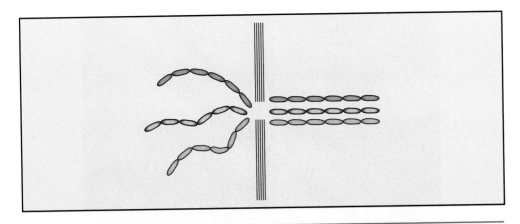

Figure 8–14 In the production of manufactured fibers, the bulk polymer is forced through small holes to form a filament in which all the polymers are aligned in the same direction.

properties in common, each may differ in physical shape, appearance, and dyeability because of modifications in basic chemical structure. Similarly, a study of more than two hundred different samples of acrylic fibers revealed that they could actually be divided into twenty-four distinguishable groups on the basis of their polymeric structure and microscopic characteristics.[7]

Textile chemists have devised numerous tests for determining the class of a fiber. However, unlike the textile chemist, the criminalist frequently does not have the luxury of having a substantial quantity of fabric to work with and must therefore select tests that will yield the most information with the least amount of material. Only a single fiber may be available for analysis, and often this may amount to no more than a minute strand recovered from a fingernail scraping of a homicide or rape victim.

A most useful physical property of fibers, from the criminalist's point of view, is that many manufactured fibers exhibit double refraction or birefringence (see pp. 110–111). Synthetic fibers are manufactured by melting a polymeric substance or dissolving it in a solvent and then forcing it through the very fine holes of a spinneret. The polymer emerges as a very fine filament, with its molecules aligned parallel to the length of the filament (see Figure 8–14). Just as the regular arrangement of atoms produces a crystal, so will the regular arrangement of the fiber's polymers cause crystallinity in the finished fiber. This crystallinity makes a fiber stiff and strong and gives it the optical property of double refraction.

Polarized white light passing through a synthetic fiber is split into two rays that are perpendicular to each other, causing the fiber to display polarization or interference colors when viewed under a polarizing microscope (see Figure 8–15). Depending on the class of fiber, each polarized plane of light has a characteristic index of refraction. This value can be determined by immersing the fiber in a fluid with a comparable refractive index and observing the disappearance of the Becke line under a polarizing microscope. Table 8–2 lists the two refractive indices of some common classes of fibers, along with their birefringence. The virtue of this technique is that a single fiber, microscopic in size, can be analyzed in a nondestructive manner.

The polymers that compose a manufactured fiber, just as in any other organic substance, selectively absorb infrared light in a characteristic pattern.

---

[7] M. C. Grieve, "Another Look at the Classification of Acrylic Fibres, Using FTIR Microscopy," *Science & Justice* 35 (1995): 179.

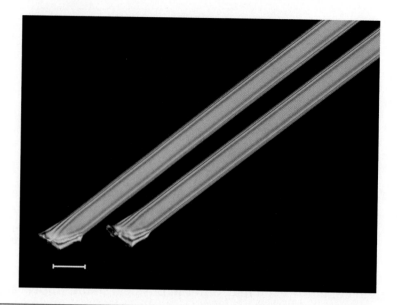

Figure 8–15 **A photomicrograph of nylon fibers displaying interference colors when observed between the crossed polars of a polarizing microscope (50×).** *Courtesy William Randle, Missouri State Highway Patrol Crime Laboratory, Jefferson City, Mo.*

Table 8–2 Refractive Indices of Common Textile Fibers

Fiber	Refractive Index		
	Parallel	Perpendicular	Birefringence
Acetate	1.478	1.477	0.001
Triacetate	1.472	1.471	0.001
Acrylic	1.524	1.520	0.004
Nylon			
Nylon 6	1.568	1.515	0.053
Nylon 6–6	1.582	1.519	0.063
Polyester			
Dacron	1.710	1.535	0.175
Kodel	1.642	1.540	0.102
Modacrylic	1.536	1.531	0.005
Rayon			
Cuprammonium rayon	1.552	1.520	0.032
Viscose rayon	1.544	1.520	0.024

Note: The listed values are for specific fibers, which explains the highly precise values given. In identification work, such precision is not practical; values within 0.02 or 0.03 of those listed will suffice.

Infrared spectrophotometry thus provides a rapid and reliable method for identifying the generic class, and in some cases the subclasses, of fibers. The infrared microspectrophotometer combines a microscope with an infrared spectrophotometer (see p. 192). Such a combination makes possible the infrared analysis of a small single-strand fiber while it is being viewed under a microscope.[8]

---

[8] M. W. Tungol et al., "Analysis of Single Polymer Fibers by Fourier Transform Infrared Microscopy: The Results of Case Studies," *Journal of Forensic Sciences* 36 (1992): 1027.

Once a fiber match has been determined, the question of the significance of such a finding is bound to be raised. In reality, no analytical technique permits the criminalist to associate a fiber strand definitively to any single garment. Furthermore, except in the most unusual circumstances, no statistical databases are available for determining the probability of a fiber's origin. Considering the mass distribution of synthetic fibers and the constantly changing fashion tastes of our society, it is highly unlikely that such data will be available in the foreseeable future. Nevertheless, one

Forensics at Work
Fatal Vision Revisited

Jeffrey MacDonald in 1995 at Sheridan, Oregon, Federal Correctional Institution.
Courtesy AP Wide World Photos

Dr. Jeffrey MacDonald was convicted in 1979 of murdering his wife and two young daughters. The events surrounding the crime and the subsequent trial were recounted in Joe McGinniss's best-selling book *Fatal Vision*. The focus of MacDonald's defense was that intruders entered his home and committed these violent acts. Eleven years after this conviction, MacDonald's attorneys filed a petition for a new trial, claiming the existence of "critical new" evidence.

The defense asserted that wig fibers found on a hairbrush in the MacDonald residence were evidence that an intruder dressed in a wig entered the MacDonald home on the day of the murder. Subsequent examination

of this claim by the FBI Laboratory focused on a blond fall frequently worn by MacDonald's wife. Fibers removed from the fall were shown to clearly match fibers on the hairbrush. The examination included the use of infrared microspectrophotometry to demonstrate that the suspect wig fibers were chemically identical to fibers found in the composition of the MacDonald fall (see Figure 8–16). Hence, although wig fibers were found at the crime scene, the source of these fibers could be accounted for—they came from Mrs. MacDonald's fall.

Another piece of evidence cited by MacDonald's lawyers was a bluish-black woolen fiber found on the body of Mrs. MacDonald. They claimed that this fiber compared to a bluish-black woolen fiber recovered from the club used to assault her. These wool fibers were central to MacDonald's defense that the "intruders" wore dark-colored clothing. Initial examination showed that the fibers were microscopically indistinguishable. However, the FBI also compared the two wool fibers by visible-light microspectrophotometry. Comparison of their spectra clearly showed that their dye compositions differed, providing no evidence of outside intruders (see Figure 8–17). Ultimately, the U.S. Supreme Court denied the merits of MacDonald's petition for a new trial.

Source: B. M. Murtagh and M. P. Malone, "Fatal Vision Revisited," *The Police Chief* (June 1993): 15.

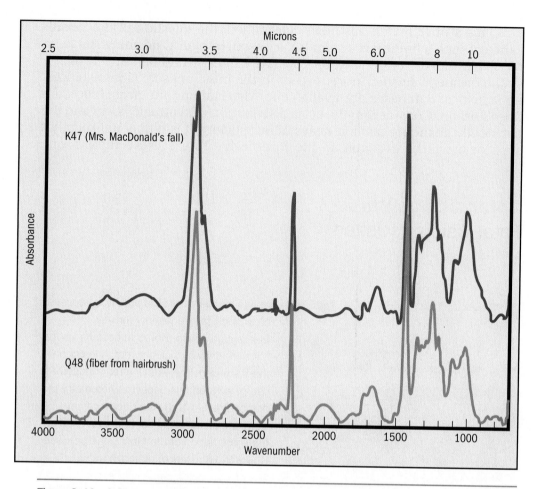

Figure 8–16 A fiber comparison made with an infrared spectrophotometer. The infrared spectrum of a fiber from Mrs. MacDonald's fall compares to a fiber recovered from a hairbrush in the MacDonald home. These fibers were identified as modacrylics, the most common type of synthetic fiber used in the manufacture of human hair goods. *Courtesy S. A. Michael Malone, FBI Laboratory, Washington, D.C.*

should not discount or minimize the significance of a fiber association. An enormous variety of fibers exists in our society. By simply looking at the random individuals we meet every day, we can see how unlikely it is to find two different people wearing identically colored fabrics (with the exception of blue denims or white cottons). There are thousands of different-colored fibers in our environment. Combine this with the fact that forensic scientists compare not only the color of fibers but also their size, shape, microscopic appearance, chemical composition, and dye content, and one can now begin to appreciate how unlikely it is to find two indistinguishable colored fibers emanating from randomly selected sources. Furthermore, the significance of a fiber association increases dramatically if the analyst can link two or more distinctly different fibers to the same object. Likewise, the associative value of fiber evidence is dramatically enhanced if it is accompanied by other types of physical evidence linking a person or object to a crime.

As with most class evidence, the significance of a fiber comparison is dictated by the circumstances of the case; by the location, number, and nature of the fibers examined; and, most important, by the judgment of an experienced examiner.

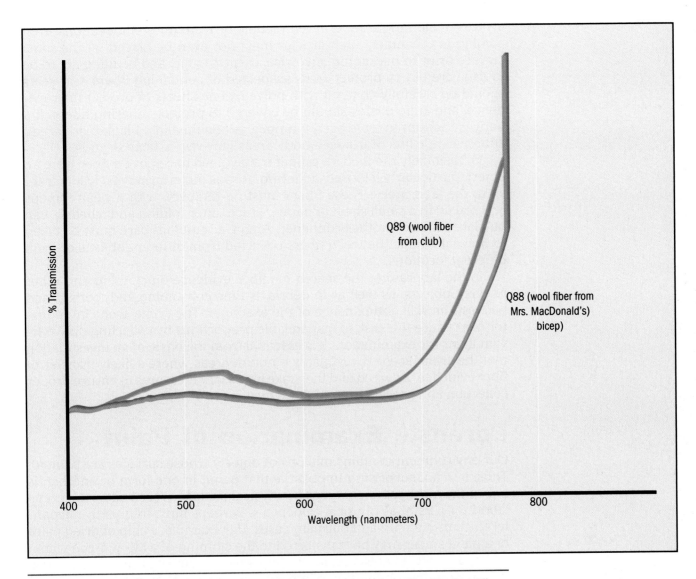

Figure 8–17 **The visible-light spectrum for the woolen fiber recovered from Mrs. MacDonald's body is clearly different from that of the fiber recovered from the club used to assault her.**
Courtesy S. A. Michael Malone, FBI Laboratory, Washington, D.C.

Collection and Preservation of Fiber Evidence

As criminal investigators have become more aware of the potential contribution of trace physical evidence to the success of their investigations, they have placed greater emphasis on conducting thorough crime-scene searches for evidence of forensic value. Their skill and determination at carrying out these tasks is tested when it comes to the collection of fiber-related evidence. Fiber evidence can be associated with virtually any type of crime. It cannot usually be seen with the naked eye and thus can be easily overlooked by someone not specifically looking for it. An investigator committed to optimizing the laboratory's chances for locating minute strands of fibers seeks to identify and preserve potential "carriers" of fiber evidence. Relevant articles of clothing should be packaged carefully in paper bags. Each article must be placed in a separate bag to avoid cross-contamination of evidence. Scrupulous care must be taken to prevent articles of clothing from different people or from different locations from coming into contact. Such articles must not even be placed on the same surface prior to packaging. Likewise, carpets, rugs, and bedding are to be folded carefully to protect areas suspected of containing fibers. Car seats should be carefully covered with polyethylene sheets to protect fiber evidence, and knife blades should be covered to protect adhering fibers. If a body is thought to have been wrapped at one time in a blanket or carpet, adhesive tape lifts of exposed body areas may reveal fiber strands.

Occasionally the field investigator may need to remove a fiber from an object, particularly if loosely adhering fibrous material may be lost in transit to the laboratory. These fibers must be removed with a clean forceps and placed in a small sheet of paper, which, after folding and labeling, can be placed inside another container. Again, scrupulous care must be taken to prevent contact between fibers collected from different objects or from different locations.

In the laboratory, the search for fiber evidence on clothing and other relevant objects, as well as in debris, is time consuming and tedious, and will test the skill and patience of the examiner. The crime-scene investigator can reduce this task to manageable proportions by collecting only relevant items for examination. It is essential from the onset of an investigation that the crime-scene investigator pinpoint areas where a likely transfer of fiber evidence occurred and then take necessary measures to ensure proper collection and preservation of these materials.

Forensic Examination of Paint

Our environment contains millions of objects whose surfaces are painted. Thus, it is not surprising to observe that paint, in one form or another, is one of the most prevalent types of physical evidence received by the crime laboratory. Paint as physical evidence is perhaps most frequently encountered in hit-and-run and burglary cases. For example, a chip of dried paint or a paint smear may be transferred to the clothing of a hit-and-run victim on impact with an automobile, or paint smears could be transferred onto a tool during the commission of a burglary. Obviously, in many situations a transfer of paint from one surface to another could impart an object with an identifiable forensic characteristic.

In most circumstances, the criminalist must compare two or more paints to establish their common origin. For example, such a comparison may associate an individual or a vehicle with the crime site. However, the criminalist need not be confined to comparisons alone. Crime laboratories often help identify the color, make, and model of an automobile by examining small quantities of paint recovered at an accident scene. Such requests, normally made in connection with hit-and-run cases, can lead to the apprehension of the responsible vehicle.

Paint spread onto a surface dries into a hard film consisting of pigments and additives suspended in a binder. Pigments impart color and hiding (or opacity) to paint and are usually mixtures of different inorganic and organic compounds added to the paint by the manufacturer to produce specific colors and properties. The binder provides the support medium for the pigments and additives and is a polymeric substance. Paint is thus composed of a binder and pigments, as well as other additives, all dissolved or dispersed in a suitable solvent. After the paint has been applied to a surface, the solvent evaporates, leaving behind a hard polymeric binder and any pigments that were suspended in it.

Forensics at Work
The Telltale Rabbit

On a cold winter's day . . . a female was found in the alleyway of an East Harlem tenement. In close proximity to the body was a California florist flower box and a plastic liner. The decedent was identified as a member of a well-known church. She was known to have been selling church literature in the buildings that surround the alley in which the body was discovered. The detectives investigating the case forwarded the flower box, plastic liner, and the decedent's clothing to the forensic science laboratory. On the box and liner were found tan wool fibers, red acrylic fibers, and navy blue wool fibers (all identified by polarized light microscopy). The three types of questioned fibers were compared microscopically with the decedent's clothing. All three were found to be consistent in all respects to the textile fibers composing the decedent's clothing (tan wool overcoat, navy blue wool/polyester blend slacks, and red acrylic sweater), thereby associating the woman with the flower box and liner. In addition, light blue nylon rug fibers and several brown-colored rabbit hairs were found on the box and liner. Similar light blue nylon rug fibers and rabbit hairs, as well as red-colored nylon rug fibers, were found on the decedent's tan wool overcoat. Neither the rabbit hairs nor the nylon rug fibers could be associated with the victim's environment (her clothing or residence).

All of this information was conveyed to the field investigators. Upon further inquiry in the neighborhood, the investigating officers learned the identification of a man who had, the day after the body was discovered, sold a full-length, brown-colored rabbit hair coat to a local man. The investigators obtained the rabbit hair coat from the purchaser. The hair composing the coat was compared microscopically to the questioned rabbit hairs found on the victim's wool coat and the flower box liner. The specimens of questioned rabbit hair were found to be consistent in all physical and microscopic characteristics to the rabbit hair composing the suspect's coat. Armed with this information, the police now had probable cause to obtain a search warrant for the suspect's apartment.

In the suspect's apartment two rugs were found. One was colored light blue and the other was red in color; both rugs were composed of nylon fibers. Samples of each rug were collected by the crime-scene unit and forwarded to the forensic science laboratory for comparison with the questioned rug fibers found on the victim's clothing, the flower box, and plastic liner. Both the questioned and known rug fibers were found to be consistent in all respects. The presence of light blue nylon rug fibers, red nylon rug fibers, and brown-colored rabbit hairs on the flower box, plastic liner, and woman's clothing enabled the author to make associations between the woman, flower box, and liner found in the alleyway with the suspect and his apartment. . . .

Further inquiry about the suspect was made in the neighborhood by the investigating officers. A witness was located who stated he saw the suspect carrying a large California flower box a day or two before the body was discovered.

From the evidence it was theorized that the woman was killed in the suspect's apartment, placed in the flower box,

continued

Forensics at Work
(continued)

brought up to the roof of the building in which the defendant resided, and thrown off the building into the alley below. On the basis of all of this evidence, the suspect was arrested, indicted, and tried for murder in the second degree. After two trials, at which extensive testimony (three days) about the trace evidence was given by the author, the defendant was found guilty of murder in the second degree and subsequently sentenced to life imprisonment.

Source: Reprinted in part by permission of the American Society of Testing and Materials from N. Petraco, "Trace Evidence—The Invisible Witness," *Journal of Forensic Sciences*, 31 (1986): 321. Copyright 1986.

One of the most common types of paint examined in the crime laboratory is finishes from automobiles. One interesting fact that is helpful in forensic characterization of automotive paint is that manufacturers apply a variety of coatings to the body of an automobile. This adds significant diversity to automobile paint and contributes to the forensic significance of automobile paint comparisons. The automotive finishing system for steel usually consists of at least four organic coatings:

Electrocoat primer. The first layer applied to the steel body of a car is the electrocoat primer. The primer, consisting of epoxy-based resins, is electroplated onto the steel body of the automobile to provide corrosion resistance. The resulting coating is uniform in appearance and thickness. The color of these electrodeposition primers ranges from black to gray.

Primer surfacer. Originally responsible for corrosion control, the surfacer usually follows the electrocoat layer and is applied before the basecoat. Primer surfacers are epoxy-modified polyesters or urethanes. The function of this layer is to completely smooth out and hide any seams or imperfections, because the colorcoat will be applied on this surface. This layer is highly pigmented. Color pigments are used to minimize color contrast between primer and topcoats. For example, a light gray primer may be used under pastel shades of a colored topcoat; a red oxide may be used under a dark-colored topcoat.

Basecoat. The next layer of paint on a car is the basecoat or colorcoat. This layer provides the color and aesthetics of the finish and represents the "eye appeal" of the finished automobile. The integrity of this layer depends on its ability to resist weather, UV radiation, and acid rain. Most commonly, an acrylic-based polymer comprises the binder system of basecoats. Interestingly, the choice of automotive pigments is dictated by toxic and environmental concerns. Thus, the use of lead, chrome, and other heavy-metal pigments has been abandoned in favor of organic-based pigments. There is also a growing trend toward pearl luster or mica pigments. Mica pigments are coated with layers of metal oxide to generate interference colors. Also, the addition of aluminum flakes to automotive paint imparts a metallic look to the paint's finish.

Figure 8–18 A stereoscopic microscope comparison of two automotive paints. The questioned paint on the left has a layer structure consistent with the contol paint on the right. *Courtesy Leica Microsystems, Inc., Buffalo, N.Y., www.leica-microsystems.com*

Clearcoat. An unpigmented clearcoat is applied to improve gloss, durability, and appearance. Most clearcoats are acrylic based, but polyurethane clearcoats are increasing in popularity. These topcoats provide outstanding etch resistance and appearance.

The microscope has traditionally been and remains the most important instrument for locating and comparing paint specimens. Considering the thousands of paint colors and shades, it is quite understandable why color, more than any other property, imparts paint with its most distinctive forensic characteristics. Questioned and known specimens are best compared side by side under a stereoscopic microscope for color, surface texture, and color layer sequence. See Figure 8–18.

The importance of layer structure for evaluating the evidential significance of paint evidence cannot be overemphasized. When paint specimens possess colored layers that match in number and sequence of colors, the examiner can begin to relate the paints to a common origin. How many layers must be matched before the criminalist can conclude that the paints come from the same source? There is no one accepted criterion. Much depends on the uniqueness of each layer's color and texture, as well as the frequency with which the particular combination of colors under investigation is observed to occur. Because no books or journals have compiled this type of information, the criminalist is left to his or her own experience and knowledge when making this decision.

Unfortunately, most paint specimens presented to the criminalist do not have a layer structure of sufficient complexity to allow them to be individualized to a single source, nor is it common to have paint chips that can be physically fitted together to prove common origin, as shown in Figure 8–19. However, the diverse chemical composition of modern paints provides additional points of comparison between specimens. Specifically, a thorough comparison of paint must include a chemical analysis of the paint's pigments, its binder composition, or both.

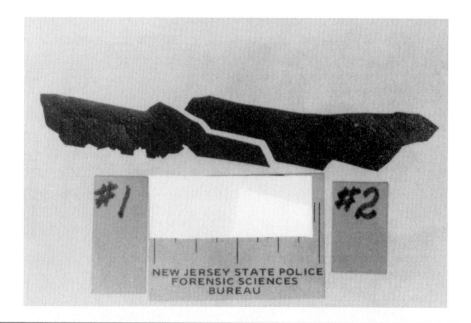

Figure 8–19   Paint chip 1 was recovered from the scene of a hit-and-run. Paint chip 2 was obtained from the suspect vehicle. *Courtesy New Jersey State Police*

The wide variation in binder formulations in automobile finishes provides particularly significant information. More important, paint manufacturers make automobile finishes in hundreds of varieties; this knowledge is most helpful to the criminalist who is trying to associate a paint chip with one car as distinguished from the thousands of similar models that have been produced in any one year. For instance, there are more than a hundred automobile production plants in the United States and Canada. Each can use one paint supplier for a particular color or vary suppliers during a model year. Although a paint supplier must maintain strict quality control over a paint's color, the batch formulation of any paint binder can vary, depending on the availability and cost of basic ingredients.

Pyrolysis gas chromatography has proven to be a particularly invaluable technique for distinguishing most paint formulations. In this process, paint chips as small as 20 micrograms are decomposed by heat into numerous gaseous products and are sent through a gas chromatograph. As shown in Figure 8–20, the polymer chain is decomposed by a heated filament, and the resultant products are swept into and through a gas chromatograph column. The separated decomposition products of the polymer emerge and are recorded. The pattern of this chromatogram or "pyrogram" distinguishes one polymer from another. The result is a pyrogram that is sufficiently detailed to reflect the chemical makeup of the binder. Figure 8–21 illustrates how the patterns produced by paint pyrograms can differentiate acrylic enamel paints removed from two different automobiles. Infrared spectrophotometry is still another analytical technique that provides information about the binder composition of paint.[9] Binders selectively absorb infrared radiation to yield a spectrum that is highly characteristic of a paint specimen.

---

[9] P. G. Rodgers et al., "The Classification of Automobile Paint by Diamond Window Infrared Spectrophotometry, Part I: Binders and Pigments," *Canadian Society of Forensic Science Journal* 9 (1976): 1; T. J. Allen, "Paint Sample Presentation for Fourier Transform Infrared Microscopy," *Vibration Spectroscopy* 3 (1992): 217.

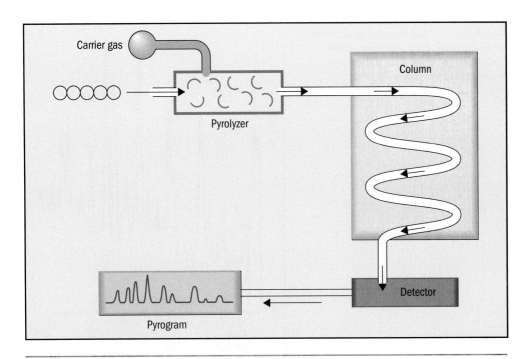

Figure 8–20 **Schematic diagram of pyrolysis gas chromatography.**

The elements that constitute the inorganic pigments of paints can be identified by a variety of techniques—emission spectroscopy, neutron activation analysis, X-ray diffraction, and X-ray spectroscopy (pp. 192–194). The emission spectrograph, for instance, can simultaneously detect fifteen to twenty elements in most automobile paints. Some of these elements are relatively common to all paints and have little forensic value; others are less frequently encountered and provide excellent points of comparison between paint specimens (see Figure 6–3).

Once a paint comparison is completed, the task of assessing the significance of the finding begins. How certain can one be that two similar paints came from the same surface? For instance, a casual observer sees countless identically colored automobiles on our roads and streets. If this is the case, what value is a comparison of a paint chip from a hit-and-run scene to paint removed from a suspect car? From previous discussions it should be apparent that far more is involved in paint comparison than matching surface paint colors. Paint layers present beneath a surface layer offer valuable points of comparison. Furthermore, forensic analysts can detect subtle differences in paint binder formulations, as well as major or minor differences in the elemental composition of paint. Obviously, these properties cannot be discerned by the naked eye.

The significance of a paint comparison was convincingly demonstrated from data gathered at the Centre of Forensic Science, Toronto, Canada.[10] Paint chips randomly taken from 260 vehicles located in a local wreck yard were compared by color, layer structure, and, when required, by infrared spectroscopy. All were distinguishable except for one pair. In statistical terms, these results signify that if a crime-scene paint sample and a paint

---

[10] G. Edmondstone, J. Hellman, K. Legate, G. L. Vardy, and E. Lindsay, "An Assessment of the Evidential Value of Automotive Paint Comparisons," *Canadian Society of Forensic Science Journal* 37 (2004): 147.

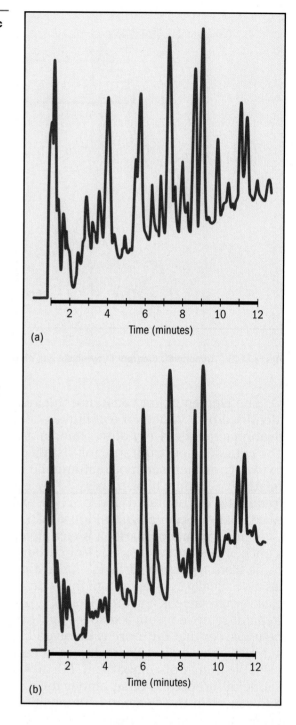

Figure 8–21 Paint pyrograms of acrylic enamel paints. (a) Paint from a Ford model and (b) paint from a Chrysler model. *Courtesy Varian Inc., Palo Alto, Calif.*

(a)

(b)

standard/reference sample removed from a suspect car compare by the previously discussed tests, the odds against the crime-scene paint originating from another randomly chosen vehicle are approximately 33,000 to one. Obviously, this type of evidence is bound to forge a strong link between the suspect car and the crime scene.

Crime laboratories are often asked to identify the make and model of a car from a very small amount of paint left behind at a crime scene. Such information is frequently of use in a search for an unknown car involved in a hit-and-run incident. Often, the questioned paint can be identified when its color is compared to color chips representing the various makes and models of manufactured cars. However, in many cases it is not possible to state the exact make or model of the car in question, since any one paint color can be found on more than one car model. For instance, General Motors may use the same paint color for several production years on cars in their Cadillac, Buick, Pontiac, and Chevrolet lines.

Color charts for automobile finishes are available from various paint manufacturers and refinishers. Starting with the 1974 model year, the Law Enforcement Standards Laboratory at the National Institute of Standards and Technology collected and disseminated to crime laboratories auto paint color samples from U.S. domestic passenger cars. This collection was distributed by Collaborative Testing Services, McLean, Virginia, through 1991. Since 1975, the Royal Canadian Mounted Police Forensic Laboratories have been systematically gathering color and chemical information on automotive paints. This computerized database, known as PDQ (Paint Data Query), allows an analyst to obtain information on paints related to automobile make, model, and year. The database contains such parameters as automotive paint layer colors, primer colors, and binder composition. A number of U.S. laboratories have access to PDQ.[11]

Collection and Preservation of Paint Evidence

As has already been noted, paint chips are most likely to be found on or near people or objects involved in hit-and-run incidents. The recovery of loose paint chips from a garment or from the road surface must be done with the utmost care to keep the paint chip intact. Paint chips may be picked up with a tweezers or scooped up with a piece of paper. Paper druggist folds and glass or plastic vials make excellent containers for paint. If the paint is smeared on or embedded in garments or objects, the investigator should not attempt to remove it; instead, it is best to package the whole item carefully and send it to the laboratory for examination.

When a transfer of paint occurs in hit-and-run situations, such as to the clothing of a pedestrian victim, uncontaminated standard/reference paint must always be collected from an undamaged area of the vehicle for comparison in the laboratory. It is particularly important that the collected paint be close to the area of the car that was suspected of being in contact with the victim. This is necessary because other portions of the car may have faded or been repainted. Standard/reference samples are always removed so as to include all the paint layers down to the bare metal. This is best accomplished by removing a painted section with a clean scalpel or knife blade. Samples 1/4 inch square are sufficient for laboratory examination. Each paint sample should be separately packaged and marked with the exact location of its recovery. When a cross-transfer of paint occurs between two vehicles, again all of the layers, including the foreign as well as

---

[11] J. L. Buckle et al., "PDQ—Paint Data Queries: The History and Technology behind the Development of the Royal Canadian Mounted Police Laboratory Services Automotive Paint Database," *Canadian Society of Forensic Science Journal,* 30 (1997): 199. An excellent discussion of the PDQ database is also available in A. Beveridge, T. Fung, and D. MacDougall, "Use of Infrared Spectroscopy for the Characterisation of Paint Fragments," in B. Caddy, ed., *Forensic Examination of Glass and Paint,* (New York: Taylor & Francis, 2001), pp. 222–233.

Forensics at Work
The CBS Murders

In the early morning hours . . . atop a lonely roof garage on the west side of Manhattan, three men were found murdered. Each man had been shot once in the back of the head. A light-colored van was seen speeding away from the scene. Hours later, in a secluded alley street on the lower east side of Manhattan, the body of a fully clothed woman was found lying face down by two dog walkers. The woman had been killed in the same manner as the men on the roof garage. The condition of the woman's body, and other evidence, made it apparent that she had been shot at the garage, and then transported to the alley.

An eyewitness to the incident stated that he saw a man shoot a woman and place her in a light-colored van. The gunman then chased down the three men who were coming to the woman's aid, and shot each one of them. Days later, the prime suspect to the killings was arrested in Kentucky, in a black-colored van.

Numerous items of evidence (over 100) were collected from the van, and forwarded to the New York City police laboratory for examination. Among the items of evidence forwarded were three sets of vacuum sweepings from the van's interior.

An autopsy of the woman produced several items of trace evidence that were removed from the victim and forwarded to the author for microscopic examination. The woman's clothing was also received by the author for trace analysis.

A prime question that arose during the investigation was: could the woman's body, which had been placed in a light-colored van at the garage, and later left in an alley on the lower east side, be associated with the black van recovered over 1000 km (600 miles) away from the scene? Microscopic analysis and comparison of the trace evidential materials found on the victim and inside the van made this association possible.

Listed in Table 1 are all the items of similar trace materials that both the victim and the van had in common.

Microscopic comparisons of the questioned human head hair present on the victim's clothing were made with known samples. Ten of the brown-colored and gray-colored Caucasian head hairs from the victim's blazer were consistent in microscopic characteristics to the defendant's known head hair sample. One chemically treated head hair found on the victim was consistent in microscopic characteristics to the known head hair sample obtained from the defendant's wife. One forcibly removed, brown-colored, Caucasian head hair that was found on the rear door of the van's interior by the Kentucky state police was found to be consistent in all characteristics with the decedent's known head hair sample.

Microscopic comparisons of the white- and brown/white-colored dog hair from the victim's clothing, and the van's interior, were made with known samples of dog hair obtained from a dog owned by the defendant's nephew, the van's previous owner. The questioned dog hairs were found to be consistent with the hair from the nephew's dog.

The white seed that was recovered from the victim's mouth by the medical

---

This case takes its title from the fact that the three male victims were employees of CBS-TV.

continued

Forensics at Work

(continued)

examiner, and the white seed that was found in the van's sweepings by the author, were forwarded to an internationally known botanist for identification and comparison. During the trial, the botanist testified that the two seeds were identical in all respects, and that although he could not identify the seed, both were either from the same species of plant, if not the same plant, probably a rare wild flower.

Sixteen gray metallic/black-colored paint chips from the victim and her clothing were compared to the gray metallic/black-colored paint removed from the van. Samples from the questioned and known sources were examined and compared by

microscopic, chemical, and instrumental means. All of the paint specimens from the van and from the victim were found to be similar in all respects.

The remaining items of trace evidence from the victim and the van were examined and compared microscopically, and where necessary, by chemical and instrumental methods. Each of the remaining types of trace evidence from the victim was found to be similar to its counterpart from the van.

Blue- and black-colored flakes of acrylic paint were found in the van's sweepings, and on the suspect's sneakers. No blue- or black-colored paint flakes were found on the victim and her clothing. During a crime

Table 1   Items of Similar Trace Evidence That Were Recovered from Both the Victim and the Van's Interior

	Source	
Trace Evidence	Victim	Van
White seed	mouth	sweepings
Paint chips gray metallic/black	hair and wool blazer	sweepings and floor
Sawdust	hair, blazer, and sheet	sweepings and misc. items

Glass fragments
  clear
  amber
  green
	wool blazer and sheet	sweepings and misc. items

Cellophane	wool blazer	floor

Urethane foam
  foam mattress
	wool blazer	sweepings, misc. items,
		  and foam mattress

Blue olefin plastic	skirt	floor

Dog hair
  brown/white
  white
	wool blazer	sweepings and misc. items

Human hair
  brown
  gray
	wool blazer	hairbrush, sweepings,
		  and misc. items

continued

Forensics at Work

(continued)

scene search of the defendant's residence in New Jersey, a large quantity of blue- and black-colored acrylic paint was found in the garage. It was apparent from the evidence present in the defendant's garage that a large rectangular shaped object had recently been painted with blue- and black-colored paint. The blue and black paint flakes from all the sources and the known blue (undercoat) and black (topcoat) paint from the van were compared by microscopic, chemical, and instrumental means. All the samples of paint were found to be consistent in every respect.

At the trial, extensive testimony concerning the collection, examination, identification, and comparison of the trace evidence from the victim and the van was given by the author, over a two-day period. When questioned about the source of the trace evidence found on the victim and her clothing, the author stated unequivocally that the trace evidence on the victim was from the defendant's van. On the basis of this evidence and other circumstantial evidence, the defendant was found guilty of all charges and sentenced to 100 years in prison.

Source: Reprinted by permission of the American Society of Testing and Materials from N. Petraco, "Trace Evidence—The Invisible Witness," *Journal of Forensic Sciences,* **31 (1986): 321. Copyright 1986.**

the underlying original paints, must be removed from each vehicle. A standard/reference sample from an adjacent undamaged area of each vehicle must also be taken in such cases. Carefully wipe the blade of any knife or scraping tool used before collecting each sample, to avoid cross-contamination of paints.

Tools used to enter buildings or safes often contain traces of paints as well as other substances such as wood and safe insulation. Care must be taken not to lose this type of trace evidence. The scene investigator should not try to remove the paint; instead, he or she should package the tool for laboratory examination. Standard/reference paint should be collected from all surfaces suspected of having been in contact with the tool. Again, all layers of paint must be included in the sample.

When the tool has left its impression on a surface, standard/reference paint is collected from an uncontaminated area adjacent to the impression. No attempt should be made to collect the paint from the impression itself. If this is done, the impression may be permanently altered and its evidential value lost.

Chapter Summary

Hair is an appendage of the skin that grows out of an organ known as the hair follicle. The length of a hair extends from its root or bulb embedded in the follicle, continues into a shaft, and terminates at a tip end. The shaft, which is composed of three layers—the cuticle, cortex, and medulla—is subjected to the most intense examination by the forensic scientist. The comparison microscope is an indispensable tool for comparing these morphological characteristics. When comparing strands of hair, the criminalist is particularly interested in matching the color, length, and diameter. A careful microscopic examination of hair reveals morphological features that can distinguish human hair from the hair of animals. Scale structure, medullary index, and medullary shape are particularly important in hair identification. Other important features for comparing hair are the presence or absence of a medulla and the distribution, shape, and color intensity of the pigment granules present in the cortex. However, microscopic hair examinations tend to be subjective and highly dependent on the skills and integrity of the analyst. Recent major breakthroughs in DNA profiling have extended this technology to the individualization of human hair. The probability of detecting DNA in hair roots is more likely for hair being examined in its anagen or early growth phase as opposed to its catagen or telogen phases. Often, when hair is forcibly removed a follicular tag, a translucent piece of tissue surrounding the hair's shaft near the root, may be present. This has proven to be a rich source of DNA associated with hair. Also, mitochondrial DNA can be extracted from the hair shaft. As a rule, all positive microscopic hair comparisons must be confirmed by DNA analysis.

The quality of fiber evidence depends on the ability of the criminalist to identify the origin of the fiber or at least to narrow the possibilities to a limited number of sources. Microscopic comparisons between questioned and standard/reference fibers are initially undertaken for color and diameter characteristics. Other morphological features that could be important in comparing fibers are striations on the surface of the fiber, the presence of delustering particles, and the cross-sectional shape of the fiber. The visible-light microspectrophotometer provides a convenient way to compare the colors of fibers through spectral patterns. Infrared spectrophotometry is a rapid and reliable tool for identifying the generic class of fibers, as is the polarizing microscope.

Paint spread onto a surface dries into a hard film consisting of pigments and additives suspended in the binder. One of the most common types of paint examined in the crime laboratory is finishes from automobiles. Automobile manufacturers normally apply a variety of coatings to the body of an automobile. Hence, the wide diversity of automotive paint contributes to the forensic significance of an automobile paint comparison. Questioned and known specimens are best compared side by side under a stereoscopic microscope for color, surface texture, and color layer sequence. Pyrolysis gas chromatography and infrared spectrophotometry are invaluable techniques for distinguishing most paint binder formulations, adding further significance to a forensic paint comparison.

Review Questions

1. Hair is an appendage of the skin, growing out of an organ known as the
   _____.

2. The three layers of the hair shaft are the _____, the _____, and the
   _____.

3. True or False: The scales of most animal hairs can be described as looking like shingles on a roof. _____

4. The _____ contains the pigment granules that impart color to hair.

5. The central canal running through many hairs is known as the _____.

6. The diameter of the medulla relative to the diameter of the hair shaft is the _____.

7. Human hair generally has a medullary index of less than _____; the hair of most animals has an index of _____ or greater.

8. Human head hairs generally exhibit (continuous, absent) medullae.

9. If a medulla exhibits a patterned shape, the hair is (human, animal) in origin.

10. The three stages of hair growth are the _____, _____, and _____ phases.

11. A single hair (can, cannot) be individualized to one person by microscopic examination.

12. In making hair comparisons, it is best to view the hairs side by side under a(n) _____ microscope.

13. _____ hairs are short and curly, with wide variation in shaft diameter.

14. It (is, is not) possible to determine when hair was last bleached or dyed.

15. True or False: The age and sex of the individual from whom a hair sample has been taken can be determined through an examination of the hair's morphological features. _____

16. Hair forcibly removed from the body (always, often) has follicular tissue adhering to its root.

17. Microscopic hair comparisons must be regarded by police and courts as presumptive in nature, and all positive microscopical hair comparisons must be confirmed by _____ typing.

18. True or False: Currently, DNA typing can individualize a single hair. _____

19. A(n) _____ hair root is a likely candidate for DNA typing.

20. A minimum collection of _____ full-length hairs normally ensures a representative sampling of head hair.

21. A minimum collection of _____ full-length pubic hairs is recommended to cover the range of characteristics present in this region of the body.

22. _____ fibers are derived totally from animal or plant sources.

23. The most prevalent natural plant fiber is _____.

24. True or False: Regenerated fibers, such as rayon and acetate, are manufactured by chemically treating cellulose and passing it through a spinneret. _____

25. Fibers manufactured solely from synthetic chemicals are classified as _____.

26. True or False: Polyester was the first synthetic fiber. _____

27. _____ are composed of a large number of atoms arranged in repeating units.

28. The basic unit of the polymer is called the _____.

29. _____ are polymers composed of thousands of amino acids linked in a highly organized arrangement and sequence.

30. True or False: A first step in the forensic examination of fibers is to compare color and diameter. _____

31. The microspectrophotometer employing _____ light is a convenient way for analysts to compare the colors of fibers through spectral patterns.

32. The dye components removed from fibers can be separated and compared by _____ chromatography.

33. Synthetic fibers possess the physical property of _____ because they are crystalline.

34. The microspectrophotometer employing _____ light provides a rapid and reliable method for identifying the generic class of a single fiber.

35. Normally, fibers possess (individual, class) characteristics.

36. The two most important components of dried paint from the criminalist's point of view are the _____ and the _____.

37. The most important physical property of paint in a forensic comparison is _____.

38. Paints can be individualized to a single source only when they have a sufficiently detailed _____.

39. The _____ layer provides corrosion resistance for the automobile.

40. "Eye appeal" of the automobile comes from the _____ layer.

41. Pyrolysis gas chromatography is a particularly valuable technique for characterizing paint's (binder, pigments).

42. Emission spectroscopy can be used to identify the (inorganic, organic) components of paint's pigments.

43. True or False: Paint samples removed for examination must always include all of the paint layers. _____

Further References

Bisbing, R. E., "The Forensic Identification and Association of Human Hair," in R. Saferstein, ed., *Forensic Science Handbook,* vol. 1, 2nd ed., Upper Saddle River, N.J.: Prentice Hall, 2002.

Caddy, B., ed., *Forensic Examination of Glass and Paint.* New York: Taylor & Francis, 2001.

Deedrick, D. W., "Hairs, Fibers, Crime, and Evidence," *Forensic Science Communications,* 2, no. 3, 2000, *www.fbi.gov/hg/lab/fsc/backissu/july2000/deedrick.htm.*

Deedrick, D. W., and S. L. Koch, "Microscopy of Hair Part I: A Practical Guide and Manual for Human Hairs," *Forensic Science Communications,* 6, no.1 (2004), *www.fbi.gov/hq/lab/fsc/backissu/jan2004/index.htm.*

Deedrick, D. W., and S. L. Koch, "Microscopy of Hair Part II: A Practical Guide and Manual for Animal Hairs," *Forensic Science Communications,* 6, no. 3, (2004), *http://www.fbi.gov/hq/lab/fsc/backissu/july2004/index.htm.*

Eyring, M. B., and B. D. Gaudette, "The Forensic Aspects of Textile Fiber Examination," in R. Saferstein, ed., *Forensic Science Handbook,* vol. 2, 2nd ed., Upper Saddle River, N.J.: Prentice Hall, 2005.

Ogle, R. R., Jr., and M. J. Fox, *Atlas of Human Hair: Microscopic Characteristics.* Boca Raton, Fla.: Taylor & Francis, 1999.

Petraco, N., and P. R. De Forest, "A Guide to the Analysis of Forensic Dust Specimens," in R. Saferstein, ed., *Forensic Science Handbook,* vol. 3. Upper Saddle River, N.J.: Prentice Hall, 1993.

Robertson, J., ed., *Forensic Examination of Hair.* New York: Taylor & Francis, 1999.

Robertson, J., and M. Grieve, eds., *Forensic Examination of Fibres,* 2nd ed., New York: Taylor & Francis, 1999.

Thornton, J. L., "Forensic Paint Examination," in R. Saferstein, ed., *Forensic Science Handbook,* vol. 1, 2nd ed., Upper Saddle River, N.J.: Prentice Hall, 2002.

Pablo Escobar, Drug Lord

In 1989, *Forbes* magazine listed Pablo Escobar as the seventh richest man in the world. Escobar began his climb to wealth as a teenage car thief in the streets of Medellin, Colombia. He eventually moved into the cocaine-smuggling business. At the peak of his power in the mid-1980s, he was shipping as much as eleven tons of cocaine per flight in jetliners to the United States. Estimates are that the Medellin cartel controlled 80 percent of the world's cocaine market and was taking in about $25 billion annually. Escobar ruthlessly ruled by the gun: murdering, assassinating, and kidnapping. He was responsible for killing three presidential candidates in Colombia, as well as the storming of the Colombian Supreme Court, which resulted in the murder of half the justices. All the while, Escobar curried favor with the Colombian general public by cultivating a Robin Hood image and distributing money to the poor. In 1991, hoping to avoid extradition to the United States, Escobar turned himself in to the Colombian government and agreed to be sent to prison. However, the prison compound could easily be mistaken for a country club. There he continued his high-flying lifestyle, trafficking by telephone and even murdering a few associates. When the Colombian government attempted to move Escobar to another jail, he escaped, again fearing extradition to the United States. Pressured by the U.S. government, Colombia organized a task force dedicated to apprehending Escobar. The manhunt for Escobar ended on December 2, 1993, when he was cornered on the roof of one of his hideouts. A shootout ensued and Escobar was fatally wounded by a bullet behind his ear.

chapter 9

Drugs

Key Terms

anabolic steriods

analgesic

confirmation

depressant

hallucinogen

microcrystalline tests

narcotic

physical dependence

psychological dependence

screening test

stimulant

Learning Objectives

After studying this chapter you should be able to:

- Compare and contrast psychological and physical dependence

- Name and classify the commonly abused drugs

- List and define the schedules of the Controlled Substances Act

- Describe the laboratory tests normally used to perform a routine drug identification analysis

- Explain the testing procedures used for forensic identification of marijuana

- Understand the proper collection and preservation of drug evidence

A *drug* can be defined as a natural or synthetic substance that is used to produce physiological or psychological effects in humans or other higher order animals. However, this colorless clinical definition does not really tell us what drugs are; in their modern context, drugs mean something different to each person. To some, drugs are a necessity for sustaining and prolonging life; to others, drugs provide an escape from the pressures of life; to still others, they are a means of ending it.

Considering the wide application and acceptance of drugs in our society, it was perhaps inevitable that a segment of our population would abuse them. During the 1960s, succeeding waves of hallucinogens, amphetamines, and barbiturates found their way out of laboratories, pharmacies, and medicine chests and into the streets. During this decade, marijuana became the most widely used illicit drug in the United States, and alcohol consumption continued to rise—today 90 million Americans drink alcohol regularly, and 10 million of these are hopelessly addicted or have severe problems in coping with their drinking habits. In the 1970s, heroin addiction emerged as a national problem, and today the United States is in the midst of an epidemic of cocaine abuse.

Drug abuse has grown from a problem generally associated with members of the lower end of the socioeconomic ladder to one that cuts across all social and ethnic classes of society. Today, approximately 23 million people in the United States use illicit drugs, including about a half million heroin addicts and nearly six million users of cocaine.

In the United States, more than 75 percent of the evidence evaluated in crime laboratories is drug related. The deluge of drug specimens has forced the expansion of existing crime laboratories and the creation of new ones. For many concerned forensic scientists, the crime laboratory's preoccupation with drug evidence represents a serious distraction from time that could be devoted to evaluating evidence related to homicides and other types of serious crimes. However, the increasing caseloads associated with drug evidence have justified the expansion of forensic laboratory services. This expansion has increased the overall analytical capabilities of crime laboratories.

Drug Dependence

In assessing the potential danger of drugs, society has become particularly conscious of their effects on human behavior. In fact, the first drugs to be regulated by law in the early years of the twentieth century were those deemed to have "habit-forming" properties. The early laws were aimed primarily at controlling opium and its derivatives, cocaine, and later marijuana. Today, it is known that the ability of a drug to induce dependence after repeated use is submerged in a complex array of physiological and social factors.

Dependence on drugs exists in numerous patterns and in all degrees of intensity, depending on the nature of the drug, the route of administration, the dose, the frequency of administration, and the individual's rate of metabolism. Furthermore, nondrug factors play an equally crucial role in determining the behavioral patterns associated with drug use. The personal characteristics of the user, his or her expectations about the drug experience, society's attitudes and possible responses, and the setting in which the drug is used are all major determinants of drug dependence.

The question of how to define and measure a drug's influence on the individual and its danger to society is difficult to assess. To this end, the nature and significance of drug dependence must be considered from two overlapping points of view: the interaction of the drug with the individual, and the drug's impact on society. It will be useful when discussing the nature of the drug experience to approach the problem from two distinctly different aspects of human behavior—psychological dependence and physical dependence.

The common denominator that characterizes all types of repeated drug use is the creation of a psychological dependence for continued use of the drug. It is important to discard the unrealistic image that all drug users are hopeless "addicts" who are social dropouts. Most users present quite a normal appearance and remain both socially and economically integrated in the life of the community.

The reasons why some people abstain from drugs while others become moderately or heavily involved are difficult if not impossible to delineate. Psychological needs arise from numerous personal and social factors that stem from the individual's desire to create a sense of well-being and to escape from reality. In some cases, the individual may be seeking relief from personal problems or stressful situations, or he or she may be trying to sustain a physical and emotional state that permits an improved level of performance. Whatever the reasons, the underlying psychological needs and the desire to fulfill them create a conditioned pattern of drug abuse.

The intensity of the psychological dependence associated with a drug's use is difficult to define and largely depends on the nature of the drug used. For drugs such as alcohol, heroin, amphetamines, barbiturates, and cocaine, there is a significant likelihood that continued use will result in a high degree of involvement. Other drugs, such as marijuana and codeine, appear to have a considerably lower potential for the development of psychological dependence. However, this does not imply that repeated abuse of drugs deemed to have a low potential for psychological dependency is safe or will always produce low psychological dependence. We have no precise way of measuring or predicting the impact of drug abuse on the individual. Even if a system could be devised for controlling the many possible variables affecting a user's response, the unpredictability of the human personality would still have to be considered; the personal inadequacies of the drug user represent the underlying motivation for drug use.

Our general knowledge of alcohol consumption should warn us of the fallacy of generalizing when attempting to describe the danger of drug abuse. Obviously, not all alcohol drinkers are psychologically addicted to the drug; most are "social" drinkers who drink in reasonable amounts and

Psychological Dependence
Conditioned use of a drug caused by underlying emotional needs.

Physical Dependence
Physiological need for a drug that has been brought about by its regular use. Dependence is characterized by withdrawal sickness when administration of the drug is abruptly stopped.

on an irregular basis. Many people have progressed beyond this stage and consider alcohol a necessary crutch for dealing with life's stresses and anxieties. However, a wide range of behavioral patterns exists among alcohol abusers, and to a large extent the degree of psychological dependency must be determined on an individual basis. Likewise, it would be fallacious to generalize that all users of marijuana can at worst develop a low degree of dependency on the drug. A wide range of factors also influence marijuana's effect, and heavy users of the drug expose themselves to the danger of developing a high degree of psychological dependency.

Where emotional well-being is the primary motive leading to repeated and intensive use of a drug, certain drugs, when taken in sufficient dose and frequency, are capable of producing physiological changes that encourage their continued use. Once the user abstains from such a drug, severe physical illness follows. The desire to avoid this *withdrawal sickness* or *abstinence syndrome* ultimately causes physical dependence, or addiction. Hence, for the addict who is accustomed to receiving large doses of heroin, the thought of abstaining and encountering body chills, vomiting, stomach cramps, convulsions, insomnia, pain, and hallucinations is a powerful inducement for continued drug use.

Interestingly, some of the more widely abused drugs have little or no potential for creating physical dependence. Drugs such as marijuana, LSD, and cocaine create strong anxieties when their repeated use is discontinued; however, no medical evidence attributes these discomforts to physiological reactions that accompany withdrawal sickness. On the other hand, use of alcohol, heroin, and barbiturates can result in development of physical dependency.

Physical dependency develops only when the drug user adheres to a regular schedule of drug intake; that is, the interval between doses must be short enough so that the effects of the drug never wear off completely. For example, the interval between injections of heroin for the drug addict probably does not exceed six to eight hours. Beyond this time the addict begins to experience the uncomfortable symptoms of withdrawal. Many users of heroin avoid taking the drug on a regular basis for fear of becoming physically addicted to its use. Similarly, the risk of developing physical dependence on alcohol becomes greatest when the consumption is characterized by a continuing pattern of daily use in large quantities.

Table 9–1 categorizes some of the more commonly abused drugs according to their effect on the body and summarizes their tendency to produce psychological dependency and to induce physical dependency with repeated use.

The social impact of drug dependence is directly related to the extent to which the user has become preoccupied with the drug. Here, the most important element is the extent to which drug use has become interwoven in the fabric of the user's life. The more frequently the drug satisfies the person's need, the greater the likelihood that he or she will become preoccupied with its use, with a consequent neglect of individual and social responsibilities. Personal health, economic relationships, and family obligations may all suffer as the drug-seeking behavior increases in frequency and intensity and dominates the individual's life. The extreme of drug dependence may lead to behavior that has serious implications for the public's safety, health, and welfare.

Drug dependence in its broadest sense involves much of the world's population. As a result, a complex array of individual, social, cultural, legal, and medical factors ultimately influence society's decision to prohibit

Table 9–1 The Potential of Some Commonly Abused Drugs to Produce Dependency with Regular Use

Drug	Psychological Dependence	Physical Dependence
Narcotics		
Morphine	High	Yes
Heroin	High	Yes
Methadone	High	Yes
Codeine	Low	Yes
Depressants		
Barbiturates (short-acting)	High	Yes
Barbiturates (long-acting)	Low	Yes
Alcohol	High	Yes
Methaqualone (Quaalude)	High	Yes
Meprobamate (Miltown, Equanil)	Moderate	Yes
Diazepam (Valium)	Moderate	Yes
Chlordiazepoxide (Librium)	Moderate	Yes
Stimulants		
Amphetamines	High	?
Cocaine	High	No
Caffeine	Low	No
Nicotine	High	Yes
Hallucinogens		
Marijuana	Low	No
LSD	Low	No
Phencyclidine (PCP)	High	No

or to impose strict controls on a drug's distribution and use. Invariably, society must weigh the beneficial aspects of the drug against the ultimate harm its abuse will do to the individual and to society as a whole. Obviously, many forms of drug dependence do not carry sufficient adverse social consequences to warrant their prohibition, as illustrated by the widespread use of such drug-containing substances as tobacco and coffee. Although heavy and prolonged use of these drugs may eventually damage body organs and injure an individual's health, there is no evidence that they result in antisocial behavior, even with prolonged or excessive use. Hence, society is willing to accept widespread use of these substances.

We are certainly all aware of the disastrous failure in the United States to prohibit the use of alcohol during the 1920s and the current debate on whether marijuana should be legalized. Each of these issues emphasizes the delicate balance between individual desires and needs and society's concern with the consequences of drug abuse; moreover, this balance is continuously subject to change and reevaluation.

Narcotic Drugs

The term narcotic is derived from the Greek word *narkotikos,* which implies a state of lethargy or sluggishness. Pharmacologists actually classify narcotic drugs as substances that bring relief from pain and produce sleep.

Narcotic
An analgesic or pain-killing substance that depresses vital body functions such as blood pressure, pulse rate, and breathing rate. Regular administration of narcotics produces physical dependence.

Unfortunately, "narcotic" has come to be popularly associated with any drug that is socially unacceptable. As a consequence of this incorrect usage, many drugs are improperly called narcotics. Furthermore, this confusion has produced legal definitions that are at variance with the pharmacological actions of many drugs. For example, until the early 1970s, most drug laws in the United States incorrectly designated marijuana as a narcotic; even now, many drug-control laws in the United States, including the federal law, classify cocaine as a narcotic drug. Pharmacologically, cocaine is actually a powerful central nervous system stimulant, possessing properties opposite to those normally associated with the depressant effects of a narcotic.

Analgesic
A drug or substance that lessens or eliminates pain.

Narcotic drugs are analgesics—that is, they relieve pain by depressing the central nervous system. Regular use of a narcotic drug leads to physical dependence, with all its dire consequences. The source of most analgesic narcotics is opium, a gummy, milky juice exuded through a cut made in the unripe pod of the poppy (*Papaver somniferum*), a plant grown mostly in parts of Asia. Opium is brownish in color and has a morphine content ranging from 4 to 21 percent.

Although morphine is readily extracted from opium, for reasons that are not totally known, most addicts prefer to use one of its derivatives, *heroin*. Heroin is made rather simply by reacting morphine with acetic anhydride or acetyl chloride (see Figure 9–1). Heroin's high solubility in water makes its street preparation for intravenous administration rather simple, for only by injection are heroin's effects almost instantaneously felt and with maximum sensitivity. To prepare the drug for injection, the addict frequently dissolves it in a small quantity of water in a spoon. The process can be speeded up by heating the spoon over a candle or several matches. The solution is then drawn into a syringe or eyedropper for injection be-

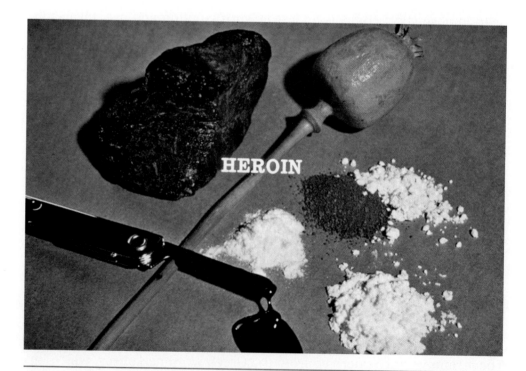

Figure 9–1 **The opium poppy and its derivatives. Shown are the poppy plant, crude and smoking opium, codeine, heroin, and morphine.** *Courtesy Pearson Education/PH College*

neath the skin. Figure 9–2 shows some of the paraphernalia typically associated with street administration of heroin. Besides being a powerful analgesic, heroin produces a "high" that is accompanied by drowsiness and a deep sense of well-being; however, the effect is short, generally lasting only three to four hours.

The content of a typical heroin bag is an excellent example of the uncertainty attached to buying illicit drugs. For many years into the 1960s and early 1970s, the average bag contained 15 to 20 percent heroin. Currently, the average purity of heroin obtained in the illicit U.S. market is approximately 35 percent. The addict rarely knows or cares what comprises the other 65 percent or so of the material. Traditionally, quinine has been the most common diluent of heroin. Like heroin, it has a bitter taste and was probably originally used to obscure the actual potency of a heroin preparation for those who wished to taste-test the material before buying it. Other diluents commonly added to heroin are starch, lactose, procaine (Novocain), and mannitol.

Codeine is also present in opium, but it is usually prepared synthetically from morphine. It is commonly used as a cough suppressant in prescription cough syrup. Codeine, only one-sixth as strong as morphine, is not an attractive street drug for addicts.

A number of narcotic drugs are not naturally derived from opium. However, because they have similar physiological effects on the body as the opium narcotics, they are commonly referred to as *opiates*. In 1995, the U.S. Food and Drug Administration approved for use the pain-killing drug *OxyContin*. The active ingredient in OxyContin is oxycodone, a synthetic closely related to morphine and heroin in its chemical structure. OxyContin is an analgesic narcotic that has effects similar to those of heroin. It is prescribed to a million patients for treatment of chronic pain, with doctors writing close to seven million OxyContin prescriptions each year. The drug is compounded with a time-release formulation that the manufacturer initially believed would reduce the risk of

Figure 9–2 Heroin paraphernalia. *Courtesy Drug Enforcement Administration*

abuse and addiction. This has not turned out to be the case. It is estimated that close to a quarter of a million individuals abuse the drug.

Because it is a legal drug that is diverted from legitimate sources, Oxy-Contin is obtained very differently than illegal drugs. Pharmacy robberies, forged prescriptions, and theft from patients with a legitimate prescription are ways in which abusers access OxyContin. Some abusers visit numerous doctors and receive prescriptions even though their medical condition may not warrant it.

Methadone is another well-known synthetic opiate. In the 1960s, scientists discovered that a person receiving methadone periodically in oral doses of 80 to 120 milligrams a day would not get high if he or she then took heroin or morphine. Clearly, although methadone is a narcotic pharmacologically related to heroin, its administration appears to eliminate the addict's desire for heroin while producing minimal side effects. Critics of the controversial methadone maintenance programs claim that methadone use is just substituting one narcotic drug for another, and supporters argue that this is the only known treatment for keeping the addict off heroin and offering some hope for eventual abstention from narcotics.

Physicians are increasingly prescribing methadone for pain relief. Unfortunately, in recent years, the wide availability of the drug for legitimate medical purposes has led to greater quantities of the drug being diverted into the illicit market. Methadone is being abused increasingly and is causing an alarming number of overdoses and deaths.

Hallucinogens

Hallucinogen
A substance that induces changes in mood, attitude, thought processes, and perceptions.

Hallucinogens are drugs that can cause marked alterations in mood, attitude, thought processes, and perceptions. Perhaps the most popular and controversial member of this class of drugs is marijuana.

Marijuana

Marijuana easily qualifies as the most widely used illicit drug in the United States today. For instance, more than 43 million Americans have tried marijuana, according to the latest surveys, and almost half that number may be regular users. Marijuana is a preparation derived from the plant *Cannabis*. Most botanists believe there is only one species of the plant, *Cannabis sativa L.* The marijuana preparation normally consists of crushed leaves mixed in varying proportions with the plant's flower, stem, and seed. See Figure 9–3. The plant secretes a sticky resin known as *hashish*. The resinous material can also be extracted from the plant by soaking in a solvent such as alcohol. On the illicit-drug market, hashish usually appears in the form of compressed vegetation containing a high percentage of resin. See Figure 9–4. A potent form of marijuana is known as *sinsemilla*. This is made from the unfertilized flowering tops of the female *Cannabis* plants, attained by removal of all male plants from the growing field at the first sign of their appearance. It follows that the production of sinsemilla requires a great deal of attention and care, and the plant is therefore cultivated on small plots.

Marijuana and its related products have been in use legally and illegally for almost three thousand years. The first reference to the medical use of marijuana is in a pharmacy book written about 2737 B.C. by the Chinese emperor Shen Nung, who recommended it for "female weakness, gout, rheumatism, malaria, beriberi, constipation and absent-mindedness." In

Figure 9–3   Several rolled marijuana cigarettes lie on a pile of crushed dried marijuana leaves next to a tobacco cigarette. *Courtesy U.S. Department of Justice, Drug Enforcement Administration*

Figure 9–4   Blocks of hashish in front of leaves and flowering tops of the marijuana plant. *Courtesy James King-Holmes, Photo Researchers, Inc.*

China, at that time and even today, the marijuana or hemp plant was also a major source of fiber for the production of rope. Marijuana's mood-altering powers probably did not receive wide attention until about 1000 B.C., when it became an integral part of Hindu culture in India. After A.D. 500, marijuana began creeping westward, and references to it began to appear in Persian and Arabian literature.

The plant was probably brought to Europe by Napoleon's soldiers when they returned from Egypt in the early years of the nineteenth century. In Europe, the drug excited the interest of many physicians who foresaw its application for the treatment of a wide range of ailments. At this time, it also found some use as a painkiller and mild sedative. In later years, these applications were either forgotten or ignored.

Marijuana was first introduced into the United States around 1920. The weed was smuggled by Mexican laborers across the border into Texas. American soldiers also brought the plant in from the ports of Havana, Tampico, and Veracruz. Although its use was confined to a small segment of the population, its popularity quickly spread from the border and Gulf states into most of the major U.S. cities. By 1937, forty-six states and the federal government had laws prohibiting the use or possession of marijuana. Under most of these laws, marijuana was subject to the same rigorous penalties applicable to morphine, heroin, and cocaine and was often erroneously designated a "narcotic."

Marijuana is a weed that grows wild under most climatic conditions. The plant grows to a height of 5 to 15 feet and is characterized by an odd number of leaflets on each leaf. Normally, each leaf contains five to nine leaflets, all having serrated or saw-tooth edges, as shown in Figure 9–5.

In 1964 scientists isolated the chemical substance largely responsible for the hallucinogenic properties of marijuana. This substance is known as *tetrahydrocannabinol*, or THC. Its discovery has allowed researchers to measure the potency of marijuana preparations and has permitted studies related to measuring the effect of marijuana's potency on individuals. The THC content of *Cannabis* varies in different parts of the plant, generally decreasing in the following sequence: resin, flowers, and leaves. Little THC is found in the stem, roots, or seeds. The potency and resulting effect of the drug fluctuate, depending on the relative proportion of these plant parts in the marijuana mixture.

The potency of marijuana depends on its form. Marijuana in the form of loose vegetation has an average THC content of about 3–4.5 percent. The

Figure 9–5 The marijuana leaf. *Courtesy Drug Enforcement Administration*

more potent sinsemilla form averages about 6–12 percent in THC content, while hashish preparations average about 2–8 percent. Another form of hashish is known as *liquid hashish* or *hashish oil*. Hashish in this form is normally a viscous substance, dark green with a tarry consistency. Liquid hashish is produced by efficiently extracting the THC-rich resin from the marijuana plant with an appropriate solvent. Liquid hashish typically varies between 8 and 20 percent in THC content. Because of its extraordinary potency, one drop of the material can produce a "high." Ordinarily a drop is placed on a regular cigarette or on a marijuana cigarette before smoking.

Any study that relates to marijuana's effect on humans must consider the potency of the marijuana preparation. An interesting insight into the relationship between dosage level and marijuana's pharmacological effect was presented in the first report of the National Commission of Marijuana and Drug Abuse:

> At low, usual "social" doses the user may experience an increased sense of well-being; initial restlessness and hilarity followed by a dreamy, carefree state of relaxation; alteration of sensory perceptions including expansion of space and time; and a more vivid sense of touch, sight, smell, taste and sound; a feeling of hunger, especially a craving for sweets; and subtle changes in thought formation and expression. To an unknowing observer, an individual in this state of consciousness would not appear noticeably different from his normal state.
>
> At higher, moderate doses these same reactions are intensified but the changes in the individual would still be scarcely noticeable to an observer. . . . At very high doses, psychotomimetic phenomena may be experienced. These include distortion of body image, loss of personal identity, sensory and mental illusions, fantasies and hallucinations.[1]

No current evidence suggests that experimental or intermittent use causes physical or psychological harm. Marijuana does not cause physical dependency. However, the risk of harm lies instead in heavy, long-term use of the drug, particularly of the more potent preparations. Heavy users can develop a strong psychological dependence on the drug. Some effects of marijuana use include increased heart rate, dry mouth, reddened eyes, impaired motor skills and concentration, and frequently hunger and an increased desire for sweets. Long-term chronic marijuana use is associated with amotivational syndrome characterized by apathy; impairment of judgment, memory, and concentration; and loss of interest in personal appearance and the pursuit of conventional goals. Accumulating evidence suggests that marijuana has potential medical uses. Two promising areas of research are marijuana's reduction of excessive eye pressure in glaucoma and lessening of nausea caused by powerful anticancer drugs. Marijuana may also be useful as a muscle relaxant.

Other Hallucinogens

A substantial number of substances of widely varying chemical compositions have become part of the drug culture because of their hallucinogenic

---

[1]*Marijuana—A Signal of Misunderstanding* (Washington, D.C.: U.S. Government Printing Office, 1972), p. 56.

properties. These include lysergic acid diethylamide (LSD), mescaline, phencyclidine (PCP), psilocybin, and methylenedioxymethamphetamine, also known as MDMA or Ecstasy.

LSD is synthesized from lysergic acid, a substance derived from ergot, which is a type of fungus that attacks certain grasses and grains. Its hallucinogenic effects were first described by the Swiss chemist Albert Hofmann after he accidentally ingested some of the material in his laboratory in 1943. The drug is very potent; as little as 25 micrograms is enough to start vivid visual hallucinations that can last for about twelve hours. The drug also produces marked changes in mood, leading to laughing or crying at the slightest provocation. Feelings of anxiety and tension almost always accompany LSD use. Although physical dependence does not develop with continued use, the individual user may be prone to flashbacks and psychotic reactions even after use is discontinued.

In recent years, abuse of phencyclidine, commonly called PCP, has grown to alarming proportions. Because this drug can be synthesized by rather simple chemical processes, it is manufactured surreptitiously for the illicit market in so-called clandestine laboratories (see Figure 9–6). These laboratories range from large, sophisticated operations to small labs located in a bathroom. Small-time operators normally have little or no training in chemistry and employ "cookbook" methods to synthesize the drug. Some of the more knowledgeable and experienced operators have been able to achieve clandestine production levels that approach a commercial level of operation.

Phencyclidine is often mixed with other drugs, such as LSD or amphetamine, and is sold as a powder ("angel dust"), capsule, or tablet, or as a liquid sprayed on plant leaves. The drug is smoked, ingested, or sniffed. Following oral intake of moderate doses (1–6 milligrams), the user first experiences feelings of strength and invulnerability, along with a dreamy sense of detachment. However, the user soon becomes unresponsive, con-

Figure 9–6   Scene from a clandestine drug laboratory. *Courtesy Drug Enforcement Administration*

fused, and agitated. Depression, irritability, feelings of isolation, audio and visual hallucinations, and sometimes paranoia accompany PCP use. Severe depression, tendencies toward violence, and suicide accompany long-term daily use of the drug. In some cases, the PCP user experiences sudden schizophrenic behavior days after the drug has been taken.

Depressants

Alcohol (Ethyl Alcohol)

Many people overlook the fact that alcohol is a drug; its major behavioral effects derive from its depressant action on the central nervous system. In the United States, the alcohol industry annually produces more than one billion gallons of spirits, wine, and beer for which 90 million consumers pay nearly $40 billion. Unquestionably, these and other statistics support the fact that alcohol is the most widely used and abused drug.

Depressant
A substance that depresses the functions of the central nervous system. Depressants calm irritability and anxiety and may induce sleep.

The behavioral patterns of alcohol intoxication vary and depend in part on such factors as social setting, amount consumed, and the personal expectation of the individual with regard to alcohol. When alcohol enters the body's bloodstream, it quickly travels to the brain, where it suppresses the brain's control of thought processes and muscle coordination.

Low doses of alcohol tend to inhibit the mental processes of judgment, memory, and concentration. The drinker's personality becomes expansive, and he or she exudes confidence. When taken in moderate doses, alcohol reduces coordination substantially, inhibits orderly thought processes and speech patterns, and slows reaction times. Under these conditions, the ability to walk or drive becomes noticeably impaired. In the next chapter, we examine in greater detail the relationship between alcohol blood levels and driving ability. Higher doses of alcohol may cause the user to become highly irritable and emotional; displays of anger and crying are not uncommon. Extremely high doses may cause an individual to lapse into unconsciousness or even a comatose state that may precede a fatal depression of circulatory and respiratory functions.

Barbiturates

Barbiturates are commonly referred to as "downers" because they relax, create a feeling of well-being, and produce sleep. Like alcohol, barbiturates suppress the vital functions of the central nervous system. Collectively, barbiturates can be described as derivatives of barbituric acid, which was first synthesized by a German chemist, Adolf Von Bayer, more than a hundred years ago. Twenty-five barbiturate derivatives are currently used in medical practice in the United States; however, five—amobarbital, secobarbital, phenobarbital, pentobarbital, and butabarbital—tend to be used for most medical applications. Slang terms for "barbs" usually stem from the color of the capsule or tablet (for example, "yellow jackets," "blue devils," and "reds").

Normally, barbiturate users take these drugs orally. The average sedative dose is about 10–70 milligrams. When taken in this fashion, the drug enters the blood through the walls of the small intestine. Some barbiturates, such as phenobarbital, are absorbed more slowly than others and are therefore classified as long-acting barbiturates. Undoubtedly, the slow action of phenobarbital accounts for its low incidence of abuse. Apparently, barbiturate abusers prefer the faster-acting ones—secobarbital, pentobarbital, and amobarbital. When taken in prescribed amounts, barbiturates are relatively safe, but in instances of extensive and prolonged use, physical dependence can develop. Since the early 1970s, a nonbarbiturate depressant, methaqualone (Quaalude), has appeared on the illicit-drug scene. Methaqualone is a powerful sedative and muscle relaxant that possesses many of the depressant properties of barbiturates.

Tranquilizers

In the past forty-five years, the use of tranquilizers has grown dramatically. Although tranquilizers can be considered depressants, they differ from barbiturates in the extent of their actions on the central nervous system. Generally, these drugs produce a relaxing tranquility without impairing high-thinking faculties or inducing sleep. Antipsychotics such as reserpine and chlorpromazine have been used to reduce the anxieties and tensions of mental patients.

A group of antianxiety drugs is commonly prescribed to deal with the everyday tensions of many healthy people. These drugs include meprobamate (Miltown), chlordiazepoxide (Librium), and diazepam (Valium). Medical evidence shows that these drugs produce psychological and physical dependency with repeated and high levels of usage. For this reason, widespread prescribing of tranquilizers as a means of overcoming the pressures and tensions of life has worried many who fear the creation of a legalized drug culture.

"Glue Sniffing"

Since the early 1960s, the practice of sniffing materials containing volatile solvents (airplane glue or model cement, for example) has grown in popularity. Within recent years, another dimension has been added to the problem with the increasing number of incidents involving the sniffing of aerosol gas propellants such as freon. All materials used in sniffing contain volatile or gaseous substances that are primarily central nervous system depressants.

Although toluene seems to be the most popular solvent to sniff, others can produce comparable physiological effects. These chemicals include naphtha, methyl ethyl ketone, gasoline, and trichloroethylene.

The usual immediate effects of sniffing are a feeling of exhilaration and euphoria combined with slurred speech, impaired judgment, and double vision. Finally, the user may experience drowsiness and stupor, with these depressant effects slowly wearing off as the user returns to a normal state. Most experts believe that users become physiologically dependent on the effects achieved by sniffing. There is, however, little evidence to suggest that solvent inhalation is addictive. But sniffers expose themselves to the danger of liver, heart, and brain damage from the chemicals they have inhaled. Even worse, sniffing of some solvents, particularly halogenated hydrocarbons, is accompanied by a significant risk of death.

Stimulants

Amphetamines

Amphetamines are a group of synthetic drugs that stimulate the central nervous system. They are commonly referred to in the terminology of the drug culture as "uppers" or "speed." Ordinary therapeutic doses of 5–20 milligrams per day, taken orally, provide a feeling of well-being and increased alertness that is followed by a decrease in fatigue and a loss of appetite. However, these apparent benefits of the drug are accompanied by restlessness and instability or apprehension, and once the stimulant effect wears off, depression may set in.

In the United States, the most serious form of amphetamine abuse stems from the intravenous injection of amphetamine or its chemical derivative, methamphetamine (see Figure 9–7). The desire for a more intense amphetamine experience is the primary motive for this route of administration. The initial sensation of a "flash" or "rush," followed by an intense feeling of pleasure, constitutes the principal appeal of the intravenous route for the "speed freak." During a "speed binge," the individual may inject 500–1,000 milligrams of amphetamines every two to three hours. Users have reported experiencing a euphoria that produces hyperactivity, with a feeling of clarity of vision as well as hallucinations. As the effect of the amphetamines wears off, the individual lapses into a period of exhaustion and may sleep continuously for one or two days. Following this, the user often experiences a prolonged period of severe depression, lasting from days to weeks.

A new smokable form of methamphetamine known as "ice" is reportedly in heavy demand in some areas of the United States. Ice is prepared by slow evaporation of a methamphetamine solution to produce large, crystal-clear "rocks." Like crack cocaine (discussed next), ice is smoked and produces effects similar to those of crack cocaine, but the effects last for a longer period of time. Once the effects of ice wear off, users often become depressed and may sleep for days. Chronic users exhibit violent destructive behavior and acute psychosis similar to paranoid schizophrenia. Repeated use of amphetamines leads to a strong psychological dependency, which encourages their continued administration.

Stimulant
A substance taken to increase alertness or activity.

Figure 9–7   Granular amphetamine beside a razor blade. *Courtesy Cordelia Molloy, Photo Researchers, Inc.*

Cocaine

Between 1884 and 1887, Sigmund Freud created something of a sensation in European medical circles by describing his experiments with a new drug. He reported a substance of seemingly limitless potential as a source of "exhilaration and lasting euphoria" that permitted "intensive mental or physical work [to be] performed without fatigue. . . . It is as though the need for food and sleep was completely banished."

The object of Freud's enthusiasm was cocaine, a drug stimulant extracted from the leaves of *Erythroxylon coca,* a plant grown in tropical Asia and the Andes mountains of South America (see Figure 9–8). At one time, cocaine had wide medical application as a local painkiller or anesthetic. However, this function has now been largely replaced by other drugs, primarily procaine and lidocaine. Cocaine is also a powerful stimulant to the central nervous system, and its effects resemble those caused by the amphetamines—namely, increased alertness and vigor, accompanied by the suppression of hunger, fatigue, and boredom. Most commonly, cocaine is sniffed or "snorted" and is absorbed into the body through the mucous membranes of the nose.

One form of cocaine that has gained widespread popularity in the drug culture is known as *crack.* The process used to make crack is simple. Ordinary cocaine is mixed with baking soda and water into a solution that is then heated in a pot. This material is then dried and broken into tiny chunks that dealers sell as crack rocks. Crack is freebase cocaine and is sufficiently volatile to be smoked, usually in glass pipes. Crack, like cocaine that is snorted, produces a feeling of euphoria by stimulating a pleasure center in the base of the brain, in an area connected to nerves that are responsible for emotions. Cocaine stimulates this pleasure center to a far greater degree than it would ever normally be stimulated. The result is euphoria—a feeling of increased energy, of being mentally more alert, of feeling really good. The faster the cocaine

Figure 9–8   Coca leaves and illicit forms of cocaine. *Courtesy Drug Enforcement Administration*

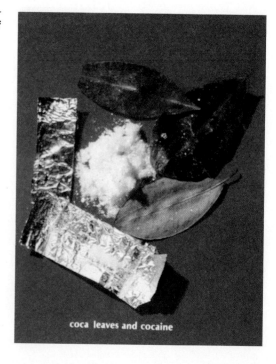

coca leaves and cocaine

level rises in the brain, the greater the euphoria, and the surest way to obtain a fast rise in the brain's cocaine level is to smoke crack. Inhaling the cocaine vapor gets a large wallop of the drug to the brain in less than fifteen seconds—about as fast as injecting it and much faster than snorting it. The dark side of crack, however, is that the euphoria fades quickly as cocaine levels drop, leaving the user feeling depressed, anxious, pleasureless. The desire to return to a euphoric feeling is so intense that crack users quickly develop a habit for the drug that is almost impossible to overcome. Only a small percentage of crack abusers will ever be cured of this drug habit.

In the United States, cocaine abuse is on the rise. Cocaine generates confidence and produces increased alertness, giving a false illusion that one is doing well at an assigned task. However, some regular users of cocaine report accompanying feelings of restlessness, irritability, and anxiety. Cocaine used chronically or at high doses can have toxic effects. Cocaine-related deaths are a result of cardiac arrest or seizures followed by respiratory arrest. Many people are apparently using cocaine to improve their ability to work and to keep going when tired. While there is no evidence of physical dependency accompanying cocaine's repeated use, abstention from cocaine after prolonged use brings on severe bouts of mental depression, which produce a very strong compulsion to resume using the drug. In fact, laboratory experiments with animals have demonstrated that of all the commonly abused drugs, cocaine produces the strongest psychological compulsions for continued use.

The United States spends millions of dollars annually in attempting to control cultivation of the coca leaf in various South American countries and to prevent cocaine trafficking into the United States. Three-quarters of the cocaine smuggled into the United States is refined in clandestine laboratories in Colombia. The profits are astronomical. Peruvian farmers may be paid $200 for enough coca leaves to make one pound of cocaine. The refined cocaine is worth $1,000 when it leaves Colombia and sells at retail in the United States for up to $20,000.

Club Drugs

The term *club drugs* refers to synthetic drugs that are used at nightclubs, bars, and raves (all-night dance parties). Substances that are often used as club drugs include, but are not limited to, MDMA (Ecstasy), GHB (gamma hydroxybutyrate), Rohypnol ("Roofies"), ketamine, and methamphetamine. These drugs have become popular at the dance scene to stimulate the rave experience. A high incidence of use has been found among teens and young adults.

The rave scene supports this type of drug use. Tablets can be easily hidden in various containers, such as Pez dispensers and other items not usually thought of as drug paraphernalia. The rave scene is often depicted as a room filled with people jumping and bouncing in unison for hours to loud rhythmic, trancelike music. The stimulatory effects of some of the club drugs allow for the users to be active for hours.

GHB and Rohypnol are central nervous system depressants that are often connected with drug-facilitated sexual assault, rape, and robbery. Effects accompanying the use of GHB include dizziness, sedation, headache, and nausea. Recreational users have reported euphoria, relaxation, disinhibition, and increased libido. Rohypnol causes muscle relaxation, loss of consciousness, and an inability to remember what happened during the hours after ingesting the drug. This is particularly a concern in a sexual assault because victims are physically unable to resist the attack. Unsuspecting victims become drowsy or dizzy. Effects are even stronger when the drug is combined with alcohol because the user experiences memory loss, blackouts, and disinhibition. Law enforcement agencies have warned multitudes of partygoers that drugs such as Rohypnol and GHB are odorless, colorless, and tasteless and so will remain undetected when slipped into a drink.

Methylenedioxymethamphetamine, also known as MDMA or Ecstasy, is the most popular drug at rave club scenes. Ecstasy is a synthetic, mind-altering drug that exhibits many hallucinogenic and amphetamine-like effects. Ecstasy was originally patented as an appetite suppressant and was later discovered to induce feelings of happiness and relaxation. Recreational drug users find that Ecstasy enhances self-awareness and decreases inhibitions. However, seizures, muscle breakdown, stroke, kidney failure, and cardiovascular system failure often accompany chronic use of Ecstasy. In addition, chronic use of Ecstasy leads to serious damage to the areas of the brain responsible for thought and memory. Ecstasy increases the heart rate and blood pressure; produces muscle tension, teeth grinding, and nausea; and causes psychological difficulties such as confusion, severe anxiety, and paranoia episodes. The drug can cause significant increases in body temperature from the combination of the drug's stimulant effect with the often hot, crowded atmosphere of a rave club.

Ketamine is primarily used in veterinary medicine as an animal anesthetic. When used by humans, the drug can cause euphoria and feelings of unreality accompanied by visual hallucinations. Ketamine can also cause impaired motor function, high blood pressure, amnesia, and mild respiratory depression.

Anabolic Steroids

Anabolic Steroids
Steroids that promote muscle growth.

Anabolic steroids are synthetic compounds that are chemically related to the male sex hormone testosterone. Testosterone has two different effects on the body. It promotes the development of secondary male characteristics (androgen effects), and it accelerates muscle growth (anabolic effects). Efforts to promote muscle growth and to minimize the hormone's androgenic effects have led to the synthesis of numerous anabolic steroids. However, a steroid free of the accompanying harmful side effects of an androgen drug has not yet been developed.

Incidence of steroid abuse first received widespread public attention when both amateur and professional athletes were discovered using these substances to enhance their performance. Interestingly, current research on male athletes given anabolic steroids has generally found little or, at best, marginal evidence of enhanced strength or performance. While the full extent of anabolic steroid abuse by the general public is not fully known, the U.S. government is sufficiently concerned to regulate the availability of these drugs to the general population and to severely punish individuals for illegal possession and distribution of anabolic steroids. In 1991, anabolic steroids were classified as controlled dangerous substances, and the Drug Enforcement Administration was given enforcement power to prevent their illegal use and distribution.

Anabolic steroids are usually taken by individuals who are unfamiliar with the harmful medical side effects. Liver cancer and other liver malfunctions have been linked to steroid use. These drugs also cause masculinizing effects in females, infertility, and diminished sex drive in males. For teenagers, anabolic steroids result in premature halting of bone growth. Anabolic steroids can also cause unpredictable effects on mood and personality, leading to unprovoked acts of anger and destructive behavior. Depression is also a frequent side effect of anabolic steroid abuse.

Drug-Control Laws

Although the previous sections have attempted to classify drugs according to their physiological effects on the body, for practical purposes of law enforcement, the legal community requires a thorough knowledge of drug classification and definitions as they are delineated by drug laws. The medical and legal definitions or classifications of a drug often bear little resemblance. The provisions of drug laws are of particular interest to the criminalist, for they may impose specific analytical requirements on drug analysis. For example, the severity of a penalty associated with the manufacture, distribution, possession, and use of a drug may depend on the weight of the drug or its concentration in a mixture. In such cases, the chemist's report must contain all information that is needed to properly charge a suspect under the provisions of the existing law.

The provisions of any drug-control law are an outgrowth of national and local law enforcement requirements and customs, as well as the result of moral and political philosophies. These factors have produced a wide spectrum of national and local drug-control laws. Although their detailed discussion is beyond the intended scope of this book, a brief description of the U.S. federal law known as the Controlled Substances Act will illustrate a legal drug classification system that has been created to prevent and control drug abuse. Many states have modeled their own drug-control laws after this act, an important step in establishing uniform drug-control laws throughout the United States.

Controlled Substances Act

The federal law establishes five schedules of classification (as outlined next) for controlled dangerous substances on the basis of a drug's potential for abuse, potential for physical and psychological dependence, and medical value. This classification system is extremely flexible in that the U.S. attorney general has the authority to add, delete, or reschedule a drug as more information becomes available. In addition, controlled dangerous substances listed in schedules I and II are subject to manufacturing quotas set by the attorney general. For example, eight billion doses of amphetamines were manufactured in the United States in 1971. In 1972, production quotas reduced amphetamine production approximately 80 percent below 1971 levels.

The criminal penalties for unauthorized manufacture, sale, or possession of controlled dangerous substances are related to the schedules as well. The most severe penalties are associated with drugs listed in schedules I and II. For example, for drugs included in schedules I and II, a first offense is punishable by up to 20 years in prison and/or a fine of

Table 9–2 Control Mechanisms of the Controlled Substances Act

Schedule	Registration	Record Keeping	Manufacturing Quotas		Distribution Restrictions	Dispensing Limits
I	Required	Separate	Yes		Order forms	Research use only
II	Required	Separate	Yes		Order forms	Rx: written; no refills
III	Required	Readily retrievable	No *but*	Some drugs limited by schedule II quotas	Records required	Rx: written or oral; with medical authorization, refills up to 5 times in 6 months
IV	Required	Readily retrievable	No *but*	Some drugs limited by schedule II quotas	Records required	Rx: written or oral; with medical authorization, refills up to 5 times in 6 months
V	Required	Readily retrievable	No *but*	Some drugs limited by schedule II quotas	Records required	Over-the-counter (Rx drugs limited to MD's order)

Source: Drug Enforcement Administration, Washington, D.C.

up to $1 million for an individual or up to $5 million for other than individuals. Table 9–2 summarizes the control mechanisms and penalties for each schedule of the Controlled Substances Act.

Schedule I. Schedule I drugs are deemed to have a high potential for abuse, have no currently accepted medical use in the United States, and/or lack accepted safety for use in treatment under medical supervision. Drugs controlled under this schedule include heroin, marijuana, methaqualone, and LSD.

Schedule II. Schedule II drugs have a high potential for abuse, a currently accepted medical use or a medical use with severe restrictions, and a potential for severe psychological or physical dependence. Schedule II drugs include opium and its derivatives not listed in schedule I, cocaine, methadone, phencyclidine (PCP), most amphetamine preparations, and most barbiturate preparations containing amobarbital, secobarbital, and pentobarbital. Dronabinol, the synthetic equivalent of the active ingredient in marijuana, has been placed in schedule II in recognition of its growing medical uses in treating glaucoma and chemotherapy patients.

Schedule III. Schedule III drugs have less potential for abuse than those in schedules I and II, a currently accepted medical use in the United States, and a potential for low or moderate physical dependence or high psychological dependence. Schedule III controls, among other substances, all barbiturate preparations (except phenobarbital) not covered under schedule II and certain codeine preparations. Anabolic steroids were added to this schedule in 1991.

| Import–Export | | Security | Manufacturer/Distributor Reports to Drug Enforcement Administration | Criminal Penalties for Individual Trafficking (First Offense) |
Narcotic	Nonnarcotic			
Permit	Permit	Vault/safe	Yes	0–20 years/$1 million
Permit	Permit	Vault/safe	Yes	0–20 years/$1 million
Permit	Declaration	Secure storage area	Yes, narcotic No, nonnarcotic	0–5 years/$250,000
Permit	Declaration	Secure storage area	Manufacturer only, narcotic No, nonnarcotic	0–3 years/$250,000
Permit to import; declaration to export	Declaration	Secure storage area	Manufacturer only, narcotic No, nonnarcotic	0–1 year/$100,000

Schedule IV. Schedule IV drugs have a low potential for abuse relative to schedule III drugs and have a current medical use in the United States; their abuse may lead to limited dependence relative to schedule III drugs. Drugs controlled in this schedule include propoxyphene (Darvon); phenobarbital; and tranquilizers such as meprobamate (Miltown), diazepam (Valium), and chlordiazepoxide (Librium).

Schedule V. Schedule V drugs must show low abuse potential, have medical use in the United States, and have less potential for producing dependence than schedule IV drugs. Schedule V controls certain opiate drug mixtures that contain nonnarcotic medicinal ingredients.

The Controlled Substances Act also stipulates that an offense involving a controlled substance analog, a chemical substance substantially similar in chemical structure to a controlled substance, shall trigger penalties as if it were a controlled substance listed in schedule I. This section is designed to combat the proliferation of so-called "designer drugs." Designer drugs are substances that are chemically related to some controlled drugs and are pharmacologically very potent. These substances are manufactured by skilled individuals in clandestine laboratories, with the knowledge that their products will not be covered by the schedules of the Controlled Substances Act. For instance, fentanyl is a powerful narcotic that is commercially marketed for medical use and is also listed as a controlled dangerous substance. This drug is about 100 times as potent as morphine. Currently, a number of substances chemically related to fentanyl have been synthesized by underground chemists and sold on the street. The first such substance encountered was sold under the street name "China White." These drugs have been responsible for more than a hundred overdose deaths in California and nearly twenty deaths in western Pennsylvania. As designer drugs, such as China White, are identified and linked to drug abuse, they are placed in appropriate schedules.

The Controlled Substances Act also reflects an effort to decrease the prevalence of clandestine drug laboratories designed to manufacture controlled substances. The act regulates the manufacture and distribution of precursors, the chemical compounds used by clandestine drug laboratories to synthesize drugs of abuse. Targeted precursor chemicals are listed in the definition section of the Controlled Substances Act. Severe penalties are provided for a person who possesses a listed precursor chemical with the intent to manufacture a controlled substance or who possesses or distributes a listed chemical knowing, or having reasonable cause to believe, that the listed chemical will be used to manufacture a controlled substance. In addition, precursors to PCP, amphetamines, and methamphetamines are enumerated specifically in schedule II, making them subject to regulation in the same manner as other schedule II substances.

Drug Identification

One only has to look into the evidence vaults of crime laboratories to appreciate the assortment of drug specimens that confront the criminalist. The presence of a huge array of powders, tablets, capsules, vegetable matter, liquids, pipes, cigarettes, cookers, and syringes is testimony to the vitality and sophistication of the illicit-drug market. If outward appearance is not evidence enough of the difficult analytical chore facing the forensic chemist, consider the complexity of the drug preparations themselves. Usually these contain active drug ingredients of unknown origin and identity, as well as additives—for example, sugar, starch, and quinine—that dilute their potency and stretch their value on the illicit-drug market. Do not forget that illicit-drug dealers are not hampered by governmental regulations that ensure the quality and consistency of a product.

When a forensic chemist picks up a drug specimen for analysis, he or she can expect to find just about anything, so all contingencies must be prepared for. The analysis must leave no room for error, because its results will have a direct bearing on the process of determining the guilt or innocence of a defendant. There is no middle ground in drug identification—either the specimen is a specific drug or it is not—and once a positive conclusion is drawn, the chemist must be prepared to support and defend the validity of the results in a court of law.

The challenge or difficulty of forensic drug identification comes in selecting analytical procedures that will ensure a specific identification of a drug. Presented with a substance of unknown origin and composition, the forensic chemist must develop a plan of action that will ultimately yield the drug's identity. This plan, or scheme of analysis, is divided into two phases. First, faced with the prospect that the unknown substance may be any one of a thousand or more commonly encountered drugs, the analyst must employ screening tests to reduce these possibilities to a small and manageable number. This objective is often accomplished by subjecting the material to a series of color tests that produce characteristic colors for the

Screening Test
A test that is nonspecific and preliminary in nature.

more commonly encountered illicit drugs. Even if these tests produce negative results, their value lies in having excluded certain drugs from further consideration.

Once the number of possibilities has been substantially reduced, the second phase of the analysis must be devoted to pinpointing and confirming the drug's identity. In an era in which crime laboratories receive voluminous quantities of drug evidence, it is impractical to subject a drug to all the chemical and instrumental tests available. Indeed, it is more realistic to look on these techniques as constituting a large analytical arsenal. The chemist, aided by training and experience, must choose tests that will most conveniently furnish the identity of a particular drug.

Forensic chemists often use a specific test (such as infrared spectrophotometry or mass spectrometry) to identify a drug substance to the exclusion of all other known chemical substances. A single test that identifies a substance is known as a confirmation. The analytical scheme sometimes consists of a series of nonspecific or presumptive tests. Each test in itself is insufficient to prove the drug's identity; however, the proper analytical scheme encompasses a combination of test results that characterize one and only one chemical substance—the drug under investigation. Furthermore, experimental evidence must confirm that the probability of any other substance responding in an identical manner to the scheme selected is so small as to be beyond any reasonable scientific certainty.

Confirmation
A single test that specifically identifies a substance.

Forensic chemists normally rely on several tests for a routine drug-identification scheme: color tests, microcrystalline tests, chromatography, spectrophotometry, and mass spectrometry.

Color Tests

Many drugs yield characteristic colors when brought into contact with specific chemical reagents. Not only do these tests provide a useful indicator of a drug's presence, but they are also used by investigators in the field to examine materials suspected of containing a drug (see Figure 9–9).[2] However, color tests are useful for screening purposes only and are never taken as conclusive identification of unknown drugs.

Five primary color test reagents are as follows:

1. *Marquis* (2 percent formaldehyde in sulfuric acid). The reagent turns purple in the presence of heroin and morphine and most opium derivatives. Marquis also becomes orange-brown when mixed with amphetamines and methamphetamines.

2. *Dillie-Koppanyi* (1 percent cobalt acetate in methanol is first added to the suspect material, followed by 5 percent isopropylamine in methanol). This is a valuable screening test for barbiturates, in whose presence the reagent turns violet-blue in color.

3. *Duquenois-Levine* (solution A is a mixture of 2 percent vanillin and 1 percent acetaldehyde in ethyl alcohol; solution B is concentrated hydrochloric acid; solution C is chloroform). This is a valuable color test

---

[2]Field-color test kits for drugs can be purchased from various commercial manufacturers.

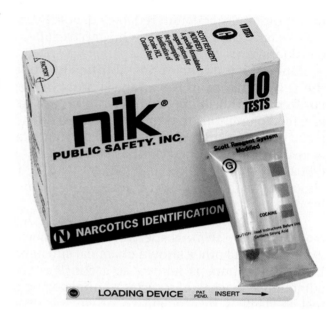

Figure 9–9 **A field color test kit for cocaine. The suspect drug is placed in the plastic pouch. Tubes containing chemicals are broken open and the color of the chemical reaction is observed.** *Courtesy Tri-Tech, Inc., Southport, N.C., www.tritechusa.com*

for marijuana, performed by adding solutions A, B, and C, respectively, to the suspect vegetation. A positive result is shown by a purple color in the chloroform layer.

4. *Van Urk* (1 percent solution of p-dimethylaminobenzaldehyde in 10 percent concentrated hydrochloric acid and ethyl alcohol). The reagent turns blue-purple in the presence of LSD. However, owing to the extremely small quantities of LSD in illicit preparations, this test is difficult to conduct under field conditions.

5. *Scott Test* (solution A is 2 percent cobalt thiocyanate dissolved in water and glycerine [1:1]; solution B is concentrated hydrochloric acid; solution C is chloroform). This is a color test for cocaine. A powder containing cocaine turns solution A blue. Upon addition of B, the blue color is transformed to a clear pink color. Upon addition of C, if cocaine is present, the blue color reappears in the chloroform layer.

Microcrystalline Tests

Microcrystalline Tests
Tests to identify specific substances by the color and morphology of the crystals formed when the substance is mixed with specific reagents.

A technique considerably more specific than color tests is the microcrystalline test. A drop of a chemical reagent is added to a small quantity of the drug on a microscopic slide. After a short time, a chemical reaction ensues, producing a crystalline precipitate. The size and shape of the crystals, under microscope examination, are highly characteristic of the drug. Crystal tests for cocaine and methamphetamine are illustrated in Figure 9–10.

Over the years, analysts have developed hundreds of crystal tests to characterize the most commonly abused drugs. These tests are rapid and often do not require the isolation of a drug from its diluents; however, because diluents can sometimes alter or modify the shape of the crystal, the examiner must develop experience in interpreting the results of the test.

Most color and crystal tests are largely empirical—that is, scientists do not fully understand why they produce the results that they do. From the forensic chemist's point of view, this is not important. When the tests

 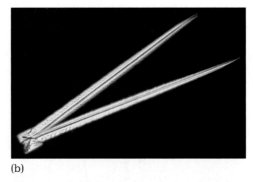

(a)   (b)

**Figure 9–10   (a) A photomicrograph of a cocaine crystal formed in platinum chloride (400×).
(b) A photomicrograph of a methamphetamine crystal formed in gold chloride (400×).** *Courtesy
David P. Blackburn, San Bernardino County Sheriff's Department, San Bernardino, Calif.*

are properly chosen and are used in proper combination, their results
constitute an analytical scheme that is characteristic for one and only
one drug.

Chromatography

Thin-layer and gas chromatography are especially well suited to the needs
of the drug analyst, because they separate drugs from their diluents while
providing for their tentative identification. The basic principles of these
techniques have already been described in Chapter 5.

Because chromatography requires a comparison of either R_f or retention-
time values between questioned and known drugs, the analyst must have
some clue to the identity of the illicit material before using these techniques.
Hence, in a typical drug analysis, chromatography accompanies and com-
plements color and crystal tests.

Spectrophotometry

Selective absorption of UV and IR light by drugs provides a valuable technique for characterizing drugs. The ultraviolet spectrum is not conclusive
for positive identification of a drug, because other materials may very
well produce an indistinguishable spectrum. Nevertheless, UV spectrophotometry is often a useful technique for establishing the *probable*
identity of a drug. For example, if an unknown substance yields a UV
spectrum that resembles that of amphetamine (see Figure 9–11), thousands of substances are immediately eliminated from consideration, and
the analyst can begin to identify the material from a relatively small
number of possibilities. A comprehensive collection of UV drug spectra
provides a ready index that can rapidly be searched in order to tentatively identify a drug or, failing that, at least to exclude certain drugs
from consideration.

Infrared spectrophotometry is one of the few analytical techniques
that can specifically identify a substance. The pattern of an infrared spectrum is unique for each compound and can thus serve as a "fingerprint"
of the compound. The combination of preliminary screening tests with a
final verification by infrared spectrophotometry offers an ideal approach
to drug identification. Unfortunately, the technique does present some

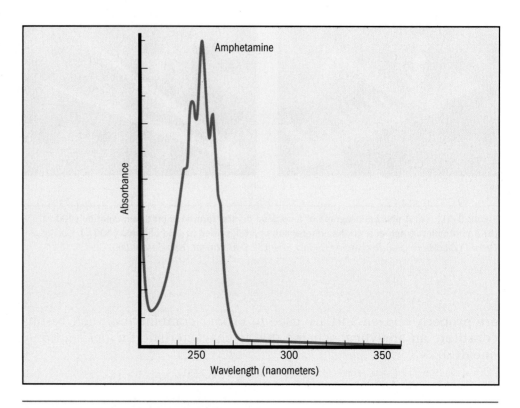

Figure 9–11   Ultraviolet spectrum of amphetamine.

problems because the substance to be identified must be as pure as possible. This requirement often necessitates lengthy purification steps to prepare the sample for IR analysis. The IR spectra of heroin and secobarbital were shown in Figure 5–19.

Mass Spectrometry

The technique of chromatography is particularly suited for analyzing illicit drugs, because it can readily separate a drug from other substances that may be present in the drug preparation. Chromatography does, however, have the drawback of not being able to provide a specific identification of the material under investigation. This deficiency has been overcome by linking the gas chromatograph to a mass spectrometer (see the discussion on pp. 150–154) to yield a very powerful combination known as *gas chromatography/mass spectrometry* (GC/MS). As a sample emerges from the gas chromatograph, it immediately enters the mass spectrometer. Here, the sample is exposed to high-energy electrons, which cause the sample molecules to fragment or break apart. With few exceptions, no two substances fragment in the same fashion; hence, this fragmentation pattern serves as a "fingerprint" of a chemical substance. The fragmentation patterns of heroin and cocaine were shown in Figure 5–21.

With data obtained from a GC/MS determination, a forensic analyst can, with one instrument, separate the components of a complex drug mixture and then unequivocally identify each substance present in the mixture (see Figure 5–20).

The Identification of Marijuana

Enforcement of laws prohibiting the sale and use of marijuana accounts for a high percentage of drug arrests in the United States. Any trial or hearing involving a seizure of marijuana requires identification of the material before the issue of guilt or innocence can be decided.

Unlike most other drugs received by the crime laboratory, marijuana (*Cannabis sativa L.*) possesses botanical features that impart identifiable characteristics. Because most marijuana specimens consist of small leaf fragments, their identification must be partially based on botanical features observed under the microscope by a trained expert. This approach is further augmented with a chemical test that will independently confirm the findings of the botanical examination.

The identification of marijuana by microscopic methods depends largely on observing short hairs shaped like "bear claws" on the upper side of the leaf (see the SEM photo in Figure 7–12). These hairs are known as *cystolithic hairs*. Further verification of the identity of marijuana is confirmed by the presence of longer, nonglandular hairs on the opposite side of the leaf.

The Duquenois-Levine color test, described earlier in this chapter, is a highly but not totally specific test for marijuana. However, when used in combination with a botanical examination, the results constitute a specific identification of marijuana. In addition, the analyst may be unable to obtain a microscopic identification of the marijuana leaf, as in the case of hashish or hashish oil. Here, the color test has to be supplemented by another examination, preferably thin-layer chromatography. This method involves separating chemical constituents found in the suspect resin on a thin-layer plate. The separated components are compared on the same plate to those obtained from a known marijuana extract, as shown in Figure 5–10. In this manner, a positive TLC comparison, used in conjunction with the Duquenois-Levine color test, constitutes a specific identification for marijuana.

Collection and Preservation of Drug Evidence

Preparation of drug evidence for submission to the crime laboratory is normally a relatively simple task, accomplished with minimal precautions in the field. The field investigator has the responsibility of ensuring that the evidence is properly packaged and labeled for delivery to the laboratory. Considering the countless forms and varieties of drug evidence seized, it is not practical to prescribe any single packaging procedure for fulfilling these requirements. Generally, common sense is the best guide in such situations, keeping in mind that the package must prevent the loss and/or cross-contamination of the contents. Often, the original container in which the drug was seized will suffice to meet these requirements. Specimens suspected of containing volatile solvents, such as those involved in glue-sniffing cases, must be packaged in an airtight container to prevent evaporation of the solvent.

All packages must be marked with sufficient information to ensure identification by the officer in future legal proceedings and to establish the chain of custody.

To aid the drug analyst, the investigator should supply any background information that may relate to a drug's identity. Analysis time can be markedly reduced when this information is at the disposal of the chemist. For the same reason, the results of drug-screening tests used in the field must also be transmitted to the laboratory. However, although these tests may indicate the presence of a drug and may help the officer establish probable cause to search and arrest a suspect, they do not offer conclusive evidence of a drug's identity.

Chapter Summary

A drug can be defined as a natural or synthetic substance that is used to produce physiological or psychological effects in humans or other higher-order animals.

Narcotic drugs are analgesics, meaning they relieve pain by depressing the central nervous system. Regular use of a narcotic drug leads to physical dependence. The most common source of narcotic drugs is opium. Morphine is readily extracted from opium and is used to synthesize heroin. Opiates, which include methadone and OxyContin (oxycodone), are not derived from opium or morphine, but they have the same physiological effects on the body as do opium narcotics. Another class of drugs is hallucinogens; marijuana is the most well-known member of this class. Hallucinogens cause marked changes in mood, attitude, thought processes, and perceptions. Marijuana is the most controversial drug in this class because its long-term effects on health are still largely unknown. Other hallucinogens include LSD, mescaline, PCP, psilocybin, and MDMA (Ecstasy).

Depressants are another class of drugs. These include alcohol (ethanol), barbiturates, tranquilizers, and various substances that can be sniffed, such as airplane glue and model cement. Stimulants include amphetamines, sometimes known as "uppers" or "speed," and cocaine, which in its free-base form is known as *crack*. The term *club drugs* refers to synthetic drugs that are used at nightclubs, bars, and raves (all-night dance parties). Substances that are often used as club drugs include, but are not limited to, MDMA (Ecstasy), GHB (gamma hydroxybutyrate), Rohypnol ("Roofies"), ketamine, and methamphetamine. Yet another category of drugs is anabolic steroids, which are synthetic compounds that are chemically related to the male sex hormone testosterone. Anabolic steroids are often abused by individuals who want to accelerate muscle growth. Federal law establishes five schedules of classification for controlled dangerous substances on the basis of a drug's potential for abuse, potential for physical and psychological dependence, and medical value.

Faced with the prospect that the unknown substance may be any one of a thousand or more commonly encountered drugs, the analyst must employ screening tests to reduce these possibilities to a small and manageable number. This objective is often accomplished by subjecting the material to a series of color tests that produce characteristic colors for the more commonly encountered illicit drugs. Once this preliminary analysis is completed, a confirmation is pursued. Forensic chemists use a specific test to identify a drug substance to the exclusion of all other known chemical substances. Typically infrared spectrophotometry or mass spectrometry is used to specifically identify a drug substance.

Review Questions

1. True or False: Underlying emotional factors are the primary motives leading to the repeated use of a drug. _____

2. Drugs such as alcohol, heroin, amphetamines, barbiturates, and cocaine can lead to a (high, low) degree of psychological dependence with repeated use.

3. The development of (psychological, physical) dependence on a drug is shown by withdrawal symptoms such as convulsions when the user stops taking the drug.

4. True or False: Abuse of barbiturates can lead to physical dependency. _____

5. True or False: Repeated use of LSD leads to physical dependency. _____

6. Physical dependency develops only when the drug user adheres to a _____ schedule of drug intake.

7. Narcotic drugs are _____ that _____ the central nervous system.

8. _____ is a gummy, milky juice exuded through a cut made in the unripe pod of the opium poppy.

9. The primary constituent of opium is _____.

10. _____ is a chemical derivative of morphine made by reacting morphine with acetic anhydride.

11. A legally manufactured drug that is chemically related to heroin and heavily abused is _____.

12. True or False: Methadone is classified as a narcotic drug, even though it is not derived from opium or morphine. _____

13. Drugs that cause marked alterations in mood, attitude, thought processes, and perceptions, are called _____.

14. _____ is the sticky resin extracted from the marijuana plant.

15. The active ingredient of marijuana largely responsible for its hallucinogenic properties is _____.

16. True or False: The potency of a marijuana preparation depends on the proportion of the various plant parts in the mixture. _____

17. The marijuana preparation with the highest THC content is _____.

18. LSD is a chemical derivative of _____, a chemical obtained from the ergot fungus that grows on certain grasses and grains.

19. The drug phencyclidine is often manufactured for the illicit-drug market in _____ laboratories.

20. Alcohol (stimulates, depresses) the central nervous system.

21. _____ are called "downers" because they depress the central nervous system.

22. Phenobarbital is an example of a (short-, long-) acting barbiturate.

23. _____ is a powerful sedative and muscle relaxant that possesses many of the depressant properties of barbiturates.

24. _____ are drugs used to relieve anxiety and tension without inducing sleep.

25. True or False: Glue sniffing stimulates the central nervous system. _____

26. _____ are a group of synthetic drugs that stimulate the central nervous system.

27. The most severe form of amphetamine abuse stems from its (oral, intravenous) administration.

28. An increasing percentage of amphetamines available on the illicit-drug market originate from _____ drug laboratories.

29. _____ is extracted from the leaf of the coca plant.

30. Traditionally, cocaine is _____ into the nostrils.

31. True or False: Cocaine is a powerful central nervous system depressant. _____

32. The two drugs usually associated with drug-facilitated sexual assaults are _____ and _____.

33. _____ steroids are designed to promote muscle growth but have harmful side effects.

34. The federal drug-control law is known as _____.

35. Federal law establishes _____ schedules of classification for the control of dangerous drugs.

36. Drugs that have no accepted medical use are placed in schedule _____.

37. Librium and Valium are listed in schedule _____.

38. True or False: Color tests are used to identify drugs conclusively. _____

39. The _____ color test reagent turns purple in the presence of heroin.

40. The _____ color test reagent turns orange-brown in the presence of amphetamines.

41. The Duquenois-Levine test is a valuable color test for _____.

42. The _____ test is a widely used color test for cocaine.

43. _____ tests tentatively identify drugs by the size and shape of crystals formed when the drug is mixed with specific reagents.

44. _____ provides a means of separating drugs from their diluents while making a tentative identification.

45. The pattern of an _____ absorption spectrum is unique for each drug and thus is a specific test for identification.

46. The gas chromatograph, in combination with the _____, can separate the components of a drug mixture and then unequivocally identify each substance present in the mixture.

47. Microscopic identification of marijuana largely depends on observing short hairs on the leaf known as _____ hairs.

48. All packages containing drugs must be marked for identification by the police officer before being sent to the laboratory in order to maintain the _____.

Further References

Bono, J. P., "Criminalistics—Introduction to Controlled Substances," in S. B. Karch, ed., *Drug Abuse Handbook*. Boca Raton, Fla.: Taylor & Francis, 1998.

Christian, D. R., Jr., "Analysis of Controlled Substances," in S. H. James and J. J. Nordby, eds., *Forensic Science: An Introduction to Scientific and Investigative Techniques, 2nd ed.* Boca Raton, Fla.: Taylor & Francis, 2005.

Siegel, J. A., "Forensic Identification of Controlled Substances," in R. Saferstein, ed., *Forensic Science Handbook,* vol. 2, 2nd ed. Upper Saddle River, N.J.: Prentice Hall, 2005.

Smith, F., and J. A. Siegel, eds., *Handbook of Forensic Drug Analysis.* Boca Raton, Fla.: Taylor & Francis, 2005.

Harold Shipman, Dr. Death

Kathleen Grundy's sudden death in 1998 was shocking news to her daughter, Angela Woodruff. Mrs. Grundy, an 81-year-old widow, was believed to be in good health when her physician, Dr. Harold Shipman, visited her a few hours before her demise. Some hours later, when friends came to her home to check on her whereabouts they found Mrs. Grundy lying on a sofa fully dressed and dead.

Dr. Shipman pronounced her dead and informed her daughter that an autopsy was not necessary. A few days later, Mrs. Woodruff was surprised to learn that a will had surfaced leaving all of Mrs. Grundy's money to Dr. Shipman. The will was immediately recognized as a forgery and led to the exhumation of Mrs. Grundy's body. A toxicological analysis of the remains revealed a lethal quantity of morphine.

In retrospect, there was good reason to suspect that Dr. Shipman was capable of foul play. In the 1970s, he was asked to leave a medical practice because of a drug abuse problem and charges that he obtained drugs by forgery and deception. However, Dr. Shipman was quickly back to practicing medicine. By 1998, local undertakers became suspicious at the number of his patients who were dying. What is more, they all seemed to be elderly women who were found sitting in a chair or lying fully clothed on a bed. As police investigated, the horror of Dr. Shipman's deeds became apparent. One clinical audit estimated that Dr. Shipman killed at least 236 of his patients over a twenty-four-year period. Most of the deaths were attributed to fatal doses of heroin or morphine. Toxicological analysis on seven exhumed bodies clearly showed significant quantities of morphine. Convicted of murder, Dr. Shipman hanged himself in his jail cell in 2004.

chapter 10

Forensic Toxicology

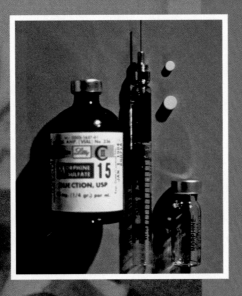

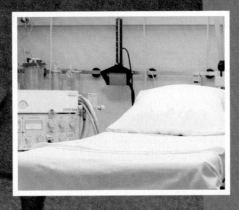

Key Terms

absorption

acid

alveoli

anticoagulant

artery

base

capillary

catalyst

excretion

fuel cell detector

metabolize

oxidation

pH scale

preservative

vein

Learning Objectives

After studying this chapter you should be able to:

- Explain how alcohol is absorbed into the bloodstream, transported throughout the body, and eliminated by oxidation and excretion

- Understand the process by which alcohol is excreted in the breath via the lungs

- Understand the concepts of infrared and fuel cell breath-testing devices for alcohol testing

- Describe commonly employed field sobriety tests to assess alcohol impairment

- List and contrast laboratory procedures for measuring the concentration of alcohol in the blood

- Relate the precautions to be taken to properly preserve blood in order to analyze its alcohol content

- Understand the significance of implied-consent laws and the *Schmerber* v. *California* case to traffic enforcement

- Describe techniques that forensic toxicologists use to isolate and identify drugs and poisons

- Appreciate the significance of finding of a drug in human tissues and organs to assessing impairment

- Understand the Drug Recognition Expert program and how to coordinate it with a forensic toxicology result

It is no secret that in spite of the concerted efforts of law enforcement agencies to prevent distribution and sale of illicit drugs, thousands die every year from intentional or unintentional administration of drugs, and many more innocent lives are lost as a result of the erratic and frequently uncontrollable behavior of individuals under the influence of drugs. But one should not automatically attribute these occurrences to the wide proliferation of illicit-drug markets. For example, in the United States alone, drug manufacturers produce enough barbiturates and tranquilizers each year to provide every man, woman, and child with about forty pills. All of the statistical and medical evidence shows ethyl alcohol, a legal over-the-counter drug, to be the most heavily abused drug in Western countries. In the United States, nearly 17,500 automobile deaths, 40 percent of all traffic deaths, are alcohol related, with a rate of injury requiring hospital treatment exceeding two million people per year. This highway death toll, as well as the untold damage to life, limb, and property, is testimony in itself to the dangerous consequences of alcohol abuse.

Because the uncontrolled use of drugs has become a worldwide problem affecting all segments of society, the role of the toxicologist has taken on new and added significance. Toxicologists detect and identify drugs and poisons in body fluids, tissues, and organs. Their services are required not only in such legal institutions as crime laboratories and medical examiners' offices; they also reach into hospital laboratories—where the possibility of identifying a drug overdose may represent the difference between life and death—and into various health facilities responsible for monitoring the intake of drugs and other toxic substances. Primary examples include performing blood tests on children exposed to leaded paints or analyzing the urine of addicts enrolled in methadone maintenance programs.

The role of the forensic toxicologist is limited to matters that pertain to violations of criminal law. However, the responsibility for performing toxicological services in a criminal justice system varies considerably throughout the United States. In systems with a crime laboratory independent of the medical examiner, this responsibility may reside with one or the other or may be shared by both. Some systems, however, take advantage of the expertise residing in governmental health department laboratories and assign this role to them. Nevertheless, whatever facility handles this work, its caseload will reflect the prevailing popularity of the drugs that are abused in the community. In most cases, this means that the forensic toxicologist handles numerous requests relating to the determination of the presence of alcohol in the body.

Toxicology of Alcohol

The Fate of Alcohol in the Body

The subject of the analysis of alcohol immediately confronts us with the primary objective of forensic toxicology—the detection and isolation of drugs in the body to determine their influence on human behavior. In the case of alcohol, however, the problem is further complicated by practical considerations. The predominant role of the automobile in our society has mandated the imposition of laws to protect the public from the drinking driver. This has meant that toxicologists have had to devise rapid and specific procedures for measuring the degree of alcohol intoxication. The methods used must be suitably designed to test hundreds of thousands of motorists annually without causing them undue physical harm or unreasonable inconvenience, while at the same time providing a reliable diagnosis that can be supported and defended within the framework of the legal system.

Alcohol, or ethyl alcohol, is a colorless liquid normally diluted with water and consumed as a beverage. Logically, the most obvious measure of intoxication would be the amount of liquor a person has consumed. Unfortunately, most arrests are made after the fact, when such information is not available to legal authorities; furthermore, even if these data could be collected, numerous related factors, such as body weight and the rate of alcohol's absorption into the body, are so variable that it would be impossible to prescribe uniform standards that would yield reliable alcohol intoxication levels.

Absorption
Passage of alcohol across the wall of the stomach and small intestine into the bloodstream.

Like any other depressant, alcohol primarily affects the central nervous system, particularly the brain. The extent of the depression is proportional to the concentration of alcohol within the nerve cells. The nerve functions most susceptible to alcohol are found in the surface areas of the forebrain. Later, as the person absorbs alcohol to a greater extent, the functions of the central and rear portions of the brain are affected. The nerve functions that are most resistant, and the last to fail, are centered in the brain's medulla, which regulates such vital functions as respiration and heart activity.

Theoretically, for a true determination of the quantity of alcohol impairing an individual's normal body functions, it would be best to remove a portion of brain tissue and analyze it for alcohol content. For obvious reasons, this cannot be done on living subjects. Consequently toxicologists concentrate on the blood, which provides the medium for circulating alcohol throughout the body, carrying it to all tissues, including the brain. Fortunately, experimental evidence supports this approach and shows blood-alcohol concentration to be directly proportional to the concentration of alcohol in the brain. From the medicolegal point of view, blood-alcohol levels have become the accepted standard for relating alcohol intake to its effect on the body.

Alcohol appears in the blood within minutes after it has been consumed and slowly increases in concentration while it is being absorbed from the stomach and the small intestine into the bloodstream. When all the alcohol has been absorbed, a maximum alcohol level is reached in the blood, and the postabsorption period begins. Then the alcohol concentration slowly decreases until a zero level is again reached.

Many factors determine the rate at which alcohol is absorbed into the bloodstream, including the total time taken to consume the drink, the alcohol content of the beverage, the amount consumed, and the quantity and type of food present in the stomach at the time of drinking. With so many variables, it is difficult to predict just how long the absorption process will require. For example, beer is absorbed more slowly than an equivalent concentration of alcohol in water, apparently because of the carbohydrates present in beer. Also, alcohol consumed on an empty stomach is absorbed faster than an equivalent amount of alcohol taken when there is food in the stomach. The longer the total time required for complete absorption to occur, the lower the peak alcohol concentration in the blood (see Figure 10–1). Depending on a combination of factors, maximum blood-alcohol concentration may not be reached until two or three hours have elapsed from the time of consumption. However, under normal social drinking conditions, it takes anywhere from thirty to ninety minutes from the time of the final drink until the absorption process is completed.

During the absorption phase, alcohol slowly enters the body's bloodstream and is carried to all parts of the body. When the absorption period is completed, the alcohol becomes distributed uniformly throughout the watery portions of the body—that is, throughout about two-thirds of the body volume. Fat, bones, and hair are low in water content and therefore contain little alcohol, whereas alcohol concentration in the rest of the body is fairly uniform. Hence, if blood is not available, as in some postmortem

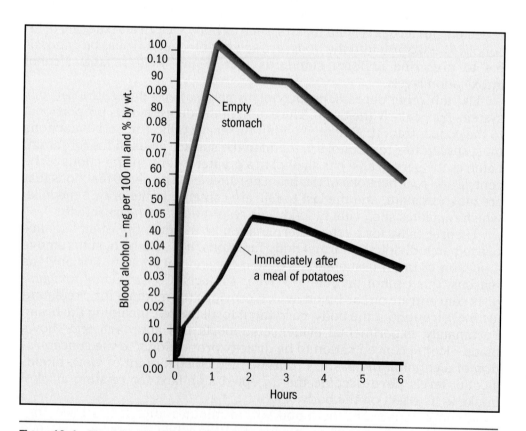

Figure 10–1 **Blood-alcohol concentrations after ingestion of 2 ounces of pure alcohol mixed in 8 ounces of water (equivalent to about 5 ounces of 80-proof vodka).** *Courtesy U.S. Department of Transportation, Washington, D.C.*

situations, a medical examiner can select a water-rich organ or fluid—for example, the brain, cerebrospinal fluid, or vitreous humor—for determining the body's alcohol content to a reasonable degree of accuracy.

As the alcohol is circulated by the bloodstream, the body begins to eliminate it. Alcohol is eliminated through two mechanisms—oxidation and excretion. Nearly all of the alcohol (95–98 percent) consumed is eventually oxidized to carbon dioxide and water. Oxidation takes place almost entirely in the liver. Here, in the presence of the enzyme alcohol dehydrogenase, the alcohol is converted into acetaldehyde and then to acetic acid. The acetic acid is subsequently oxidized in practically all parts of the body to carbon dioxide and water.

The remaining alcohol is excreted unchanged in the breath, urine, and perspiration. Most significantly, the amount of alcohol exhaled in the breath is in direct proportion to the concentration of alcohol in the blood. This observation has had a tremendous impact on the technology and procedures used for blood-alcohol testing. The development of instruments to reliably measure breath for its alcohol content has made possible the testing of millions of people in a rapid, safe, and convenient manner.

The fate of alcohol in the body is therefore relatively simple— namely, absorption into the bloodstream, distribution throughout the body's water, and finally, elimination by oxidation and excretion. The elimination or "burn-off" rate of alcohol varies in different individuals; 0.015 percent w/v (weight per volume) per hour seems to be average once the absorption process is complete.[1] However, this figure is an average that varies by as much as 30 percent among individuals.

Alcohol in the Circulatory System

The extent to which an individual may be under the influence of alcohol is usually determined by measuring the quantity of alcohol present in the blood system. Normally, this is accomplished in one of two ways: (1) by direct chemical analysis of the blood for its alcohol content and (2) by measurement of the alcohol content of the breath. In either case, the significance and meaning of the results can better be understood when the movement of alcohol through the circulatory system is studied.

Humans, like all vertebrates, have a closed circulatory system, which consists basically of a heart and numerous arteries, capillaries, and veins. An artery is a blood vessel carrying blood away from the heart, and a vein is a vessel carrying blood back toward the heart. Capillaries are tiny blood vessels that interconnect the arteries with the veins. The exchange of materials between the blood and the other tissues takes place across the thin walls of the capillaries. A schematic diagram of the circulatory system is shown in Figure 10–2.

Let us now trace the movement of alcohol through the human circulatory system. After alcohol is ingested, it moves down the esophagus into the stomach. About 20 percent of the alcohol is absorbed through the stomach walls into the portal vein of the blood system. The remaining alcohol passes into the blood through the walls of the small intestine. Once in the blood, the alcohol is carried to the liver, where its destruction starts

Oxidation
The combination of oxygen with other substances to produce new products.

Excretion
Elimination of alcohol from the body in an unchanged state; alcohol is normally excreted in breath and urine.

Artery
A blood vessel that carries blood away from the heart.

Vein
A blood vessel that transports blood toward the heart.

Capillary
A tiny blood vessel across whose walls exchange of materials between the blood and the tissues takes place; receives blood from arteries and carries it to veins.

---

[1] In the United States, laws that define blood-alcohol levels almost exclusively use the unit *percent weight per volume*—percent w/v. Hence, 0.015 percent w/v is equivalent to 0.015 grams of alcohol per 100 milliliters of blood, or 15 milligrams of alcohol per 100 milliliters.

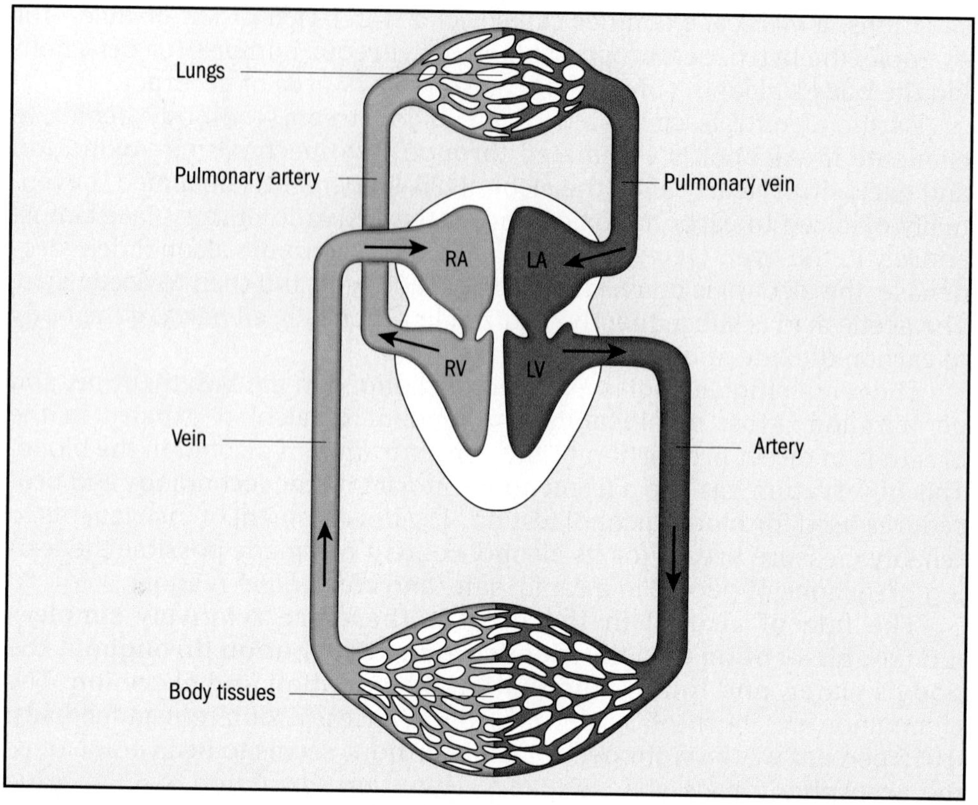

Figure 10–2 Simplified diagram of the human circulatory system. Dark vessels contain oxygenated blood; light vessels contain deoxygenated blood.

as the blood (carrying the alcohol) moves up to the heart. The blood enters the upper right chamber of the heart, called the right atrium (or auricle), and is forced into the lower right chamber of the heart, known as the right ventricle. Having returned to the heart from its circulation through the tissues, the blood at this time contains very little oxygen and much carbon dioxide. Consequently, the blood must be pumped up to the lungs, through the pulmonary artery, to be replenished with oxygen.

The respiratory system bridges with the circulatory system in the lungs, so that oxygen can enter the blood and carbon dioxide can leave it. As shown in Figure 10–3(a), the pulmonary artery branches into capillaries lying close to tiny pear-shaped sacs called alveoli. There are about 250 million alveoli in the lungs, all located at the ends of the bronchial tubes. The bronchial tubes connect to the windpipe (trachea), which leads up to the mouth and nose [see Figure 10–3(b)]. At the surface of the alveolar sacs, blood flowing through the capillaries comes in contact with fresh oxygenated air in the sacs. A rapid exchange now proceeds to take place between the fresh air in the sacs and the spent air in the blood. Oxygen passes through the walls of the alveoli into the blood while carbon dioxide is discharged from the blood into the air [see Figure 10–3(a)]. If, during this exchange, alcohol or any other volatile substance is in the blood, it too will pass into the alveoli. During breathing, the carbon dioxide and alcohol are expelled through the nose and mouth, and the alveoli sacs are replenished with fresh oxygenated air breathed into the lungs, allowing the process to begin all over again.

The distribution of alcohol between the blood and alveolar air is similar to the example of a gas dissolved in an enclosed beaker of water, as

Alveoli

Small sacs in the lungs through whose walls air and other vapors are exchanged between the breath and the blood.

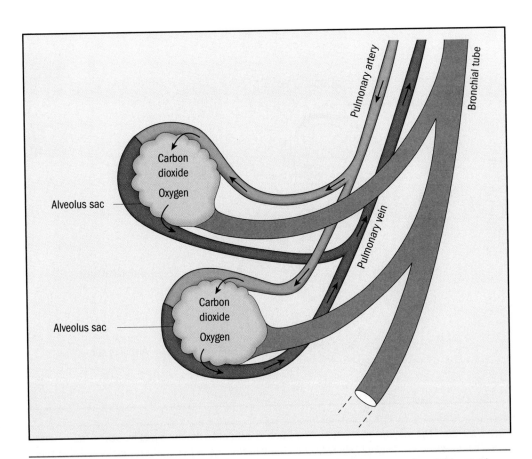

Labels in figure: Pulmonary artery, Bronchial tube, Alveolus sac, Carbon dioxide, Oxygen, Pulmonary vein, Alveolus sac, Carbon dioxide, Oxygen

Figure 10–3a Gas exchange in the lungs. Blood flows from the pulmonary artery into vessels that lie close to the walls of the alveoli sacs. Here the blood gives up its carbon dioxide and absorbs oxygen. The oxygenated blood leaves the lungs via the pulmonary vein and returns to the heart.

described on pp. 133–134. Here again, one can use Henry's law to explain how the alcohol divides itself between the air and blood. Henry's law may now be restated as follows: **When a volatile chemical (alcohol) is dissolved in a liquid (blood) and is brought to equilibrium with air (alveolar breath), there is a fixed ratio between the concentration of the volatile compound (alcohol) in air (alveolar breath) and its concentration in the liquid (blood), and this ratio is constant for a given temperature.**

The temperature at which the breath leaves the mouth is normally 34°C. **At this temperature, experimental evidence has shown that the ratio of alcohol in the blood to alcohol in alveoli air is approximately 2,100 to 1. In other words, 1 milliliter of blood will contain nearly the same amount of alcohol as 2,100 milliliters of alveolar breath. Henry's law thus becomes a basis for relating breath to blood-alcohol concentration.**

Now let's return to the circulating blood. After emerging from the lungs, the oxygenated blood is rushed back to the upper left chamber of the heart (left atrium) by the pulmonary vein. When the left atrium contracts, it forces the blood through a valve into the left ventricle, which is the lower left chamber of the heart. The left ventricle then pumps the freshly oxygenated blood into the arteries, which carry the blood to all parts of the body. Each of these arteries, in turn, branches into smaller arteries, which eventually connect with the numerous tiny capillaries embedded in the tissues. Here the alcohol moves out of the blood and into the

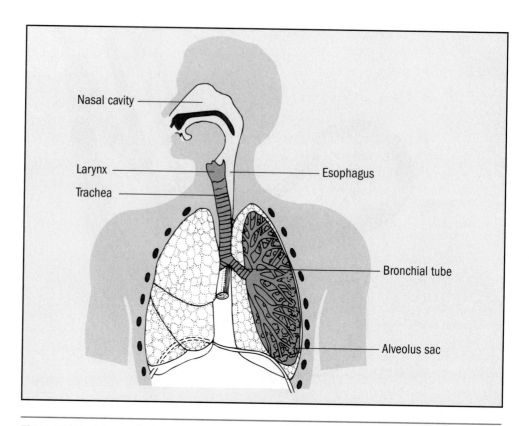

Figure 10–3b The respiratory system. The trachea connects the nose and mouth to the bronchial tubes. The bronchial tubes divide into numerous branches that terminate in the alveoli sacs in the lungs.

tissues. The blood then runs from the capillaries into tiny veins that fuse to form larger veins. These veins eventually lead back to the heart to complete the circuit.

During absorption, the concentration of alcohol in the arterial blood is considerably higher than the concentration of alcohol in the venous blood. One typical study revealed a subject's arterial blood-alcohol level to be 41 percent higher than the venous level thirty minutes after the last drink.[2] This difference is thought to exist because of the rapid diffusion of alcohol into the body tissues from venous blood during the early phases of absorption. Because the administration of a blood test requires drawing venous blood from the arm, this test is clearly to the advantage of a subject who may still be in the absorption stage. However, once absorption is complete, the alcohol becomes equally distributed throughout the blood system.

A breath test reflects the alcohol concentration in the pulmonary artery. Breath-test results obtained during the absorption phase may be higher than results obtained from a simultaneous direct analysis of venous blood. However, the former are more reflective of the concentration of alcohol reaching the brain and therefore more accurately reflect the effects

---

[2] R. B. Forney et al., "Alcohol Distribution in the Vascular System: Concentrations of Orally Administered Alcohol in Blood from Various Points in the Vascular System and in Rebreathed Air during Absorption," *Quarterly Journal of Studies on Alcohol* 25 (1964): 205.

of alcohol on the subject. Again, once absorption is complete, the difference between a blood test and a breath test should be minimal.

Breath-Test Instruments

From a practical point of view, the idea of drawing blood from a vein to test motorists suspected of being under the influence of alcohol simply does not provide a convenient method for monitoring alcoholic drivers. Having the suspect transported to a location where a medically qualified person can draw blood would be costly and time consuming, considering the hundreds of tests that the average police department must conduct every year. Thus, breath analysis serves a very useful purpose in providing an easily obtainable specimen along with a rapid and accurate result. A breath tester is simply a device for collecting and measuring the alcohol content of alveolar breath. The first successful commercial breath-test device, known as *the Breathalyzer,* was developed in 1954 by R. K. Borkenstein, who was a captain in the Indiana State Police. The Breathalyzer required the subject to blow into a disposable mouthpiece that led into a metal cylinder. The last portion of breath (alveolar breath) was trapped in the cylinder. The amount of breath collected in this manner was 52.5 milliliters, or 1/40 of 2,100 milliliters.[3] We have already seen that the amount of alcohol in 2,100 milliliters of alveolar breath approximates that in 1 milliliter of blood. Hence, in essence, the Breathalyzer was designed to measure alcohol concentration present in 1/40 of a milliliter of blood.

The quantity of alcohol in the trapped breath was measured by passing the breath into a glass ampoule containing potassium dichromate, sulfuric acid, and water. Any alcohol in the breath immediately dissolves in the dichromate solution and is oxidized to acetic acid. In the oxidation process, potassium dichromate is also destroyed. The extent of this destruction is measured by the Breathalyzer and is related to the quantity of alcohol passed into the ampoule.

Basically, the Breathalyzer is a spectrophotometer (see Chapter 5) designed to measure the absorption of light passing through the potassium dichromate solution at a single wavelength. A schematic diagram of a Breathalyzer is shown in Figure 10–4. To better understand its operation, let's examine what is happening in the ampoule when alcohol is converted to acetic acid. Whenever a chemical reaction occurs between two or more substances, chemists use a chemical equation as a shorthand method to describe the changes taking place. The equation serves two purposes: it identifies the participants, and it describes the quantitative aspects of the reaction.

The following equation depicts the chemical reaction taking place in the ampoule:

$$2K_2Cr_2O_7 + 3C_2H_5OH + 8H_2SO_4 \rightarrow$$

potassium dichromate $\qquad$ ethyl alcohol $\qquad$ sulfuric acid $\qquad$ yields

$$2Cr_2(SO_4)_3 + 2K_2SO_4 + 3CH_3COOH + 11H_2O$$

chromium sulfate $\qquad$ potassium sulfate $\qquad$ acetic acid $\qquad$ water

---

[3] Actually, the collection cylinder is designed to hold 56.5 milliliters of breath. This is because, having left the mouth at 34°C, the breath will expand when heated to 50°C in the cylinder. Furthermore, added breath is needed to compensate for the air that remains in the delivery tube leading to the test ampoule.

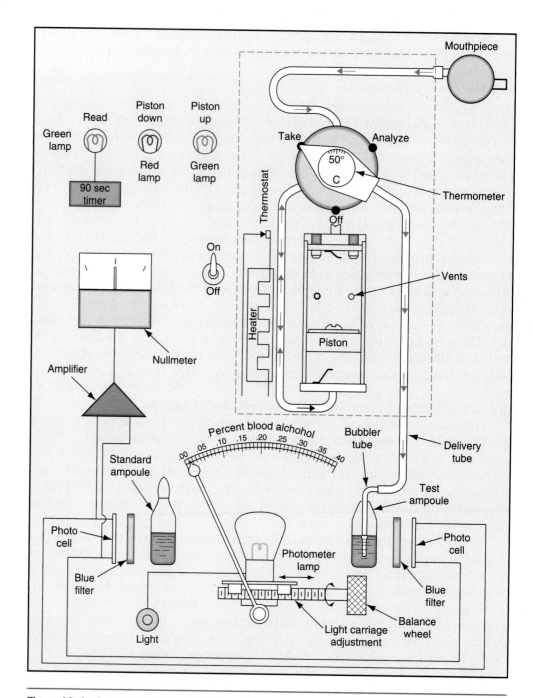

Figure 10–4   Schematic diagram of a Breathalyzer. *Courtesy Draeger Safety, Inc., Breathalyzer Division, Durango, Colo.*

From this chemical equation, we can see that there is always a fixed relationship between the number of potassium dichromate molecules reacting with the alcohol. Two molecules of potassium dichromate always combine with three molecules of ethyl alcohol. Hence, determining the amount of potassium dichromate consumed is an indirect way of determining the quantity of alcohol originally present. Silver nitrate is also present in the Breathalyzer ampoule; however, this substance acts only as a **catalyst** to speed up the rate of reaction between potassium dichromate and ethyl alcohol. As a catalyst, silver nitrate undergoes no net change itself during the reaction.

Catalyst

A substance that accelerates the rate of a chemical reaction but is not itself permanently changed by the reaction.

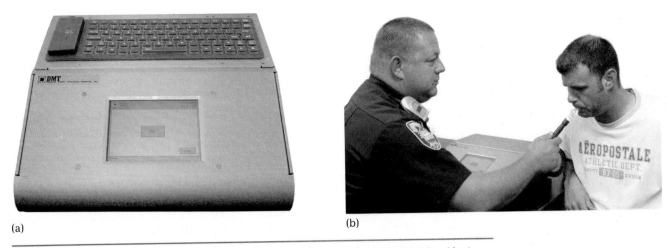

(a)

(b)

Figure 10–5 **(a) An infrared breath-testing instrument—the Data Master DMT. (b) A subject blowing into the DMT breath tester.** *Courtesy National Patent Analytical Systems, Inc., Mansfield, Ohio, www.npas.com*

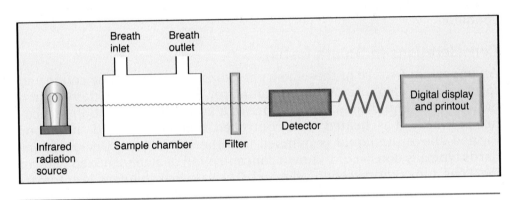

Figure 10–6 **Schematic diagram of an infrared breath-testing instrument.**

Starting in the 1970s, the Breathalyzer was phased out and replaced by the computerized breath-alcohol instruments that dominate the field today. Interestingly, these instruments still have one thing in common with the old Breathalyzer: they measure the alcoholic content of alveolar breath. Like the Breathalyzer, they assume that the ratio of alcohol in the blood to alcohol in alveoli air is 2,100 to 1 at a mouth temperature of 34°C. Unlike the Breathalyzer, modern breath testers are free of chemicals. Most of these devices aim beams of infrared radiation at the sample cell containing the alveolar breath to detect and measure alcohol.

An evidential testing instrument that incorporates the principle of infrared light absorption is shown in Figure 10–5. In principle, these instruments operate no differently from the spectrophotometers described on pp. 147–149. Any alcohol in the subject's breath is passed into the instrument's breath chamber. As shown in Figure 10–6, a beam of infrared light is aimed through the chamber. A filter is used to select a wavelength of infrared light at which alcohol will absorb. As the infrared light passes through the chamber, it interacts with the alcohol and causes the light to decrease in intensity. The decrease in light intensity is measured by a photoelectric detector that gives a signal proportional to the concentration of alcohol present in the collected breath sample. This information is processed by an electronic microprocessor, and the percent blood-alcohol concentration is displayed on a digital readout. Also, the blood-alcohol level is printed on a card to produce a permanent record of the test result. Most infrared breath testers aim a second infrared beam into the same chamber to check for acetone or other chemical interferences on the breath. If the instrument detects differences in the relative response of the two infrared radiations that does not conform to ethyl alcohol, the operator is immediately informed of the presence of an "interferant."

Fuel Cell Detector
A detector in which chemical reactions produce electricity.

Another approach for measuring alcohol in breath is to use a fuel cell detector. A fuel cell converts a fuel and an oxidant into an electrical current. In evidential breath-testing devices that use this concept, breath alcohol is the fuel and atmospheric oxygen is the oxidant. Alcohol is converted in the fuel cell into acetic acid, generating a current that is proportional to the quantity of alcohol present in the breath.

Infrared and fuel-cell-based breath testers are microprocessor controlled so that all an operator has to do is press a start button and the instrument automatically moves through a sequence of steps that produce a printout of the subject's test results. These instruments also perform self-diagnostic tests to ascertain whether the instrument is in proper operating condition.

Considerations in Breath Testing

An important feature of these instruments is that they can be connected to an external alcohol standard or simulator in the form of either a liquid or a gas. The liquid simulator comprises a known concentration of alcohol in water. It is heated to a controlled temperature and the vapor formed above the liquid is pumped into the instrument. Dry-gas standards typically consist of a known concentration of alcohol mixed with an inert gas and compressed in cylinders. The external standard is automatically sampled by the breath-test instrument before and/or after the subject's breath sample is taken and recorded. Thus the operator can check the accuracy of the instrument against the known alcohol standard.

The key to the accuracy of a breath-testing device is to ensure that the unit measures the alcohol in the alveolar breath (deep-lung breath) of the subject. This is typically accomplished by programming the unit to accept no less than 1.5 liters of breath from the subject. Also, the subject must blow for a minimum time (such as 6 seconds) with a minimum breath flow rate (such as 3 liters per minute).

Another feature of these instruments is the *slope detector*. As the subject blows into the instrument, the breath-alcohol concentration initially will rise steadily as a function of time. The instrument accepts a breath sample only when consecutive breath measurements show little or no rate of change in breath alcohol concentration. This approach ensures that the breath sample being measured is alveolar or deep-lung breath and thus most closely relates to the true blood-alcohol concentration of the subject being tested.

A breath-test operator must take other steps to ensure that the breath-test result truly reflects the actual blood-alcohol concentration of the subject. A major consideration is to avoid measuring "mouth alcohol" resulting from regurgitation, belching, or recent intake of an alcoholic beverage. Also, the recent gargling of an alcohol-containing mouthwash can lead to the presence of mouth alcohol. As a result, the alcohol concentration detected in the exhaled breath is higher than the concentration in the alveolar breath. To avoid this possibility, the operator must not allow the subject to take any foreign material into his or her mouth for a minimum of fifteen to twenty minutes prior to the breath test. Likewise, the subject should be observed not to have belched or regurgitated during this period of time. Mouth alcohol has been shown to dissipate after fifteen to twenty minutes from its inception.

Independent measurement of duplicate breath samples taken within a few minutes of each other is another extremely important check of the integrity of the breath test. Acceptable agreement between the two tests taken minutes apart significantly reduces the possibility of errors arising from the operator, mouth alcohol, instrument component failures, and spurious electric signals.

Field Sobriety Testing

A police officer who suspects that an individual is under the influence of alcohol usually conducts a series of preliminary tests before ordering the suspect to submit to an evidential breath or blood test. **These preliminary, or field sobriety, tests are normally performed to ascertain the degree of the suspect's physical impairment and whether an evidential test is justified.** Field sobriety tests usually consist of a series of psychophysical tests and a preliminary breath test (if such devices are authorized and available for use). A portable handheld roadside breath tester is shown in Figure 10–7. This pocket-sized device weighs 5 ounces and uses a fuel cell to measure the alcohol content of a breath sample. The fuel cell absorbs the alcohol from the breath sample, oxidizes it, and produces an electrical current proportional to the breath-alcohol content. This instrument can typically perform for three to five years before the fuel cell needs to be replaced. Breath-test results obtained with devices such as those shown in Figure 10–7 must be considered preliminary and nonevidential in nature. They should only establish probable cause for requiring an individual to submit to a more thorough breath or blood test.

Horizontal-gaze nystagmus, walk and turn, and the one-leg stand constitute a series of reliable and effective psychophysical tests. Horizontal-gaze nystagmus is an involuntary jerking of the eye as it moves

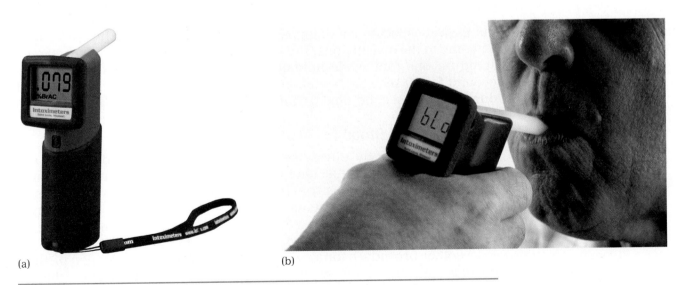

(a) (b)

Figure 10–7 (a) The Alco-Sensor FST. (b) A subject blowing into the roadside tester device.
Courtesy Intoximeters, Inc., St. Louis, Mo., www.intox.com

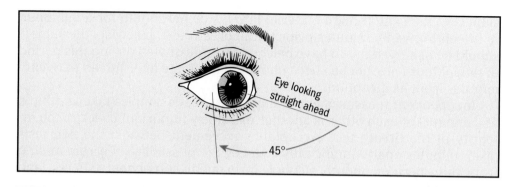

Figure 10–8   When a person's blood-alcohol level is in the range of 0.10 percent, jerking of the eye during the horizontal-gaze nystagmus test begins before the eyeball has moved 45 degrees to the side.

to the side. A person experiencing nystagmus is usually unaware that the jerking is happening and is unable to stop or control it. The subject being tested is asked to follow a penlight or some other object with his or her eye as far to the side as the eye can go. The more intoxicated the person is, the less the eye has to move toward the side before jerking or nystagmus begins. Usually, when a person's blood-alcohol concentration is in the range of 0.10 percent, the jerking begins before the eyeball has moved 45 degrees to the side (see Figure 10–8). Higher blood-alcohol concentration causes jerking at smaller angles. Also, if the suspect has taken a drug that also causes nystagmus (such as phencyclidine, barbiturates, and other depressants), the nystagmus onset angle may occur much earlier than would be expected from alcohol alone.

Walk and turn and the one-leg stand are divided-attention tasks, testing the subject's ability to comprehend and execute two or more simple instructions at one time. The ability to understand and simultaneously carry out more than two instructions is significantly affected by increasing blood-alcohol levels. Walk and turn requires the suspect to maintain balance while standing heel-to-toe and at the same time listening to and comprehending the test instructions. During the walking stage, the suspect must walk a straight line, touching heel-to-toe for nine steps, then turn around on the line and repeat the process. The one-leg stand requires the suspect to maintain balance while standing with heels together listening to the instructions. During the balancing stage, the suspect must stand on one foot while holding the other foot several inches off the ground for 30 seconds; simultaneously, the suspect must count out loud during the 30-second time period.

The Analysis of Blood for Alcohol

Gas chromatography offers the toxicologist the most widely used approach for determining alcohol levels in blood. Under proper gas chromatographic conditions, alcohol can be separated from other volatiles in the blood. By comparing the resultant alcohol peak area to ones obtained with known blood-alcohol standards, the investigator can calculate the alcohol level with a high degree of accuracy (see Figure 10–9).

Another procedure for alcohol analysis involves the oxidation of alcohol to acetaldehyde. This reaction is carried out in the presence of the enzyme alcohol dehydrogenase and the coenzyme nicotin-amide-adenine

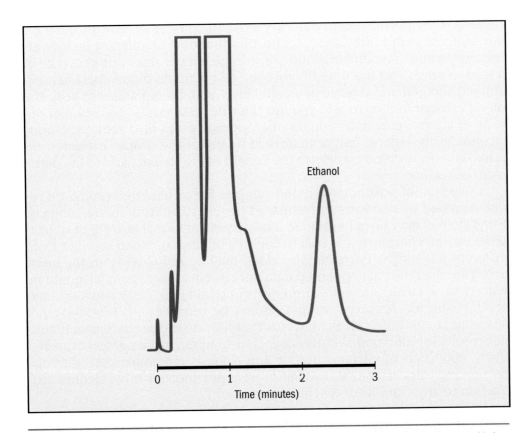

Figure 10–9   Gas chromatogram showing ethyl alcohol (ethanol) in whole blood. *Courtesy Varian Inc., Palo Alto, Calif.*

dinucleotide (NAD). As the oxidation proceeds, NAD is converted into another chemical species, NADH. The extent of this conversion is measured spectrophotometrically and is related to alcohol concentration. This approach to blood-alcohol testing is normally associated with instruments used in a clinical or hospital setting. On the other hand, forensic laboratories normally use gas chromatography for determining blood-alcohol content.

Collection and Preservation of Blood

Blood must always be drawn under medically accepted conditions by a qualified individual. It is important to apply a nonalcoholic disinfectant before the suspect's skin is penetrated with a sterile needle or lancet, to negate any argument that an alcoholic disinfectant may have inadvertently contributed to a falsely high blood-alcohol result. Nonalcoholic disinfectants such as aqueous benzalkonium chloride (Zepiran), aqueous mercuric chloride, or povidone-iodine (Betadine) are recommended for this purpose.

Once blood is removed from an individual, it is best preserved sealed in an airtight container after adding an anticoagulant and a preservative. The blood should be stored in a refrigerator until delivery to the toxicology laboratory. The addition of an anticoagulant, such as EDTA or potassium oxalate, prevents clotting; a preservative, such as sodium fluoride, inhibits the growth of microorganisms capable of destroying alcohol.

Anticoagulant
A substance that prevents coagulation or clotting of blood.

Preservative
A substance that stops the growth of microorganisms in blood.

One study performed to determine the stability of alcohol in blood removed from living individuals found that the most significant factors affecting alcohol's stability in blood are storage temperature, the presence of a preservative, and the time of storage.[4] Not a single blood specimen examined showed an increase in alcohol level with time. Failure to keep the blood refrigerated or to add sodium fluoride resulted in a substantial decline in alcohol concentration. Longer storage times also reduced blood-alcohol levels. Hence, failure to adhere to any of the proper preservation requirements for blood works to the benefit of the suspect and to the detriment of society.

Collection of postmortem blood samples for alcohol determination requires added precautions as compared to collection from living subjects. Ethyl alcohol may be generated in a deceased individual as a result of bacterial action. Therefore, it is best to collect a number of blood samples from different body sites. For example, blood may be removed from the heart and from the femoral (leg) and cubital (arm) veins. Each sample should be placed in a clean, airtight container containing an anticoagulant and sodium fluoride preservative and should be refrigerated. Blood-alcohol levels attributed solely to alcohol consumption should result in nearly similar results for all blood samples collected from the same person. Alternatively, collection of vitreous humor and urine is recommended. Vitreous humor and urine usually do not suffer from postmortem ethyl alcohol production to any significant extent.

Alcohol and the Law

Constitutionally, every state in the United States is charged with establishing and administering statutes regulating the operation of motor vehicles. Although such an arrangement might encourage diverse laws defining permissible blood-alcohol levels, this has not been the case. Both the American Medical Association and the National Safety Council have exerted considerable influence in convincing the states to establish uniform and reasonable blood-alcohol standards.

Between 1939 and 1964, thirty-nine states and the District of Columbia enacted legislation that followed the recommendations of the American Medical Association and the National Safety Council in specifying that a person with a blood-alcohol concentration in excess of 0.15 percent w/v was to be considered under the influence of alcohol.[5] However, continued experimental studies have since shown that there is a clear correlation between drinking and driving impairment for blood-alcohol levels much below 0.15 percent w/v. As a result of these studies, in 1960 the American Medical Association and in 1965 the National Safety Council recommended lowering the presumptive level at which an individual was considered to be under the influence of alcohol to 0.10 percent w/v. All the states, as well as the District of Columbia and most possessions of the United States, have complied with this recommendation. In fact, all states have now established *per se laws,* meaning that any individual meeting or

---

[4] G. A. Brown et al., "The Stability of Ethanol in Stored Blood," *Analytica Chemica Acta* 66 (1973): 271.

[5] 0.15 percent w/v is equivalent to 0.15 grams of alcohol per 100 milliliters of blood, or 150 milligrams per 100 milliliters.

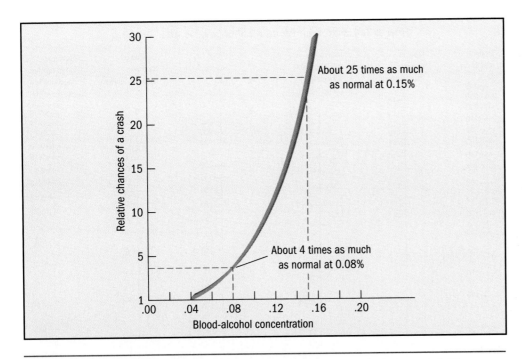

Figure 10–10   **Diagram of increased driving risk in relation to blood-alcohol concentration.**
Courtesy U.S. Department of Transportation, Washington, D.C.

exceeding a defined blood-alcohol level (usually 0.08 percent) shall be deemed intoxicated. No other proof of alcohol impairment is necessary. As shown in Figure 10–10, one is about four times as likely to become involved in an automobile accident at the 0.08 percent level as compared to a sober individual. At the 0.15 percent level, the chances are 25 times as much for involvement in an automobile accident as compared to a sober driver. The reader can *estimate* the relationship of blood-alcohol levels to body weight and the quantity of 80-proof liquor consumed by referring to Figure 10–11.

The trend toward lowering the impairment level continues; in 1972, the Committee on Alcohol and Drugs of the National Safety Council suggested that a blood concentration of 0.08 percent w/v indicates impairment in driving performance. In 1992, the U.S. Department of Transportation (DOT) recommended that states adopt 0.08 percent blood-alcohol concentration as the legal measure of drunk driving. This recommendation was enacted into federal law in 2000. The 0.08 percent level applies only to noncommercial drivers, as the federal government has set the maximum allowable blood-alcohol concentration for commercial truck and bus drivers at 0.04 percent.

Several Western countries have also set 0.08 percent w/v as the blood-alcohol level above which it is an offense to drive a motor vehicle. Those countries include Canada, Italy, Switzerland, and the United Kingdom. Finland, France, Germany, Ireland, Japan, the Netherlands, and Norway have a 0.05 percent limit. Australian states have adopted a 0.05 percent blood-alcohol concentration level. Sweden has lowered its blood-alcohol concentration limit to 0.02 percent.

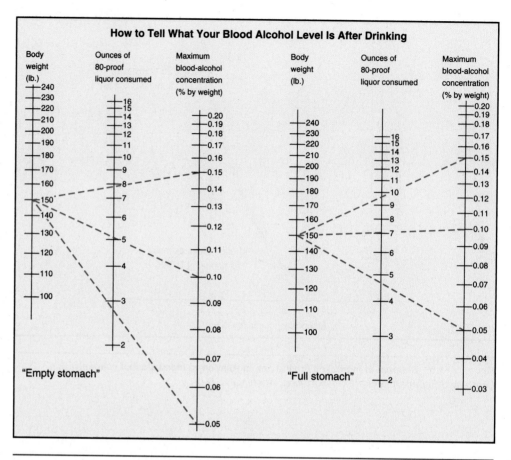

Figure 10–11 To use this diagram, lay a straightedge across your weight and the number of ounces of liquor you've consumed on an empty or full stomach. The point where the edge hits the right-hand column is your maximum blood-alcohol level. The rate of elimination of alcohol from the bloodstream is approximately 0.015 percent per hour. Therefore, to calculate your actual blood-alcohol level, subtract 0.015 from the number in the right-hand column for each hour from the start of drinking.

To prevent a person's refusal to take a test for alcohol intoxication on the constitutional grounds of self-incrimination, the National Highway Traffic Safety Administration recommended an "implied consent" law. By 1973, all the states had complied with this recommendation. In accordance with this statute, operating a motor vehicle on a public highway automatically carries with it the stipulation that the driver must either submit to a test for alcohol intoxication if requested or lose his or her license for some designated period—usually six months to one year.

The leading case relating to the constitutionality of collecting a blood specimen for alcohol testing, as well as for obtaining other types of physical evidence from a suspect without consent, is *Schmerber* v. *California*.[6] While being treated at a Los Angeles hospital for injuries sustained in an automobile collision, Schmerber was arrested for driving under the influence of alcohol. A physician took a blood sample from Schmerber at the direction of the police, over the objection of the defendant. On appeal to the U.S. Supreme Court, the defendant argued

---

[6] 384 U.S. 757 (1966).

that his privilege against self-incrimination had been violated by the introduction of the results of the blood test at his trial. The Court ruled against the defendant, reasoning that the Fifth Amendment only prohibits compelling a suspect to give "testimonial" evidence that may be self-incriminating; being compelled to furnish "physical" evidence, such as fingerprints, photographs, measurements, and blood samples, the Court ruled, was not protected by the Fifth Amendment.

The Court also addressed the question of whether Schmerber was subjected to an unreasonable search and seizure by the taking of a blood specimen without a search warrant. The Court upheld the blood removal, reasoning in this case that the police were confronted with an emergency situation. By the time police officials would have obtained the warrant, the blood levels would have declined significantly as a result of natural body elimination processes. In effect, the evidence would have been destroyed. The Court also emphasized that the blood specimen was taken in a medically accepted manner and without unreasonable force.

This opinion in no way condones warrantless taking of blood for alcohol or drug testing under all circumstances. The reasonableness of actions a police officer may take to compel an individual to yield evidence can be judged only on a case-by-case basis.

The Role of the Toxicologist

Once the forensic toxicologist ventures beyond the analysis of alcohol, he or she encounters an encyclopedic maze of drugs and poisons. Even a cursory discussion of the problems and handicaps imposed on toxicologists is enough to develop a sense of appreciation for their accomplishments and ingenuity. The toxicologist is presented with body fluids and/or organs and asked to examine them for the presence of drugs and poisons. If he or she is fortunate, which is not often, some clue to the type of toxic substance present may develop from the victim's symptoms, a postmortem pathological examination, an examination of the victim's personal effects, or the nearby presence of empty drug containers or household chemicals. Without such supportive information, the toxicologist must use general screening procedures with the hope of narrowing thousands of possibilities to one.

If this task does not seem monumental, consider that the toxicologist is not dealing with drugs at the concentration levels found in powders and pills. By the time a drug specimen reaches the toxicology laboratory, it has been dissipated and distributed throughout the body. Where the drug analyst may have gram or milligram quantities of material to work with, the toxicologist must be satisfied with nanogram or at best microgram amounts, acquired only after careful extraction from body fluids and organs.

Furthermore, the body is an active chemistry laboratory, and no one can appreciate this observation more than a toxicologist. Few substances enter and completely leave the body in the same chemical state. The drug that is injected is not always the substance extracted from the body tissues. Therefore, a thorough understanding of how the body alters or metabolizes the chemical structure of a drug is essential in detecting its presence. It would, for example, be futile and frustrating to search exhaustively for heroin in the human body. This drug is almost immediately

WebExtra 10.1

Calculate Your Blood Alcohol Level

www.prenhall.com/Saferstein

WebExtra 10.2

See How Alcohol Affects Your Behavior

www.prenhall.com/Saferstein

Metabolize
To transform a chemical in the body to another chemical to facilitate its elimination from the body.

metabolized to morphine on entering the bloodstream. Even with this information, the search may still prove impossible unless the examiner also knows that only a small percentage of morphine is excreted unchanged in urine. For the most part, morphine becomes chemically bonded to body carbohydrates before elimination in urine. Thus, successful detection of morphine requires that its extraction be planned in accordance with a knowledge of its chemical fate in the body.

Last, when and if the toxicologist has surmounted all of these obstacles and has finally detected, identified, and quantitated a drug or poison, he or she must assess the substance's toxicity. Fortunately, there is published information relating to the toxic levels of most drugs; however, when such data are available, their interpretation must assume that the victim's physiological behavior agrees with that of the subjects of previous studies. In some cases, such an assumption may not be entirely valid without knowing the subject's case history. No experienced toxicologist would be surprised to find an individual tolerating a toxic level of a drug that would have killed most other people.

Toxicology is made infinitely easier once it is recognized that the toxicologist's capabilities are directly dependent on the input received from the attending physician, medical examiner, and police investigator. It is a tribute to forensic toxicologists, who must often labor under conditions that do not afford such cooperation, that they can achieve such a high level of proficiency.

Generally, with a deceased person, the medical examiner decides what biological specimens must be shipped to the toxicology laboratory for analysis. However, a living person suspected of being under the influence of a drug presents a completely different problem, and few options are available. When possible, both blood and urine are taken from any suspected drug user. The entire urine void is collected and submitted for toxicological analysis. Preferably, two consecutive voids should be collected in separate specimen containers. When a licensed physician or registered nurse is available, a sample of blood should also be collected. The amount of blood taken depends on the type of examination to be conducted. Comprehensive toxicological tests for drugs and poisons can conveniently be carried out on a minimum of 10 cc of blood. A determination solely for the presence of alcohol will require much less—approximately 5 cc of blood. However, many therapeutic drugs, such as tranquilizers and barbiturates, when taken in combination with a small, nonintoxicating amount of alcohol, produce behavioral patterns resembling alcohol intoxication. For this reason, the toxicologist must be given an adequate amount of blood so he or she will have the option of performing a comprehensive analysis for drugs in cases of low alcohol concentrations.

Techniques Used in Toxicology

For the toxicologist, the upsurge in drug use and abuse has meant that the overwhelming majority of fatal and nonfatal toxic agents are drugs. Not surprisingly, a relatively small number of drugs—namely, those discussed in Chapter 9—comprise nearly all the toxic agents encountered. Of these, alcohol, marijuana, and cocaine normally account for 90 percent or more of the drugs encountered in a typical toxicology laboratory.

Like the drug analyst, the toxicologist must devise an analytical scheme to detect, isolate, and identify a toxic substance. The first chore is to selectively remove and isolate drugs and other toxic agents from the biological materials submitted as evidence. Because drugs constitute a large portion of the toxic materials found, a good deal of effort must be devoted to their extraction and detection. The procedures are numerous, and a useful description of them would be too detailed for this text. We can best understand the underlying principle of drug extraction by observing that many drugs fall into the categories of acids and bases.

Although several definitions exist for these two classes, a simple one states that an acid is a compound that sheds a hydrogen ion (or a hydrogen atom minus its electron) with reasonable ease. Conversely, a base is a compound that can pick up a hydrogen ion shed by an acid. The idea of acidity and basicity can be expressed in terms of a simple numerical value that relates to the concentration of the hydrogen ion (H^+) in a liquid medium such as water. Chemists use the pH scale to do this. This scale runs from 0 to 14:

$$\text{pH} = 0 \quad 1 \quad 2 \quad 3 \quad 4 \quad 5 \quad 6 \quad 7 \quad 8 \quad 9 \quad 10 \quad 11 \quad 12 \quad 13 \quad 14$$
$\leftarrow$ Increasing acidity—Neutral—Increasing basicity $\rightarrow$

Normally, water is neither acid nor basic—in other words, it is neutral, with a pH of 7. However, when an acidic substance—for example, sulfuric acid or hydrochloric acid—is added to the water, it adds excess hydrogen ions, and the pH value becomes less than 7. The lower the number, the more acidic the water. Similarly, when a basic substance—for example, sodium hydroxide or ammonium hydroxide—is added to water, it removes hydrogen ions, thus making water basic. The more basic the water, the higher its pH value.

By controlling the pH of a water solution into which blood, urine, or tissues are dissolved, the toxicologist can conveniently control the type of drug that is recovered. For example, acid drugs are easily extracted from an acidified water solution (pH less than 7) with organic solvents such as chloroform. Similarly, basic drugs are readily removed from a basic water solution (pH greater than 7) with organic solvents. This simple approach gives the toxicologist a general technique for extracting and categorizing drugs. Some of the more commonly encountered drugs may be classified as follows:

Acid Drugs	Basic Drugs
Barbiturates	Phencyclidine
Acetylsalicylic acid (aspirin)	Methadone
	Amphetamines
	Cocaine

Once the specimen has been extracted and divided into acidic and basic fractions, the toxicologist can identify the drugs present. The strategy for identifying abused drugs entails a two-step approach: *screening* and *confirmation* (see Figure 10–12). A screening test is normally employed to give the analyst quick insight into the likelihood that a specimen contains a drug substance. This test allows a toxicologist to examine a large number of specimens within a short period of time for a wide range of drugs.

Acid
A compound capable of donating a hydrogen ion (H^+) to another compound.

Base
A compound capable of accepting a hydrogen ion (H^+).

pH Scale
A scale used to express the basicity or acidity of a substance. A pH of 7 is neutral; lower values are acidic and higher values are basic.

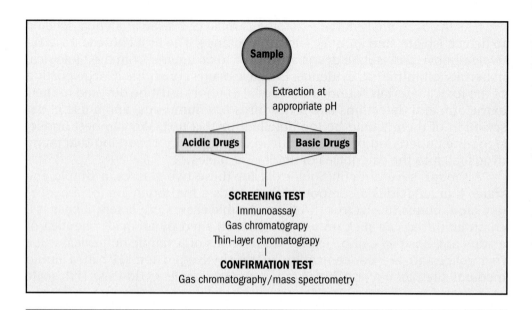

Figure 10–12 Biological fluids and tissues are extracted for acidic and basic drugs by controlling the pH of a water solution in which they are dissolved. Once this is accomplished, the toxicologist analyzes for drugs by using screening and confirmation test procedures.

Any positive results from a screening test are tentative at best and must be verified with a confirmation test.

The three most widely used screening tests are thin-layer chromatography (TLC), gas chromatography (GC), and immunoassay. The techniques of GC and TLC have already been described on pp. 135–138 and 138–142, respectively. Immunoassay has proven to be a useful screening tool in toxicology laboratories. Its principles are very different from any of the analytical techniques we have discussed so far. Basically, immunoassay is based on specific drug antibody reactions. We will learn about this concept in Chapter 12. The primary advantage of immunoassay is its ability to detect small concentrations of drugs in body fluids and organs. In fact, this technique provides the best approach for detecting the low drug levels normally associated with smoking marijuana.

The necessity of eliminating the possibility that a positive screening test may be due to a substance's having a close chemical structure to an abused drug requires the toxicologist to follow up a positive screening test with a confirmation test. Because of the potential impact of the results of a drug finding on an individual, only the most conclusive confirmation procedures should be used. **Gas chromatography/mass spectrometry is generally accepted as the confirmation test of choice.** The combination of gas chromatography and mass spectrometry provides the toxicologist with a one-step confirmation test of unequaled sensitivity and specificity (see pp. 150–153). As shown in Figure 10–13, the sample is separated into its components by the gas chromatograph. When the separated sample component leaves the column of the gas chromatograph, it enters the mass spectrometer, where it is bombarded with high-energy electrons. This bombardment causes the sample to break up into fragments, producing a fragmentation pat-

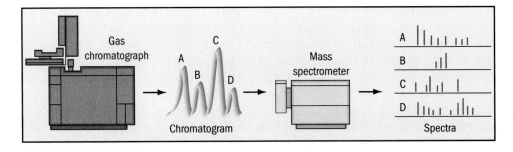

Figure 10–13 **The combination of the gas chromatograph and the mass spectrometer enables forensic toxicologists to separate the components of a drug mixture and provides specific identification of a drug substance.**

tern or mass spectrum for each sample. For most compounds, the mass spectrum represents a unique "fingerprint" pattern that can be used for identification.

There is tremendous interest in drug-testing programs conducted not only in criminal matters but for industry and government as well. Urine testing for drugs is becoming common for job applicants and employees in the workplace. Likewise, the U.S. military has an extensive drug urine-testing program for its members. Many urine-testing programs rely on private laboratories to perform the analyses. In any case, when the test results form the basis for taking action against an individual, both a screening and confirmation test must be incorporated into the testing protocol to ensure the integrity of the laboratory's conclusions.

The forensic toxicologist only occasionally encounters a group of poisons known as *heavy metals*. These include arsenic, bismuth, antimony, mercury, and thallium. To screen for many of these metals, the investigator may dissolve the suspect body fluid or tissue in a hydrochloric acid solution and insert a copper strip into the solution (the Reinsch test). The appearance of a silvery or dark coating on the copper indicates the presence of a heavy metal. Such a finding must be confirmed by the use of analytical techniques suitable for inorganic analysis—namely, atomic absorption spectrophotometry, emission spectroscopy, or X-ray diffraction.

Carbon monoxide still represents one of the most common poisons encountered in a forensic laboratory. When carbon monoxide enters the human body, it is primarily absorbed by the red blood cells, where it combines with hemoglobin to form carboxyhemoglobin. An average red blood cell contains about 280 million molecules of hemoglobin. Oxygen normally combines with hemoglobin, which transports the oxygen throughout the body. However, if a high percentage of the hemoglobin combines with carbon monoxide, not enough is left to carry sufficient oxygen to the tissues, and death by asphyxiation quickly follows.

There are two basic methods for measuring the concentration of carbon monoxide in the blood. Spectrophotometric methods examine the visible spectrum of blood to determine the amount of carboxyhemoglobin relative to oxyhemoglobin or total hemoglobin; or a volume of blood can be treated with a reagent to liberate the carbon monoxide, which is then measured by gas chromatography.

The amount of carbon monoxide in blood is generally expressed as "percent saturation." This represents the extent to which the available hemoglobin has been converted to carboxyhemoglobin. The transition from normal or occupational levels of carbon monoxide to toxic levels is not sharply defined. It depends, among other things, on the age, health, and general fitness of each individual. In a healthy middle-aged individual, a carbon monoxide blood saturation greater than 50 to 60 percent is considered fatal. However, in combination with alcohol or other depressants, fatal levels may be significantly lower. For instance, a carbon monoxide saturation of 35 to 40 percent may prove fatal in the presence of a blood-alcohol concentration of 0.20 percent w/v. Interestingly, chain smokers may have a constant carbon monoxide level of 8 to 10 percent from the carbon monoxide in cigarette smoke.

Inhaling automobile fumes is a relatively common way to commit suicide. A garden or vacuum cleaner hose is often used to connect the tailpipe with the vehicle's interior, or the engine is allowed to run in a closed garage. A level of carbon monoxide sufficient to cause death accumulates in five to ten minutes in a closed single-car garage.

The level of carbon monoxide in the blood of a victim found dead at the scene of a fire is significant in ascertaining whether foul play has occurred. High levels of carbon monoxide in the blood prove that the victim breathed the combustion products of the fire and was alive when the fire began. Many attempts at covering up a murder by setting fire to a victim's house or car have been uncovered in this manner.

The Significance of Toxicological Findings

Once a drug is found and identified, the toxicologist assesses its influence on the behavior of the individual. Interpreting the results of a toxicology find is one of the toxicologist's more difficult chores. Recall that many of the world's countries have designated a specific blood-alcohol level at which an individual is deemed under the influence of alcohol. These levels were established as a result of numerous studies conducted over several years to measure the effects of alcohol levels on driving performance. However, no such legal guidelines are available to the toxicologist who must judge how a drug other than alcohol affects an individual's performance or physical state.

For many drugs, blood concentration levels are readily determined and can be used to *estimate* the pharmacological effects of the drug on the individual. Often, when dealing with a living person, the toxicologist has the added benefit of knowing what a police officer may have observed about an individual's behavior and motor skills, as well as the outcome of a drug influence evaluation conducted by a police officer trained to be a drug recognition expert (discussed shortly). For a deceased person, drug levels in various body organs and tissues provide additional information about the individual's state at the time of death. However, before conclusions can be drawn about a drug-induced death, other factors must also be considered, including the age, physical condition, and tolerance of the drug user. With prolonged use of a drug, an individual may become less responsive to a drug's effects and tolerate blood-drug concentrations that would kill a casual drug user. Therefore, knowledge of an individual's history of drug use is important in evaluating drug concentrations. Another consideration is additive or synergistic effects of the interaction of two or more drugs, which may produce a highly intoxicated or comatose state even though none of the drugs alone is present at high or toxic levels. The combination of alcohol with tranquilizers or narcotics is a common example of a potentially lethal drug combination.

The concentration of a drug present in urine is a poor indicator of how extensively an individual's behavior or state is influenced by the drug. Urine is formed outside the body's circulatory system, and consequently drug levels can build up in it over a long period. Some drugs are found in the urine one to three days after they have been taken and long after their effects on the user have disappeared. Nevertheless, the value of this information should not be discounted. Urine drug levels, like blood levels, are best used by law enforcement authorities and the courts to corroborate other investigative and medical findings regarding an individual's condition. Hence, for an individual who is arrested for suspicion of being under the influence of a drug, a toxicologist's determinations supplement the observations of the arresting officer, including the results of a drug influence evaluation (discussed next). For a deceased person, the responsibility for establishing a cause of death rests with the medical examiner or coroner. However, before a conclusive determination is made, the examining physician depends on the forensic toxicologist to demonstrate the presence or absence of a drug or poison in the tissues or body fluids of the deceased. Only through the combined efforts of the toxicologist and the medical examiner (or coroner) can society be assured that death investigations achieve high professional and legal standards.

The Drug Recognition Expert

While recognizing alcohol-impaired performance is an expertise generally accorded to police officers by the courts, recognizing drug-induced intoxication is much more difficult and generally not part of police training. During the 1970s, the Los Angeles Police Department developed and tested a series of clinical and psychophysical examinations that a trained police officer could use to identify and differentiate between types of drug impairment. This program has evolved into a national program to train police as *drug recognition experts*. Normally, a three- to five-month training program is required to certify an officer as a drug recognition expert (DRE).

The DRE program incorporates standardized methods for examining suspects to determine whether they have taken one or more drugs. The process is systematic and standard; to ensure that each subject has been tested in a routine fashion, each DRE must complete a standard Drug Influence Evaluation form (see Figure 10–14). The entire drug evaluation takes approximately thirty to forty minutes. The components of the twelve-step process are summarized in Table 10–1.

The DRE evaluation process can suggest the presence of the following seven broad categories of drugs:

1. Central nervous system depressants

2. Central nervous system stimulants

3. Hallucinogens

4. Phencyclidine

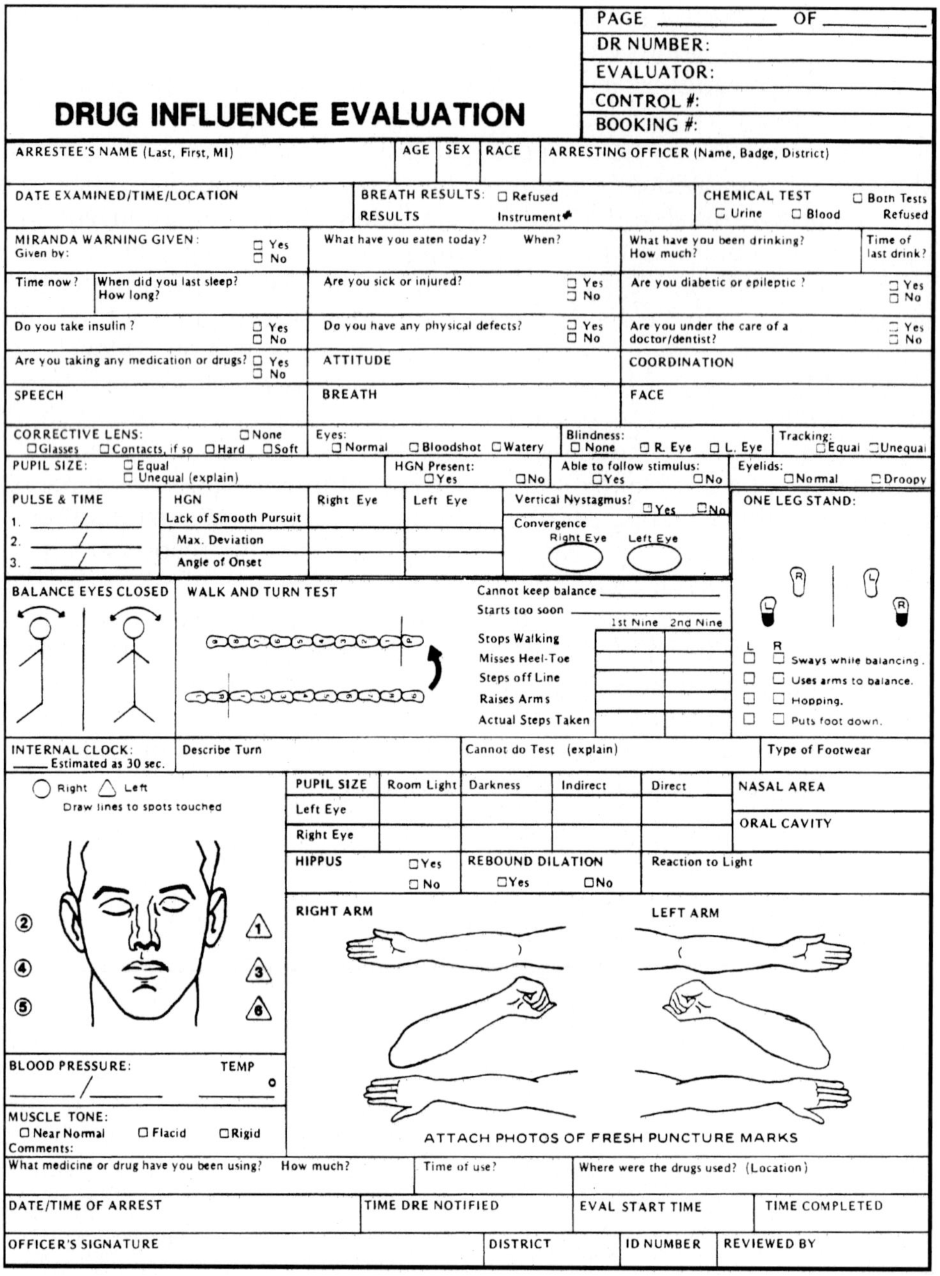

DRUG INFLUENCE EVALUATION

PAGE _____ OF _____
DR NUMBER:
EVALUATOR:
CONTROL #:
BOOKING #:

ARRESTEE'S NAME (Last, First, MI) | AGE | SEX | RACE | ARRESTING OFFICER (Name, Badge, District)

DATE EXAMINED/TIME/LOCATION | BREATH RESULTS: ☐ Refused | CHEMICAL TEST ☐ Both Tests
RESULTS Instrument ✔ | ☐ Urine ☐ Blood Refused

MIRANDA WARNING GIVEN: ☐ Yes ☐ No | What have you eaten today? When? | What have you been drinking? How much? | Time of last drink?
Given by:

Time now? When did you last sleep? How long? | Are you sick or injured? ☐ Yes ☐ No | Are you diabetic or epileptic? ☐ Yes ☐ No

Do you take insulin? ☐ Yes ☐ No | Do you have any physical defects? ☐ Yes ☐ No | Are you under the care of a doctor/dentist? ☐ Yes ☐ No

Are you taking any medication or drugs? ☐ Yes ☐ No | ATTITUDE | COORDINATION

SPEECH | BREATH | FACE

CORRECTIVE LENS: ☐ None | Eyes: ☐ Normal ☐ Bloodshot ☐ Watery | Blindness: ☐ None ☐ R. Eye ☐ L. Eye | Tracking: ☐ Equal ☐ Unequal
☐ Glasses ☐ Contacts, if so ☐ Hard ☐ Soft

PUPIL SIZE: ☐ Equal ☐ Unequal (explain) | HGN Present: ☐ Yes ☐ No | Able to follow stimulus: ☐ Yes ☐ No | Eyelids: ☐ Normal ☐ Droopy

PULSE & TIME | HGN | Right Eye | Left Eye | Vertical Nystagmus? ☐ Yes ☐ No | ONE LEG STAND:
1. ___ / ___ | Lack of Smooth Pursuit | | | Convergence
2. ___ / ___ | Max. Deviation | | | Right Eye Left Eye
3. ___ / ___ | Angle of Onset

BALANCE EYES CLOSED | WALK AND TURN TEST | Cannot keep balance _____
| | Starts too soon _____ | 1st Nine 2nd Nine
| | Stops Walking
| | Misses Heel-Toe | L R
| | Steps off Line | ☐ ☐ Sways while balancing.
| | Raises Arms | ☐ ☐ Uses arms to balance.
| | Actual Steps Taken | ☐ ☐ Hopping.
| | | ☐ ☐ Puts foot down.

INTERNAL CLOCK: _____ Estimated as 30 sec. | Describe Turn | Cannot do Test (explain) | Type of Footwear

☐ Right △ Left Draw lines to spots touched

| PUPIL SIZE | Room Light | Darkness | Indirect | Direct | NASAL AREA
Left Eye
Right Eye | | | | | ORAL CAVITY
HIPPUS ☐ Yes ☐ No | REBOUND DILATION ☐ Yes ☐ No | Reaction to Light

RIGHT ARM | LEFT ARM

② ④ ⑤ | ① ③ ⑥

ATTACH PHOTOS OF FRESH PUNCTURE MARKS

BLOOD PRESSURE: ___/___ | TEMP ___°

MUSCLE TONE: ☐ Near Normal ☐ Flacid ☐ Rigid
Comments:

What medicine or drug have you been using? | How much? | Time of use? | Where were the drugs used? (Location)

DATE/TIME OF ARREST | TIME DRE NOTIFIED | EVAL START TIME | TIME COMPLETED

OFFICER'S SIGNATURE | DISTRICT | ID NUMBER | REVIEWED BY

Figure 10–14 Drug Influence Evaluation form.

5. Inhalants

6. Narcotic analgesics

7. Cannabis

The DRE program is not designed to be a substitute for toxicological testing. The toxicologist can often determine that a suspect has a particular drug in his or her body. But the toxicologist often cannot infer with reasonable certainty that the suspect was impaired at a specific time. On the

Table 10–1 Components of the Drug Recognition Process

1. *The Breath-Alcohol Test.* By obtaining an accurate and immediate measurement of the suspect's blood-alcohol concentration, the drug recognition expert (DRE) can determine whether alcohol may be contributing to the suspect's observable impairment and whether the concentration of alcohol is sufficient to be the sole cause of that impairment.

2. *Interview with the Arresting Officer.* Spending a few minutes with the arresting officer often enables the DRE to determine the most promising areas of investigation.

3. *The Preliminary Examination.* This structured series of questions, specific observations, and simple tests provides the first opportunity to examine the suspect closely. It is designed to determine whether the suspect is suffering from an injury or from another condition unrelated to drug consumption. It also affords an opportunity to begin assessing the suspect's appearance and behavior for signs of possible drug influence.

4. *The Eye Examination.* Certain categories of drugs induce nystagmus, an involuntary, spasmodic motion of the eyeball. Nystagmus is an indicator of drug-induced impairment. The inability of the eyes to converge toward the bridge of the nose also indicates the possible presence of certain types of drugs.

5. *Divided-Attention Psychophysical Tests.* These tests check balance and physical orientation and include the walk and turn, the one-leg stand, the Romberg balance, and the finger-to-nose.

6. *Vital Signs Examinations.* Precise measurements of blood pressure, pulse rate, and body temperature are taken. Certain drugs elevate these signs; others depress them.

7. *Dark Room Examinations.* The size of the suspect's pupils in room light, near-total darkness, indirect light, and direct light is checked. Some drugs cause the pupils to either dilate or constrict.

8. *Examination for Muscle Rigidity.* Certain categories of drugs cause the muscles to become hypertense and quite rigid. Others may cause the muscles to relax and become flaccid.

9. *Examination for Injection Sites.* Users of certain categories of drugs routinely or occasionally inject their drugs. Evidence of needle use may be found on veins along the neck, arms, and hands.

10. *Suspect's Statements and Other Observations.* The next step is to attempt to interview the suspect concerning the drug or drugs he or she has ingested. Of course, the interview must be conducted in full compliance of the suspect's constitutional rights.

11. *Opinions of the Evaluator.* Using the information obtained in the previous ten steps, the DRE is able to make an informed decision about whether the suspect is impaired by drugs and, if so, what category or combination of categories is the probable cause of the impairment.

12. *The Toxicological Examination.* The DRE should obtain a blood or urine sample from the suspect for laboratory analysis in order to secure scientific, admissible evidence to substantiate his or her conclusions.

other hand, the DRE can supply credible evidence that the suspect was impaired at a specific time and that the nature of the impairment was consistent with a particular family of drugs. But the DRE program usually cannot determine which specific drug was ingested. Proving drug intoxication requires a coordinated effort and the production of competent data from both the DRE and the forensic toxicologist.

Chapter Summary

Toxicologists detect and identify the presence of drugs and poisons in body fluids, tissues, and organs. A major branch of forensic toxicology deals with the measurement of alcohol in the body for matters that pertain to violations of criminal law. Alcohol appears in the blood within minutes after it has been taken by mouth and slowly increases in concentration while it is being absorbed from the stomach and the small intestine into the bloodstream. When all the alcohol has been absorbed, a maximum alcohol level is reached in the blood and the postabsorption period begins. Then the alcohol concentration slowly decreases until a zero level is again reached. Alcohol is eliminated from the body through oxidation and excretion. Oxidation takes place almost entirely in the liver, while alcohol is excreted unchanged in the breath, urine, and perspiration. The extent to which an individual is under the influence of alcohol is usually determined by measuring the quantity of alcohol in the blood or the breath. Breath testers that operate on the principle of infrared light absorption are becoming increasingly popular within the law enforcement community.

Many types of breath testers analyze a set volume of breath. The sampled breath is exposed to infrared light. The degree of interaction of the light with alcohol in the breath sample allows the instrument to measure a blood alcohol concentration in breath. These breath-testing devices operate on the principle that the ratio between the concentration of alcohol in deep-lung or alveolar breath and its concentration in blood is fixed. Most breath-test devices have set the ratio of alcohol in the blood to alcohol in alveolar air at 2,100 to 1.

Law enforcement officers typically use field sobriety tests to estimate a motorist's degree of physical impairment by alcohol and whether an evidential test for alcohol is justified. The horizontal-gaze nystagmus test, walk and turn, and the one-leg stand are all reliable and effective psychophysical tests.

Gas chromatography is the most widely used approach for determining alcohol levels in blood. Blood must always be drawn under medically accepted conditions by a qualified individual. A nonalcoholic disinfectant must be applied before the suspect's skin is penetrated with a sterile needle or lancet. Once blood is removed from an individual, it is best preserved sealed in an airtight container after adding an anticoagulant and a preservative.

The forensic toxicologist must devise an analytical scheme to detect, isolate, and identify toxic drug substances. Once the drug has been extracted from appropriate biological fluids, tissues, and organs, the forensic toxicologist can identify the drug substance. The strategy for identifying abused drugs entails a two-step approach: screening and confirmation. A screening test gives the analyst quick insight into the likelihood that a specimen contains a drug substance. Positive results from a screening test are tentative at best and must be verified with a confirmation test. The most widely used screening tests are thin-layer chromatography, gas chromatography, and immunoassay. Gas chromatography/mass spectrometry is generally accepted as the confirmation test of choice. Once the drug is extracted and identified, the toxicologist may be required to judge the drug's effect on an individual's natural performance or physical state. The Drug Recognition Expert program incorporates standardized methods for examining automobile drivers suspected of being under the influence of drugs. But the DRE program usually cannot determine which specific drug was ingested. Hence, reliable data from both the DRE and the forensic toxicologist are required to prove drug intoxication.

Review Questions

1. The most heavily abused drug in the Western world is _____.

2. True or False: Toxicologists are employed only by crime laboratories. _____

3. The amount of alcohol in the blood (is, is not) directly proportional to the concentration of alcohol in the brain.

4. True or False: Blood levels have become the accepted standard for relating alcohol intake to its effect on the body. _____

5. Alcohol consumed on an empty stomach is absorbed (faster, slower) than an equivalent amount of alcohol taken when there is food in the stomach.

6. Under normal drinking conditions, alcohol concentration in the blood peaks in _____ to _____ minutes.

7. In the postabsorption period, alcohol is distributed uniformly among the _____ portions of the body.

8. Alcohol is eliminated from the body by _____ and _____.

9. Ninety-five to 98 percent of the alcohol is _____ to carbon dioxide and water.

10. Oxidation of alcohol takes place almost entirely in the _____.

11. The amount of alcohol exhaled in the _____ is directly proportional to the concentration of alcohol in the blood.

12. Alcohol is eliminated from the blood at an average rate of _____ percent w/v.

13. Alcohol is absorbed into the blood from the _____ and _____.

14. A(n) _____ carries blood away from the heart; a(n) _____ carries blood back to the heart.

15. The _____ artery carries deoxygenated blood from the heart to the lungs.

16. Alcohol passes from the blood capillaries into the _____ sacs in the lungs.

17. One milliliter of blood contains the same amount of alcohol as approximately _____ milliliters of alveolar breath.

18. When alcohol is being absorbed into the blood, the alcohol concentration in venous blood is (higher, lower) than that in arterial blood.

19. The Breathalyzer and similar devices are designed to measure the alcohol content of _____ breath.

20. Most modern breath testers use _____ radiation to detect and measure alcohol in the breath.

21. To avoid the possibility of "mouth alcohol" the operator of a breath tester must not allow the subject to take any foreign materials into the mouth for _____ minutes prior to the test.

22. Alcohol can be separated from other volatiles in blood and quantitated by the technique of _____.

23. Roadside breath testers that utilize a _____ detector are becoming increasingly popular with the law enforcement community.

24. True or False: Portable handheld roadside breath testers for alcohol provide evidential test results. _____

25. Usually, when a person's blood-alcohol concentration is in the range of 0.10 percent, horizontal-gaze nystagmus begins before the eyeball has moved _____ degrees to the side.

26. When drawing blood for alcohol testing, the suspect's skin must first be wiped with a _____ disinfectant.

27. Failure to add a preservative, such as sodium fluoride, to blood removed from a living person may lead to a(n) (decline, increase) in alcohol concentration.

28. Most states have established _____ percent w/v as the impairment limit for blood-alcohol concentration.

29. In the case of _____, the Supreme Court ruled that taking nontestimonial evidence, such as a blood sample, did not violate a suspect's Fifth Amendment rights.

30. Heroin is changed upon entering the body into _____.

31. The body fluids _____ and _____ are both desirable for the toxicological examination of a living person suspected of being under the influence of a drug.

32. A large number of drugs can be classified chemically as _____ and _____.

33. Water with a pH value (less, greater) than 7 is basic.

34. Barbiturates are classified as _____ drugs.

35. Drugs are extracted from body fluids and tissues by carefully controlling the _____ of the medium in which the sample has been dissolved.

36. The technique of _____ is based on specific drug antibody reactions.

37. Both _____ and _____ tests must be incorporated into the drug-testing protocol of a toxicology laboratory to ensure the correctness of the laboratory's conclusions.

38. The gas _____ combines with hemoglobin in the blood to form carboxyhemoglobin, thus interfering with the transportation of oxygen in the blood.

39. The amount of carbon monoxide in blood is usually expressed as _____.

40. True or False: Blood levels of drugs can alone be used to draw definitive conclusions about the effects of a drug on an individual. _____

41. Interaction of alcohol and barbiturates in the body can produce a(n) _____ effect.

42. The level of a drug present in the urine is by itself a (good, poor) indicator of how extensively an individual is affected by a drug.

43. Urine and blood drug levels are best used by law enforcement authorities and the courts to _____ other investigative and medical findings pertaining to an individual's condition.

44. The _____ program incorporates standardized methods for examining suspects to determine whether they have taken one or more drugs.

Further References

Benjamin, David M., "Forensic Pharmacology," in R. Saferstein, ed., *Forensic Science Handbook,* vol. 3. Upper Saddle River, N.J.: Prentice Hall, 1993.

Caplan, Y. H., and J. R. Zettl, "The Determination of Alcohol in Blood and Breath," in R. Saferstein, ed., *Forensic Science Handbook,* vol. 1, 2nd ed., Upper Saddle River, N.J.: Prentice Hall, 2002.

Couper, F. J. and B. K. Logan, *Drugs and Human Performance.* Washington, D.C.: National Highway Traffic Safety Administration, 2004, www.nhtsa.dot.gov/people/injury/research/job185drugs/technical-page.htm.

Fenton, John J., *Toxicology: A Case-Oriented Approach.* Boca Raton, Fla.: Taylor & Francis, 2002.

Garriott, James C., ed., *Medicolegal Aspects of Alcohol,* 4th ed. Tucson, Ariz.: Lawyers & Judges, 2004.

Karch, S. B., ed., *Drug Abuse Handbook.* Boca Raton, Fla.: Taylor & Francis, 1998.

Levine, B., ed., *Principles of Forensic Toxicology,* 2nd ed. Washington, D.C.: AACC Press, 2003.

The Oklahoma City Bombing

It was the biggest act of mass murder in U.S. history. On a sunny spring morning in April 1995, a Ryder rental truck pulled into the parking area of the Alfred P. Murrah federal building in Oklahoma City. The driver stepped down from the truck's cab and casually walked away. Minutes later, the truck exploded into a fireball, unleashing enough energy to destroy the building and kill 168 people, including 19 children and infants in the building's day care center. Later that morning, an Oklahoma Highway Patrol officer pulled over a beat-up 1977 Mercury Marquis being driven without a license plate. On further investigation, the driver, Timothy McVeigh, was found to be in possession of a loaded firearm and charged with transporting a firearm.

At the explosion site, remnants of the Ryder truck were located and the truck was quickly traced to a renter—Robert Kling, an alias for Timothy McVeigh. Coincidentally, the rental agreement and McVeigh's driver's license both used the address of McVeigh's friend, Terry Nichols.

Outrage at the destruction of the Branch Davidian compound at Waco had spurred McVeigh and Nichols into planning the destruction of the federal building. Investigators later recovered McVeigh's fingerprint on a receipt for 2,000 pounds of ammonium nitrate, a basic explosive ingredient. Forensic analysts also located PETN residues on the clothing McVeigh wore on the day of his arrest. PETN is a component of detonating cord. A jury took three days to decide McVeigh's guilt and then sentenced McVeigh to die by lethal injection.

chapter 11

Forensic Aspects of **Arson** and **Explosion** Investigations

Key Terms

accelerant
black powder
combustion
deflagration
detonating cord
detonation
endothermic reaction
energy
exothermic reaction
explosion
flammable range
flash point
glowing combustion
heat of combustion
high explosive
hydrocarbon
ignition temperature
low explosive
modus operandi
oxidation
oxidizing agent
primary explosive
pyrolysis
safety fuse
secondary explosive
smokeless powder (double-base)
smokeless powder (single-base)
spontaneous combustion

Modus Operandi
An offender's pattern of operation.

Arson and explosions often present complex and difficult circumstances to investigate. Normally, these incidents are committed at the convenience of a perpetrator who has thoroughly planned the criminal act and has left the crime scene long before any official investigation is launched. Furthermore, proving commission of the offense is more difficult because of the extensive destruction that frequently dominates the crime scene. The contribution of the criminalist is only one aspect of a comprehensive and difficult investigative process that must establish a motive, the modus operandi, and a suspect.

The criminalist's function is rather limited; usually he or she is expected only to detect and identify relevant chemical materials collected at the scene and to reconstruct and identify igniters or detonating mechanisms. Although a chemist can identify trace amounts of gasoline or kerosene in debris, no scientific test can determine whether an arsonist has used a pile of rubbish or paper to start a fire. Furthermore, a fire can have many accidental causes, including faulty wiring, overheated electric motors, improperly cleaned and regulated heating systems, and cigarette smoking—which usually leave no chemical traces. Thus, the final determination of the cause of a fire or explosion must consider numerous factors and requires an extensive on-site investigation. The ultimate determination must be made by an investigator whose training and knowledge have been augmented by the practical experiences of fire and explosion investigation.

The Chemistry of Fire

Humankind's early search to explain the physical concepts underlying the behavior of matter always bestowed a central and fundamental role on fire. To ancient Greek philosophers, fire was one of the four basic elements from which all matter was derived. The alchemist thought of fire as an instrument of transformation, to be used for changing one element into another. One ancient recipe expresses its mystical power as follows: "Now the substance of cinnabar is such that the more it is heated, the more exquisite are its sublimations. Cinnabar will become mercury, and passing through a series of other sublimations, it is again turned into cinnabar, and thus it enables man to enjoy eternal life."

Today, we know of fire not as an element of matter but as a transformation process during which oxygen is united with some other substance to produce noticeable quantities of heat and light (a flame). Therefore, any insight into why and how a fire is initiated and sustained must begin with the knowledge of the fundamental chemical reaction of fire—oxidation.

Oxidation
The combination of oxygen with other substances to produce new substances.

In a simple description of oxidation, oxygen combines with other substances to produce new products. Thus, we may write the chemical equation for the burning of methane gas, a major component of natural gas, as follows:

$$CH_4 \quad + \quad 2O_2 \quad \longrightarrow \quad CO_2 \quad + \quad 2H_2O$$

methane   oxygen yields carbon dioxide   water

However, not all oxidation proceeds in the manner that one associates with fire. For example, oxygen combines with many metals to form oxides. Thus, iron forms a red-brown iron oxide, or rust, as follows:

$$4Fe \quad + \quad 3O_2 \quad \longrightarrow \quad 2Fe_2O_3$$

iron   oxygen yields iron oxide

Yet chemical equations do not give us a complete insight into the oxidation process. We must consider other factors to understand all of the implications of oxidation or, for that matter, any other chemical reaction. When methane unites with oxygen, it burns; but the mere mixing of methane and oxygen will not produce a fire, nor, for example, will gasoline burn when it is simply exposed to air. However, light a match in the presence of any one of these fuel–air mixtures (assuming proper proportions) and you have an instant fire. What are the reasons behind these differences? Why do some oxidations proceed with the outward appearances that we associate with a fire while others do not? Why do we need a match to initiate some oxidations while others proceed at room temperature? The explanation lies in a fundamental but abstract concept—energy.

Energy can be defined as the capacity for doing work. Energy takes many forms, such as heat energy, electrical energy, mechanical energy, nuclear energy, light energy, and chemical energy. For example, when methane is burned, the stored chemical energy in methane is converted to energy in the form of heat and light. This heat may be used to boil water or to provide high-pressure steam to turn a turbine. This is an example of converting chemical energy to heat energy to mechanical energy. The turbine can then be used to generate electricity, transforming mechanical energy to electrical energy. Electrical energy may then be used to turn a motor. In other words, energy can enable work to be done; heat is energy.

The quantity of heat from a chemical reaction comes from the breaking and formation of chemical bonds. Methane is a molecule composed of one carbon atom bonded with four hydrogen atoms:

$$\begin{array}{c} H \\ | \\ H-C-H \\ | \\ H \end{array}$$

An oxygen molecule forms when two atoms of the element oxygen bond:

$$O=O$$

In chemical changes, atoms are not lost but merely redistributed during the chemical reaction; thus, the products of methane's oxidation will be carbon dioxide:

$$O=C=O$$

and water:

$$H-O-H$$

Energy

The combined ability or potential of a system or material to do work. Some forms of energy are heat energy, chemical energy, and electrical energy.

This rearrangement, however, means that the bonds holding the atoms together must be broken and new bonds formed. We now have arrived at a fundamental observation in our dissection of a chemical reaction—that molecules must absorb energy to break apart their chemical bonds, and that they liberate energy when their bonds are reformed. The amount of energy needed to break a bond and the quantity of energy liberated when a bond is formed are characteristic of the type of chemical bond involved. Hence, a chemical reaction involves a change in energy content; energy is going in and energy is given off. The quantities of energies involved are different for each reaction and are determined by the participants of the chemical reaction.

All oxidation reactions, including the combustion of methane, are examples of reactions in which more energy is liberated than what is required to break the various bonds. This excess energy is liberated as heat and often as light and is known as the heat of combustion. Such reactions are said to be exothermic. Table 11–1 summarizes the heats of combustion of some important fuels in fire investigation.

Although we will not be concerned with them, some reactions require more energy than they will eventually liberate. These reactions are known as endothermic reactions.

Thus, all reactions require an energy input to start them. We can think of this requirement as an invisible energy barrier between the reactants and the products of a reaction (see Figure 11–1). The higher this barrier, the more energy required to initiate the reaction. Where does this initial energy come from? There are many sources of energy; however, for the purpose of this discussion we need to look at only one—heat.

The energy barrier in the conversion of iron to rust is relatively small, and it can be surmounted with the help of heat energy present in the surrounding environment at normal outdoor temperatures. Not so for methane or gasoline; these energy barriers are quite high, and a high temperature must be applied to start the oxidation of these fuels. Hence, before any fire can result, the temperature of these fuels must be raised to a value that will

Combustion
Rapid combination of oxygen with another substance accompanied by the production of noticeable heat and light.

Heat of Combustion
The heat liberated during combustion.

Exothermic Reaction
A chemical transformation in which heat energy is liberated.

Endothermic Reaction
A chemical transformation in which heat energy is absorbed from the surroundings.

Table 11–1 Heats of Combustion of Fuels

Fuel	Heat of Combustion[a]
Crude oil	19,650 Btu/gal
Diesel fuel	19,550 Btu/lb
Gasoline	19,250 Btu/lb
Methane	995 Btu/cu ft
Natural gas	128–1,868 Btu/cu ft
Octane	121,300 Btu/gal
Wood	7,500 Btu/lb
Coal, bituminous	11,000–14,000 Btu/lb
Anthracite	13,351 Btu/lb

[a]Btu (British thermal unit) is defined as the quantity of heat required to raise the temperature of 1 pound of water 1°F at or near its point of maximum density.

Source: John D. DeHaan, *Kirk's Fire Investigation*, 2nd ed. Upper Saddle River, N.J.: Prentice Hall, 1983.

allow the heat energy input to exceed the energy barrier. Table 11–2 shows that this temperature, known as the ignition temperature, is quite high for common fuels. Once the combustion starts, enough heat is liberated to keep the reaction going by itself. In essence, the fire becomes a chain reaction, absorbing a portion of its own liberated heat to generate even more heat. The fire will burn until either the oxygen or the fuel is exhausted.

Normally, a lighted match provides a convenient igniter of fuels. However, the fire investigator must also consider other potential sources of ignition—for example, electrical discharges, sparks, and chemicals—while reconstructing the initiation of a fire. All of these sources have temperatures in excess of what is needed to meet the ignition temperature requirements of most fuels.

Although the liberation of energy explains many important features of oxidation, it does not completely explain all characteristics of the reaction. Obviously, although all oxidations liberate energy, they are not all accompanied by the presence of a flame; witness the oxidation of iron to rust. Therefore, one other important consideration will make our understanding of oxidation and fire complete: **the rate or speed at which the reaction takes place.**

We can picture a chemical reaction, such as oxidation, taking place when molecules combine or collide with one another. Essentially, the faster the molecules move, the greater the number of collisions between them

Ignition Temperature
The minimum temperature at which a fuel will spontaneously ignite.

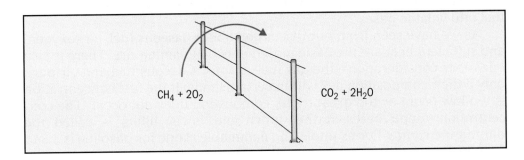

Figure 11–1 An energy barrier must be hurdled before reactants such as methane and oxygen can combine with one another to form the products of carbon dioxide and water.

Table 11–2 Ignition Temperatures of Some Common Fuels	
Fuel	Ignition Temperature, °F
Acetone	869
Benzene	928
Fuel oil #2	495
Gasoline (low octane)	536
Kerosene (fuel oil #1)	410
n-Octane	428
Petroleum ether	550
Turpentine	488

Source: John D. DeHaan, *Kirk's Fire Investigation*, 5th ed. Upper Saddle River, N.J.: Prentice Hall, 2002.

and the faster the rate of reaction. Many factors influence the rate of these collisions. In our description of fire and oxidation, we consider only two: the physical state of the fuel and the temperature.

A fuel achieves a reaction rate with oxygen sufficient to produce a flame only when it is in the gaseous state, for only in this state can molecules collide frequently enough to support a flaming fire. This remains true whether the fuel is a solid such as wood, paper, cloth, or plastic, or a liquid such as gasoline or kerosene. How then does a liquid or solid maintain a gaseous reaction? In the case of a liquid fuel, the temperature must be high enough to vaporize the fuel. The vapor that forms burns when it mixes with oxygen and combusts as a flame. The flash point is the *lowest* temperature at which a liquid gives off sufficient vapor to form a mixture with air that will support combustion. Once the flash point is reached, the fuel can be ignited by some outside source of temperature to start a fire. The ignition temperature is always considerably higher than the flash point. For example, gasoline has a flash point of $-50°F$; however, an ignition temperature of $495°F$ is needed to start a gasoline fire. With a solid fuel, the process of generating vapor is more complex. Wood, or any other solid fuel, burns only when it is exposed to heat that is hot enough to decompose the solid into gaseous products. This chemical breakdown of solid material is known as pyrolysis. The numerous gaseous products of pyrolysis combine with oxygen to produce a fire. Here again, fire can be described as a chain reaction. A match or other source of heat initiates the pyrolysis of the solid fuel, the gaseous products react with oxygen in the air to produce heat and light, and this heat in turn pyrolyzes more solid fuel into volatile gases.

As we have seen from our discussion about gaseous fuel, air (oxygen) and sufficient heat are the basic ingredients of a flaming fire. There is also one other consideration—the gas fuel–air mix. Gaseous fuel and air burn only if their composition lies within certain limits. If the fuel concentration is too low (lean) or too great (rich), combustion does not occur. The concentration range between the upper and lower limits is called the flammable range. For example, the flammable range for gasoline is 1.3 to 6.0 percent.

Although a flaming fire can be supported only by a gaseous fuel, in some instances a fuel can burn without the presence of a flame. Witness a burning cigarette or the red glow of hot charcoals. These are examples of a phenomenon known as glowing combustion or *smoldering*. Here, combustion is taking place on the surface of a solid fuel in the absence of heat high enough to pyrolyze the fuel. Interestingly, this phenomenon generally ensues long after the flames have gone out. Wood, for example, tends to burn with a flame until all of its pyrolyzable components have been expended; however, wood's carbonaceous residue continues to smolder long after the flame has extinguished itself.

We may now consider the conversion of iron to rust as an example of an extremely slow oxidation process, a situation that exists because of the inability of the iron atoms to achieve a gaseous state. For this reason, the combination of oxygen with iron to produce rust is restricted to the surface area of the metal exposed to air, a limitation that severely reduces the rate of reaction. On the other hand, the reaction of methane and oxygen is an example of oxidation in which all the reactants are in the gaseous state. Hence, this reaction proceeds rapidly, as reflected by the production of noticeable quantities of heat and light (a flame).

Flash Point
The minimum temperature at which a liquid fuel produces enough vapor to burn.

Pyrolysis
The decomposition of organic matter by heat.

Flammable Range
The entire range of possible gas or vapor fuel concentrations in air that are capable of burning.

Glowing Combustion
Burning at the fuel–air interface. Examples are a red-hot charcoal or a burning cigarette.

Most typically, the rate of a chemical reaction increases when the temperature is raised. The magnitude of the increase in rate with temperature varies from one reaction to another and also from one temperature range to another. For most reactions, a 10°C (18°F) rise in temperature doubles or triples the reaction rate. This observation explains in part why burning is so rapid. As the fire spreads, it raises the temperature of the fuel–air mixture, thus increasing the rate of reaction; this in turn generates more heat, again increasing the rate of reaction. Only when the fuel or oxygen is depleted will this vicious cycle come to a halt.

One rather interesting phenomenon often invoked by arson suspects as being the cause of a fire is spontaneous combustion. Actually, the conditions under which spontaneous combustion can develop are rather limited and rarely account for the cause of a fire. Spontaneous combustion is the result of a natural heat-producing process in poorly ventilated containers or areas. For example, hay stored in barns provides an excellent growing medium for bacteria whose activities generate heat. If the hay is not properly ventilated, the heat builds to a level that supports other types of heat-producing chemical reactions in the hay. Eventually, as the heat rises, the ignition temperature of hay is reached, spontaneously setting off a fire.

Another known example of spontaneous combustion involves the ignition of improperly ventilated containers containing rags soaked with certain types of highly unsaturated oils, such as linseed oil. Heat can build up to the point of ignition as a result of a slow heat-producing chemical oxidation between the air and the oil. Of course, storage conditions must encourage the accumulation of the heat over a prolonged period of time. However, spontaneous combustion does not occur with hydrocarbon lubricating oils, and it is not expected to occur with most household fats and oils.

Until now we have referred only to oxidation reactions that rely on air as the sole source of oxygen. However, we need not restrict ourselves to this type of situation. For example, explosives are substances that undergo a rapid exothermic oxidation reaction, producing large quantities of gases. This sudden buildup of gas pressure constitutes an explosion. Detonation occurs so rapidly that oxygen in the air cannot participate in the reaction; thus, many explosives must have their own source of oxygen. Chemicals that supply oxygen are known as oxidizing agents. One such agent is found in black powder, a low explosive, which is composed of a mixture of the following chemical ingredients:

> 75 percent potassium nitrate (KNO_3)
> 15 percent charcoal (C)
> 10 percent sulfur (S)

In this combination, oxygen containing potassium nitrate acts as an oxidizing agent for the charcoal and sulfur fuels. As heat is applied to black powder, oxygen is liberated from potassium nitrate and simultaneously combines with charcoal and sulfur to produce heat and gases (symbolized by ↑), as represented in the following chemical equation:

$$3C \quad + \quad S \quad + \quad 2KNO_3 \quad \longrightarrow \quad 3CO_2\uparrow \quad + \quad N_2\uparrow \quad + \quad K_2S$$

| carbon | sulfur | potassium nitrate | yields | carbon dioxide | nitrogen | potassium sulfide |

Spontaneous Combustion
A fire caused by a natural heat-producing process in the presence of sufficient air and fuel.

Oxidizing Agent
A substance that supplies oxygen to a chemical reaction.

Some explosives have their oxygen and fuel components combined within one molecule. For example, the chemical structure of nitroglycerin, the major constituent of dynamite, combines carbon, hydrogen, nitrogen, and oxygen:

$$
\begin{array}{ccc}
\text{H} & \text{H} & \text{H} \\
| & | & | \\
\text{H} - \text{C} - \text{C} - \text{C} - \text{H} \\
| & | & | \\
\text{NO}_2 & \text{NO}_2 & \text{NO}_2
\end{array}
$$

When nitroglycerin detonates, large quantities of energy are released as the molecule decomposes, and the oxygen recombines to produce large volumes of carbon dioxide, nitrogen, and water.

In summary, three requirements must be satisfied if combustion is to be initiated and sustained:

1. A fuel must be present.

2. Oxygen must be available in sufficient quantity to combine with the fuel.

3. Heat must be applied to initiate the combustion, and sufficient heat must be generated to sustain the reaction.

Searching the Fire Scene

The arson investigator should begin examining a fire scene for signs of arson as soon as the fire has been extinguished. Time is constantly working against the arson investigator. Most arsons are started with petroleum-based accelerants such as gasoline or kerosene. Any petroleum residues that remain after the fire is extinguished may evaporate within a few days or even hours. Furthermore, safety and health conditions may necessitate that cleanup and salvage operations begin as quickly as possible. Once this occurs, a meaningful investigation of the fire scene will be impossible.

The need to begin an *immediate* investigation of the circumstances surrounding a fire even takes precedence over the requirement to obtain a search warrant to enter and search the premises. The Supreme Court, in explaining its position on this issue, stated in part:

> . . . Fire officials are charged not only with extinguishing fires, but with finding their causes. Prompt determination of the fire's origin may be necessary to prevent its recurrence, as through the detection of continuing dangers such as faulty wiring or a defective furnace. Immediate investigation may also be necessary to preserve evidence from intentional or accidental destruction. And, of course, the sooner the officials complete their duties, the less will be their subsequent interference with the privacy and the recovery efforts of the victims. For these reasons, officials need no warrant to remain in a building for a reasonable time to investigate the cause of a blaze after it has been extinguished. And if the warrantless entry to put out the fire and determine its cause is constitutional, the warrantless seizure of evidence while inspecting the premises for these purposes also is constitutional. . . .

In determining what constitutes a reasonable time to investigate, appropriate recognition must be given to the exigencies that confront offi-

Accelerant
Any material used to start or sustain a fire. The most common accelerants are combustible liquids.

Figure 11-2 Irregularly shaped pattern on the ground resulting from a poured ignitable liquid. *Courtesy Franklin County Crime Scene Unit, North Carolina*

cials serving under these conditions, as well as to individuals' reasonable expectations of privacy.[1]

A search of the fire scene must focus on finding the fire's origin, which will prove most productive in any search for an accelerant or ignition device. In a search to determine the specific point of origin of a fire, the investigator may uncover telltale signs of arson. For instance, there may be evidence of separate and unconnected fires or the use of "streamers" to spread the fire from one area to another. For example, the arsonist may have spread a trail of gasoline or paper to cause the fire to move rapidly from one room to another. Additionally, the presence of containers capable of holding an accelerant or the finding of an ignition device ranging in sophistication from a candle to a time-delay device certainly will arouse suspicions of an arson-caused fire. Another telltale sign of arson is the existence of an irregularly shaped pattern on a floor or on the ground (see Figure 11-2) resulting from pouring an accelerant onto the surface. Investigators should simultaneously look for signs of breaking and entering and theft, and they should begin interviewing any eyewitnesses to the fire.

There are no fast and simple rules for identifying a fire's origin. Normally, a fire tends to move in an upward direction, and thus the probable origin is most likely closest to the lowest point that shows the most intense characteristics of burning. Sometimes as the fire burns upward, a V-shaped pattern forms against a vertical wall, as shown in Figure 11-3. However, many factors can contribute to the deviation of a fire from normal behavior. Prevailing drafts and winds; secondary fires due to collapsing floors and roofs; the physical arrangement of the burning structure; stairways and elevator shafts; holes in the floor, wall, or roof; and the effects of the firefighter in suppressing the fire are all factors that the knowledgeable fire investigator must consider before determining conclusive

---

[1] *Michigan v. Tyler,* 436 U.S. 499 (1978).

Figure 11–3 **Typical V patterns illustrating upward movement of the fire.** *Courtesy John Lentini*

findings. Because flammable liquids always flow to the lowest point, more severe burning found on the floor than on the ceiling may indicate the presence of an accelerant. If a flammable liquid was used, charring is expected to be more intense on the bottom of furniture, shelves, and other items rather than the top.

Once located, the point of origin should be protected to permit careful investigation. As at any crime scene, nothing should be touched or moved before notes, sketches, and photographs are taken. An examination must also be made for possible accidental causes, as well as for evidence of arson. The most common materials used by an arsonist to ensure the rapid spread and intensity of a fire are gasoline and kerosene or, for that matter, any volatile flammable liquid. Fortunately, only under the most ideal conditions will combustible liquids be entirely consumed during a fire. When the liquid is poured over a large area, it is highly likely that a portion of it will seep into a porous surface, such as cracks in the floor, upholstery, rags, plaster, wallboards, or carpet, where enough of it remains unchanged that it can be detected in the crime laboratory. In addition, when a fire is extinguished with water, the rate of evaporation of volatile fluids may be slowed, because water cools and covers materials through which the combustible liquid may have soaked. Fortunately, the presence of water does not interfere with laboratory methods used to detect and characterize flammable liquid residues.

The fire investigator's search for traces of flammable liquid residues may be aided by the use of a highly sensitive portable vapor detector or "sniffer" (see Figure 11–4). This device can rapidly screen suspect materials for the presence of volatile residues by sucking in the air surrounding the questioned sample. The air is passed over a heated filament; if a combustible vapor is present, it oxidizes and immediately increases the temperature of the filament. The rise in filament temperature is then registered as a deflection on the detector's meter. Of course, such a device is not a conclusive test for a flammable vapor, but it does provide the investigator with an excellent screening device for checking suspect samples at the fire scene. Another approach is to use dogs that have been trained and conditioned to recognize the odor of hydrocarbon accelerants.

The first fire-research laboratory in the United States has recently become operational. The Fire Research Laboratory, constructed by the U.S. government and located in Maryland, performs research on the determina-

Figure 11–4 Portable hydrocarbon detector. *Courtesy Sirchie Finger Print Laboratories, Inc., Youngsville, N.C., www.sirchie.com*

tion of fire origin and cause, fire growth and spread, and fire-scene reconstruction. This facility provides investigators and researchers with the tools necessary to reconstruct and test key aspects of most fire scenarios encountered by fire investigators in the field. The laboratory can perform anything from small-scale fire tests to full-scale testing of residential structures. It has several large test cells (rooms) where full-scale test fires can be conducted.

Collection and Preservation of Arson Evidence

As a matter of routine, two to three quarts of ash and soot debris must be collected at the point of origin of a fire when arson is suspected. The collection should include all porous materials and all other substances thought likely to contain flammable residues. These include such things as wood flooring, rugs, upholstery, and rags. Specimens are to be immediately packaged in airtight containers so no loss of possible residues can occur through evaporation. New, clean paint cans with friction lids are good containers because they are low cost, airtight, and unbreakable and are available in a variety of sizes (see Figure 11–5). Wide-mouthed glass jars are also useful for packaging suspect specimens, provided that they contain airtight lids. Cans and jars should be filled one-half to two-thirds full, leaving an air space in the container above the debris. Large bulky samples should be cut to size at the scene as needed so that they will fit into available containers. Plastic polyethylene bags are not suitable for packaging specimens because they react with hydrocarbons and permit volatile hydrocarbon vapors to be depleted.

The collection of all materials suspected of containing volatile liquids must be accompanied by a thorough sampling of similar but uncontaminated control specimens from another area of the fire scene. This is known as *substrate control*. For example, if an investigator collects carpeting at the point of origin, he or she must sample the same carpet from another part of the room, where it can be reasonably assumed that no flammable substance was placed. In the laboratory, the criminalist checks the substrate control to be sure that it is free of any flammables. This procedure reduces the possibility and subsequent argument that the carpet was exposed to a flammable liquid such as a cleaning solution during normal maintenance. In addition, laboratory tests on the unburned control material may help analyze the breakdown products from the material's exposure to intense heat during the fire. This is because common materials such as plastic floor tiles, carpet, linoleum, and adhesives can produce volatile

Figure 11–5 Various sizes of paint cans suitable for collecting debris at fire scenes. *Courtesy Sirchie Finger Print Laboratories, Inc., Youngsville, N.C., www.sirchie.com*

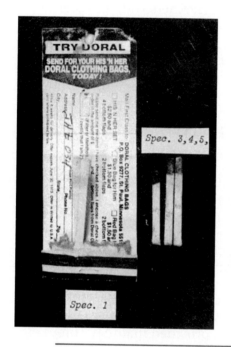

Figure 11–6 Three matches (Spec. 3, 4, 5) discarded at the scene of an arson are each shown to fit into a matchbook (Spec. 1) found in the suspect's possession. Such evidence provides a strong link between the crime scene and the suspect. *Courtesy New Jersey State Police*

hydrocarbons when they are burned. These breakdown products can sometimes be mistaken for an accelerant.

Fluids found in open bottles or cans must be collected and sealed. Even when such containers appear empty, the investigator is wise to seal and preserve them in case they contain trace amounts of liquids or vapors. At the same time, a thorough search of the scene should be undertaken for igniters. The most common igniter is a match. Normally, the match is completely consumed during a fire and is impossible to locate. However, there have been cases in which, by force of habit, matches have been extinguished and tossed aside only to be recovered later by the investigator. This evidence may prove valuable if the criminalist can successfully fit the match to a book found in the possession of a suspect, as shown in Figure 11–6. In addition, an arsonist can construct many other types of devices to start a fire. These include a burning cigarette, firearms, ammunition, a mechanical match striker, electrical sparking devices, and a

Figure 11–7   Removal of vapor from an enclosed container prior to gas chromatographic analysis.

"Molotov cocktail." Relatively complex mechanical devices are much more likely to survive the fire for later discovery. The broken glass and wick of the Molotov cocktail, if recovered, must be preserved as well.

One important piece of evidence is the clothing of the suspect perpetrator. If this individual is arrested within a few hours of initiating the fire, residual quantities of the accelerant may still be present in the clothing. As we will see in the next section, the forensic laboratory can detect extremely small quantities of accelerant materials, making the examination of a suspect's clothing a feasible investigative approach. Each item of clothing should be placed in a separate airtight container, preferably a new, clean paint can.

The arson investigator must also be aware that accelerants present in soil and vegetation can be rapidly degraded by bacterial action. Freezing samples containing soil or vegetation is an effective way to prevent this degradation.

Analysis of Flammable Residues

Criminalists are nearly unanimous in judging the gas chromatograph to be the most sensitive and reliable instrument for detecting and characterizing flammable residues. Most arsons are initiated by petroleum distillates such as gasoline and kerosene; these liquids are actually composed of a complex mixture of **hydrocarbons**. Basically, the gas chromatograph separates the hydrocarbon components and produces a chromatographic pattern characteristic of a particular petroleum product.

The easiest way to recover accelerant residues from fire-scene debris is to heat the airtight container in which the sample is sent to the laboratory. When the container is heated, any volatile residue present in the debris is driven off and trapped in the container's enclosed airspace. The vapor or *headspace* is removed with a syringe, as shown in Figure 11–7. When the vapor is injected into the gas chromatograph, it is separated into its components, and each peak is recorded on the chromatogram. The identity of the volatile residue is determined when the pattern of the resultant chromatogram is compared to patterns produced by known petroleum products.

Hydrocarbon
Any compound consisting only of carbon and hydrogen.

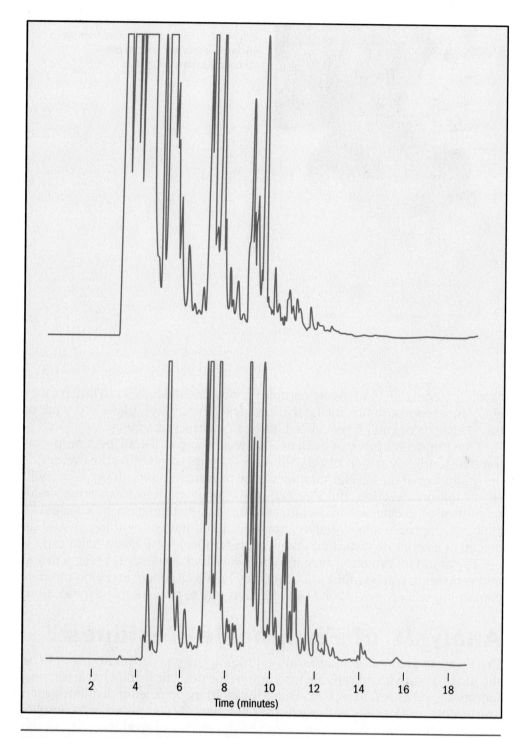

Figure 11–8 **(top) Gas chromatograph of vapor from a genuine gasoline sample.** *(bottom)* **Gas chromatograph of vapor from debris recovered at a fire site. Note the similarity of the known gasoline to vapor removed from the debris.** *Courtesy New Jersey State Police*

For example, in Figure 11–8, a gas chromatographic analysis of debris recovered from a fire site shows a chromatogram similar to a known gasoline standard, thus proving the presence of gasoline. In the absence of any recognizable pattern, the individual peaks can be identified when the investigator compares their retention times to known hydrocarbon standards (such as hexane, benzene, toluene, and xylenes). At present, it is not possible to determine the brand name of a gasoline sample by gas chromatogra-

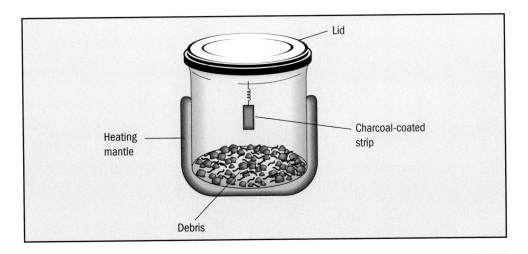

Figure 11–9 **Apparatus for accelerant recovery by vapor concentration. The vapor in the enclosed container is exposed to charcoal, a chemical absorbent, where it is trapped for later analysis.**

phy or any other technique. Fluctuating gasoline markets and exchange agreements among the various oil companies preclude this possibility.

One major disadvantage of the headspace technique described earlier is that the size of the syringe limits the volume of vapor that can be removed from the container and injected into the gas chromatograph. To overcome this deficiency, many crime laboratories have begun to augment the headspace technique with a method called *vapor concentration*. One setup for accomplishing this analysis is shown in Figure 11–9. A charcoal-coated strip, similar to that used in environmental monitoring badges, is placed within the container holding the debris that has been collected from the fire scene.[2] The container is then heated to about 60°C for about one hour. At this temperature, a significant quantity of accelerant vaporizes into the container airspace. The charcoal absorbs the accelerant vapor that it comes in contact with. In this manner, over a short period of time, a significant quantity of the accelerant will be trapped and concentrated onto the charcoal strip. Once the heating procedure is complete, the analyst removes the charcoal strip from the container and recovers the accelerant from the strip by washing it with a small volume of solvent (carbon disulfide). The solvent is then injected into the gas chromatograph for analysis. The major advantage of using vapor concentration with gas chromatography is its extreme sensitivity. By absorbing the accelerant into a charcoal strip, the forensic analyst can increase the sensitivity of accelerant detection at least a hundredfold over the conventional headspace technique.

An examination of Figure 11-8 shows that identifying an accelerant, such as gasoline, by gas chromatography is an exercise in pattern recognition. Typically, a forensic analyst compares the pattern generated by the sample to chromatograms from accelerant standards obtained under the same conditions. The pattern of gasoline, as with many other accelerants, can easily be placed in a searchable library. But on occasion, discernible

---

[2] R. T. Newman et al., "The Use of Activated Charcoal Strips for Fire Debris Extractions by Passive Diffusion. Part 1: The Effects of Time, Temperature, Strip Size, and Sample Concentration," *Journal of Forensic Sciences* 41 (1996): 361.

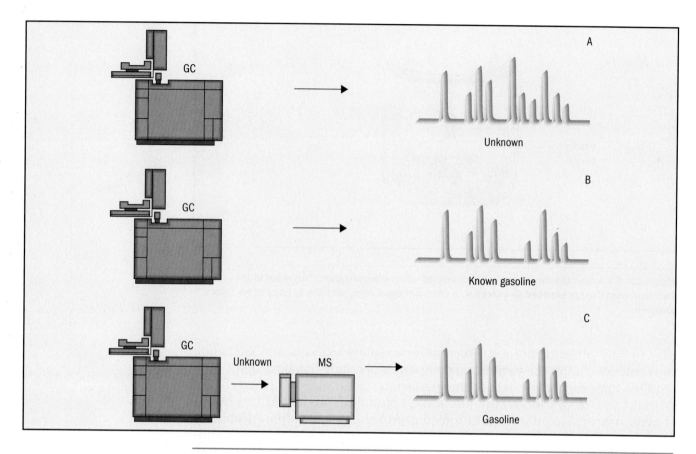

Figure 11–10 Chromatogram of a residue sample collected at a fire scene (A) shows a pattern somewhat like that of gasoline (B). However, a definitive conclusion that the unknown contained gasoline could be obtained only after extraneous peaks were eliminated from the unknown by the use of GC/MS (C).

patterns are not attainable by gas chromatography. There may be a mixture of accelerants, or the accelerant residue may be mixed with heat-generated breakdown products of materials burning at the fire scene, making a gas chromatographic pattern difficult if not impossible to interpret. In these cases, gas chromatography combined with mass spectrometry (see pp. 150–153) has proven to be a valuable technique for solving difficult problems in the detection of accelerant residues.

Complex chromatographic patterns can be simplified by passing the separated components emerging from the gas chromatographic column through a mass spectrometer. As each component enters the mass spectrometer, it is fragmented into a collection of ions. The analyst can then control which ions will be detected and which ones will go unnoticed. In essence, the mass spectrometer acts as a filter allowing the analyst to see only the peaks associated with the ions selected for a particular accelerant. In this manner, the chromatographic pattern can be simplified by eliminating extraneous peaks that may obliterate the pattern.[3] The process is illustrated in Figure 11–10.

[3] M. W. Gilbert, "The Use of Individual Extracted Ion Profiles versus Summed Extracted Ion Profiles in Fire Debris Analysis," *Journal of Forensic Sciences* 43 (1998): 871.

Types of Explosives

The ready accessibility of potentially explosive laboratory chemicals, dynamite, and, in some countries, an assortment of military explosives has provided the criminal element of society with a lethal weapon. Although politically motivated bombings have received considerable publicity worldwide, in the United States most bombing incidents are perpetrated by isolated individuals rather than by organized terrorists. Unfortunately for society, explosives have become an attractive weapon to criminals bent on revenge, destruction of commercial operations, or just plain mischief.

Most bombing incidents involve the use of homemade explosives and incendiary devices. The design of such weapons is limited only by the imagination and ingenuity of the bomber. Like arson investigation, bomb investigation requires close cooperation of a group of highly specialized individuals trained and experienced in bomb disposal, bomb-site investigation, forensic analysis, and criminal investigation. The criminalist must detect and identify explosive chemicals recovered from the crime scene as well as identify the detonating mechanisms. This special responsibility concerns us for the remainder of this chapter.

Like fire, an explosion is the product of combustion accompanied by the creation of gases and heat. However, the distinguishing characteristic of an explosion is the rapid rate at which the reaction proceeds. The sudden buildup of expanding gas pressure at the origin of the explosion produces the violent physical disruption of the surrounding environment. Consider, for example, the effect of confining an explosive charge to a relatively small, closed container. On detonation, the explosive almost instantaneously produces large volumes of gases that exert enormously high pressures on the interior walls of the container. In addition, the heat energy released by the explosion expands the gases, causing them to push on the walls with an even greater force. If we could observe the effects of an exploding lead pipe in slow motion, we would first see the pipe's walls stretch and balloon under pressures as high as several hundred tons per square inch. Finally, the walls would fragment and fly outward in all directions. This flying debris or shrapnel constitutes a great danger to life and limb in the immediate vicinity.

On release from confinement, the gaseous products of the explosion suddenly expand and compress layers of surrounding air as they move outward from the origin of the explosion. This blast effect, or outward rush of gases, at a rate that may be as high as 7,000 miles per hour creates an artificial gale that can overthrow walls, collapse roofs, and disturb any object in its path. If a bomb is sufficiently powerful, more serious damage will be inflicted by the blast effect than by fragmentation debris.

The speed at which explosives decompose varies greatly from one to another and permits their classification as high **and** low explosives. In a low explosive, this speed is called the *speed of deflagration* (burning). This is characterized by very rapid oxidation that produces heat, light, and a subsonic pressure wave. In a high explosive, it is called the *speed of detonation*. Detonation refers to the creation of a supersonic shock wave within the explosive charge. This shock wave causes the chemical bonds of the explosive charge to break apart, leading to the new instantaneous buildup of heat and gases.

Low explosives, such as black and smokeless powders, decompose relatively slowly at rates that vary up to 1,000 meters per second. Because of their slow burning rates, they produce a propelling or throwing action that

Explosion
A chemical or mechanical action resulting in the rapid expansion of gases.

High Explosive
An explosive with a velocity of detonation greater than 1,000 meters per second. Examples include dynamite and RDX.

Low Explosive
An explosive with a velocity of detonation less than 1,000 meters per second. Examples include black powder and smokeless powder.

Deflagration
A very rapid oxidation reaction accompanied by the generation of a low-intensity pressure wave that can disrupt the surroundings.

Detonation
An extremely rapid oxidation reaction accompanied by a violent disruptive effect and an intense, high-speed shock wave.

makes them suitable as propellants for ammunition or skyrockets. However, the danger of this group of explosives must not be underestimated, because when any one of them is confined to a relatively small container, it can explode with a force as lethal as that of any known explosive. High explosives include dynamite, TNT, PETN, and RDX. They detonate almost instantaneously at rates from 1,000 to 8,500 meters per second, producing a smashing or shattering effect on their target.

Low Explosives

The most widely used explosives in the low-explosive group are black powder and smokeless powder. The popularity of these two explosives is enhanced by their accessibility to the public. Both are available in any gun store, and black powder can easily be made from ingredients purchased at any chemical supply house as well. Black powder is a relatively stable mixture of potassium nitrate or sodium nitrate, charcoal, and sulfur. Unconfined, it merely burns; it is used as a medium for carrying a flame to an explosive charge. A safety fuse usually consists of black powder wrapped in a fabric or plastic casing. When ignited, a sufficient length of fuse will burn at a rate slow enough to allow a person adequate time to leave the site of the pending explosion. Black powder, like any other low explosive, becomes explosive and lethal only when it is confined.

The only ingredients required for a low explosive are fuel and a good oxidizing agent. Thus, the oxidizing agent potassium chlorate, for example, when mixed with sugar, produces a popular and accessible explosive mix. When it is confined to a small container—for example, a pipe—and ignited by the flame of a safety fuse, this mixture can explode with a force equivalent to a stick of 40 percent dynamite. Some other commonly encountered ingredients that may be combined with chlorate to produce an explosive are carbon, sulfur, starch, phosphorus, and magnesium filings. Chlorate mixtures may also be ignited by the heat generated from a chemical reaction. For instance, sufficient heat can be generated to initiate combustion when concentrated sulfuric acid comes in contact with a sugar–chlorate mix.

The safest and most powerful low explosive is smokeless powder. This explosive usually consists of nitrated cotton or nitrocellulose (single-base powder) or nitroglycerin mixed with nitrocellulose (double-base powder). The powder is manufactured in a variety of grain sizes and shapes, depending on the desired application.

Another form of low explosive is created when a considerable quantity of natural gas escapes into a confined area and mixes with a sufficient amount of air. If ignited, this mixture results in simultaneous combustion and sudden production of large volumes of gases and heat. In a building, walls are forced outward by the expanding gases, causing the roof to fall into the interiors, and objects are thrown outward and scattered in erratic directions with no semblance of pattern.

Mixtures of air and a gaseous fuel will explode or burn only within a limited concentration range. For example, the concentration limits for methane in air range from 5.3 to 13.9 percent. In the presence of too much air, the fuel becomes too diluted and does not respond to efforts to ignite it; on the other hand, if the fuel becomes too concentrated, ignition is prevented because there is not enough oxygen to support the combustion. Mixtures at or near the upper concentration limit ("rich" mixtures) explode; however, some gas remains unconsumed because there is not enough oxygen to complete the combustion. As air rushes back into the

Black Powder
Normally, a mixture of potassium nitrate, carbon, and sulfur in the ratio 75/15/10.

Safety Fuse
A cord containing a core of black powder. It is used to carry a flame at a uniform rate to an explosive charge.

Smokeless Powder (Single-Base)
An explosive consisting of nitrocellulose.

Smokeless Powder (Double-Base)
An explosive consisting of a mixture of nitrocellulose and nitroglycerin.

origin of the explosion, it combines with the residual hot gas and a fire is produced that is characterized by a *whoosh* sound. This fire is often more destructive than the explosion that preceded it. Mixtures near the lower end of the limit ("lean" mixtures) generally cause an explosion without accompanying damage due to fire.

High Explosives

The sensitivity of a high explosive provides a convenient basis for its classification into two groups. The first group, primary explosives, are ultra-sensitive to heat, shock, or friction, and under normal conditions detonate violently instead of burning. For this reason, they are used to detonate other explosives through a chain reaction and are often referred to as *primers*. Primary explosives provide the major ingredient of a blasting cap and include lead azide, lead styphnate, and diazodinitrophenol. Because of their extreme sensitivity, these explosives are rarely used as the main charge of a homemade bomb.

Primary Explosive
A high explosive that is easily detonated by heat or shock.

The second group, secondary explosives, are relatively insensitive to heat, shock, or friction, and normally burn rather than detonate if they are ignited in small quantities in open air. This group comprises the majority of high explosives used for commercial and military blasting. Some common examples of noninitiating explosives are dynamite, TNT (trinitrotoluene), PETN (pentaerythritol tetranitrate), RDX (cyclotrimethylenetrinitramine), and tetryl (2,4,6-trinitrophenylmethylnitramine).

Secondary Explosive
A high explosive that normally must be detonated by a primary explosive.

It is an irony of history that the prize most symbolic of humanity's search for peace—the Nobel Peace Prize—should bear the name of the developer of one of our most lethal discoveries—dynamite. In 1867, the Swedish chemist Alfred Nobel, searching for a method to desensitize nitroglycerin, found that when kieselguhr, a variety of diatomaceous earth, absorbed a large portion of nitroglycerin, it became far less sensitive but still retained its explosive force. Nobel later decided to use pulp as an absorbent because kieselguhr was a heat-absorbing material. Thus, pulp dynamite was the beginning of what is now known as the straight dynamite series, the gradations of which are specified according to the percentage of nitroglycerin used. These dynamites are used when a quick shattering action is desired. Present-day straight dynamites also include sodium nitrate, which furnishes oxygen for complete combustion, along with a small percentage of a stabilizer—for example, calcium carbonate. The strength rating of a straight dynamite is designated by the weight percentage of nitroglycerin in the formula: a 40 percent straight dynamite contains 40 percent, a 60 percent grade contains 60 percent, and so forth. However, the concept that the actual blasting power developed by different strengths is in direct proportion to the percentage markings is erroneous. A 60 percent straight dynamite, rather than being three times as strong as a 20 percent, is only one and one-half times as strong.

In recent years, nitroglycerin-based dynamite has all but disappeared from the industrial explosives market. Commercially, these explosives have been replaced mainly by *ammonium nitrate–based explosives,* that is, *water gels, emulsions,* and *ANFO explosives.* These explosives mix oxygen-rich ammonium nitrate with a fuel to form a low-cost and very stable explosive. Typically, water gels have a consistency resembling that of set gelatin or gel-type toothpaste. They are characterized by their water-resistant nature and are employed for all types of blasting under wet conditions. These explosives are based on formulations of ammonium nitrate and sodium nitrate gelled with a natural polysaccharide such as guar gum. Commonly, a combustible material such as aluminum is mixed into the gel to serve as the explosive's fuel.

Emulsion explosives differ from gels in that they consist of two distinct phases, an oil phase and a water phase. In these emulsions, a droplet of a supersaturated solution of ammonium nitrate is surrounded by a hydrocarbon serving as a fuel. A typical emulsion consists of water, one or more inorganic nitrate oxidizers, oil, and emulsifying agents. Commonly, emulsions contain micron-sized glass, resin, or ceramic spheres known as *microspheres* or *microballoons*. The size of these spheres controls the explosive's sensitivity and detonation velocity.

Ammonium nitrate soaked in fuel oil is an explosive known as *ANFO*. Such commercial explosives are inexpensive and safe to handle and have found wide applications in blasting operations in the mining industry. Ammonium nitrate in the form of fertilizer makes a readily obtainable ingredient for homemade explosives. Indeed, in an incident related to the 1993 bombing of New York City's World Trade Center, the FBI arrested five men during a raid on their hideout in New York City, where they were mixing a "witches' brew" of fuel oil and an ammonium nitrate–based fertilizer.

Triacetone triperoxide (TATP) is a homemade explosive that has been used as an improvised explosive by terrorist organizations in Israel and other Middle Eastern countries. It is prepared by reacting the common ingredients of acetone and hydrogen peroxide in the presence of an acid catalyst such as hydrochloric acid. TATP is a friction- and impact-sensitive explosive that is extremely potent when confined in a container such as a pipe. The 2005 London transit bombings were caused by TATP-based explosives and provide ample evidence that terrorist cells have moved TATP outside the Middle East. A London bus destroyed by one of the TATP bombs is shown in Figure 11–11.

No discussion of high explosives would be complete without a mention of military high explosives. In many countries outside the United

Figure 11–11   A London bus destroyed by a TATP-based bomb. *Courtesy AP Wide World Photos*

States, the accessibility of high explosives to terrorist organizations makes them very common constituents of homemade bombs. RDX, the most popular and powerful military explosive, is often encountered in the form of a pliable plastic of doughlike consistency known as *composition C–4* (a U.S. military designation).

TNT was produced and used on an enormous scale during World War II and may be considered the most important military bursting charge explosive. Alone or in combination with other explosives, it has found wide application in shells, bombs, grenades, demolition explosives, and propellant compositions. Interestingly, military "dynamite" contains no nitroglycerin but is actually composed of a mixture of RDX and TNT. Like other military explosives, TNT is rarely encountered in bombings in the United States.

PETN is used by the military in TNT mixtures for small-caliber projectiles and grenades. Commercially, the chemical is used as the explosive core in a detonating cord or *primacord*. Instead of the slower-burning safety fuse, a detonating cord is often used to connect a series of explosive charges so that they will detonate simultaneously.

Unlike low explosives, bombs made of high explosives must be detonated by an initiating explosion. In most cases, detonators are blasting caps composed of copper or aluminum cases filled with lead azide as an initiating charge and PETN or RDX as a detonating charge. Blasting caps can be initiated by means of a burning safety fuse or by an electrical current (see Figure 11–12).

Detonating Cord
A cordlike explosive containing a core of high-explosive material, usually PETN; also called primacord.

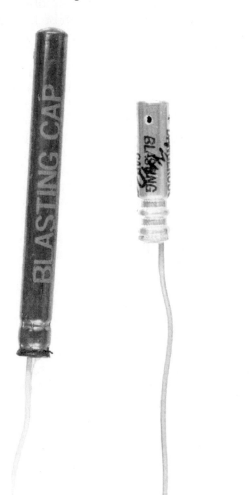

Figure 11–12 **Blasting caps. The left and center caps are initiated by an electrical current; the right cap is initiated by a safety fuse.**

Homemade bombs camouflaged in packages, suitcases, and the like are usually initiated with an electrical blasting cap wired to a battery. An unlimited number of switching-mechanism designs have been devised for setting off these devices; clocks and mercury switches are favored. Bombers sometimes prefer to employ outside electrical sources. For instance, most automobile bombs are detonated when the ignition switch of a car is turned on.

Collection and Analysis of Explosives

The most important step in the detection and analysis of explosive residues is the collection of appropriate samples from the explosion scene. Invariably, undetonated residues of the explosive remain at the site of the explosion. The detection and identification of these explosives in the laboratory depends on the bomb-scene investigator's skill and ability to recognize and sample the areas most likely to contain such materials.

The most obvious characteristic of a high or contained low explosive is the presence of a crater at the origin of the blast. Once the crater has been located, all loose soil and other debris must immediately be removed from the interior of the hole and preserved for laboratory analysis. Other good sources of explosive residues are objects located near the origin of detonation. Wood, insulation, rubber, and other soft materials that are readily penetrated often collect traces of the explosive. However, nonporous objects near the blast must not be overlooked. For instance, residues can be found on the surfaces of metal objects near the site of an explosion. Material blown away from the blast's origin should also be recovered because it, too, may retain explosive residues. All personnel involved in searching the bomb scene must take appropriate measures to avoid contaminating the scene, including dressing in disposable gloves, shoe covers, and overalls.

The entire area must be systematically searched, with great care given to recovering any trace of a detonating mechanism or any other item foreign to the explosion site. Wire-mesh screens are best utilized for sifting through debris. In pipe-bomb explosions, particles of the explosive are frequently found adhering to the pipe cap or to the pipe threads, as a result of either being impacted into the metal by the force of the explosion or being deposited in the threads during the construction of the bomb. **One approach for screening objects for the presence of explosive residues in the field or the laboratory is the ion mobility spectrometer (IMS).** A portable IMS is shown in Figure 11–13.

This handheld detector uses a vacuum to collect explosive residues from suspect surfaces. Alternatively, the surface suspected of containing explosive residues is wiped down with a Teflon-coated fiberglass disc and the collected residues are then drawn into the spectrometer off the disc. Once in the IMS, the explosive residues are vaporized by the application of heat. These vaporized substances are exposed to a beam of electrons or beta rays (see p. 172) emitted by radioactive nickel and converted into electrically charged molecules or ions. The ions are then allowed to move through a tube (drift region) under the influence of an electric field. A schematic diagram of an IMS is shown in Figure 11–14. Ions move at different speeds depending on their size and structure. The preliminary identification of an explosive residue can be made by noting the time it takes the explosive to move through the tube. Used as a screening tool, this method rapidly detects a full range of explosives, even at low detection lev-

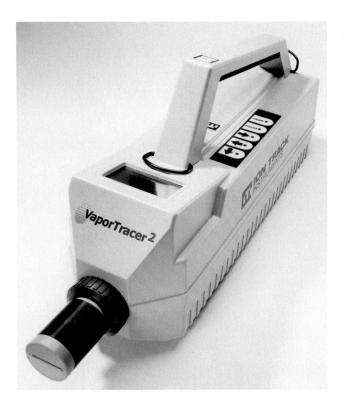

Figure 11–13 **A portable ion mobility spectrometer used to rapidly detect and tentatively identify trace quantities of explosives.** *Courtesy GE Ion Track, Wilmington, Mass. 01887*

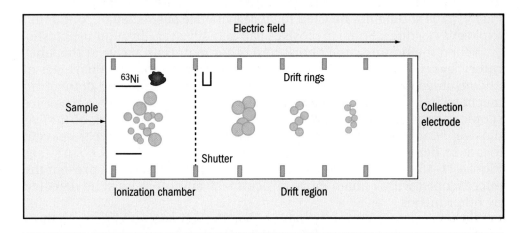

Figure 11–14 **Schematic diagram of an ion mobility spectrometer. A sample is introduced into an ionization chamber, where bombardment with radioactive particles emitted by an isotope of nickel converts the sample to ions. The ions move into a drift region where ion separation occurs based on the speed of the ions as they move through an electric field.**

els. However, all results need to be verified through confirmatory tests. The IMS can detect plastic explosives as well as commercial and military explosives. More than 10,000 portable and full-size IMS units are currently used at airport security checkpoints, and more than 50,000 handheld IMS analyzers have been deployed for chemical-weapons monitoring in various armed forces.

All materials collected for examination by the laboratory must be placed in airtight sealed containers and labeled with all pertinent information. Soil and other soft loose materials are best stored in metal air-

Figure 11–15 Samples of smokeless powders.

tight containers such as clean paint cans. Debris and articles collected from different areas are to be packaged in separate airtight containers. Plastic bags should not be used to store evidence suspected of containing explosive residues. Some explosives can actually seep through the plastic.

When the bomb-scene debris and other materials arrive at the laboratory, everything is first examined microscopically to detect particles of unconsumed explosive. Portions of the recovered debris and detonating mechanism, if found, are carefully viewed under a low-power stereoscopic microscope in a painstaking effort to locate particles of the explosive. Black powder and smokeless powder are relatively easy to locate in debris because of their characteristic shapes and colors (see Figure 11–15). However, dynamite and other high explosives present the microscopist with a much more difficult task and often must be detected by other means.

Following microscopic examination, the recovered debris is thoroughly rinsed with acetone. The high solubility of most explosives in acetone ensures their quick removal from the debris. Once collected, the acetone extract is concentrated and analyzed using color spot tests, thin-layer chromatography (TLC), high-performance liquid chromatography (HPLC; see p. 138), and gas chromatography/mass spectrometry (see pp. 150–153). The presence of an explosive will be indicated by a well-defined spot on a TLC plate with an R_f value corresponding to a known explosive—for example, nitroglycerin, RDX, or PETN. The high sensitivity of HPLC also makes it very useful for analyzing trace evidence of explosives. The HPLC operates at room temperature and hence does not cause explosives, many of which are temperature sensitive, to decompose during their analysis. When a water-gel explosive containing ammonium nitrate or a low explosive is suspected, the debris should be rinsed with water so that water-soluble substances (such as nitrates and chlorates) will be extracted. Table 11–3 lists a number of simple color tests the examiner can perform

Table 11–3 Color Spot Tests for Common Explosives

Substance	Reagent		
	Griess[a]	Diphenylamine[b]	Alcoholic KOH[c]
Chlorate	No color	Blue	No color
Nitrate	Pink to red	Blue	No color
Nitrocellulose	Pink	Blue-black	No color
Nitroglycerin	Pink to red	Blue	No color
PETN	Pink to red	Blue	No color
RDX	Pink to red	Blue	No color
TNT	No color	No color	Red
Tetryl	Pink to red	Blue	Red-violet

[a]Griess reagent: Solution 1—Dissolve 1 g sulfanilic acid in 100 mL 30% acetic acid. Solution 2—Dissolve 0.5 g N-(1-napthyl) ethylenediamine in 100 mL methyl alcohol. Add solutions 1 and 2 and a few milligrams of zinc dust to the suspect extract.

[b]Diphenylamine reagent: Dissolve 1 g diphenylamine in 100 mL concentrated sulfuric acid.

[c]Alcoholic KOH reagent: Dissolve 10 g of potassium hydroxide in 100 mL absolute alcohol.

on the acetone and water extracts to screen for the presence of organic and inorganic explosives, respectively.

When sufficient quantities of explosives are recoverable, confirmatory tests may be performed by either infrared spectrophotometry or X-ray diffraction. The former produces a unique "fingerprint" pattern for an organic explosive, as shown by the IR spectrum of RDX in Figure 11–16. The latter provides a unique diffraction pattern for inorganic substances, as exemplified by the diffraction patterns for potassium nitrate and potassium chlorate, shown in Figure 6-11.

An explosive "taggant" program has been proposed to further enhance a bomb-scene investigator's chances of recovering useful evidence at a postexplosion scene. Under this proposal, tiny color-coded chips the size of sand grains would be added to commercial explosives during their manufacture. Some of these chips would be expected to survive an explosion and be capable of recovery at explosion scenes. To aid in their recovery, the chips are made both fluorescent and magnetic sensitive. Hence, investigators can search for taggants at the explosion site with magnetic tools and ultraviolet light.

The taggant chip is arranged in a color sequence that indicates where the explosive was made and when it was produced (see Figure 11–17). With this knowledge, the explosive can be traced through its distribution chain to its final legal possessor. The taggant colors are readily observed and are read with the aid of a low-power microscope.

There are no plans to institute a taggant program for commercial explosives in the United States. In Europe, only Switzerland has adopted a taggant program; thus, it is extremely doubtful that taggants will be found in any significant number of bombing incidents in the foreseeable future. Interestingly, the International Civil Aviation Organization has mandated that a volatile taggant be added to plastic explosives during their manufacture in order to facilitate the detection of these explosives. Programs are now under way to tag commercial C–4 with the volatile chemical known as DMNB (2,3-dimethyl-2,3-dinitrobutane).

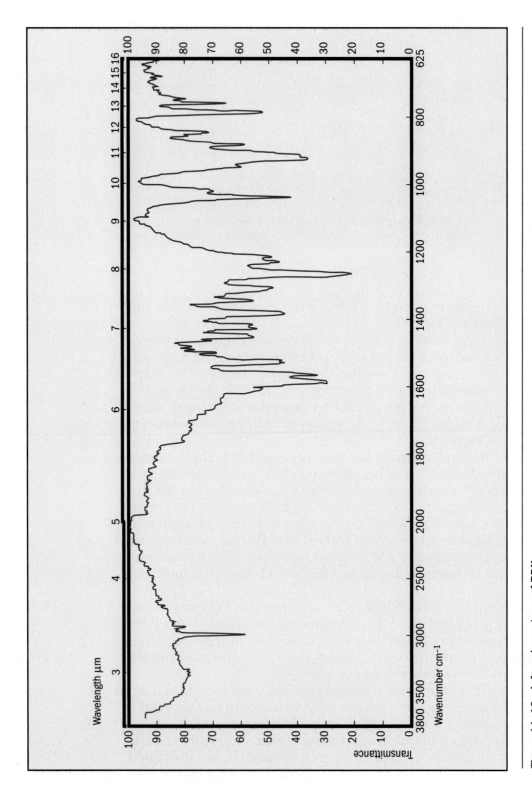

Figure 11–16   Infrared spectrum of RDX.

Forensic Aspects of Arson and Explosion Investigations **337**

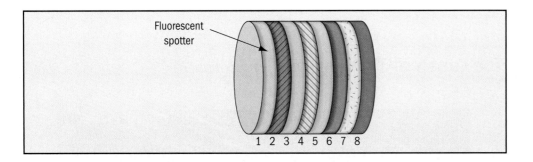

Figure 11–17   Cross-section of a taggant. The color sequence of the recovered taggant is observed with the aid of a low-power microscope. The colors are then matched to a color code to yield information about the plant of manufacture, production lot, and purchasers of the explosive material.

Forensics at Work
The Crash of TWA Flight 800

Though the crash of TWA Flight 800 was ultimately not proven to be an act of terrorism, the initial investigation revealed the difficulties investigators can expect to encounter in recovering explosive residues at bombing scenes. For example, in spite of the large quantities of explosive used, investigators encountered extreme difficulties in recovering explosive residues at both the World Trade Center (1993) and Oklahoma federal building bombing sites.

The Search: The TWA Plane Crash
Three weeks after the Atlantic Ocean swallowed a flaming Boeing 747, investigators continue to explore a prevailing theory that the downfall of Trans World Airlines Flight 800 was caused by a bomb. But their complicated mission is made all the more complex by the very water in which much of the plane rests.

Investigators say they are still concerned that the extended submersion in saltwater might have an effect on telltale chemical traces that a bomb would have left on airplane aluminum, plastic containers, luggage—and anything else from the jumbo jet's front end, where, investigators theorize, the explosion that downed the aircraft took place. More than 80 percent of the airplane remains scattered on the ocean floor, 120 feet down.

Their worry has heightened the sense of urgency in recovering debris from the water, said Joseph Cantamessa Jr., an F.B.I. special agent in charge. "It's the reason we have been so impatient about getting the evidence in the lab for testing."

Christopher Ronay, the former head of the Federal Bureau of Investigation's explosives unit and now president of the Institute of Makers of Explosives in Washington, D.C., said investigators have cause for concern. "Your explosive residue," he said, "adheres to all sorts of

continued

Forensics at Work
The Crash of TWA Flight 800 *(continued)*

FBI agents and New York State police guard the reconstruction of TWA Flight 800.
Source: Mark Lennihan, AP Wide World Photos

materials—to carpet fibers and upholstery and plastics, and it can be trapped in the surface material through all sorts of means. And certainly water washes away some kinds of residues."

But the July 17 explosion of Flight 800, which killed all 230 people on board, remains a puzzle in many pieces. As Mr. Ronay and others point out, the airplane may or may not have been brought down by a bomb. And if a bomb was the cause, the explosive material could have been one of several kinds. And depending on the kind of explosive, ocean water could either wash away the chemical residue or have little effect.

Dr. Jesse L. Beauchamp, a chemistry professor at the California Institute of Technology in Pasadena, said: "It goes without saying that any traces of explosives that were present on wreckage

would likely be partially removed—not entirely removed—by continued exposure to saltwater. But it depends on the type of explosives."

Mr. Ronay, who helped coordinate the bureau's successful investigation into the fatal explosion of Pan Am Flight 103 over Lockerbie, Scotland, in 1988, expressed confidence in the F.B.I. laboratory's sophisticated equipment and in Tom Thurman, his successor as chief of the explosives unit and the case agent in the Lockerbie investigation.

Mr. Thurman and his team of forensic specialists have been examining the recovered airplane debris at a hangar in Calverton, L.I. In general they are concentrating on two avenues of inquiry: finding any explosive's chemical residue, and searching for pockmarks, tearing and other signs found on items that were

continued

Forensics at Work
The Crash of TWA Flight 800 *(continued)*

near the explosion, often called "witness material."

In an explosion, a chemical reaction transforms the explosive material into gas. But some of that material is merely scattered, albeit in microscopic fragments. And that is what the forensic investigator seeks.

"There's almost always some residue," said Dr. Jimmie Oxley, a professor of chemistry at the University of Rhode Island. "And you look for something abnormal in the chemical analysis, something that shouldn't be there."

Dr. Oxley, who is a consultant to the F.B.I. and the Bureau of Alcohol, Tobacco and Firearms, said that investigators undoubtedly are rinsing airplane parts with an organic solvent to see if there is organic material that would not normally be present. "If you found traces of a military explosive such as RDX, which is not water soluble, it would have no reason for possibly being there," she said. "So now you have positive evidence."

But the ocean presents another variable. "On the other hand, if you never find anything at all, you can't draw any conclusions," Dr. Oxley said. "Now you've got to look at a lot of other things. There are explosive materials that could have been used that are water soluble. There is ammonium nitrate fuel oil, which is water soluble except for the oil. And this stuff has been bathing down there for a long time."

Even in the case of ammonium nitrate fuel oil, or ANFO, the material used in last year's deadly bombing of a Federal building in Oklahoma City, the investigators would expect to find traces of insoluble materials used to detonate the mixture.

Investigators in Calverton are using tools such as a gas chromatograph, which separates organic components, and a mass spectrometer, which identifies each component by its molecular weight. But Mr. Ronay said that more in-depth analysis is being done at the F.B.I. laboratory in Washington where, he said, there are specific instruments to use on specific explosives.

"Their equipment is so sensitive that it can track material in parts per trillion," he said. "I don't think a shark can smell blood in the water to that degree."

Still, Mr. Ronay acknowledged the difficulty that his former colleagues face. "It's such a big, big project," he said. "And you might never find the right piece."

That would force investigators to focus on the other avenue of inquiry—the hunt for a specific kind of tear in metal, or the pitting in a piece of luggage that might have been near the source of an explosion.

"If they never find the residue, the experts will probably characterize the damage and make some estimates regarding the kind of explosive that was used," Mr. Ronay said. "But if you find residue, you don't need to guess."

Source: Dan Barry, "Saltwater's Ill Effects Depend on Bomb Type," *New York Times*, August 7, 1996, p. B-5. Copyright © 1996 by the New York Times Company. Reprinted with permission.

Chapter Summary

The arson investigator needs to begin examining a fire scene for signs of arson as soon as the fire has been extinguished. The search of the fire scene must focus on finding the fire's origin. Some telltale signs of arson include evidence of separate and unconnected fires, the use of "streamers" to spread the fire from one area to another, and evidence of severe burning found on the floor as opposed to the ceiling of a structure. At the suspect point of origin of a fire, porous materials should be collected and stored in airtight containers.

When a fire occurs, oxygen combines with a fuel to produce noticeable quantities of heat and light (flames). If combustion is to be initiated and sustained, a fuel must be present, oxygen must be available, heat must be applied to initiate the combustion, and sufficient heat must be generated to sustain the reaction. A fuel achieves a reaction rate with oxygen sufficient to sustain a fire only when it is in the gaseous state.

In the laboratory, the gas chromatograph is the most sensitive and reliable instrument for detecting and characterizing flammable residues. Most arsons are initiated by petroleum distillates such as gasoline and kerosene. The gas chromatograph separates the hydrocarbon components and produces a chromatographic pattern characteristic of a particular petroleum product. By comparing select gas chromatographic peaks recovered from fire-scene debris to known flammable liquids, a forensic analyst may be able to identify the accelerant used to initiate the fire.

Explosives are substances that undergo a rapid oxidation reaction with the production of large quantities of gases. This sudden buildup of gas pressure constitutes an explosion. The speed at which explosives decompose permits their classification as high or low explosives. The most widely used low explosives are black powder and smokeless powder. Among the high explosives, primary explosives are ultrasensitive to heat, shock, or friction and provide the major ingredients found in blasting caps. Secondary explosives normally constitute the main charge of a high explosive. Nitroglycerin-based dynamite has all but disappeared from the industrial explosive market and has been replaced by ammonium nitrate–based explosives (such as water gels, emulsions, and ANFO explosives). In many countries outside the United States, the accessibility of military high explosives to terrorist organizations makes them very common constituents of homemade bombs. RDX is the most popular and powerful of the military explosives.

The entire bomb site must be systematically searched with great care given to recovering any trace of a detonating mechanism or any other item foreign to the explosion site. Objects located at or near the origin of the explosion must be collected for laboratory examination. Typically, in the laboratory, debris collected at explosion scenes is examined microscopically for unconsumed explosive particles. Recovered debris may also be thoroughly rinsed with organic solvents and analyzed by testing procedures that include color spot tests, thin-layer chromatography, high-performance liquid chromatography, and gas chromatography/mass spectrometry.

Review Questions

1. True or False: The absence of chemical residues always rules out the possibility of arson. _____

2. The combination of oxygen with other substances to produce new chemical products is called _____.

3. True or False: All oxidation reactions produce noticeable quantities of heat and light. _____

4. _____ is the capacity for doing work.

5. Burning methane for the purpose of heating water to produce steam in order to drive a turbine is an example of converting _____ energy to _____ energy.

6. The quantity of heat evolved from a chemical reaction arises out of the _____ and _____ of chemical bonds.

7. Molecules must (absorb, liberate) energy to break their bonds and (absorb, liberate) energy when their bonds are reformed.

8. All oxidation reactions (absorb, liberate) heat.

9. Reactions that liberate heat are said to be _____.

10. Excess heat energy liberated by an oxidation reaction is called the _____.

11. A chemical reaction in which heat is absorbed from the surroundings is said to be _____.

12. True or False: All reactions require an energy input to start them. _____

13. The minimum temperature at which a fuel burns is known as the _____ temperature.

14. A fuel achieves a sufficient reaction rate with oxygen to produce a flame only in the (gaseous, liquid) state.

15. The lowest temperature at which a liquid fuel produces enough vapor to burn is the _____.

16. _____ is the chemical breakdown of a solid material to gaseous products.

17. _____ is a phenomenon in which a fuel burns without the presence of a flame.

18. The rate of a chemical reaction (increases, decreases) as the temperature rises.

19. _____ describes a fire caused by a natural heat-producing process.

20. Oxidizing agents supply _____ to a chemical reaction.

21. Three ingredients of black powder are _____, _____, and _____.

22. True or False: An immediate search of a fire scene can commence without obtaining a search warrant. _____

23. A search of the fire scene must focus on finding the fire's _____.

24. True or False: The probable origin of a fire is most likely closest to the lowest point that shows the most intense characteristics of burning. _____

25. The collection of debris at the origin of a fire should include all (porous, nonporous) materials.

26. _____ containers must be used to package all materials suspected of containing hydrocarbon residues.

27. The most sensitive and reliable instrument for detecting and characterizing flammable residues is the (gas chromatograph, infrared spectrophotometer).

28. The identity of a volatile petroleum residue is determined by the (size, pattern) of its gas chromatogram.

29. True or False: The major advantage of using the vapor concentration technique in combination with gas chromatography is its extreme sensitivity for detecting volatile residues from fire-scene evidence. _____

30. True or False: A forensic analyst typically compares the gas chromatographic pattern generated from a fire scene sample to a library of patterns in order to identify the accelerant. _____

31. The criminalist (can, cannot) identify gasoline residues by brand name.

32. Rapid combustion accompanied by the creation of large volumes of gases describes a(n) _____.

33. Explosives that decompose at relatively slow rates are classified as _____ explosives.

34. _____ explosives detonate almost instantaneously to produce a smashing or shattering effect.

35. The most widely used low explosives are _____ and _____.

36. A low explosive becomes explosive and lethal only when it is _____.

37. True or False: Air and a gaseous fuel burn when mixed at any concentration range. _____

38. High explosives can be classified as either _____ or _____ explosives.

39. The blasting power of different dynamite strengths (is, is not) in direct proportion to the weight percentage of nitroglycerin.

40. True or False: The most common commercial explosives incorporate ammonium nitrate. _____

41. The most widely used explosive in the military is _____.

42. The explosive core in detonating cord is _____.

43. A high explosive is normally detonated by a(n) _____ explosive contained within a blasting cap.

44. An obvious characteristic of a high explosive is the presence of a(n) _____ at the origin of the blast.

45. The most important step in detecting explosive residues is the _____ of appropriate samples from the explosion scene.

46. Unconsumed explosive residues may be detected in the laboratory through a careful _____ examination of the debris.

47. Debris recovered from the site of an explosion is routinely rinsed with _____ in an attempt to recover high-explosive residues.

48. Once collected, the acetone extract is initially analyzed by _____, _____, and _____.

49. The technique of _____ produces a unique absorption spectrum for an organic explosive.

50. The technique of _____ provides a unique diffraction pattern for the identification of the inorganic constituents of explosives.

Further References

Almirall, J. R., and K. G. Furton, eds., *Fire Scene Evidence*. Boca Raton, Fla.: Taylor & Francis, 2004.

DeHaan, John D., *Kirk's Fire Investigation*, 5th ed. Upper Saddle River, N.J.: Prentice Hall, 2002.

Lentini, J.J., *Scientific Protocols for Fire Investigation*. Boca Raton, Fla.: Taylor & Francis, 2006.

Midkiff, C. R., "Arson and Explosive Investigation," in R. Saferstein, ed., *Forensic Science Handbook,* vol. 1, 2nd ed. Upper Saddle River, N.J.: Prentice Hall, 2002.

Midkiff, C. R., "Laboratory Examination of Arson Evidence," in S. M. Gerber and R. Saferstein, eds., *More Chemistry and Crime.* Washington, D.C.: American Chemical Society, 1997.

NFPA 921 Guide for Fire and Explosion Investigations, Quincy, Mass.: National Fire Protection Association, 2004.

Thurman, J.T., *Practical Bomb Scene Investigation.* Boca Raton, Fla.: Taylor & Francis, 2006.

Yinon, J., *Forensic and Environmental Detection of Explosives.* West Sussex, England: Wiley, 1999.

The Sam Sheppard Case—A Trail of Blood

Convicted in 1954 of bludgeoning his wife to death, Dr. Sam Sheppard achieved celebrity status when the storyline of TV's *The Fugitive* was apparently modeled on his efforts to seek vindication for the crime he professed not to have committed.

Dr. Sheppard, a physician, claimed he was dozing on his living room couch when his pregnant wife, Marilyn, was attacked. Sheppard's story was that he quickly ran upstairs to stop the carnage, but was knocked unconscious briefly by the intruder. The suspicion that fell on Dr. Sheppard was fueled by the revelation that he was having an adulterous affair. At trial, the local coroner testified that a pool of blood on Marilyn's pillow contained the impression of a "surgical instrument." After Sheppard had been imprisoned for ten years, the U.S Supreme Court set aside his conviction due to the "massive, pervasive, and prejudicial publicity" that had attended his trial.

In 1966, the second Sheppard trial commenced. This time, the same coroner was forced to back off from his insistence that the bloody outline of a surgical instrument was present on Marilyn's pillow. However, a medical technician from the coroner's office now testified that blood on Dr. Sheppard's watch was from blood spatter, indicating that Dr. Sheppard was wearing the watch in the presence of the battering of his wife. The defense countered with the expert testimony of eminent criminalist Dr. Paul Kirk. Dr. Kirk concluded that blood spatter marks in the bedroom showed the killer to be left-handed. Dr. Sheppard was right-handed.

Dr. Kirk further testified that Sheppard stained his watch while attempting to obtain a pulse reading. After less than twelve hours of deliberation, the jury failed to convict Sheppard. But the ordeal had taken its toll. Four years later Sheppard died, a victim of drug and alcohol abuse.

chapter 12

Forensic Serology

Key Terms

acid phosphatase
agglutination
allele
antibody
antigen
antiserum
aspermia
chromosome
deoxyribonucleic acid (DNA)
egg
enzyme
erythrocyte
gene
genotype
hemoglobin
heterozygous
homozygous
hybridoma cells
iso-enzymes
locus
luminol
monoclonal antibodies
oligospermia
phenotype
plasma
polyclonal antibodies
polymorphism
precipitin
serology
serum
sperm
X chromosome
Y chromosome
zygote

Learning Objectives

After studying this chapter you should be able to:

- List the A-B-O antigens and antibodies found in the blood for each of the four blood types: A, B, AB, and O

- Understand and describe how whole blood is typed

- List and describe forensic tests used to characterize a stain as blood

- Understand the concept of antigen–antibody interactions and how it is applied to species identification and drug identification

- Explain the differences between monoclonal and polyclonal antibodies

- Contrast chromosomes and genes

- Learn how the Punnett square is used to determine the genotypes and phenotypes of offspring

- List the laboratory tests necessary to characterize seminal stains

- Explain how suspect blood and semen stains are to be properly preserved for laboratory examination

- Describe the proper collection of physical evidence in a rape investigation

In 1901, Karl Landsteiner announced one of the most significant discoveries of the twentieth century—the typing of blood—a finding that twenty-nine years later earned him a Nobel Prize. For years physicians had attempted to transfuse blood from one individual to another. Their efforts often ended in failure because the transfused blood tended to coagulate in the body of the recipient, causing instantaneous death. Landsteiner was the first to recognize that all human blood was not the same; instead, he found that blood is distinguishable by its group or type. Out of Landsteiner's work came the classification system that we call the *A-B-O system*. Now physicians had the key for properly matching the blood of a donor to a recipient. One blood type cannot be mixed with a different blood type without disastrous consequences. This discovery, of course, had important implications for blood transfusion and the millions of lives it has since saved. Meanwhile, Landsteiner's findings had opened up a completely new field of research in the biological sciences. Others began to pursue the identification of additional characteristics that could further differentiate blood. By 1937, the Rh factor in blood was demonstrated, and shortly thereafter, numerous blood factors or groups were discovered. More than a hundred different blood factors have been shown to exist. However, the ones in the A-B-O system are still the most important for properly matching a donor and recipient for a transfusion.

Until the early 1990s, forensic scientists focused on blood factors, such as A-B-O, as offering the best means for linking blood to an individual. What made these factors so attractive to the forensic scientist was that in theory no two individuals, except for identical twins, could be expected to have the same combination of blood factors. In other words, blood factors are controlled genetically and have the potential of being a highly distinctive feature for personal identification. What makes this observation so relevant is the high frequency of occurrence of bloodstains at crime scenes, especially crimes of the most serious nature—that is, homicides, assaults, and rapes. Consider, for example, a transfer of blood, between the victim and assailant during a struggle; that is, the victim's blood is transferred to the suspect's garment or vice versa. If the criminalist could individualize human blood by identifying all of its known factors, the result would be evidence of the strongest kind for linking the suspect to the crime scene.

The advent of DNA technology has dramatically altered the approach of forensic scientists toward individualization of bloodstains and other biological evidence. The search for genetically controlled blood factors in bloodstains has been abandoned in favor of characterizing biological evidence by select regions of our deoxyribonucleic acid (DNA). The individualization of dried blood and other biological evidence, now a reality, has significantly altered the role that crime laboratories play in criminal investigations. As we will learn in the next chapter, the high sensitivity of DNA analysis has even altered the type of materials collected from crime scenes in the search for DNA. The next chapter is devoted to discussing recent breakthroughs in associating blood and semen stains with a single individual through characterization of DNA. This chapter focuses on underlying biological concepts that forensic scientists historically relied on as they sought to characterize and individualize biological evidence prior to the dawning of the age of DNA.

DNA
Abbreviation for deoxyribonucleic acid—the molecules carrying the body's genetic information. DNA is double stranded in the shape of a double helix.

The Nature of Blood

Antigens and Antibodies

The word *blood* actually refers to a highly complex mixture of cells, enzymes, proteins, and inorganic substances. The fluid portion of blood is called plasma. Plasma is composed principally of water and accounts for 55 percent of blood content. Suspended in the plasma are solid materials consisting chiefly of cells—that is, red blood cells (erythrocytes), white blood cells (leukocytes), and platelets. The solid portion of blood accounts for 45 percent of its content. Blood clots when a protein in the plasma known as *fibrin* traps and enmeshes the red blood cells. If one were to remove the clotted material, a pale yellowish liquid known as serum would be left.

Plasma
The fluid portion of unclotted blood.

Erythrocyte
A red blood cell.

Serum
The liquid that separates from the blood when a clot is formed.

Obviously, considering the complexity of blood, any discussion of its function and chemistry would have to be extensive, extending beyond the scope of this text. It is certainly far more relevant at this point to concentrate our discussion on the blood components that are directly pertinent to the forensic aspects of blood identification—the red blood cells and the blood serum.

Functionally, red blood cells transport oxygen from the lungs to the body tissues and in turn remove carbon dioxide from tissues by transporting it back to the lungs, where it is exhaled. However, for reasons unrelated to the red blood cell's transporting mission, on the surface of each cell are millions of characteristic chemical structures called antigens. Antigens impart blood-type characteristics to the red blood cells. Blood antigens are grouped into systems depending on their relationship to one another. More than fifteen blood antigen systems have been identified to date; of these, the A-B-O and Rh systems are the most important.

Antigen
A substance, usually a protein, that stimulates the body to produce antibodies against it.

If an individual is type A, this simply indicates that each red blood cell has A antigens on its surface; similarly, all type B individuals have B antigens; and the red blood cells of type AB contain both A and B antigens. Type O individuals have neither A nor B antigens on their cells. Hence, the presence or absence of the A and B antigens on the red blood cells determines a person's blood type in the A-B-O system.

Another important blood antigen has been designated as the Rh factor, or D antigen. People with the D antigen are said to be *Rh positive;*

those without this antigen are *Rh negative*. In routine blood banking, the presence or absence of the three antigens—A, B, and D—must be determined in testing for the compatibility of the donor and recipient.

Serum is important because it contains certain proteins known as antibodies. **The fundamental principle of blood typing is that for every antigen, there exists a specific antibody.** Each antibody symbol contains the prefix *anti-,* followed by the name of the antigen for which it is specific. Hence, anti-A is specific only for A antigen, anti-B for B antigen, and anti-D for D antigen. The serum-containing antibody is referred to as the antiserum, meaning a serum that reacts against something (antigens).

An antibody reacts only with its specific antigen and no other. Thus, if serum containing anti-B is added to red blood cells carrying the B antigen, the two immediately combine, causing the antibody to attach itself to the cell. Antibodies are normally *bivalent*—that is, they have two reactive sites. This means that each antibody can simultaneously be attached to antigens located on two different red blood cells. This creates a vast network of cross-linked cells usually seen as clumping or agglutination (see Figure 12–1).

Let's look a little more closely at this phenomenon. In normal blood, shown in Figure 12–2(a), antigens on red blood cells and antibodies coexist without destroying each other because the antibodies present are not specific toward any of the antigens. However, suppose a foreign serum added to the blood introduces a new antibody. The occurrence of a specific antigen–antibody reaction immediately causes the red blood cells to link together, or agglutinate, as shown in Figure 12–2(b).

Evidently, nature has taken this situation into account, for when we examine the serum of type A blood, we find anti-B and no anti-A. Similarly, type B blood contains only anti-A, type O blood has both anti-A and anti-B, and type AB blood contains neither anti-A nor anti-B. The antigen and antibody components of normal blood are summarized in the following table:

Blood Type	Antigens on Red Blood Cells	Antibodies in Serum
A	A	Anti-B
B	B	Anti-A
AB	AB	Neither anti-A nor anti-B
O	Neither A nor B	Both anti-A and anti-B

The reasons for the fatal consequences of mixing incompatible blood during a transfusion should now be quite obvious. For example, transfusing type A blood into a type B patient will cause the natural anti-A in the blood of the type B patient to react promptly with the incoming A antigens, resulting in agglutination. In addition, the incoming anti-B of the donor will react with the B antigens of the patient.

Blood Typing

The term serology is used to describe a broad scope of laboratory tests that use specific antigen and serum antibody reactions. The most widespread application of serology is the typing of whole blood for its A-B-O identity. In determining the A-B-O blood type, only two antiserums are needed—anti-A and anti-B. For routine blood typing, both of these antiserums are commercially available.

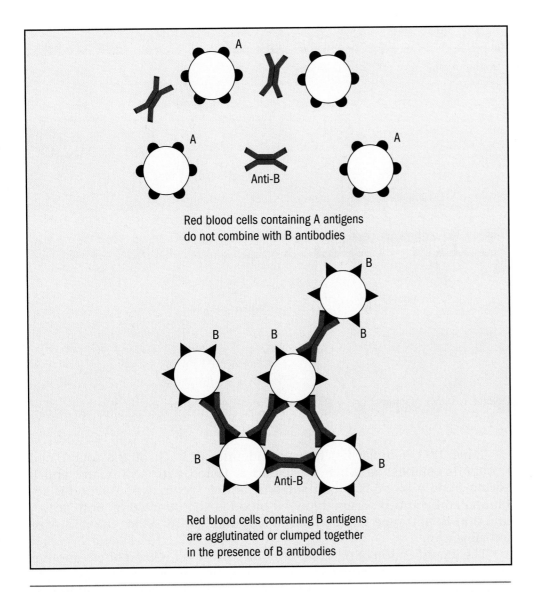

Red blood cells containing A antigens
do not combine with B antibodies

Red blood cells containing B antigens
are agglutinated or clumped together
in the presence of B antibodies

Figure 12–1

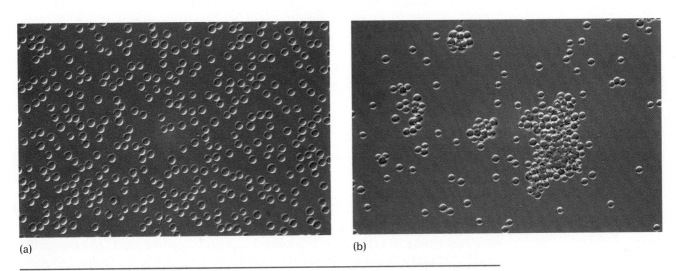

(a)

(b)

**Figure 12–2   (a) Microscopic view of normal red blood cells (500×). (b) Microscopic view of
agglutinated red blood cells (500×).** *Courtesy J.C. Revy, Phototake NYC*

Table 12–1	Identification of Blood with Known Antiserum		
Anti-A Serum + Whole Blood	Anti-B Serum + Whole Blood	Antigen Present	Blood Type
+	−	A	A
−	+	B	B
+	+	A and B	AB
−	−	Neither A nor B	O

Note: + shows agglutination; − shows absence of agglutination.

Table 12–2	Identification of Blood with Known Cells		
A Cells + Blood	B Cells + Blood	Antibody Present	Blood Type
+	−	Anti-A	B
−	+	Anti-B	A
+	+	Both anti-A and anti-B	O
−	−	Neither anti-A nor anti-B	AB

Note: + shows agglutination; − shows absence of agglutination.

Table 12–1 summarizes how the identity of each of the four blood groups is established when the blood is tested with anti-A and anti-B serum. Type A blood is agglutinated by anti-A serum; type B blood is agglutinated by anti-B serum; type AB blood is agglutinated by both anti-A and anti-B; and type O blood is not agglutinated by either the anti-A or anti-B serum.

The identification of natural antibodies present in blood offers another route to the determination of blood type. Testing blood for the presence of anti-A and anti-B requires using red blood cells that have known antigens. Again, these cells are commercially available. Hence, when A cells are added to a blood specimen, agglutination occurs only in the presence of anti-A. Similarly, B cells agglutinate only in the presence of anti-B. All four A-B-O types can be identified in this manner by testing blood with known A and B cells, as summarized in Table 12–2.

The population distribution of blood types varies with location and race throughout the world. In the United States, a typical distribution is as follows:

O	A	B	AB
43%	42%	12%	3%

Immunoassay Techniques

The concept of a specific antigen–antibody reaction is finding application in other areas unrelated to the blood typing of individuals. Most significantly, this approach has been extended to the detection of drugs in blood and urine. Antibodies that react with drugs do not naturally exist; however, they can be produced in animals such as rabbits by first combining the

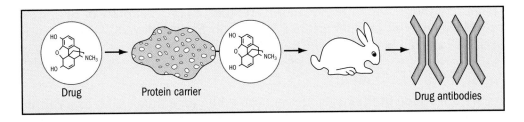

Figure 12–3

drug with a protein and injecting this combination into the animal. This drug–protein complex acts as an antigen stimulating the animal to produce antibodies (see Figure 12–3). The recovered blood serum of the animal will contain antibodies that are specific or nearly specific to the drug.

A number of immunological assay techniques are commercially available for detecting drugs through an antigen–antibody reaction. One such technique, the *enzyme-multiplied immunoassay technique (EMIT)*, has gained widespread popularity among toxicologists because of its speed and high sensitivity for detecting drugs in urine. A typical EMIT analysis begins by adding to a subject's urine antibodies that bind to the drug being measured. For example, if someone's urine is being checked for the presence of methadone, one would add methadone antibodies to the urine. Any methadone present in the urine immediately combines with these antibodies. Then enzyme-labeled methadone is added to the urine. Methadone antibodies that did not interact with the methadone now combine with the enzyme-labeled methadone. The quantity of enzyme-labeled methadone left uncombined is then measured, and this value is related to the concentration of methadone originally present in the urine.

One of the most frequent uses of EMIT in forensic laboratories has been for screening the urine of suspected marijuana smokers. In marijuana, THC is considered the primary pharmacologically active agent (see p. 256). To facilitate its elimination, the body converts THC to a series of substances or metabolites that are more readily excreted. The major THC metabolite found in urine is a substance called *THC-9-carboxylic acid*. Antibodies against this metabolite are prepared for EMIT testing. Normally, the urine of marijuana smokers contains THC-9-carboxylic acid in a very small quantity (less than one-millionth of a gram); however, this level is readily detected by EMIT.

The greatest problem with detecting marijuana in urine is interpretation. While smoking marijuana will result in the detection of THC metabolite, it is very difficult to determine when the individual actually used marijuana. In individuals who smoke marijuana frequently, detection is possible within two to five days after the last use of the drug. However, some individuals may yield positive results up to ten days after the last use of marijuana. Though EMIT is currently a popular immunoassay technique in forensic laboratories, other immunoassay procedures are commercially available. For example, *radioimmunoassay (RIA)* uses drugs labeled with radioactive tags. Whether using an enzyme tag as in EMIT or a radioactive tag as in RIA, the analyst must be cautious because immunoassay techniques are not totally specific for any drug. Substances with a chemical structure similar to the drug in question may cross-react with the antibody to give a false-positive reaction. Hence, positive immunoassay tests must always be confirmed by another reliable analytical procedure. The issue of specificity, along with other questions relating to the reliability of RIA, was raised during the murder trial of Dr. Mario E. Jascalevich, which is described in detail at the end of Chapter 1.

Monoclonal Antibodies

As we have seen in the previous section, when an animal, such as a rabbit or mouse, is injected with an antigen, the animal responds by producing antibodies designed to bind to the invading antigen. However, the process of producing antibodies designed to respond to foreign antigens is complex. For one, an antigen typically has structurally different sites to which an antibody may bind. So when the animal is actively producing attack antibodies it produces a series of different antibodies, all of which are designed to attack some particular site on the antigen of interest. These antibodies are known as polyclonal antibodies. However, the disadvantage of polyclonal antibodies is that an animal can produce antibodies that vary in composition over time. As a result, different batches of polyclonals may vary in their specificity and their ability to bind to a particular antigen site.

As the technologies associated with forensic science have grown in importance, a need has developed, in some instances, to have access to antibodies that are more uniform in their composition and attack power than the traditional polyclonals. This is best accomplished by adopting a process in which an animal will produce antibodies designed to attack one and only one site on an antigen. Such antibodies are known as monoclonal antibodies. How can such monoclonals be produced? The process begins by injecting a mouse with the antigen of interest. In response, the mouse's spleen cells will produce antibodies to fight off the invading antigen. The spleen cells are removed from the animal and are fused to fast-growing blood cancer cells to produce hybridoma cells. The hybridoma cells are then allowed to multiply and are screened for their specific antibody activity. The hybridoma cells that bear the antibody activity of interest are then selected and cultured. The rapidly multiplying cancer cells linked to the selected antibody cells produce identical monoclonal antibodies in a limitless supply (see Figure 12–4).

Monoclonal antibodies are being incorporated into commercial forensic test kits with increasing frequency. Many immunoassay test kits for drugs of abuse are being formulated with monoclonal antibodies. Also, a recently introduced test for seminal material that incorporates a monoclonal antibody has found wide popularity in crime laboratories (see pp. 369–370).

As a side note, in 1999 the U.S. Food and Drug Administration approved a monoclonal drug treatment for cancer. Rituxin is a nontoxic monoclonal antibody designed to attack and destroy cancerous white blood cells containing an antigen designated as CD20. Other monoclonal drug treatments are in the pipeline. Monoclonals are finally beginning to fulfill their long-held expectation as medicine's version of the "magic bullet."

Polyclonal Antibodies
Antibodies produced by injecting animals with a specific antigen. A series of antibodies are produced responding to a variety of different sites on the antigen.

Monoclonal Antibodies
A collection of identical antibodies that interact with a single antigen site.

Hybridoma Cells
Fused spleen and tumor cells. Used to produce identical monoclonal antibodies in a limitless supply.

Forensic Characterization of Bloodstains

The criminalist must answer the following questions when examining dried blood: (1) Is it blood? (2) From what species did the blood originate? (3) If the blood is of human origin, how closely can it be associated with a particular individual?

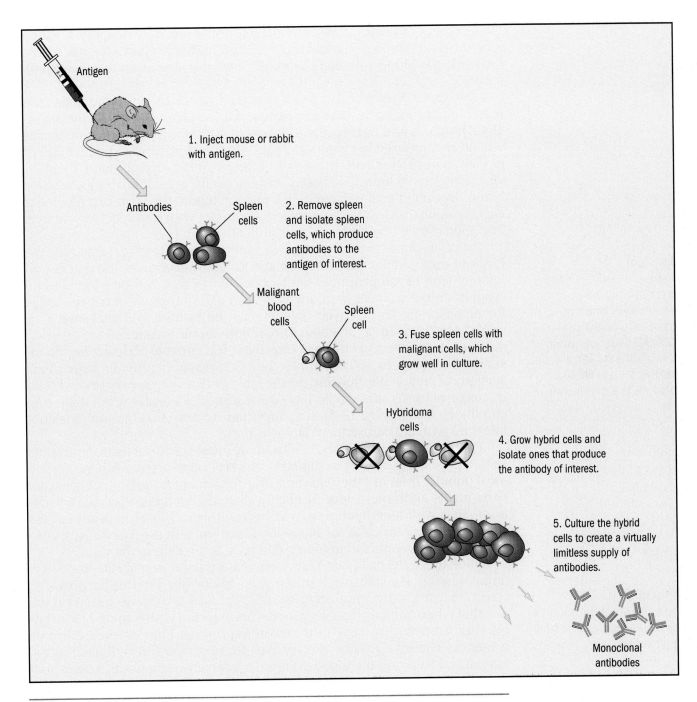

Figure 12–4 Steps required to produce monoclonal antibodies.

The determination of blood is best made by means of a preliminary color test. For many years, the most commonly used test for this purpose was the *benzidine color test;* however, because benzidine has been identified as a known carcinogen, its use has generally been discontinued, and the chemical phenolphthalein is usually substituted in its place (this test is also known as the *Kastle-Meyer color test*).[1] Both the benzidine and Kastle-Meyer color tests are based on the observation that blood hemoglobin possesses peroxidase-like activity. Peroxidases are enzymes that accelerate

Hemoglobin
A red blood cell protein that transports oxygen in the bloodstream; it is responsible for the red color of blood.

[1] M. Cox, "A Study of the Sensitivity and Specificity of Four Presumptive Tests for Blood," *Journal of Forensic Sciences* 36 (1991): 1503.

the oxidation of several classes of organic compounds by peroxides. When a bloodstain, phenolphthalein reagent, and hydrogen peroxide are mixed together, the blood's hemoglobin will cause the formation of a deep pink color.

The Kastle-Meyer test is not a specific test for blood; some vegetable materials, for instance, may turn Kastle-Meyer pink. These substances include potatoes and horseradish. However, it is unlikely that such materials will be encountered in criminal situations, and thus from a practical point of view, a positive Kastle-Meyer test is highly indicative of blood. Field investigators have found Hemastix strips a useful presumptive field test for blood. Designed as a urine dipstick test for blood, the strip can be moistened with distilled water and placed in contact with a suspect bloodstain. The appearance of a green color is indicative of blood.

Another important presumptive identification test for blood is the luminol test.[2] Unlike the benzidine and Kastle-Meyer tests, the reaction of luminol with blood produces light rather than color. By spraying luminol reagent onto a suspect item, investigators can quickly screen large areas for bloodstains. The sprayed objects must be located in a darkened area while being viewed for the emission of light (luminescence).

The luminol test is extremely sensitive—it is capable of detecting bloodstains diluted up to 300,000 times. For this reason, spraying large areas such as carpets, walls, flooring, or the interior of a vehicle may reveal blood traces or patterns that would have gone unnoticed under normal lighting conditions (see Figure 12–5). It is important to note that luminol does not interfere with any subsequent DNA testing.[3]

The identification of blood can be made more specific if microcrystalline tests are performed on the material. Several tests are available; the two most popular ones are the *Takayama* and *Teichmann tests*. Both of these depend on the addition of specific chemicals to the blood so that characteristic crystals with hemoglobin derivatives will form. Crystal tests are far less sensitive than color tests for blood identification and are more susceptible to interference from contaminants that may be present in the stain.

Once the stain has been characterized as blood, the serologist determines whether the stain is of human or animal origin. For this purpose, the standard test used is the precipitin test. Precipitin tests are based on the fact that when animals (usually rabbits) are injected with human blood, antibodies form that react with the invading human blood to neutralize its presence. The investigator can recover these antibodies by bleeding the animal and isolating the blood serum. This serum contains antibodies that specifically react with human antigens. For this reason, the serum is known as *human antiserum*. In the same manner, by injecting rabbits with the blood of other known animals, virtually any kind of animal antiserum can be produced. Currently, antiserums are commercially available for humans and for a variety of commonly encountered animals—for example, dogs, cats, and deer.

A number of techniques have been devised for performing precipitin tests on bloodstains. The classic method is to layer an extract of the bloodstain on top of the human antiserum in a capillary tube. Human blood, or for

Luminol
The most sensitive chemical test that is capable of presumptively detecting bloodstains diluted up to 300,000 times. Its reaction with blood emits light and thus requires the result to be observed in a darkened area.

Precipitin
An antibody that reacts with its corresponding antigen to form a precipitate.

---

[2] The luminol reagent is prepared by mixing 0.1 grams 3-amino-phthalhydrazide and 5.0 grams sodium carbonate in 100 milliliters distilled water. Before use, 0.7 grams sodium perborate is added to the solution.

[3] A. M. Gross et al., "The Effect of Luminol on Presumptive Tests and DNA Analysis Using the Polymerase Chain Reaction," *Journal of Forensic Sciences* 44 (1999): 837.

(a)

(b)

Figure 12–5 **(a) A section of a linoleum floor photographed under normal light. This floor was located in the residence of a missing person. (b) Same section of the floor shown in (a) after spraying with luminol. A circular pattern was revealed. Investigators concluded that the circular blood pattern was left by the bottom of a bucket carried about during the cleaning up of the blood. A small clump of sponge, blood, and hair was found near where this photograph was taken.** *Courtesy North Carolina State Bureau of Investigation*

that matter, any protein of human origin in the extract, reacts specifically with antibodies present in the antiserum, as indicated by the formation of a cloudy ring or band at the interface of the two liquids (see Figure 12–6).

Another method, called *gel diffusion,* takes advantage of the fact that antibodies and antigens diffuse or move toward one another on an agar gel–coated plate. The extracted bloodstain and the human antiserum are placed in separate holes opposite each other on the gel. If the blood is of human origin, a line of precipitation will form where the antigens and antibodies meet. Similarly, the antigens and antibodies can be induced to move toward one another under the influence of an electrical field. In the *electrophoretic method* (see pp. 142–146), an electrical potential is applied to the gel medium; a specific antigen–antibody reaction is denoted by a line of precipitation formed between the hole containing the blood extract and the hole containing the human antiserum (see Figure 12–7).

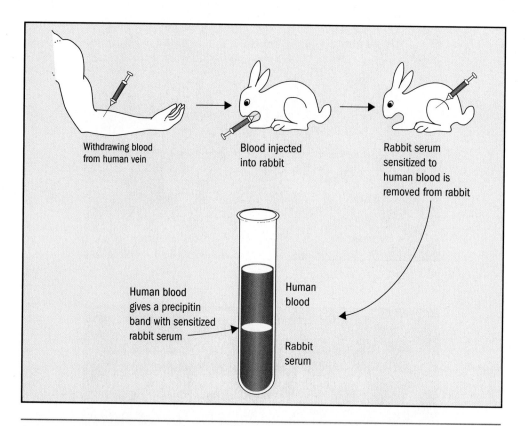

Figure 12–6

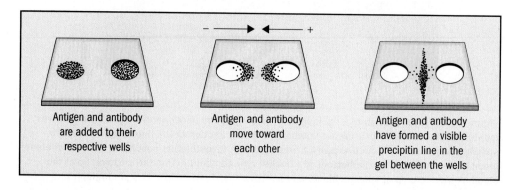

Antigen and antibody are added to their respective wells

Antigen and antibody move toward each other

Antigen and antibody have formed a visible precipitin line in the gel between the wells

Figure 12–7

The precipitin test is very sensitive and requires only a small amount of blood for testing. Human bloodstains dried for ten to fifteen years and longer may still give a positive precipitin reaction. Even extracts of tissue from mummies four to five thousand years old have given positive reactions with this test. Furthermore, human bloodstains diluted by washing in water and left with only a faint color may still yield a positive precipitin reaction (see Figure 12–8).

Once it has been determined that the bloodstain is of human origin, an effort must be made to associate or disassociate the stain with a particular individual. Until the mid-1990s, routine characterization of bloodstains included the determination of A-B-O types; however, the widespread use of

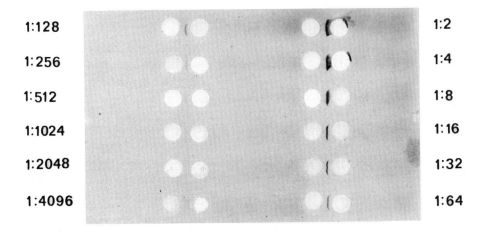

Figure 12–8 **Results of the precipitin test of dilutions of human serum up to 1 in 4,096 against a human antiserum. A reaction is visible for blood dilutions up to 1 in 256.** *Courtesy Millipore Biomedica, Acton, Mass.*

DNA profiling or typing has relegated this subject to one of historical interest only.

In addition to the A and B antigens discussed earlier, other substances found in the red blood cell were widely investigated until the mid-1990s as forensic scientists sought to individualize bloodstains. These other substances are called enzymes. Enzymes are proteins that have important functions in regulating many of the body's chemical reactions. In the past, forensic serologists were particularly interested in enzymes that exist in different forms, or are polymorphic. These enzymes can actually be separated into protein components called iso-enzymes. Again, the advent of DNA analysis has reduced this approach for characterizing biological stains to one of historical interest only.

Let's look at one such enzyme, PGM, in order to understand how forensic serologists use this marker to characterize biological evidence. The iso-enzymes of PGM (phosphoglucomutase) can be separated from one another by electrophoresis (see pp. 142–146). What is interesting and most important about this separation is the observation that everyone does not have the same PGM iso-enzymes. Actually, as shown in Figure 12–9, there are three common variations or types of PGM: PGM 1, PGM 2-1, and PGM 2. These variations are distributed unevenly throughout the population: PGM 1 is present in approximately 58 percent of the population; PGM 2-1 in 36 percent; and PGM 2 in 6 percent. Thus, identification of the PGM type in a dried bloodstain provides the forensic serologist with added statistical information with which to reduce the number of possible sources of the bloodstain. Numerous polymorphic enzymes in red blood cells provide potential markers for determining blood origin. Also, a number of polymorphic proteins have been found in blood serum. However, from a practical point of view, only enzymes and proteins that are capable of surviving the drying and aging processes are of any value to the forensic serologist.

Because antigens, enzymes, and proteins occur independently of one another, the probability of a dried bloodstain having a particular combination of these factors is determined by the product of their distribution in the population (see p. 75). For example, if a bloodstain is found to be

Enzyme
A type of protein that acts as a catalyst for certain specific reactions.

Polymorphism
The existence of more than one form of a genetic trait.

Iso-enzymes
Multiple molecular forms of an enzyme, each having the same or very similar enzyme activities.

type A, then such a stain could have originated from approximately 42 percent of the population. Now, if it is also determined that this stain contains PGM 1, then its origin can be narrowed to 24 percent of the population (42% × 58% = 24%). Obviously, the more factors a serologist can find in a stain, the smaller its frequency of occurrence in a population. Hence, forensic researchers have made extensive efforts at uncovering blood factors that are identifiable in bloodstains (see Table 12–3).

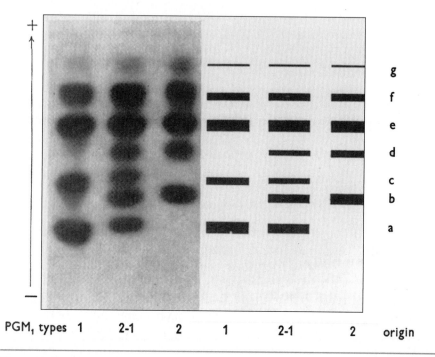

Figure 12–9   Photograph and diagram of the separation of PGM iso-enzymes accomplished by electrophoresis. PGM can be grouped into one of three types—1, 2-1, and 2—according to band patterns. *Reproduced from Harry Harris,* The Principles of Human Biochemical Genetics, *2nd ed. New York: North-Holland, 1975, p. 61*

Table 12–3 Blood Enzymes and Proteins Used to Discriminate Bloodstains	
Blood Factor	**Abbreviation**
Adenosine deaminase	ADA
Adenylate kinase	AK
Carbonic anhydrase II	CA II
Erythrocyte acid phosphatase	EAP
Esterase D	EsD
Glucose-6-phosphate dehydrogenase	G6PD
Glyoxylase I	GLO I
Group-specific component	Gc
Haptoglobin	Hp
Peptidase A	Pep A
Phosphoglucomutase	PGM
6-Phosphogluconate dehydrogenase	6PGD
Transferrin	Tf

Stain Patterns of Blood

The crime-scene investigator must not overlook the fact that the location, distribution, and appearance of bloodstains and spatters may be useful for interpreting and reconstructing the events that must have occurred to have produced the bleeding. A thorough analysis of the significance of the position and shape of blood patterns with respect to their origin and trajectory is exceedingly complex and requires the services of an examiner who is experienced in such determinations. Most important, the interpretation of bloodstain patterns necessitates carefully planned control experiments using surface materials comparable to those found at the crime scene.

A number of observations and conclusions have important implications for any investigator who seeks to trace the direction, dropping distance, and angle of impact of a bloodstain. Some of them can be summarized as follows:

1. Surface texture is of paramount importance in the interpretation of bloodstain patterns, and correlations between standards and unknowns are valid only if identical surfaces are used. In general, the harder and less porous the surface, the less spatter results. The effect of surface is shown in Figure 12–10.

2. The direction of travel of blood striking an object may be discerned by the stain's shape. The pointed end of a bloodstain always faces its direction of travel. In Figure 12–11, the bloodstain pattern was produced by several droplets of blood that were traveling from left to right before striking a flat level surface.

3. It is possible to determine the impact angle of blood on a flat surface by measuring the degree of circular distortion of the stain. A drop of blood striking a surface at right angles gives rise to a nearly circular stain; as the angle decreases, the stain becomes elongated in shape. This progressive elongation is evident in Figure 12–12.

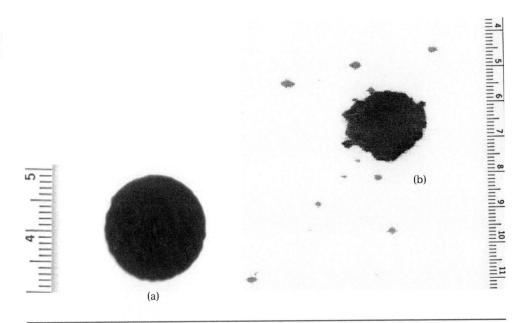

Figure 12–10 **(a) Bloodstain from a single drop of blood that struck a glass surface after falling 24 inches. (b) Bloodstain from a single drop of blood that struck a cotton muslin sheet after falling 24 inches.** *Courtesy A. Y. Wonder*

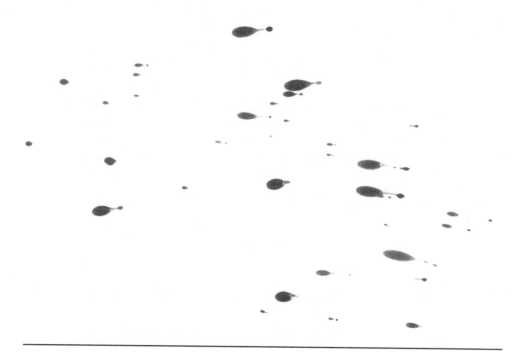

Figure 12–11 **Bloodstain pattern produced by droplets of blood that were traveling from left to right.** *Courtesy A. Y. Wonder*

Figure 12–12 **The higher pattern is of a single drop of human blood that fell 24 inches and struck a hard, smooth cardboard at 50 degrees. The lower pattern is of a single drop of human blood that fell 24 inches and struck a hard, smooth cardboard at 15 degrees.** *Courtesy A. Y. Wonder*

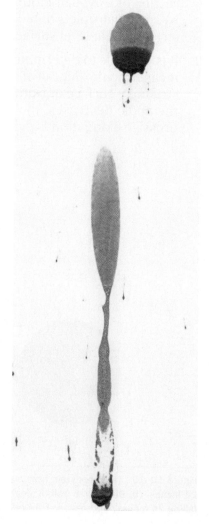

4. The origin of a blood spatter in a two-dimensional configuration can be established by drawing straight lines through the long axis of several individual bloodstains. The intersection or area of convergence of the lines represents the area from which the blood emanated (see Figure 12–13).

An example of the utility of blood spatter formations in performing crime-scene reconstruction is illustrated in Figures 12–14 through 12–16. This case relates to an elderly male who was found lying dead on his living-room floor. He had been beaten about the face and head, then stabbed in the chest and robbed. The reconstruction of bloodstains found on the interior front door and the adjacent wall documented that the victim was beaten about the face with a fist and struck on the back of the head with his cane. A suspect was apprehended three days later, and he was found to have an acute fracture of the right hand. When he was confronted with the bloodstain evidence, the suspect admitted striking the victim, first with his fist, then with a cane, and finally stabbing him with a kitchen knife. The suspect pleaded guilty to three first-degree felonies.

Web-Extra 12-1
See How Blood Stain Patterns are Formed
www.prenhall.com/Saferstein

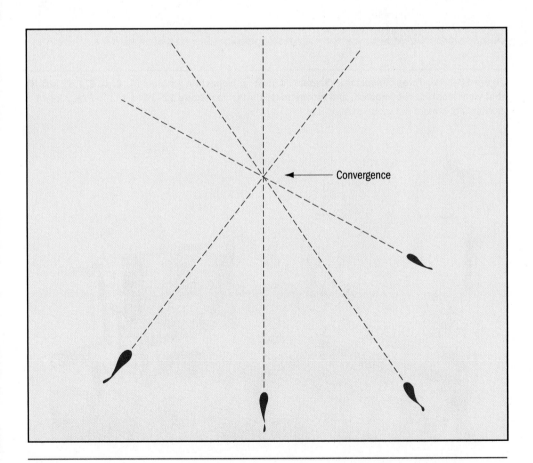

Figure 12–13 Illustration of stain convergence on a two-dimensional plane. Convergence represents the area from which the stains emanated. *Courtesy Judith Bunker, J. L. Bunker & Assoc., Ocoee, Fla.*

Figure 12–14a Three-dimensional diagram illustrating bloodstain patterns (A, B, C, E, F, G, and H) that were located, documented, and reconstructed. Also see Figure 12–16 (a–c). *Courtesy Judith Bunker, J.L. Bunker & Assoc., Ocoee, FLa.*

Figure 12–14b Crime-scene photograph of bloodstained areas. *Courtesy Sarasota County (Fla.) Sheriff's Department*

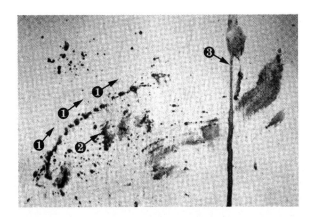

Figure 12–14c Detail photograph of bloodstains designated A, B, and C on the wall adjacent to the interior door. Positions of impact spatter from blows that were inflicted to victim's face are indicated in Figure 12–16(a). Arrow no 1 points to cast-off pattern directed left to right as blood was flung from the perpetrator's fist while inflicting blows. Arrow no. 2 points to three repetitive transfer impression patterns directed left to right as the perpetrator's bloodstained hand contacted the wall as the fist blows were being inflicted on the victim. Arrow no. 3 points to blood flow from the victim's wounds as he slumped against the wall. *Courtesy Judith Bunker, J.L. Bunker & Assoc., Ocoee, Fla.*

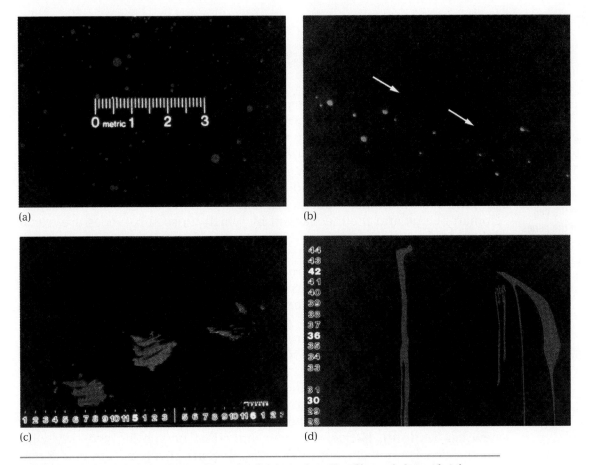

(a)

(b)

(c)

(d)

Figure 12–15 (a) Laboratory test pattern showing impact spatter. Size and shape of stains demonstrate forceful impact 90 degrees to target. (b) Laboratory test pattern illustrating cast-off pattern directed left to right from a right overhead swing. (c) Laboratory test pattern showing repetitive transfer impression pattern produced by a bloodstained hand moving left to right across the target. (d) Laboratory test patterns illustrating vertical flow patterns. Left pattern represents stationary source; right pattern produced by left-to-right motion. *Courtesy Judith Bunker, J.L. Bunker & Assoc., Ocoee, Fla.*

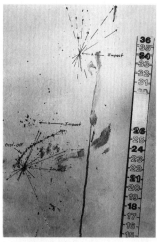
(a) Patterns A, B, C

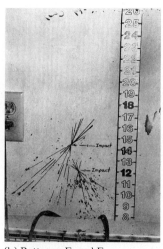
(b) Patterns E and F

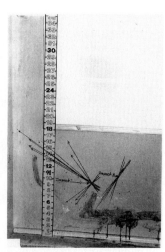
(c) Patterns G and H

Figure 12–16 **(a) Convergence of impact spatter patterns associated with beating by fist. (b) Convergence of impact spatter associated with victim falling to the floor while bleeding from the nose. (c) Convergence of impact spatter associated with victim while face down at the door, being struck with a cane.** *Courtesy Judith Bunker, J.L. Bunker & Assoc., Ocoee, Fla.*

Principles of Heredity

Transmission of Our Traits

All of the antigens and polymorphic enzymes and proteins that have been described in previous sections are genetically controlled traits. That is, they are inherited from parents and become a permanent feature of a person's biological makeup from the moment he or she is conceived. Determining the identity of these traits, then, not only provides us with a picture of how one individual compares to or differs from another, but gives us an insight into the basic biological substances that determine our overall makeup as human beings and the mechanism by which those substances are transmitted from one generation to the next.

Hereditary material is transmitted via microscopic units called **genes**. The gene is the basic unit of heredity. Each gene by itself or in concert with other genes controls the development of a specific characteristic in the new individual; the genes determine the nature and growth of virtually every body structure.

The genes are positioned on **chromosomes**, threadlike bodies that appear in the nucleus of every body cell. See Figure 12–17. All human cells contain forty-six chromosomes, mated in twenty-three pairs. The only exceptions are the human reproductive cells, the **egg** and **sperm**, which contain only twenty-three unmated chromosomes. During fertilization, a sperm and egg combine so that each contributes chromosomes to form the new cell (**zygote**). Hence, the new individual begins life properly with twenty-three mated chromosome pairs. Because the genes are positioned on the chromosomes, the new individual inherits genetic material from each parent.

Actually, two dissimilar chromosomes are involved in the determination of sex. The egg cell always contains a long chromosome known as the X chromosome; but the sperm cell may contain either a short chromo-

Gene
A unit of inheritance consisting of a DNA segment located on a chromosome.

Chromosome
A rodlike structure in the cell nucleus, along which the genes are located. It is composed of DNA surrounded by other material, mainly proteins.

Egg
The female reproductive cell.

Sperm
The male reproductive cell.

Zygote
The cell arising from the union of an egg and a sperm cell.

X Chromosome
The female sex chromosome.

Web-Extra 12-2

Learn About the Chromosomes Present in Our Cells

www.prenhall.com/Saferstein

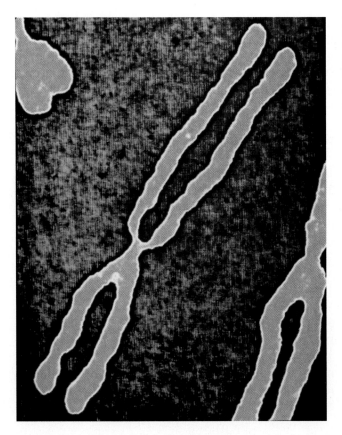

Figure 12–17 Computer-enhanced photomicrograph image of human chromosomes. *Courtesy Alfred Pasieka, Science Photo Library, Photo Researchers, Inc.*

some, known as the Y chromosome, or a long X chromosome. When an X-carrying sperm fertilizes an egg, the new cell is XX and develops into a female. A Y-carrying sperm produces an XY fertilized egg and develops into a male. Because the sperm cell ultimately determines the nature of the chromosome pair, we can say that the father biologically determines the sex of the child.

Just as chromosomes come together in pairs, so do the genes they bear. The position a gene occupies on a chromosome is its locus. Genes that govern a given characteristic are similarly positioned on the chromosomes inherited from the mother and father. Thus, a gene for eye color on the mother's chromosome will be aligned with a gene for eye color on the corresponding chromosome inherited from the father. Alternative forms of genes that influence a given characteristic and are aligned with one another on a chromosome pair are known as alleles. Another simple example of allele genes in humans is that of blood types belonging to the A-B-O system. Inheritance of the A-B-O type is best described by a theory that utilizes three genes designated A, B, and O.

A gene pair made up of two similar genes—for example, AA and BB—is said to be homozygous; a gene pair made up of two different genes—AO, for example—is said to be heterozygous. If the chromosome inherited from the father carries the A gene and the chromosome inherited from the mother carries the same gene, the offspring would have an AA combination. Similarly, if one chromosome contains the A gene and the other has the O gene, the genetic makeup of the offspring would be AO.

Y Chromosome
The male sex chromosome.

Locus
The physical location of a gene on a chromosome.

Allele
Any of several alternative forms of a gene located at the same point on a particular pair of chromosomes. For example, the genes determining the blood types A and B are alleles.

Homozygous
Having two identical allelic genes on two corresponding positions of a pair of chromosomes.

Heterozygous
Having two different allelic genes on two corresponding positions of a pair of chromosomes.

Web-Extra 12-3
Learn About the Structure of Our Genes
www.prenhall.com/Saferstein

Genotype
The particular combination of genes present in the cells of an individual.

Phenotype
The physical manifestation of a genetic trait such as shape, color, and blood type.

When an individual inherits two similar genes from his or her parents, there is no problem in determining the blood type of that person. Hence, an AA combination will always be type A, a BB type B, and an OO type O. However, when two different genes are inherited, one gene will be dominant. It can be said that the A and B genes are *dominant* and that the O gene is always *recessive*—that is, its characteristics remain hidden. For instance, with an AO combination, A is always dominant over O, and the individual will be typed as A. Similarly, a BO combination is typed as B. In the case of AB, the genes are codominant, and the individual's blood type will be AB. The recessive characteristics of O appear only when both recessive genes are present. Hence, the combination OO is typed simply as O.

A pair of allele genes together constitutes the **genotype** of the individual. However, no laboratory test can determine an individual's A-B-O genotype. For example, a person's outward characteristic, or **phenotype**, may be that of type A, but this does not tell us whether his or her genotype is AA or AO. The genotype can be determined only by studying the family history of the individual. If the genotypes of both parents are known, that of their possible offspring can be forecast.

An easy way to figure this out is to construct a *Punnett square*. To do this, write along a horizontal line the two genes of the male parent, and in the vertical column write the two kinds of female genes present, as shown. In our example, we assume the male parent is type O and therefore has to be an OO genotype; the female parent is type AB and can be only an AB genotype:

Father's
genotype

	O	O
A		
B		

Mother's genotype

Next, write in each box the corresponding gene contributed from the female and then from the male. The squares will contain all the possible genotype combinations that the parents can produce in their offspring:

	O	O
A	AO	AO
B	BO	BO

Hence, in this case, 50 percent of the offspring are likely to be AO and the other 50 percent BO. These are the only genotypes possible from this combination. Because O is recessive, 50 percent of the offspring will probably be type A and 50 percent type B. **From this example, we can see that no blood group gene can appear in a child unless it is present in at least one of the parents.**

In the same way, the genotypes of parents determine the identity of all blood group systems as well as the polymorphic enzymes and proteins of

Web-Extra 12-4
See How Genes Position Themselves on a Chromosome Pair
www.prenhall.com/Saferstein

their offspring. For example, an individual whose blood carries the enzyme EAP-BA has two allelic genes determining this trait. One gene corresponds to EAP-B, the other to EAP-A. When paired, these genes are codominant.

Paternity Testing

Although the genotyping of blood factors has useful applications for studying the transmission of blood characteristics from one generation to the next, it has no direct relevance to criminal investigations. It does, however, have important implications in disputed-paternity cases, which are normally encountered in civil, not criminal, courts.

Many cases of disputed paternity can be resolved when the suspected parents and the offspring are related according to their blood group systems. For instance, in the previous example, had the child been type AB, the suspected father would have been cleared. A type O father and a type AB mother cannot have a type AB child. On the other hand, if the child had been type A or type B, the most that could be said is that the suspect may have been the father; this does not mean that he *is* the father, just that he is not excluded based on blood typing. Obviously, many other males also have type O blood. Of course, the more blood group systems that are tested, the better the chances of excluding an innocent male from involvement. Conversely, if no discrepancies are found between offspring and suspect father, the more certain one can be that the suspect is indeed the father. In fact, routine paternity testing involves characterizing blood factors other than A-B-O. For example, the HLA (human leukocyte antigen) test relies on identifying a complex system of antigens on white blood cells. If a suspect cannot be excluded as fathering a child after this test is performed, the chances are better than 90 percent that he is the father. Currently, paternity testing laboratories have implemented DNA test procedures that can raise the odds of establishing paternity beyond 99 percent.

Forensic Characterization of Semen

Many cases received in a forensic laboratory involve sexual offenses, making it necessary to examine exhibits for the presence of seminal stains.

The normal male releases 2.5 to 6 milliliters of seminal fluid during an ejaculation. Each milliliter contains 100 million or more spermatozoa, the male reproductive cells. Forensic examination of articles for seminal stains can actually be considered a two-step process. First, before any tests can be conducted, the stain must be located. Considering the number and soiled condition of outergarments, undergarments, and possible bedclothing submitted for examination, this may prove to be an arduous task. Once located, the stain will have to be subjected to tests that will prove its identity; it may even be tested for the blood type of the individual from whom it originated.

Often, seminal stains are readily visible on a fabric because they exhibit a stiff, crusty appearance. However, reliance on such appearance for locating the stain is at best unreliable and is useful only when the stain is present in a rather obvious area. Certainly, if the fabric has been

Web-Extra 12-5
See How Genes Define Our Genetic Makeup
www.prenhall.com/Saferstein

Acid Phosphatase
An enzyme found in high concentration in semen.

washed or contains only minute quantities of semen, visual examination of the article offers little chance of detecting the stain. The best way to locate and characterize a seminal stain is to perform the *acid phosphatase color test.*

Acid phosphatase is an enzyme that is secreted by the prostate gland into seminal fluid. Its concentrations in seminal fluid are up to 400 times greater than those found in any other body fluid. Its presence can easily be detected when it comes in contact with an acidic solution of sodium alpha naphthylphosphate and Fast Blue B dye. Also, 4-methyl umbelliferyl phosphate (MUP) fluoresces under UV light when it comes in contact with acid phosphatase.

The utility of the acid phosphatase test is apparent when it becomes necessary to search numerous garments or large fabric areas for seminal stains. If a filter paper is simply moistened with water and rubbed lightly over the suspect area, acid phosphatase, if present, is transferred to the filter paper. Then, when a drop or two of the sodium alpha naphthylphosphate and Fast Blue B solution are placed on the paper, the appearance of a purple color indicates the acid phosphatase enzyme. In this manner, any fabric or surface can be systematically searched for seminal stains. If it is necessary to search extremely large areas—for example, a bedsheet or carpet—the article can be tested in sections, narrowing the location of the stain with each successive test. Alternatively, the garment under investigation can be pressed against a suitably sized piece of moistened filter paper. The paper is then sprayed with MUP solution. Semen stains appear as strongly fluorescent areas under UV light. A negative reaction can be interpreted as meaning the absence of semen. Although some vegetable and fruit juices (such as cauliflower and watermelon), fungi, contraceptive creams, and vaginal secretions give a positive response to the acid phosphatase test, none of these substances normally reacts with the speed of seminal fluid. A reaction time of less than 30 seconds is considered a strong indication of the presence of semen.

Semen can be unequivocally identified by the presence of spermatozoa. When spermatozoa are located through a microscope examination, the stain is definitely identified as having been derived from semen. Spermatozoa are slender, elongated structures 50–70 microns long, each with a head and a thin flagellate tail (see Figure 12–18). The criminalist can normally locate them by immersing the stained material in a small volume of water. Rapid stirring of the liquid transfers a small percentage of the spermatozoa present into the water. A drop of the water is dried onto a microscope slide, then stained and examined under a compound microscope at a magnification of approximately 400×.[4]

Considering the extremely large number of spermatozoa found in seminal fluid, one would think the chance of locating one would be very good; however, this is not always true. One reason is that spermatozoa are bound tightly to cloth materials.[5] Also, spermatozoa are extremely brittle when

[4] J. P. Allery et al., "Cytological Detection of Spermatozoa: Comparison of Three Staining Methods," *Journal of Forensic Sciences* 46 (2001): 349.

[5] In one study, only a maximum of 4 sperm cells out of 1,000 could be extracted from a cotton patch and observed under the microscope. Edwin Jones (Ventura County Sheriff's Department, Ventura, Calif.), personal communication.

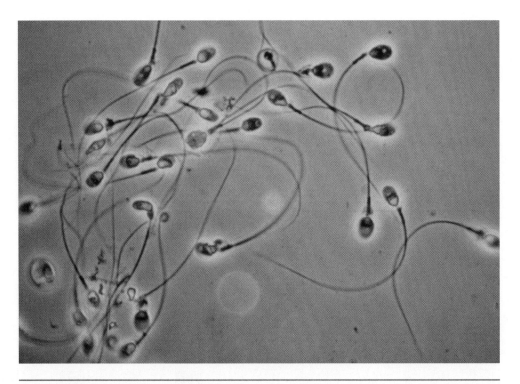

Figure 12–18 Photomicrograph of human spermatozoa (300×). *Courtesy John Walsh, Photo Researchers, Inc.*

dry and easily disintegrate if the stain is washed or when the stain is rubbed against another object, as can happen frequently in the handling and packaging of this type of evidence. Furthermore, sexual crimes may involve males who have an abnormally low sperm count, a condition known as oligospermia, or they may involve individuals who have no spermatozoa at all in their seminal fluid (aspermia). Significantly, aspermatic individuals are increasing in numbers due to the growing popularity of vasectomies.

Forensic analysts often must examine stains or swabs that they suspect contain semen (because of the presence of acid phosphatase) but that yield no detectable spermatozoa. How, then, can one unequivocally prove the presence of semen? The solution to this problem came with the discovery in the 1970s of a protein called *p30* or *prostate specific antigen (PSA)*. Under the analytical conditions employed in forensic laboratories, p30 is unique to seminal plasma.

When p30 is isolated and injected into a rabbit, it stimulates the production of polyclonal antibodies (anti-p30). The sera collected from these immunized rabbits can then be used to test suspected semen stains. As shown in Figure 12–19, the stain extract is placed in one well of an electrophoretic plate and the anti-p30 in an opposite well. When an electric potential is applied, the antigens and antibodies move toward each other. The formation of a visible line midway between the two wells shows the presence of p30 in the stain and proves that the stain was seminal in nature.

A more elegant approach to identifying PSA (p30) involves placing an extract of a questioned sample on a porous membrane in the presence of a monoclonal PSA antibody that is linked to a dye. If PSA is present in

Oligospermia
An abnormally low sperm count.

Aspermia
The absence of sperm; sterility in males.

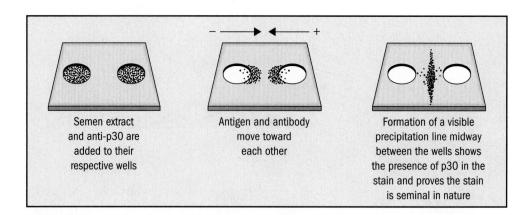

Figure 12–19

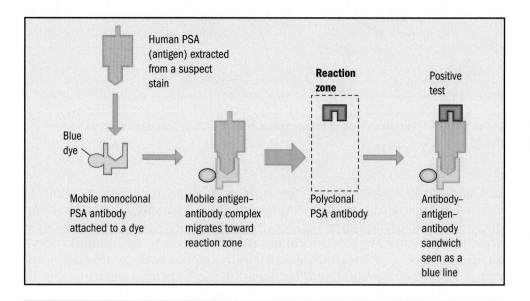

Figure 12–20   An antibody–antigen–antibody sandwich or complex is seen as a colored band. This signifies the presence of PSA in the extract of a stain and positively identifies human semen.

the extract, a PSA antigen–monoclonal PSA antibody complex forms. This complex then migrates along the membrane, where it interacts with a polyclonal PSA antibody imbedded in the membrane. The antibody–antigen–antibody "sandwich" that forms will be apparent by the presence of a colored line (see Figure 12–20). This monoclonal antibody technique is about a hundred times more sensitive for detecting PSA than the one described in the previous paragraph.[6]

---

[6] J. Kearsey, H. Louie, and H. Poon, "Validation Study of the Onestep ABAcard® PSA Test Kit for RCMP Casework," *Canadian Society of Forensic Science Journal* 34 (2001): 63; S. J. Denison, E. M. Lopes, L. D'Costa, and J. C. Newman, "Positive Prostate-Specific Antigen (PSA) Results in Semen-Free Samples," *Canadian Society of Forensic Science Journal* 37 (2004): 197.

Once the material under examination is proven to be semen, the next task is to attempt to associate the semen as closely as possible with a single individual. As we will learn in Chapter 13, forensic scientists can link seminal material to one individual with DNA technology. Just as important is the knowledge that this technology can exonerate many of those wrongfully accused of sexual assault.

Collection of Rape Evidence

Seminal constituents on a rape victim are important evidence that sexual intercourse has taken place, but their absence does not necessarily mean that a rape did not occur. Physical injuries such as bruises or bleeding tend to confirm that a violent assault did take place. Furthermore, the forceful physical contact between victim and assailant may result in a transfer of physical evidence—blood, semen, hairs, and fibers. The presence of such physical evidence will help forge a vital link in the chain of circumstances surrounding a sexual crime.

To protect this kind of evidence, all the outer- and undergarments from the involved parties should be carefully removed and packaged separately in paper (not plastic) bags. Place a clean bedsheet on the floor and lay a clean paper sheet over it. The victim must remove her shoes before standing on the paper. Have the person disrobe while standing on the paper in order to collect any loose foreign material falling from the clothing. Collect each piece of clothing as it is removed and place the items in separate paper bags to avoid cross-contamination of physical evidence. Carefully fold the paper sheet so that all foreign materials are contained inside.

If it is deemed appropriate, bedding, or the object on which the assault took place, should be submitted to the laboratory for processing. Items suspected of containing seminal stains must be handled carefully. Folding an article through the stain may cause it to flake off, as will rubbing the stained area against the surface of the packaging material. If, under unusual circumstances, it is not possible to transport the stained article to the laboratory, the stained area should be cut out and submitted with an unstained piece as a substrate control.

In the laboratory, analysts try to link seminal material to a donor(s) using DNA typing. Because an individual may transfer his or her DNA types to a stain through perspiration, investigators must handle stained articles with care, minimizing direct personal contact. The evidence collector must wear disposable latex gloves when such evidence must be touched.

The rape victim must undergo a medical examination as soon as possible after the assault. At this time, the appropriate items of physical evidence are collected by trained personnel. Evidence collectors should have an evidence-collection kit from the local crime laboratory (see Figure 12–21).

The following items of physical evidence are to be collected:

1. *Pubic combings.* Place a paper towel under the buttocks and comb the pubic area for loose or foreign hairs.

2. *Pubic hair standard/reference samples.* Cut fifteen to twenty full-length hairs from the pubic area at the skin line.

Figure 12–21a Victim rape collection kit showing the kit envelope, kit instructions, medical history and assault information forms, and foreign materials collection bag. *Courtesy Tri-Tech, Inc., Southport, N.C., www.tritechusa.com*

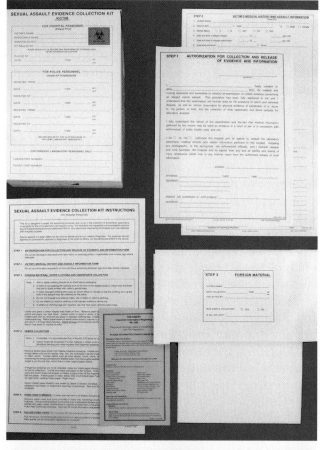

Figure 12–21b Victim rape collection kit showing collection bags for outer clothing, underpants, debris, pubic hair combings, pubic hair standard/reference samples, vaginal swabs, and rectal swabs. *Courtesy Tri-Tech, Inc., Southport, N.C., www.tritechusa.com*

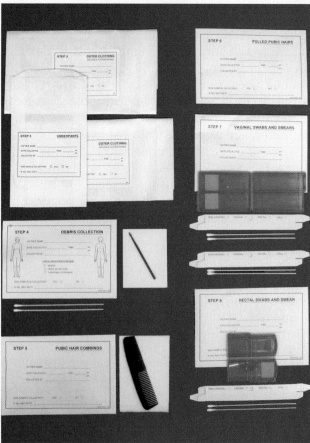

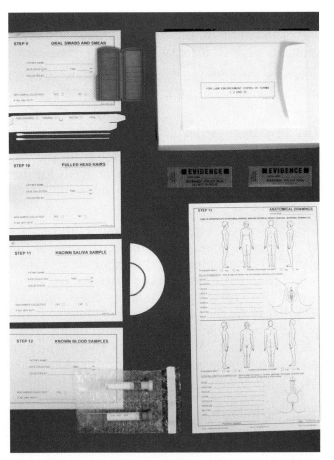

Figure 12–21c Victim collection rape kit showing collection bags for oral swabs and smear, pulled head hair standard/reference, known saliva sample, known blood samples, and anatomical drawings. *Courtesy Tri-Tech, Inc., Southport, N.C., www.tritechusa.com*

3. *External genital dry-skin areas.* Swab with at least one dry swab and one moistened swab.

4. *Vaginal swabs and smear.* Using two swabs simultaneously, carefully swab the vaginal area and let the swabs air-dry before packaging. Using two additional swabs, repeat swabbing procedure and smear the swabs onto separate microscope slides, allowing them to air-dry before packaging.

5. *Cervix swabs.* Using two swabs simultaneously, carefully swab the cervix area and let the swabs air-dry before packaging.

6. *Rectal swabs and smear.* To be taken when warranted by case history. Using two swabs simultaneously, swab the rectal canal, smearing one of the swabs onto a microscope slide. Allow both samples to air-dry before packaging.

7. *Oral swabs and smear.* To be taken if oral–genital contact occurred. Use two swabs simultaneously to swab the buccal area and gum line. Using both swabs, prepare one smear slide. Allow both swabs and the smear to air-dry before packaging.

8. *Head hairs.* Cut at skin line a minimum of five full-length hairs from each of the following scalp locations: center, front, back, left side, and right side. It is recommended that a total of at least fifty hairs be cut and submitted to the laboratory.

9. **Blood sample.**   Collect at least 20 milliliters in a vacuum tube containing the preservative EDTA. The blood sample can be used for DNA typing as well as for toxicological analysis if required.

10. **Fingernail scrapings.**   Scrape the undersurface of the nails with a dull object over a piece of clean paper to collect debris. Use separate paper, one for each hand.

11. **All clothing.**   Package as described earlier.

12. **Urine specimen.**   Collect 30 milliliters or more of urine from the victim for the purpose of conducting a drug toxicological analysis for Rohypnol, GHB, and other substances associated with drug-facilitated sexual assaults (see pp. 263–264).

Often during the investigation of a sexual assault, the victim reports that a perpetrator engaged in biting, sucking, or licking of areas of the victim's body. As we will learn in the next chapter, the tremendous sensitivity associated with DNA technology offers investigators the opportunity to identify a perpetuator's DNA types from saliva residues collected off the skin. The most efficient way to recover saliva residues from the skin is to first swab the suspect area with a rotating motion using a cotton swab moistened with distilled water. A second, dry swab which is then rotated over the skin to recover the moist remains on the skin's surface from the wet swab. The swabs are air-dried and packaged together as a single sample.[7]

If a suspect is apprehended, the following items are routinely collected:

1. *All clothing* and any other items believed to have been worn at the time of assault.

2. *Pubic hair combings.*

3. *Pulled head and pubic hair standard/reference samples.*

4. *Penile swab* within twenty-four hours of assault when appropriate to case history.

5. A blood sample or buccal swab (see p. 414) for DNA typing purposes.

The advent of DNA profiling has forced investigators to rethink what items are evidential with respect to a sexual assault. As we will learn in Chapter 13, DNA levels in the range of one-billionth of a gram are now routinely characterized in crime laboratories. In the past, scant attention was paid to the underwear recovered from a male who was suspected of being involved in a sexual assault. From a practical point of view, the presence of seminal constituents on a man's underwear had little or no investigative value. Today, the high sensitivity of DNA analysis has created new areas of investigation. Experience now tells us that it is possible to establish a link between a victim and her assailant by analyzing biological material recovered from the interior front surface of a male suspect's underwear. This is especially important when investigations have failed to yield the presence of a suspect's DNA on exhibits recovered from the victim.

---

[7] D. Sweet et al., "An Improved Method to Recover Saliva from Human Skin: The Double Swab Technique," *Journal of Forensic Sciences* 42 (1997): 320.

Forensic Brief

A common mode of DNA transfer occurs when skin cells from the walls of the victim's vagina are transferred onto the suspect during intercourse. Subsequent penile contact with the inner surface of the suspect's underwear often leads to the recovery of the female victim's DNA from the underwear's inner surface. The power of DNA is aptly illustrated in a case in which the female victim of a rape had consensual sexual intercourse with a male partner prior to being assaulted by a different male. DNA extracted from the inside front area of the suspect's underwear revealed a female DNA profile matching that of the victim. The added bonus in this case was finding male DNA on the same underwear which matched that of the consensual partner.

Source: Gary G. Verret, "Sexual Assault Cases with No Primary Transfer of Biological Material from Suspect to Victim: Evidence of Secondary and Tertiary Transfer of Biological Material from Victim to Suspect's Undergarments," *Proceedings of the Canadian Society of Forensic Science,* Toronto, Ontario, November 2001.

The persistence of seminal constituents in the vagina may become a factor when trying to ascertain the time of an alleged sexual attack. While the presence of spermatozoa in the vaginal cavity provides evidence of intercourse, important information regarding the time of sexual activity can be obtained from the knowledge that motile or living sperm generally survive up to four to six hours in the vaginal cavity of a living person. However, a successful search for motile sperm requires a microscopic examination of a vaginal smear immediately after it is taken from the victim.

A more extensive examination of vaginal collections is later made at a forensic laboratory. Nonmotile sperm may be found in a living female for up to three days after intercourse and occasionally up to six days later. However, intact sperm (sperm with tails) are not normally found sixteen hours after intercourse but have been found as late as seventy-two hours after intercourse. The likelihood of finding seminal acid phosphatase in the vaginal cavity markedly decreases with time following intercourse, with little chance of identifying this substance forty-eight hours after intercourse.[8] Hence, with the possibility of the prolonged persistence of both spermatozoa and acid phosphatase in the vaginal cavity after intercourse, investigators should determine when and if voluntary sexual activity last occurred prior to the sexual assault. This information will be useful for evaluating the significance of finding these seminal constituents in the female victim. Blood or buccal swabs for DNA analysis are to be taken from any consensual partner having sex with the victim within seventy-two hours of the assault.

---

[8] Anne Davies and Elizabeth Wilson, "The Persistence of Seminal Constituents in the Human Vagina," *Forensic Science* 3 (1974): 45.

Another significant indicator of recent sexual activity is p30. This semen marker normally is not detected in the vaginal cavity beyond twenty-four hours following intercourse.[9]

Chapter Summary

The term *serology* describes a broad scope of laboratory tests that use specific antigen and serum antibody reactions. An antibody reacts or agglutinates only with its specific antigen. The identity of each of the four A-B-O blood groups can be established by testing the blood with anti-A and anti-B sera. The concept of specific antigen–antibody reactions has been applied to immunoassay techniques for detecting drugs of abuse in blood and urine. When an animal is injected with an antigen its body produces a series of different antibodies, all of which are designed to attack some particular site on the antigen of interest. This collection of antibodies is known as polyclonal antibodies. Alternately, a more uniform and specific collection of antibodies designed to combine with a single antigen site can be manufactured. Such antibodies are known as *monoclonals*.

The criminalist must answer the following questions when examining dried blood: (1) Is it blood? (2) From what species did the blood originate? (3) If the blood is of human origin, how closely can it be associated to a particular individual? The determination of blood is best made by means of a preliminary color test. A positive result from the Kastle-Meyer color test is highly indicative of blood. Alternatively, the luminol test is used to search out trace amounts of blood located at crime scenes. The precipitin test uses antisera normally derived from rabbits that have been injected with the blood of a known animal to determine the species origin of a questioned bloodstain. Prior to the advent of DNA typing, bloodstains were linked to a source by A-B-O typing and the characterization of polymorphic blood enzymes and proteins. This approach has now been supplanted by the newer DNA technology.

The crime-scene investigator must remember that the location, distribution, and appearance of bloodstains and spatters may be useful for interpreting and reconstructing the events that produced the bleeding. Surface texture and the stain's shape, size, and location must be considered when determining the direction, dropping distance, and angle of impact of a bloodstain.

Many cases sent to a forensic laboratory involve sexual offenses, making it necessary to examine exhibits for the presence of seminal stains. The best way to locate and characterize a seminal stain is to perform the acid phosphatase color test. Semen can be unequivocally identified by the presence of either spermatozoa or p30, a protein unique to seminal plasma. Forensic scientists can link seminal material to an individual by DNA typing. The rape victim must undergo a medical examination as soon as pos-

---

[9] J. Kearsey, H. Louie, and H. Poon, "Validation Study of the Onestep ABAcard® PSA Test Kit for RCMP Casework," *Canadian Society of Forensic Science Journal* 34 (2001): 63.

sible after the assault. At that time clothing, hairs, and vaginal and rectal swabs can be collected for subsequent laboratory examination. If a suspect is apprehended within twenty-four hours of the assault, it may be possible to detect the victim's DNA on the male's underwear or on a penile swab of the suspect.

Review Questions

1. Karl Landsteiner discovered that blood can be classified by its _____.
2. True or False: No two individuals, except for identical twins, can be expected to have the same combination of blood types or antigens. _____
3. _____ is the fluid portion of unclotted blood.
4. The liquid that separates from the blood when a clot is formed is called the _____.
5. _____ transport oxygen from the lungs to the body tissues and carry carbon dioxide back to the lungs.
6. On the surface of red blood cells are chemical substances called _____, which impart blood type characteristics to the cells.
7. Type A individuals have _____ antigens on the surface of their red blood cells.
8. Type O individuals have (both, neither) A and B antigens on their red blood cells.
9. The presence or absence of the _____ and _____ antigens on the red blood cells determines a person's blood type in the A-B-O system.
10. The D antigen is also known as the _____ antigen.
11. Serum contains proteins known as _____, which destroy or inactivate antigens.
12. An antibody reacts with (any, only a specific) antigen.
13. True or False: Agglutination describes the clumping together of red blood cells by the action of an antibody. _____
14. Type B blood contains _____ antigens and anti-_____ antibodies.
15. Type AB blood has (both, neither) anti-A (and, nor) anti-B.
16. A drug–protein complex can be injected into an animal to form specific _____ for that drug.
17. The term _____ describes the study of antigen–antibody reactions.
18. Type AB blood (is, is not) agglutinated by both anti-A and anti-B serum.
19. Type B red blood cells agglutinate when added to type (A, B) blood.
20. Type A red blood cells agglutinate when added to type (AB, O) blood.
21. An immunological assay technique used to detect the presence of minute quantities of drugs in blood and urine is _____.
22. The distribution of type A blood in the United States is approximately (42, 15) percent.
23. The distribution of type AB blood in the United States is approximately (12, 3) percent.
24. (All, Most) blood hemoglobin has peroxidase-like activity.
25. For many years, the most commonly used color test for identifying blood was the _____ color test.
26. _____ reagent reacts with blood, causing it to luminesce.

27. Blood can be characterized as being of human origin by the _____ test.

28. Antigens and antibodies (can, cannot) be induced to move toward each other under the influence of an electrical field.

29. Antibodies designed to interact with a specific antigen site are (monoclonal, polyclonal).

30. True or False: Hybridoma cells are used to produce antigens designed to attack one and only one site on an antibody. _____

31. _____ are proteins that have important functions in regulating many of the body's chemical reactions.

32. Enzymes that exist in different forms in a population are (polymorphic, monomorphic).

33. Protein and enzyme components can be separated and typed by the technique of _____.

34. True or False: The shape of bloodstains may provide useful information regarding the direction, dropping distance, and angle of impact of spattered blood. _____

35. The basic unit of heredity is the _____.

36. Genes are positioned on threadlike bodies called _____.

37. All cells in the human body, except the reproductive cells, have _____ pairs of chromosomes.

38. The sex of an offspring is always determined by the (mother, father).

39. Genes that influence a given characteristic and are aligned with one another on a chromosome pair are known as _____.

40. When a pair of allelic genes is identical, the genes are said to be (homozygous, heterozygous).

41. A (phenotype, genotype) is an observable characteristic of an individual.

42. The combination of genes present in the cells of an individual is called the _____.

43. A gene (will, will not) appear in a child when it is present in one of the parents.

44. A type B individual may have the genotype _____ or the genotype _____.

45. A type AB mother and type AB father will have offspring of what possible genotypes?

46. A type AB mother and type AB father will have offspring of what possible phenotypes?

47. The _____ color test is used to locate and characterize seminal stains.

48. Semen is unequivocally identified by the microscopic appearance of _____.

49. Males with a low sperm count have a condition known as (oligospermia, aspermia).

50. The protein _____ is unique to seminal plasma.

51. True or False: DNA may be transferred to an object through the medium of perspiration. _____

52. True or False: Seminal constituents may remain in the vagina for up to six days after intercourse. _____

Further References

Bevel, T., and R. M. Gardner, *Bloodstain Pattern Analysis—With an Introduction to Crime Scene Reconstruction,* 2nd ed. Boca Raton, Fla.: Taylor & Francis, 2002.

James, S. H., P. E. Kish, and T. P. Sutton, *Principles of Bloodstain Pattern Analysis: Theory and Practice.* Boca Raton, Fla.: Taylor & Francis, 2005.

Jones, E. L., Jr., "The Identification and Individualization of Semen Stains," in R. Saferstein, ed., *Forensic Science Handbook,* vol. 2, 2nd ed. Upper Saddle River, N.J.: Prentice Hall, 2005.

Shaler, R. C., "Modern Forensic Biology," in R. Saferstein, ed., *Forensic Science Handbook,* vol. 1, 2nd ed. Upper Saddle River, N.J.: Prentice Hall, 2002.

Whitehead, P. H., "A Historical Review of the Characterization of Blood and Secretion Stains in the Forensic Laboratory—Part One: Bloodstains," *Forensic Science Review* 5 (1993): 35.

Wonder, A., *Blood Dynamics.* Burlington, Mass.: Elsevier Academic Press, 2001.

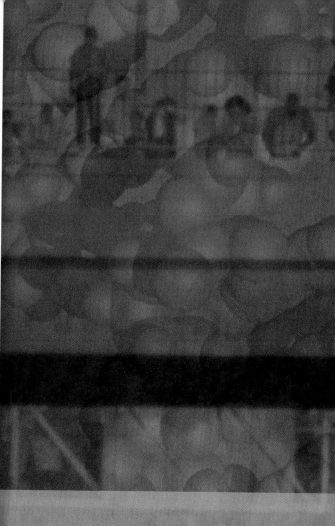

BK4013970 06-17-94

LOS ANGELES POLICE · JAIL DIV

O.J. Simpson—A Mountain of Evidence

On June 12, 1994, police arrived at the home of Nicole Simpson only to view a horrific scene. The bodies of O. J. Simpson's estranged wife and her friend Ron Goldman were found on the path leading to the front door of Nicole's home. Both bodies were covered in blood and had suffered deep knife wounds. Nicole's head was nearly severed from her body. This was not a well-planned murder. A trail of blood led away from the murder scene. Blood was found in O. J. Simpson's Bronco. Blood drops were on O. J.'s driveway and in the foyer of his home. A blood-soaked sock was located in O. J. Simpson's bedroom, and a bloodstained glove rested outside his residence.

As DNA was extracted and profiled from each bloodstained article, a picture emerged that seemed to irrefutably link Simpson to the murders. A trail of DNA leaving the crime scene was consistent with O. J.'s profile, as was the DNA found entering Simpson's home. Simpson's DNA profile was found in the Bronco along with that of both victims. The glove contained the DNA profiles of Nicole and Ron, and the sock had Nicole's DNA profile. At trial, the defense team valiantly fought back. Miscues in evidence collection were craftily exploited. The defense strategy was to paint a picture of, not only an incompetent investigation, but one that was tinged with dishonest police planting evidence. The strategy worked. O. J. Simpson was acquitted of murder.

chapter 13

DNA The Indispensable Forensic Science Tool

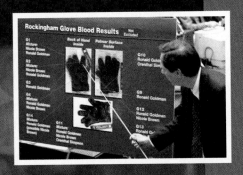

Key Terms

amelogenin gene
amino acids
buccal cells
chromosome
complementary base
   pairing
deoxyribonucleic acid (DNA)
electrophoresis
epithelial cells
human genome
hybridization
low copy number
mitochondria
multiplexing
nucleotide
picogram
polymer
polymerase chain reaction
   (PCR)
primer
proteins
replication
restriction enzymes
restriction fragment length
   polymorphisms (RFLPs)
sequencing
short tandem repeat (STR)
substrate control
tandem repeat
Y-STRs

Learning Objectives

After studying this chapter you should be able to:

- Name the parts of a nucleotide and explain how they are linked together to form DNA

- Understand the concept of base pairing as it relates to the double-helix structure of DNA

- Contrast DNA strands that code for the production of proteins with strands that contain repeating base sequences

- Explain the technology of polymerase chain reaction (PCR) and how it applies to forensic DNA typing

- Contrast the newest DNA-typing technique, short tandem repeats (STRs), with previous DNA-typing technologies

- Describe the difference between nuclear and mitochondrial DNA

- Understand the use of DNA computerized databases in criminal investigation

- List the necessary procedures for the proper preservation of bloodstained evidence for laboratory DNA analysis

DNA
Abbreviation for deoxyribonucleic acid—the molecules carrying the body's genetic information. DNA is double stranded in the shape of a double helix.

The discovery of **deoxyribonucleic acid (DNA)**, the deciphering of its structure, and the decoding of its genetic information were turning points in our understanding of the underlying concepts of inheritance. Now, with incredible speed, as molecular biologists unravel the basic structure of genes, we can create new products through genetic engineering and develop diagnostic tools and treatments for genetic disorders. For a number of years, these developments were of seemingly peripheral interest to forensic scientists. All that changed when, in 1985, what started out as a more or less routine investigation into the structure of a human gene led to the discovery that portions of the DNA structure of certain genes are as unique to each individual as fingerprints. Alec Jeffreys and his colleagues at Leicester University, England, who were responsible for these revelations, named the process for isolating and reading these DNA markers *DNA fingerprinting*. As researchers uncovered new approaches and variations to the original Jeffreys technique, the terms *DNA profiling* and *DNA typing* came to be applied to describe this relatively new technology. This discovery caught the imagination of the forensic science community, for forensic scientists have long desired to link with certainty biological evidence such as blood, semen, hair, or tissue to a single individual. Although conventional testing procedures had gone a long way toward narrowing the source of biological materials, individualization remained an elusive goal. Now DNA typing has allowed forensic scientists to accomplish this goal. The technique is still relatively new, but in the few years since its introduction, DNA typing has become routine in public crime laboratories and has been made available to interested parties through the services of a number of skilled private laboratories. In the United States, courts have overwhelmingly admitted DNA evidence and accepted the reliability of its scientific underpinnings.

What Is DNA?

Chromosome
A rodlike structure in the cell nucleus, along which the genes are located. It is composed of DNA surrounded by other material, mainly proteins.

Inside each of 60 trillion cells in the human body are strands of genetic material called **chromosomes**. Arranged along the chromosomes, like beads on a thread, are nearly 25,000 genes. **The gene is the fundamental unit of heredity. It instructs the body cells to make proteins that determine everything from hair color to our susceptibility to diseases.** Each gene is actually composed of DNA specifically designed to carry out a single body function. Interestingly, although DNA was first discovered in 1868, scientists were slow to understand and appreciate its fundamental role in inheritance. Painstakingly, researchers developed evidence that DNA was probably the substance by which genetic instructions are passed from one generation to the next. But the major breakthrough in comprehending how DNA works did not occur until the early 1950s, when two researchers, James Watson and Francis Crick, deduced the structure of DNA. It turns out that DNA is an extraordinary molecule skillfully designed to carry out the task of controlling the genetic traits of all living cells, plant and animal.

Before examining the implications of Watson and Crick's discovery, let's see how DNA is constructed. DNA is a polymer. As we learned in Chapter 8, a polymer is a very large molecule made by linking a series of repeating units. In this case, the units are known as nucleotides. A nucleotide is composed of a sugar molecule, a phosphorus-containing group, and a nitrogen-containing molecule called a *base*.

Figure 13–1 shows how nucleotides can be strung together to form a DNA strand. In this figure, S designates the sugar component, which is joined with a phosphate group to form the backbone of the DNA strand. Projecting from the backbone are the bases. The key to understanding how DNA works is to appreciate the fact that only four types of bases are associated with DNA: adenine, cytosine, guanine, and thymine. To simplify our discussion of DNA, we will designate each of these bases by the first letter of their names. Hence, *A* will stand for adenine, *C* will stand for cytosine, *G* will stand for guanine, and *T* will represent thymine. Again, notice in Figure 13–1 how the bases project from the backbone of DNA. Also, although this figure shows a DNA strand of four bases, keep in mind that in

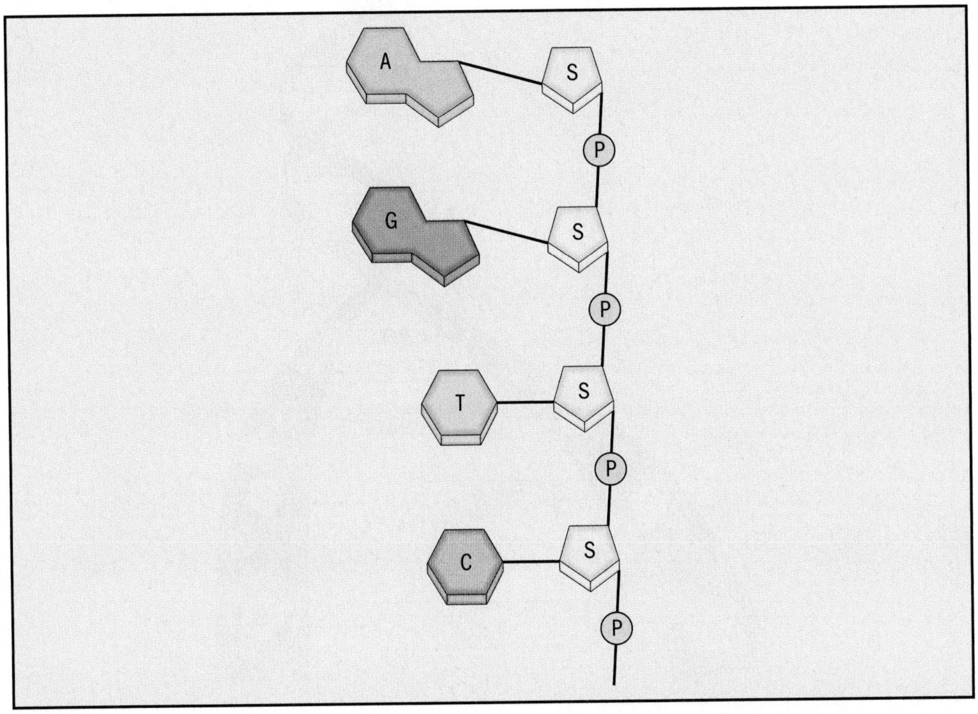

Polymer
A substance composed of a large number of atoms. These atoms are usually arranged in repeating units, or monomers.

Nucleotide
The unit of DNA consisting of one of four bases—adenine, guanine, cytosine, or thymine—attached to a phosphate-sugar group.

Figure 13–1 How nucleotides can be linked to form a DNA strand. S designates the sugar component, which is joined with phosphate groups (P) to form the backbone of DNA. Projecting from the backbone are four bases: *A*, adenine; *G*, guanine; *T*, thymine; and *C*, cytosine.

theory there is no limit to the length of the DNA strand; in fact, a DNA strand can be composed of a long chain with millions of bases.

The information just discussed was well known to Watson and Crick by the time they set about to detail the structure of DNA. Their efforts led to the discovery that the DNA molecule is actually composed of two DNA strands coiled into a *double helix*. This can be thought of as resembling two wires twisted around each other. As these researchers manipulated scale models of DNA strands, they realized that the only way the bases on each strand could be properly aligned with each other in a double-helix configuration was to place base *A* opposite *T* and *G* opposite *C*. Watson and Crick had solved the puzzle of the double helix and presented the world with a simple but elegant picture of DNA (see Figure 13–2).

The only arrangement possible in the double-helix configuration was the pairing of bases *A* to *T* and *G* to *C*, a concept that has become known as complementary base pairing. Although *A–T* and *G–C* pairs are always required, there are no restrictions on how the bases are to be sequenced on a DNA strand. Thus, one can observe the sequences *T–A–T–T* or *G–T–A–A* or *G–T–C–A*. When these sequences are joined with their opposite number in a double-helix configuration, they pair as follows:

Complementary Base Pairing

The specific pairing of base *A* with *T* and base *C* with *G* in double-stranded DNA.

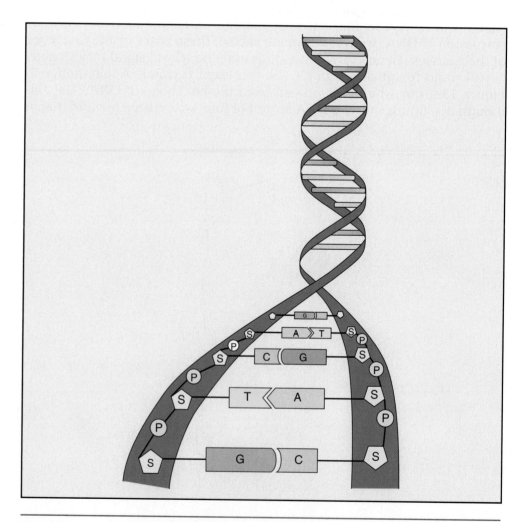

Figure 13–2 A representation of a DNA double helix. Notice how bases G and C pair with each other, as do bases A and T. This is the only arrangement in which two DNA strands can align with each other in a double-helix configuration.

```
T A T T        G T A A        G T C A
| | | |        | | | |        | | | |
A T A A        C A T T        C A G T
```

Any base can follow another on a DNA strand, which means that the possible number of different sequence combinations is staggering! Consider that the average human chromosome has DNA containing 100 million base pairs. All of the human chromosomes taken together contain about three billion base pairs. From these numbers, we can begin to appreciate the diversity of DNA and hence the diversity of living organisms. DNA is like a book of instructions. The alphabet used to create the book is simple enough: *A, T, G,* and *C.* The order in which these letters are arranged defines the role and function of a DNA molecule.

WebExtra 13.1

What Is DNA?
www.prenhall.com/Saferstein

DNA at Work

The inheritable traits that are controlled by DNA arise out of its ability to direct the production of complex molecules called proteins. Proteins are actually made by linking a combination of amino acids. Although thousands of proteins exist, they can all be derived from a combination of up to twenty known amino acids. The sequence of amino acids in a protein chain determines the shape and function of the protein. Let's look at one example: The protein hemoglobin is found in our red blood cells. It carries oxygen to our body cells and removes carbon dioxide from these cells. One of the four amino acid chains of "normal" hemoglobin is shown in Figure 13–3(a). Studies of individuals afflicted with sickle-cell anemia show that this inheritable disorder arises from the presence of "abnormal" hemoglobin in their red blood cells. An amino acid chain for "abnormal" hemoglobin is shown in Figure 13–3(b). Note that the sole difference between

Proteins
Polymers of amino acids that play basic roles in the structures and functions of living things.

Amino Acids
The building blocks of proteins. There are twenty common amino acids. Amino acids are linked to form a protein. The types of amino acids and the order in which they're linked determine the character of each protein.

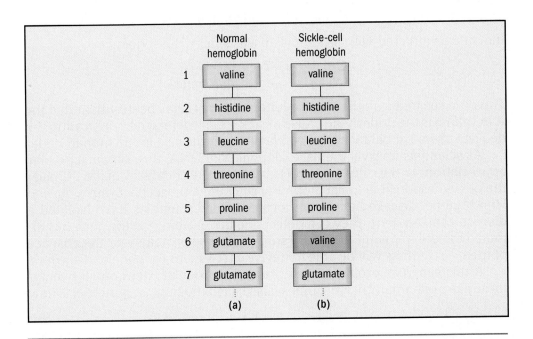

Figure 13–3 **(a) A string of amino acids composes one of the protein chains of hemoglobin. (b) Substitution of just one amino acid for another in the protein chain results in sickle-cell hemoglobin.**

"normal" and "abnormal" or sickle-cell hemoglobin arises from the substitution of one amino acid for another in the protein chain.

The genetic information that determines the amino acid sequence for every protein manufactured in the human body is stored in DNA in a genetic code that relies on the sequence of bases along the DNA strand. The alphabet of DNA is simple—*A, T, G,* and *C*—but the key to deciphering the genetic code is to know that each amino acid is coded by a sequence of three bases. Thus, the amino acid alanine is coded by the combination *C–G–T;* the amino acid aspartate is coded by the combination *C–T–A;* and the amino acid phenylalanine is coded by the combination *A–A–A.* With this code in hand, we can now see how the amino acid sequence in a protein chain is determined by the structure of DNA. Consider the DNA segment

$$-C–G–T–C–T–A–A–A–A–C–G–T–$$

The triplet code contained within this segment translates into

$$[C–G–T] – [C–T–A] – [A–A–A] – [C–G–T]$$
alanine   aspartate   phenylalanine   alanine

or the protein chain

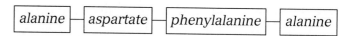

Interestingly, this code is not restricted to humans. Almost all living cells studied to date use the same genetic code as the language of protein synthesis.[1]

If we look at the difference between "normal" and sickle-cell hemoglobin (see Figure 13–3), we see that the latter is formed by substituting one amino acid (valine) for another (glutamate). Within the DNA segment that codes for the production of normal hemoglobin, the letter sequence is

$$-[C–C–T]–[G–A–G]–[G–A–G]-$$
proline   glutamate   glutamate

Individuals afflicted with sickle-cell disease carry the sequence

$$-[C–C–T]–[G–T–G]–[G–A–G]-$$
proline   valine   glutamate

Thus, we see that a single base or letter change (*T* has been substituted for *A* in valine) is the underlying cause of sickle-cell anemia, demonstrating the delicate chemical balance between health and disease in the human body.

As scientists unravel the base sequences of DNA, they obtain a greater appreciation for the roles that proteins play in the chemistry of life. Already the genes responsible for hemophilia, Duchenne muscular dystrophy, and Huntington's disease have been located. Once scientists have isolated a disease-causing gene, they can determine the protein that the gene has directed the cell to manufacture. By studying these proteins—or the absence of them—scientists will be able to devise a treatment for genetic disorders.

A thirteen-year project to determine the order of bases on all twenty-three pairs of human chromosomes (also called the **human genome**) is now

Human Genome
The total DNA content found within the nucleus of a cell. In humans, it is composed of approximately three billion base pairs of genetic information.

---

[1] Instructions for assembling proteins are actually carried from DNA to another region of the cell by ribonucleic acid (RNA). RNA is directly involved in the assembly of the protein utilizing the genetic code it received from DNA.

complete. Knowing where on a specific chromosome DNA codes for the production of a particular protein is useful for diagnosing and treating genetic diseases. This information is crucial for understanding the underlying causes of cancer. Also, comparing the human genome with that of other organisms will help us understand the role and implications of evolution.

Replication of DNA

Once the double-helix structure of DNA was discovered, it became apparent how DNA duplicated itself prior to cell division. The concept of base pairing in DNA suggests the analogy of positive and negative photographic film. Each strand of DNA in the double helix has the same information; one can make a positive print from a negative or a negative from a positive. DNA replication begins with the unwinding of the DNA strands in the double helix. Each strand is then exposed to a collection of free nucleotides. Letter by letter, the double helix is re-created as the nucleotides are assembled in the proper order, as dictated by the principle of base pairing (*A* with *T* and *G* with *C*). The result is the emergence of two identical copies of DNA where before there was only one (see Figure 13–4). A cell can now pass on its genetic identity when it divides.

Replication
The synthesis of new DNA from existing DNA.

Many enzymes and proteins are involved in the process of unwinding the DNA strands, keeping the two DNA strands apart, and assembling the new DNA strands. For example, DNA *polymerases* are enzymes that assemble a new DNA strand in the proper base sequence determined by the original or parent DNA strand. DNA polymerases also "proofread" the growing DNA double helices for mismatched base pairs, which are replaced with correct bases.

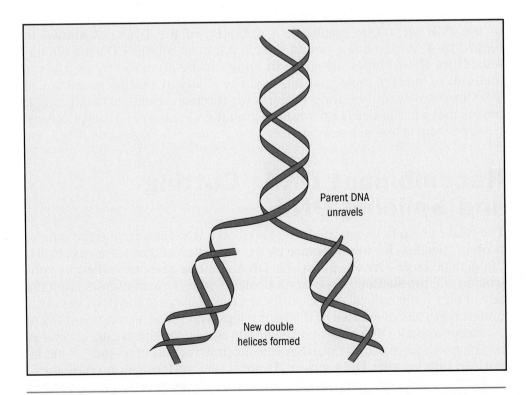

Parent DNA
unravels

New double
helices formed

Figure 13–4   Replication of DNA. The strands of the original DNA molecule are separated, and two new strands are assembled.

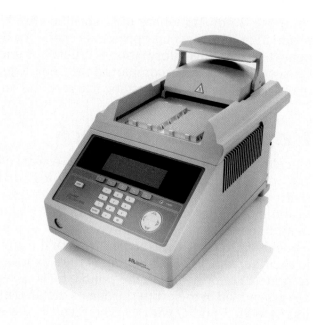

Figure 13–5 **The DNA Thermal Cycler, an instrument that automates the rapid and precise temperature changes required to copy a DNA strand. Within a matter of hours, DNA can be multiplied a millionfold.** *Courtesy Applied Biosystems, Foster City, Calif.*

Polymerase Chain Reaction (PCR)
A technique for replicating or copying a portion of a DNA strand outside a living cell. This technique leads to millions of copies of the DNA strand.

Until recently, the phenomenon of DNA replication appeared to be only of academic interest to forensic scientists interested in DNA for identification purposes. However, this changed when researchers perfected the technology of using DNA polymerases to copy a DNA strand located outside a living cell. This relatively new laboratory technique is known as polymerase chain reaction (PCR). Small quantities of DNA or broken pieces of DNA found in crime-scene evidence can be copied with the aid of a DNA polymerase. The copying process can be accomplished in an automated fashion using a DNA Thermal Cycler (see Figure 13–5). Each cycle of the PCR technique results in a doubling of the DNA, as shown in Figure 13–4. Within a few hours, thirty cycles can multiply DNA a billionfold. Once DNA copies are in hand, they can be analyzed by any of the methods of modern molecular biology. The ability to multiply small bits of DNA opens new and exciting avenues for forensic scientists to explore. It means that sample size is no longer a limitation in characterizing DNA recovered from crime-scene evidence.

Recombinant DNA: Cutting and Splicing DNA

The relationship between the base letters on a DNA strand and the type of protein specified for manufacture by the sequence of these letters is called the *genetic code*. Once a particular DNA site has been identified as controlling the production of a certain protein, molecular biologists can take advantage of the natural chemical-producing abilities of the DNA site. This undertaking has given rise to the technology known as *recombinant DNA*.

Restriction Enzymes
Chemicals that act as scissors to cut DNA molecules at specific locations.

Recombinant DNA relies on the ability of certain chemicals, known as restriction enzymes, to cut DNA into fragments that can later be incorporated into another DNA strand. Restriction enzymes can be thought of as highly specialized scissors that cut a DNA molecule when it recognizes a specific sequence of bases. At present, more than 150 restriction enzymes are commercially available. Thus, molecular biologists have a great deal of

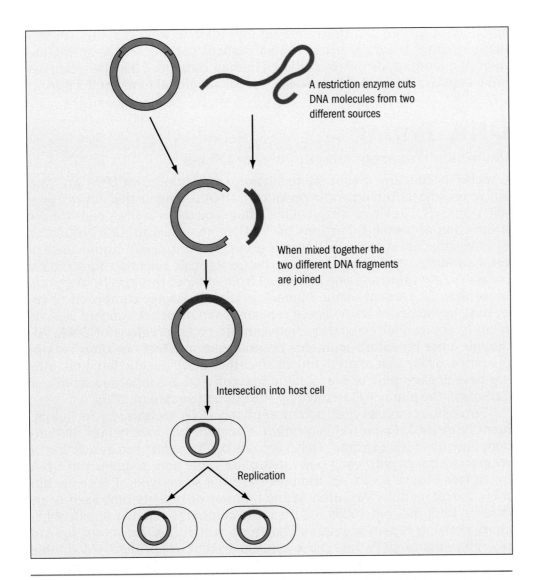

A restriction enzyme cuts DNA molecules from two different sources

When mixed together the two different DNA fragments are joined

Intersection into host cell

Replication

Figure 13–6   The joining of DNA from two different sources via recombinant DNA technology.

flexibility in choosing the portion of a DNA strand they wish to cut out. Once a portion of the DNA strand has been cut out with the aid of a restriction enzyme, the next step in the recombinant DNA process is to insert the isolated DNA segment into a foreign DNA strand (normally, bacterium DNA is selected). Many types of bacteria contain DNA shaped in a circle. A restriction enzyme is used to cut open the circular DNA; then the foreign DNA is spliced in to re-form the circle (see Figure 13–6). The newly fashioned DNA is reintroduced into the bacterial cells. As the bacteria multiply rapidly in their usual fashion, copies of altered DNA are passed on to all descendants.

The commercial implications of recombinant DNA technology are enormous. For example, the gene that produces human growth hormone has been introduced into goldfish and carp, and the gene that produces growth hormone in rainbow trout has been introduced into carp. In each case, the gene-altered fish have grown significantly faster and larger than their natural relatives. If altered bacteria are infused with the DNA segment that makes human insulin, for example, the bacteria make human insulin. Because bacteria multiply so rapidly, it is not long before significant amounts of insulin can be recovered and used to treat diabetes. In this manner, other naturally occurring substances can be produced in commercial quantities for the treatment of human ailments. Likewise, plant genetic engineering holds promise for increasing global food production.

DNA Typing

Restriction Fragment Length Polymorphisms

Geneticists concerned with the technology of recombinant DNA are usually interested in finding and reproducing DNA segments that control protein synthesis. However, not all of the letter sequences in DNA code for the production of proteins. Portions of the DNA molecule contain sequences of letters that are repeated numerous times. The origin and significance of these tandem repeats is a mystery, but to forensic scientists they offer a means of distinguishing one individual from another through *DNA typing*. More than 30 percent of the human genome is largely composed of repeating segments of DNA. These repeating sequences or tandem repeats seem to act as filler or spacers between the coding regions of DNA. Although these repeating segments do not seem to affect our outward appearance, or for that matter control any other basic genetic function, they are nevertheless part of our genetic makeup and are inherited from our parents in the manner illustrated by the Punnett square (p. 366).

Forensic scientists first began applying DNA technology to human identity in 1985. From the beginning, attention has focused on the tandem repeats of the genome. These repeats can be visualized as a string of connected boxes with each box having the same core sequence of DNA bases (see Figure 13–7). All humans have the same type of repeats, but there is tremendous variation in the number of repeats that each of us has. Up until the mid-1990s, the forensic community aimed its efforts at characterizing repeat segments known as restriction fragment length polymorphisms (RFLPs). These repeats are cut out of the DNA double helix by a restriction enzyme that acts like a pair of scissors. A number of different RFLPs were selected by the forensic science community for performing DNA typing. Typically a core sequence is fifteen to thirty-five bases long and repeats itself up to one thousand times.

Let's examine some DNA strands with regions of repeating base sequences to see how this process works. Figure 13–8 illustrates a portion of a pair of chromosomes. Note that each chromosome is composed of two DNA strands wrapped in a double-helix configuration. Each chromosome has a region that contains repeating bases. For the sake of simplicity in illustrating the RFLP method, we assume that the core repeat is

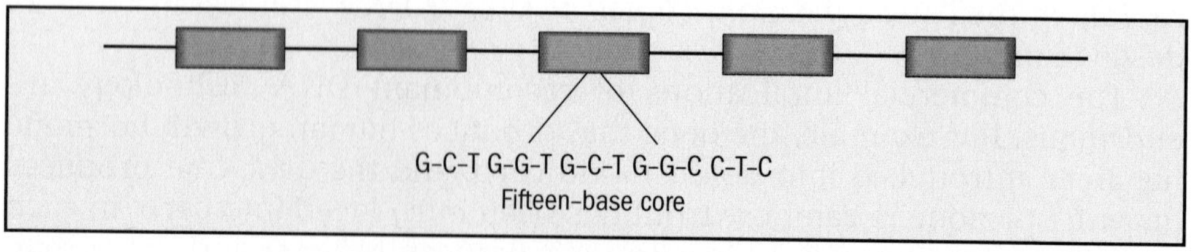

Tandem Repeat
A region of a chromosome that contains multiple copies of a core DNA sequence that are arranged in a repeating fashion.

Restriction Fragment Length Polymorphisms (RFLP)
Different fragment lengths of base pairs that result from cutting a DNA molecule with restriction enzymes.

G–C–T G–G–T G–C–T G–G–C C–T–C
Fifteen-base core

Figure 13–7 **A DNA segment consisting of a series of repeating DNA units. In this illustration, the fifteen-base core can repeat itself hundreds of times. The entire DNA segment is typically hundreds to thousands of bases long.**

only three bases long having a sequence *T–A–G*. Note an important distinction between the two chromosomes: the chromosome on the left has three repeating sequences of *T–A–G*, while the one on the right has two repeating sequences of *T–A–G*. As with any genetic trait, these repeating sequences were inherited from the parents. In this example, one parent contributed the chromosome containing the three repeating sequences, and the other parent passed on the chromosome containing the two repeating sequences.

The key to understanding DNA typing lies in the knowledge that within the world's population, numerous possibilities exist for the number of times a particular sequence of base letters can repeat itself on a DNA strand. The possibilities become even greater when one deals with two chromosomes, each containing different lengths of repeating sequences. During RFLP typing, restriction enzymes cut up chromosomes into hundreds of fragments, some containing repeating sequences from the DNA molecule. In our example, shown in Figure 13–8, the chromosome pair, when cut, will yield two different fragment lengths of *T–A–G*. The length differences associated with DNA strands or RFLPs allow forensic scientists to distinguish one person from another. In actuality, these strands are relatively long, often consisting of thousands of bases. Once the DNA molecules have been cut up by the restriction enzyme, the resulting fragments must be sorted out. This is accomplished by separating the fragments by electrophoresis (pp. 142–149). DNA from various sources, cut up by re-

Electrophoresis
A technique for separating molecules through their migration on a support medium while under the influence of an electrical potential.

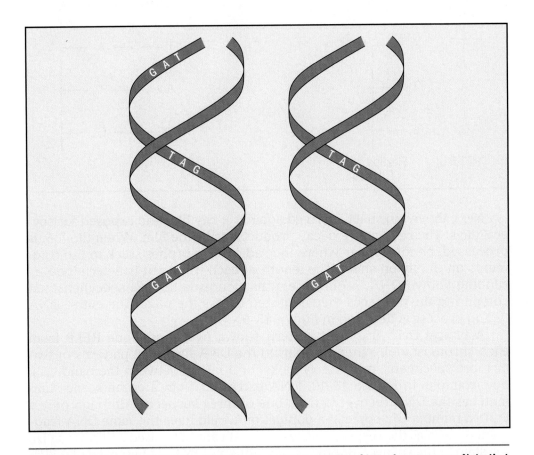

Figure 13–8 Intertwined strands of DNA representing segments of two chromosomes. Note that the chromosome segment on the left contains three repeating sequences of *T–A–G*, while the chromosome segment on the right has two repeating sequences of *T–A–G*.

striction enzymes, is placed in separate lanes on an electrophoretic gel and subjected to an electric field. During the electrophoretic process, the DNA fragments migrate across a gel-coated plate. The smaller DNA fragments move faster along the plate than do the larger fragments (see Figure 5–12). Once the electrophoresis process is completed, the double-stranded fragments of DNA are chemically treated so that the strands separate from each other. The fragments are then transferred to a nylon membrane in much the same way as one would transfer an ink line onto a blotter. This transfer process is called *Southern blotting,* named after its developer, Edward Southern. To visualize the separated RFLPs, the nylon sheet is treated with radioactively labeled probes containing a base sequence complementary to the RFLPs being identified (a process called hybridization).

In our example, we aim to identify RFLPs composed of a repeating string of letters spelling *T–A–G.* Hence, the appropriate probes would have the complementary letter sequence *A–T–C,* as shown in the following diagram, so that the probes can specifically bind to the desired RFLP. (Note: The asterisk designates a radioactive label.)

Hybridization

The process of joining two complementary strands of DNA to form a double-stranded molecule.

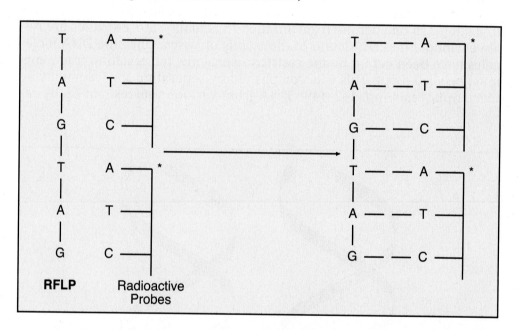

Next, the nylon sheet is placed against X-ray film and exposed for several days. The radioactive decay products strike the film. When the film is processed, bands appear where the radioactive probes stuck to the fragments on the nylon sheet. The length of each fragment is determined by running known DNA fragment lengths alongside the test specimens and comparing the distances they migrated across the plate. The entire DNA typing process is depicted in Figure 13–9.

A typical DNA fragment pattern shows two bands (one RFLP from each chromosome). When comparing the DNA fragment patterns of two or more specimens, one merely looks for a match between the band sets. For example, in Figure 13–10, DNA extracted from a crime-scene stain matches the DNA recovered from one of three suspects. Although only a limited number of people in a population would have the same DNA fragment pattern as the suspect, this test in itself cannot be used to individualize the stain to the suspect. But by using additional DNA probes, each of which recognizes different repeating DNA segments (other than *T–A–G*), a high degree of discrimination or even near individualization can be achieved. For

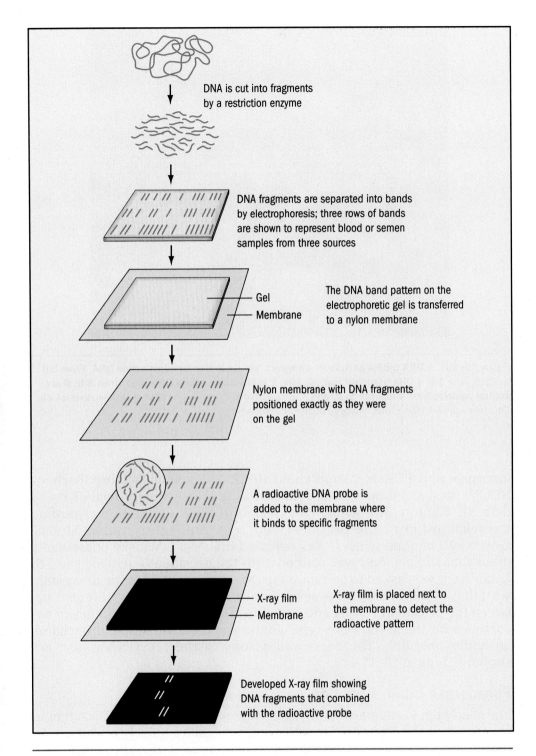

DNA is cut into fragments
by a restriction enzyme

DNA fragments are separated into bands
by electrophoresis; three rows of bands
are shown to represent blood or semen
samples from three sources

— Gel

— Membrane

The DNA band pattern on the
electrophoretic gel is transferred
to a nylon membrane

Nylon membrane with DNA fragments
positioned exactly as they were
on the gel

A radioactive DNA probe is
added to the membrane where
it binds to specific fragments

— X-ray film

— Membrane

X-ray film is placed next to
the membrane to detect the
radioactive pattern

Developed X-ray film showing
DNA fragments that combined
with the radioactive probe

Figure 13–9   The DNA RFLP typing process.

example, if each probe selected yielded a DNA type having a frequency of occurrence of one in one hundred in a population, then four different probes would have a combined frequency of one in 100 million (1/100 × 1/100 × 1/100 × 1/100).

RFLP DNA typing has the distinction of being the first scientifically accepted protocol in the United States used for the forensic characterization of DNA. However, its utility has been short lived. New technology

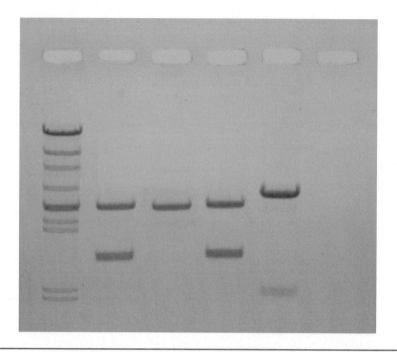

Figure 13–10   A DNA profile pattern of a suspect and its match to crime-scene DNA. From left to right, lane 1 is a DNA standard marker; lane 2 is the crime-scene DNA; and lanes 3 to 5 are control samples from suspects 1, 2, and 3, respectively. Crime-scene DNA matches suspect #2. *Courtesy Edvotek, The Biotechnology Education Company*

incorporating PCR has supplanted RFLP. In its short history, perhaps RFLP's most startling impact related to the impeachment trial of President Bill Clinton. The whole complexion of the investigation regarding the relationship of the president with a White House intern, Monica Lewinsky, changed when it was revealed that Ms. Lewinsky possessed a dress that she claimed was stained with the president's semen. The FBI Laboratory was asked to compare the DNA extracted from the dress stain with that of the president. A seven-probe RFLP match was obtained between the president's DNA and the stain. The combined frequency of occurrence for the seven DNA types found was nearly one in eight trillion, an undeniable link. The dress and a copy of the FBI DNA report are shown in Figure 13–11.

Polymerase Chain Reaction

For nearly ten years starting in 1985, RFLP was the dominant DNA typing procedure in the United States. However, its utility quickly ended by the mid-1990s. What caused this change? The answer is quite simple: the emergence of a revolutionary and elegant technique known as polymerase chain reaction. Put simply, PCR is a technique designed to copy or multiply DNA strands. For the forensic scientist, who is often presented with minute quantities of materials, the opportunity to multiply the quantity of sample available for analysis was too good to pass up.

PCR is the outgrowth of knowledge gained from an understanding of how DNA strands naturally replicate within a cell. The most important feature of PCR is knowing that an enzyme called *DNA polymerase* can be directed to synthesize a specific region of DNA. In a relatively straight forward manner, PCR can be used to repeatedly duplicate or amplify a strand

FEDERAL BUREAU OF INVESTIGATION
WASHINGTON, D. C. 20535

Report of Examination

Examiner Name: ████████████	Date:	08/17/98
Unit: **DNA Analysis 1**	Phone No.:	202-324-4409
FBI File No.: **29D-OIC-LR-35063**	Lab No.:	980730002 S BO
		980803100 S BO

Results of Examinations:

Deoxyribonucleic acid (DNA) profiles for the genetic loci
D2S44, D17S79, D1S7, D4S139, D10S28, D5S110 and D7S467 were
developed from HaeIII-digested high molecular weight DNA
extracted from specimens K39 and Q3243-1(a semen stain removed
from specimen Q3243). Based on the results of these seven
genetic loci, specimen K39 (CLINTON) is the source of the DNA
obtained from specimen Q3243-1, to a reasonable degree of
scientific certainty.

No DNA-RFLP examinations were conducted on specimen Q3243-
2 (a semen stain removed from specimen Q3243).

BLACK — 1,440,000,000,000
CAUC — 7,870,000,000,000
SEH — 3,140,000,000,000
SWH — 943,000,000,000

DNAU1 - Page 1 of 1

This Report Is Furnished For Official Use Only

Q3243

Figure 13–11   The dress and the FBI Report of Examination for a semen stain located on the dress.

of DNA millions of times. As an example, let's consider a segment of DNA
that we want to duplicate by PCR:

$$-G-T-C-T-C-A-G-C-T-T-\textbf{C-C-A-G}-$$
$$-\textbf{C-A-G}-A-G-T-C-G-A-A-G-G-T-C-$$

To perform PCR on this DNA segment, short sequences of DNA on each
side of the region of interest must be identified. In the example shown
here, the short sequences are designated by boldface letters in the DNA
segment. These short DNA segments must be available in a pure form
known as a primer if the PCR technique is going to work.

Primer

A short strand of DNA used to
target a region of DNA for
replication by PCR.

The first step in the PCR process is to heat the DNA strands to about 94°C. At this temperature, the double-stranded DNA molecules separate completely:

–G–T–C–T–C–A–G–C–T–T–C–C–A–G–

–C–A–G–A–G–T–C–G–A–A–G–G–T–C–

The second step is to add the primers to the separated strands and allow the primers to combine or hybridize with the strands by lowering the test-tube temperature to about 60°C.

–G–T–C–T–C–A–G–C–T–T–C–C–A–G–
C–A–G–A

                                        C–C–A–G
–C–A–G–A–G–T–C–G–A–A–G–G–T–C–

The third step is to add the DNA polymerase and a mixture of free nucleotides (*G, A, T, C*) to the separated strands. When the test tube is heated to 72°C, the polymerase enzyme directs the rebuilding of a double-stranded DNA molecule, extending the primers by adding the appropriate bases, one at a time, resulting in the production of two complete pairs of double-stranded DNA segments.

–G–T–C–T–C–A–G–C–T–T–C–C–A–G–
C–A–G–A–G–T–C–G–A–A–G–G–T–C–

–G–T–C–T–C–A–G–C–T–T–C–C–A–G
–C–A–G–A–G–T–C–G–A–A–G–G–T–C–

This completes the first cycle of the PCR technique, and the outcome is a doubling of the number of DNA strands—that is, from one to two. The cycle of heating, cooling, and strand rebuilding is then repeated, resulting again in a doubling of the DNA strands. On completion of the second cycle, four double-stranded DNA molecules will have been created from the original double-stranded DNA sample. Typically, twenty-eight to thirty-two cycles are carried out to yield almost a billion copies of the original DNA molecule. Each cycle takes less than two minutes to perform.

Why couldn't the PCR technology be applied to RFLP DNA typing? Simply put, the RFLP strands are too long, often containing thousands of bases. PCR is best used with DNA strands that are no longer than a couple of hundred bases. The obvious solution to this problem is to characterize DNA strands that are much shorter than RFLPs. Another advantage in moving to shorter DNA strands is that they would be expected to be more stable and less subject to degradation brought about by adverse environmental conditions. The long RFLP strands tend to break apart under adverse conditions not uncommon at crime scenes.

From the forensic scientist's viewpoint, PCR offers another distinct advantage in that it can amplify minute quantities of DNA, thus overcoming the limited sample-size problem often associated with crime-scene evidence. With PCR, less than one-billionth of a gram of DNA is required for analysis. Consequently, PCR can characterize DNA extracted from small quantities of blood, semen, and saliva. The extraordinary sensitivity of PCR allows forensic analysts to characterize small quantities of DNA that could never be detected by RFLP. For instance, PCR has been applied to the identification of saliva residues found on envelopes, stamps, soda cans, and cigarette butts.

WebExtra 13.2

Click on "Amplification" and Follow the PCR Process Through Five Cycles

www.prenhall.com/Saferstein

Short Tandem Repeats (STRs)

Out with the Old, In with the New   The latest method of DNA typing, short tandem repeat (STR) analysis, has emerged as the most successful and widely used DNA profiling procedure. **STRs are locations (loci) on the chromosome that contain short sequence elements that repeat themselves within the DNA molecule.** They serve as helpful markers for identification because they are found in great abundance throughout the human genome. STRs normally consist of repeating sequences of three to seven bases; the entire strand of an STR is also very short, less than 450 bases long. These strands are significantly shorter than those encountered in the RFLP procedure. This means that STRs are much less susceptible to degradation and can often be recovered from bodies or stains that have been subject to extreme decomposition. Also, because of their shortness, STRs are an ideal candidate for multiplication by PCR, thus overcoming the limited-sample-size problem often associated with crime-scene evidence. Only one-billionth of a gram or less of DNA is fifty to one hundred times less than normally required for RFLP analysis.

To understand the utility of STRs in forensic science, let's look at one commonly used STR known as TH01. This DNA segment contains the repeating sequence A–A–T–G. Seven TH01 variants have been identified in the human genome. These variants contain five to eleven repeats of A–A–T–G. Figure 13–12 illustrates two such TH01 variants, one containing six repeats and the other containing eight repeats of A–A–T–G.

During a forensic examination, TH01 is extracted from biological materials and amplified by PCR in the manner described on pp. 394–396. The ability to copy an STR means that extremely small amounts of the molecule can be detected and analyzed. Once the STRs have been copied or amplified, they are separated on an electrophoretic gel. By examining the

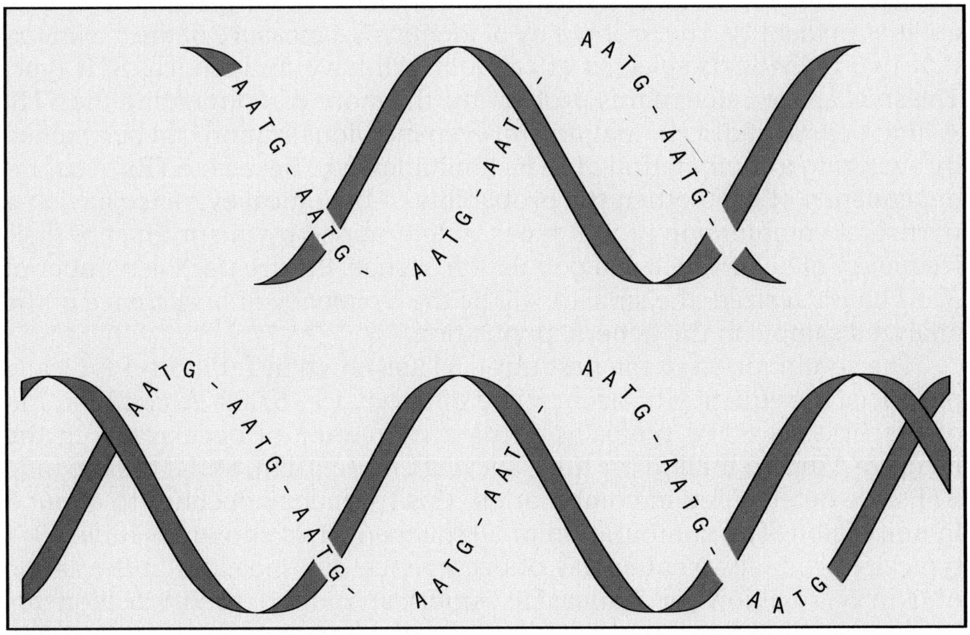

Short Tandem Repeat (STR)
A region of a DNA molecule that contains short segments consisting of three to seven repeating base pairs.

Figure 13–12   Variants of the short tandem repeat TH01. The upper DNA strand contains six repeats of the sequence A–A–T–G; the lower DNA strand contains eight repeats of the sequence A–A–T–G. This DNA type is designated as TH01 6,8.

distance the STR has migrated on the electrophoretic plate, one can determine the number of *A–A–T–G* repeats in the STR. Every person has two STR types for TH01, one inherited from each parent. Thus, for example, one may find in a semen stain TH01 with six repeats and eight repeats. This combination of TH01 is found in approximately 3.5 percent of the population.

What makes STRs so attractive to forensic scientists is that hundreds of different types of STRs are found in human genes. The more STRs one can characterize, the smaller will be the percentage of the population from which these STRs can emanate. This gives rise to the concept of multiplexing. Using the technology of PCR, one can simultaneously extract and amplify a combination of different STRs. For example, one system on the commercial market is the STR Blue Kit.[2] This kit provides the necessary materials for the coamplification and detection of three STRs *(triplexing)*—D3S1358, vWA, and FGA. The design of the system ensures that the size of the STRs does not overlap, thereby allowing each marker to be viewed clearly on an electrophoretic gel, as shown in Figure 13–13. In the United States, the forensic science community has standardized on thirteen STRs for entry into a national database known as the Combined DNA Index System (CODIS).

One important concept to grasp in understanding STR technology is that when an STR is selected for analysis not only must the identity and number of core repeats be defined, but the sequence of bases flanking the repeats must also be known. This knowledge allows commercial manufacturers of STR typing kits to prepare the correct primers to delineate the STR segment to be amplified by PCR. Figure 13–14 illustrates how appropriate primers are used to define the region of DNA to be amplified. Also, a mix of different primers aimed at different STRs will be used to simultaneously amplify a multitude of STRs (multiplexing). In fact, one STR kit on the commercial market can simultaneously make copies of fifteen different STRs.

The thirteen CODIS STRs are listed in Table 13–1 along with their probabilities of identity. The probability of identity is a measure of the likelihood that two individuals selected at random will have an identical STR type. The smaller the value of this probability, the more discriminating the STR. A high degree of discrimination and even individualization can be attained by analyzing a combination of STRs (multiplexing). Because STRs occur independently of each other, the probability of biological evidence having a particular combination of STR types is determined by the product of their frequency of occurrence in a population. Hence, the greater the number of STRs characterized, the smaller will be the frequency of occurrence of the analyzed sample in the general population.

The combination of the first three STRs shown in Table 13–1 typically produces a frequency of occurrence of about 1 in 5,000. A combination of the first six STRs typically yields a frequency of occurrence in the range of 1 in two million for the Caucasian population, and if the top nine STRs are determined in combination, this frequency declines to about 1 in one billion. The combination of all thirteen STRs shown in Table 13–1 typically produces frequencies of occurrence that measure in the range of 1 in 575 trillion for Caucasian Americans and 1 in 900 trillion for

Multiplexing
A technique that simultaneously detects more than one DNA marker in a single analysis.

WebExtra 13.3
See the 13 CODIS STRs and Their Chromosomal Positions
www.prenhall.com/Saferstein

---

[2] Applied Biosystems, 850 Lincoln Centre Drive, Foster City, Calif. 94404.

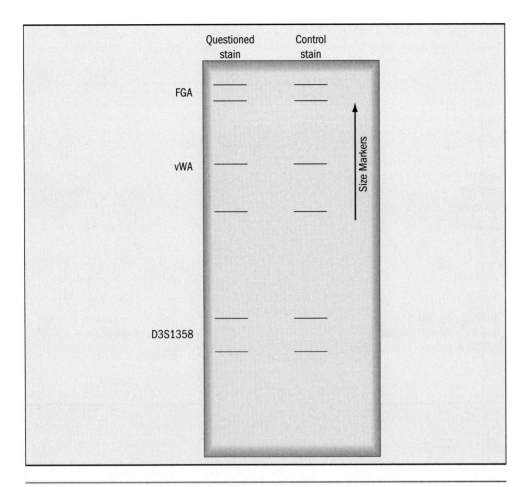

Figure 13–13 Triplex system containing three loci: FGA, vWA, and D3S1358, indicating a match between the questioned and the standard/reference stains.

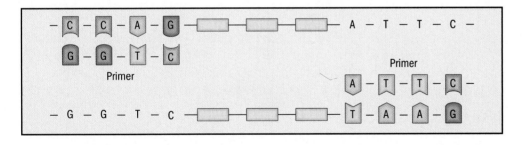

Figure 13–14 Appropriate primers flanking the repeat units of a DNA segment must be selected and put in place in order to initiate the PCR process.

African-Americans. Importantly, a number of commercially available kits readily allow forensic scientists to profile STRs in the kinds of combinations cited here.

The separation of STRs can typically be carried out on a flat gel-coated electrophoretic plate, as depicted in Figures 5–12 and 13–13. However, with the advent and success of STR analysis, the need to reduce analysis time and to automate the sampling and data collection procedures has led to the emergence of *capillary electrophoresis* as the preferred technology

WebExtra 13.4

See How to Calculate the Frequency of Occurrence of a DNA Profile

www.prenhall.com/Saferstein

Table 13–1	The Thirteen CODIS STRs and Their Probability of Identities	
STR	**African-American**	**U.S. Caucasian**
D3S1358	0.094	0.075
vWA	0.063	0.062
FGA	0.033	0.036
THO1	0.109	0.081
TPOX	0.090	0.195
CSF1PO	0.081	0.112
D5S818	0.112	0.158
D13S317	0.136	0.085
D7S820	0.080	0.065
D8S1179	0.082	0.067
D21S11	0.034	0.039
D18S51	0.029	0.028
D16S539	0.070	0.089

Source: *The Future of Forensic DNA Testing: Predictions of the Research and Development Working Group.* Washington, D.C.: National Institute of Justice, Department of Justice, 2000, p. 41.

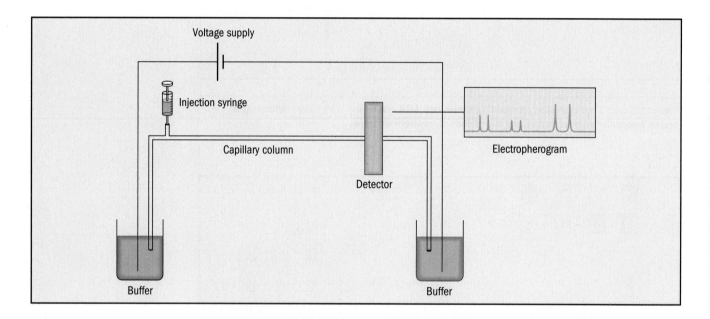

Figure 13–15 Capillary electrophoresis technology has evolved from the traditional flat gel electrophoresis approach. The separation of DNA segments is carried out on the interior wall of a glass capillary tube that is kept at a constant voltage. The size of the DNA fragments determines the speed at which they move through the column. This figure illustrates the separation of three sets of STRs (triplexing).

for the characterization of STRs. Capillary electrophoresis is carried out in a thin glass column rather than on the surface of a coated-glass plate. As illustrated in Figure 13–15, each end of the column is immersed in a reservoir of buffer liquid that also holds electrodes (coated with platinum) to supply high-voltage energy. The column is coated with a gel polymer, and the DNA-containing sample solution is injected into one end of the column with a syringe. The STR fragments then move through the column under the influence of an electrical potential at a speed that is related to the length of the STR fragments. The other end of the column is connected to a detector that tracks the separated STRs as they emerge from the column. As the DNA peaks pass through the detector, they are recorded on a display known as an electropherogram.

Manufacturers of commercial STR kits typically used by crime laboratories provide analysts with one additional piece of useful information along with STR types: the sex of the DNA contributor. The focus of attention here is the amelogenin gene located on both the X and Y chromosomes (see pp. 364–365). This gene, which is actually the gene for tooth pulp, has an interesting characteristic in that it is shorter by six bases in the X chromosome than in the Y chromosome. Hence, when the amelogenin gene is amplified by PCR and separated by electrophoresis, males, who have an X and a Y chromosome, show two bands; females, who have two X chromosomes, have just one band. Typically, these results are obtained in conjunction with STR types.

Y-STRs Another tool in the arsenal of the DNA analyst is the ability to type STRs located on the Y chromosome. The Y chromosome is male specific and is always paired with the X chromosome. More than twenty different Y-STR markers have been identified, and a commercial kit allows for the characterization of 17 Y-chromosome STRs. When can it be advantageous to seek out Y-STR types? Generally, Y-STRs are useful when one is confronted with blood, saliva, or a vaginal swab that is a mix originating from more than one male. For example, Y-STRs prove useful when multiple males are involved in a sexual assault.

Keep in mind that STR types derived from the Y chromosome originate only from this single male chromosome. A female or XX subject does *not* contribute any DNA information. Also, unlike a conventional STR analysis that is derived from two chromosomes and typically shows two bands or peaks, a Y-STR has only one band or peak for each STR type. For example, the traditional STR DNA pattern may prove to be overly complex in the case of a vaginal swab containing the semen of two males. Each STR type would be expected to show four bands, two bands from each male. Also complicating the appearance of the DNA profile may be the presence of DNA from skin cells emanating from the walls of the vagina. In this circumstance, homing in on the Y chromosome greatly simplifies the appearance and interpretation of the DNA profile. Thus, when presented with a DNA mixture of two males and one female, each STR type would be expected to show six bands. However, the same mixture subjected to Y-STR analysis would show only two bands (one band for each male) for each Y-STR type.

STR DNA typing has become an essential and basic investigative tool in the law enforcement community. The technology has progressed at a rapid rate and in only a few years has surmounted numerous legal challenges to become vital evidence for resolving violent crimes and sex offenses. DNA evidence is impartial, implicating the guilty and exonerating the innocent. Significantly, about 25 percent of the DNA examinations conducted by the FBI Laboratory since 1989 have excluded suspects identified by police as the source of DNA evidence collected from the crime scene. In a number of well-publicized cases, DNA evidence has exonerated individuals who have been wrongly convicted and imprisoned for the commission of a crime (see Figure 13–16). The importance

WebExtra 13.5
Understand the Operational Principles of Capillary Electrophoresis
www.prenhall.com/Saferstein

Amelogenin Gene
A genetic locus useful for determining gender.

WebExtra 13.6
See the Electropherogram Record from One Individual's DNA
www.prenhall.com/Saferstein

Y-STRs
Short tandem repeats located on the human Y chromosome. Their utility in forensic science is that they originate only from a male donor of DNA.

WebExtra 13.7
An Animation Depicting Y-STRs
www.prenhall.com/Saferstein

After 24 Years in Prison, Man Has a Reason to Smile

By SHAILA DEWAN

MARIETTA, Ga., Dec. 7—It is rare to see a prison inmate with a life sentence who cannot stop grinning. Thus, when presented with a DNA mixture of two males and one female, each STR type would be expected to show six bands. However, the same mixture subjected to Y-STR analysis would show only two bands (one band for each male) for each Y-STR type.

But that was Robert Clark Jr. on Wednesday, the day before his conviction for rape, robbery and kidnapping was expected to be vacated on the strength of a DNA test that showed he was not the rapist.

After 24 years in prison—one of the longest incarcerations served by the 164 people who have been exonerated by DNA testing—Mr. Clark, 45, was buoyant at the prospect of seeing his siblings, children and the five grandchildren he did not have when he was sentenced in 1982.

"I still got a little life in me," he said.

Though wrenching, Mr. Clark's story is not so different from that of others who were wrongfully convicted. What is stunning about it is the fact that the man who the authorities now believe was the real rapist, Floyd Antonio Arnold, was in early reach of the police at the time.

The DNA test that exonerated Mr. Clark started a chain reaction that revealed not just Mr. Clark's innocence, but a series of law-enforcement bungles. Those missteps allowed Mr. Arnold to commit violent crimes repeatedly and, very nearly, to walk out of prison, where he is serving time for cruelty to children, at the end of January, despite the fact that his DNA matches that found in Mr. Clark's case and two other previously unsolved rapes.

"This is the worst case of tunnel vision that we've seen in the history of the Innocence Project," said Peter J. Neufeld, a co-founder of the project, which has been instrumental in DNA exonerations and which is handling Mr. Clark's case.

At 21, Mr. Clark was living with his mother and 5-year-old son in southwestern Atlanta. He worked as a roofer and had no criminal record, save a juvenile burglary charge. One day an acquaintance, Mr. Arnold, lent him a car. Because the car was not hotwired and Mr. Arnold had the keys, Mr. Clark said, he did not think the car was stolen.

But the car had belonged to Patricia J. Tucker, 29, who had been getting into the driver's seat in a Kentucky Fried Chicken parking lot where she was carjacked, kidnapped, taken to the woods and raped three times. At Mr. Clark's trial, the sole defense witness identified Mr. Arnold in the courtroom and testified she had seen him driving the car before Mr. Clark was arrested with it.

But Ms. Tucker testified that Mr. Clark had been her attacker, even though she had initially described him as 5-foot-7 and Mr. Clark was 6-foot-1. The detective in the case told the jury that he never investigated Mr. Arnold because Mr. Clark had initially lied to officers about where he had gotten the car, then switched his story. The judge sentenced Mr. Clark to life.

When Mr. Clark heard that, he interrupted, saying: "Your Honor, they had Tony here. I can't put him on the stand. He'll tell you I didn't do nothing but drive the car two weeks later. Y'all got him right here."

"Mr. Clark, you have had your trial," the jury admonished. "Just remain silent."

Mr. Arnold went on to commit a string of felonies, including burglary, gun possession and sodomy. In 2001, he was charged with multiple counts of child molesting in a case prosecutors say involved a 13-year-old female relative. He pleaded guilty to a lesser charge, cruelty to children, for which he is now serving time.

Meanwhile, Mr. Clark wrote birthday cards to his children and letters to anyone he thought might be able to help with his case.

When his mother came to visit, he would lay his head in her lap and sleep. When her kidneys failed, he asked to be locked up in solitary confinement so he could be alone to grieve. She died last year, before he gained his freedom. "She knew I got the court order I needed," Mr. Clark said, smiling again.

Finally, the Innocence Project took his case, and a DNA test was done on the evidence. In November, the results showed that the attacker was not Mr. Clark. The district attorney in Cobb County, Pat Head, ran the DNA profile against the criminal offender database. A match came back: Mr. Arnold.

But there was more, said Ted Staples, the manager of forensic biology for the Georgia Bureau of Investigation. The printout showed that in 2003, when Mr. Arnold's DNA was first added to the database, it matched that in two other rapes, in Fulton and DeKalb Counties.

No action was taken against Mr. Arnold, who will finish his current sentence on Jan. 31.

Mr. Staples said the police in those jurisdictions were notified at the time by phone and letter. But a spokesman for the Fulton County Police Department said it did not know of the match until last week. It has put a hold on Mr. Arnold so he cannot be released.

In DeKalb, Detective Sgt. K. D. Johnson, of the DeKalb County Police Department's youth and sex crimes unit, acknowledged that the department was notified in 2003, but said that the information had slipped through the cracks. "It had gone through several different detectives who have since been transferred to other departments," Sergeant Johnson said. "We're trying to figure out who had it and when."

For his part, Mr. Clark stands to get some restitution from the state, which has paid $1.5 million to two other exonerated men. But, he said, he is thinking more about his 5-year-old granddaughter, Alexis, than how much he might be owed. "They owe me an apology," he said. "They done messed my life up." And he smiled.

---

of DNA analyses in criminal investigations has also placed added burdens on crime laboratories to improve their quality-assurance procedures and to ensure the correctness of their results. A number of well-publicized instances have occurred where the accuracy of DNA tests conducted by government-funded laboratories have been called into question.

Mitochondrial DNA

Typically, when one describes DNA in the context of a criminal investigation, the subject is assumed to be the DNA in the nucleus of a cell. Actually, a human cell contains two types of DNA—nuclear and mitochondrial. The first constitutes the twenty-three pairs of chromosomes in the nuclei of our cells. Each parent contributes to the genetic makeup of these chromosomes. Mitochondrial DNA (mtDNA), on the other hand, is found outside the nucleus of the cell and is inherited solely from the mother.

Mitochondria are cell structures found in all human cells. They are the power plants of the body, providing about 90 percent of the energy that the body needs to function. A single mitochondrion contains several loops of DNA, all of which are involved in energy generation. Further, because each cell in our bodies contains hundreds to thousands of mitochondria, there are hundreds to thousands of mtDNA copies in a human cell. This compares to just one set of nuclear DNA located in that same cell. Thus, forensic scientists are offered enhanced sensitivity and the opportunity to characterize mtDNA when nuclear DNA is significantly degraded, such as in charred remains, or when nuclear DNA may be present in a small quantity (such as in a hair shaft). Interestingly, when authorities cannot obtain a reference sample from an individual who may be long deceased or missing, an mtDNA reference sample can be obtained from any maternally related relative. However, all individuals of the same maternal lineage will be indistinguishable by mtDNA analysis.

While mtDNA analysis is significantly more sensitive than nuclear DNA profiling, forensic analysis of mtDNA is more rigorous, time consuming, and costly than nuclear DNA profiling. For this reason, only a handful of public and private forensic laboratories receive evidence for this type of determination. The FBI Laboratory has imposed strict limitations on the type of cases in which it will apply mtDNA technology.

As was previously discussed, nuclear DNA is composed of a continuous linear strand of nucleotides (*A, T, G,* and *C*). On the other hand, mtDNA is constructed in a circular or loop configuration. Each loop contains enough (approximately 16,569) *A, T, G,* and *C* to make up thirty seven genes involved in mitochondrial energy generation. Two regions of mtDNA have been found to be highly variable in the human population. These two regions have been designated hypervariable region I (HV1) and hypervariable region II (HV2), as shown in Figure 13–17. As indicated previously, the process for analyzing HV1 and HV2 is tedious. It involves generating many copies of these DNA hypervariable regions by PCR and then determining the order of the *A–T–G–C* bases constituting the hypervariable regions. This process is known as sequencing. The FBI Laboratory, the Armed Forces DNA Identification Laboratory, and other laboratories have collaborated to compile an mtDNA population database containing the base sequences from HV1 and HV2.

Mitochondria
Small structures located outside the nucleus of a cell. These structures supply energy to the cell. Maternally inherited DNA is found in each mitochondrion.

WebExtra 13.8
See How We Inherit Our Mitochondrial DNA
www.prenhall.com/Saferstein

Sequencing
A procedure used to determine the order of the base pairs that constitute DNA.

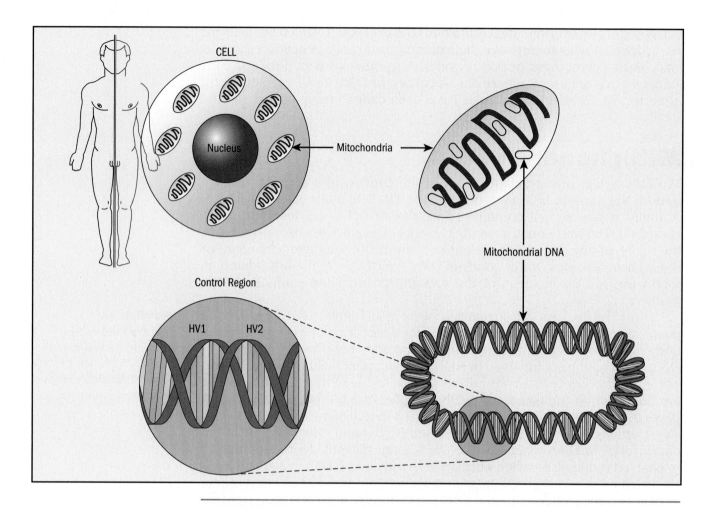

Figure 13–17 Every cell in the body contains hundreds of mitochondria, which provide energy to the cell. Each mitochondrion contains numerous copies of DNA shaped in the form of a loop. Distinctive differences between individuals in their mitochondrial DNA makeup are found in two specific segments of the control region on the DNA loop known as HV1 and HV2.

Once the sequences of the hypervariable regions from a case sample are obtained, most laboratories simply report the number of times these sequences appear in the mtDNA database maintained by the FBI. The mtDNA database contains about five thousand sequences. This approach permits an assessment of how common or rare an observed mtDNA sequence is in the database. Interestingly, many of the sequences that have been determined in case work are unique to the existing database, and many types are present at frequencies no greater than 1 percent in the database. Thus it is often possible to demonstrate how uncommon a particular mitochondrial DNA sequence is. However, even under the best of circumstances, mtDNA typing does not approach STR analysis in its discrimination power. Thus, mtDNA analysis is best reserved for samples for which nuclear DNA typing is simply not possible.

The first time mtDNA was admitted as evidence in a U.S. court was in 1996 in the case of *State of Tennessee* v. *Paul Ware*. Here, mtDNA was used to link two hairs recovered from the crime scene to the defendant. Interestingly, in this case, blood and semen evidence was absent. Mitochondrial DNA analysis also plays a key role in the identification of human

WebExtra 13.9

Look Into the Structure of Mitochondrial DNA and See How It Is Used for DNA Typing
www.prenhall.com/Saferstein

Forensics at Work
Outrage: The O. J. Simpson Verdict

To distill this case down to its irreducible minimum (and temporarily ignoring all the other evidence pointing inexorably to Simpson's guilt), if your blood is found at the murder scene, as Simpson's was conclusively proved to be by DNA tests, that's really the end of the ball game. There is nothing more to say. (And in this case, not only was Simpson's blood found at the murder scene, but the victims' blood was found inside his car and home.) I mean, to deny guilt when your blood is at the murder scene is the equivalent of a man being caught by his wife *in flagrante* with another woman and saying to her (quoting comedian Richard Pryor), "Who are you going to believe? Me or your lying eyes?"

At the crime scene there were five blood drops leading away from the slain bodies of Nicole Brown Simpson and Ronald Goldman toward the rear alley, four of which were immediately to the *left* of bloody size-12 shoe prints (Simpson's shoe size). This indicated, of course, that the killer had been wounded on the left side of his body. And the morning after the murders, Simpson was observed by the police to be wearing a bandage on his left middle finger. When the bandage was removed that afternoon, it was seen that he had a deep cut on the knuckle of the finger.

DNA (deoxyribonucleic acid) is the genetic material found in all human cells that carries the coded messages of heredity unique (with the exception of identical twins) to each individual. DNA, then, is our genetic fingerprint. Each of the approximately 100 trillion cells in a human body contains twenty-three pairs of chromosomes—one of each pair coming from one's father, the other from the mother—which contain DNA molecules. In criminal cases, DNA can be extracted from samples of blood, semen, saliva, skin, or hair follicles found at a crime scene and then compared to DNA drawn from a suspect to determine if there is a "match." DNA testing is a new forensic science, first used in Great Britain in 1985 and in the United States in 1987.

DNA tests on all five blood drops and on three bloodstains found on the rear gate at the crime scene showed that all of this blood belonged to Simpson. Two DNA tests were used: PCR (polymerase chain reaction) and RFLP (restrictive fragment length polymorphism). The PCR test is less precise than the RFLP, but can be conducted on much smaller blood samples as well as samples that have degenerated ("degraded") because of bacteria and/or exposure to the elements. PCR tests were conducted on four out of the five blood drops. Three showed that only one out of 240,000 people had DNA with the markers found in the sample. (A marker is a gene that makes up one portion of the DNA molecule, and the more markers in the sample, the more comparison tests can be conducted, and hence the greater the exclusion of other humans.) The fourth blood drop had markers which one out of 5200 people could have. Simpson was one of these people. The fifth blood drop had sufficient markers for an RFLP test, and showed that only one out of 170 million people had DNA with those markers. Again, Simpson's blood did. The richest sample was on the rear gate, and an RFLP test showed that only one out of 57 billion people had those markers. Simpson was one of them. In other words,

continued

just on the blood evidence alone, there's only a one out of 57 billion chance that Simpson is innocent. Fifty-seven billion is approximately ten times the current population of the entire world.

Now I realize that Igor in Kiev, Gino in Naples, Colin down Johannesburg way, and Kartac on Pluto might have the same DNA as O. J. Simpson. If you're a skeptic I wouldn't blame you if you checked to see if Igor, Gino, Colin, or Kartac was in Brentwood on the night of the murders, used to beat Nicole within an inch of her life, had blood all over his car, driveway, and home on the night of the murders, had no alibi, and, if charged with the murders, would refuse to take the witness stand to defend himself. Who knows—maybe Simpson isn't the murderer after all. Maybe Igor or one of the others is. You should definitely check this out. And while you're checking it out, someone should be checking you into the nearest mental ward.

To elaborate on the irreducible minimum mentioned earlier, there are only three possible explanations other than guilt for one's blood being found at the murder scene, and all three are preposterous on their face. One is that Simpson left his blood there on an earlier occasion. When Simpson was interrogated by LAPD detectives on the afternoon after these murders, he said he had not cut himself the last time he was at the Bundy address a week earlier. But even without that, how can one believe that on some prior occasion Simpson bled, not just on the Bundy premises, but at the precise point on the premises where the murders occurred? In fact, so farfetched is this possibility that even the defense attorneys,

whose stock-in-trade during the trial was absurdity, never proffered it to the jury.

And here, not only was Simpson's blood found at the murder scene, but there were the four drops of Simpson's blood found just to the left of the killer's bloody shoe prints leaving the murder scene. If there is someone who isn't satisfied even by this, I would suggest that this book is perhaps not for you, that you think about pursuing more appropriate intellectual pursuits, such as comic strips. When I was a kid, one of my favorites was *Mandrake the Magician.* You might check to see if Mandrake is still doing his thing.

The second possibility is that Simpson cut himself while killing Ron Goldman and Nicole Brown in self-defense—that is, either Ron or Nicole or both together unleashed a deadly assault on Simpson, and he either took out a knife he had on his own person or wrestled Ron's or Nicole's knife away, and stabbed the two of them to death. This, of course, is just too insane to talk about. Again, even the defense attorneys, who apparently possess the gonads of ten thousand elephants, never suggested this possibility. It should be added parenthetically that if such a situation had occurred, Simpson wouldn't have had any reason to worry, since self-defense is a justifiable homicide, a complete defense to murder.

The third and final possibility is that the LAPD detectives planted Simpson's blood not just at the murder scene but to the left of the bloody shoe prints leaving the scene. This is not as insane a proposition as the first two, but only because there are degrees of everything in life. It is still an insane possibility, and if any reader is silly

Forensics at Work
Outrage: The O. J. Simpson Verdict *(continued)*

enough to believe that the LAPD detectives decided to frame someone they believed to be innocent of these murders (Simpson) and actually planted his blood all over the murder scene (and, of course, planted the victims' blood in Simpson's car and home), again, this book is probably not for that reader. This book is for people who are very angry that a brutal murderer is among us—with a smile on his face, no less—and want to know how this terrible miscarriage of justice could have occurred. . . .

Let me point out to those who believe in the "possible" existence of either of the aforementioned three innocent possibilities for Simpson's blood being found at the murder scene, that the prosecution only has the burden of proving guilt beyond a *reasonable* doubt, not beyond all possible doubt. So it isn't necessary to have all possible doubts of guilt removed from one's mind in order to reach a conclusion of guilt. Only reasonable doubts of guilt have to be removed. Of course, in this case, *no* doubt remains of Simpson's guilt. . . .

There perhaps is no better example of the phenomenon of people seeing what they expect to see working to the prosecution's very definite disadvantage than the situation with one of the defense's expert witnesses, Dr. Henry Lee. Lee, director of the Connecticut State Forensic Science Laboratory, is reputed to be the preeminent dean of American forensic scientists, the "top forensic sleuth," as it were. But I think we all know by now how suspect reputations can be, and if Lee's testimony in the Simpson case is any indication at all of his abilities, he is nothing short of incompetent. At best, he's

an example of how Mark Twain once described an expert: "Just some guy from out of town." The problem is that the jury couldn't see through the bloated reputation of Dr. Lee, and the prosecution, in its summation, never exposed Lee so the jurors could see the emperor without his clothing on.

There were two particular areas in which Lee's testimony, if believed by the jury, was very damaging to the prosecution. One, he testified that he found four small bloodstains on a paper bindle enclosing seven cotton swatches containing blood removed from one of the blood drops (Item 47) to the left of a bloody shoe print leaving the Bundy murder scene (later identified as Simpson's blood by DNA testing). Lee couldn't figure out how the blood could have leaked onto the paper when the swatches had been left out to dry overnight prior to their being packaged. The fact that there was no assurance the blood on all seven swatches had dried completely by the time they were wrapped, or that the subsequently frozen swatches did not leak the blood later in the summer when they were thawed out for DNA testing, or that there was not some other innocent explanation (in virtually every case there are questions, the innocent answers to which are simply never learned) did not deter Lee from saying there was "something wrong," a term that resonated with the jurors during their deliberations. The implication the defense sought to convey, of course, was that the answer lay in evil LAPD conspirators who crept into the LAPD lab in the middle of the night and planted and tampered with the blood evidence.

Lee also testified that he found three key "imprints" on the terra-cotta walkway at

continued

Forensics at Work
Outrage: The O. J. Simpson Verdict *(continued)*

the crime scene which he himself photographed when he went to the scene on June 25, 1994. They did not match the many size-12 Bruno Magli bloody shoe prints at the scene which the prosecutors said belonged to Simpson. One was definitely a shoe print, he testified, one was a "parallel line imprint," and the other he simply called an "imprint." The latter two "could be" shoe prints, he said, raising the inference of a second assailant. This, of course, challenged the prosecution's position that Simpson was the lone killer, and hence challenged their conception of the entire case against him.

Lee also found bloody "parallel line imprint" patterns on the envelope found at the murder scene containing the glasses belonging to Nicole's mother which she had left at the Mezzaluna restaurant earlier in the evening and which Ron Goldman was returning when he was murdered, on a small, triangular piece of paper near the bodies, and on Ron Goldman's jeans. Lee testified that all of these imprints could possibly be partial shoe prints, and since he concluded they were not from the Bruno Maglis or Ron Goldman's shoes, the defense suggested they came from the shoe of the second assailant.

But William Bodziak, the FBI's senior expert on shoe prints, and the former chairman of the footwear and tire section of the International Association for Identification, later debunked all of Lee's conclusions. Bodziak told me he went back to the Bundy crime scene with copies of photographs Lee had taken on June 25 to examine the shoe print and the other two imprints on the walkway which Lee said

"could be" shoe prints. What he found was astonishing. With blown-up color photographs, he pointed out to the jury that one of the imprints (the parallel line one) on the walkway Lee had photographed and testified to was actually tool (trowel) marks made by the workers in the laying of the cement years earlier, and the other imprint was a shoe print from one of these workers which was a permanent indentation in the concrete (ridges, depressions) that Bodziak felt with his own hands.

As to the bloody "parallel line imprint" patterns on the envelope, paper, and jeans Lee had suggested could possibly have come from the shoes of a second assailant, Bodziak said that none of them were shoe prints. The parallel line imprints on the right leg of Ron Goldman's blue jeans were too erratic to be shoe prints and also had no borders representing the edge of any heel or sole. They appeared to be consistent with having been made by a swiping or brushing motion against the jeans by a sleeve from Goldman's long-sleeved shirt, which was thick and roughly textured. Bodziak testified that he found a "striking similarity between the ribbed design on the shirt [taken from test impressions]" and the bloody imprint on the shirt. (FBI special agent Douglas Deedrick, an expert on fiber evidence, had previously testified that the bloody imprint on the jeans appeared to have come from fiber such as that on Goldman's shirt.) As to the small ("half the size of one's thumb") bloody imprint on the envelope, it too was not a part of a shoe print, again having no borders, being too erratic, and the patterns being so fine and small as to

Forensics at Work
Outrage: The O. J. Simpson Verdict *(continued)*

be uncharacteristic of any shoe sole or heel Bodziak had ever seen. Bodziak testified that the parallel lines were consistent with a "fabric" pattern, and could have come from the jeans or shirt of Goldman. Bodziak also testified that the bloody imprint on the piece of paper wasn't a shoe print, and even if it had been, it would have had to come from the shoe of a tiny child.

Lee demonstrated further incompetence in the forensic technique he employed to reach his conclusions. He made no test impressions of Ron Goldman's Levi jeans and shirt (although photographs were taken of the small piece of paper, the LAPD criminalists did not collect it). This was shocking to Bodziak. He testified: "You could look at the fabric on my sleeves with a magnifying glass, but because of its three-dimensional quality, you could not determine what the exact pattern would look like in a test impression. It is absolutely essential to make test impressions for comparison purposes. It is the *only* way that you can make a valid comparison."

Lee, stung and wounded by the obvious repudiation of his conclusions by the FBI's shoe print expert (Lee's specialty is not shoe prints), told reporters from his laboratory in Connecticut that although he stuck to his conclusions, "I'm sorry I ever got involved in the Simpson case," and said he would probably resist any defense subpoena to return to Los Angeles to defend himself and his conclusions.

As it turned out, he didn't have to defend or rehabilitate himself. His reputation was enough for the jury, which should have been skeptical of every single one of his conclusions once his shoe print and imprint testimony was proved to be claptrap. The foreperson of the jury, Armanda Cooley, said in the book she coauthored on the case, *Madam Foreman:* "Dr. Henry Lee was a very impressive gentleman. Highly intelligent, world-renowned. I had a lot of respect for Dr. Lee." Lee's discredited testimony hadn't lessened his stature in Cooley's mind one iota. Juror Lionel (Lon) Cryer told the *Los Angeles Times* right after the verdict that the jury viewed Lee as "the most credible witness" of all at the trial. Cryer repeated Lee's statement that "there was something wrong," saying the jury took these words back to the jury room with them. "Dr. Lee had a lot of impact on a lot of people," he added.

remains. An abundant amount of mtDNA is generally found in skeletal re-mains. Importantly, mtDNA reference samples are available from family members sharing the same mother, grandmother, great-grandmother, and so on. One of the most publicized cases performed on human remains was the identification of the individual buried in the tomb of the Vietnam War's unknown soldier. The remains lying in the tomb were believed to belong to First Lt. Michael J. Blassie, whose A-37 warplane was shot down near An Loc, South Vietnam, in 1972. In 1984, the U.S. Army Central Identification Laboratory failed to identify the remains by physical characteristics, personal artifacts, or blood-typing results from hairs. The remains were subsequently placed in the tomb. In 1998, at the insistence of the Blassie family, the remains were disinterred for the purpose of performing mtDNA analysis and comparing the results to references from seven families thought to be associated with the case. The remains in the tomb were subsequently analyzed and confirmed to be consistent with DNA from Lt. Blassie's family.

Forensic Brief

In the fall of 1979, a 61-year-old patient wandered away from a U.S. Department of Veterans Affairs medical facility. Despite an extensive search, authorities never located the missing man. More than ten years later, a dog discovered a human skull in a wooded area near the facility. DNA Analysis Unit II of the FBI Laboratory received the case in the winter of 1999.

The laboratory determined that the mitochondrial DNA profile from the missing patient's brother matched the mitochondrial DNA profile from the recovered skull and provided the information to the local medical examiner. Subsequently, the remains were declared to be those of the missing patient and returned to the family for burial.

Source: *FBI Law Enforcement Bulletin* **78** (2002): 21.

The Combined DNA Index System (CODIS)

Perhaps the most significant investigative tool to arise from a DNA typing program allows crime laboratories to compare DNA types recovered from crime-scene evidence to those of convicted sex offenders and other convicted criminals. This capability is of tremendous value to investigators in cases in which the police have not been able to identify a suspect. All fifty states have legislatively mandated collection of DNA samples from convicted offenders of particular crimes and establishment of DNA databases for law enforcement purposes. CODIS (Combined DNA Index System) is a computer software program developed by the FBI that maintains local, state, and national databases of DNA profiles from convicted offenders, unsolved crime-scene evidence, and profiles of missing people. CODIS software enables local, state, and national crime laboratories to compare DNA profiles electronically. Thousands of matches have linked serial crimes to each other and have solved crimes by allowing investigators to match crime-scene evidence to known convicted offenders. As mentioned earlier, in the United States the forensic science community has currently standardized on thirteen STRs for entry into CODIS. The CODIS concept has already had a significant impact on police investigations in various states, as shown by the following brief.

Forensic Brief

In 1990, a series of brutal attacks on elderly victims occurred in Goldsboro, North Carolina, by an unknown individual dubbed the Night Stalker. During one such attack in March, an elderly woman was brutally raped and almost murdered. Her daughter's early arrival home saved the woman's life. The suspect fled, leaving behind materials intended to ignite the residence and the victim in an attempt to conceal the crime. In July 1990, another elderly woman was brutally raped and murdered in her home. Three months later, a third elderly woman was raped and stabbed to death. Her husband was also murdered. Their house was burned in an attempt to cover up the crime, but fire and rescue personnel pulled the bodies from the house before it was engulfed in flames.

DNA analysis of biological evidence collected from vaginal swabs from each victim enabled authorities to conclude that the same perpetrator had committed all three crimes. However, there was no suspect.

More than ten years after the commission of these crimes, law enforcement authorities retested the biological evidence from all three cases using newer DNA technology and entered the DNA profiles into North Carolina's DNA database. The DNA profile developed from the crime-scene evidence was thus compared to thousands of convicted-offender profiles already in the database.

In April 2001, a "cold hit" was made with an individual in the convicted-offender DNA database. The perpetrator had been convicted of shooting into an occupied dwelling, an offense that requires inclusion in the North Carolina DNA database. The suspect was brought into custody for questioning and was served with a search warrant to obtain a sample of his blood. That sample was analyzed and compared to the crime-scene evidence, confirming the DNA database match. When confronted with the DNA evidence, the suspect confessed to all three crimes.

Source: National Institute of Justice, "Using DNA to Solve Cold Cases," NIJ special report, 2002, *http://www.ojp.usdoj.gov/nij/pubs-sum/194197.htm*

Collection and Preservation of Biological Evidence for DNA Analysis

Since the early 1990s, the advent of DNA profiling has vaulted biological crime-scene evidence to a stature of importance that is eclipsed only by the fingerprint. In fact, the high sensitivity of DNA determinations has even changed the way police investigators define biological evidence. Just how sensitive is STR profiling? Forensic analysts using currently accepted protocols can reach sensitivity levels as low as 125 picograms. Interestingly, a human cell has an estimated 7 picograms of DNA, which means that only eighteen DNA-bearing cells are needed to obtain an STR profile. However, modifications in the technology can readily extend the level of detection down to nine cells. A quantity of DNA that is below the normal level of detection is defined as a low copy number. With this technology in hand, the horizon of the criminal investigator extends beyond the traditional dried

Picogram
One-trillionth of a gram, or 0.000000000001 gram.

Low Copy Number
Fewer than eighteen DNA-bearing cells.

blood or semen stain to include stamps and envelopes licked with saliva, a cup or can that has touched a person's lips, chewing gum, the sweat band of a hat, or a bedsheet containing dead skin cells. Likewise, skin or epithelial cells transferred onto the surface of a weapon, the interior of a glove, or a pen have yielded DNA results.[3]

Epithelial Cells
The outer layer of skin cells. These DNA-bearing cells often fall off or are rubbed off onto objects retrieved from crime scenes.

The ultimate sensitivity goal in forensic DNA analysis is profiling DNA extracted from one human cell. Such an accomplishment seems close to fruition. Researchers have reported obtaining STR profiles from one or two cells and have successfully profiled DNA from single dermal ridge fingerprints.[4] While it's premature to imply that this technology, or a comparable one, is eligible for admission in criminal trials, one cannot exclude its utilization in criminal and forensic intelligence investigations. Table 13–2 illustrates the power of DNA as a creator of physical evidence.

However, before investigators become enamored with the wonders of DNA, they should first realize that the crime scene must be treated in the traditional manner. Before the collection of evidence begins, biological evidence should be photographed close up and its location relative to the entire crime scene recorded through notes, sketches, and photographs. If the shape and position of bloodstains may provide information about the circumstances of the crime, an expert must immediately conduct an on-the-spot evaluation of the blood evidence. The significance of the position and shape of bloodstains can best be ascertained when the expert has an on-site overview of the entire crime scene and can better reconstruct the movement of the individuals involved. No attempt should be made to disturb the blood pattern before this phase of the investigation is completed.

The evidence collector must handle all body fluids and biologically stained materials with a minimum amount of personal contact. All body fluids must be assumed to be infectious; hence, wearing disposable latex gloves while handling the evidence is required. Latex gloves also significantly reduce the possibility that the evidence collector will contaminate the evidence. These gloves should be changed frequently during the evidence-collection phase of the investigation. Safety considerations and avoidance of contamination also call for the wearing of face masks, shoe covers, and possibly coveralls.

Blood has great evidential value when a transfer between a victim and suspect can be demonstrated. For this reason, all clothing from both victim and suspect should be collected and sent to the laboratory for examination. This procedure must be followed even when the presence of blood on a garment does not appear obvious to the investigator. Laboratory search procedures are far more revealing and sensitive than any that can be conducted at the crime scene. In addition, blood should also be searched for in less-than-obvious places. For example, the criminal may have wiped his or her hands on materials not readily apparent to the investigator. Investigators should look for towels, handkerchiefs, or rags that may have been used and then hidden, and should also examine floor cracks or other crevices that may have trapped blood.

---

[3] R. A Wickenheiser, "Trace DNA: A Review, Discussion of Theory, and Application of the Transfer of Trace Quantities through Skin Contact," *Journal of Forensic Sciences* 47 (2002): 442.

[4] E. K. Hanson and J. Ballantyne, "Whole Genome Amplification Strategy for Forensic Genetic Analysis Using Single or Few Cell Equivalents of Genomic DNA," *Analytical Biochemistry* 346 (2005): 246.

Table 13–2 Location and Sources of DNA at Crime Scenes

Evidence	Possible Location of DNA on the Evidence	Source of DNA
baseball bat or similar weapon	handle, end	sweat, skin, blood, tissue
hat, bandanna, or mask	inside	sweat, hair, dandruff
eyeglasses	nose or ear pieces, lens	sweat, skin
facial tissue cotton swab	surface area	mucus, blood, sweat, semen, ear wax
dirty laundry	surface area	blood, sweat, semen
toothpick	tips	saliva
used cigarette	cigarette butt	saliva
stamp or envelope	licked area	saliva
tape or ligature	inside/outside surface	skin, sweat
bottle, can, or glass	sides, mouthpiece	saliva, sweat
used condom	inside/outside surface	semen, vaginal or rectal cells
blanket, pillow, sheet	surface area	sweat, hair, semen, urine, saliva
"through and through" bullet	outside surface	blood, tissue
bite mark	person's skin or clothing	saliva
fingernail, partial fingernail	scrapings	blood, sweat, tissue

Source: National Institute of Justice, U.S. Department of Justice.

Biological evidence should not be packaged in plastic or airtight containers, because accumulation of residual moisture could contribute to the growth of DNA-destroying bacteria and fungi. **Each stained article should be packaged separately in a paper bag or a well-ventilated box.** If feasible, the entire stained article should be packaged and submitted for examination. If this is not possible, dried blood is best removed from a surface with a sterile cotton-tipped swab lightly moistened with distilled water from a dropper bottle. A portion of the unstained surface material near the recovered stain must likewise be removed or swabbed and placed in a separate package. This is known as a substrate control. The forensic examiner might use the substrate swab to confirm that the results of the tests performed were brought about by the stain and not by the material on which it was deposited. However, this practice is normally not necessary when DNA determinations are carried out in the laboratory. One point is critical, and that is that the collected swabs must not be packaged in a wet state. After the collection is made, the swab must be air-dried for approximately five to ten minutes. Then it is best to place it in a swab box (see Figure 13–18), which has a circular hole to allow air circulation. The swab box can then be placed in a paper or manila envelope.

All packages containing biological evidence should be refrigerated or stored in a cool location out of direct sunlight until delivery to the laboratory. However, one common exception is blood mixed with soil. Microbes present in soil rapidly degrade DNA. Therefore, blood in soil must be stored in a clean glass or plastic container and immediately frozen.

Substrate Control
An unstained object adjacent to an area on which biological material has been deposited.

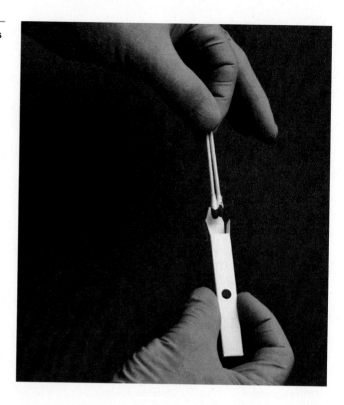

Figure 13–18 Air-dried swabs are placed in a swab box for delivery to the forensic laboratory. *Courtesy Tri-Tech, Inc., Southport, N.C., www.tritechusa.com*

Biological evidence attains its full forensic value only when an analyst can compare each of its DNA types to known DNA samples collected from victims and suspects. For this purpose, at least 7 cc of whole blood should be drawn from individuals by a qualified medical person. The blood sample should be collected in a sterile vacuum tube containing the preservative *EDTA* (ethylenediamine tetraacetic acid). In addition to serving as a preservative, EDTA inhibits the activity of enzymes that degrade DNA. The tubes must be kept refrigerated (not frozen) while awaiting transportation to the laboratory. In addition to blood, other options exist for obtaining standard/reference DNA specimens. The least intrusive method for obtaining a DNA standard/reference, one that nonmedical personnel can readily use, is the *buccal swab*. Cotton swabs are placed in the subject's mouth and the inside of the cheek is vigorously swabbed, resulting in the transfer of buccal cells onto the swab (see Figure 13–19).

If an individual is not available to give a DNA standard/reference sample, some interesting alternatives are available to evidence collectors, including a toothbrush, combs and hairbrushes, a razor, soiled laundry, used cigarette butts, and earplugs. Any of these items may contain a sufficient quantity of DNA for typing purposes. Interestingly, as investigators worked to identify the remains of victims of the World Trade Center attack on September 11, 2001, the families of the missing were requested to supply the New York City DNA Laboratory with these types of items in an effort to match recovered DNA with human remains.

One key concern during the collection of a DNA-containing specimen is contamination. Contamination can occur by introducing foreign DNA through coughing or sneezing onto a stain during the collection process, or there can be a transfer of DNA when items of evidence are incorrectly placed in contact with each other during packaging. Fortunately, an examination of DNA band patterns in the laboratory readily reveals the presence of contamination. For example, with an STR, one will expect to

Buccal Cells
Cells derived from the inner cheek lining.

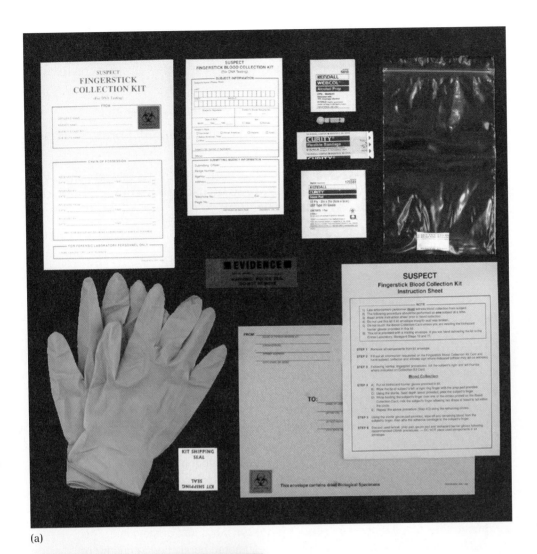

(a)

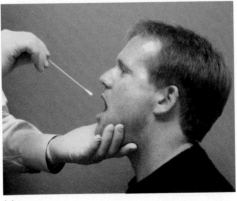

(b)   (c)

Figure 13–19 A buccal swab collection kit is designed for use by nonmedical personnel. The cotton-tipped swabs are placed in the subject's mouth and the inside of the cheek is vigorously swabbed, resulting in the transfer of buccal cells onto the cotton bulb of the swab. The kit is then delivered to the forensic laboratory. *Courtesy Tri-Tech, Inc., Southport, N.C., www.tritechusa.com*

see a two-band pattern. More than two bands suggest a mixture of DNA from more than one source.

Crime-scene investigators can take some relatively simple steps to minimize contamination of biological evidence:

1. Change gloves before handling each new piece of evidence.

2. Collect a substrate control for possible subsequent laboratory examination.

3. Pick up small items of evidence such as cigarette butts and stamps with clean forceps. Disposable forceps are to be used so that they can be discarded after a single evidence collection.

4. Always package each item of evidence in its own well-ventilated container.

Forensic Brief

A woman alleged that she had been held against her will and sexually assaulted by a male friend in an apartment. During the course of the assault, a contact lens was knocked from the victim's eye. After the assault, she escaped, but due to fear from threats made by her attacker, she did not report the assault to the police for three days. When the police examined the apartment, they noted that it had been thoroughly cleaned. A vacuum cleaner bag was seized for examination and several pieces of material resembling fragments of a contact lens were discovered within the bag.

In the laboratory, approximately 20 nanograms of human DNA was recovered from the contact lens fragments. Cells from both the eyeball and the interior of the eyelids are naturally replaced every six to twenty-four hours. As such, both are potential sources for the DNA found. The DNA profile originating from the fragments matched the victim, thus corroborating the victim's account of the crime. The estimated population frequency of occurrence for the nine matching STRs are approximately 1 in 850 million. The suspect subsequently pleaded guilty to the offense.

STR Locus	Victim's DNA Type	Contact Lens
D3S1358	15,18	15,18
FGA	24,25	24,25
vWA	17,17	17,17
THO1	6,7	6,7
F13A1	5,6	5,6
fes/fps	11,12	11,12
D5S818	11,12	11,12
D13S317	11,12	11,12
D7S820	10,12	10,12

Source: R. A. Wickenheiser and R. M. Jobin, "Comparison of DNA Recovered from a Contact Lens Using PCR DNA Typing," *Canadian Society of Forensic Science Journal* 32 (1999): 67.

A common occurrence at crime scenes is to suspect the presence of blood, but not be able to observe any with the naked eye. In these situations, the common test of choice is luminol (see p. 354). Interestingly, luminol does not inhibit the ability to detect and characterize STRs.[5] Therefore, luminol can be used to locate traces of blood and areas that have been washed nearly free of blood without compromising the potential for DNA typing.

Chapter Summary

Portions of the DNA structure are as unique to each individual as fingerprints. The gene is the fundamental unit of heredity. Each gene is actually composed of DNA specifically designed to control the genetic traits of our cells. DNA is constructed as a very large molecule made by linking a series of repeating units called nucleotides. Four types of bases are associated with the DNA structure: adenine (*A*), guanine (*G*), cytosine (*C*), and thymine (*T*). The bases on each strand are properly aligned in a double-helix configuration. As a result, adenine pairs with thymine and guanine pairs with cytosine. This concept is known as base pairing. The order of the bases is what distinguishes different DNA strands.

Portions of the DNA molecule contain sequences of bases that are repeated numerous times. To a forensic scientist, these tandem repeats offer a means of distinguishing one individual from another through DNA typing. Length differences associated with relatively long repeating DNA strands are called restriction fragment length polymorphisms (RFLPs) and form the basis for one of the first DNA-typing procedures. Once the DNA molecules have been cut up by a restriction enzyme, the resulting fragments are sorted out by electrophoresis. A typical DNA fragment pattern shows two bands (one RFLP from each chromosome). When comparing the DNA fragment patterns of two or more specimens, one merely looks for a match between the band sets.

Polymerase chain reaction (PCR) is the outgrowth of knowledge gained from an understanding of how DNA strands naturally replicate within a cell. PCR offers a distinct advantage in that it can amplify minute quantities of DNA. PCR technology cannot be applied to RFLP DNA typing. The RFLP strands are too long, often numbering in the thousands of bases. PCR is best used with DNA strands that are no longer than a couple of hundred bases. Another advantage in moving to shorter DNA strands is that they would be expected to be more stable and less subject to degradation brought about by adverse environmental conditions. The long RFLP strands tend to break apart under the adverse conditions not uncommon at crime scenes.

The latest method of DNA typing, short tandem repeat (STR) analysis, has emerged as the most successful and widely used DNA-profiling procedure. STRs are locations on the chromosome that contain short sequences that repeat themselves within the DNA molecule. They serve as useful markers for identification because they are found in great abundance throughout the human genome. STRs normally consist of repeating

---

[5] A. M. Gross et al., "The Effect of Luminol on Presumptive Tests and DNA Analysis Using the Polymerase Chain Reaction," *Journal of Forensic Sciences* 44 (1999): 837.

sequences three to seven bases long, and the entire strand of an STR is also very short, less than 450 bases long. This means that STRs are much less susceptible to degradation and may often be recovered from bodies or stains that have been subjected to extreme decomposition. Also, because of their shortness, STRs are ideal candidates for multiplication by PCR, thus overcoming the limited-sample-size problem often associated with crime-scene evidence. What makes STRs so attractive to forensic scientists is that hundreds of different types of STRs are found in human genes. The more STRs one can characterize, the smaller the percentage of the population from which a particular combination of STRs can emanate. This gives rise to the concept of multiplexing. Using the technology of PCR, one can simultaneously extract and amplify a combination of different STRs. Currently, U.S. crime laboratories have standardized on thirteen STRs. With STR, as few as 125 picograms of DNA are required for analysis. This is one-hundredth the amount normally required for RFLP analysis.

Another type of DNA used for individual characterization is mitochondrial DNA. Mitochondrial DNA is located outside the cell's nucleus and is inherited from the mother. However, mitochondrial DNA typing does not approach STR analysis in its discrimination power and thus is best reserved for samples, such as hair, for which STR analysis may not be possible.

Bloodstained evidence should not be packaged in plastic or airtight containers because accumulation of residual moisture could contribute to the growth of blood-destroying bacteria and fungi. Each stained article should be packaged separately in a paper bag or in a well-ventilated box.

WebExtra 13.10

DNA Forensics
www.prenhall.com/Saferstein

Review Questions

1. The fundamental unit of heredity is the _____.
2. Each gene is actually composed of _____, specifically designed to carry out a single body function.
3. A(n) _____ is a very large molecule made by linking a series of repeating units.
4. A(n) _____ is composed of a sugar molecule, a phosphorus-containing group, and a nitrogen-containing molecule called a base.
5. DNA is actually a very large molecule made by linking a series of _____ to form a natural polymer.
6. _____ different bases are associated with the makeup of DNA.
7. Watson and Crick demonstrated that DNA is composed of two strands coiled into the shape of a(n) _____.
8. The structure of DNA requires the pairing of base A to _____ and base G to _____.
9. The base sequence *T–G–C–A* can be paired with the base sequence _____ in a double-helix configuration.
10. The inheritable traits that are controlled by DNA arise out of DNA's ability to direct the production of _____.
11. _____ are derived from a combination of up to twenty known amino acids.
12. The production of an amino acid is controlled by a sequence of _____ bases on the DNA molecule.
13. True or False: Enzymes known as DNA polymerase assemble new DNA strands into a proper base sequence during replication. _____
14. True or False: DNA can be copied outside a living cell. _____

15. Recombinant DNA relies on the ability of chemicals known as _____ to cut DNA into fragments.

16. True or False: All of the letter sequences in DNA code for the production of proteins. _____

17. In RFLP DNA typing, restriction enzymes are used to cut out (repeating, random) sequences from the DNA molecule.

18. In RFLP DNA typing, restriction enzymes are used to cut out sequences of DNA with different (widths, lengths).

19. DNA fragments can be sorted according to their size by the technique of _____.

20. In the RFLP DNA typing process, DNA fragments are transferred to a nylon membrane by a process called _____ blotting.

21. True or False: In the RFLP DNA typing process, a radioactively labeled probe is used to visualize the separated DNA fragments. _____

22. The probe complementary to the base sequence *T–A–G* has the letter sequence _____.

23. In RFLP DNA typing, a typical DNA pattern shows (two, three) bands.

24. True or False: Specimens amenable to DNA typing are blood, semen, body tissues, and hair. _____

25. Short DNA segments containing repeating sequences of three to seven bases are called _____.

26. True or False: The longer the DNA strand, the less susceptible it is to degradation. _____

27. The short length of STRs allows them to be replicated by _____.

28. The concept of (CODIS, multiplexing) involves simultaneous detection of more than one DNA marker.

29. DNA fragments can be separated and identified by (gas chromatography, capillary electrophoresis).

30. The amelogenin gene shows two bands for a (male, female) and one band for a (male, female).

31. Y-STR typing is useful when one is confronted with a DNA mixture containing more than one (male, female) contributor.

32. Mitochondrial DNA is inherited from the (mother, father).

33. True or False: Mitochondrial DNA is more plentiful in the human cell than is nuclear DNA. _____

34. (Two, Four) regions of mitochondrial DNA have been found to be highly variable in the human population.

35. True or False: Polymerase chain reaction is a part of the process used in the forensic analysis of RFLP, STRs, and mitochondrial DNA. _____

36. The national DNA database in the United States has standardized on _____ STRs for entry into the database.

37. True or False: Y-STR data is normally entered into the CODIS database collection. _____.

38. Small amounts of blood are best submitted to a crime laboratory in a (wet, dry) condition.

39. True or False: Airtight packages make the best containers for blood-containing evidence. _____

40. Whole blood collected for DNA typing purposes must be placed in a vacuum containing the preservative _____.

41. A typical STR DNA type emanating from a single individual shows a (one, two, three)-band pattern.

Further References

Butler, J. M., *Forensic DNA Typing,* 2nd ed. Burlington, Mass.: Elsevier Academic Press, 2005.

Inman, K., and N. Rudin, *An Introduction to Forensic DNA Analysis,* 2nd ed. Boca Raton, Fla.: Taylor & Francis, 2002.

Isenberg, A. R., "Forensic Mitochondrial DNA Analysis," in R. Saferstein, ed., *Forensic Science Handbook,* vol. 2, 2nd ed. Upper Saddle River, N.J.: Prentice Hall, 2005.

Isenberg, A. R., and J. M. Moore, "Mitochondrial DNA Analysis at the FBI Laboratory," *Forensic Science Communications* 1, no. 2 (1999), *http//www.fbi.gov/programs/lab/fsc/current/backissu.htm.*

Kobilinsky, L., "Deoxyribonucleic Acid Structure and Function—A Review," in R. Saferstein, ed., *Forensic Science Handbook,* vol. 3. Upper Saddle River, N.J.: Prentice Hall, 1993.

Sensabaugh, G. F., and E. T. Blake, "DNA Analysis in Biological Evidence: Application of the Polymerase Chain Reaction," in R. Saferstein, ed., *Forensic Science Handbook,* vol. 3. Upper Saddle River, N.J.: Prentice Hall, 1993.

Case Study
The Forensic Community's Response to September 11

On September 11, Brion Smith was home in Frederick, Md., enjoying a vacation day when the news flashed across his television screen—the World Trade Center (WTC) buildings had been struck by two hijacked airplanes. Minutes later, a third plane struck the Pentagon while a fourth later crashed in a field in Somerset County, Pa. Acting on impulse, Smith, chief deputy medical examiner for the DNA Division of the Office of the Armed Forces Medical Examiner (OAFME), immediately gathered his things and headed in to work. "Your first inclination, of course, is to go to the crash site," he says, "however, a DNA person has little utility outside of the laboratory." . . .

World Trade Center

Marie Samples, an assistant director in the Department of Forensic Biology in the Office of Chief Medical Examiner (OCME) in New York, was sitting in a management meeting when a co-worker poked his head in and delivered the horrific news. "When someone tells you that the WTCs have just collapsed, you don't ever fathom that happening," says Samples. "I don't think it sunk in with me until I got home."

Overseeing mass tragedies is nothing new to the OCME. In 1990, the lab handled the Happy Land Social Club fire in which 87 people died; then in 1993, they handled the *Golden Venture* tragedy in which 286 Chinese immigrants drowned when their boat went aground off the coast of New Jersey. The OCME has about 90 experienced technicians on staff who perform various tasks, including examining physical evidence; conducting DNA

extractions; and overseeing DNA quantitation, amplification, and finally, DNA typing.

"Our first thought was that we would be able to handle the samples in-house," says Samples. But as the estimates of the number of bodies at the WTC site continued to pile up—initial reports were as high as 7000—those plans quickly changed. "We've handled big disasters in the past, but this was nothing like we've ever seen," exclaims Samples. Although the OCME has the largest DNA analysis lab in the country, the thought of tackling a project with that many unknown and presumed dead presented other problems for Samples and her lab. "We had two big responsibilities that were clashing," she says, "our commitment to serve the criminal justice system in New York for the cases we normally handle—sexual assaults, homicides, etc.—and our role as a support lab for the medical examiners in determining the cause of death." She goes on to say, "We knew we couldn't do both of

Wilder Damian Smith
Staff editor for *Analytical Chemistry*

United Flight 175, hijacked by terrorists, crashes into 2 World Trade Center.
Courtesy Robert Clark, Aurora & Quanta Productions Inc.

them well at the same time, so we decided to contract out the DNA typing work."

As the search and rescue mission for the victims of the WTC collapse became a recovery mission, more problems faced the forensic community. At Ground Zero—the name given to the site of the collapsed WTC buildings—literally millions of human remains were lying scattered deep beneath the tons of twisted metal and shattered cement. "We have to remember that when those towers fell, they turned into giant shredders," says Kevin McElfresh, a senior scientist with BODE Technologies. The smoldering fires, the exposure to the outside weather, and the estimated amount of time it would take to remove the debris—a year, by some calculations—also presented problems for the chemists. "At least in the [1999] Swiss Air crash, the remains were in the water at the bottom of the ocean in four degree water; even though they were down there for three months, we were still able to extract DNA to generate full profiles," says Benoit Leclair, senior scientist with Myriad Genetics. . . .

Some 7 months later, remains were still being collected and taken to Fresh Kills, an abandoned 3000-acre landfill on Staten Island, N.Y., that has been reincarnated as the country's largest "rake-and-sift" DNA lab. There, workers meticulously pick through bits of concrete, rocks, and other rubble in search of the tiniest remnants of human tissue, teeth, and even hair to aid in the identification process. The OCME extracts the DNA from each of the remains recovered, and those extracts are then shipped off to the respective companies for DNA typing and profiling.

To handle the profiling, the OCME contracted the services of three companies: Myriad Genetics, Celera Genomics, and BODE Technologies. Blood and tissue samples recovered from the site are being sent to Myriad Genetics, based in Salt Lake City, Utah. The company is using the technique of short tandem repeats (STR) on the recovered

tissues. "I would refer to this as data mining," says Leclair. STR is a technique that focuses on 13 loci found over the 23 pairs of chromosomes that make up a human's genome. After polymerase chain reaction (PCR) amplification, the newly formed DNA fragments are separated by capillary electrophoresis. Myriad had worked with the New York State Police prior to September 11, performing similar analysis on New York's rape kits.

When blood and tissue samples are not available from the WTC site for DNA typing, forensic scientists often have to turn to another source: bones. BODE Technical Group, a Virginia-based company, is overseeing the bone analysis of the victims. Its lab has about 70 employees, and one of its two specialized units is devoted to forensic analysis. The company participated in the forensic identification of the 88 victims in the Alaska Air crash in 2000. Currently, it has received over 7000 samples from the WTC site.

When the tissue samples are severely burned or degraded, a process called mitochondrial DNA (mtDNA) analysis often has to be done; because this was the case with some of the recovered remains from Ground Zero, the OCME contracted the Rockville, Md., company Celera Genomics to oversee the mtDNA analyses of the WTC victims. However, Celera, a business under the Applera Corp., was an unusual choice. "Unlike BODE and Myriad," says Heather Kowalski, Celera's director of corporate communications, "[Celera] didn't have a forensic part to our business before this tragedy occurred." Celera is known mainly for its work on the Human Genome Project and as a high-throughput sequencing company.

In preparation for the incoming samples, Celera built four new forensic laboratories in the span of two months and hired Rhonda Roby to oversee the forensics program. Before that, Roby worked as a forensic scientist for Applied Biosystems (AB), which is also a business unit of Applera, and which has a Human

Identification Group and experience working with the forensic community. Despite the novelty of the project, Roby wasn't intimidated. "As scientists, we knew we had something to offer, and Applera wanted to do it right," says Roby. "Celera offers expertise in high-throughput sequencing and bioinformatics capabilities, and Applied Biosystems offers expertise as the inventors of the sequencing chemistry, software and instruments, and a team of forensic scientists from the Human Identification Group."

Quality Control

After DNA profiles are obtained, the results are then shipped back to the New York State Police Laboratory in Albany, N.Y. There, the information is stored in a specially modified version of the FBI's Combined DNA Index System (CODIS) database.

The original CODIS database stores the DNA information of convicted felons and is used to match that information in prosecution cases. This new version of the database uses the same DNA comparison

Courtesy AP/Wide World Photos

software, but only for purposes of matching the September 11 DNA profiles to those of the recovered victims' blood samples submitted by their relatives, and to the DNA information obtained from the victims' toothbrushes, hair, soiled laundry, and used cigarette butts. Also, as part of the OCME's quality control efforts, BODE is also repeating 5% of the mtDNA analysis that Celera conducts.

Sample Analysis

Medical and legal issues have to be considered when determining how much of a sample is needed to yield identifying information. The condition of the recovered body parts determines which type of analysis—nuclear (nucDNA) or mtDNA—is performed.

NucDNA analysis is the most commonly used because it's faster, the genome is found in the cell's nucleus, and the DNA has alleles from each parent. In nucDNA analysis, the DNA fragments are analyzed and amplified using PCR. The profile from the nucDNA is then obtained and used to match and verify a victim. However, this type of analysis usually requires a lot of sample. "The problem," says Smith, "is that despite having a large amount of sample, sometimes there are only three grams of usable tissue available for analysis; and that is often totally exhausted during analysis."

MtDNA analysis is somewhat different. Mitochondria are abundant in the cell's cytoplasm, but the mtDNA only comes from the mother. The high number of mtDNA genomes in the cell increases the likelihood of successful PCR amplification. However, mtDNA analysis is more difficult to perform than nucDNA, more time consuming, and very expensive.

The second issue facing analysts is more humanitarian. "We can't tell someone, 'The good news was that it was him; the bad news is that he's all gone'," says Smith. Most families would rather have some remains of their loved one to take home, even if it is just a small piece.

"There isn't one of our people that doesn't understand that there is a family in dire need to know what happened to their loved one," says McElfresh. The scientists use every piece of information they can to find answers. "What gets to me the most is that when it's late and you have a set of records in front of you and what you are looking at is the reconstruction of a person's life through the eyes and the contributions of their family," he says. The resolve of the scientists, says Smith, is evident every day. "With this project, I've seen people so driven that they are standing with their eyes shut and you have to tell them to go home," he says.

The Pentagon and Somerset

Civilian plane crashes are normally assigned to the Federal Aviation Administration (FAA) and the National Transportation Safety Board (NTSB). However, the DNA Division of the OAFME— a federal lab based in Rockville, Md., with two forensic facilities—handled the remains from the Pentagon and the Somerset County, Pa., sites. "We [NTSB] don't have DNA analysis capability," says Frank Ciaccio, chief of forensic sciences and a forensic anthropologist for the NTSB.

In 1996, the NTSB established a memorandum of understanding with the Department of Defense that recommends to local coroners that they use the services of the Armed Forces DNA Identification Laboratory (AFDIL)—the first facility of the OAFME—for DNA analysis. Under the terms of that agreement, the Armed Forces Institute of Pathology (AFIP) simply had to be invited to perform the DNA identifications of the crash victims by the local coroner, and that is what happened in the Pentagon and Somerset cases.

Previously, the AFDIL had performed DNA casework on the victims of the 1999 Egypt Air and the 2000 Alaska Air plane crashes. The AFDIL has 30 technicians divided into 6 teams that specialize in mtDNA analysis and a smaller group that handles all the

nucDNA casework. The mtDNA section of the AFDIL was created in 1991 and has been instrumental in the identification of the recovered remains of American servicemen from the Korean War. To date, the AFDIL has received over 2000 samples for typing from the Pentagon and Somerset crashes.

The second OAFME facility, called the Armed Forces Repository of Specimen Samples for the Identification of Remains, houses blood-stained cards for all active duty, reserve, and National Guard military personnel. These filter paper cards are refrigerated and contain each person's name, social security number, date of birth, and two quarter-size spots of blood. In the Pentagon and Somerset crashes, about 50 of the victims were active duty American servicemen.

Were They Prepared?

"We have the largest DNA lab in the country, and even we couldn't handle [the WTC] caseload," says Samples. "It's hard for a lab to try to prepare for something along the lines of New York when it isn't likely to happen." (Sample's lab also had 12 new lab technicians start work on September 10.)

Learning from previous crashes, Smith's lab implemented a few critical changes. "We found that by having a DNA collection team [at the crash site], they could collect the tissue sample after it has been taken from the body and tag it with a number and bar code onsite before it gets back to the lab," he says. Creating better software in the chain of custody was also important. "For the Pentagon and Somerset crashes we set up two computer systems, one at the Dover Air Force Base and the other in Somerset County for the Pennsylvania crash."

Smith believes experience is the best teacher. "The thing we were missing in the Egypt and Alaska Air crashes was how to compare hundreds of DNA profiles obtained from the evidence with hundreds of DNA reference profiles," he says. "The hardest part of the project was sorting, comparing, matching, and reporting the data, so there was clearly a role for automation."

Need for New Technology

Although forensic technology has advanced, Leclair believes it still is always a step behind the last disaster. "We have the DNA typing tools to tackle a disaster such as Swiss Air only as a result of the TWA 800 disaster," states Leclair. Back in the late 1980s, DNA analysis was all done using a variable number of tandem repeats or restriction fragment-length polymorphisms, which required an enormous amount of sample and analysis time.

Today, most labs are using PCR to analyze DNA. "PCR has been the biggest addition to forensic technology," says McElfresh. "I can't imagine dealing with something the magnitude of this [WTC buildings and Pentagon] with that old technology."

But the tragedies of September 11, say some forensic scientists, should be a wake-up call to the community. "Considering the magnitude of the New York disaster, one can readily see the need for powerful bioinformatics tools," states Leclair.

Roby believes that robotics and more advanced automation are the technologies of the future for forensics. "What may come out of [September 11] is that we are using robotic systems and automation, and we may be able to advance forensic sciences with the scientific technology that is available in other areas with these systems," she says. Samples agrees. "We had thought about using the robotics system before, but our caseload had never justified using them."

Justifying new technology, and finding the time to develop it, seem to be the biggest obstacles. "I think the forensic community could have handled the caseload of the WTC buildings without robotics and automation," says Roby, "but the question is how long would it have taken?"

James Earl Ray: Conspirator or Lone Gunman?

Since his arrest in 1968 for the assassination of Dr. Martin Luther King, Jr., endless speculation has swirled around the motives and connections of James Earl Ray. Ray was a career criminal who was serving time for armed robbery when he escaped from the Missouri State Prison almost one year prior to the assassination. On April 3, 1968, Ray arrived in Memphis, Tennessee. The next day he rented a room at Bessie Brewer's Rooming House, which was situated across the street from the Lorraine Motel where Dr. King was staying.

At 6:00 P.M., Dr. King left his second-story motel room and stepped onto the balcony of the Lorraine Motel. As King turned toward his room, a shot rang out, striking the civil rights activist. Nothing could be done to revive him and Dr. King was pronounced dead at 7:05 P.M. As the assailant ran on foot from Bessie Brewer's, he left a blanket-covered package in front of a nearby building and then drove off in a white Mustang. The package was later shown to contain a high-powered rifle equipped with a scope, a radio, some clothes, a pair of binoculars, a couple of beer cans, and a receipt for the binoculars. Almost a week after the shooting, the white Mustang was found abandoned in Atlanta, Georgia.

Fingerprints later identified as James Earl Ray's were found in the Mustang, on the rifle, on the binoculars, and on a beer can. In 1969, Ray entered a guilty plea in return for a sentence of ninety-nine years. While a variety of conspiracy theories surround this crime, the indisputable fact is that a fingerprint put the rifle that killed Martin Luther King, Jr., in the hands of James Earl Ray.

chapter 14

Fingerprints

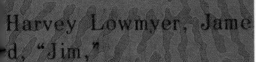

Key Terms

anthropometry

arch

digital imaging

fluoresce

iodine fuming

latent fingerprint

livescan

loop

ninhydrin

Physical Developer

pixel

plastic print

portrait parlé

ridge characteristics
(minutiae)

sublimation

Super Glue fuming

visible print

whorl

Learning Objectives

After studying this chapter you should be able to:

- Know the common ridge characteristics of a fingerprint

- List the three major fingerprint patterns and their respective subclasses

- Distinguish visible, plastic, and latent fingerprints

- Describe the concept of an automated fingerprint identification system (AFIS)

- List the techniques for developing latent fingerprints on porous and nonporous objects

- Describe the proper procedures for preserving a developed latent fingerprint

Portrait Parlé

A verbal description of a perpetrator's physical characteristics and dress provided by an eyewitness.

Anthropometry

A system of identification of individuals by measurement of parts of the body, developed by Alphonse Bertillon.

History of Fingerprinting

Since the beginnings of criminal investigation, police have sought an infallible means of human identification. The first systematic attempt at personal identification was devised and introduced by a French police expert, Alphonse Bertillon, in 1883. The Bertillon system relied on a detailed description (portrait parlé) of the subject, combined with full-length and profile photographs and a system of precise body measurements known as anthropometry.

The use of anthropometry as a method of identification rested on the premise that the dimensions of the human bone system remained fixed from age 20 until death. Skeleton sizes were thought to be so extremely diverse that no two individuals could have exactly the same measurements. Bertillon recommended routine taking of eleven measurements of the human anatomy. These included height, reach, width of head, and length of the left foot (see Figure 1–1).

For two decades, this system was considered the most accurate method of identification. But in the first years of the new century, police began to appreciate and accept a system of identification based on the classification of finger ridge patterns known as *fingerprints*. Today, the fingerprint is the pillar of modern criminal identification.

Evidence exists that the Chinese used the fingerprint to sign legal documents as far back as three thousand years ago. However, whether this practice was performed for ceremonial custom or as a means of personal identity remains a point of conjecture lost to history. In any case, the examples of fingerprinting in ancient history are ambiguous, and the few that exist did not contribute to the development of fingerprinting techniques as we know them today.

Several years before Bertillon began work on his system, William Herschel, an English civil servant stationed in India, started the practice of requiring natives to sign contracts with the imprint of their right hand, which was pressed against a stamp pad for the purpose. The motives for Herschel's requirement remain unclear; he may have envisioned fingerprinting as a means of personal identification or just as a form of the Hindu custom that a trace of bodily contact was more binding than a signature on a contract. In any case, he did not publish anything about his activities until after a Scottish physician, Henry Fauld, working in a hospital in Japan, published his views on the potential application of fingerprinting to personal identification.

In 1880, Fauld suggested that skin ridge patterns could be important for the identification of criminals. He told about a thief who left his fingerprint on a whitewashed wall, and how in comparing these prints with those of a suspect, he found that they were quite different. A few days later another suspect was found whose fingerprints compared with those on the wall. When confronted with this evidence, the individual confessed to the crime.

Fauld was convinced that fingerprints furnished infallible proof of identification. He even offered to set up at his own expense a fingerprint bureau at Scotland Yard to test the practicality of the method. But his offer was rejected in favor of the Bertillon system. This decision was reversed less than two decades later.

The extensive research into fingerprinting conducted by another Englishman, Francis Galton, provided the needed impetus that made police agencies aware of its potential application. In 1892, Galton published his classic textbook *Finger Prints,* the first book of its kind on the subject. In his book, he discussed the anatomy of fingerprints and suggested methods for recording them. Galton also proposed assigning fingerprints to three pattern types—loops, arches, and whorls. Most important, the book demonstrated that no two prints were identical and that an individual's prints remained unchanged from year to year. At Galton's insistence, the British government adopted fingerprinting as a supplement to the Bertillon system.

The next step in the development of fingerprint technology was the creation of classification systems capable of filing thousands of prints in a logical and searchable sequence. Dr. Juan Vucetich, an Argentinian police officer fascinated by Galton's work, devised a workable concept in 1891. His classification system has been refined over the years and is still widely used today in most Spanish-speaking countries. In 1897, another classification system was proposed by an Englishman, Sir Edward Richard Henry. Four years later, Henry's system was adopted by Scotland Yard. Today, most English-speaking countries, including the United States, use some version of Henry's classification system to file fingerprints.

Early in the twentieth century, Bertillon's measurement system began to fall into disfavor. Its results were highly susceptible to error, particularly when the measurements were taken by people who were not thoroughly trained. The method was dealt its most severe and notable setback in 1903 when a convict, Will West, arrived at Fort Leavenworth prison. A routine check of the prison files startlingly revealed that a William West, already in the prison, could not be distinguished from the new prisoner by body measurements or even by photographs. In fact, the two men looked just like twins, and their measurements were practically the same. Subsequently, fingerprints of the prisoners clearly distinguished them.

In the United States, the first systematic and official use of fingerprints for personal identification was adopted by the New York City Civil Service Commission in 1901. The method was used for certifying all civil service applications. Several American police officials received instruction in fingerprint identification at the 1904 World's Fair in St. Louis from representatives of Scotland Yard. After the fair and the Will West incident, fingerprinting began to be used in earnest in all major cities of the United States. In 1924, the fingerprint records of the Bureau of Investigation and Leavenworth were merged to form the nucleus of the identification records of the new Federal Bureau of Investigation. The FBI has the largest collection of fingerprints in the world. By the beginning of World War I, England and practically all of Europe had adopted fingerprinting as their primary method of identifying criminals.

In 1999, the admissibility of fingerprint evidence was challenged in the case of *United States* v. *Byron C. Mitchell* in the Eastern District of Pennsylvania. The defendant's attorneys argued that fingerprints could not be proven unique under the guidelines cited in *Daubert* (see pp. 17–18). Government experts vigorously disputed this claim. After a four-and-a-half-day *Daubert* hearing, the judge upheld the admissibility of fingerprints as scientific evidence and ruled that (1) human friction ridges are unique and permanent and (2) human friction ridge skin arrangements are unique and permanent.

Fundamental Principles of Fingerprints

First Principle: A Fingerprint Is an Individual Characteristic; No Two Fingers Have Yet Been Found to Possess Identical Ridge Characteristics

The acceptance of fingerprint evidence by the courts has always been predicated on the assumption that no two individuals have identical fingerprints. Early fingerprint experts consistently referred to Galton's calculation, showing the possible existence of 64 billion different fingerprints, to support this contention. Later, researchers questioned the validity of Galton's figures and attempted to devise mathematical models to better approximate this value. However, no matter what mathematical model one refers to, the conclusions are always the same: The probability for the existence of two identical fingerprint patterns in the world's population is extremely small.

Not only is this principle supported by theoretical calculations, but just as important, it is verified by the millions of individuals who have had their prints classified during the past 110 years—no two have ever been found to be identical. The FBI has nearly 50 million fingerprint records in its computer database and has yet to find an identical image belonging to two different people.

Ridge Characteristics (Minutiae)
Ridge endings, bifurcations, enclosures, and other ridge details, which must match in two fingerprints in order for their common origin to be established.

The individuality of a fingerprint is not determined by its general shape or pattern but by a careful study of its ridge characteristics (also known as minutiae). The identity, number, and relative location of characteristics such as those illustrated in Figure 14–1 impart individuality to a fingerprint. If two prints are to match, they must reveal characteristics that not only are identical but have the same relative location to one another in a print. In a judicial proceeding, a point-by-point comparison must be demonstrated by the expert, using charts similar to the one shown in Figure 14–2, in order to prove the identity of an individual.

If an expert were asked to compare the characteristics of the complete fingerprint, no difficulty would be encountered in completing such an assignment; the average fingerprint has as many as 150 individual ridge characteristics. However, most prints recovered at crime scenes are partial impressions, showing only a segment of the entire print. Under these circumstances, the expert can compare only a small number of ridge characteristics from the recovered print to a known recorded print. For years, experts have debated how many ridge comparisons are necessary to identify two fingerprints as the same. Numbers that range from eight to sixteen have been suggested as being sufficient to meet the criteria of individuality. However, the difficulty in establishing such a minimum is that no com-

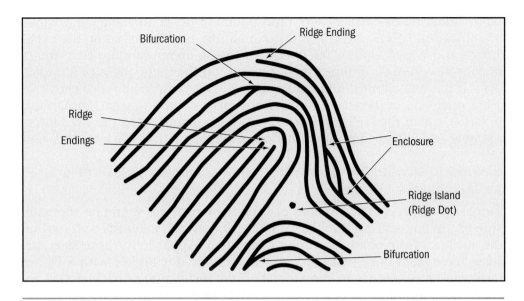

Figure 14–1   Fingerprint ridge characteristics. *Courtesy Sirchie Finger Print Laboratories, Inc., Youngsville, N.C., www.sirchie.com*

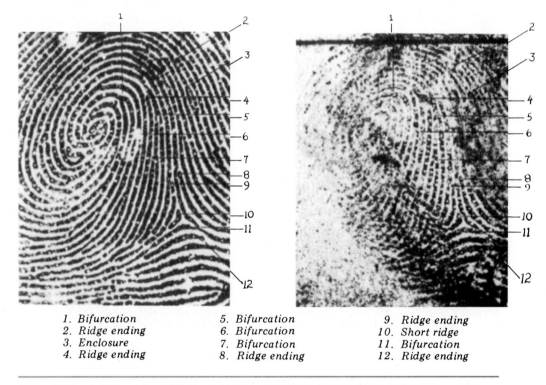

1. Bifurcation	5. Bifurcation	9. Ridge ending
2. Ridge ending	6. Bifurcation	10. Short ridge
3. Enclosure	7. Bifurcation	11. Bifurcation
4. Ridge ending	8. Ridge ending	12. Ridge ending

Figure 14–2   A fingerprint exhibit illustrating the matching ridge characteristics between the crime-scene print and an inked impression of one of the suspect's fingers. *Courtesy New Jersey State Police.*

prehensive statistical study has ever been undertaken to determine the frequency of occurrence of different ridge characteristics and their relative locations. Until such a study is undertaken and completed, no meaningful guidelines can be established for defining the uniqueness of a fingerprint.

In 1973, the International Association for Identification, after a three-year study of this question, concluded that "no valid basis exists for requiring a predetermined minimum number of friction ridge characters which must be present in two impressions in order to establish positive identification." Hence, the final determination must be based on the experience and knowledge of the expert, with the understanding that others may profess honest differences of opinion on the uniqueness of a fingerprint if the question of minimal number of ridge characteristics exists. In 1995, members of the international fingerprint community at a conference in Israel issued the Ne'urim Declaration, which supported the 1973 International Association for Identification resolution.

Second Principle: A Fingerprint Remains Unchanged During an Individual's Lifetime

Fingerprints are a reproduction of friction skin ridges found on the palm side of the fingers and thumbs. Similar friction skin can also be found on the surface of the palms and soles of the feet. Apparently, these skin surfaces have been designed by nature to provide our bodies with a firmer grasp and a resistance to slippage. A visual inspection of friction skin reveals a series of lines corresponding to hills (ridges) and valleys (grooves). The shape and form of the skin ridges are what one sees as the black lines of an inked fingerprint impression.

Actually, skin is composed of layers of cells. Those nearest the surface make up the outer portion of the skin known as the *epidermis,* and the inner skin is known as the *dermis.* A cross-section of skin (see Figure 14–3) reveals a boundary of cells separating the epidermis and dermis. The shape of this boundary, made up of *dermal papillae,* determines the form and pattern of the ridges on the surface of the skin. Once the dermal papillae develop in the human fetus, the ridge patterns remain unchanged throughout life except to enlarge during growth.

Each skin ridge is populated by a single row of pores that are the openings for ducts leading from the sweat glands. Through these pores, perspiration is discharged and deposited on the surface of the skin. Once the

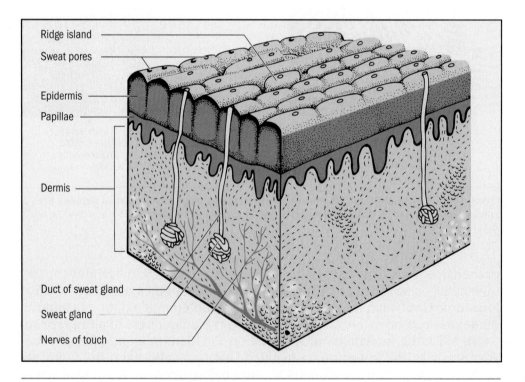

Figure 14–3 Cross-section of human skin.

finger touches a surface, perspiration, along with oils that may have been picked up by touching the hairy portions of the body, is transferred onto that surface, thereby leaving an impression of the finger's ridge pattern (a fingerprint). Prints deposited in this manner are invisible to the eye and are commonly referred to as latent fingerprints.

Although it is impossible to change one's fingerprints, there has been no lack of effort on the part of some criminals to obscure them. If an injury reaches deeply enough into the skin and damages the dermal papillae, a permanent scar will form. However, for this to happen, such a wound would have to penetrate 1 to 2 millimeters beneath the skin's surface. Indeed, efforts at intentionally scarring the skin can only be self-defeating, for it would be totally impossible to obliterate all of the ridge characteristics on the hand, and the presence of permanent scars merely provides new characteristics for identification.

Perhaps the most publicized attempt at obliteration was that of the notorious gangster John Dillinger, who tried to destroy his own fingerprints by applying a corrosive acid to them. Prints taken at the morgue after he was shot to death, compared with fingerprints recorded at the time of a previous arrest, proved that his efforts had been fruitless (see Figure 14–4).

Third Principle: Fingerprints Have General Ridge Patterns That Permit Them to Be Systematically Classified

All fingerprints are divided into three classes on the basis of their general pattern: loops, whorls, and arches. Sixty to 65 percent of the population have loops, 30 to 35 percent have whorls, and about 5 percent have arches. These three classes form the basis for all ten-finger classification systems presently in use.

A typical loop pattern is illustrated in Figure 14–5. A loop must have one or more ridges entering from one side of the print, recurving, and exiting from the same side. If the loop opens toward the little finger, it is called an *ulnar loop;* if it opens toward the thumb, it is a *radial loop.* The pattern area of the loop is surrounded by two diverging ridges known as *type lines.* The ridge point at or nearest the type-line divergence and located at or directly in front of the point of divergence is known as the *delta.*

Latent Fingerprint
A fingerprint made by the deposit of oils and/or perspiration. It is invisible to the naked eye.

Loop
A class of fingerprints characterized by ridge lines that enter from one side of the pattern and curve around to exit from the same side of the pattern.

Whorl
A class of fingerprints that includes ridge patterns that are generally rounded or circular in shape and have two deltas.

Arch
A class of fingerprints characterized by ridge lines that enter the print from one side and flow out the other side.

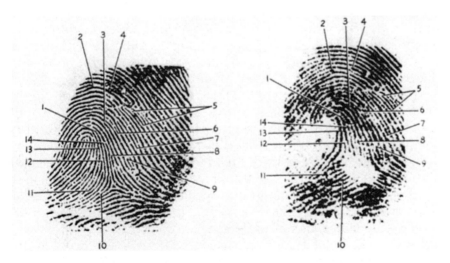

Figure 14–4   The right index finger impression of John Dillinger, before scarification on the left and afterward on the right. Comparison is proved by the fourteen matching ridge characteristics. *Courtesy Institute of Applied Science, Youngsville, N.C.*

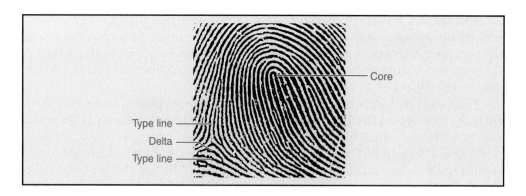

Figure 14–5 **Loop pattern.**

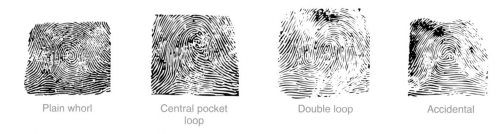

Plain whorl   Central pocket loop   Double loop   Accidental

Figure 14–6 **Whorl patterns.**

To many, a fingerprint delta resembles the silt formation that builds up as a river flows into the entrance of a lake—hence, the analogy to the geological formation known as a delta. All loops must have one delta. The *core,* as the name suggests, is the approximate center of the pattern.

Whorls are actually divided into four distinct groups, as shown in Figure 14–6: plain, central pocket loop, double loop, and accidental. All whorl patterns must have type lines and at least two deltas. A plain whorl and a central pocket loop have at least one ridge that makes a complete circuit. This ridge may be in the form of a spiral, oval, or any variant of a circle. If an imaginary line drawn between the two deltas contained within these two patterns touches any one of the spiral ridges, the pattern is a plain whorl. If no such ridge is touched, the pattern is a central pocket loop.

As the name implies, the double loop is made up of two loops combined into one fingerprint. Any whorl classified as an accidental either contains two or more patterns (not including the plain arch) or is a pattern not covered by other categories. Hence, an accidental may consist of a combination loop and plain whorl or loop and tented arch.

Arches, the least common of the three general patterns, are subdivided into two distinct groups: plain arches and tented arches, as shown in Figure 14–7. The plain arch is the simplest of all fingerprint patterns; it is formed by ridges entering from one side of the print and exiting on the opposite side. Generally, these ridges tend to rise in the center of the pattern, forming a wavelike pattern. The tented arch is similar to the plain arch except that instead of rising smoothly at the center, there is a sharp upthrust or spike, or the ridges meet at an angle that is less than 90 degrees.[1] Arches do not have type lines, deltas, or cores.

---

[1] A tented arch is also any pattern that resembles a loop but lacks one of the essential requirements for classification as a loop.

Plain   Tented

Figure 14–7 Arch patterns.

With a knowledge of basic fingerprint pattern classes, we can now begin to develop an appreciation for fingerprint classification systems. However, the subject is far more complex than can be described in a textbook of this nature. The student seeking a more detailed treatment of the subject would do well to consult the references cited at the end of the chapter.

Classification of Fingerprints

The original Henry system, as it was adopted by Scotland Yard in 1901, converted ridge patterns on all ten fingers into a series of letters and numbers arranged in the form of a fraction. However, the system as it was originally designed could accommodate files of up to only 100,000 sets of prints; thus, as collections grew in size, it became necessary to expand the capacity of the classification system. In the United States, the FBI, faced with the problem of filing ever-increasing numbers of prints, expanded its classification capacity by modifying and adding additional extensions to the original Henry system. These modifications are collectively known as the *FBI system* and are used by most agencies in the United States today.

The Primary Classification

Although we will not discuss all of the different divisions of the FBI system, a description of just one part, the primary classification, will provide an interesting insight into the process of fingerprint classification.

The primary classification is part of the original Henry system and provides the first classification step in the FBI system. Using this classification alone, all of the fingerprint cards in the world could be divided into 1,024 groups. The first step in obtaining the primary classification is to pair up fingers, placing one finger in the numerator of a fraction, the other in the denominator. The fingers are paired in the following sequence:

$$\frac{\text{R. Index}}{\text{R. Thumb}} \quad \frac{\text{R. Ring}}{\text{R. Middle}} \quad \frac{\text{L. Thumb}}{\text{R. Little}} \quad \frac{\text{L. Middle}}{\text{L. Index}} \quad \frac{\text{L. Little}}{\text{L. Ring}}$$

The presence or absence of the whorl pattern is the basis for determination of the primary classification. If a whorl pattern is found on any finger of the first pair, it is assigned a value of 16; on the second pair, a value of 8; on the third pair, a value of 4; on the fourth pair, a value of 2; and on the last pair, a value of 1. Any finger with an arch or loop pattern is assigned a value of 0.

After values for all ten fingers are obtained in this manner, they are totaled, and 1 is added to both the numerator and denominator. The fraction thus obtained is the primary classification. For example, if the right index and right middle fingers are whorls and all the others are loops, the primary classification is

$$\frac{16 + 0 + 0 + 0 + 0 + 1}{0 + 8 + 0 + 0 + 0 + 1} = \frac{17}{8}$$

Approximately 25 percent of the population falls into the 1/1 category; that is, all their fingers have either loops or arches.

A fingerprint classification system cannot in itself unequivocally identify an individual; it merely provides the fingerprint examiner with a number of candidates, all of whom have an indistinguishable set of prints in the system's file. The identification must always be made by a final visual comparison of the suspect print's and file print's ridge characteristics; only these features can impart individuality to a fingerprint. Although ridge patterns impart class characteristics to the print, the type and position of ridge characteristics give it its individual character.

Automated Fingerprint Identification Systems

The Henry system and its subclassifications have proven to be a cumbersome system for storing, retrieving, and searching for fingerprints, particularly as fingerprint collections grow in size. Nevertheless, until the emergence of fingerprint computer technology, this manual approach was the only viable method for the maintenance of fingerprint collections. Since 1970, technological advances have made possible the classification and retrieval of fingerprints by computers. Automated Fingerprint Identification Systems (AFISs) have proliferated throughout the law enforcement community. In 1999, the FBI initiated full operation of the Integrated Automated Fingerprint Identification System (IAFIS), the largest AFIS in the United States, which links state AFIS computers with the FBI database. This database contains nearly 50 million fingerprint records. However, an AFIS can come in all sizes ranging from the FBI's to independent systems operated by cities, counties, and other agencies of local government. Unfortunately, these local systems often are not linked to the state's AFIS system due to differences in software configurations.

The heart of AFIS technology is the ability of a computer to scan and digitally encode fingerprints so that they can be subject to high-speed computer processing. **The AFIS uses automatic scanning devices that convert the image of a fingerprint into digital minutiae that contain data showing ridges at their points of termination (ridge endings) and the branching of ridges into two ridges (bifurcations).** The relative position and orientation of the minutiae are also determined, allowing the computer to store each fingerprint in the form of a digitally recorded geometric pattern. The computer's search algorithm determines the degree of correlation between the location and relationship of the minutiae for both the search and file prints. In this manner, a computer can make thousands of fingerprint comparisons in a second; for example, a set of ten fingerprints can be searched against a file of 500,000 ten-finger prints (ten-prints) in about eight-tenths of a second. During the search for a match, the computer uses a scoring system that assigns prints to each of the criteria set by an operator. When the search is complete, the computer produces a list of file prints that have the closest correlation to the search prints. All of the selected prints are then examined by a trained fingerprint expert, who makes the final verification of the print's identity. Thus, the AFIS makes no final decisions on the identity of a fingerprint, leaving this function to the eyes of a trained examiner.

The speed and accuracy of ten-print processing by AFIS have made possible the search of single latent crime-scene fingerprints against an entire file's print collection. Prior to the AFIS, police were usually restricted to comparing crime-scene fingerprints against those of known suspects. The impact of the AFIS on no-suspect cases has been dramatic. Minutes after California's AFIS network received its first assignment, the computer scored a direct hit by identifying an individual who had committed fifteen murders, terrorizing the city of Los Angeles. Police estimate that it would have taken a single technician, manually searching the city's 1.7 million print cards, sixty-seven years to come up with the perpetrator's prints. With the AFIS, the search took approximately twenty minutes. In its first year of operation, San Francisco's AFIS computer conducted 5,514 latent fingerprint searches and achieved 1,001 identifications—a hit rate of 18 percent. This compares to the previous year's average of 8 percent for manual latent print searches.

As an example of how an AFIS computer operates, one system has been designed to automatically filter out imperfections in a latent print, enhance its image, and create a graphic representation of the fingerprint's ridge endings and bifurcations and their direction. The print is then computer searched against file prints. The image of the latent print and a matching file print are then displayed side by side on a high-resolution video monitor as shown in Figure 14–8. The matching latent and file prints are then verified and charted by a fingerprint examiner at a video workstation.

Figure 14–8 **A side-by-side comparison of a latent print against a file fingerprint is conducted in seconds and their similairity rating (SIM) is displayed on the upper-left portion of the screen.**
Courtesy Sirchie Finger Print Laboratories, Inc., Youngsville, N.C., www.sirchie.com

AFIS has fundamentally changed the way criminal investigators operate, allowing them to spend less time developing suspect lists and more time investigating the suspects generated by the computer. However, investigators must be cautioned against overreliance on a computer. Sometimes a latent print does not make a hit because of the poor quality of the file print. To avoid these potential problems, investigators must still print all known suspects in a case and manually search these prints against the crime-scene prints.

AFIS computers are available from several different suppliers. Each system scans fingerprint images and detects and records information about minutiae (ridge endings and bifurcations); however, they do not all incorporate exactly the same features, coordinate systems, or units of measure to record fingerprint information. These software incompatibilities often mean that, although state systems can communicate with the FBI's IAFIS, they may not communicate with each other directly. Likewise, local and state systems frequently cannot share information with each other. Many of these technical problems will be resolved as more agencies follow transmission standards developed by the National Institute of Standards and Technology and the FBI.

The sterotypical image of a booking officer rolling inked fingers onto a standard ten-print card for ultimate transmission to a database has, for the most part, been replaced with digital-capture devices (livescan) that eliminate ink and paper. The livescan captures the image on each finger and the palms as they are lightly pressed against a glass platen. These livescan images can then be sent to the AFIS database electronically, so that within minutes the booking agency can enter the fingerprint record into the AFIS database and search the database for previous entries of the same individual. See Figure 14–9.

Livescan
An inkless device that captures the digital images of fingerprints and palm prints and electronically transmits the images to an AFIS.

Figure 14–9 Livescan technology enables law enforcement to print and compare a subject's fingerprints rapidly, without inking the fingerprints. *Printrac International*

Forensics at Work
The Mayfield Affair

On March 11, 2004, a series of ten explosions at four sites occurred on commuter trains traveling to or near the Atocha train station in Madrid, Spain. The death toll from these explosions was nearly 200, with more than 1,500 injured. On the day of the attack, a plastic bag was found in a van previously reported as stolen. The bag contained copper detonators like those used on the train bombs. On March 17 the FBI received electronic images of latent fingerprints that were recovered from the plastic bag. A search was initiated on the FBI's IAFIS. A senior fingerprint examiner encoded seven minutiae points from the high-resolution image of one suspect latent fingerprint and initiated an IAFIS search matching the print to Brandon Mayfield.

Mayfield's prints were in the FBI's central database because they had been taken when he joined the military, where he served for eight years before being honorably discharged as a second lieutenant. After a visual comparison of the suspect and file prints, the examiner concluded a "100 percent match." The identification was verified by a retired FBI fingerprint examiner with more than thirty years of experience who was under contract with the bureau, as well as by a court-appointed independent fingerprint examiner (see Figure 14–10).

Mayfield, age 37, a Muslim convert, was arrested on May 6 on a material witness warrant. The U.S. Attorney's Office came up with a list of Mayfield's potential ties to Muslim terrorists, which they included in the affidavit they presented to the federal judge who ordered his arrest and detention. The document also said that while no travel records were found for Mayfield, "It is believed that Mayfield may have traveled under a false or fictitious

name." On May 24, after the Spaniards had linked the print from the plastic bag to an Algerian national, Mayfield's case was thrown out. The FBI issued him a highly unusual official apology, and his ordeal became a stunning embarrassment to the United States government.

As part of its corrective-action process, the FBI formed an international committee of distinguished latent-print examiners and forensic experts. Their task was to review the analysis performed by the FBI Laboratory and make recommendations that would help prevent this type of error in the future. The committee came up with some startling findings and observations (available at *http://www.fbi.gov/hq/lab/fsc/ backissu/jan2005/special_report/2005_ special_report.htm*).

The committee members agreed that "the quality of the images that were used to make the erroneous identification was not a factor. . . . the identification is filled with dissimilarities that were easily observed when a detailed analysis of the latent print was conducted."

They further stated,

> the power of the IAFIS match, coupled with the inherent pressure of working an extremely high-profile case, was thought to have influenced the initial examiner's judgment and subsequent examination. . . . The apparent mindset of the initial examiner after reviewing the results of the IAFIS search was that a match did exist; therefore, it would be reasonable to assume that the other characteristics must match as well. In the absence of a detailed analysis of the print, it

continued

Forensics at Work
The Mayfield Affair (continued)

can be a short distance from finding only seven characteristics sufficient for plotting, prior to the automated search, to the position of 12 or 13 matching characteristics once the mind-set of identification has become dominant. . . .

Once the mind-set occurred with the initial examiner, the subsequent examinations were tainted. . . . because of the inherent pressure of such a high-profile case, the power of an IAFIS match in conjunction with the similarities in the candidate's print, and the knowledge of the previous examiners' conclusions (especially since the initial examiner was a highly respected supervisor with many years of experience), it was concluded that subsequent examinations were incomplete and inaccurate. To disagree was not an expected response. . . . when the individualization had been made by the examiner, it became increasingly difficult for others in the agency to disagree.

The committee went on to make a number of quality-assurance recommendations to help avoid a recurrence of this type of error.

The Mayfield incident has also been the subject of an investigation by the Office of the Inspector General (OIG), U.S. Department of Justice (*http://www.usdoj. gov/oig/special/s0601/final.pdf*). The OIG investigation concluded that a "series of systemic issues" in the FBI Laboratory contributed to the Mayfield misidentification. The report noted that the FBI has made significant procedural modifications to help prevent similar errors in the future, and strongly supported the FBI's decision to undertake research to develop more objective standards for fingerprint identification.

An internal review of the FBI Latent Print Unit conducted in the aftermath of the Mayfield affair has resulted in the implementation of revisions in training, as well as in the decision-making process when determining the comparative value of a latent print, along with more stringent verification policies and procedures (Smrz, M.A., et al., *J. Forensic Identification, 56*, 402–34, 2006).

The impact of the Mayfield affair on fingerprint technology as currently practiced and the weight courts will assign to fingerprint matches remain open questions.

Methods of Detecting Fingerprints

Through common usage, the term *latent fingerprint* has come to be associated with any fingerprint discovered at a crime scene. Sometimes, however, prints found at the scene of a crime are quite visible to the eye, and the word *latent* is a misnomer. Actually, there are three kinds of crime-scene prints: **Visible prints** are made by fingers touching a surface after the ridges have been in contact with a colored material such as blood, paint, grease, or ink; **plastic prints** are ridge impressions left on a soft material such as putty, wax, soap, or dust; and *latent* or *invisible prints* are impressions caused by the transfer of body perspiration or oils present on finger ridges to the surface of an object.

Visible Print
A fingerprint made when the finger deposits a visible material such as ink, dirt, or blood onto a surface.

Plastic Print
A fingerprint impressed in a soft surface.

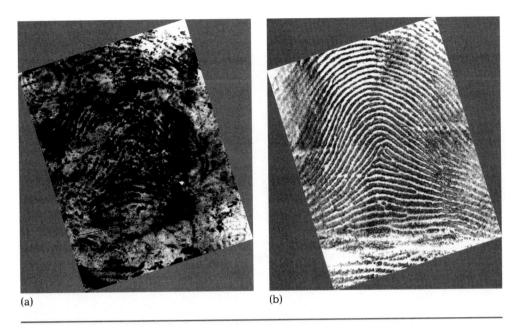

(a)   (b)

Figure 14–10 **(a) Questioned print recovered in connection with the Madrid bombing investigation. (b) File print of Brandon Mayfield.** *Courtesy www.onin.com/fp/problemidents. html#madrid.*

Locating visible or plastic prints at the crime scene normally presents little problem to the investigator, because these prints are usually distinct and visible to the eye. Locating latent or invisible prints is obviously much more difficult and requires the use of techniques to make the print visible. Although the investigator can choose from several methods for visualizing a latent print, the choice depends on the type of surface being examined.

Hard and nonabsorbent surfaces (such as glass, mirror, tile, and painted wood) require different development procedures from surfaces that are soft and porous (such as papers, cardboard, and cloth). Prints on the former are preferably developed by the application of a powder or treatment with Super Glue, whereas prints on the latter generally require treatment with one or more chemicals.

Sometimes the most difficult aspect of fingerprint examination is the location of prints. Recent advances in fingerprint technology have led to the development of an ultraviolet image converter for the purpose of detecting latent fingerprints. This device, called the Reflected Ultraviolet Imaging System (RUVIS), can locate prints on most nonabsorbent surfaces without the aid of chemical or powder treatments (see Figure 14–11). RUVIS detects the print in its natural state by aiming UV light at the surface suspected of containing prints. When the UV light strikes the fingerprint, the light is reflected back to the viewer, differentiating the print from its background surface. The transmitted UV light is then converted into visible light by an image intensifier. Once located in this manner, the crime-scene investigator can develop the print in the most appropriate fashion. See Figure 14–12.

Fingerprint powders are commercially available in a variety of compositions and colors. These powders, when applied lightly to a nonabsorbent surface with a camel's-hair or fiberglass brush, readily adhere to perspiration

Figure 14–11 **A Reflected Ultraviolet Imaging System allows an investigator to directly view surfaces for the presence of untreated latent fingerprints.** *Courtesy Sirchie Finger Print Laboratories, Inc., Youngsville, N.C., www.sirchie.com*

Figure 14–12 **Using a Reflected Ultraviolet Imaging System with the aid of a UV lamp to search for latent fingerprints.** *Courtesy Sirchie Finger Print Laboratories, Inc., Youngsville, N.C., www.sirchie.com*

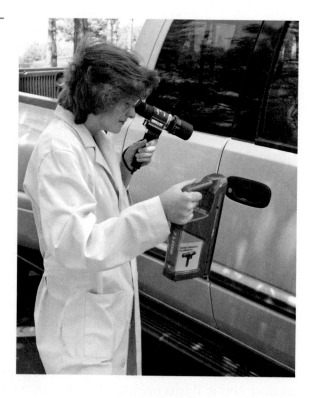

residues and/or deposits of body oils left on the surface (see Figure 14–13). Experienced examiners find that gray and black powders are adequate for most latent-print work; the examiner selects the powder that affords the best color contrast with the surface being dusted. Hence, the gray powder, composed of an aluminum dust, is used on dark-colored surfaces. It is also applied to mirrors and metal surfaces that are polished to a mirrorlike finish, because these surfaces photograph as black. The black powder, composed basically of black carbon or charcoal, is applied to white or light-colored surfaces.

Other types of powders are available for developing latent prints. A magnetic-sensitive powder can be spread over a surface with a magnet in the form of a Magna Brush. A Magna Brush does not have any bristles to come in contact with the surface, so there is less chance that the print will be destroyed or damaged. The magnetic-sensitive powder comes in black and gray and is especially useful on such items as finished leather and

Figure 14–13 Developing a latent fingerprint on a surface by applying a fingerprint powder with a fiberglass brush. *Courtesy Sirchie Finger Print Laboratories, Inc., Youngsville, N.C., www.sirchie.com*

Figure 14–14 A heated fuming cabinet. *Courtesy Sirchie Finger Print Laboratories, Inc., Youngsville, N.C., www.sirchie.com*

rough plastics, where the minute texture of the surface tends to hold particles of ordinary powder. Fluorescent powders are also used to develop latent fingerprints. These powders fluoresce under ultraviolet light. By photographing the fluorescence pattern of the developing print under UV light, it is possible to avoid having the color of the surface obscure the print.

Of the several chemical methods used for visualizing latent prints, iodine fuming is the oldest. Iodine is a solid crystal that, when heated, is transformed into a vapor without passing through a liquid phase; such a transformation is called sublimation. Most often, the suspect material is placed in an enclosed cabinet along with iodine crystals (see Figure 14–14). As the crystals are heated, the resultant vapors fill the chamber and combine with

Iodine Fuming
A technique for visualizing latent fingerprints by exposing them to iodine vapors.

Sublimation
A physical change from the solid directly into the gaseous state.

constituents of the latent print to make it visible. The reasons why latent prints are visualized by iodine vapors are not yet fully understood. Many believe that the iodine fumes combine with fatty oils; however, there is also convincing evidence that the iodine may actually interact with residual water left on a print from perspiration.[2] Unfortunately, iodine prints are not permanent and begin to fade once the fuming process is stopped. Therefore, the examiner must photograph the prints immediately on development in order to retain a permanent record. Also, iodine-developed prints can be fixed with a 1 percent solution of starch in water, applied by spraying. The print turns blue and lasts for several weeks to several months.

Another chemical used for visualizing latent prints is ninhydrin. The development of latent prints with ninhydrin depends on its chemical reaction to form a purple-blue color with amino acids present in trace amounts in perspiration. Ninhydrin (triketohydrindene hydrate) is commonly sprayed onto the porous surface from an aerosol can. A solution is prepared by mixing the ninhydrin powder with a suitable solvent, such as acetone or ethyl alcohol; a 0.6 percent solution appears to be effective for most applications. Generally, prints begin to appear within an hour or two after ninhydrin application; however, weaker prints may be visualized after twenty-four to forty-eight hours. The development can be hastened if the treated specimen is heated in an oven or on a hot plate at a temperature of 80–100°C. The ninhydrin method has developed latent prints on paper as old as fifteen years.

Physical Developer is a third chemical mixture used for visualizing latent prints. Physical Developer is a silver nitrate–based liquid reagent. The procedure for preparing and using Physical Developer is described in Appendix IV. This method has gained wide acceptance by fingerprint examiners, who have found it effective for visualizing latent prints that remain undetected by the previously described methods. Also, this technique is very effective for developing latent fingerprints on porous articles that may have been wet at one time.

For most fingerprint examiners, the chemical method of choice is ninhydrin. Its extreme sensitivity and ease of application have all but eliminated the use of iodine for latent-print visualization. However, when ninhydrin fails, development with Physical Developer may provide identifiable results. Application of Physical Developer washes away any traces of proteins from an object's surface; **hence, if one wishes to use all of the previously mentioned chemical development methods on the same surface, it is necessary to first fume with iodine, follow this treatment with ninhydrin, and then apply Physical Developer to the object.**

In the past, chemical treatment for fingerprint development was reserved for porous surfaces such as paper and cardboard. However, since 1982, a chemical technique known as Super Glue fuming has gained wide popularity for developing latent prints on nonporous surfaces such as metals, electrical tape, leather, and plastic bags.[3] See Figure 14–15. Super Glue is approximately 98–99 percent cyanoacrylate ester, a chemical that actually interacts with and visualizes a latent fingerprint. Cyanoacrylate ester fumes can be created when Super Glue is placed on absorbent cotton

---

Ninhydrin
A chemical reagent used to develop latent fingerprints on porous materials by reacting with amino acids in perspiration.

Physical Developer
A silver nitrate–based reagent formulated to develop latent fingerprints on porous surfaces.

Super Glue Fuming
A technique for visualizing latent fingerprints on nonporous surfaces by exposing them to cyanoacrylate vapors; named for the commercial product Super Glue.

---

[2] J. Almag, Y. Sasson, and A. Anati, "Chemical Reagents for the Development of Latent Fingerprints II: Controlled Addition of Water Vapor to Iodine Fumes—A Solution to the Aging Problem," *Journal of Forensic Sciences* 24 (1979): 431.

[3] F. G. Kendall and B. W. Rehn, "Rapid Method of Super Glue Fuming Application for the Development of Latent Fingerprints," *Journal of Forensic Sciences* 28 (1983): 777.

Figure 14–15 Super Glue fuming a nonporous metallic surface in the search for latent fingerprints.
Courtesy Sirchie Finger Print Laboratories, Inc., Youngsville, N.C., www.sirchie.com

treated with sodium hydroxide. The fumes can also be created by heating the glue. The fumes and the evidential object are contained within an enclosed chamber for up to six hours. Development occurs when fumes from the glue adhere to the latent print, usually producing a white-appearing latent print. Interestingly, small enclosed areas, such as the interior of an automobile, have been successfully processed for latent prints with fumes from Super Glue. Through the use of a small handheld wand, cyanoacrylate fuming is now easily done at a crime scene or in a laboratory setting. The wand heats a small cartridge containing cyanoacrylate. Once heated, the cyanoacrylate vaporizes, allowing the operator to direct the fumes onto the suspect area (see Figure 14–16).

One of the most exciting and dynamic areas of research in forensic science today is the application of chemical techniques to the visualization of latent fingerprints. Changes are occurring very rapidly as researchers uncover a variety of processes applicable to the visualization of latent fingerprints. Interestingly, for many years progress in this field was minimal, and fingerprint specialists traditionally relied on three chemical techniques—iodine, ninhydrin, and silver nitrate—to reveal a hidden fingerprint. Then Super Glue fuming extended chemical development to prints deposited on nonporous surfaces. The first hint of things to come was the discovery that latent fingerprints could be visualized by exposure to laser light. This laser method took advantage of the fact that perspiration contains a variety of components that fluoresce when illuminated by laser light. Fluorescence occurs when a substance absorbs light and reemits the light in wavelengths longer than the illuminating source. Importantly, substances that emit light or fluoresce are more readily seen with either the naked eye or through photography than are non-light-emitting materials. The high sensitivity of fluorescence serves as the underlying principle of many of the new chemical techniques used to visualize latent fingerprints.

Fluoresce
To emit visible light when exposed to light of a shorter wavelength.

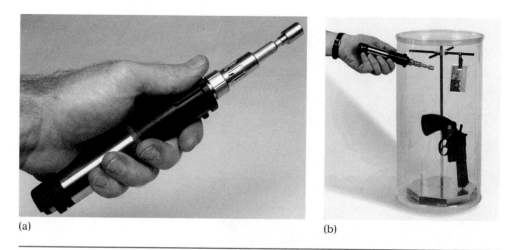

(a)   (b)

Figure 14–16   (a) A handheld fuming wand uses disposable cartridges containing cyanoacrylate The wand is used to develop prints at the crime scene and (b) in the laboratory. *Courtesy Sirchie Finger Print Laboratories, Inc., Youngsville, N.C., www.sirchie.com*

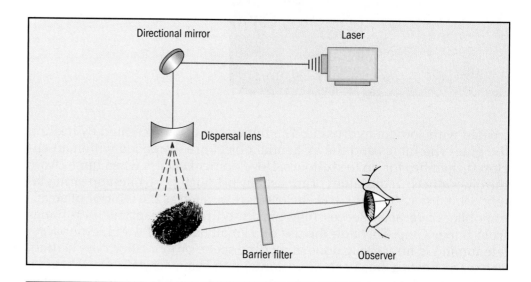

Figure 14–17   Schematic depicting latent-print detection with the aid of a laser. A fingerprint examiner, wearing safety goggles containing optical filters, examines the specimen being exposed to the laser light. The filter absorbs the laser light and permits the wavelengths at which latent-print residues fluoresce to pass through to the eyes of the wearer. *Courtesy Federal Bureau of Investigation, Washington, D.C.*

The earliest use of fluorescence to visualize fingerprints came with the direct illumination of a fingerprint with argon–ion lasers. This laser type was chosen because its blue-green light output induced some of the perspiration components of a fingerprint to fluoresce (see Figure 14–17). The major drawback of this approach is that the perspiration components of a fingerprint are often present in quantities too minute to observe even with the aid of fluorescence. The fingerprint examiner, wearing safety goggles containing optical filters, visually examines the specimen being exposed to the laser light. The filters absorb the laser light and permit the wavelengths at which latent-print residues fluoresce to pass through to the eyes of the wearer. The filter also protects the operator against eye damage from scattered or reflected laser light. Likewise, latent-print residue producing sufficient fluorescence can be photographed by placing this same filter across

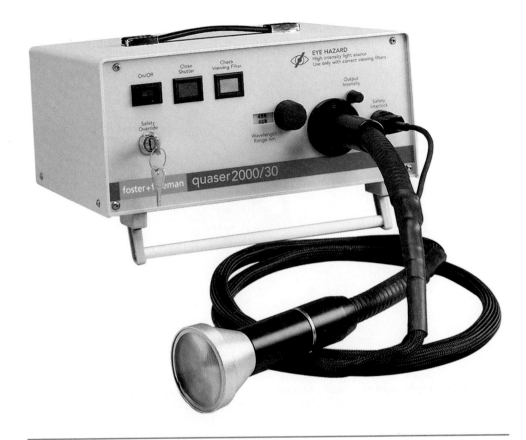

Figure 14–18   An alternate light source system incorporating a high-intensity light source.
Courtesy Foster & Freeman Limited, Worcesterhire, U.K., www.fosterfreeman.co.uk

the lens of the camera. Examination of specimens and photography of the fluorescing latent prints are carried out in a darkened room.

The next advancement in latent-fingerprint development occurred with the discovery that fingerprints could be treated with chemicals that would induce fluorescence when exposed to laser illumination. For example, the application of zinc chloride after ninhydrin treatment or the application of the dye rhodamine 6G after Super Glue fuming caused fluorescence and increased the sensitivity of detection on exposure to laser illumination. The discovery of numerous chemical developers for visualizing fingerprints through fluorescence quickly followed. This knowledge set the stage for the next advance in latent-fingerprint development—the *alternate light source*.

With the advent of chemically induced fluorescence, lasers were no longer needed to induce fingerprints to fluoresce through their perspiration residues. High-intensity light sources or alternate light sources have proliferated and all but replaced laser lights. See Figure 14–18. High-intensity quartz halogen or xenon-arc light sources can be focused on a suspect area through a fiber-optic cable. This light can be passed through several filters, giving the user more flexibility in selecting the wavelength of light to be aimed at the latent print. Alternatively, lightweight, portable alternate light sources that use light-emitting diodes (LEDs) are also commercially available (see Figure 14–19). In most cases, these light sources have proven to be as effective as laser light in developing latent prints, and they are commercially available at costs significantly below those of laser illuminators. Furthermore, these light sources are portable and can be readily taken to any crime scene.

Figure 14–19   Lightweight hand-held alternate light source that uses an LED light source.
Courtesy Foster & Freeman Limited, Worcestershire, U.K., www.fosterfreeman.co.uk

A large number of chemical treatment processes are available to the fingerprint examiner (see Figure 14–20), and the field is in a constant state of flux. Selection of an appropriate procedure is best left to technicians who have developed their skills through casework experience. Newer chemical processes include a substitute for ninhydrin called DFO (1,8-diazafluoren-9-one). This chemical visualizes latent prints on porous materials when exposed to an alternate light source. DFO has been shown to develop 2.5 times more latent prints on paper than ninhydrin. 1,2-indanedione is also emerging as a potential reagent for the development of latent fingerprints on porous surfaces. 1,2-indanedione gives both good initial color and strong fluorescence when reacted with amino acids derived from prints and thus has the potential to provide in one process what ninhydrin and DFO can do in two different steps. Dye combinations known as RAM, RAY, and MRM 10 when used in conjunction with Super Glue fuming have been effective in visualizing latent fingerprints by fluorescence. A number of chemical formulas useful for latent-print development are listed in Appendix IV.

Studies have demonstrated that common fingerprint-developing agents do not interfere with DNA-testing methods used for characterizing bloodstains.[4] Nonetheless, in cases involving items with material adhering to their

---

[4] C. Roux et al., "A Further Study to Investigate the Effect of Fingerprint Enhancement Techniques on the DNA Analysis of Bloodstains," *Journal of Forensic Identification* 49 (1999): 357; C. J. Frégeau et al., "Fingerprint Enhancement Revisited and the Effects of Blood Enhancement Chemicals on Subsequent Profiler Plus™ Fluorescent Short Tandem Repeat DNA Analysis of Fresh and Aged Bloody Fingerprints," *Journal of Forensic Sciences* 45 (2000): 354; P. Grubwieser et al., "Systematic Study on STR Profiling on Blood and Saliva Traces after Visualization of Fingerprints," *Journal of Forensic Sciences* 48 (2003): 733.

(a)

(b)

(c)

(d)

Figure 14–20 **(a) Latent fingerprint visualized by cyanoacrylate fuming. (b) Fingerprint treated with cyanoacrylate and a blue/green fluorescent dye. (c) Fingerprint treated with cyanoacrylate and rhodamine 6G fluorescent dye. (d) Fingerprint treated with cyanoacrylate and the fluorescent dye combination RAM.** *(b) Courtesy 3M Corp., Austin Texas*

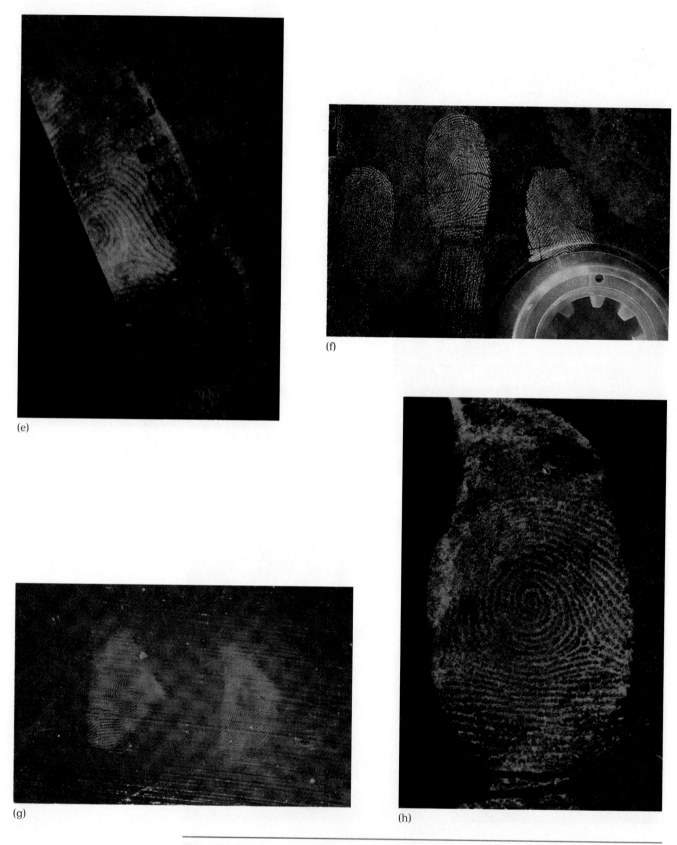

Figure 14–20 *(cont'd.)* **(e) Fingerprint visualized by the fluorescent chemical DFO. (f) Fingerprint visualized by Redwop fluorescent fingerprint powder. (g) A bloody fingerprint detected by laser light without any chemical treatment. (h) A bloody fingerprint detected by laser light after spraying with merbromin and hydrogen peroxide.** *(f) Courtesy Melles Griot Inc., Carlsbad, Calif. All other photographs courtesy of North Carolina State Bureau of Investigation, Raleigh, N.C.*

surfaces and/or items that will require further laboratory examinations, fingerprint processing should not be performed at the crime scene. Rather, the items should be submitted to the laboratory, where they can be processed for fingerprints in conjunction with other necessary examinations.

Preservation of Developed Prints

Once the latent print has been visualized, it must be permanently preserved for future comparison and possible use in court as evidence. A photograph must be taken before any further attempts at preservation. Any camera equipped with a close-up lens will do; however, many investigators prefer to use a camera specially designed for fingerprint photography. Such a camera comes equipped with a fixed focus to take photographs on a 1:1 scale when the camera's open eye is held exactly flush against the print's surface (see Figure 14–21). In addition, photographs must be taken to provide an overall view of the print's location with respect to other evidential items at the crime scene.

Once photographs have been secured, one of two procedures is to be followed. If the object is small enough to be transported without destroying the print, it should be preserved in its entirety; the print should be covered with cellophane so it will be protected from damage. On the other hand, prints on large immovable objects that have been developed with a powder can best be preserved by "lifting." The most popular type of lifter is a broad adhesive tape similar to clear adhesive tape. When the powdered surface is covered with the adhesive side of the tape and pulled up, the powder is transferred to the tape. Then the tape is placed on a properly labeled card that provides a good background contrast with the powder.

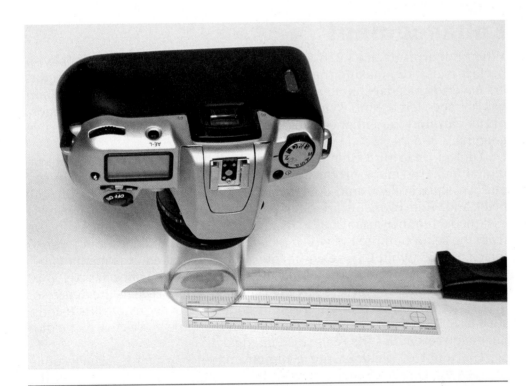

Figure 14–21   Camera fitted with an adapter designed to give an approximate 1:1 photograph of a fingerprint. *Courtesy Sirchie Finger Print Laboratories, Inc., Youngsville, N.C., www.sirchie.com*

Figure 14–22 **"Lifting" a fingerprint.** *Courtesy Sirchie Finger Print Laboratories, Inc., Youngsville, N.C., www.sirchie.com*

A variation of this procedure is the use of an adhesive-backed clear plastic sheet attached to a colored cardboard backing. Before it is applied to the print, a celluloid separator is peeled from the plastic sheet to expose the adhesive lifting surface. The tape is then pressed evenly and firmly over the powdered print and pulled up (see Figure 14–22). The sheet containing the adhering powder is now pressed against the cardboard backing to provide a permanent record of the fingerprint.

Digital Imaging for Fingerprint Enhancement

When fingerprints are lifted from a crime scene, they are not usually in perfect condition, making the analysis that much more difficult. Computers have advanced technology in most fields, and fingerprint identification has not been left behind. With the help of digital imaging software, fingerprints can now be enhanced for the most accurate and comprehensive analysis.

Digital imaging is the process by which a picture is converted into a digital file. The image produced from this digital file is composed of numerous square electronic dots called pixels. Images composed of only black and white elements are referred to as *grayscale images*. Each pixel is assigned a number according to its intensity. The grayscale image is made from the set of numbers to which a pixel may be assigned, ranging from 0 (black) to 255 (white). Once an image is digitally stored, it is manipulated by computer software that changes the numerical value of each pixel, thus altering the image as directed by the user. *Resolution* reveals the degree of detail that can be seen in an image. It is defined in terms of dimensions, such as 800×600 pixels. The larger the numbers, the more closely the digital image resembles the real-world image.

The input of pictures into a digital imaging system is usually done through the use of scanners, digital cameras, and video cameras. After the picture is changed to its digital image, several methods can be employed to enhance the image. The overall brightness of an image, as well as the

Digital Imaging
A process through which a picture is converted into a series of square electronic dots known as pixels. The picture is manipulated by computer software that changes the numerical value of each pixel.

Pixel
A square electronic dot that is used to compose a digital image.

contrast between the image and the background, can be adjusted through contrast-enhancement methods. One approach used to enhance an image is *spatial filtering*. Several types of filters produce various effects. A low-pass filter is used to eliminate harsh edges by reducing the intensity difference between pixels. A second filter, the high-pass filter, operates by modifying a pixel's numerical value to exaggerate its intensity difference from that of its neighbor. The resulting effect increases the contrast of the edges, thus providing a high contrast between the elements and the background. Frequency analysis, also referred to as *frequency Fourier transform* (FFT), is used to identify periodic or repetitive patterns such as lines or dots that interfere with the interpretation of the image. These patterns are diminished or eliminated to enhance the appearance of the image. Interestingly, the spacings between fingerprint ridges are themselves periodic. Therefore, the contribution of the fingerprint can be identified in FFT mode and then enhanced. Likewise, if ridges from overlapping prints are positioned in different directions, their corresponding frequency information is at different locations in FFT mode. The ridges of one latent print can then be enhanced while the ridges of the other are suppressed.

Color interferences also pose a problem when analyzing an image. For example, a latent fingerprint found on paper currency or a check may be difficult to analyze because of the distracting colored background. With the imaging software, the colored background can simply be removed to make the image stand out (see Figure 14–23). If the image itself is a particular color, such as a ninhydrin-developed print, the color can be isolated and enhanced to distinguish it from the background.

Digital imaging software also provides functions in which portions of the image can be examined individually. With a scaling and resizing tool, the user can select a part of an image and resize it for a closer look. This function operates much like a magnifying glass, helping the examiner view fine details of an image.

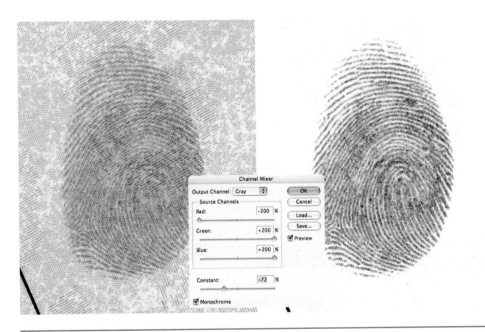

Figure 14–23 **A fingerprint being enhanced in Adobe Photoshop. In this example, on the left is the original scan of an inked fingerprint on a check. On the right is the same image after using Adobe Photoshop's Channel Mixer to eliminate the green security background.** *Courtesy Imaging Forensics, Fountain Valley, Calif., www.imagingforensics.com*

Case # 05-01234

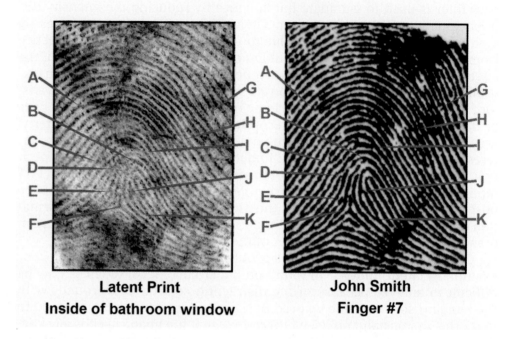

Latent Print
Inside of bathroom window

John Smith
Finger #7

Figure 14–24 **Current imaging software allows fingerprint analysts to prepare a fingerprint comparison chart. The fingerprint examiner can compare prints side by side and display important features that are consistent between the fingerprints. The time needed to create a display of this sort digitally is about thirty to sixty minutes.** *Courtesy Imaging Forensics, Fountain Valley, Calif., www.imagingforensics.com*

An important and useful tool, especially for fingerprint identification, is the compare function. This specialized feature places two images side by side and allows the examiner to chart the common features on both images simultaneously (see Figure 14–24). The zoom function is used in conjunction with the compare tool. As the examiner zooms into a portion of one image, the software automatically zooms into the second image for comparison.

Although digital imaging is undoubtedly an effective tool for enhancing and analyzing images, it is only as useful as the images it has to work with. If the details do not exist on the original images, the enhancement procedures are not going to work. The benefits of digital enhancement methods are apparent when weak images are made more distinguishable.

Chapter Summary

Fingerprints are a reproduction of friction skin ridges found on the palm side of the fingers and thumbs. The basic principles underlying the use of fingerprints in criminal investigations are that (1) a fingerprint is an individual characteristic because no two fingers have yet been found to possess identical ridge characteristics; (2) a fingerprint remains unchanged during an individual's lifetime; and (3) fingerprints have general ridge patterns that permit them to be systematically classified. All fingerprints are divided into three classes on the basis of their general pattern: loops, whorls, and arches. Fingerprint classification systems are based on knowledge of fingerprint pattern classes. The individuality of a fingerprint is not determined by its general shape or pattern, but by a careful study of its ridge characteristics. The expert must demonstrate a point-by-point comparison in order to prove the identity of an individual. AFIS aids this process by converting the image of a fingerprint into digital minutiae that contain data showing ridges at their points of termination (ridge endings) and their branching into two ridges (bifurcations). A single fingerprint can be searched against the FBI AFIS digital database of 50 million fingerprint records in a matter of minutes.

Once the finger touches a surface, perspiration, along with oils that may have been picked up by touching the hairy portions of the body, is transferred onto that surface, thereby leaving an impression of the finger's ridge pattern (a fingerprint). Prints deposited in this manner are invisible to the eye and are commonly referred to as latent or invisible fingerprints.

Visible prints are made when fingers touch a surface after the ridges have been in contact with a colored material such as blood, paint, grease, or ink. Plastic prints are ridge impressions left on a soft material, such as putty, wax, soap, or dust. Latent prints deposited on hard and nonabsorbent surfaces (such as glass, mirror, tile, and painted wood) are preferably developed by the application of a powder; prints on porous surfaces (such as paper and cardboard) generally require treatment with a chemical. Examiners use various chemical methods to visualize latent prints, such as iodine fuming, ninhydrin, and Physical Developer. Super Glue fuming develops latent prints on nonporous surfaces, such as metals, electrical tape, leather, and plastic bags. Development occurs when fumes from the glue adhere to the print, usually producing a white latent print.

The high sensitivity of fluorescence serves as the underlying principle of many of the new chemical techniques used to visualize latent fingerprints. Fingerprints are treated with chemicals that induce fluorescence when exposed to a high-intensity light or an alternate light source.

Once the latent print has been visualized, it must be permanently preserved for future comparison and for possible use as court evidence. A photograph must be taken before any further attempts at preservation are made. If the object is small enough to be transported without destroying the print, it should be preserved in its entirety. Prints on large immovable objects that have been developed with a powder are best preserved by "lifting" with a broad adhesive tape.

Review Questions

1. The first systematic attempt at personal identification was devised and introduced by _____.

2. A system of identification relying on precise body measurements is known as _____.

3. The fingerprint classification system used in most English-speaking countries was devised by _____.

4. True or False: The first systematic and official use of fingerprints for personal identification in the United States was adopted by the New York City Civil Service Commission. _____

5. The individuality of a fingerprint (is, is not) determined by its pattern.

6. A point-by-point comparison of a fingerprint's _____ must be demonstrated in order to prove identity.

7. _____ are a reproduction of friction skin ridges.

8. The form and pattern of skin ridges are determined by the (epidermis, dermal papillae).

9. A permanent scar forms in the skin only when an injury damages the _____.

10. Fingerprints (can, cannot) be changed during a person's lifetime.

11. The three general patterns into which fingerprints are divided are _____, _____, and _____.

12. The most common fingerprint pattern is the _____.

13. Approximately 5 percent of the population has the _____ fingerprint pattern.

14. A loop pattern that opens toward the thumb is known as a(n) (radial, ulnar) loop.

15. The pattern area of the loop is enclosed by two diverging ridges known as _____.

16. The ridge point nearest the type-line divergence is known as the _____.

17. All loops must have (one, two) delta(s).

18. The approximate center of a loop pattern is called the _____.

19. If an imaginary line drawn between the two deltas of a whorl pattern touches any of the spiral ridges, the pattern is classified as a (plain whorl, central pocket loop).

20. The simplest of all fingerprint patterns is the _____.

21. Arches (have, do not have) type lines, deltas, and cores.

22. The presence or absence of the _____ pattern is used as a basis for determining the primary classification in the Henry system.

23. The largest category (25 percent) in the primary classification system is (1/1, 1/2).

24. A fingerprint classification system (can, cannot) unequivocally identify an individual.

25. True or False: Computerized fingerprint search systems match prints by comparing the position of bifurcations and ridge endings. _____

26. A fingerprint left by a person with soiled or stained fingertips is called a _____.

27. _____ fingerprints are impressions left on a soft material.

28. Fingerprint impressions that are not readily visible are called _____.

29. Fingerprints on hard and nonabsorbent surfaces are best developed by the application of a(n) _____.

30. Fingerprints on porous surfaces are best developed with _____ treatment.

31. _____ vapors chemically combine with fatty oils or residual water to visualize a fingerprint.

32. The chemical _____ visualizes fingerprints by its reaction with amino acids.

33. Chemical treatment with _____ visualizes fingerprints on porous articles that may have been wet at one time.

34. True or False: A latent fingerprint is first treated with Physical Developer followed by ninhydrin. _____

35. A chemical technique known as _____ is used to develop latent prints on nonporous surfaces such as metal and plastic.

36. _____ occurs when a substance absorbs light and reemits the light in wavelengths longer than the illuminating source.

37. High-intensity light sources known as _____ are effective in developing latent fingerprints.

38. Once a fingerprint has been visualized, it must be preserved by _____.

39. The image produced from a digital file is composed of numerous square electronic dots called _____.

40. A (high-pass filter, frequency Fourier transform analysis) is used to identify repetitive patterns such as lines or dots that interfere with the interpretation of a digitized fingerprint image.

Further References

Cowger, James E., *Friction Ridge Skin.* Boca Raton, Fla.: Taylor & Francis, 1992.

Komarinski, Peter, *Automated Fingerprint Identification Systems (AFIS),* Burlington, Mass.: Elsevier Academic Press, 2005.

Lee, H. C., and R. E. Gaensleen, eds., *Advances in Fingerprint Technology,* 2nd ed. Boca Raton, Fla.: Taylor & Francis, 2001.

Lennard, C., M. Margot, C. Stoilovic, and C. Champod, eds., *Fingerprints and Other Ridge Skin Impressions,* Boca Raton, Fla.: Taylor & Francis, 2004.

U.S. Department of Justice, *The Science of Fingerprints.* Washington, D.C.: U.S. Government Printing Office, 1990.

The Beltway Snipers

During a three-week period in October 2002, ten people were killed and three others were wounded as two snipers terrorized the region in and around the Baltimore–Washington metropolitan area. The arrest of John Allen Muhammad, 41, and Lee Boyd Malvo, 17, ended the ordeal. The semiautomatic .223-caliber rifle seized from them was ultimately linked by ballistic tests to eight of the ten killings. The car that Muhammad and Malvo were driving had been specially configured with one hole in the trunk through which a rifle barrel could protrude, so that a sniper could shoot from inside a slightly ajar trunk.

The major break in the case came when a friend of Muhammad's called police suggesting that Muhammad and his friend Malvo were the likely snipers. Muhammad's automobile records revealed numerous traffic stops in the Beltway area during the time of the shootings. Another break in the case came when Malvo called a priest to boast of a killing weeks before in Montgomery, Alabama. Investigators traced the claim to a recent liquor store holdup that left one person dead. Fortunately, the perpetrator of this crime left a latent fingerprint at the murder scene. Authorities quickly tracked the print to Malvo, a Jamaican citizen, through his fingerprints on file with the Immigration and Naturalization Service. A description of Muhammad's car was released to the media, leading to tips from alert citizens who noticed the car parked in a rest area with both occupants asleep.

The motive for the shooting spree was believed to be a planned plot to extort $10 million from local and state governments. Muhammad was sentenced to death and Malvo is currently serving life imprisonment without parole.

chapter 15

Firearms, Tool Marks, and Other Impressions

Key Terms

bore

breechblock

caliber

choke

distance determination

ejector

extractor

firearms identification

gauge

Greiss test

grooves

lands

rifling

Learning Objectives

After studying this chapter you should be able to:

- Describe techniques for rifling a barrel

- Recognize the class and individual characteristics of bullets and cartridge cases

- Understand the use of the comparison microscope to compare bullets and cartridge cases

- Explain the concept of the NIBIN database

- Explain the procedure for determining how far a weapon was fired from a target

- Identify the laboratory tests for determining whether an individual has fired a weapon

- Explain the forensic significance of class and individual characteristics to the comparison of toolmark, footwear, and tire impressions

- List some common field reagents used to enhance bloody footprints

Just as natural variations in skin ridge patterns and characteristics provide a key to human identification, minute random markings on surfaces can impart individuality to inanimate objects. Structural variations and irregularities caused by scratches, nicks, breaks, and wear permit the criminalist to relate a bullet to a gun; a scratch or abrasion mark to a single tool; or a tire track to a particular automobile. Individualization, so vigorously pursued in all other areas of criminalistics, is frequently attainable in firearms and tool mark examination.

Although a portion of this chapter will be devoted to the comparison of surface features for the purposes of bullet identification, a complete description of the services and capabilities of the modern forensic firearms laboratory cannot be restricted to just this one subject, important as it may be. The high frequency of shooting cases means that the science of firearms identification must extend beyond mere comparison of bullets to include knowledge of the operation of all types of weapons, restoration of obliterated serial numbers on weapons, detection and characterization of gunpowder residues on garments and around wounds, estimation of muzzle-to-target distances, and detection of powder residues on hands. Each of these functions will be covered in this chapter.

Firearms Identification
A discipline mainly concerned with determining whether a bullet or cartridge was fired by a particular weapon. It is not to be confused with ballistics, which is the study of a projectile in motion.

Grooves
The cut or low-lying portions between the lands in a rifled bore.

Rifling
The spiral grooves formed in the bore of a firearm barrel that impart spin to the projectile when it is fired.

Bore
The interior of a firearm barrel.

Lands
The raised portion between the grooves in a rifled bore.

Bullet Comparisons

The inner surface of the barrel of a gun leaves its markings on a bullet passing through it. These markings are peculiar to each gun. Hence, if one bullet found at the scene of a crime and another test-fired from a suspect's gun show the same markings, the suspect is linked to the crime. Because these inner surface striations are so important for bullet comparison, it is important to know why and how they originate.

The gun barrel is produced from a solid bar of steel that has been hollowed out by drilling. The microscopic drill marks left on the barrel's inner surface are randomly irregular and in themselves impart a uniqueness to each barrel. However, the manufacture of a barrel requires the additional step of impressing its inner surface with spiral grooves, a step known as rifling. The surfaces of the original bore remaining between the grooves are called lands (see Figure 15–1). As a fired bullet travels through a barrel, it engages the rifling grooves; these grooves then guide the bullet through the barrel, giving it a rapid spin. This is done because a spinning bullet does not tumble end over end on leaving the barrel, but remains instead on a true and accurate course.

The diameter of the gun barrel, sketched in Figure 15–2, measured between opposite lands, is known as the caliber of the weapon. Caliber is normally recorded in hundredths of an inch or in millimeters—for example, .22 caliber and 9 mm. Actually, the term *caliber,* as it is commonly applied, is not an exact measurement of the barrel's diameter; for example, a .38-caliber weapon might actually have a bore diameter that ranges from 0.345 to 0.365 inch.

Before 1940, barrels were rifled by having one or two grooves at a time cut into the surface with steel hook cutters. The cutting tool was rotated as it passed down the barrel, so that the final results were grooves spiraling either to the right or left. However, as the need for increased speed in the manufacture of weapons became apparent, newer techniques were developed that were far more suitable for the mass production of weapons. The broach cutter, shown in Figure 15–3, consists of a series of concentric steel rings, with each ring slightly larger than the preceding one. As the broach passes through the barrel, it simultaneously cuts all grooves into the barrel at the required depth. The broach rotates as it passes through the barrel, giving the grooves their desired direction and rate of twist.

In contrast to the broach, the button process involves no cuttings. A steel plug or "button" impressed with the desired number of grooves is forced under extremely high pressures through the barrel. A single pass of the button down the barrel compresses the metal to create lands and

Caliber
The diameter of the bore of a rifled firearm. The caliber is usually expressed in hundredths of an inch or millimeters—for example, .22 caliber and 9 mm.

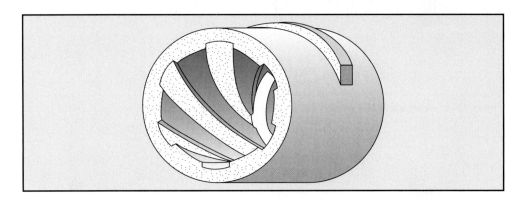

Figure 15–1   Interior view of a gun barrel, showing the presence of lands and grooves.

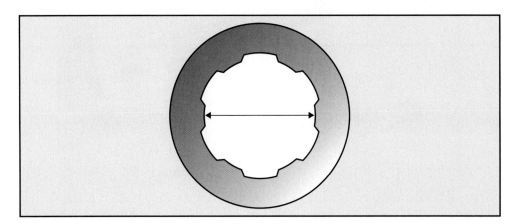

Figure 15–2   Cross-section of a barrel with six grooves. The diameter of the bore is the caliber.

grooves on the barrel walls that are negative forms of those on the button. The button rotates to produce the desired direction and rate of twist (see Figure 15–4).

Like the button process, the mandrel rifling or hummer forging process involves no cutting of metal. A mandrel is a rod of hardened steel machined so its form is the reverse impression of the rifling it is intended to produce. The mandrel is inserted into a slightly oversized bore, and the barrel is compressed with hammering or heavy rollers into the mandrel's form.

Every firearms manufacturer chooses a rifling process that is best suited to meet the production standards and requirements of its product. Once the choice is made, however, the class characteristics of the weapon's barrel will remain consistent; each will have the same number of lands and

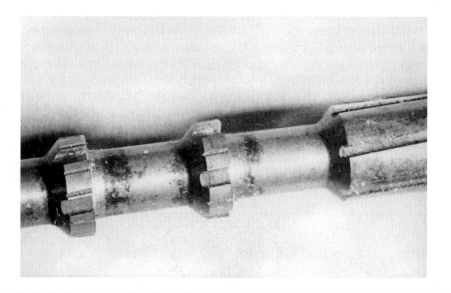

Figure 15–3   A segment of a broach cutter. *Courtesy New Jersey State Police*

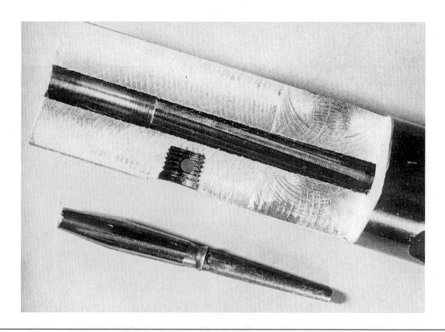

Figure 15–4   *(top)* Cross-section of a .22-caliber rifled barrel. *(bottom)* A button used to produce the lands and grooves in the barrel. *Courtesy New Jersey State Police*

grooves, with the same approximate width and direction of twist. For example, .32-caliber Smith & Wesson revolvers have five lands and grooves twisting to the right. On the other hand, Colt .32-caliber revolvers exhibit six lands and grooves twisting to the left. Although these class characteristics permit the examiner to distinguish one type or brand name of weapon from another, they do not impart individuality to any one barrel; no class characteristic can do this.

If one could cut a barrel open lengthwise, a careful examination of the interior would reveal the existence of fine lines, or *striations*, many running the length of the barrel's lands and grooves. These striations are impressed into the metal as the negatives of minute imperfections found on the rifling cutter's surface, or they are produced by minute chips of steel pushed against the barrel's inner surface by a moving broach cutter. The random distribution and irregularities of these markings are impossible to duplicate exactly in any two barrels. **No two rifled barrels, even those manufactured in succession, have identical striation markings.** These striations form the individual characteristics of the barrel.

As the bullet passes through the barrel, its surface is impressed with the rifled markings of the barrel. The bullet emerges from the barrel carrying the impressions of the bore's interior surface; these impressions reflect both the class and individual characteristics of the barrel (see Figure 15–5). Because there is no practical way of making a direct comparison between the markings on the fired bullet and those found within a

Figure 15–5   A bullet is impressed with the rifling markings of the barrel when it emerges from the weapon. *Courtesy New Jersey State Police*

barrel, the examiner must obtain test bullets fired through the suspect barrel for comparison. To prevent damage to the test bullet's markings and to facilitate the bullet's recovery, test firings are normally made into a recovery box filled with cotton or into a water tank.

The number of lands and grooves, and their direction of twist, are obvious points of comparison during the initial stages of the examination. Any differences in these class characteristics immediately eliminate the possibility that both bullets traveled through the same barrel. A bullet with five lands and grooves could not possibly have been fired from a weapon of like caliber with six lands and grooves, nor could one having a right twist have come through a barrel impressed with a left twist. If both bullets carry the same class characteristics, the analyst must begin to match the striated markings on both bullets. This can be done only with the assistance of the comparison microscope (see Chapter 7).

Modern firearms identification began with the development and use of the comparison microscope. This instrument is the most important tool at the disposal of the firearms examiner. The test and evidence bullets are mounted on cylindrical adjustable holders beneath the objective lenses of the microscope, each pointing in the same direction (see Figure 15–6). Both bullets are observed simultaneously within the same field of view, and the examiner rotates one bullet until a well-defined land or groove

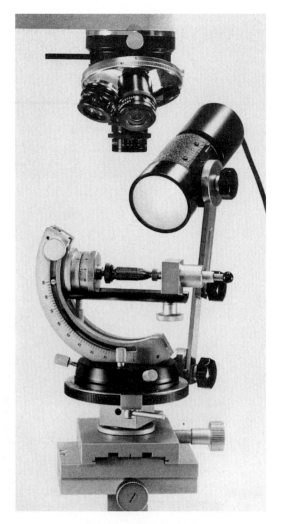

Figure 15–6   A bullet holder beneath the objective lens of a comparison microscope. *Courtesy Leica Microsystems, Buffalo, N.Y., www.leica-microsystems.com*

comes into view. Once the striation markings are located, the other bullet is rotated until a matching region is found. Not only must the lands and grooves of the test and evidence bullet have identical widths, but the longitudinal striations on each must coincide. When a matching area is located, the two bullets are simultaneously rotated to obtain additional matching areas around the periphery of the bullets. Figure 15–7 shows a typical photomicrograph of a bullet match as viewed under a comparison microscope.

Unfortunately, the firearms examiner rarely encounters a perfect match all around the bullet's periphery. The presence of grit and rust can alter the markings on bullets fired through the same barrel. More commonly, recovered evidence bullets may become so mutilated and distorted on impact as to yield only a small area with intact markings. Furthermore, striation markings on a barrel are not permanent structures; they are subject to continuing change and alteration through wear as succeeding bullets traverse the length of the barrel. Fortunately, in most cases, these changes are not dramatic and do not prevent the matching of two bullets fired by the same weapon. As with fingerprint comparison, there are no hard-and-fast rules governing the minimum number of points required for a bullet comparison. The final opinion must be based on the judgment, experience, and knowledge of the expert.

Frequently, the firearms examiner receives a spent bullet without an accompanying suspect weapon and is asked to determine the caliber and possible make of the weapon. If a bullet appears not to have lost its metal, its weight may be one factor in determining its caliber. In some instances, the number of lands and grooves, the direction of twist, and the widths of

Figure 15–7   Photomicrograph of two bullets through a comparison microscope. The test bullet is on the right; the questioned bullet is on the left. *Courtesy Philadelphia Police Department Laboratory*

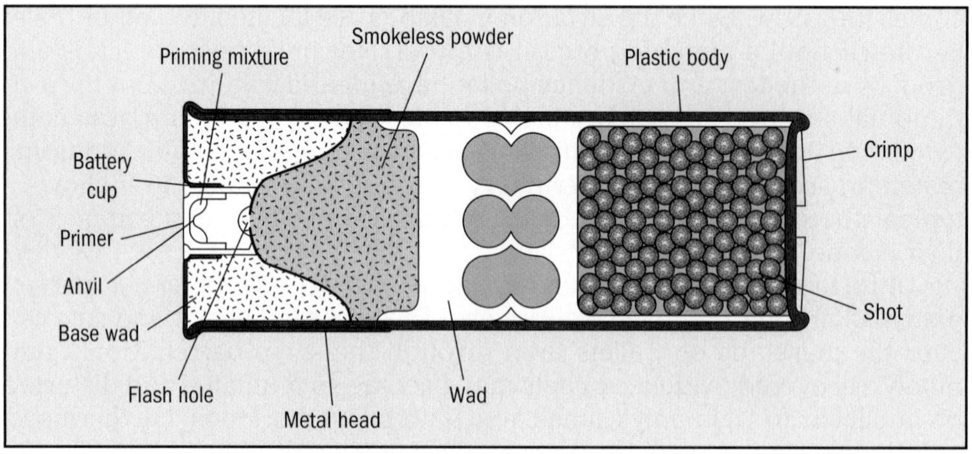

Figure 15–8 Cross-section of a loaded shotgun shell.

lands and grooves are useful class characteristics for eliminating certain makes of weapons from consideration. For example, a bullet that has five lands and grooves and twists to the right could not come from a weapon manufactured by Colt, because Colts are not manufactured with these class characteristics. Sometimes a bullet has rifling marks that set it apart from most other manufactured weapons, as in the case of Marlin rifles. These weapons are rifled by a technique known as *microgrooving* and may have eight to twenty-four grooves impressed into their barrels; few other weapons are manufactured in this fashion. In this respect, the FBI maintains a record known as the General Rifling Characteristics File. This file contains listings of class characteristics, such as land and groove width dimensions, for known weapons. It is periodically updated and distributed to the law enforcement community to help identify rifled weapons from retrieved bullets.

WebExtra 15.1
Practice Matching Bullets with the Aid of a 3-D Interactive Illustration
www.prenhall.com/Saferstein

Gauge
Size designation of a shotgun, originally the number of lead balls with the same diameter as the barrel that would make a pound. For example, a 12-gauge shotgun would have a bore diameter of a lead ball 1/12 pound in weight. The only exception is the .410 shotgun, in which bore size is 0.41 inch.

WebExtra 15.2
3-D Shotshell Illustrations
www.prenhall.com/Saferstein

Unlike rifled firearms, a shotgun has a smooth barrel. It therefore follows that projectiles passing through a shotgun barrel are not impressed with any characteristic markings that can later be related back to the weapon. Shotguns generally fire small lead balls or pellets contained within a shotgun shell (see Figure 15–8). A paper or plastic wad pushes the pellets through the barrel on ignition of the cartridge's powder charge. By weighing and measuring the diameter of the shot recovered at a crime scene, the examiner can usually determine the size of shot used in the shell. The size and shape of the recovered wad may also reveal the gauge of the shotgun used and, in some instances, may indicate the manufacturer of the fired shell.

The diameter of the shotgun barrel is expressed by the term **gauge**.[1] The higher the gauge number, the smaller the barrel's diameter. For example, a 12-gauge shotgun has a bore diameter of 0.730 inch as contrasted to 0.670 inch for a 16-gauge shotgun. The exception to this rule is the .410-gauge shotgun, which refers to a barrel 0.41 inch in diameter.

[1] Originally, the number of lead balls with the same diameter as the barrel would make a pound. For example, a 20-gauge shotgun has an inside diameter equal to the diameter of a lead ball that weighs 1/20 of a pound.

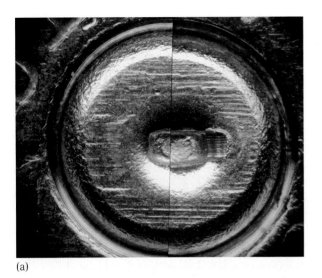
(a)

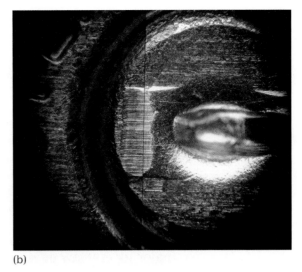
(b)

Figure 15–9 Comparison microscope photomicrograph showing a match between (a) firing pin impressions and (b) the breechblock markings on two shells. *Courtesy Ronald Welsh, Bureau of Forensic Services, Central Valley Laboratory, Ripon, Calif.*

Cartridge Cases

The act of pulling a trigger releases the weapon's firing pin, causing it to strike the primer, which in turn ignites the powder. The expanding gases generated by the burning gunpowder propel the bullet forward through the barrel, simultaneously pushing the spent cartridge case or shell back with equal force against the breechblock. As the bullet is marked by its passage through the barrel, the shell is also impressed with markings by its contact with the metal surfaces of the weapon's firing and loading mechanisms. As with bullets, these markings can be reproduced in test-fired cartridges to provide distinctive points of comparison for individualizing a spent shell to a rifled weapon or shotgun.

The shape of the firing pin is impressed into the relatively soft metal of the primer on the cartridge case, revealing the minute distortions of the firing pin. These imperfections may be sufficiently random to individualize the pin impression to a single weapon. Similarly, the cartridge case, in its rearward thrust, is impressed with the surface markings of the breechblock. The breechblock, like any machined surface, is populated with random striation markings that become a highly distinctive signature for individualizing its surface. Other distinctive markings that may appear on the shell as a result of metal-to-metal contact are caused by the ejector and extractor mechanism and the magazine or clip, as well as by imperfections on the fire chamber walls. Photomicrographs in Figure 15–9 reveal a comparison of the firing pin and breechblock impressions on evidence and test-fired shells.

Firing pin, breechblock, extractor, and ejector marks may also be impressed onto the surface of the brass portion of shells fired by a shotgun. These impressions provide points for individualizing the shell to a weapon that are just as valuable as cartridge cases discharged from a rifled firearm. Furthermore, in the absence of a suspect weapon, the size and shape of a firing pin impression and/or the position of ejector marks in relationship to extractor and other markings may provide some clue to the type or make of the weapon that may have fired the questioned shell, or at least may eliminate a large number of possibilities.

Breechblock
The rear part of a firearm barrel.

WebExtra 15.3
3-D Revolver Cartridge Illustrations
www.prenhall.com/Saferstein

WebExtra 15.4
3-D Pistol Cartridge Illustrations
www.prenhall.com/Saferstein

WebExtra 15.5
3-D Rifle Cartridge Illustrations
www.prenhall.com/Saferstein

Ejector
The mechanism in a firearm that throws the cartridge or fired case from the firearm.

Extractor
The mechanism in a firearm by which a cartridge or a fired case is withdrawn from the chamber.

WebExtra 15.6
View Animations to Illustrate the Firing Process and the Extraction/Ejection Process of a Semiautomatic Pistol
www.prenhall.com/Saferstein

Automated Firearms Search Systems

The use of firearms, especially semiautomatic weapons, during the commission of a crime has significantly increased throughout the United States. Because of the expense of such firearms, the likelihood that a specific weapon will be used in multiple crimes has risen. The advent of computerized imaging technology has made possible the storage of bullet and cartridge surface characteristics in a manner analogous to the storage of automated fingerprint files (see pp. 436–438). Using this concept, crime laboratories can be networked, allowing them to share information on bullets and cartridges retrieved from several jurisdictions. The effort to build a national computerized database for firearms evidence in the United States had a rather confusing and inefficient start in the early 1990s. Two major federal law enforcement agencies, the FBI and the ATF, offered the law enforcement community competing and incompatible computerized systems. The automated search system developed for the FBI was known as *DRUGFIRE*. This system emphasized the examination of unique markings on the cartridge casings expended by the weapon. The specimen was analyzed through a microscope attached to a video camera. The magnification allowed for a close-up view to identify individual characteristics. The image was captured by a video camera, digitized, and stored in a database. Although DRUGFIRE emphasized cartridge-case imagery, the images of highly characteristic bullet striations could also be stored in a like manner for comparisons.

The *Integrated Ballistic Identification System (IBIS),* developed for the Bureau of Alcohol, Tobacco, Firearms and Explosives, processed digital microscopic images of identifying features found on both expended bullets and cartridge casings. IBIS incorporated two software programs: Bulletproof, a bullet-analyzing module, and Brasscatcher, a cartridge-case-analyzing module. A schematic diagram of Bulletproof's operation is depicted in Figure 15–10.[2]

In 1999, members of the FBI and ATF joined forces to introduce the *National Integrated Ballistics Information Network (NIBIN)* program to the discipline of firearms examination. NIBIN guides and assists federal, state, and local laboratories interested in housing an automated search system. The new unified system, incorporates both DRUGFIRE and IBIS technologies available in prior years. ATF has the overall responsibility for the system sites, while the FBI is responsible for the communications network. Agencies using the new IBIS technology produce database files from bullets and cartridge casings retrieved from crime scenes or test fires from retrieved firearms. More than two hundred law enforcement agencies worldwide have adapted to this technology.

The success of the system has been proven with more than 800,000 images compiled; nationwide, law enforcement agencies have connected more than 11,000 bullets and casings to more than one crime (see Figure 15–11). For example, in a recent case, a Houston security guard was shot and killed during a botched armed robbery. A bullet and

---

[2] R. E. Tontarski, Jr., and R. M. Thompson, "Automated Firearms Evidence Comparison: A Forensic Tool for Firearms Identification—An Update," *Journal of Forensic Sciences* 43 (1998): 641.

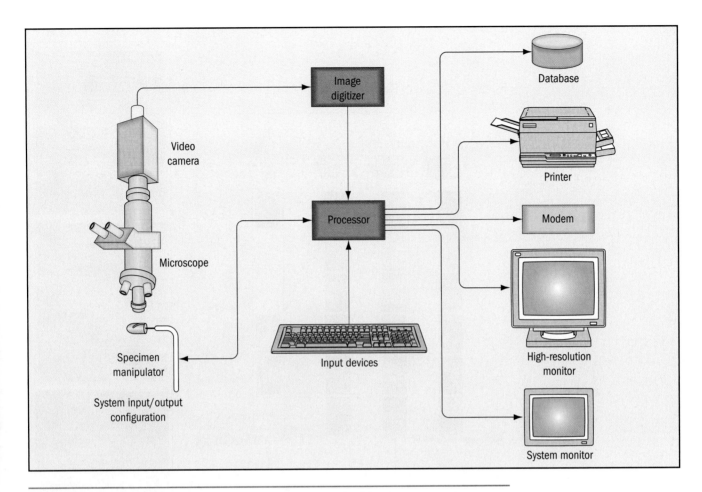

Figure 15–10   Bulletproof configuration. The sample is mounted on the specimen manipulator and illuminated by the light source from a microscope. The image is captured by a video camera and digitized. This digital image is then stored in a database, available for retrieval and comparison. The search for a match includes analyzing the width of land and groove impressions along with both rifling and individual characteristics. The Brasscatcher software uses the same system configuration but emphasizes the analysis of expended cartridge casings rather than the expended bullets. *Courtesy Forensic Technology (WAI) Inc., Côte St-Luc, Quebec, Canada*

.40-caliber Smith and Wesson cartridge casing were recovered and imaged into NIBIN. Earlier that day, a robbery-turned-double-homicide left two store clerks dead. Again, two bullets and two .40-caliber Smith and Wesson cartridge casings were recovered. Once they were processed into NIBIN, a correlation was found with the murder of the security officer and a separate aggravated robbery that occurred two weeks prior. All three crimes were linked with a firearm believed to be a .40-caliber Smith and Wesson pistol. Further investigation into the use of a victim's credit card aided police in locating two suspects. In the possession of one suspect was a .40-caliber Smith and Wesson pistol. Once retrieved, the gun was test-fired and imaged into NIBIN. The casing from the test-fired weapon matched the evidence obtained in the robbery and the aggravated robbery-homicides. The associations were verified by traditional firearms examination comparisons performed by a firearms examiner. Before this computerized technology was developed, it would have taken years, or may have been impossible, to link all of these shootings to one single firearm. In another example, the ATF laboratory in Rockville, Maryland, received 1,466 cartridge casings from the Ovcara mass burial

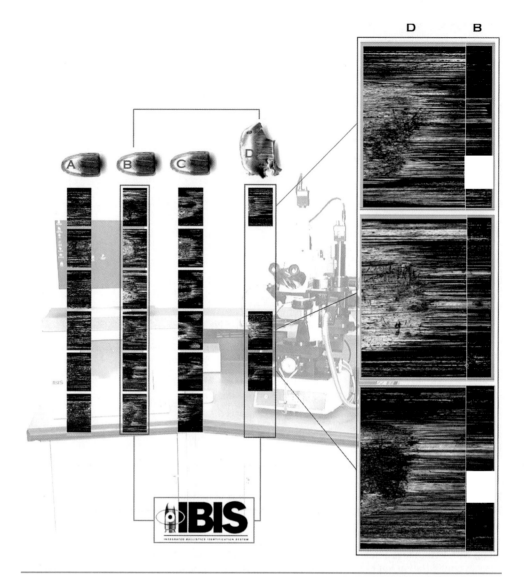

Figure 15–11   **Bullets A, B, C, and D were acquired in the IBIS database at different times from different crime scenes. D is a fragmented bullet that had only three land impressions available for acquisition. Upon the entry of bullet D, IBIS found a potential matching candidate in the database: B. On the far right, bullet D is compared to bullet B using the IBIS imaging software. Finally, a forensic firearms examiner using the actual evidence under a conventional comparison microscope will confirm the match between B and D.** *Courtesy Forensic Technology WAI Inc.*

site in Bosnia. After processing and imaging profiles for all casings, the examiners determined that eighteen different firearms were used at the site. With the help of NIBIN technology and competent examiners, jurists were able to try and convict an individual for war crimes.

NIBIN serves only as a screening tool for firearms evidence. A computerized system does not replace the skills of the firearms examiner. NIBIN can screen hundreds of unsolved firearms cases and may narrow the possibilities to several firearms. However, the final comparison will be made by the forensic examiner through traditional microscopic methods.

Participating crime laboratories in the United States are building databases of bullet and cartridge cases found at crime scenes and those fired in tests of guns seized from criminals. As these databases come online and prove their usefulness in solving crimes, law enforcement officials and the political community are scrutinizing the feasibility of scaling this concept up to create a system of *ballistic fingerprinting*. This system would entail the capture and storage of appropriate markings on bullets and cartridges test-fired from handguns and rifles before they are sold to the public. Questions regarding who will be responsible for collecting the images and details of how they will be stored are but two of many issues to be determined. The concept of ballistic fingerprinting is an intriguing one for the law enforcement community and promises to be explored and debated intensely in the future.

Gunpowder Residues

In incidents involving gunshot wounds, it is often necessary to determine the distance from which the weapon was fired. Frequently, in incidents involving a shooting death, the individual apprehended and accused pleads self-defense as the motive for the attack. Such claims are fertile grounds for **distance determinations**, because finding the proximity of the parties involved in the incident is necessary to establish the facts of the incident. Similarly, careful examination of the wounds of suicide victims usually reveals characteristics associated with a very close-range gunshot wound. The absence of such characteristics is a strong indication that the wound was not self-inflicted and signals the possibility of foul play.

Distance Determination
The process of determining the distance between the firearm and a target, usually based on the distribution of powder patterns or the spread of a shot pattern.

Modern ammunition is propelled toward a target by the expanding gases created by the ignition of smokeless powder or nitrocellulose in a cartridge. Under ideal circumstances, all of the powder would be consumed in the process and converted into the rapidly expanding gases. However, in practice the powder is never totally burned. When a firearm is discharged, unburned and partially burned particles of gunpowder in addition to smoke are propelled out of the barrel along with the bullet toward the target. If the muzzle of the weapon is sufficiently close, these products are deposited onto the target. The distribution of gunpowder particles and other discharge residues around the bullet hole permits an assessment of the distance from which a handgun or rifle was fired.

The accuracy of a distance determination varies according to the circumstances of the case. When the investigator is unable to recover a suspect weapon, the best that the examiner can do is to state whether a shot could have been fired within some distance interval from the target. More exact opinions are possible only when the examiner has the suspect weapon in hand and has knowledge of the type of ammunition used in the shooting.

The precise distance from which a handgun or rifle has been fired must be determined by careful comparison of the powder-residue pattern on the victim's clothing or skin against test patterns made when the suspect weapon is fired at varying distances from a target. A white cloth or a fabric comparable to the victim's clothing may be used as a test target (see Figure 15–12). Because the spread and density of the residue pattern vary widely between weapons and ammunition, such a comparison is significant only when it is made with the suspect weapon and suspect ammunition, or with ammunition of the same type and make. By comparing the test and evidence patterns, the examiner may find enough similarity in shape and density on which to judge the distance from which the shot was fired.

Without the weapon, the examiner is restricted to looking for recognizable characteristics around the bullet hole. Such findings are at best approximations made as a result of general observations and the examiner's

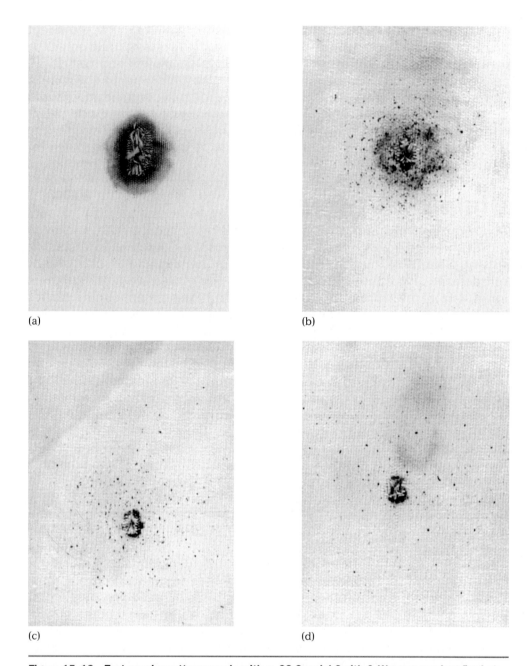

(a)

(b)

(c)

(d)

Figure 15–12   Test powder patterns made with a .38 Special Smith & Wesson revolver fired at the following distances from the target: (a) contact, (b) 6 inches, (c) 12 inches, and (d) 18 inches. *Courtesy New Jersey State Police*

experience. However, some noticeable characteristics should be sought. For instance, when the weapon is held in contact with or less than 1 inch from the target, a heavy concentration of smokelike vaporous lead usually surrounds the bullet entrance hole. Often, loose fibers surrounding a contact hole show scorch marks from the flame discharge of the weapon, and some synthetic fibers may show signs of being melted as a result of the heat from the discharge. Furthermore, the blowback of muzzle gases may produce a stellate (star-shape) tear pattern around the hole. Such a hole is invariably surrounded by a rim of a smokelike deposit of vaporous lead (see Figure 15–13).

A halo of vaporous lead (smoke) deposited around a bullet hole normally indicates a discharge 12 to 18 inches or less from the target. The

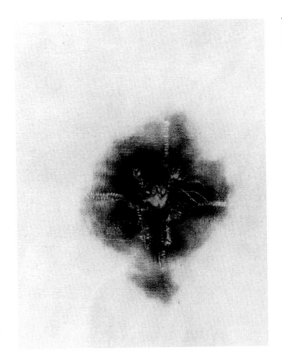

Figure 15–13 A contact shot. *Courtesy New Jersey State Police*

presence of scattered specks of unburned and partially burned powder grains without any accompanying soot can often be observed at distances up to approximately 25 inches. Occasionally, however, scattered gunpowder particles are noted at a firing distance as far out as 36 inches. With ball powder ammunition, this distance may be extended to 6 to 8 feet. Finally, a weapon that has been fired more than 3 feet from a target usually does not deposit any powder residues onto the target's surface. In these cases, the only visual indication that the hole was made by a bullet is a dark ring, known as *bullet wipe,* around the perimeter of the entrance hole. Bullet wipe consists of a mixture of carbon, dirt, lubricant, primer residue, and lead wiped off the bullet's surface as it passes through the target. Again, in the absence of a suspect weapon, these observations are general guidelines for estimating target distances. Numerous factors—barrel length, caliber, type of ammunition, and type and condition of the weapon fired—influence the amount of gunpowder residue deposited on a target.

When garments or other evidence relevant to a shooting are received in the crime laboratory, the surfaces of all items are first examined microscopically for gunpowder residue. These particles may be identifiable by their characteristic colors, sizes, and shapes. However, the absence of visual indications does not preclude the possibility that gunpowder residue is present. Sometimes the lack of color contrast between the powder and garment or the presence of heavily encrusted deposits of blood can obscure the visual detection of gunpowder. Often, an infrared photograph of the suspect area overcomes the problem. Such a photograph may enhance the contrast, thus revealing vaporous lead and powder particles deposited around the hole (see Figure 15–14). In other situations, this may not help, and the analyst must use chemical tests to detect gunpowder residues.

Nitrites are one type of chemical product that results from the incomplete combustion of smokeless (nitrocellulose) powder. One test method for locating powder residues involves transferring particles embedded on the target surface to chemically treated gelatin-coated photographic paper. This procedure is known as the Greiss test. The examiner presses the

Greiss Test

A chemical test used to develop patterns of gunpowder residues around bullet holes.

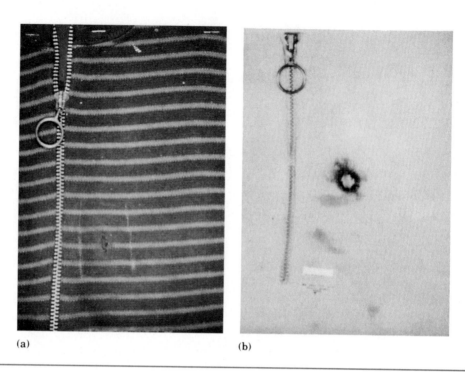

(a)   (b)

Figure 15–14   (a) A shirt bearing a powder stain, photographed under normal light. (b) Infrared photograph of the same shirt. *Courtesy New Jersey State Police*

photographic paper onto the target with a hot iron; once the nitrite particles are on the paper, they are made easily visible by chemical treatment.[3] In addition, comparing the developed nitrite pattern to nitrite patterns obtained from test firings at known distances can be useful in determining the shooting distance from the target. A second chemical test is then performed to detect any trace of lead residue around the bullet hole. The questioned surface is sprayed with a solution of sodium rhodizonate, followed by a series of oversprays with acid solutions. This treatment causes lead particles to exhibit a pink color, followed by a blue-violet color.

The determination of firing distances involving shotguns must again be related to test firings performed with the suspect weapon, using the same type of ammunition known to be used in the crime. In the absence of a weapon, the muzzle-to-target distance can be estimated by measuring the spread of the discharged shot. With close-range shots varying in distance up to 4 to 5 feet, the shot charge enters the target as a concentrated mass, producing a hole somewhat larger than the bore of the barrel. As the distance increases, the pellets progressively separate and spread out. Generally speaking, the spread in the pattern made by a 12-gauge shotgun increases 1 inch for each yard of distance. Thus, a 10-inch pattern would be produced at approximately 10 yards. Of course, this is only a rule of thumb; normally, a great number of variables can affect the shot pattern. Other factors to consider include the barrel length, the size and quantity of the pellets fired, the quantity of powder charge used to propel the pellets, and the choke of the gun under examination. Choke is the degree of constriction placed at the muzzle end of the barrel. The greater the choke, the narrower the shotgun pattern and the faster and farther the pellets will travel.

Choke

An interior constriction placed at or near the muzzle end of a shotgun's barrel to control shot dispersion.

---

[3] P. C. Maiti, "Powder Patterns around Bullet Holes in Bloodstained Articles," *Journal of the Forensic Science Society* 13 (1973): 197.

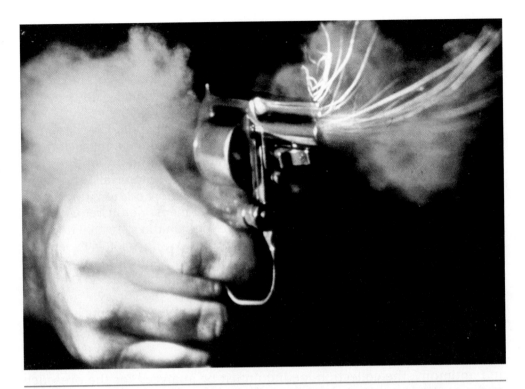

Figure 15–15 **When a handgun is fired, gunpowder and primer residues are normally blown back toward the hand of the shooter.** *Courtesy Centre for Forensic Sciences, Toronto, Canada*

Primer Residues on the Hands

The firing of a weapon not only propels residues toward the target, but also blows gunpowder and primer residues back toward the shooter (see Figure 15–15). As a result, traces of these residues are often deposited on the firing hand of the shooter, and their detection can provide valuable information as to whether an individual has recently fired a weapon.

Early efforts at demonstrating powder residues on the hands centered on chemical tests that could detect unburned gunpowder or nitrates. For many years, the *dermal nitrate test* enjoyed popularity. It required the application of hot paraffin or wax to the suspect's hand with a paintbrush. After drying into a solid crust, the paraffin was removed and tested with diphenylamine. A blue color was taken as an indication of a positive reaction for nitrates (see Table 11–3). However, the dermal nitrate test has fallen into disfavor with law enforcement agencies, owing mainly to its lack of specificity. Common materials such as fertilizers, cosmetics, urine, and tobacco all give positive reactions that are indistinguishable from that obtained for gunpowder by this test.

Efforts to identify a shooter now center on the detection of primer residues deposited on the hand of a shooter at the time of firing. With the exception of most .22-caliber ammunition, primers currently manufactured contain a blend of lead styphnate, barium nitrate, and antimony sulfide. Residues from these materials are most likely to be deposited on the thumb web and the back of the firing hand of a shooter, because these areas are closest to gases escaping along the side or back of the gun during discharge. In addition, individuals who handle a gun without firing it may have primer residues deposited on the palm of the hand coming in contact with the weapon. However, with the handling of a used firearm, the passage of time, and the resumption of normal activities following a shooting, gunshot residues from the back of the hand are frequently redistributed to other areas, including the palms. Therefore, it is not unusual to find higher levels of barium and antimony on the palms than on the backs of the hands of known shooters. Another possibility is the deposition of significant levels of barium and antimony on the hands of an individual who is near a firearm when it is discharged.

Determination of whether a person has fired or handled a weapon or has been near a discharged firearm is normally made by measuring the presence and possibly the amount of barium and antimony on the relevant portions of the suspect's hands. A variety of materials and techniques are used for removing these residues. The most popular approach, and certainly the most convenient for the field investigator, requires the application of an adhesive tape or adhesive to the hand's surface in order to remove any adhering residue particles. Another approach is to remove any residues present by swabbing both the firing and nonfiring hands with cotton that has been moistened with 5 percent nitric acid. The front and back of each hand are separately swabbed. All four swabs, along with a moistened control, are then forwarded to the crime laboratory for analysis (see Appendix II for a detailed description of residue collection procedures).

In any case, once the hands are treated for the collection of barium and antimony, the collection medium must be analyzed for the presence of these elements. High barium and antimony levels on the suspect's hand(s) strongly indicate that the person fired or handled a weapon or was near a firearm when it was discharged. Because these elements are normally present after a firing in small quantities (less than 10 micrograms), only the most sensitive analytical techniques can be used to detect them.

Unfortunately, even though most specimens submitted for this type of analysis have been from individuals strongly suspected of having fired a gun, there has been a low rate of positive findings. The major difficulty appears to be the short time that primer residues remain on the hands. These residues are readily removed by intentional or unintentional washing, rubbing, or wiping of hands. In fact, one study convincingly demonstrated that it is very difficult to detect primer residues on cotton hand swabs taken as soon as two hours after firing a weapon.[4] Hence, some laboratories do not accept cotton hand swabs taken from living subjects six or more hours after a firing has occurred. In cases that involve suicide victims, a higher rate of positives for the presence of gunshot residue is obtained when the hand swabbing is conducted before the person's body is moved or when the hands are protected by paper bags.[5] However, hand swabbing or the application of an adhesive cannot be used to detect firings with most .22-caliber rim-fire ammunition. Such ammunition may contain only barium or neither barium nor antimony in its primer composition.

Neutron activation analysis and flameless atomic absorption spectrophotometry (see Chapter 6) are analytical methods that have demonstrated a sensitivity high enough to be suitable for detecting barium and

[4] J. W. Kilty, "Activity after Shooting and Its Effect on the Retention of Primer Residues," *Journal of the Forensic Sciences* 29 (1975): 219.

[5] G. E. Reed et al., "Analysis of Gunshot Residue Test Results in 112 Suicides," *Journal of Forensic Sciences* 35 (1990): 62.

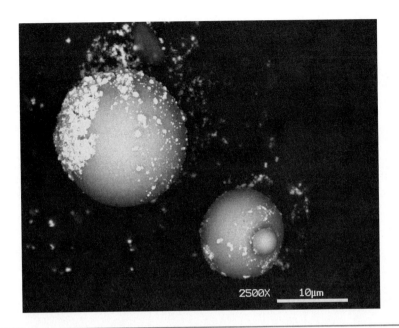

Figure 15–16   An SEM view of gunshot residue particles. *Courtesy Jeol USA Inc., Peabody, Mass., www.jeol.usa.com*

antimony in gunshot residues in hand swabs. However, the need for access to a neutron source, expensive counting equipment, and extensive regulatory requirements limit neutron activation analysis technology to a small number of crime laboratories. On the other hand, flameless atomic absorption spectrophotometry (see pp. 168–169) can be purchased at a cost well within the budgets of most crime laboratories, and a number of laboratories use this instrument to detect barium and antimony on a shooter's hands.

Most laboratories possessing gunshot residue detection capabilities require the application of an adhesive to the shooter's hands.[6] Microscopic primer and gunpowder particles on the adhesive are then located with the aid of a scanning electron microscope (SEM). These particles have a characteristic size and shape that readily distinguish them from other contaminants present on the hands (see Figure 15–16). When the SEM is linked to an X-ray analyzer (see pp. 192–194), an elemental analysis of the particles can be conducted. A finding of a select combination of elements (lead, barium, and antimony) confirms that the particles were indeed primer residue (see Figure 15–17). Appendix II contains a detailed description of the SEM residue collection procedure.

The major advantage of the SEM approach for primer residue detection is its enhanced specificity over hand swabbing. The SEM characterizes primer particles by their size and shape as well as by their chemical composition. Unfortunately, the excessive operator time required to search out and characterize gunshot residue has deterred this technique's use. The availability of automated particle search and identification systems for use with scanning electron microscopes may overcome this problem. Results of work performed with automated systems

---

[6] G. M. Woiten et al., "Particle Analysis for the Detection of Gunshot Residue, I: Scanning Electron Microscopy/Energy Dispersive X-Ray Characterization of Hand Deposits from Firing," *Journal of Forensic Sciences* 24 (1979): 409.

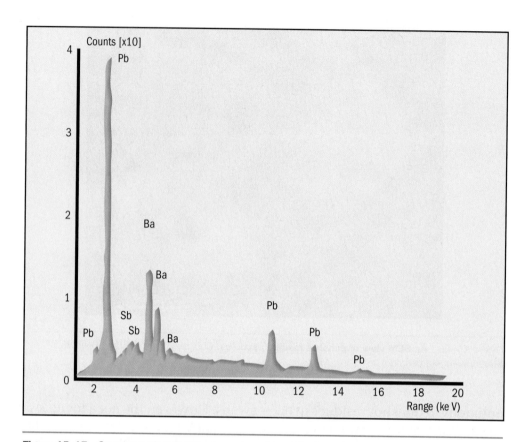

Figure 15–17   Spectrum showing the presence of lead, barium, and antimony in gunshot residue. *Courtesy Jeol USA Inc., Peabody, Mass., www.jeolusa.com*

show it to be significantly faster than a manual approach for searching out gunshot residue particles.[7]

Serial Number Restoration

Today, many manufactured items, including automobile engine blocks and firearms, are impressed with a serial number for identification. Increasingly, the criminalist is asked to restore such a number when it has been removed or obliterated by grinding, rifling, or punching.

Serial numbers are usually stamped on a metal body or frame, or on a plate, with hard steel dies. These dies strike the metal surface with a force that allows each digit to sink into the metal at a prescribed depth. Serial numbers can be restored because the metal crystals in the stamped zone are placed under a permanent strain that extends a short distance beneath the original numbers. When a suitable etching agent is applied, the strained area dissolves faster than the unaltered metal, thus revealing the etched pattern in the form of the original numbers. How-

[7] R. S. White and A. D. Owens, "Automation of Gunshot Residue Detection and Analysis by Scanning Electron Microscopy/Energy Dispersive X-Ray Analysis (SEM/EDX)," *Journal of Forensic Sciences* 32 (1987): 1595; W. L. Tillman, "Automated Gunshot Residue Particle Search and Characterization," *Journal of Forensic Sciences* 32 (1987): 62.

ever, if the zone of strain has been removed, or if the area has been impressed with a different strain pattern, the number usually cannot be restored.

Before any treatment with the etching reagent, the obliterated surface must be thoroughly cleaned of dirt and oil and polished to a mirrorlike finish. The reagent is swabbed onto the surface with a cotton ball. The choice of etching reagent depends on the type of metal surface being worked on. A solution of hydrochloric acid (120 mL), copper chloride (90 g), and water (100 ml) generally works well for steel surfaces.

Collection and Preservation of Firearms Evidence

Firearms

The Hollywood image of an investigator picking up a weapon by its barrel with a pencil or stick in order to protect fingerprints must be avoided. This practice only disturbs powder deposits, rust, or dirt lodged in the barrel, and consequently may alter the striation markings on test-fired bullets. If recovery of latent fingerprints is a primary concern, hold the weapon by the edge of the trigger guard or by the checkered portion of the grip, which usually does not retain identifiable fingerprints.

The most important consideration in handling a weapon is safety. Before any weapon is sent to the laboratory, all precautions must be taken to prevent an accidental discharge of a loaded weapon in transit. In most cases, it will be necessary to unload the weapon. If this is done, a record should first be made of the weapon's hammer and safety position; likewise, the location of all fired and unfired ammunition in the weapon must be recorded. When a revolver is recovered, the chamber position in line with the barrel should be indicated by a scratch mark on the cylinder. Each chamber is designated with a number on a diagram, and as each cartridge or casing is removed, it should be marked to correspond to the numbered chambers in the diagram. Knowledge of the cylinder position of a cartridge casing may be useful for later determination of the sequence of events, particularly in shooting cases, when more than one shot was fired. Place each round in a separate box or envelope. If the weapon is an automatic, the magazine must be removed and checked for prints and the chamber then emptied.

As with any other type of physical evidence recovered at a crime scene, firearms evidence must be marked for identification and a chain of custody must be established. Therefore, when a firearm is recovered, an identification tag should be attached to the trigger guard. The tag should be marked to show appropriate identifying data, including the weapon's serial number, make and model, and the investigator's initials. The firearm itself may be further identified by being marked directly with a sharp-pointed scriber in an inconspicuous area of the weapon—for example, the inside of the trigger guard. This practice will avoid any permanent defacement of the weapon.

When a weapon is recovered from an underwater location, no effort must be made to dry or clean it. Instead, the firearm should be transported to the laboratory in a receptacle containing enough of the same water necessary to keep it submerged. This procedure prevents rust from developing during transport.

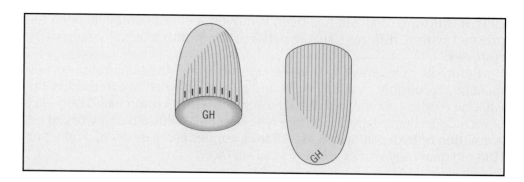

Figure 15–18   Discharged evidence bullets should be marked on the base or nose. When there is more than one bullet, a number should accompany the initials. *Never* mark bullets on the side.

Ammunition

Protection of class and individual markings on bullets and cartridge cases must be the primary concern of the field investigator. Thus, extreme caution is needed when removing a lodged bullet from a wall or other object. If the bullet's surface is accidentally scratched during this operation, valuable striation markings could be obliterated. It is best to free bullets from their target by carefully breaking away the surrounding support material while avoiding direct contact with the projectile.

Bullets recovered at the crime scene are scribed with the investigator's initials, either on the base or the nose of the bullet (see Figure 15–18). Again, obliteration of any striation markings on the bullet must be scrupulously avoided. If the bullet is badly deformed and there is no apparent place for identification, it should just be placed in a container that is appropriately marked for identification. In any case, the investigator must protect the bullet by wrapping it in tissue paper before placing it in a pillbox or an envelope for shipment to the crime laboratory. In handling the bullet, the investigator should be conscious of the possibility that minute traces of evidence, such as paint and fibers, may be adhering to the bullet. Care must be taken to leave these trace materials intact. Similarly, a fired casing must be identified so as to avoid destroying marks impressed on it from the weapon. The investigator's initials should be placed near the outside or inside mouth of the shell (see Figure 15–19). Discharged shells from shotguns are initialed with ink or indelible pencil on the paper or plastic tube remaining on the shell or on the metal nearest the mouth of the shell. In addition, when semiautomatic or automatic weapons have been fired, the ejection pattern of the casings can help establish the relationship of the suspect to his or her victim. For this reason, the exact location of the place from which a shell casing was recovered is important information that must be noted by the investigator.

In incidents involving shotguns, any wads recovered are to be packaged and sent to the laboratory. An examination of the size and composition of the wad may reveal information about the type of ammunition used and the gauge of the shotgun.

Gunpowder Deposits

The clothing of a firearms victim must be carefully preserved so as to prevent damage or disruption to powder residues deposited around a bullet or shell hole. The cutting or tearing of clothing in the area of the holes must be avoided as the clothing is being removed. All wet clothing should be air-

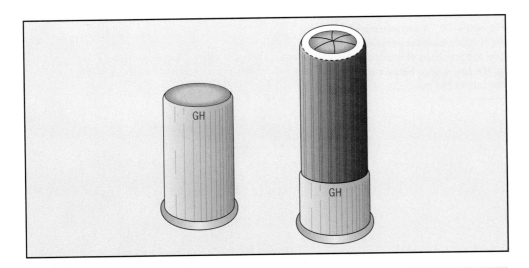

Figure 15–19   Discharged evidence shells should be marked on the outside or inside, as close as possible to the mouth of the shell. Discharged shotgun shells should be marked on the brass, close to the paper or plastic. *Never* mark the shells where the firing pin strikes the primer.

dried out of direct sunlight and then folded carefully so as not to disrupt the area around the bullet hole. Each item should be placed in a separate paper bag.

Tool Marks

A *tool mark* is any impression, cut, gouge, or abrasion caused by a tool coming into contact with another object. Most often, tool marks are encountered at burglary scenes that involve forcible entry into a building or safe. Generally, these marks occur as indented impressions into a softer surface or as abrasion marks caused by the tool cutting or sliding against another object.

Typically, an indented impression is left on the frame of a door or window as a result of the prying action of a screwdriver or crowbar. A careful examination of these impressions can reveal important class characteristics—that is, the size and shape of the tool. However, they rarely reveal any significant individual characteristics that could permit the examiner to individualize the mark to a single tool. Such characteristics, when they do exist, usually take the form of discernible random nicks and breaks that the tool has acquired through wear and use (Figure 15–20).

Just as the machined surfaces of a firearm are impressed with random striations during its manufacture, the edges of a pry bar, chisel, screwdriver, knife, or cutting tool likewise display a series of microscopic irregularities that look like ridges and valleys. Such markings are left as a result of the machining processes used to cut and finish tools. The shape and pattern of such minute imperfections are further modified by damage and wear during the life of the tool. Considering the unending variety of patterns that the hills and valleys can assume, it is highly unlikely that any two tools will be identical. Hence, these minute imperfections impart individuality to each tool.

If the edge of a tool is scraped against a softer surface, it may cut a series of striated lines that reflect that pattern of the tool's edge. Markings left in this manner are compared in the laboratory through a comparison

Figure 15–20   A comparison of a tool mark with a suspect screwdriver. Note how the presence of nicks and breaks on the tool's edge helps individualize the tool to the mark. *Courtesy New Jersey State Police*

microscope with test tool marks made from the suspect tool. The result can be a positive comparison, and hence a definitive association of the tool with the evidence mark, when a sufficient quantity of striations match between the evidence and test markings.

One of the major problems associated with tool mark comparisons is the difficulty in duplicating in the laboratory the tool mark left at the crime scene. A thorough comparison requires the preparation of a series of test marks obtained by applying the suspect tool at various angles and pressures to a soft metal surface (lead is commonly used). This approach gives the examiner ample opportunity to duplicate many of the details of the original evidence marking. A photomicrograph of a typical tool mark comparison is illustrated in Figure 15–21.

Whenever practical, the entire object or the part of the object bearing a tool mark should be submitted to the crime laboratory for examination. When removal of the tool mark is impractical, the only recourse is to photograph the marked area to scale and make a cast of the mark. Under these circumstances, liquid silicone casting material has been found to be the most satisfactory for reproducing most of the fine details of the mark. See Figure 15–22. However, even under the most optimum conditions, the clarity of many of the tool mark's minute details will be lost or obscured in a photograph or cast. Of course, this will reduce the chance of individualizing the mark to a single tool.

The crime-scene investigator must never attempt to fit the suspect tool into the tool mark. Any contact between the tool and the marked surface may alter the mark and will, at the least, raise serious questions about the integrity of the evidence. The suspect tool and mark must be packaged in separate containers, with every precaution taken to avoid contact between the tool or mark and another hard surface. Failure to properly protect the tool or mark from damage could result in the destruction of its individual

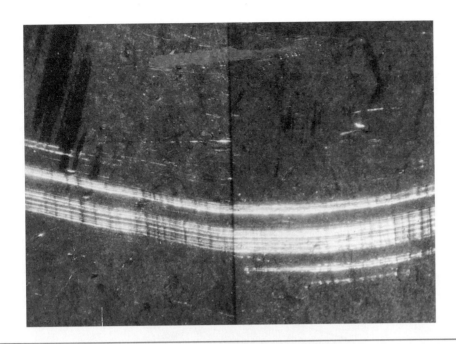

Figure 15–21   A photograph of a tool mark comparison seen under a comparison microscope.
Courtesy Leica Microsystems, Buffalo, N.Y., www.leica-microsystems.com

(a)   (b)

Figure 15–22   (a) Casting a tool mark impression with a silicone-based putty. (b) Impression alongside suspect tool. *Courtesy Sirchie Finger Print Laboratories, Inc., Youngsville, N.C., www.sirchie.com*

characteristics. Furthermore, the tool or its impression may contain valuable trace evidence. Chips of paint adhering to the mark or tool provide perhaps the best example of how the transfer of trace physical evidence can occur as a result of using a tool to gain forcible entry into a building. Obviously, the presence of trace evidence greatly enhances the evidential value of the tool or its mark and requires special care in handling and packaging the evidence to avoid losing or destroying these items.

Other Impressions

From time to time, impressions of another kind are left at a crime scene. This evidence may take the form of a shoe, tire, or fabric impression and may be as varied as a shoe impression left on a piece of paper at the scene of a burglary (Figure 15–23), a hit-and-run victim's garment that has come into violent contact with an automobile (Figure Figure 15–24), or the impression of a bloody shoe print left on a floor or carpet at a homicide scene (Figure 15–25).

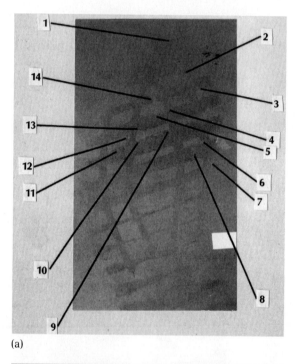

(a)

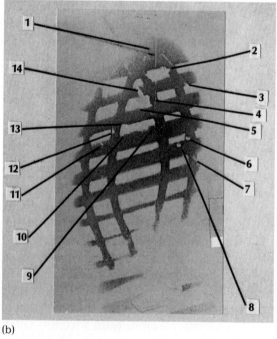

(b)

Figure 15–23   (a) Impression of shoe found at a crime scene. (b) Test impression made with suspect shoe. A sufficient number of points of comparison exist to support the conclusion that the suspect shoe left the impression at the crime scene.

Figure 15–24 A small child was found dead at the edge of a rural road near a railroad crossing, the victim of a hit-and-run driver. A local resident was suspected, but he denied any knowledge of the incident. The investigating officer noted what appeared to be a fabric imprint on the bumper of the suspect's automobile. The weave pattern of the clothing of the deceased was compared with the imprint on the bumper and was found to match. When the suspect was confronted with this information, he admitted his guilt. *Courtesy Centre for Forensic Sciences, Toronto, Canada*

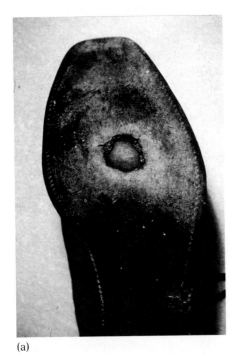

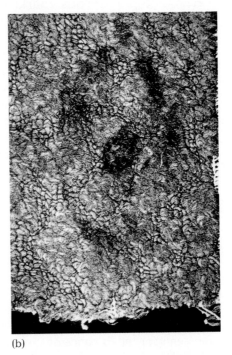

(a) (b)

Figure 15–25 A bloody imprint of a shoe was found on the carpet in the home of a homicide victim (b). The suspect's shoe, shown in (a), made the impression. Note the distinctive impression of the hole present in the shoe's sole. *Courtesy Dade County Crime Lab, Miami, Fla.*

The primary consideration in collecting impressions at the crime scene is the preservation of the impression or its reproduction for later examination in the crime laboratory. Before any impression is moved or otherwise handled, it must be photographed (a scale should be included in the picture) to show all the observable details of the impression. Several shots should be taken directly over the impression as well as at various angles around the impression. The skillful use of side lighting for illumination will help highlight many ridge details that might otherwise remain obscured. Photographs should also be taken to show the position of the questioned impression in relation to the overall crime scene.

Although photography is an important first step in preserving an impression, it must be considered merely a backup procedure that is available to the examiner if the impression is damaged before reaching the crime laboratory. Naturally, it is preferable for the examiner to receive the original impression for comparison to the suspect shoe, tire, garment, and so forth. In most cases when the impression is on a readily recoverable item, such as glass, paper, or floor tile, little or no difficulty is presented in transporting the evidence intact to the laboratory.

If an impression is encountered on a surface that cannot be submitted to the laboratory, the investigator may be able to preserve the print in a manner that is analogous to lifting a fingerprint. This is especially true of impressions made in light deposits of dust or dirt. A lifting material large enough to lift the entire impression should be used. Carefully place the lifting material over the entire impression. Use a fingerprint roller to eliminate any air pockets before lifting the impression off the surface.

A more exotic approach to lifting and preserving dust impressions involves the use of a portable electrostatic lifting device.[8] The principle employed is similar to that of creating an electrostatic charge on a comb and using the comb to lift small pieces of tissue paper. A mylar sheet of film is placed on top of the dust mark, and the film is pressed against the impression with the aid of a roller. The high-voltage electrode of the electrostatic unit is then placed in contact with the film while the unit's earth electrodes are placed against a metal plate (earth plate) (see Figure 15–26). A charge difference develops between the mylar film and the surface below the dust mark so that the dust is attached to the lifting film. In this manner, dust prints on chairs, walls, floors, and the like can be transferred to the mylar film. Floor surfaces up to 40 feet long can be covered with a mylar sheet and searched for dust impressions. The electrostatic lifting technique is particularly helpful in recovering barely visible dust prints on colored surfaces. Dust impressions can also be enhanced through chemical development (see Figure 15–27).[9]

When shoe and tire marks are impressed into soft earth at a crime scene, their preservation is best accomplished by photography and casting.[10] Class I dental stone, a form of gypsum, is widely recommended for

---

[8] See R. Milne, "Electrostatic Lifting of Marks at Crime Scenes and the Development of Pathfinder," *Science & Justice* 38 (1998): 135.

[9] B. Glattstein, Y. Shor, N. Levin, and A. Zeichner, "pH Indicators as Chemical Reagents for the Enhancement of Footwear Marks," *Journal of Forensic Sciences* 41 (1996): 23.

[10] D. S. Hilderbrand and M. Miller, "Casting Materials—Which One to Use?" *Journal of Forensic Identification* 45 (1995): 618.

Figure 15–26 **Electrostatic lifting of a dust impression off a floor using an electrostatic unit.**
Courtesy Sirchie Finger Print Laboratories, Inc., Youngsville, N.C., www.sirchie.com

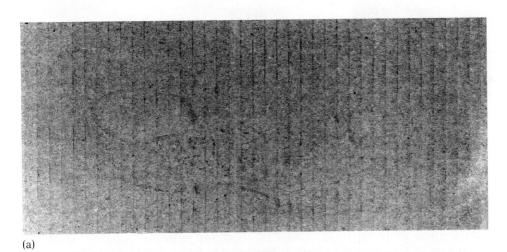

(a)

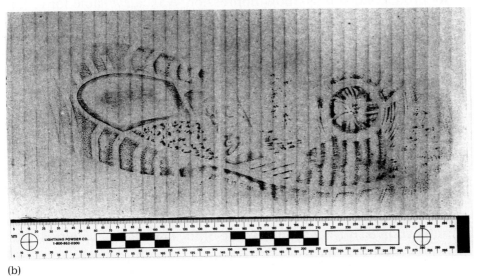

(b)

Figure 15–27 **(a) A dust impression of a shoe print on cardboard before enhancement. (b) Shoe print after chemical enhancement with Bromophenol Blue and exposure to water vapor.** *Courtesy Division of Identification and Forensic Science, Israel Police Headquarters, Jerusalem, Israel*

(a)   (b)   (c)

Figure 15–28   (a) Shoe impression in mud. (b) Cast of shoe impression. (c) Shoe suspected of leaving muddy impression. *Courtesy Sirchie Finger Print Laboratories, Inc., Youngsville, N.C., www.sirchie.com*

making casts of shoe and tire impressions. A series of photographs clearly illustrating the steps to be carried out in the casting of an impression may be found at *www.sccja.org/csr-cast.htm*. The cast should be allowed to air-dry for twenty-four to forty-eight hours before it is shipped to the forensic science laboratory for examination. Figure 15–28 illustrates a cast made from a shoe print in mud. The cast compares to the suspect shoe. An aerosol product known as Snow Impression Wax is available for casting snow impressions.[11] The recommended procedure is to spray three light coats of the wax at an interval of one to two minutes between layers and then let it dry for ten minutes. A viscous mixture of Class I dental stone is then poured onto the wax-coated impression. After the casting material has hardened, the cast can be removed.

A number of chemicals can be used to develop and enhance footwear impressions made with blood. In areas where a bloody footwear impression is very faint or where the subject has tracked through blood leaving a trail of bloody impressions, chemical enhancement can visualize latent or nearly invisible blood impressions (see Figure 15–29). A number of chemical formulas useful for bloody footwear impression development are listed in Appendix V.

A number of blood enhancement chemicals have been examined for their impact on STR DNA typing. None of the chemicals examined had a

---

[11] Available from Sirchie Finger Print Laboratories, Inc., Youngsville, N.C.

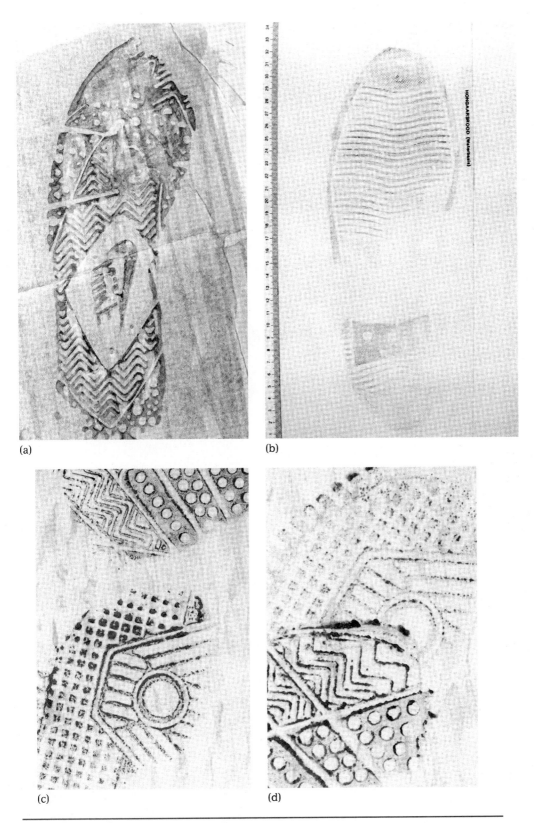

(a)

(b)

(c)

(d)

Figure 15–29   (a) Bloody footprint on cardboard treated with amido black. (b) Bloody footprint treated with Hungarian Red dye. (c) Bloody footprint visualized with leucocrystal violet. (d) Bloody footprint enhanced with patent blue. *(a) Courtesy Dwane S. Hilderbrand and David P. Coy, Scottsdale Police Crime Laboratory, Scottsdale, Ariz. (b) Courtesy ODV Inc., South Paris, Maine. (c–h) Courtesy William Bodziak, FBI Laboratory*

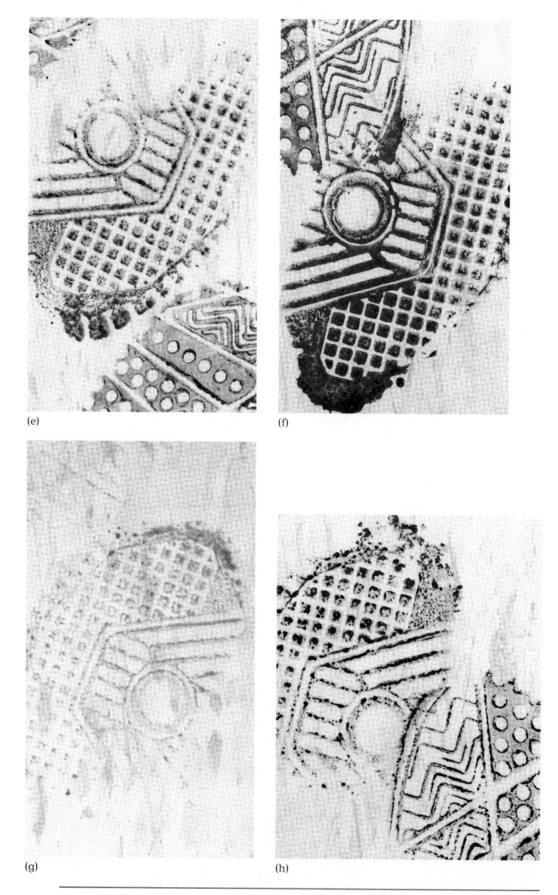

(e)

(f)

(g)

(h)

Figure 15–29 *(cont'd.)* (e) Bloody foot impression treated with amido black. (f) Bloody footprint visualized with fushin acid dye. (g) Bloody foot impression visualized with tartrazine. (h) Bloody footprint treated with diaminobenzidine.

deleterious effect, on a short-term basis, on the ability to carry out STR DNA typing on the blood.[12]

Whatever the circumstances, the laboratory procedures used for examining any type of impression remain the same. Of course, a comparison is possible only when an item suspected of having made the impression is recovered. Test impressions may be necessary to compare the characteristics of the suspect item with the evidence impression. The evidential value of the impression is determined by the number of class and individual characteristics that the examiner finds. Agreement with respect to size, shape, or design may permit the conclusion that the impression could have been made by a particular shoe, tire, or garment; however, one cannot entirely exclude other possible sources from having the same class characteristics. More significant is the existence of individual characteristics arising out of wear, cuts, gouges, or other damage. A sufficient number or the uniqueness of such points of comparison support a finding that both the evidence and test impressions originated from one and only one source.

When tire tread impressions are left at a crime scene, the laboratory can examine the design of the impression and possibly determine the style and/or manufacturer of the tire. This may be particularly helpful to investigators when a suspect tire has not yet been located.

New computer software may be able to help the forensic scientist make shoe print comparisons. For example, an automated shoe print identification system developed in England, called Shoeprint Image Capture and Retrieval (SICAR), incorporates multiple databases to search known and unknown footwear files for comparison against footwear specimens. Using the system, an impression from a crime scene can be compared to a reference database to find out what type of shoe caused the imprint. That same impression can also be searched in the suspect and crime databases to reveal whether that shoe print matches the shoes of a person who has been in custody or the shoe prints left behind at another crime scene. When matches are made during the searching process, the images are displayed side by side on the computer screen (see Figure 3–5).

An excellent resource for shoe print and tire impression examiners is a Web site that has been assembled by the Chesapeake area shoe print and tire track examiners at *http://members.aol.com/varfee/mastssite/*. The Web site's goal is to enable examiners to enhance their footwear or tire track impression examinations by providing references, databases, and links to manufacturers, experts, vendors, trade associations, and professional societies connected to these forensic disciplines.

Human bite mark impressions on skin and foodstuffs have proven to be important items of evidence for convicting defendants in a number of homicide and rape cases in recent years. If a sufficient number of points of similarity between test and suspect marks are present, a forensic odontologist may conclude that a bite mark was made by one particular individual (see Figure 15–30).

WebExtra 15.7

Casting a Footwear Impression
www.prenhall.com/Saferstein

---

[12] C. J. Frégeau et al., "Fingerprint Enhancement Revisited and the Effects of Blood Enhancement Chemicals on Subsequent Profiler Plus™ Fluorescent Short Tandem Repeat DNA Analysis of Fresh and Aged Bloody Fingerprints," *Journal of Forensic Sciences* 45 (2000): 354.

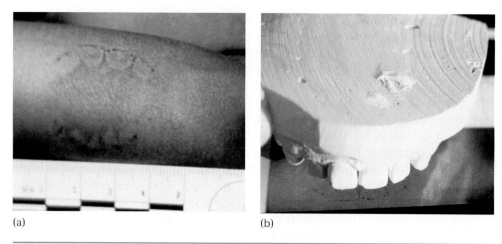

(a)

(b)

Figure 15–30 **(a) Bite mark impression on the victim's fore-arm. (b) Upper dental model from the teeth of the suspect matches the individual teeth characteristics of the bite marks.** *Courtesy Haskin Askin, D.D.S., Chief Forensic Odontologist, City of Philadelphia, Pa.*

Chapter Summary

Structural variations and irregularities caused by scratches, nicks, breaks, and wear permit the criminalist to relate a bullet to a gun; a scratch or abrasion mark to a single tool; or a tire track to a particular automobile. The manufacture of a barrel requires impressing its inner surface with spiral grooves, a step known as rifling. The surfaces of the original bore remaining between the grooves are called lands. No two rifled barrels, even those manufactured in succession, have identical striation markings. These striations form the individual characteristics of the barrel. The inner surface of the barrel of a gun leaves its striation markings on a bullet passing through it. The number of lands and grooves and their direction of twist are obvious points of comparison during the initial stages of an examination. Any differences in these class characteristics immediately eliminate the possibility that both bullets traveled through the same barrel.

The comparison microscope is the most important tool to a firearms examiner. Two bullets can be observed and compared simultaneously within the same field of view. Not only must the lands and grooves of the test and evidence bullet have identical widths, but the longitudinal striations on each must coincide. The firing pin, breechblock, and ejector and extractor mechanism also offer a highly distinctive signature for individualization of cartridge cases. The advent of computerized imaging technology has made possible the storage of bullet and cartridge surface characteristics in a manner analogous to automated fingerprint files. However, the final comparison will be made by the forensic examiner through traditional microscopic methods.

The distribution of gunpowder particles and other discharge residues around a bullet hole permits an assessment of the distance from which a handgun or rifle was fired. The firing of a weapon not only propels residues toward the target, but also blows gunpowder and primer residues back toward the shooter. As a result, traces of these residues are often deposited on the firing hand of the shooter, and their detection can provide valuable information as to whether an individual has recently fired a weapon. Examiners measure the amount of barium and antimony on the relevant portion of the suspect's hands or characterize the morphology of particles containing these elements to determine whether a person has fired or handled a weapon, or was near a discharged firearm.

Increasingly, the criminalist is asked to restore a serial number that has been obliterated by grinding, rifling, or punching. Restoration of serial numbers is possible through chemical etching because the metal crystals in the stamped zone are placed under a permanent strain that extends a short distance beneath the original numbers.

A tool mark is any impression, cut, gouge, or abrasion caused by a tool coming into contact with another object. Hence any minute imperfections on a tool impart individuality to that tool. The shape and pattern of such imperfections are further modified by damage and wear during the life of the tool. The comparison microscope is used to compare crime-scene toolmarks with test impressions made with the suspect tool. When shoe and tire marks are impressed into soft earth at a crime scene, their preservation is best accomplished by photography and casting. In areas where a bloody footwear impression is very faint or where the subject has tracked through blood, leaving a trail of bloody impressions, chemical enhancement can visualize latent or nearly invisible blood impressions. A sufficient number of points of comparison or the uniqueness of such points support a finding that both the questioned and test impressions originated from one and only one source.

Review Questions

1. The _____ is the original part of the bore left after rifling grooves are formed.
2. The diameter of the gun barrel is known as its _____.
3. The number of lands and grooves is a(n) (class, individual) characteristic of a barrel.
4. The (individual, class) characteristics of a rifled barrel are formed by striations impressed into the barrel's surface.
5. The most important instrument for comparing bullets is the _____.
6. True or False: On bullets fired in succession from the same weapon, all of the individual characteristics are always identical. _____
7. It is (always, sometimes) possible to determine the make of a weapon by examining a bullet it fired.
8. A shotgun has a (rifled, smooth) barrel.
9. The diameter of a shotgun barrel is expressed by the term _____.
10. True or False: Shotgun pellets can be individualized to a single weapon. _____
11. A cartridge case (can, cannot) be individualized to a single weapon.
12. True or False: The shape of the indentation caused by the firing pin may be a characteristic peculiar to a firearm. _____

13. True or False: The distribution of gunpowder particles and other discharge residues around a bullet hole permits an approximate determination of the distance from which the gun was fired. _____

14. True or False: Without the benefit of a weapon, an examiner can make an exact determination of firing distance. _____

15. A halo of vaporous lead (smoke) deposited around a bullet hole normally indicates a discharge _____ to _____ inches from the target.

16. A(n) _____ photograph may help visualize gunpowder deposits around a target.

17. True or False: One test method for locating powder residues involves transferring particles embedded on the target surface to chemically treated photographic paper. _____

18. As a rule of thumb, the spread in the pattern made by a 12-gauge shotgun increases one inch for every _____ of distance from the target.

19. Current methods for identifying a shooter rely on the detection of (primer, gunpowder) residues on the hands.

20. Determining whether an individual has fired a weapon is done by measuring the elements _____ and _____ present on the hands.

21. True or False: Firings with all types of ammunition can be detected by hand swabbings with nitric acid. _____

22. True or False: Restoration of serial numbers is possible because in the stamped zone the metal is placed under a permanent strain that extends beneath the original numbers. _____

23. It (is, is not) proper to insert a pencil into the barrel when picking up a crime-scene gun.

24. Recovered bullets are initialed on either the _____ or _____ of the bullet.

25. True or False: Cartridge cases are best marked at the base of the shell. _____

26. The clothing of the victim of a shooting must be handled so as to prevent disruption of _____ around bullet holes.

27. A(n) _____ is any impression caused by a tool coming into contact with another object.

28. Tool marks compare only when a sufficient number of _____ match between the evidence and test markings.

29. A wear pattern can impart (class, individual) characteristics to a shoe.

30. Shoe and tire marks impressed into soft earth at a crime scene are best preserved by _____ and _____.

Further References

An Introduction to Forensic Firearm Identification, www.firearmsid.com.

Bodziak, William J., *Footwear Impression Evidence,* 2nd ed. Boca Raton, Fla.: Taylor & Francis, 1999.

McDonald, Peter, *Tire Imprint Evidence.* Boca Raton, Fla.: Taylor & Francis, 1989.

Rowe, Walter F., "Firearms Identification," in R. Saferstein, ed., *Forensic Science Handbook,* vol. 2, 2nd ed., Upper Saddle River, N.J.: Prentice Hall, 2005.

Schehl, S. A., "Firearms and Toolmarks in the FBI Laboratory," *Forensic Science Communications* 2, no. 2 (2000), http://www.fbi.gov/hq/lab/fsc/backissu/april2000/schehl1.htm.

The Unabomber

In 1978, a parcel addressed to a Northwestern University professor exploded as it was being opened by a campus security officer. This was the first of a series of bomb-containing packages sent to universities and airlines. The perpetrator was dubbed UN (university) A (airlines) BOM; hence, *the Unabomber.* The explosives were usually housed in a pipe within a wooden box. The explosive ingredients generally were black powder, smokeless powder, or an ammonium nitrate mix. The box was filled with metal objects to create a shrapnel effect on explosion. The device typically had the initials "FC" punched into it. The first Unabomber fatality came in 1985. The Unabomber surfaced again in 1993, mailing bombs to two university professors. Their injuries were not fatal, but his next two attacks did result in fatalities.

In 1995, the case took an unexpected turn when the Unabomber promised to end his mad spree if his 35,000-page typewritten "Manifesto" sent to the *New York Times* and *The Washington Post* were published. The *Manifesto* proved to be a long, rambling rant against technology, but it offered valuable clues that broke the case. David Kaczynski realized that the *Manifesto's* writing style and the philosophy it espoused closely resembled that of his brother Ted. Linguistic experts carefully pored over the *Manifesto's* content. Ted Kaczynski was arrested in Montana in 1996. Inside his ramshackle cabin were writings similar to the *Manifesto,* three manual typewriters, and bomb-making materials. Forensic document examiners matched the typewritten *Manifesto* to one of the typewriters recovered from the cabin.

chapter 16

Document and Voice Examination

Key Terms

charred document

erasure

exemplar

indented writings

infrared luminescence

natural variations

obliteration

questioned document

voiceprint

Questioned Document
Any document about which some issue has been raised or that is the subject of an investigation.

Ordinarily, the work of the document examiner involves examining of handwriting and typescript to ascertain the source or authenticity of a questioned document. However, document examination is not restricted to a mere visual comparison of words and letters. The document examiner must know how to use the techniques of microscopy, photography, and even such analytical methods as chromatography to uncover successfully all efforts, both brazen and subtle, designed to change the content or meaning of a document. Alterations of documents through overwriting, erasures, or the more obvious crossing out of words must be recognized and characterized as efforts to alter or obscure the original meaning of a document. The document examiner uses his or her special skills to reconstruct the written contents of charred or burned paper or to uncover the meaning of indented writings found on a paper pad after the top sheet has been removed.

Any object that contains handwritten or typewritten markings whose source or authenticity is in doubt may be referred to as a **questioned document**. Such a broad definition covers all of the written and printed materials we normally encounter in our daily social and business activities. Letters, checks, drivers' licenses, contracts, wills, voter registrations, passports, petitions, and even lottery tickets are the more common specimens received in crime laboratories to be examined. However, we need not restrict our examples to paper documents. Questioned documents may include writings or other markings found on walls, windows, doors, or any other objects.

Document examiners possess no mystical powers or scientific formulas for identifying the authors of writings. They apply knowledge gathered through years of training and experience to recognize and compare the individual characteristics of questioned and known authentic writings. For this purpose, the gathering of documents of known authorship or origin is critical to the outcome of the examination. Collecting known writings may entail considerable time and effort, and their collection may be further hampered by uncooperative or missing witnesses. However, the uniqueness of handwriting makes this type of physical evidence, like fingerprints, one of few definitive individual characteristics available to the investigator, a fact that certainly justifies an extensive investigative effort.

Handwriting Comparisons

Document experts continually testify that no two individuals write exactly alike. This is not to say that there cannot be marked resemblances between two individuals' handwritings, because many factors make up the total character of a person's writing. Perhaps the most obvious feature of handwriting to the layperson is its general style. As children we all learn to write by attempting to copy letters that match a standard form or style shown to us by our teachers. The style of writing acquired by the learner is that which is fashionable for the particular time and locale. In the United States, for example, the two most widely used systems are the Palmer method, first introduced in 1880, and the Zaner-Blosser method, introduced in about 1895. To some extent, both of these systems are taught in nearly all fifty states.

The early stages that accompany the learning and practicing of handwriting are characterized by a conscious effort on the part of the student to copy standard letter forms. It is not surprising that many pupils in a handwriting class tend at first to have writing styles that are similar to one another, with minor differences attributable to skill in copying. However, as initial writing skills improve, a child normally reaches the stage where the nerve and motor responses associated with the act of writing become subconscious. The individual's writing now begins to take on innumerable habitual shapes and patterns that distinguish it from all others. The document examiner looks for these unique writing traits.

The unconscious handwriting of two different individuals can never be identical. Individual variations associated with mechanical, physical, and mental functions make it extremely unlikely that all of these factors can be exactly reproduced by any two people. Thus, variations are expected in angularity, slope, speed, pressure, letter and word spacings, relative dimensions of letters, connections, pen movement, writing skill, and finger dexterity. Furthermore, many other factors besides pure handwriting characteristics should be considered. The arrangement of the writing on the paper may be as distinctive as the writing itself. Margins, spacings, crowding, insertions, and alignment are all results of personal habits. Spelling, punctuation, phraseology, and grammar can be personal and, if so, combine to individualize the writer.

In a problem involving the authorship of handwriting, all characteristics of both the known and questioned documents must be considered and compared. Dissimilarities between the two writings are a strong indication of two writers, unless these differences can logically be accounted for by the facts surrounding the preparation of the documents. Because any single characteristic, even the most distinctive one, may be found in the handwriting of other individuals, no single handwriting characteristic can by itself be taken as the basis for a positive comparison. The final conclusion must be based on a sufficient number of common characteristics between the known and questioned writings to effectively preclude the chance of their having originated from two different sources.

What constitutes a sufficient number of personal characteristics? Here again, there are no hard-and-fast rules for making such a determination. The expert examiner can make this judgment only in the context of each particular case.

When the examiner receives a reasonable amount of known handwriting for comparison, there is usually little difficulty in finding sufficient evidence to determine the source of a questioned document. Frequently, however, circumstances may prevent a positive conclusion or may permit only the expression of a qualified opinion. Such situations usually develop when an insufficient number of known writings are made available for comparison. Although nothing may be found that definitely points to the questioned and known handwriting being of a different origin, not enough personal characteristics may be present in the known writings that are consistent with the questioned materials.

Difficulties may also arise when the examiner receives questioned writings containing only a few words, all deliberately written in a crude, unnatural form or all very carefully written and thought out so as to disguise the writer's natural style—a situation usually encountered with threatening or obscene letters. It is extremely difficult to compare handwriting that has been very carefully prepared to a document written with such little thought for structural details that it contains only the subconscious writing habits of the writer. However, although it may be relatively easy to change one's writing habits for a few words or sentences, the task of maintaining such an effort grows more difficult with each additional word. When an adequate amount of writing is available to the examiner, the attempt at total disguise may fail. This was illustrated in the attempt by Clifford Irving to forge letters in the name of the late industrialist Howard Hughes in order to obtain lucrative publishing contracts for Hughes's life story. Figure 16–1 shows the forged signatures of Howard Hughes along with Clifford Irving's known writings. By comparing these signatures, document examiner R. A. Cabbane of the U.S. Postal Inspection Service detected many examples of Irving's personal characteristics in the forged signatures. For example, note the formation of the letter *r* in the word *Howard* on lines 1 and 3, as compared with the composite on line 6. Observe the manner in which the terminal stroke of the letter *r* tends to terminate with a little curve at the baseline of Irving's writing and the forgery. Notice the way the bridge of the *w* drops in line 1 and also in line 6. Also, observe the similarity in the formation of the letter *g* as it appears on line 1 as compared with the second signature on line 5.

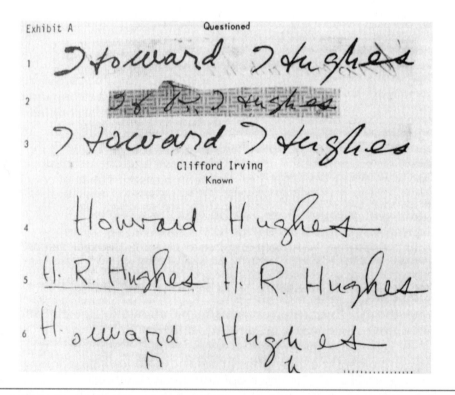

Figure 16–1   Forged signatures of Howard Hughes and examples of Clifford Irving's writing.
Reprinted by permission of the American Society for Testing and Materials from the Journal of Forensic Sciences, copyright 1975

The document examiner must also be aware that writing habits may be altered beyond recognition by the influence of drugs or alcohol. Under these circumstances, it may be impossible to obtain known writings of a suspect written under conditions comparable to those at the time the questioned document was prepared.

Collection of Handwriting Exemplars

It should be fairly obvious by now that collection of an adequate number of known writings (exemplars) is most critical for determining the outcome of a comparison. Generally, known writings of the suspect furnished to the examiner should be as similar as possible to the questioned document. This is especially true with respect to the writing implement and paper. Styles and habits may be somewhat altered if a person switches from a pencil to a ballpoint pen or to a fountain pen. The way the paper is ruled, or the fact that it is unruled, may also affect the handwriting of a person who has become particularly accustomed to one type or the other. Known writings should also contain some of the words and combinations of letters present in the questioned document.

The known writings must be adequate in number to show the examiner the range of natural variations in a suspect's writing characteristics. No two specimens of writing prepared by one person are ever identical in every detail. Variation is an inherent part of natural writing. In fact, a signature forged by tracing an authentic signature can often be detected even if the original and tracing coincide exactly, because no one ever signs two signatures exactly alike.

Many sources are available to the investigator for establishing the authenticity of the writings of a suspect. An important consideration in selecting sample writings is the age of the genuine document relative to the questioned one. It is important to try to find standards that date closely in time to the questioned document. For most typical adults, basic writing changes are comparatively slow. Therefore, material written within two or three years of the disputed writing is usually satisfactory for comparison; as the age difference between the genuine and unknown specimens becomes greater, the standard tends to become less representative.

Despite the many potential sources of handwriting exemplars, it may be difficult or impossible to obtain an adequate set of collected standards. In these situations, handwriting may have to be obtained voluntarily or under court order from the suspect. There is ample case law to support the constitutionality of taking handwriting specimens. In the case of *Gilbert* v. *California,*[1] the Supreme Court upheld the taking of handwriting exemplars before the appointment of counsel. The Court also reasoned that handwriting samples are identifying physical characteristics that lie outside the protection privileges of the Fifth Amendment. Furthermore, in the case of *United States* v. *Mara,*[2] the Supreme Court ruled that taking a handwriting sample did not constitute an unreasonable search and seizure of a person and hence did not violate Fourth Amendment rights.

Exemplar
An authentic sample used for comparison purposes, such as handwriting.

Natural Variations
Normal deviations found between repeated specimens of an individual's handwriting or any printing device.

---

[1] 388 U.S. 263 (1967).
[2] 410 U.S. 19 (1973).

As opposed to nonrequested specimens (written without the thought that they may someday be used in a police investigation), requested writing samples may be consciously altered by the writer. However, the investigator can take certain steps to minimize attempts at deception. The requirement of several pages of writing normally provides enough material that is free of attempts at deliberate disguise or nervousness for a valid comparison. In addition, the writing of dictation yields exemplars that best represent the suspect's subconscious style and characteristics.

Other steps that can be taken to minimize a conscious writing effort, as well as to ensure conditions approximating those of the questioned writing, can be summarized as follows:

1. The writer should be allowed to write sitting comfortably at a desk or table and without distraction.

2. The suspect should not under any conditions be shown the questioned document or be told how to spell certain words or what punctuation to use.

3. The suspect should be furnished a pen and paper similar to those used in the questioned document.

4. The dictated text should be the same as the contents of the questioned document, or at least should contain many of the same words, phrases, and letter combinations found in the document. In handprinting cases, the suspect must not be told whether to use uppercase (capital) or lowercase (small) lettering. If after writing several pages the writer fails to use the desired type of lettering, he or she can then be instructed to include it. Altogether, the text must be no shorter than a page.

5. Dictation of the text should take place at least three times. If the writer is trying to disguise the writing, noticeable variations should appear among the three repetitions. Discovering this, the investigator must insist on continued repetitive dictation of the text.

6. Signature exemplars can best be obtained when the suspect is required to combine other writings with a signature. For example, instead of compiling a set of signatures alone, the writer might be asked to fill out completely twenty to thirty separate checks or receipts, each of which includes a signature.

7. Before requested exemplars are taken from the suspect, a document examiner should be consulted and shown the questioned specimens.

Typescript Comparisons

One mechanical writing device the document examiner encounters is the typewriter, although it is not as prevalent as it used to be. Examiners are most often asked the following two questions about typewriters: (1) Can the make and model of the typewriter used to type the questioned document be identified? (2) Can a particular suspect typewriter be identified as having prepared the questioned document?

To answer the first question, the examiner must have access to a complete reference collection of past and present typefaces used by typewriter manufacturers. The two most popular typeface sizes are pica (10 letters to the inch) and elite (12 letters to the inch). Although a dozen manufacturers may use a pica or an elite typeface, many of these are readily distinguishable when the individual type character's style, shape, and size are compared.

As is true for any mechanical device, use of a typewriter will result in wear and damage to the machine's moving parts. These changes occur both randomly and irregularly, thereby imparting individual characteristics to the typewriter. Variations in vertical and horizontal alignment (characters are too high or low or too far left or right of their correct position) and perpendicular misalignment of characters (characters leaning to the left or to the right), as well as defects in each typeface, are most valuable for proving the identity of a typewriter (see Figure 16–2).

The widespread use of business and personal computers is creating a series of new problems to challenge the skills of the document examiner. Personal computers use daisy wheel, dot-matrix, ink-jet, and laser printers. More and more, the document examiner encounters problems involving these machines, which often produce typed copies that have only inconspicuous defects.

Associating a particular typewriter with a typewritten document requires comparing the questioned document to exemplars prepared from the suspect typewriter. As with handwriting, collection of proper standards is the foundation of such comparisons. In this respect, it is preferable if the investigator can directly supply the document examiner with the questioned typewriter. This arrangement gives the examiner the opportunity to prepare an adequate number of exemplars and also allows direct examination of the machine's typefaces. If the investigator has to prepare standards from the questioned machine, a minimum of one copy in full word-for-word order of the questioned typewriting must be obtained.

Another area of investigation relates to the ribbon. An examination of the type impressions left on a ribbon may reveal the portion of the ribbon on which a particular text was typed.

When the suspect typewriter is not available for examination, the investigator must gather known writings that have been typed on the suspect machine. Ideally, material should be selected that contains many of the same combinations of letters and words found on the questioned document. The individual defects that characterize a typewriter develop and change as the machine is used; some may have changed between the preparation of the questioned and standard material. Hence, if many specimens are available, those prepared near the time of the disputed document should be collected.

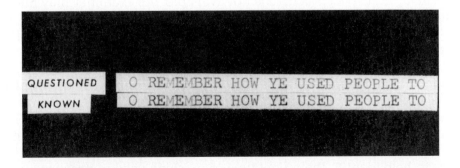

Figure 16–2   A portion of a typewriting comparison points to the conclusion that the same machine typed both specimens. Besides the similarity in the design and size of type, note the light impression consistently made by the letter *M*. Also, the letter *E* slants to the right, almost touching *D* in the word *USED* in both specimens. *Courtesy New Jersey State Police*

Photocopier, Printer, and Fax Examination

With the emergence of digital technology, document examiners are confronted with a new array of machines capable of creating documents subject to alteration or fraudulent use. In the cases of photocopiers, fax machines, and computer printers, an examiner may need to identify the make and model of a machine that may have been used in printing a document. Alternatively, the examiner may need to compare a questioned document with test samples printed from a suspect machine. Typically, the examiner generates approximately ten samples through each machine to obtain a sufficient representation of a photocopier's characters. A side-by-side comparison is then made between the questioned document and the printed exemplars to compare markings produced by the machine.

Transitory defect marks originating from random debris on the glass platen, inner cover, or mechanical portions of a copier produce images. These images are often irregularly shaped and sometimes form distinctive patterns. Thus, they become points of comparison as the document examiner attempts to link the document to suspect copiers. The gradual change, shift, or duplication of these marks may aid the examiner in dating the document.

In analyzing computer printouts and faxes, examiners use the same approach for comparing the markings on a questioned document to exemplar documents generated by a suspect machine. These markings include all possible transitory patterns arising from debris and other extraneous materials. Interestingly, fax machines print a header known as the *transmitting terminal identifier* (TTI) at the top of each fax page. For the document examiner, the TTI is a very important point of comparison. The header and the document's text should have different type styles. TTIs can be fraudulently prepared and placed in the appropriate position on a fax copy. However, a microscopic examination of the TTI's print quickly reveals significant characteristics that distinguish it from a genuine TTI. In determining the fax machine's model type, the examiner most often begins by analyzing the TTI type style. The fonts of that line are determined by the sending machine. The number of characters, their style, and their position in the header are best evaluated through a collection of TTI fonts organized into a useful database. One such database is maintained by the American Society of Questioned Document Examiners.

When the suspect machine is not available, the examiner may need to analyze the document's class characteristics to identify the make and model of the machine. It is important to identify the printing technology, the type of paper, the type of toner or ink used, the chemical composition of the toner, and the type of toner-to-paper fusing method used in producing the document. Examination of the toner usually involves microscopic analysis to characterize its surface morphology, followed by identification of the inorganic and organic components of the toner. These results separate model types into categories based on their mechanical and printing characteristics. Typically, document examiners access databases to help identify the model type of machine used to prepare a questioned document. The resulting list of possibilities produced by the database hopefully reduces the number of potential machines to a manageable number. Obviously, once a suspect machine is identified, the examiner must perform a side-by-side comparison of questioned and exemplar printouts as described previously.

Computer printer model determination requires an extensive analysis of the specific printer technology and type of ink used. Visual and microscopic techniques provide useful information in determining the technology and toner used. Generally, printers are categorized as impact and nonimpact printers by the mechanism of their toner application. Nonimpact printers, such as ink-jet and laser printers, and impact printers, such as thermal and dot-matrix printers, all have characteristic ways of printing documents. Character shapes, toner differentiation, and toner application methods are easily determined with a low-power microscope and help the examiner narrow the possibilities of model type.

Alterations, Erasures, and Obliterations

Documents are often altered or changed after preparation so that their original intent may be hidden or so that a forgery may be perpetrated. Documents can be changed in several ways, and for each way, the application of a special discovery technique is necessary.

One of the most common ways to alter a document is to try to erase parts of it, using an India rubber eraser, sandpaper, razor blade, or knife to remove writing or type by abrading or scratching the paper's surface. All such attempts at erasure disturb the upper fibers of the paper. These changes are apparent when the suspect area is examined under a microscope using direct light or by allowing the light to strike the paper obliquely from one side (side lighting). Although microscopy may reveal whether an erasure has been made, it does not necessarily indicate the original letters or words present. Sometimes so much of the paper has been removed that identifying the original contents is impossible.

Erasure
The removal of writing, typewriting, or printing from a document. It is normally accomplished by either chemical means or an abrasive instrument.

In addition to abrading the paper, the perpetrator may also choose to obliterate words with a chemical erasure. In this case, strong oxidizing agents are placed over the ink, producing a colorless reaction product. Although such an attempt may not be noticeable to the naked eye, examination under the microscope reveals a discoloration on the treated area of the paper. Sometimes examination of the document under ultraviolet or infrared lighting reveals the chemically treated portion of the paper. Interestingly, examination of documents under ultraviolet light may also reveal the presence of fluorescent ink markings that go unnoticed in room light, as seen in Figure 16–3.

Some inks, when exposed to blue-green light, absorb the radiation and reradiate infrared light. This phenomenon is known as infrared luminescence. Thus, if an alteration is made to a document with ink differing from the original, it can sometimes be detected by illuminating the document with blue-green light and using infrared-sensitive film to record the light emanating from the document's surface. In this fashion, any differences in the luminescent properties of the inks are observed (see Figure 16–4). Infrared luminescence has also revealed writing that has been erased. Such writings may be recorded by invisible residues of the original ink that remain embedded in the paper even after an erasure.

Infrared Luminescence
A property exhibited by some dyes that emit infrared light when exposed to blue-green light.

Figure 16–3 (a) A twenty-dollar bill as it appears under room light. (b) The bill illuminated with ultraviolet light reveals ink writing. *Courtesy Sirchie Finger Print Laboratories, Inc., Youngsville, N.C., www.sirchie.com*

(a)

(b)

Obliteration

The blotting out or smearing over of writing or printing to make the original unreadable.

Another important application of infrared photography arises from the observation that inks may differ in their ability to absorb infrared light. Thus, illuminating a document with infrared light and recording the light reflected off the document's surface with infrared-sensitive film may enable the examiner to differentiate inks of a dissimilar chemical composition (see Figure 16–5).

Intentional obliteration of writing by overwriting or crossing out is seldom used for fraudulent purposes because of its obviousness. Nevertheless, such cases may be encountered in all types of documents. Success at permanently hiding the original writing depends on the material used to cover the writing. If it is done with the same ink as was used to write the original material, recovery will be difficult if not impossible. However, if the two inks are of a different chemical composition, photography with infrared-sensitive film may reveal the original writing. Infrared radiation may pass through the upper layer of writing while being absorbed by the underlying area (see Figure 16–6).

Close examination of a questioned document sometimes reveals crossing strokes or strokes across folds of perforations in the paper that are not in a sequence that is consistent with the natural preparation of the document. Again, these differences can be shown by microscopic or photographic scrutiny.

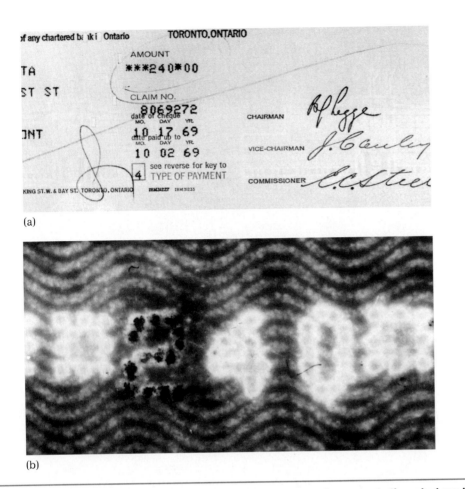

(a)

(b)

Figure 16–4 Part of a check stolen from a government agency as it appears to the naked eye is shown in (a). An infrared luminescence photograph was prepared of the amount figures at a magnification of 10× in (b). This clearly shows that the number 2 was added with a different ink. The accused pleaded guilty. *Courtesy Centre of Forensic Sciences, Toronto, Canada*

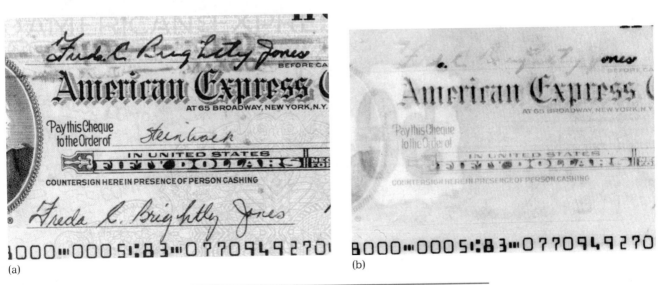

(a)

(b)

Figure 16–5 (a) This photograph, taken under normal illumination, shows the owner of an American Express check to be "Freda C. Brightly Jones." Actually, this signature was altered. The check initially bore the signature "Fred C. Brightly Jr." (b) This photograph taken under infrared illumination, using infrared-sensitive film, clearly shows that the check was altered by adding *a* to *Fred* and *ones* to *Jr*. The ink used to commit these changes is distinguishable because it absorbs infrared light, whereas the original ink does not. *Courtesy New Jersey State Police*

(a)

(b)

Figure 16–6 **(a) A photograph showing an area of a document that has been blacked out with a heavy layer of ink overwriting. (b) In this photograph, the covering ink has been penetrated by infrared photography to reveal the original writing.** *Courtesy Centre of Forensic Sciences, Toronto, Canada*

Charred Document
Any document that has become darkened and brittle through exposure to fire or excessive heat.

Infrared photography sometimes reveals the contents of a document that has been accidentally or purposely charred in a fire. Another way to decipher **charred documents** involves reflecting light off the paper's surface at different angles in order to contrast the writing against the charred background (see Figure 16–7).

Figure 16–7 **Decipherment of charred papers seized in the raid of a suspected bookmaking establishment. The charred documents were photographed with reflected light.** *Courtesy New Jersey State Police*

Digital image processing is the method by which the visual quality of digital pictures is improved or enhanced. *Digitizing* is the process by which the image is stored in memory. This is commonly done by scanning an image with a flatbed scanner or a digital camera and converting the image by computer into an array of digital intensity values called *pixels,* or picture elements (see p. 452). Once the image has been digitized, an image editing program such as Adobe Photoshop is used to adjust the image. An image may be enhanced through lightening,

ORIGINAL

EXCLUSION

LEVELS

SCREEN

CURVES

REPLACE COLOR

Figure 16–8 This composite demonstrates the various changes that can be applied to a digitized image in order to reveal information that has been obscured. Using a photo editor (Adobe Photoshop) the original was duplicated and pasted as a second layer. Colors were changed in selected areas of the image using the "screen" and "exclusion" options. "Replace color" allows the user to choose a specific color or range of colors and lighten, darken, or change the hue of the colors selected. "Level" and "curves" tools can adjust the lightest and darkest color ranges and optimize contrast, highlights, and shadow detail of the image for additional clarity. *Courtesy Lt. Robert J. Garrett, Middlesex County Prosecutor's Office, N.J.*

darkening, and color and contrast controls. An example of how the technology is applied to forensic document examination is shown in Figures 16–8 and 16–9.

Other Document Problems

Indented Writings

Impressions left on papers positioned under a piece of paper that has been written on.

Indented writings are the partially visible depressions on a sheet of paper underneath the one on which the visible writing was done. Such depressions are due to the application of pressure on the writing instrument

(a)

(b)

Figure 16–9   (a) Receipts have been used in investigations to establish a victim's whereabouts, provide suspects with alibis, and substantiate a host of personal conduct. Unfortunately, many times due to wear, age, or poor printing at the register, the receipt may be unreadable. This can be corrected using photo-editing software. In this example, the original toll receipt was scanned at the highest color resolution, which allows more than 16 million colors to be reproduced. The image was then manipulated, revealing the printed details, by adjusting the lightest and darkest levels and the color content of the image. (b) Invoices may contain details about a transaction that are important to an investigation. The copy that ships with the merchandise may have that information blocked out. This information may be recovered using digital imaging. The left figure shows the original shipping ticket. The right figure shows the information revealed after replacing the color of the blocking pattern. *Courtesy Lt. Robert J. Garrett, Middlesex County Prosecutor's Office, N.J.*

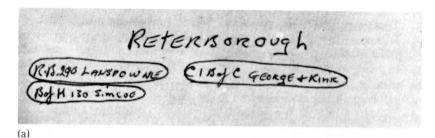

(a)

(b)

Figure 16–10 **A suspected forger was arrested. In his car, police found written lists of the victims he intended to defraud. Some of these writings are shown in (a). A writing pad found in his house had indentations on the top page of the pad shown in (b). These indentations corresponded to the writings found in the car, further linking the suspect to the writings.**
Courtesy Centre of Forensic Sciences, Toronto, Canada

and would appear as a carbon copy of a sheet if carbon paper had been inserted between the pages.

Indented writings have proved to be valuable evidence. For example, the top sheet of a bookmaker's records may have been removed and destroyed, but it still may be possible to determine the writing by the impressions left on the pad. These impressions may contain incriminating evidence supporting the charge of illegal gambling activities. When paper is studied under oblique or side lighting, its indented impressions are often readable (see Figure 16–10). An innovative approach to visualizing indented writings has been developed at the London College of Printing in close consultation with the Metropolitan Police Forensic Science Laboratory.[3] The method involves applying an electrostatic charge to the surface of a polymer film that has been placed in contact with a questioned document, as shown in Figure 16–11. Indented impressions on the document are revealed by applying a toner powder to the charged film. For many documents examined by this process, clearly readable images have been produced from impressions that could not be seen or were barely visible under normal illumination. An instrument that develops indented writings by electrostatic detection is commercially available and is routinely used by document examiners.

A study of the chemical composition of writing ink present on documents may verify whether known and questioned documents were prepared by the same pen. A nondestructive approach to comparing ink lines is accomplished with a visible microspectrophotometer (see pp.189–192).[4] A case example illustrating the application of this approach to ink analysis

---

[3] D. M. Ellen, D. J. Foster, and D. J. Morantz, "The Use of Electrostatic Imaging in the Detection of Indented Impressions," *Forensic Science International* 15 (1980): 53.

[4] P. W. Pfefferli, "Application of Microspectrophotometry in Document Examination," *Forensic Science International* 23 (1983): 129.

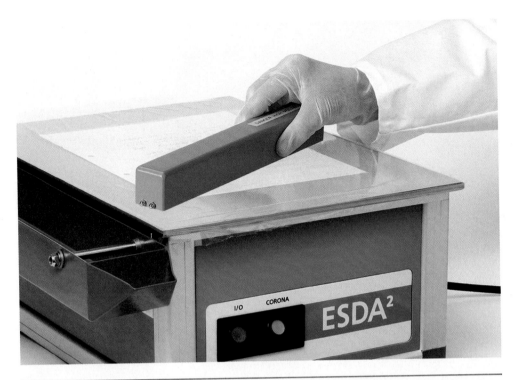

Figure 16–11   An electrostatic detection apparatus (ESDA) works by applying an electrostatic charge to a document suspected of containing indented writings. The indentations are then visualized by the application of charge-sensitive toner. *Courtesy Foster and Freeman Limited, Worcestershire, U.K., www.fosterfreeman.co.uk*

appears in Figure 7–10. Thin-layer chromatography is also suitable for ink comparisons. Most commercial inks, especially ballpoint inks, are actually mixtures of several organic dyes. These dyes can be separated on a properly developed thin-layer chromatographic plate. The separation pattern of the component dyes is distinctly different for inks with different dye compositions and thus provides many points of comparison between a known and a questioned ink.

Ink can be removed from paper with a hypodermic needle with a blunted point to punch out a small sample from a written line. About ten plugs or microdots of ink are sufficient for chromatographic analysis. The United States Secret Service and the Internal Revenue Service maintain the United States International Ink Library. This collection includes more than 8,5000 inks which date back to the 1920s. Each year new pen and ink formulations are added to this reference collection. These inks have been systematically cataloged according to dye patterns developed by thin-layer chromatography (TLC; see Figure 16–12). On several occasions, this approach has been used to prove that a document has been fraudulently backdated. For example, in one instance, it was possible to establish that a document dated 1958 was backdated because a dye identified in the questioned ink had not been synthesized until 1959.

To further aid forensic chemists in ink-dating matters, several ink manufacturers, at the request of the U.S. Treasury Department, voluntarily tag their inks during the manufacturing process. The tagging program allows inks to be dated to the exact year of manufacture by changing the tags annually.

Another area of inquiry for the document examiner is the paper on which a document is written or printed. Paper is often made from cellulose fibers found in wood and fibers recovered from recycled paper products. The most common features associated with a paper examination are general appearance, color, weight, and watermarks. Other areas of examination include fiber identification and the characterization of additives, fillers, and pigments present in the paper product.

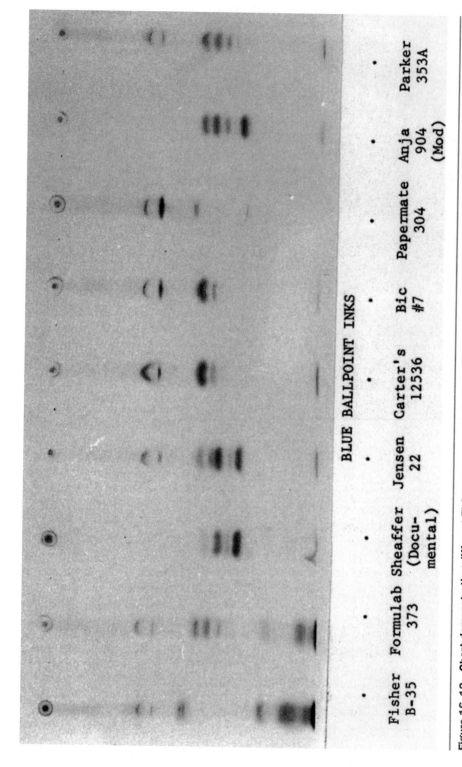

Figure 16–12 Chart demonstrating different TLC patterns of blue ballpoint inks. *Courtesy Alcohol, Tobacco, Firearms and Explosives Laboratory, U.S. Department of Justice, Washington, D.C.*

Voice Examination

The Sound Spectrograph

In this era of telephone, radio, and tape-recorded communications, the human voice may often prove to be valuable evidence for associating an individual with a criminal act. The telephoned bomb threat, obscene phone call, or tape-recorded kidnap ransom message have all become frequent enough occurrences to warrant the interest of law enforcement officials in scientific techniques capable of transforming the voice into a form suitable for personal identification. To this end, a good deal of research and casework has been generated as a result of the development of the *sound spectrograph;* an instrument that converts speech into a visual graphic display.

The sound spectrograph was first developed at Bell Telephone Laboratories in 1941 during research devoted to studying speech signals as they related to communications services. During World War II, the instrument was used for intelligence purposes to identify the voices broadcast by German military communications. Following the war and during his employment with the company, a Bell System engineer, Lawrence Kersta, worked with this new technique and became convinced that voice spectrograms, or **voiceprints**, as he called them, could provide a valuable means of personal identification.

Kersta contended that each voice has its own unique quality and character, arising out of individual variations in the vocal mechanism (see Figure 16–13). The probability that any two individuals have the same size vocal cavities (throat, nasal, and two oral cavities formed by positioning the tongue) and coordinate their articulators (lips, teeth, tongue, soft palate, and jaw muscles) in a like manner is so small as to make the human voice a unique personal trait. According to Kersta, the voiceprint is simply a graphic display of the unique characteristics of the voice.

Voiceprint
A pictorial representation of the frequency, duration, and amplitude of human voice sounds.

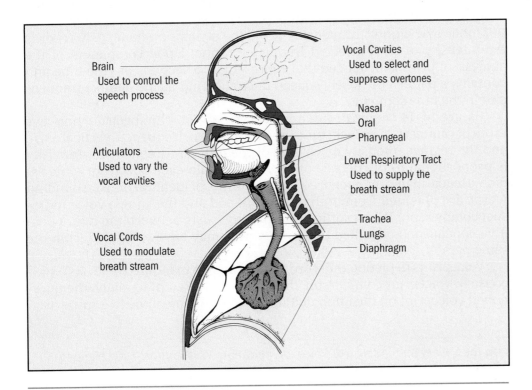

Figure 16–13   Schematic of the vocal mechanism.

As a result of Kersta's claim, the sound spectrograph has attracted great interest among criminal investigators. Many law enforcement laboratories have purchased the instrument, and various courts have been asked to accept its results as evidence of an individual's participation in a crime. However, there are still conflicting opinions in the courts as to whether the voiceprint has gained a sufficient degree of "general acceptance" within the scientific community to satisfy its admissibility as scientific evidence. A detailed report on voiceprints by the National Academy of Science concluded that

> the degree of accuracy and the corresponding error rates of aural-visual voice identification vary widely from case to case, depending upon several conditions including the properties of the voices involved, the conditions under which the voice samples were made, the characteristics of the equipment used, the skill of the examiner making the judgments, and the examiner's knowledge about the case.[5]

The National Academy's concern that there is no adequate scientific basis for legal authorities to judge the reliability of voice spectrographic comparisons was addressed by a 1986 FBI study.[6] A survey of two thousand voice identification comparisons made by FBI examiners under actual forensic conditions found that meaningful decisions were made in only 34.8 percent of the requested comparisons, with observed error rates of 0.31 percent for false identifications and 0.53 percent for false eliminations. Because the error rates were determined from direct feedback from field investigators, which may not always be correct, these percentages represent minimum error rates. An error rate of 1 percent would seem to be realistic under typical case conditions.

The analog sound spectrograph converts the sound of a voice into a visual display called a *spectrogram* or *voiceprint*. The selected frequencies are converted into electrical energy and are recorded by a stylus on specially prepared chart paper. As the drum revolves, the variable filter moves to higher and higher frequencies while the stylus simultaneously records the intensity of each selected frequency range. Upon completion of the analysis, a print is produced that represents 2.5 seconds of tape time and contains a pattern of closely spaced lines showing all the audible frequencies in the tape segment.

Figure 16–14 demonstrates a typical voiceprint. The spectrum portrays three parameters of speech: time (horizontal axis), frequency (vertical axis), and the relative intensity or volume of the different frequencies. Intensity is proportional to the degree of darkness within each spectrographic region. Hence, in this manner, frequency patterns of identical or like-sounding words are obtained from both the questioned and the known voice for visual comparison. When sufficient similarity exists between the two, a positive conclusion is justified that both voices may have emanated from the same person.

Voiceprints depicting the word *you* are shown in Figure 16–15. As an exercise in voiceprint comparison, the reader can attempt to match the questioned voiceprint on the upper left to the voice of one of the five suspects.

---

[5] *On the Theory and Practice of Voice Identification.* Washington, D.C.: National Academy of Sciences, 1979.

[6] B. E. Koenig, "Spectrographic Voice Identification: A Forensic Survey," *Journal of the Acoustical Society of America* 79 (1986): 2088.

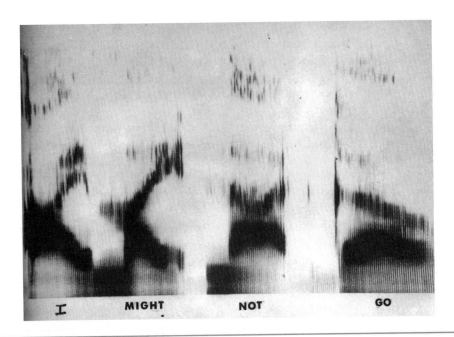

Figure 16–14   A voiceprint. *Courtesy New Jersey State Police*

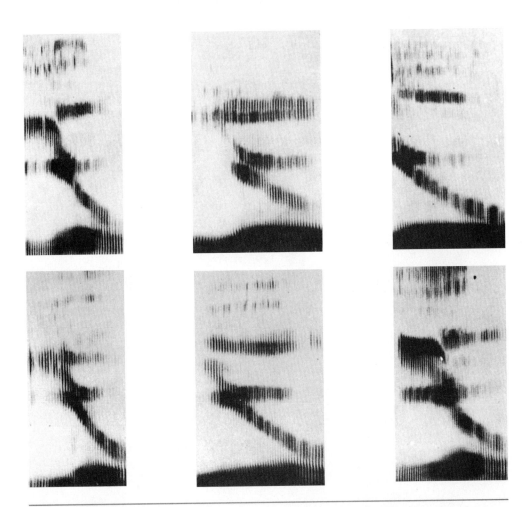

Figure 16–15   A questioned voiceprint and voiceprints of five male speakers uttering the word *you.* **Match the questioned voiceprint on the upper left to the voiceprint of one of the five suspects. (The upper left and lower right voiceprints are of the same person.)**

The recent introduction of the computerized sound spectrograph (see Figure 16–16) simplifies the work for today's examiners. This valuable tool allows multiple sound spectrograms to be displayed simultaneously and permits CD-quality playback of each recording. The reproducibility of the spectrograms by the computerized system is no different from the analog system, but offers many effective ways of analyzing recordings without compromising much sample preparation time. Common techniques used by examiners can be completed effortlessly with digital cuts and other editing features available with a computer. Simple acts such as adjusting of the recording's time alignment and range of frequency can aid in making a comparison. Furthermore, the examiner can remove much of the background noise that might lessen the recording's usefulness.

Examiners apply both aural and visual techniques when comparing two voice samples. A common way of performing aural analysis is to repeatedly re-record the selected segment. During the visual analysis, the spectrograms are placed side by side for rapid comparison. Only those that contain identical texts are compared and are digitally displayed for overall pattern recognition and identifiable features. Finally, the examiner can classify the recording into one of the following seven categories as recommended by the American Board of Recorded Evidence:

1. A positive identification with more than twenty matching speech sounds

2. A probable identification with more than fifteen matching sounds and no unexplained differences

3. A possible identification with more than ten matching sounds and no unexplained differences

4. An inconclusive decision mainly due to a poor recording

5. A possible elimination with ten or more sounds that do not match

Figure 16–16 A sound spectrograph. *Courtesy KayPENTAX., Lincoln Park, N.J.*

6. A probable elimination with fifteen or more sounds that do not match

7. A positive elimination with twenty or more sounds that do not match

Notable applications of voiceprint technology have increased public awareness of this technique. For example, voiceprints played a part in Howard Hughes's refutation of Clifford Irving's purported autobiography of Hughes. A few days after McGraw-Hill and *Life* magazine announced their intent to publish Irving's work, Hughes Tool Company officials arranged for a telephone interview between the reclusive Howard Hughes in the Bahamas and a group of newspaper, radio, and TV reporters assembled in Los Angeles. At the request of one of the major TV networks, spectrographic comparisons of the voice from the Bahamas were made against a known sample of Hughes's voice recorded in 1947. The results proved beyond a doubt that the reporters had been conversing with Howard Hughes and not with an impostor. Irving was eventually found guilty of forging the "Hughes autobiography."

In another case, a perpetrator called the police to report that he had killed a woman and to reveal the location of the body. He gave his name as that of an acquaintance. During the course of the investigation, the man whose name was used was eliminated as the caller, and the perpetrator was identified through voiceprint comparisons. Based on that identification, the impostor was found guilty and sentenced to prison.

Present use of forensic voiceprint technology is limited to a relatively small number of active examiners. Legal barriers to the admission of this evidence exist in many jurisdictions. This situation will likely remain unchanged until a consensus develops among the practitioners of this technology with regard to minimum education and experience for spectrographic examiners and a minimum set of uniform criteria for defining and evaluating voiceprint comparisons.

Chapter Summary

Any object with handwriting or print whose source or authenticity is in doubt may be referred to as a questioned document. Document examiners apply knowledge gathered through years of training and experience to recognize and compare the individual characteristics of questioned and known authentic writings. For this purpose, gathering documents of known authorship or origin is critical to the outcome of the examination. Many factors compose the total character of a person's writing. The unconscious handwriting of two different individuals can never be identical. Furthermore, the writing style of one individual may be altered beyond recognition by the influence of drugs or alcohol. The collection of an adequate number of known writings is critical for determining the outcome of a handwriting comparison. Known writing should contain some of the words and combinations of letters present in the questioned document.

The two requests most often made of the examiner in connection with the examination of typewriters and printing devices are to determine whether the make and model of the typewriter and printing devices used to prepare the questioned document can be identified and whether a particular suspect typewriter or printing device can be identified as having prepared the questioned document. The individual type character's style, shape, and size are compared to a complete reference collection of past and present typefaces. As is true for any mechanical device, use of a printing device results in wear and damage to the machine's moving parts. These changes occur both randomly and irregularly, thereby imparting individual characteristics to the printing device. The document examiner has to deal with problems involving business and personal computers, which often produce printed copies that have only subtle defects.

Document examiners must deal with evidence that has been changed in several ways, such as through alterations, erasures, and obliterations. Indented writings have proved to be valuable evidence. It may be possible to determine what was written by the impressions left on a paper pad. Applying an electrostatic charge to the surface of a polymer film that has been placed in contact with a questioned document visualizes indented writings. A study of the chemical composition of writing ink on documents may verify whether known and questioned documents were prepared by the same pen.

The human voice may prove to be valuable evidence for associating an individual with a criminal act. The probability that any two individuals have the same size vocal cavities (throat, nasal, and two oral cavities formed by positioning the tongue) and coordinate their articulators (lips, teeth, tongue, soft palate, and jaw muscles) in a like manner is so small as to make the human voice a unique personal trait. The sound spectrograph is an instrument that converts speech into a visual graphic display. Courts have been asked to accept its results as evidence of an individual's participation in a crime. However, there are still conflicting opinions in the courts as to whether the voiceprint has gained a sufficient degree of general acceptance within the scientific community to satisfy its admissibility as scientific evidence.

Review Questions

1. Any object that contains handwriting or typescript and whose source or authenticity is in doubt is referred to as a (n)_____.

2. Variations in mechanical, physical, and mental functions make it (likely, unlikely) that the writing of two different individuals can be distinguished.

3. In a problem involving the authorship of handwriting, all characteristics of both the _____ and _____ documents must be considered and compared.

4. True or False: A single handwriting characteristic can by itself be taken as a basis for a positive comparison. _____

5. True or False: Normally, known writings need not contain words and combinations of letters present in the questioned document. _____

6. As the age difference between genuine and unknown specimens becomes greater, the standard tends to become (more, less) representative of the unknown.

7. In the case of _____, the Supreme Court held handwriting to be nontestimonial evidence not protected by Fifth Amendment privileges.

8. When requested writing is being given by a suspect, care must be taken to minimize a (n) _____ writing effort.

9. Random wear and damage to a typewriter impart it with _____ characteristics.

10. Examination of a document under _____ or _____ lighting may reveal chemical erasures of words or numbers.

11. Some inks, when exposed to blue-green light, absorb _____ radiation and emit light.

12. Handwriting containing inks of different chemical compositions may be distinguished by photography with _____ film.

13. _____ writings are partially visible impressions appearing on a sheet of paper underneath the one on which the visible writing was done.

14. Many ink dyes can be separated by the technique of _____ chromatography.

15. The _____ was first developed at Bell Telephone Laboratories in 1941.

16. The sound spectrograph converts sound into a visual display called a (n) _____.

17. True or False: Voices analyzed by the sound spectrograph have been widely accepted as evidence in U.S. courts.

Further References

Brunelle, Richard L., "Questioned Document Examination," in R. Saferstein, ed., *Forensic Science Handbook,* vol. l, 2nd ed., Upper Saddle River, N.J.: Prentice Hall, 2002.

Ellen, David, *The Scientific Examination of Documents—Methods and Techniques,* 3rd ed. Boca Raton, Fla.: Taylor & Francis, 2006.

Held, D.A. E., "Handwriting, Typewriting, Shoeprints, and Tire Treads: FBI Laboratory's Questioned Documents Unit," *Forensic Science Communications,* 3, no.2, (2001), *http://www.fbi.gov/hq/lab/fsc/backissu/april2001/held.htm.*

Hilton, Ordway, *Scientific Examination of Questioned Documents,* rev. ed. Boca Raton, Fla.: Taylor & Francis, 1992.

Levinson, Jay, *Questioned Documents—A Lawyer's Handbook.* San Diego: Academic Press, 2001.

McDermott, Michael C., and T. Owen, "Voice Identification: The Aural/Spectrographic Method," www.owlinvestigations.com/forensic_articles/.

Bill Thomas Killman
1684 S. Oldmanor
Wichita. KS. 67218

The Wichita Eagle & Be
Pub. Co. Inc.
825 E. Douglas
Wichita, KS. 67202

The BTK Killer

Dennis Rader was arrested in February 2005 and charged with committing ten murders since 1974 in the Wichita, Kansas, area. The killer, whose nickname stands for "bind, torture, kill," hadn't murdered since 1991, but resurfaced in early 2004 by sending a letter to a local newspaper taking credit for a 1986 slaying. Included with the letter were a photocopy of the victim's driver's license and three photos of her body. The BTK killer was back to his old habit of taunting the police. Three months later another letter surfaced. This time the letter detailed some of the events surrounding BTK's first murder victims. In 1974, he strangled Joseph and Julie Otero along with two of their children. Shortly after

those murders occurred, BTK sent a letter to a local newspaper in which he gave himself the name BTK. In December 2004, a package found in a park contained the driver's license of another BTK victim along with a doll whose hands were bound with pantyhose and who was covered with a plastic bag.

The major break in the case came when BTK sent a message on a floppy disk to a local TV station. "Erased" information on the disk was recovered and restored by forensic computer specialists, and the disk was traced to the Christ Lutheran Church in Wichita. The disk was then quickly linked to Dennis Rader, the church council president. The long odyssey of the BTK killer was finally over.

chapter 17

Computer
Forensics

By Andrew W. Donofrio

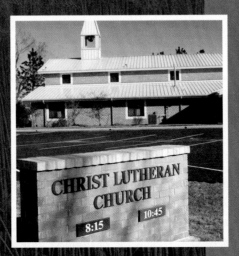

Key Terms

bit

byte

central processing unit (CPU)

cluster

file slack

hard disk drive (HDD)

hardware

latent data

Message Digest 5 (MD5)/secure hash algorithm (SHA)

motherboard

operating system (OS)

partition

RAM slack

random-access memory (RAM)

sector

software

swap file

temporary files

unallocated space

visible data

Learning Objectives

After studying this chapter you should be able to:

- List and describe the hardware and software components of a computer

- Understand the difference between read-only memory and random-access memory

- Describe how a hard disk drive is partitioned

- Describe the proper procedure for preserving computer evidence at a crime scene

- Understand the difference between and location of visible and latent data

- List the areas of the computer that will be examined to retrieve forensic data

Since the 1990s, few fields have progressed as rapidly as computer technology. Computers are no longer a luxury, nor are they in the hands of just a select few. Technology and electronic data are a part of everyday life and permeate all aspects of society. Consequently, computers have become increasingly important as sources of evidence in an ever-widening spectrum of criminal activities.

Investigators frequently encounter computers and other digital devices in all types of cases. As homicide investigators sift for clues they may inquire whether the method for a murder was researched on the Internet; whether signs of an extramarital affair can be found in e-mail or remnants of instant messages, which might provide motive for a spouse killing or murder for hire; or whether threats were communicated to the victim prior to a murder by an obsessed stalker. Arson investigators want to know whether financial records on a computer might provide a motive in an arson-for-profit fire. A burglary investigation would certainly be aided if law enforcement determined that the proceeds from a theft were being sold online—perhaps through eBay or a similar online auction site.

Accessibility to children and the perception of anonymity has given sexual predators a way to seek out child victims online. The vulnerability of computers to hacker attacks is a constant reminder of security issues surrounding digitally stored data. Finally, the fact that computers control most of our critical infrastructure makes technology an appetizing target for would-be terrorists.

Computer forensics involves the preservation, acquisition, extraction, analysis, and interpretation of computer data. Although this is a simple definition, it gets a bit more complicated. Part of this complication arises from technology itself. More and more devices are capable of storing electronic data: cell phones, personal digital assistants (PDAs), iPods, digital cameras, flash memory cards, smart cards, jump drives, and many others. Methods for extracting data from these devices each present unique challenges.

Andrew W. Donofrio is a Detective Sergeant with the Prosecutor's Office in Bergen County, New Jersey, and is a leading computer forensics examiner for Bergen County, with more than 18 years experience in the field of law enforcement. He has conducted more than 500 forensic examinations of computer evidence and frequently lectures on the subject throughout the state, as well as teaching multi-day courses on computer forensics and investigative topics at police academies and colleges in New Jersey. Det. Sgt. Donofrio writes regularly on Internet-related and computer forensics issues for a number of law enforcement publications and has appeared as a guest expert on Internet-related stories on MSNBC.

There are, however, sound forensic practices that apply to all these devices. The most logical place to start to examine these practices is with the most common form of electronic data: the personal computer.

From Input to Output: How Does the Computer Work?

Hardware versus Software

Before we get into the nuts and bolts of computers, we must establish the important distinction between hardware and software. Hardware comprises the physical components of the computer: the computer chassis, monitor, keyboard, mouse, hard disk drive, random-access memory (RAM), and central processing unit (CPU), and so on (see Figure 17–1). The list is much more extensive, but generally speaking, if it is a computer component or peripheral that you can see, feel, and touch, it is hardware.

Software, conversely, is a set of instructions compiled into a program that performs a particular task. Software consists of programs and applications that carry out a set of instructions on the hardware. Operating systems (Windows, Mac OS, Linux, Unix), word-processing programs (Microsoft Word, WordPerfect), web-browsing applications (Internet Explorer, Netscape Navigator, Firefox), and accounting applications (Quicken, QuickBooks, Microsoft Money) are all examples of software. It is important

Hardware
The physical components of a computer: case, keyboard, monitor, motherboard, RAM, HDD, mouse, and so on. Generally speaking, if it is a computer component you can touch, it is hardware.

Software
A set of instructions compiled into a program that performs a particular task. Software consists of programs and applications that carry out a set of instructions on the hardware.

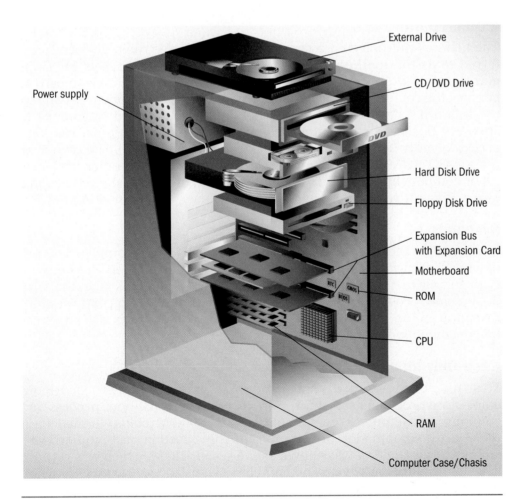

- External Drive
- CD/DVD Drive
- Power supply
- Hard Disk Drive
- Floppy Disk Drive
- Expansion Bus with Expansion Card
- Motherboard
- ROM
- CPU
- RAM
- Computer Case/Chasis

Figure 17–1 Cutaway diagram of a personal computer showing the tangible hardware components of a computer system. *Courtesy Tim Downs*

not to confuse software with the physical media that it comes on. When you buy an application such as Microsoft Office, it comes on a compact disc (CD). The CD containing this suite of applications is typically referred to as software, but this is technically wrong. The CD is external computer media that contains the software; it is a container for and a medium to load the set of instructions onto the hard disk drive (the hardware).

Computer Case/Chassis

The case is the physical box holding the fixed internal computer components in place. Cases come in many shapes and sizes: a full upright tower chassis, a slim desktop model sitting on the desktop, or an all-in-one monitor/computer case like the iMac. For our purposes, the term *system unit* is probably most appropriate when describing a chassis seized as evidence. The term *system unit* accurately references the chassis, including the motherboard and other internal components.

Power Supply

The term *power supply* is actually a misnomer, because it doesn't actually supply power—the power company does that. Rather, a computer's power supply converts power from the wall outlet to a usable format for the computer and its components. Different power supplies have different wattage ratings. The use, or more specifically the components, of the computer dictate the appropriate power supply.

Motherboard

Motherboard
The main system board of a computer (and many other electronic devices). It delivers power, data, and instructions to the computer's components. Every component in the computer connects to the motherboard, either directly or indirectly.

The main circuit board in a computer (or other electronic devices) is referred to as the **motherboard**. Motherboards contain sockets for chips and slots for add-on cards. Examples of add-on cards are a video card to connect the computer to the monitor, a network card or modem to connect to an internal network or the Internet, and a sound card to connect to speakers. Sockets on the motherboard typically accept things like random-access memory (RAM) or the central processing unit (CPU). The keyboard, mouse, CD-ROM drives, floppy disk drives, monitor, and other peripherals or components connect to the motherboard in some fashion through a direct wired or wireless connection.

System Bus

Contained on the motherboard, the system bus is a vast complex network of wires that carry data from one hardware device to another. This network is analogous to a complex highway. Data is sent along the bus in the form of ones and zeros (or, more appropriately stated, as electrical impulses representing an "on" or "off" state—this two-state computing is also known as *binary computing*).

Read-Only Memory (ROM)

This rather generic term describes special chips on the motherboard. ROM chips store programs called *firmware*, used to start the boot process and configure a computer's components. Today's ROM chips, termed *flash ROM*, are a combination of two types of chips used in past motherboard technologies. The first was known as the *system ROM*, which was responsible for booting the system and handling the "assumed" system hardware present in the computer. As the system ROM, generally speaking, could not be altered, and because as technology matured changes to the "assumed" hardware were more common, a different type of chip was introduced. The *complementary metal-oxide semiconductor* (CMOS) was a separate chip that allowed the user to exercise setup control over several system components. Regardless of how this technology is present on the motherboard, it can be referred to as the BIOS, for *basic input-output system*. The operation of the BIOS is relevant to several computer forensic procedures, particularly the boot sequence. It is the set of routines associated with the BIOS in ROM that initiates the booting process and enables the computer to communicate with various devices in the system such as disk drives, keyboard, monitor, and printer. As will become clear later, it is important not to boot the actual computer under investigation to the original hard disk drive. This would cause changes to the data, thus compromising the integrity of evidence. The BIOS allows investigators to control the boot process to some degree.

Central Processing Unit (CPU)

The central processing unit (CPU), also referred to as a processor, is essentially the brain of the computer. It is the main (and typically the largest) chip that plugs into a socket on the motherboard. The CPU is the part of the computer that actually computes. Basically, all operations performed by the computer are run through the CPU. The CPU carries out the program steps to perform the requested task. That task can range from opening and working in a Microsoft Word document to performing advanced mathematical algorithms. CPUs come in various shapes, sizes, and types. Intel Pentium chips and Advanced Micro Devices (AMD) chips are among the most common.

Central Processing Unit (CPU)
The main chip within the computer; also referred to as the brain of the computer. This microprocessor chip handles most of the operations (code and instructions) of the computer.

Random-Access Memory (RAM)

This is one of the most widely mentioned types of computer memory. Random-access memory (RAM) takes the burden off the computer's processor and hard disk drive (HDD). If the computer had to access the HDD each time it wanted data, it would run slowly and inefficiently. Instead the computer, aware that it may need certain data at a moment's notice, stores the data in RAM. It is helpful to envision RAM as chips that create a large spreadsheet, with each cell representing a memory address that the CPU can use as a reference to retrieve data. RAM is referred to as *volatile memory* because it is not permanent; its contents undergo constant change and are forever lost once power is taken away from the computer. RAM takes the physical form of chips that plug into the motherboard; SIMMs (Single Inline Memory Modules), DIMMs (Dual Inline Memory Modules), and SDRAM (Synchronous Dynamic Random-Access Memory) are just a few of the types of chips. Today's computers come with various denominations of RAM: 256 MB (megabytes), 512 MB, and 1 GB (gigabyte) are the most common.[1]

Random-Access Memory (RAM)
The volatile memory of the computer, when power is turned off, its contents are lost. Programs and instructions are loaded into RAM while they are in use.

Input Devices

Input devices are used to get data into the computer or to give the computer instructions. Input devices constitute part of the "user" side of the computer. Examples include the keyboard, mouse, joystick, and scanner.

---

[1] A megabyte (MB) is approximately one million bytes (discussed later in the chapter), a gigabyte (GB) is approximately one billion bytes, or 1,000 megabytes.

Figure 17–2 **An inside view of the platter and read/write head of a hard disk drive.** *Courtesy Corbis RF*

Output Devices

Output devices are equipment through which data is obtained from the computer. Output devices are also part of the "user" side of the computer, and provide the results of the user's tasks. They include the monitor, printer, and speakers.

Hard Disk Drive (HDD)

Hard Disk Drive (HDD)
Typically the main storage location within the computer. It consists of magnetic platters contained in a case (usually 3.5″ in a desktop computer and 2.5″ in a laptop). The HDD is usually where the operating system, applications, and user data are stored.

Generally speaking, the hard disk drive (HDD) is the primary component of storage in the personal computer (Figure 17–2). It typically stores the operating system (Windows, Mac OS, Linux, Unix), the programs (Microsoft Word, Internet Explorer, Open Office for Linux, and so on) and data files created by the user (documents, spreadsheets, accounting information, the company database, and so on). Unlike RAM, the HDD is permanent storage and retains its information even after the power is turned off. HDDs work off a controller that is typically part of the motherboard, but sometimes takes the form of an add-on (expansion) card plugged into the motherboard. The most common types of HDD controllers are integrated drive electronics (IDE), small computer system interface (SCSI), and serial ATA (SATA). Each HDD type has a different interface that connects it to the controller. Regardless of the type of controller, the data is basically stored in the same fashion. HDDs are mapped (formatted) and have a defined layout. They are logically divided into sectors, clusters, tracks, and cylinders. (See the section titled "How Data Is Stored" for further information).

Other Common Storage Devices

Although the HDD is the most common storage device for the personal computer, many others exist. Methods for storing data and the layout of that data can vary from device to device. A CD-ROM, for example, uses a different technology and format for writing data than a floppy disk or USB thumb drive. Fortunately, regardless of the differences among devices, the same basic forensic principals apply for acquiring the data. Common storage devices include the following:

CD-R/RW (compact disc-record/rewrite) and DVD-R/RW (DVD-record/rewrite). Compact discs (CDs) and digital video discs (DVDs) are two of the most common forms of storing external data. They are used to store everything from music and video to data files. A largely plastic disc with an aluminum layer is read by laser light in the CD/DVD reader. Different CDs are encoded in different ways, making the job of the forensic examiner difficult at times.

Floppy Disks. Though "floppies" are not as common as they once were, forensic examiners still encounter the 3.5-inch floppy disk. Floppy disks can be used to boot an operating system or to store data. They are constructed of hard plastic with a thin plastic disk on the inside. That thin plastic disk is coated with a magnetic iron oxide material. The disk is mapped and stores data in a similar fashion to the hard disk drive. By today's standards, floppy disks don't hold much data.

Zip Disks. Similar in structure to floppy disks, Zip disks hold a much larger amount of data. They come in several storage capacities, each with their own drive.

USB Thumb Drives and Smart Media Cards. These devices can store a large amount of data—some as much as 4 GB. They are known as solid-state storage devices because they have no moving parts. Smart media cards are typically found in digital cameras and PDAs, while USB thumb drives come in many shapes, sizes, and storage capacities.

Tapes. Tapes come in many different formats: 4 mm, 8 mm and storage capacities. Each typically comes with its own hardware reader and sometimes a proprietary application to read and write its contents. Tapes are typically used for backup purposes and consequently have great forensic potential.

Network Interface Card (NIC)

Very rarely do we find a computer today that doesn't have a NIC. Whether they are on a local network or the Internet, when computers need to communicate with each other, they typically do so through a NIC. NICs come in many different forms: add-on cards that plug into the motherboard, hard-wired devices on the motherboard, add-on cards (PCMCIA) for laptops, and universal serial bus (USB) plug-in cards, to name a few. Some are wired cards, meaning they need a physical wired connection to participate on the network, and others are wireless, meaning they receive their data via radio waves.

Putting It All Together

A person approaches the computer, sits down, and presses the power button. The power supply wakes up and delivers power to the motherboard and all of the hardware connected to the computer. At this point the flash ROM chip on the motherboard (the one that contains the BIOS) conducts a power-on self test (POST) to make sure everything is working properly.

The flash ROM also polls the motherboard to check the hardware that is attached and follows its programmed boot order, thus determining from what device it should boot. Typically the boot device is the HDD, but it can also be a floppy disk, CD, or USB drive. If it is the HDD, the HDD is then sent control. It locates the first sector of its disk (known as the master boot record), determines its layout (partition(s)), and boots an operating system (Windows, Mac OS, Linux, Unix). The person is then presented with a computer work environment, commonly referred to as a desktop. Now ready to work, the user double-clicks an icon on the desktop, such as a Microsoft Word shortcut, to open the program and begin to type a document. The CPU processes this request, locates the Microsoft Word program on the HDD (using a predefined map of the drive called a *file system table*), carries out the programming instructions associated with the application, loads Microsoft Word into RAM via the system bus, and sends the output to the monitor by way of the video controller, which is either located on or attached to the motherboard. The user then begins to type, placing the data from the keyboard into RAM. At the end, the user might print the document or simply save it to the HDD for later retrieval. If printed, the data is taken from RAM, processed by the CPU, placed in a format suitable for printing, and sent through the system bus to the external port where the printer is connected. If the document is saved, the data is taken from RAM, processed by the CPU, passed to the HDD controller (IDE, SCSI, or SATA) by way of the system bus, and written to a portion of the HDD. The HDD's file system table is updated so it knows where to retrieve that data later. In actuality, the boot process is more complex than the way it has been described above and requires the forensic examiner to possess an in-depth knowledge of its process.

The preceding example illustrates how three components perform the majority of the work: the CPU, RAM, and system bus. The example can get even more complicated as the user opens more applications and performs multiple tasks simultaneously (*multitasking*). Several tasks can be loaded into RAM at once and the CPU is capable of juggling them all. This allows for the multitasking environment and the ability to switch back and forth between applications. All of this is orchestrated by the operating system and is written in the language of the computer—ones and zeros. The only detail missing, and one that is important from a forensic standpoint, is a better understanding of how data is stored on the hard disk drive (see Figure 17–2).

How Data Is Stored

Operating System (OS)
The software that provides the bridge between the system hardware and the user. The OS lets the user interact with the hardware and manages the file system and applications. Some examples are Windows (XP, 2000), Linux, and Mac OS.

Partition
A contiguous set of blocks that are defined and treated as an independent disk.

Before beginning to understand how data is stored on a hard disk drive (HDD), it is first important to understand the role of the operating system (OS). An OS, such as Windows, Mac OS, Linux, or Unix, is the bridge between the human user and the computer's electronic components. It provides the user with a working environment and facilitates interaction with the system's components. Each OS supports certain types of file systems that store data in different ways, but some support the methods of others. Generally speaking, before an OS can write to a HDD it must first be formatted. But even before it can be formatted, a partition must be defined. A partition is nothing more than a contiguous set of blocks that are defined and treated as an independent disk. This means that a hard disk drive can hold several partitions, making a single HDD appear as several disks. Partitioning a drive can be thought of as dividing a container that begins as nothing more than four sides with empty space on the inside. We then cut a hole in the front of it and place inside two drawers con-

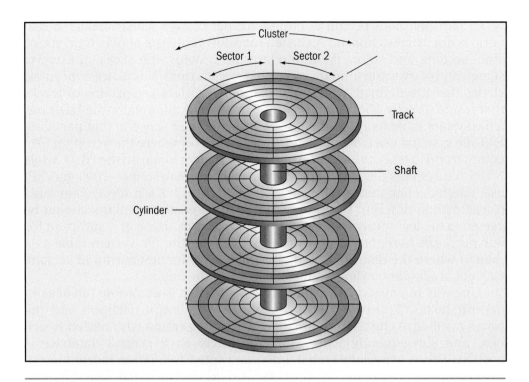

Figure 17–3 Partitions of a hard disk drive

taining the hardware to open and close them. We have just created a two-drawer filing cabinet and defined each drawer as contiguous blocks of storage. A partitioning utility such as Disk Manager or fdisk defines the drawer or drawers (partitions) that will later hold the data on the HDD. Just as the style, size, and shape of a filing cabinet drawer can vary, so too can partitions. After a hard drive is partitioned, it is typically formatted. (At this point it is a high-level format, not to be confused with low-level format, which is generally done by the manufacturer of the HDD.) The formating process initializes portions of the HDD and creates the structure of the file system. The file system can be thought of as the system for storing and locating data on a storage device; but more on this in a bit. Some of the file system types are FAT12 (typically on floppy disks), FAT16 (older DOS and older Windows partitions), FAT32 (Windows file systems), NTFS (most current Windows systems—2000 and XP), EXT2 and EXT3 (Linux systems), and HPFS (some Macintosh systems).

Each of these file systems has a different way of storing, retrieving, and allocating data. So, in summary, it can be said that a drive is prepared in three processes: low-level formatting (typically done by the manufacturer, dividing the platters into tracks and sectors), partitioning (accomplished through a utility such as fdisk or Disk Manager, defining a contiguous set of blocks), and formatting (initializing portions of the disk and creating the file system structure). Although a bit more technical and detailed, at the conclusion of these processes, the drive is logically defined. We say "logically" because no real divisions are made. If you were to crack open the HDD before or after partitioning and formatting, to the naked eye the platters would look the same. As shown in Figure 17–3, HDDs contain several platters stacked vertically which are logically divided into sectors, clusters, tracks, and cylinders. **Sectors** are typically 512 bytes in size (a **byte** is eight bits; a **bit** is a single one or zero). **Clusters** are groups of sectors; their size is defined by the file system, but they are always in sector multiples of two. (Although an

Sector
The smallest addressable unit of data by a hard disk drive; generally consists of 512 bytes.

Byte
A group of eight bits.

Bit
Short for *binary digit*; Taking the form of either a one or a zero, it is the smallest unit of information on a machine.

Cluster
A group of sectors in multiples of two. Cluster size varies from file system to file system and is typically the minimum space allocated to a file.

NTFS partition does permit a one-sector-per-cluster scenario, such a scenario is not usually chosen.) A cluster, therefore, consists of two, four, six, or eight sectors, and so on. (With modern file systems, the user can exercise some control over the amount of sectors per cluster.) Tracks are concentric circles that are defined around the platter. Cylinders are groups of tracks that reside directly above and below each other. Additionally, the HDD has a file system table (map) of the layout of the defined space in that partition. FAT file systems use a *file allocation table* (which is where the acronym *FAT* comes from) to track the location of files and folders (data) on the HDD, while NTFS file systems (used by most current Windows systems—2000 and XP) use, among other things, a *master file table (MFT)*. Each file system table tracks data in different ways, and computer forensic examiners should be versed in the technical nuances of the HDDs they examine. It is sufficient for our purposes here, however, to merely visualize the file system table as a map to where the data is located. This map uses the numbering of sectors, clusters, tracks, and cylinders to keep track of the data.

One way to envision a partition and file system is as a room full of safe-deposit boxes. The room itself symbolizes the entire partition and the boxes symbolize clusters of data. In order to determine who rented which box, and subsequently where their property is, a central database is needed. This is especially true if a person rented two boxes located in opposite ends of the room (noncontiguous data on the HDD). The database tracking the locations of the safe-deposit boxes is much like a file system table tracking the location of data within the clusters. This example is also useful to understand the concept of reformatting a HDD. If the database managing the locations of the safe-deposit boxes were wiped out, the property in them would still remain; we just wouldn't know what was where. So too with the hard disk drive. If a user were to wipe the file system table clean—for example, by reformatting it—the data itself would not be gone. Both the database tracking the locations of the safe-deposit boxes and the file system table tracking the location of the data in the cluster are maps—not the actual contents. (Exceptions exist with some file systems, such as an NTFS file system, which stores data for very small files right in its file system table, known as the master file table).

Processing the Electronic Crime Scene

Processing the electronic crime scene has a lot in common with processing a traditional crime scene. The investigator must first ensure that the proper legal requirements (search warrant, consent, and so on) have been met so that the scene can be searched and the evidence seized. The investigator should then devise a plan of approach based on the facts of the case and the physical location. The scene should be documented in as much detail as possible before disturbing any evidence, and before the investigator lays a finger on any computer components. Of course there are circumstances in which an investigator might have to act quickly and pull a plug before documenting the scene, such as when data is in the process of being deleted.

Crime-scene documentation is accomplished through two actions: sketching and photographing. The electronic crime scene is no different.

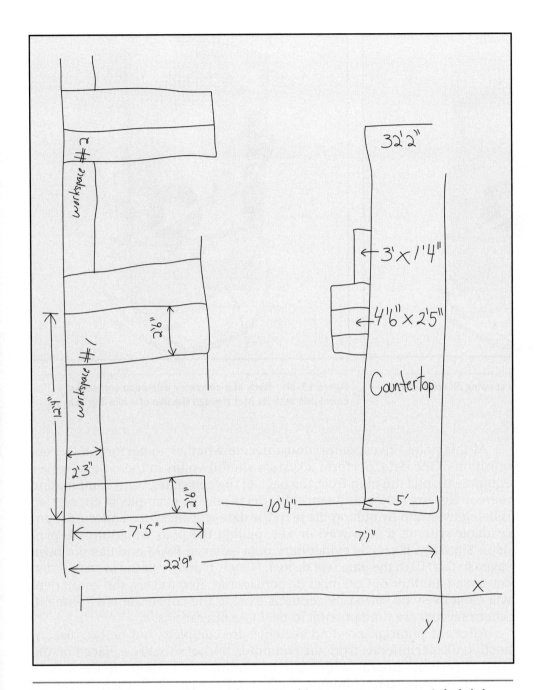

Figure 17–4   Rough sketch made at a crime scene with necessary measurements included.

The scene should be sketched in a floor plan fashion (see Figure 17–4) and then overall photographs of the location taken. In the case of a network, a technical network sketch should also be included if possible. After taking photographs of the overall layout, close-up photographs should be shot. A close-up photograph of any running computer monitor should be taken. All the connections to the main system unit, such as peripheral devices (keyboard, monitor, speakers, mouse, and so on), should be photographed. If necessary, system units should be moved delicately and carefully to facilitate the connections photograph. (See Figure 17–5a). Close-up photographs of equipment serial numbers should be taken if practical.

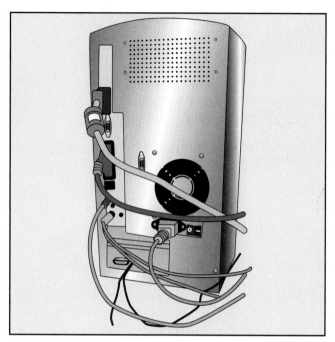

Figure 17–5a Back of a computer showing all connections.

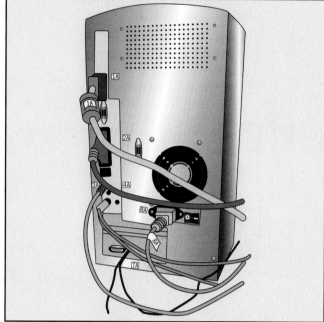

Figure 17–5b Back of a computer with each component correlated with its port through the use of a labeling scheme.

At this point, investigators must decide whether to perform a live acquisition of the data, perform a system shutdown (as in the case of server equipment), pull the plug from the back of the computer,[2] or a combination thereof. Several factors influence this decision. For example, if encryption is being used and by pulling the plug the data will encrypt, rendering it unreadable without a password or key, pulling the plug would not be prudent. Similarly, if crucial evidentiary data exists in RAM and has not been saved to the HDD, the data will be lost. Hence, if power to the system is discontinued another option must be considered. Regardless, the equipment will most likely be seized. Exceptions exist in the corporate environment, where servers are fundamental to business operations.

After the photographs and sketches are complete, but before disconnecting the peripherals from the computer, a label should be placed on the cord of each peripheral, with a corresponding label placed on the port to which it is connected. A numbering scheme should be devised to identify the system unit if several computers are at the scene (Figure 17–5b). The combination of sketching, photographing, and labeling should adequately document the scene, prevent confusion of which component went with which system unit, and facilitate reconstruction if necessary for lab or courtroom purposes.

Forensic Image Acquisition

Now that the items have been seized, the data needs to be obtained for analysis. The number of electronic items that potentially store evidentiary

---

[2] Pulling the plug should always be done by removing the plug from the back of the computer. If the plug is removed from the wall, a battery backup (UPS) might be in place, causing an alert to the system and keeping the unit powered on.

data are too vast to cover in this section. The hard disk drive will be used as an example, but the same "best practices" principles apply for other electronic devices as well.

Throughout the entire process, the computer forensic examiner must use the least intrusive method. The goal in obtaining data from a HDD is to do so without altering even one bit of data. Because booting a HDD to its operating system changes many files and could potentially destroy evidentiary data, obtaining data is generally accomplished by removing the HDD from the system and placing it in a laboratory forensic computer so that a forensic image can be created. However, the BIOS of the seized computer sometimes interprets the geometry of the HDD differently than the forensic computer does. In these instances, the image of the HDD must be obtained using the seized computer. Regardless, the examiner must ensure that the drive to be analyzed is in a "write-blocked," read-only state when creating the forensic image. Furthermore, the examiner needs to be able to prove that the forensic image he or she obtained includes every bit of data and caused no changes (writes) to the HDD. To this end, a sort of fingerprint of the drive is taken before and after imaging. This fingerprint is taken through the use of a Message Digest 5 (MD5), Secure Hash Algorithm (SHA), or similar validated algorithm. Before imaging the drive the algorithm is run and a 32-character alphanumeric string is produced based on the drive's contents. The algorithm is then run against the resulting forensic image; if nothing changed, the same alphanumeric string is produced, thus demonstrating that the image is all-inclusive of the original contents and that nothing was altered in the process.

A forensic image of the data on a HDD (and the same holds true for floppy disks, CDs, DVDs, tapes, flash memory devices, and any other storage medium) is merely an exact duplicate of the entire contents of the drive. In other words, all portions of the drive are copied from the first bit (one or zero) to the last. Why would investigators want to copy what appears to be blank or unused portions of the HDD? The answer is simple: to preserve latent data, discussed later in the chapter. It suffices to say here that data exists in areas of the drive that are, generally speaking, unknown and inaccessible to most end users. This data can be valuable as evidence. Therefore, a forensic image—one that copies every single bit of information on the drive—is necessary.[3] A forensic image differs from a backup or standard copy in that it takes the entire contents, not only data the operating system is aware of.

Many forensic software packages come equipped with a method to obtain the forensic image. The most popular software forensic tools—EnCase, Forensic Toolkit (FTK), Forensic Autopsy (Linux-based freeware), and SMART (Linux-based software by ASR Data)—all include a method to obtain a forensic image. All produce self-contained image files that can then be interpreted and analyzed. They also allow image compression to conserve storage. The fact that self-contained, compressed files are the result of forensic imaging allows many images from different cases to be stored on the same forensic storage drive. This makes case management and storage much easier (see Figure 17–6).

Message Digest 5 (MD5)/Secure Hash Algorithm (SHA)
A software algorithm used to "fingerprint" a file or contents of a disk; used to verify the integrity of data. In forensic analysis it is typically used to verify that an acquired image of suspect data was not altered during the process of imaging.

---

[3] In this instance, *bit* is both metaphorical and literal. Every bit of information is needed, so we must get it all. So too every bit, as in the smallest unit of data storage—a one or a zero—must be imaged.

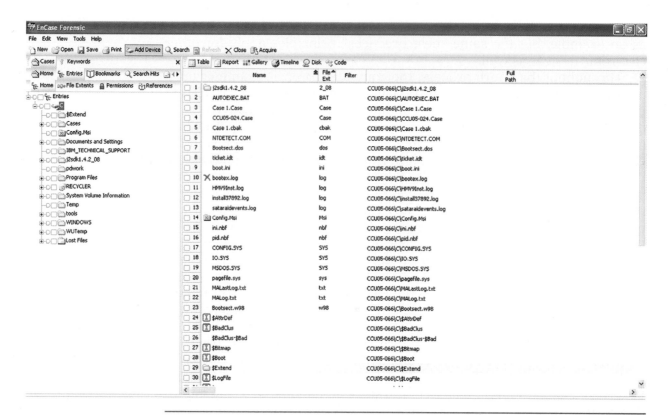

Figure 17–6   Screen shot of Encase Software. Encase is a common forensic sofware application capable of imaging and assisting in the analysis of data. *Courtesy of Encase, www.encase.com*

Analysis of Electronic Data

Analysis of electronic data is virtually limitless and bound only to the level of skill of the examiner. The more familiar an examiner is with computers, operating systems, application software, data storage, and a host of other disciplines, the more prepared he or she will be to look for evidentiary data. Because computers are vast and complex, discussing each area, file, directory, log, or computer process that could potentially contain evidentiary data is beyond the scope of one chapter—and may be beyond the scope of an entire book. What follows are some of the more common areas of analysis. While reading this section, reflect on your own knowledge of computers and consider what other data might be of evidentiary value and where it might be found.

Evidentiary Data

Visible Data

Visible Data
All data that the operating system is presently aware of, and thus is readily accessible to the user.

The category of visible data includes all information that the operating system is presently aware of, and thus is readily accessible to the user. Here we present several common types of visible data considered in many investigations. This list is by no means exhaustive and can include any information that has value as evidence.

Data/Work Product Files.   One place to find evidence is in documents or files produced by the suspect. This category is extremely broad and can include data from just about any software program. Microsoft Word and

WordPerfect word-processing programs typically produce text-based files such as typed documents and correspondence. These programs, and a host of other word-processing programs, have replaced the typewriter. They are common sources of evidence in criminal cases, particularly those involving white-collar crime.

Also relevant in white-collar crime and similar financial investigations are any data related to personal and business finance. Programs such as QuickBooks and Peachtree accounting packages can run the entire financial portion of a small to midsize business. Similarly, it is not uncommon to find personal bank account records in the computer that are managed with personal finance software such as Microsoft Money and Quicken. Moreover, criminals sometimes use these programs as well as spreadsheet applications to track bank accounts stolen from unsuspecting victims. Computer forensic examiners should familiarize themselves with these programs, the ways in which they store data, and methods for extracting and reading the data.

Advances in printer technology have made high-quality color printing both affordable and common in many homes. While this is a huge benefit for home office workers and those interested in graphic arts, the technology has been used for criminal gain. Counterfeiting and check and document fraud are easily perpetrated by most home computer users. All that is required is a decent ink-jet printer and a scanner. Including the computer, a criminal could set up a counterfeiting operation for less than $1500. Examiners must learn the graphics and photo-editing applications used for nefarious purposes. Being able to recognize the data produced by these applications and knowing how to display the images is key to identifying the evidence.

Swap File Data.   When an application is running, the program and the data being accessed are loaded into RAM. A computer's RAM is much faster than the "read" speed of the hard disk drive, and that's why the programs are loaded here—for fast access and functioning. RAM, however, has its limits. Some computers have 256 MB of RAM, others 512 MB, and still others as much as a gigabyte or two. Regardless of the amount, though, most operating systems (Windows, Linux, and so on) are programmed to conserve RAM when possible. This is where the swap file comes in. The operating system attempts to keep only data and applications that are presently being used in RAM. Other applications that were started, but are currently waiting for user attention, may be swapped out of RAM and written to the swap space on the hard disk drive.[4] For example, a manager of a retail store may want to type a quarterly report based on sales. The manager starts Microsoft Word and begins his report. Needing to incorporate sales figure data from a particular spreadsheet, he opens Microsoft Excel. Depending on what is running on the computer, the original Word document may be swapped from RAM to the swap space on the HDD to free up space for Excel. As the manager goes back and forth between the programs (and maybe checks his e-mail in between) this swapping continues. Data that is swapped back and forth is sometimes left behind in the swap space. Even as this area is constantly changed, some of the data is orphaned in unallocated space, an area of the HDD discussed later in this chapter.

Swap File
A file or defined space on the HDD used to conserve RAM. Data is swapped (paged) to this file/space to free RAM for applications that are in use.

---

[4] Actually, the more appropriate term is probably *paging* as opposed to *swapping*. This is because entire programs are typically not swapped in and out of memory to the swap space; rather, *pages* of memory are placed there.

Swap file or space can be defined as a particular file or even a separate HDD partition, depending on the operating system and file system type (FAT, NTFS, EXT2, and so on). For Windows systems either the swap file *Win386.sys* or *pagefile.sys* is used, depending on the specific Windows version and file system type. Linux systems can create partitions just for swapping data in and out of RAM. Data in the swap space can be read by examining the HDD through forensic software or a utility that provides a binary view, such as Norton Disk Editor or WinHex (see Figure 17–7).

Temporary Files. Any user who has suffered a sudden loss of power in the middle of typing a document can attest to the value of a temporary file. Most programs automatically save a copy of the file being worked on in a temporary file. After typing a document, working on a spreadsheet, or working on a slide presentation, the user can save the changes, thus promoting the temporary copy to an actual file. This is done as a sort of backup on the fly. If the computer experiences a sudden loss of power or other catastrophic failure, the temporary file can be recovered, limiting the amount of data lost. The loss is limited because the temporary file is not updated in real time. Rather, it is updated periodically (typically defaulted to every ten minutes in most programs), depending on the application's settings. Temporary files can sometimes be recovered during a forensic examination. Additionally, some of the data that may have been orphaned from a previous version may be recoverable, if not the complete file. This is true even when a document has been typed and printed, but never saved. The creation of the temporary file makes it possible for some of this "unsaved" data to be recovered during analysis.

Another type of temporary file valuable to the computer investigator is the print spool file. When a print job is sent to the printer a spooling process delays the sending of the data to the printer. This happens so the application can continue to work while the printing takes place in the background. To facilitate this, a temporary print spool file is created; this file typically includes the data to be printed and information specific to the printer. There are different methods for accomplishing this, and thus the files created as a

Temporary Files
Files temporarily written by an application to perform a function. For applications, such as Microsoft Word and Excel, temporary files are created to provide a "backup" copy of the work product should the computer experience a catastrophic failure.

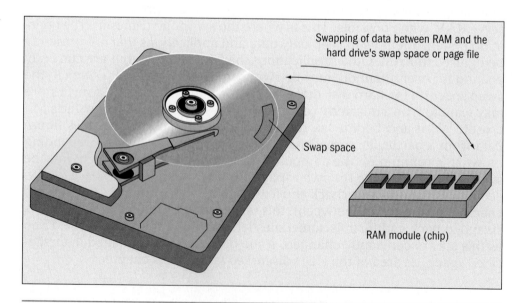

Figure 17–7   As user switches between applications and performs multiple tasks, data is swapped back and forth between RAM and the computer's hard drive. This area on the hard drive is referred to as either *swap space* **or a** *paging file.*

result of this process vary. It is sometimes possible to view the data in a readable format from the files created during the spooling process.

Latent Data

The term latent data includes data that are obfuscated (not necessarily intentionally) from a user's view. It includes areas of files and disks that are typically not apparent to the computer user, but contain data nonetheless. Latent data are one of the reasons a forensic image of the media is created. If a standard copy were all that was produced, only the logical data (that which the operating system is aware of) would be captured. Getting every bit of data ensures that potentially valuable evidence in latent data is not missed.

Once the all-inclusive forensic image is produced, how is the latent data viewed? Utilities that allow a user to examine a hard disk drive on a binary (ones and zeros) level are the answer. Applications such as Norton Disk Editor and WinHex provide this type of access to a hard disk drive or other computer media. Thus these applications, sometimes also referred to as *hex editors* (for the hexadecimal shorthand of computer language), allow all data to be read on the binary level independent of the operating system's file system table. Utilities such as these can write to the media under examination, thus changing data. Consequently, a software or hardware write-blocker should be used. A more common option in data forensics is to use specialized forensic examination software. EnCase and Forensic Toolkit for Windows and SMART and Forensic Autopsy for Linux are examples of forensic software. Each allows a search for evidence on the binary level and provides automated tools for performing common forensic processing techniques. Examiners should be cautious, however, about relying too heavily on automated tools. To merely use an automated tool without understanding what is happening in the background and why evidentiary data might exist in particular locations would severely impede the ability to testify to the findings.

Slack Space. Slack space can really be divided into two separate areas—**file slack** and **RAM slack**. Before we can begin to understand the concept of either, we must return to how files are stored. To illustrate this concept it is best to use the example of a simple Windows partition. Recall that a partition system is nothing more than a contiguous set of blocks that are defined and treated as an independent disk. Remember that although the smallest unit of data measure is one bit (either a one or a zero), a HDD cannot address or deal with such a small unit. In fact, not even a byte (eight bits) can be addressed. Rather, the smallest unit of addressable space by a HDD is the sector. Sectors are groups of bytes and can vary in size depending on the media; HDDs typically group sectors in 512-byte increments, while CD-ROMs allocate 2048 bytes per sector. Even though the sector is the smallest addressable unit by the HDD, the operating system and the file system on the HDD view it a bit differently. File systems may mandate a minimum amount of space allocated to each file. This returns us to the concept of clusters.

As you may recall, clusters are groups of sectors used to store files and folders. The cluster is the minimum storage unit defined and used by the logical partition. These clusters are maintained by the tables or bitmaps of the file system. (Remember, the tables and bitmaps—FAT, NTFS, EXT2— are similar to databases that track safe-deposit boxes, letting us know

Latent Data
Areas of files and disks that are typically not apparent to the computer user (and often not to the operating system), but contain data nonetheless.

where to find things.) It is because of the minimum addressable sector of the HDD and the minimum unit of storage requirement of the volume that we have slack space.

If the minimum addressable unit of the HDD is 512 bytes, what happens if the file is only 100 bytes? In this instance there are 412 bytes of slack space. It does not end here, however, because of the minimum cluster requirement. Minimum cluster allocation must be defined in a sector multiple of two. Thus a cluster must be a minimum of two, four, six, or eight sectors, and so on. So, if we return to our initial example of the 100-byte file and apply it to a two-sector-per-cluster (1024 bytes) volume requirement, we now isolate 1024 bytes (two sectors) of storage space for a 100-byte file. The remaining 924 bytes would be slack space (see Figure 17–8).

To illustrate this point, let us expand on the concept of safe-deposit boxes. The bank offers safe-deposit boxes of a particular size. This is the equivalent of the HDD's clusters. A person wanting to place only a deed to a house in the box gets the same size box as a person who wants to stuff it full of cash. The former would have empty space should he or she desire to place additional items in the box. This empty space is the equivalent of slack space. But what if the box becomes full and the person needs more space? That person must then get a second box. Similarly, if a file grows to fill one cluster and beyond, a second cluster (and subsequent clusters as needed) is allocated. The remaining space in the second cluster is slack space. This continues as more and more clusters are allocated depending on file size and file growth.

This example is a bit of an oversimplification because there are actually two types of slack space: RAM slack and file slack. RAM slack occupies the space from where the actual (logical) data portion of the file ends to where the first allocated sector in the cluster terminates. File slack, therefore, occupies the remaining space of the cluster. Let us go back to the 100-byte file with the two-sector-per-cluster minimum requirement. Following the end of the logical data (the end of the 100 bytes), the remaining 412 bytes of that

RAM Slack

The area beginning at the end of the logical file and terminating at the end of that sector. In some older operating systems this area is padded with information in RAM.

File Slack

The area that begins at the end of the last sector that contains logical data and terminates at the end of the cluster.

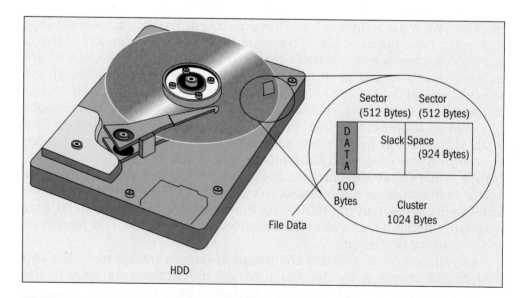

Figure 17–8   **Slack space illustrated in a two-sector cluster. Cluster sizes are typically greater than two sectors, but two sectors are displayed here for simplicity.**

sector is RAM slack; the additional 512 bytes completing the cluster is then file slack. See Figure 17–9 for a visual depiction. The question now becomes: What can I expect to find in slack space and why is this important? The answer: junk—valuable junk.

RAM slack is a concept that was more relevant in older operating systems. Remember that the minimum amount of space the HDD can address is the 512-byte sector. Therefore if the file size is only 100 bytes, the remaining space must be padded. Some operating systems pad this area with data contained in RAM. This could include Web pages, passwords, data files, or other data that existed in RAM when the file was written. Modern Windows operating systems pad this space with zeros, but some examinations may still yield valuable data in this area.

File slack, on the other hand, can contain a lot of old, orphaned data. To illustrate this point, let's take the 100-byte file example a bit further. Let's say that prior to the 100-byte file being written to the HDD and occupying one cluster (two sectors totaling 1024 bytes), a 1,000-byte file occupied this space but was deleted by the user. Understanding that when a file is "deleted" the data still remains behind, so it is probably a safe bet that data from the original 1000-byte file remains in the slack space of the new 100-byte file now occupying this cluster. This is just one example of why data exists in file slack and why it might be valuable as evidence.

In one final attempt to illustrate this point, let us again build on our safe-deposit box analogy. If a person rents two safe-deposit boxes—each box representing a sector and combined representing a cluster—and that person places the deed to his house in the first box, the remaining space of that first box would be analogous to RAM slack. The space in the second box would be the equivalent of file slack. The only difference is that unlike the empty spaces of the safe-deposit box, the slack space of the file most likely contains data that might be valuable as evidence.

The data contained in RAM and file slack is not really the concern of the operating system. As far as the OS is concerned, this space is empty and therefore ready to be used. Until that happens, however, an examination

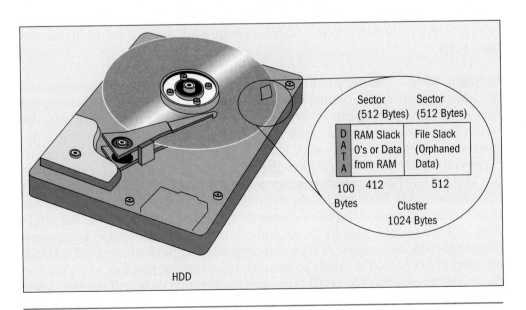

Figure 17–9   File slack.

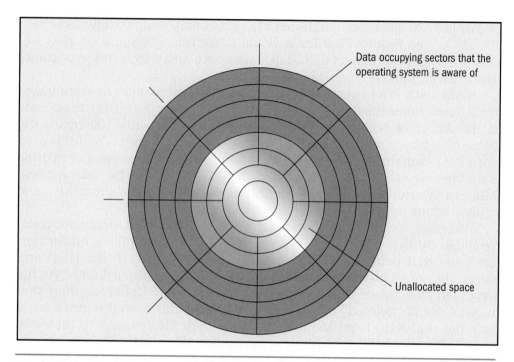

Data occupying sectors that the operating system is aware of

Unallocated space

Figure 17–10 Simplistic view of a hard drive platter demonstrating the concept of unallocated space.

with one of the aforementioned tools will allow a look into these areas, thus revealing the orphaned data. The same is true for unallocated space.

Unallocated Space

The area of the HDD that the operating system (file system table) sees as empty (containing no logical files) and ready for data. Simply stated, it is the unused portion of the HDD, but is not necessarily empty.

Unallocated Space.   Latent evidentiary data also resides in **unallocated space**. What is unallocated space, how does data get in there, and what is done to access this space? If we have a 80 GB hard drive and only half of the hard drive is filled with data, then the other half, or 40 GB, is unallocated space (see Figure 17–10.) Returning to our safe-deposit box analogy, if the entire bank of safe-deposit boxes contains 100 boxes, but only 50 are currently in use, then the other 50 would be the equivalent of unallocated space. The HDD's unallocated space typically contains a lot of useful data. The constant shuffling of files on the HDD causes data to become orphaned in unallocated space as the logical portion of the file is rewritten to other places. Some examples of how data is orphaned may help.

Defragmenting.   Defragmenting a HDD involves moving noncontiguous data back together. Remember that the HDD has minimum space reservation requirements. Again, if the file requires only 100 bytes of space, the operating system might allocate much more than that for use. If the file grows past what has been allocated for it, another cluster is required. If, however, a different file occupies the next cluster in line, then the operating system will have to find another place for that first file on the drive. In this scenario, the file is said to be *fragmented* because data for the same file is contained in noncontiguous clusters. In the case of the HDD, the shuffling of files causes data to be orphaned in unallocated space. Ultimately fragmentation of numerous files can degrade the performance of a HDD, causing the read/write heads to have to traverse the platters to locate the data. Defragmenting the HDD takes noncontiguous data and rearranges it so it is in contiguous clusters. Building yet again on our safe-deposit box analogy, if a renter eventually needs to store more property than his original box can hold, the bank will rent him a second box. If, however, all the boxes around his are occupied and the only free one is in another section of the room, then his property is "fragmented." The bank would have to "defrag" the safe-deposit boxes to get the property of users with more than one box into adjacent boxes.

Swap File/Swap Space. Recall that a computer uses the HDD to maximize the amount of RAM by constantly swapping data in and out of RAM to a predetermined location on the HDD, thus freeing valuable RAM. The constant read and write operations of RAM cause a constant change in the swap file—*WIN386.swp* or *pagefile.sys* in Windows—or swap space on a Linux system. Data can become orphaned in unallocated space from this constant swapping to and from the HDD.

Deleted Files. The deletion of files is another way that data becomes orphaned in unallocated space. Data from deleted files can manifest itself in different ways during a forensic examination. The actions that occur when a file is deleted vary among file systems. What is fairly consistent, though, is that generally speaking the data is not gone. For example, consider what happens when a user or program deletes a file in a Windows operating system with a FAT file system. When a file is deleted the first character in the file's directory entry (its name) is replaced with the Greek letter sigma. When the sigma replaces the first character, the file is no longer viewable through conventional methods and the operating system views the space previously occupied by the file as available. The data, however, is still there.

This example doesn't account for the actions of the Windows Recycle Bin. When the Windows operating system is set up to merely place the deleted file in the Recycle Bin, the original directory entry is deleted and one is created in the Recycle folder for that particular user. The new Recycle folder entry is linked to another file, the *info* or *info2* file, which includes some additional data, such as the location of the file prior to its deletion should the user wish to restore it to that location. Detailed discussions of the function of the Recycle Bin are beyond the scope of this chapter, but suffice it to say that even when the Recycle Bin is emptied the data usually remains behind until overwritten. Moreover, Windows NTFS partitions and Linux EXT partitions handle deleted files differently, but in both cases data typically remains.

What if a new file writes data to the location of the original file? Generally speaking, the data is gone. This is, of course, unless the new file only partially overwrites the original. In this instance we return to the unallocated space orphaned data scenario: If a file that occupied two clusters is deleted, and a new file overwrites one of the clusters, then the data in the second cluster is orphaned in unallocated space. Of course yet a third file can overwrite the second cluster entirely, but until then the data remains in unallocated space. Let us once again look to our safe-deposit box analogy. If, for example, the owner of two safe-deposit boxes stopped renting them, the bank would list them as available. If the owner didn't clean them out, the contents would remain unchanged. If a new owner rented one of the boxes, the contents from the former owner would be replaced with the new owner's possessions. The second box would therefore still contain orphaned contents from its previous owner. The contents would remain in this "unallocated box" space until another renter occupies it.

Chapter Summary

Computers have permeated society and are used in countless ways with innumerable applications. Similarly, the role of electronic data in investigative work has realized exponential growth in the last decade. Users of computers and other electronic data storage devices leave footprints and data trails behind. Computer forensics involves the preservation, acquisition, extraction, analysis, and interpretation of computer data. In today's world of technology, many devices are capable of storing data and could thus be grouped into the field of computer forensics.

The central processing unit (CPU) is the brain of the computer—the main chip responsible for doing the actual computing. Random-access memory (RAM) is volatile memory containing data that is forever lost when the power is turned off. Programs are loaded into RAM because of its faster read speed. The hard disk drive (HDD) is typically the primary location of data storage within the computer. Different operating systems map out HDDs differently and examiners must be familiar with the file system they are examining. Evidence exists in many different locations and in numerous forms on a HDD. This evidence can be grouped into two major categories: visible and latent data.

Visible data is data that the operating system is aware of, and consequently is easily accessible to the user. From an evidentiary standpoint, it can encompass any type of user-created data, such as word-processing documents, spreadsheets, accounting records, databases, and pictures. Temporary files, created by programs as a sort of backup on the fly, can also prove valuable as evidence. Finally, data in the swap space (used to conserve the valuable RAM within the computer system) can yield evidentiary visible data.

Latent data, on the other hand, is data that the operating system typically is not aware of. Evidentiary latent data can exist in both RAM slack and file slack. RAM slack is the area from the end of the logical file to the end of the sector. File slack is the remaining area from the end of the final sector containing logical data to the end of the cluster. Another area where latent data might be found is in unallocated space. Unallocated space is space on a HDD that the operating system sees as empty and ready for data. The constant shuffling of data through deletion, defragmentation, and swapping is one of the ways data is orphaned in latent areas. Finally, when a user deletes files the data typically remains behind. Deleted files are therefore another source of latent data to be examined during forensic analysis.

Computer file systems and data structures are vast and complex. Therefore, areas of forensic analysis are almost limitless and constrained only by the knowledge and skill of the examiner. With a working knowledge of a computer's function, how they are utilized, and how they store data, an examiner is on his or her way to begin to locate the evidentiary data.

Review Questions

1. Computer forensics involves the _____, _____, _____, and _____ of computer data.

2. True or False: Hardware comprises the physical components of the computer. _____

3. _____ is a set of instructions compiled into a program that performs a particular task.

4. (ROM, RAM) chips store programs used to start the boot process.

5. The term used to describe the chassis, including the motherboard and any other internal components of a personal computer, is _____.

6. True or False: The motherboard is a complex network of wires that carry data from one hardware device to another. _____

7. True or False: The first thing you should do when you encounter a computer system in a forensic investigation is to connect the power supply and boot the system. _____

8. RAM is referred to as volatile memory because it is not _____.

9. The brain of the computer is referred to as the _____.

10. The _____ is the primary component of storage in the personal computer.

11. Personal computers typically communicate with each other through a(n) _____.

12. The computer's _____ permits the user to manage files and applications.

13. A hard drive's partitions are typically divided into _____, _____, _____, and _____.

14. A(n) _____ is a single one or zero in the binary system, and the smallest term in the language of computers.

15. A(n) _____ is a group of eight bits.

16. A group of sectors, always units in multiples of two, is called a(n) _____.

17. An exact duplicate of the entire contents of a hard disk drive is known as a(n) _____.

18. All data readily available to a computer user is known as _____ data.

19. A(n) _____ file is created when data is moved from RAM to the hard disk drive to conserve space.

20. Most programs automatically save a copy of a file being worked on into a(n) _____ file.

21. The existence of _____ data is why a forensic image of the media is created.

22. The smallest unit of addressable space on a hard disk drive is the _____.

23. The two types of slack space are _____ slack and _____ slack.

24. _____ slack is the area from the end of the logical to the end of the sector.

25. The portion of a disk that does not contain stored data is called _____.

26. True or False: Defragmenting a hard disk drive involves moving noncontiguous data back together. _____

27. True or False: A portion of a "deleted" file may be found in a computer's unallocated space. _____

Further References

Britz, M. T., *Computer Forensics and Cyber Crime*. Upper Saddle River, N.J.: Prentice Hall, 2004.

Casey, E., *Digital Evidence and Computer Crimes*, 2nd ed., San Diego: Elsevier Academic Press, 2004.

Kruse, W. G., and J. G. Heiser, *Computer Forensics—Incident Response Essentials*. Boston: Addison-Wesley, 2001.

Nelson, B., A. Phillips, F. Enfinger, and C. Steuart, *Guide to Computer Forensics and Investigations*, 2nd ed. Boston: Thomson Course Technology, 2005.

Case Study 1
Computer Forensic Analysis Answers the Question "Arson or Accident?"

Brief

The home of John Smith was destroyed by a fire, which was later determined not to be an accident, but rather the result of arson. During the fire Smith's wife, Jane, died. Investigators learn that insurance policies taken against both the home and the life of Jane Smith were recently increased. Smith stands to receive a very large monetary settlement. This fact, and problems with his purported alibi at the time of the fire, makes him the primary suspect. Smith has steadfastly denied the existence of the insurance policies and offers that his wife must have recently changed the policies. Further investigation discloses that the couple did not possess a home computer but that Smith uses a computer at work. After applying for and receiving a search warrant for Smith's workplace, the arson investigator seizes the computer system unit from underneath Smith's desk, which he found in a powered-off condition.

Furthermore, during the execution of the search warrant, the company's computer administrator tells investigators that the computer was used only by Smith. The computer system unit is submitted for forensic analysis.

Analysis Request

Locate any incriminating or exculpatory evidentiary data with respect to Smith's knowledge of changes in his insurance policy. Locate any evidentiary data with respect to motive for the crimes of arson and/or homicide.

Forensic Image Acquisition

1. The computer system was documented and its chassis was opened and a single IDE/ATA hard disk drive (HDD) was located and documented. The HDD was removed from the system and the computer system unit was booted to the BIOS setup program. The system date and time were verified.

2. The HDD was then placed in a forensic workstation, connected to the system using a hardware write-blocking device

Courtesy of Peter Arnold, Inc.

to ensure that the suspect HDD was not altered in any way.

3. A forensic image of the HDD was acquired using EnCase Version 5. The integrity of this image was verified using the MD5 algorithm inherent in the EnCase program. (A date and time analysis was done on all the files, revealing no dates later than the date of the execution of the search warrant).

Analysis

1. Deleted files were recovered.

2. All files, including dates and times, logical and physical sizes, and complete location path, were documented by the EnCase program.

3. User accounts were documented: two default accounts (*Administrator* and *Guest*, SID 500 and 501 respectively) and one user account (*jsmith*).

4. The operating system and file system type were documented: Windows 2000 using an NTFS partition.

5. Keyword text searches, derived from the text of letters received by the insurance company, were conducted.

6. All Microsoft Word documents (.doc and .rtf) were examined.

7. All text documents were examined.

8. Print spool files were examined.

Findings

1. A file titled *insurance1.doc* was located in the directory *C:\Documents and Settings\jsmith\junk*. The directory structure *C:\Documents and Settings\jsmith* coincides with a default directory for the user name *jsmith*, which would have been established with that account. The subdirectory *junk* was then added by a user of the *jsmith* account. The text in this file is the same as the one received by the insurance company requesting an increase in homeowner's insurance.

2. Text found in unallocated space matches sections of text in a second letter received by the insurance company requesting an increase in life insurance for Jane Smith.

3. A file titled ~ *WRL1604.tmp* was found in the directory *C:\Documents and Settings\jsmith\junk*. The file matches that of a temporary Microsoft Word file and contains text matching sections of text in the letter received by the insurance company requesting an increase in life insurance for Jane Smith.

4. A file titled *46127a.SPL* was located in the directory *C:\windows\system32\spool\printers*. This file appears to be a print spool file. This file, when viewed as an Enhanced Meta File (EMF), revealed a document exact in composition and similar in layout to the letter received by the insurance company requesting an increase in life insurance for Jane Smith. An EMF is a type of spool file created during the printing process and can be viewed as a Windows picture file in the forensic software.

Conclusion

Based on the forensic examination of the computer data submitted in this case, it can be stated within a reasonable degree of scientific certainty that a user of this computer had knowledgeable interaction with letters very similar in content, composition, and structure to the evidentiary letters submitted as reference for analysis.

Case Study 2
Counterfeiting and Fraud: A Forensic Computer Investigation

Brief

A detective submits a computer laptop for examination and explains that it was seized in connection with a case of counterfeiting and fraud. According to the detective, patrol officers happened upon a large sport-utility vehicle, occupied by one male driver, parked in the lot of a local mall. According to the officers, the driver and the circumstances appeared suspicious. After investigating further, the officers located a laptop computer, color printer, and scanner in the rear of the vehicle. All equipment was hooked up and running. Additionally, the officers located gift certificates for one of the stores within the mall, which apparently were printed inside the vehicle. Finally, two $100 bills bearing exactly the same serial number were located in the driver's wallet. In response to questioning, the driver admitted using the system to print bogus gift certificates and counterfeit cash, which he then redeemed inside the mall. Prior to submission at the computer forensics laboratory, the equipment was processed for fingerprints at the state Bureau of Criminal Identification (BCI).

Analysis Request

Locate any evidentiary data with respect to the crimes of counterfeiting and fraud. Demonstrate any connection between the recovered printed documents and the electronic equipment seized from the vehicle.

Forensic Image Acquisition

1. The computer system was documented and its case was opened and a single IDE hard disk drive (HDD) was located and documented. The HDD was removed from the system and the computer system unit was booted to the BIOS setup program. The system date and time were verified.

2. The HDD was then placed in a forensic workstation, connected to the system using a hardware write-blocking device to ensure that the suspect HDD was not altered in any way.

3. A forensic image of the HDD was acquired using EnCase Version 5. The integrity of this image was verified using the MD5 algorithm inherent in the EnCase program. A date and time analysis was done on all the files, revealing no dates later than the date of the execution of the search warrant.

Analysis

1. Deleted files were recovered.

2. All files, including dates and times, logical and physical sizes, and complete location path, were documented by the EnCase program.

3. The operating system and file system type were documented: Windows XP using an NTFS file system.

4. All graphics files were viewed, including ones previously deleted.

Courtesy Getty Images, Inc.

5. A graphics finder script was run against unallocated space. The script searched this area to locate file signatures of known graphics files.

6. All print spool files were located and examined.

Findings

1. A file titled *100front.jpg* was located in the directory *C:\Documents and Settings\user1\My Documents*. This file is an image of the front of a $100 bill. The serial number on this image matched the serial number of the suspected counterfeit $100 bills found on the suspect.

2. A file titled *100back.jpg* was located in the directory *C:\Documents and Settings\user1\My Documents*. This file is an image of the back of a $100 bill.

3. A file titled *GapGiftCert1.jpg* was located in the directory *C:\Documents and Settings\user1\My Documents*. This file is an image of the front of a gift certificate for The Gap, a retail store.

4. A file titled *GapGiftCert2.jpg* was located in the directory *C:\Documents and Settings\user1\My Documents*. This file is an image of the back of a gift certificate for The Gap, a retail store.

5. A file titled *thumbs.db* was located in the directory *C:\Documents and Settings\user1\My Documents*. This file, when viewed as a compound file, displayed several images, namely the images in items 1–4.

6. In the folder *C:\Documents and Settings\User1\My Recent Documents,* link files were found to the following:

   a. *C:\Documents and Settings\user1\My Documents\100front.jpg*

   b. *C:\Documents and Settings\user1\My Documents\100back.jpg*

   c. *C:\Documents and Settings\user1\My Documents\GapGiftCert1.jpg*

   d. *C:\Documents and Settings\user1\My Documents\GapGiftCert2.jpg*

7. The submitted scanner and printer were connected to a laboratory computer system and the aforementioned evidentiary files were copied onto the HDD of that system. Several printouts of the images were made. Additionally, test items were scanned and printed. All exemplars produced from the laboratory computer system were submitted to the state Bureau of Criminal Identification. The original counterfeit currency and gift certificates were also submitted to BCI for comparison to the exemplars. BCI was asked to locate any distinguishing characteristics produced by the printer and scanner submitted in this case.

Conclusion

Based on the forensic examination of the computer data submitted in this case, it can be stated within a reasonable degree of scientific certainty that a user of this computer knowingly produced counterfeit currency and counterfeit gift certificates.

Scott Peterson: A Case of Circumstantial Evidence

Scott Peterson was charged with the murder of his pregnant wife, Laci, and her unborn son, Conner. On the surface, this young couple lived a happy and content lifestyle in Modesto, California. The 30-year-old Peterson had married his college sweetheart, Laci, a 27-year-old substitute teacher. She was about one month away from delivering her first child. Scott Peterson had told investigators that he had last seen his wife on December 24, 2002, at 9:30 a.m. when he left home for a fishing trip off San Francisco Bay. The decomposed remains of Laci washed ashore in April 2003, not far from where Scott Peterson said he had gone fishing on the day she vanished. Peterson said she was dressed in a white top and black pants when he last saw her, but Laci's body was found with khaki pants. Her sister recalled that Laci was wearing khaki pants the night before her disappearance.

Peterson claimed that he had gone fishing for sturgeon or striped bass, but the police investigation revealed that he failed to bring the appropriate fishing rod and lines to catch such fish. Further revelations surfaced when it became known that Scott was having an affair with another woman. A search of Scott's warehouse led to the recovery of a black hair on a pair of pliers resting in Scott's boat. A mitochondrial DNA profile of the hair was consistent with Laci's DNA. Scott Peterson was charged with murder and convicted and currently awaits his fate on death row.

Visit WebExtra 18.1 to view the evidence that prosecutors presented to convict Scott Peterson.

chapter **18**

Forensic Science and the Internet

By Andrew W. Donofrio and Richard Saferstein

KEY TERMS

bookmark

broadband

browser

cookies

domain

download

e-mail

firewall

hacking

hypertext

Internet cache

Internet history

Internet protocol

Internet service provider (ISP)

mailing list

modem

newsgroups

router

search engine

uniform resource locator (URL)

VoIP (voiceover Internet protocol)

Wi-Fi

Today, one cannot read a newspaper or turn on the television without seeing some reference to the Internet. The Internet, often referred to as the "information superhighway," is a medium for people to communicate with others and to access millions of pieces of information on computers located anywhere on the globe. No subject or profession remains untouched by the Internet, including forensic science. Every week many new pages of information are added to the Internet on the subject of forensic science, providing instant access to updated forensic science news and information. The Internet brings together forensic scientists from all parts of the world, linking them into one common electronic community.

The Internet was developed in 1969 by the U.S. Department of Defense with the purpose of providing a connection between computers in different locations. The project, called ARPANET, originated from a group of scientists and engineers funded by the Pentagon's Advanced Research Projects Agency (ARPA). Their idea was based on the premise that the network would still operate even if part of the connection failed. The first successful link was established between computers housed at UCLA and Stanford Research Institute. Shortly thereafter, USC–Santa Barbara and University of Utah computers were added to the system. In 1972, more than twenty sites were connected on the system when the first electronic mail (e-mail) message was sent. In the 1980s, this network of interconnected computers grew with the establishment of the National Science Foundation Network (NSFNet), which encompassed five supercomputing centers across the United States. At about the same time, regional networks were formed around the United States for the purpose of accessing NSFNet. By 1989, ARPANET had closed down and NSFNet, along with its regional networks, began to mushroom into a worldwide network known as the Internet.[1]

WebExtra 18.1

The Scott Peterson Case
www.prenhall.com/Saferstein

What Is the Internet?

The Internet can be defined as a "network of networks." A single network consists of two or more computers that are connected in some fashion to share information; the Internet connects thousands of these networks so

---

[1] An excellent history of the Internet is found in Katie Hefner and Matthew Lyon, *Where Wizards Stay Up Late: The Origins of the Internet* (New York: Simon & Schuster, 1996).

information can be exchanged worldwide. Connections are sometimes made through a modem, a device that allows computers to exchange and transmit information through telephone lines. A modem passes digital information through a series of steps to convert it to analog signals that can be passed over a telephone line. The process is reversed when the modem converts analog signals coming in from the phone line. Modems transfer information at a rate of bits per second (bps). Obviously, a modem with high-speed capabilities will ensure a faster connection on the Internet. Currently, a modem that transmits at 56,000 bits (or 56 kilobits) per second is recommended for convenience and reasonable connection speed. This speed is roughly equivalent to transmitting 1,000 to 2,000 words per second. The trend, however, is to offer Internet users even higher-speed broadband connections to websites. Digital subscriber line (DSL) service is available from phone companies in many regions. DSL carries digital information on your regular telephone line without disturbing voice traffic. These lines can carry up to 1.1 megabits per second. Alternatively, one may opt to transmit over a TV cable line. Cable modems offer speeds comparable to DSL. Once your computer is hooked into a DSL or cable line you now have an additional option to link other computers in your home or office, through either network wire (typically Ethernet) or high-frequency radio waves via a wireless or Wi-Fi connection. A device called a router serves as a sort of splitter, designed to link computers and manage traffic between them. The router, whether wired or wireless, allows computers to share a connection to the Internet. The advantage of Wi-Fi technology is that it avoids messy wires. Once you have positioned a router in your home or office, another option awaits you—voice over Internet protocol (VoIP). The IP (Internet Protocol) portion of VoIP is the bloodline of the Internet—but more on that later.

A broadband Internet connection can send and receive the human voice in a manner indistinguishable from a traditional telephone line. If you're in the range of a router, your Wi-Fi phone (cost about $150) can operate like a traditional cell phone. Unlimited-calling plans are commercially available for $20–25 per month.

It is quite astonishing to think that there is no overriding network controlling the Internet. Rather, various larger, higher-level networks are connected through *network access points*. Many large Internet service providers (ISPs) (Verizon, AOL, Yahoo) connect to each other through these network access points. The ISP's customers can then connect to the network by connecting to the bank of modems or the cable/DSL connected routers present at the Internet service provider location and thus be connected to all the other networks. Because this places many individual computers on the network, an address system is needed so that all the data traveling on the network can get to its intended location.

On the Internet, the address is known as an Internet protocol (IP) address. This is derived from the protocol suite (transmission-control protocol/Internet protocol—TCP/IP) that defines how traffic is to be presented and transmitted over the Internet. TCP/IP is nothing more than a set of rules on how manufacturers and developers of both hardware and software must configure their products if they want to send traffic over the Internet. With all of the different computer manufacturers and software developers, some rules are necessary if computers are to successfully communicate on a global network. Just as any human language needs rules for people to communicate successfully, so does the language of computers. Computers that participate on the Internet, therefore,

Modem
A device that connects a computer to another computer through a phone line.

Broadband
Describes any kind of Internet connection with a download speed of more than 56 kilobits per second.

Wi-Fi
Technology that uses high-frequency radio signals to transmit and receive data over the Internet. Allows for a wireless connection to the Internet.

Router
A device that manages traffic between computers belonging to a network, enabling them to share a connection to the Internet.

VoIP (Voice Over Internet Protocol)
Transmission of the human voice over the Internet, usually through a telephone.

Internet Service Provider (ISP)
A company that provides connections to the Internet.

Internet Protocol
The set of rules used to transmit packets of data over the Internet and route them to their destination.

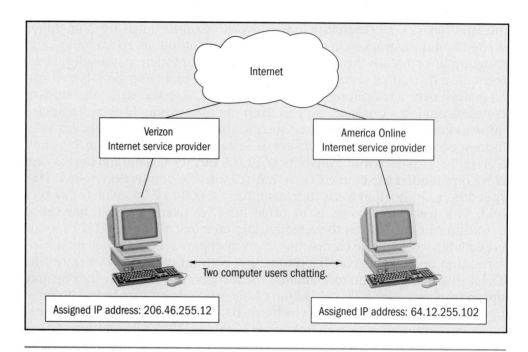

Figure 18–1   Two computers communicating by sending data to each other's IP address via the Internet. An IP address is assigned to each computer by their respective Internet service providers (ISPs).

must be provided with an IP address from the Internet service provider to which they connect. IP addresses take the form ###.###.###.###, where, generally speaking, the ### can be any number from 0 to 255. A typical IP address might look like this: 66.94.234.13. Not only do these IP addresses provide the means by which data can be routed to the appropriate location, but they also provide the means by which most Internet investigations are conducted (see Figure 18–1).

Once a computer is connected to the Internet, it becomes a node on this network of networks. **Domains** are human-readable names, such as www.nytimes.com, assigned to an IP address. Thus, www.nytimes.com is the registered name for the *New York Times*. A domain name usually consists of two or more labels separated by dots. The rightmost label is the *top-level domain*. Following are the most common abbreviations by which a top-level domain name is identified on the Internet:

Domain

A human readable name and abbreviation for a website—for example, com, org, or gov are common abbreviations.

   .gov—government
   .mil—military
   .edu—educational institution
   .com—commercial providers
   .org—nonprofit organizations

To the left of the top-level domain is the subdomain; thus, nytimes is a subdomain of the .com domain. For the purpose of e-mail, the name of an individual at the *New York Times* may be added before the subdomain and the @ sign is used to separate them. An e-mail address may read as: Johndoe@nytimes.com.

At this point you may be wondering: If everything on the Internet uses an IP address to route data to the correct location, how can we use

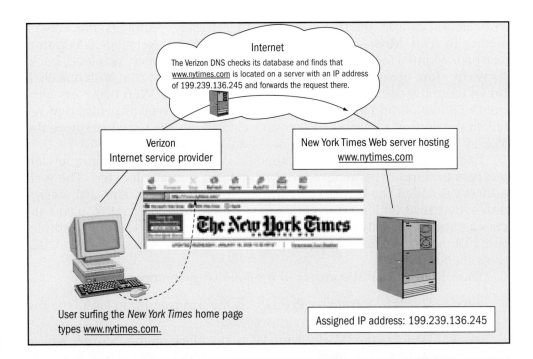

Figure 18–2   **A user wishing to visit the *New York Times* website types the user-friendly web address www.nytimes.com. Because all traffic on the Internet is routed by IP address, the web address needs to be resolved to the IP address. This is done by the user's ISP's domain name system (DNS).**

web addresses and e-mail addresses to access websites and send e-mail? The answer, although technically complex, is quite simple. Understanding the apparent limitations of the human mind to remember numbers, developers created the concept of the domain name system (DNS). *Domain name systems* are essentially large databases distributed over the Internet that relate domain names to their actual IP address. For instance, a person who wants to read the *New York Times* online only needs to know the web address. Even if the user is unsure of the actual address, the most logical place to start would obviously be www.newyorktimes.com or www.nytimes.com (both of which will work, by the way). In actuality, however, the address is 199.239.137.245. This can be verified by typing that IP address directly into your web browser where you would normally type the web address. Domain name systems makes it much easier for us to navigate the Web, but for investigative purposes it is important to realize that no names exist on the Internet; rather it's all about the IP address (see Figure 18–2).

Where to Go on the Internet

The World Wide Web

The most popular area of the Internet is the World Wide Web. Also known as WWW, W3, or the web, it is a collection of documents, called *webpages*, that are stored in the computers connected to the Internet throughout the world. Web browsers, such as Netscape Navigator and Microsoft Internet Explorer, are programs that allow the user to explore

Browser
A program that allows access to websites.

information stored on the Web and to retrieve webpages the viewer wishes to read. Most browsers, such as the popular Netscape Navigator, perform within a toolbar interface. Various functions such as reload, back, forward, stop, open, and print appear on the toolbar so that with one click on an icon, the user can easily navigate the Internet. Web browsers permit the downloading and capture of documents, as well as printing of selected portions of websites. A browser also allows the user to explore the World Wide Web and newsgroups.

Each webpage is stored in a specific website that has a unique web address that indicates where the document is actually located. The web address is called the **uniform resource locator (URL)**. The URL designates the site at which information is stored on the Internet. You can access a page by directly entering the URL into your browser. For example, the FBI has a website that can be accessed by typing in its URL: *www.fbi.gov*.

The URL for the FBI consists of the following components:

http://—Hypertext Transfer Protocol is the programming language the browser uses to locate and read webpages.

www.—Denotes the World Wide Web, the place on the Internet where the information is located.

fbi.—Designates the subdomain or server; in this case, for the Federal Bureau of Investigation.

gov—Designates the domain name.

Upon entering the FBI website, you are confronted with a multitude of services and information provided by the FBI, such as an overview of the bureau's operation, information regarding ongoing investigations, reports concerning crime statistics, and even a list of the ten most-wanted fugitives. The Internet has made browsing or exploring the Web easy through the existence of **hypertext**. Hypertext is not hard to find because it is highlighted with a different color within the webpage. When selected, hypertext enables the user to jump to another webpage related to the subject at hand. For example, if a user is interested in examining the FBI's Law Enforcement Bulletin webpage, one would merely look on the FBI's home page and search for the term *Law Enforcement Bulletin*. The user is immediately transferred to a hypertext page where, with a click of the mouse, one is taken to the website. This website has the URL *www.fbi.gov/publications/leb/leb.htm*, where *leb.htm* designates a document on the FBI website. Another FBI publication available online is *Forensic Science Communications*. This quarterly online forensic science journal presents technical articles, technical notes, case reports, and review articles in a paperless format.

The advantage of using hypertext is that the user can quickly switch back and forth between related webpages without having to retype the URL or start over at the beginning of the search. The existence of hypertext makes the Internet user-friendly and has given rise to the expressions *browsing* and *surfing the net*. Users can navigate from one website of the Internet to another, browsing at leisure through a succession of documents. Another quick way to reach a site is to designate it as a bookmark or favorite place. Most browsers allow the user to customize a list of favorite websites for easy access with one click (see Figure 18–3).

Uniform Resource Locator (URL)
A standard method by which Internet sites are addressed.

Hypertext
Links to other websites. The linked document is displayed by clicking on a highlighted word or icon.

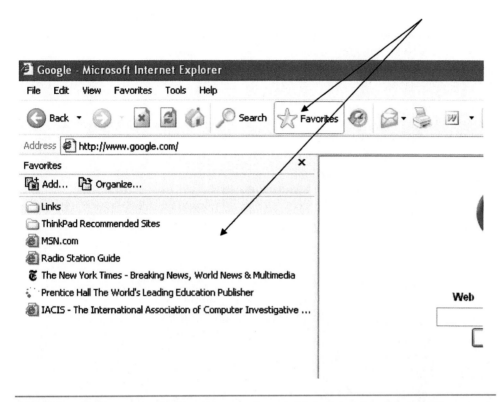

Figure 18–3 **Bookmarks or favorite places can be saved for quick access in most web browsers.**

Hundreds of new sites are added every day, providing Internet users with a staggering amount of information. You may wish to explore popular website locations by using the list of the Top 100 Classic Websites compiled by *PC Magazine* (*http://www.pcmag.com*) (see Table 18–1). The *PC Magazine* Top 100 Classic Websites list includes sites related to business and finance, computing, news, entertainment, online shopping, and reference sources. This list opens a gateway to exploring the diversity of the World Wide Web. For example, you can easily visit Expedia.com, a popular site for those interested in finding information on traveling. Through this site you can book flights, hotel rooms, and cruises and plan most any type of vacation. The Amazon.com website provides one of the largest bookstores on the Internet. Here the user can search by keyword, author, subject, or title to locate or purchase books on any topic imaginable. You can even ask Amazon.com to e-mail you when books related to your personal interests arrive in stock.

A favorite site of the author is the Switchboard website www.switchboard.com. This site is devoted to helping users locate long-lost friends or contact relatives who are spread across the country. A database of names, phone numbers, addresses, and e-mail addresses can easily be searched with a variety of options. Another interesting website that can be helpful to the user is the MapQuest website (*http://www.mapquest.com*). Here the user designates a location and the site generates a map, accompanied by directions explaining which roads to follow to best travel to that location. A fun site is BlueMountain.com (*www.bluemountain.com*), where the user can compose, personalize, and send greeting cards for all sorts of occasions.

Table 18–1 PC Magazine's Top 100 Classic Websites

AAPS: PC and Mobile

AvantGo
www.avantgo.com

Homestead
www.homestead.com

Mailblocks
www.mailblocks.com

MSN Hotmail
www.hotmail.com

Shutterfly
www.shutterfly.com

Vindigo
www.vindigo.com

WebEx
www.webex.com

Yahoo! Groups
groups.yahoo.com

Business and Finance

Bloomberg.com
www.bloomberg.com

Internal Revenue Service
www.irs.gov

MSN Money
www.moneycentral.msn.com

SmartMoney.com
www.smartmoney.com

The Motley Fool
www.fool.com

TheStreet.com
www.thestreet.com

U.S. Securities and Exchange
Commission
www.sec.gov

Careers

Dice.com
www.dice.com

Monster.com
www.monster.com

Yahoo! HotJobs
hotjobs.yahoo.com

Computing

Annoyances.org
www.annoyances.org

Answers that Work
www.answersthatwork.com

Digital Photography Review
www.dpreview.com

EarthWeb
www.earthweb.com

eWeek
www.eweek.com

ExtremeTech
www.extremetech.com

Java Technology
www.java.sun.com

PalmGear.com
www.palmgear.com

PC Magazine
www.pcmag.com

Slashdot
slashdot.org

Technology Review
www.technologyreview.com

W3Schools
www.w3schools.com

Webopedia
www.webopedia.com

**Current Events and News You
Can Use**

Electronic Privacy Information Center
www.epic.org

IEEE Virtual Museum
www.ieee-virtual-museum.org

NASA
www.nasa.gov

Project Vote Smart
www.vote-smart.org

World Health Organization
www.who.int

Lifestyle and Fun

Citysearch
www.citysearch.com

Discovery Kids
kids.discovery.com

Epicurious
www.epicurious.com

HowStuffWorks
www.howstuffworks.com

ifilm
www.ifilm.com

National Geographic Society
www.nationalgeographic.com

Nickelodeon Online
www.nick.com

Pogo
www.pogo.com

Smithsonian Institution
www.si.edu

Yahoo! Games
games.yahoo.com

News and Entertainment

AMG All Music Guide
www.allmusic.com

BBC News
www.bbc.co.uk

CNN
www.cnn.com

E! Online
www.eonline.com

ESPN.com
www.espn.com

Internet Archive
www.archive.org

Internet Movie Database (IMDb)
www.imdb.com

Slate
www.slate.com

The New York Times on the Web
www.nytimes.com

NPR
www.npr.org

The Onion
www.theonion.com

RollingStone.com
www.rollingstone.com

Salon.com
www.salon.com

ScienceDaily
www.sciencedaily.com

Television Without Pity
www.televisionwithoutpity.com

Wired News
www.wired.com

Security and the Net

Broadbandreports.com
dslreports.com

CERT Coordination Center
www.cert.org

Table 18–1 *Continued*

GetNetWise *www.getnetwise.org*	Google *www.google.com*	Netflix *www.netflix.com*
Gibson Research Corp. *www.grc.com*	iVillage.com *www.ivillage.com*	Overstock.com *www.overstock.com*
Internet Traffic Report *www.internettrafficreport.com*	Librarians' Internet Index *www.lii.org*	PriceGrabber.com *www.pricegrabber.com*
Netcraft *news.netcraft.com*	The Library of Congress *www.loc.gov*	Shopping.com *www.shopping.com*
SecurityFocus *www.securityfocus.com*	MSN Encarta *encarta.msn.com*	Surprise.com *www.surprise.com*
TrendMicro *www.trendmicro.com*	Nolo.com *www.nolo.com*	Techbargains.com *www.techbargains.com*
Search, Reference, and Portals	WebMD *www.webmd.com*	**Travel**
About.com *www.about.com*	Yahoo! *www.yahoo.com*	Expedia *www.expedia.com*
Centers for Disease Control and Prevention *www.cdc.gov*	**Shopping**	Fodors *www.fodors.com*
Dictionary.com *dictionary.reference.com*	Amazon.com *www.amazon.com*	Frommers.com *www.frommers.com*
Encyclopaedia Britannica *www.britannica.com*	CarsDirect.com *www.carsdirect.com*	Lonely Planet *www.lonelyplanet.com*
FedStats *www.fedstats.gov*	ConsumerReview.com *www.consumerreview.com*	Orbitz *www.orbitz.com*
FirstGov.gov *www.firstgov.gov*	eBay *www.ebay.com*	Travelocity *www.travelocity.com*

Search Engines

Sifting through the enormous amount of information on the World Wide Web can often resemble looking for a needle in a haystack. As the Internet grows, so does the need for automated search tools. Several directories and indexes known as search engines help users search the Internet for a particular topic. Typically, a user enters a keyword or phrase into a search engine to locate sites on the Internet that are relevant to a particular subject. The number of search engines continues to change with new technology, as faster, newer tools are adopted and slower, older ones are phased out. Interestingly, search engines have taken on a new look, becoming portals offering a wide variety of Internet services in addition to their traditional search functions. Some of the more popular search engines, along with their URLs, are listed here:

Search Engine

A website devoted to searching for information on the Internet using keywords.

Search Engine	URL
Yahoo!	*www.yahoo.com*
Google	*www.google.com*
MSN	*www.msn.com*
Dogpile	*www.dogpile.com*
Lycos	*www.lycos.com*

The reader can also find a multitude of search engines at www. easysearcher.com/index.html. Most search engines contain tools called *spiders* or *crawlers* that search the Web seeking titles, subjects, and keywords to index the contents of individual webpages. Through search engines, the user can locate relevant webpages containing a particular piece of information on the Internet. When the user types in keywords and phrases related to the needed information, the search engines search their databases and list all the pages involving the keyword selection. Because each search engine has different capabilities, it is recommended that multiple search engines be used when researching a subject. For example, in compiling this edition, the author had the occasion to search on the term "Roger Severs" and found a variety of search engine matches:

Search Engine	No. of Matches
Google	43
Yahoo	31
Lycos	30
Dogpile	19
MSN	16

Automated search tools called *meta-engines* load a query into several of the Internet's leading search engines to compile a single list of results. One example of a meta-engine is MetaCrawler (*www.metacrawler.com*).

Electronic Mail and Mailing Lists

E-mail
Electronic mail.

The service that is most commonly used in conjunction with the Internet is electronic mail. Also called e-mail, this communication system can transport messages across the world in a matter of seconds. In order to use e-mail, users must acquire an e-mail address, usually through an Internet service provider or a free e-mail server. Like regular postal mail, you will need an address to receive mail, and you will need to know a recipient's address to send messages. These messages are stored in an individualized mailbox that can be opened electronically at your convenience. Another interesting feature is that one can attach a file to an e-mail so that the recipient can download the attached file. The file can then be saved and stored on the recipient's computer. A file may consist of text, pictures, music, or video. For example, a text file can be viewed and modified by means of a word-processing program.

Download
The transfer of a file through an Internet connection from a remote computer to a user's computer.

Mailing List
A list of people with a common interest who receive all the e-mails sent to the list.

Also, having an e-mail account provides the opportunity to receive information through mailing lists. A mailing list is a discussion group for a selected topic in which related messages are sent directly to your mailbox through e-mail. For example, Forens-L is a mailing list dedicated to the discussion of forensic medicine and forensic science that provides a quick, useful way to exchange ideas or share information about forensics with people of similar interests around the world. General information about the mailing list is at http://geradts.com/mailman/listinfo/forens_geradts.com.

Newsgroups
Large bulletin board systems that consist of several thousand specialized discussion groups. Messages are posted to a bulletin board via e-mail for others to read.

Newsgroups

Another service much like mailing lists involves newsgroups. Like a mailing list, a newsgroup is devoted to a particular topic. Whereas a mailing list, however, is usually managed by a single site, a newsgroup networks many sites that are set up by local Internet service providers. The result is that a newsgroup joins together a significantly larger audience compared to a mailing list. A newsgroup is analogous to a bulletin board where articles (messages) are posted by subscribers. When you connect to a newsgroup, you have the ability to quickly scan through a list of article titles, selecting only those that interest you. To find a newsgroup of interest, you can explore Usenet, an index of the available newsgroups. The index can be located through search engines such as Google. Usenet can be searched through keywords in the same manner in which the World Wide Web is explored. For example, entering the keyword *law enforcement* into Usenet produces a list of articles from any of the newsgroups containing that keyword. The articles are hypertext so that with a click of the mouse, you can read the article instantaneously. A useful website (www.google.com/grphp?hl=en) lists newsgroups in hypertext so that the newsgroup can be accessed directly from the World Wide Web. Commercial services such as AOL allow the user to subscribe to a newsgroup and provide the program that will keep track of how many articles are available, which ones you have read, and which ones you have not read.

Exploring Forensic Science on the World Wide Web

There are no limits to the amount or type of information that can be found on the Internet. The fields of law enforcement and forensic science have not been left behind by advancing computer technology. Extensive information about forensic science is available on the Internet. The types of webpages range from simple explanations of the different fields of forensics to intricate details of crime-scene reconstruction. You can also find information on which colleges offer programs for degrees in forensics or pages posted by law enforcement agencies that detail their activities, as well as possible employment opportunities. Table 18–2 lists a number of websites available in the forensic science field.

Reddy's Forensic Home Page (*www.forensicpage.com*) is a valuable starting point and a must for those with an interest in forensic science on the Internet. This site is a collection of forensic webpages listed under categories such as new links in forensics; general forensic information sources, associations, colleges, and societies; literature and journals; forensic laboratories; general webpages; forensic-related mailing lists and newsgroups; universities; conferences; and various forensic fields of expertise. Another website offering a multitude of information related to forensic science is Zeno's Forensic Webpage (*forensic.to/forensic.html*). Here you can find links to forensic education and expert consultation, as well as a wealth of information concerning specific fields of forensic science. A comprehensive and useful website for those interested in law enforcement is the Police Officer's Internet Directory (*www.officer.com*). This comprehensive collection of criminal justice resources is organized into easy-to-read subdirectories that relate to topics such as law enforcement agencies, police association and organization sites, criminal justice organizations, law research pages, and police mailing-list directories.

Table 18–2 Forensic Science Web Sites*

- *American Academy of Forensic Sciences*—professional society dedicated to the application of science to the law and committed to the promotion of education in the forensic sciences.
- *American Board of Forensic Entomology*—provides information about the field's history, case studies, and professional status.
- *American Board of Forensic Toxicology Inc.*—working to establish and revise as necessary standards of qualification for those who practice forensic toxicology.
- *American College of Forensic Examiners (ACFE)*—dedicated to members of the forensic community. Also provides links to help people find expert witnesses in the forensic field.
- *American Society of Crime Laboratory Directors (ASCLD)*—nonprofit professional society devoted to the improvement of crime laboratory operations through sound management practices.
- *American Society of Questioned Document Examiners*—online references, technical notes on handwriting identification, and other areas of professional interest to the forensic document analyst.
- *ASCLD: Laboratory Accreditation Board*—offers the general public and users of laboratory services a means of identifying those laboratories which have demonstrated that they meet established standards.
- *Association for Crime Scene Reconstruction (ACSR)*—members are law enforcement investigators, forensic experts, and educators.
- *Association of Firearm and Tool Mark Examiners*—defines standards and ethics for individual workers in the field of firearms and toolmark examination.
- *California Association of Criminalists*—membership is offered to those who are presently employed as laboratory scientists and are professionally engaged in one or more fields directly related to the forensic sciences.
- *Canadian Society of Forensic Science*—includes journal abstracts, history, and meeting information.
- *European Association for Forensic Entomology*—created in May 2002 in Rosny sous Bois, France, to promote forensic entomology in Europe.
- *Forensic Science Service*
- *Forensic Science Society*—provides information on careers, conferences, and publications.
- *International Association for Identification*—professional association for those engaged in forensic identification, investigation, and scientific examination.
- *International Association of Bloodstain Pattern Analysis*—organization of forensic experts promoting education, establishing training standards, and encouraging research in the field of bloodstain pattern analysis.
- *International Association of Forensic Toxicologists*
- *International Organisation on Electronic Evidence (IOCE)*—formed to develop international principles for the procedures relating to digital evidence.
- *National Forensic Science Technology Center*—dedicated to supporting forensic science laboratories to achieve the highest possible quality of operations.
- *Natural Resources DNA Profiling and Forensic Centre*—undertakes research on natural populations of animals and plants for the purpose of providing information to managers charged with conserving biodiversity and ensuring the sustainable use of Canada's biological resources.
- *Society of Forensic Toxicologists*

*Web sites are hypertexted at *http://dir.yahoo.com/Science/Forensics/Organizations/?o=a.*

Table 18–2 *Continued*

- *Southern Association of Forensic Scientists*—organization of professional forensic scientists.
- *Southern California Association of Fingerprint Officers*—an association for scientific investigation and identification.
- *U.S. Department of Justice: National Commission on the Future of DNA Evidence*—working to maximize the value of forensic DNA evidence in the criminal justice system.
- *Vidocq Society*—forensic experts who meet in the shadow of Independence Hall to investigate and solve unsolved homicides.

Websites You May Wish to Explore

The Internet contains hundreds of webpages for the reader who is interested in introductory information on forensic science and criminal investigation. The list on the pages that follow contains websites that serve such a purpose.

An Introduction to Forensic Firearm Identification.   This website contains an extensive collection of information relating to the identification of firearms. An individual can explore in detail how to examine bullets, cartridge cases, and clothing for gunshot residues and suspect shooters' hands for primer residues. Information on the latest technology involving the automated firearms search system IBIS can also be found on this site.

Carpenter's Forensic Science Resources.   This site provides a bibliography with hypertext references pertaining to different aspects of criminal investigations involving forensic evidence. For example, the user can find references about DNA, fingerprints, hairs, fibers, and questioned documents as they relate to crime scenes and assist investigations. This website is an excellent place to start a research project in forensic science.

Crime Scene Investigation.   For those who are interested in learning the process of crime-scene investigation, this site provides detailed guidelines and information regarding crime-scene response and collection and preservation of evidence. For example, information concerning packaging and analysis of bloodstains, seminal fluids, hairs, fibers, paint, glass, firearms, documents, and fingerprints can be found through this website. This website explains the importance of inspecting the crime scene and the impact forensic evidence has on the investigation.

Crimes and Clues.   Users interested in learning about the forensic aspects of fingerprinting will find this a useful and informative website. The site covers the history of fingerprints, as well as subjects pertaining to the development of latent fingerprints. The user will also find links to other websites covering a variety of subjects pertaining to crime-scene investigation, documentation of the crime scene, and expert testimony.

Interactive Investigator–Détective Interactif.   This is an outstanding site. Visitors can obtain general information and an introduction to the main aspects of forensic science from a database on the subject. They can also explore actual evidence gathered from notorious crime scenes. Users will be able to employ deductive skills and forensic knowledge while playing an interactive game in which they must help Detective Wilson and Detective Marlow solve a gruesome murder.

The Chemical Detective.   This site offers descriptions of relevant forensic science disciplines. Topics such as fingerprint, fire and arson, and DNA analysis are described in informative layperson's terms. Case histories describe the application of forensic evidence to criminal investigations. Emphasis is placed on securing and documenting the crime scene. The site directs the reader to other important forensic links.

Questioned Document Examination.   This basic, informative webpage answers frequently asked questions concerning document examination, explains the application of typical document examinations, and details the basic facts and theory of handwriting and signatures. There are also links to noted document examination cases for the user to read and recognize the real-life application of forensic document examination.

Forensic Analysis of Internet Data

It's important from the investigative standpoint to be familiar with the evidence left behind from a user's Internet activity. A forensic examination of a computer system reveals quite a bit of data about a user's Internet activity. The data described next would be accessed and examined using the forensic techniques outlined in Chapter 17.

Internet Cache

Evidence of web browsing typically exists in abundance on the user's computer. Most web browsers (Internet Explorer, Netscape, and Firefox) use a caching system to expedite web browsing and make it more efficient. This was particularly true in the days of dial-up Internet access. When a user accesses a website, such as the *New York Times* home page, the data is fed from that server (in this example the *New York Times*), via the Internet service provider, over whatever type of connection the user has, to his or her computer. If that computer is accessing the Internet via a dial-up connection, the transfer of the *New York Times* home page may take a while, because the data transfer rate and capabilities (bandwidth) of the telephone system is limited. Even with the high-speed access of a DSL line or cable connection, conservation of bandwidth is always a consideration. Taking that into account, web browsers store (cache) portions of the pages visited onto the local hard disk drive. This way, if the page is revisited, portions of it can be reconstructed more quickly from this saved data, rather than having to pull it yet again from the Internet and use precious bandwidth.

This **Internet cache** is a potential source of evidence for the computer investigator. Portions of, and in some cases, entire visited webpages can be reconstructed. Even if deleted, these cached files can often be recovered (see the section on deleted data in Chapter 17). Investigators must know how to search for this data within the particular web browser used by a suspect.

Internet Cache

Portions of visited webpages placed on the local hard disk drive to facilitate quicker retrieval once revisited.

Internet Cookies

Cookies provide another area where potential evidence can be found. To appreciate the value of cookies you must first understand how they get onto the computer and their intended purpose. Cookies are placed on the local hard disk drive by websites the user has visited, if the user's web browser (such as Netscape Navigator or Internet Explorer) is set to allow this to happen. Netscape Navigator stores cookies in a *cookies.txt* file and Microsoft Internet Explorer places cookies in a dedicated directory. The website uses cookies to track certain information about its visitors. This information can be anything from history of visits and purchasing habits to passwords and personal information used to recognize the user for later visits. Consider a user who registers for an account at the Barnes and Noble bookstore website, and then returns to the same site from the same computer a few days later. The site will then display "Welcome, *Your User Name.*" This data is retrieved from the cookie file placed on the user's hard disk drive by the website during the initial visit and registration with the site.

It is helpful to think of cookies almost like a "Caller ID" for websites. The site recognizes and retrieves information about the visitor, as when a salesman recognizes the caller from a Caller ID display and quickly pulls the client's file. Cookie files can be a valuable source of evidence. In Internet Explorer, they take the form of plain text files, which can typically be opened with a standard text viewer or word-processing program, revealing part of the data. The existence of the files themselves, regardless of the information contained within, can be of evidentiary value to show a history of web visits. A typical cookie may resemble the following: rsaferstein@forensic-science.txt. From this we can surmise that someone using the local computer login *rsaferstein* accessed the forensic science website. It is possible that the cookie was placed there by an annoying pop-up ad, but considered against other evidence in the computer data, the presence of this cookie may be of corroborative value.

Cookies
Files placed on a computer from a visited website; they are used to track visits and usage of that site.

Internet History

Most web browsers track the history of webpage visits for the computer user. This is probably done merely for a matter of convenience. Like the "recent calls" list on a cell phone, the Internet history provides an accounting of sites most recently visited, with some storing weeks' worth of visits. Users can go back and access sites they recently visited just by going through the browser's history. Most web browsers store this information in one particular file; Internet Explorer uses the *index.dat* file. On a Windows system, an *index.dat* file is created for each login user name on the computer. The history file can be located and read with most popular computer forensic software packages. It displays the uniform resource locator (URL) of each website, along with the date and time the site was accessed. An investigation involving Internet use almost always includes an examination of Internet history data.

In some respects, the term "*Internet* history" is wrong because it doesn't encompass all of its functions. Several browsers—Internet Explorer, for one—store other valuable evidence independent of Internet access. It is not uncommon to see files accessed over a network listed in the history. Similarly, files accessed on external media, such as floppy disks, CDs, or thumb drives, may also appear in the history. Regardless, the Internet history data is a valuable source of evidence worthy of examination (see Figure 18–4).

Internet History
An accounting of websites visited. Different browsers store this information in different ways.

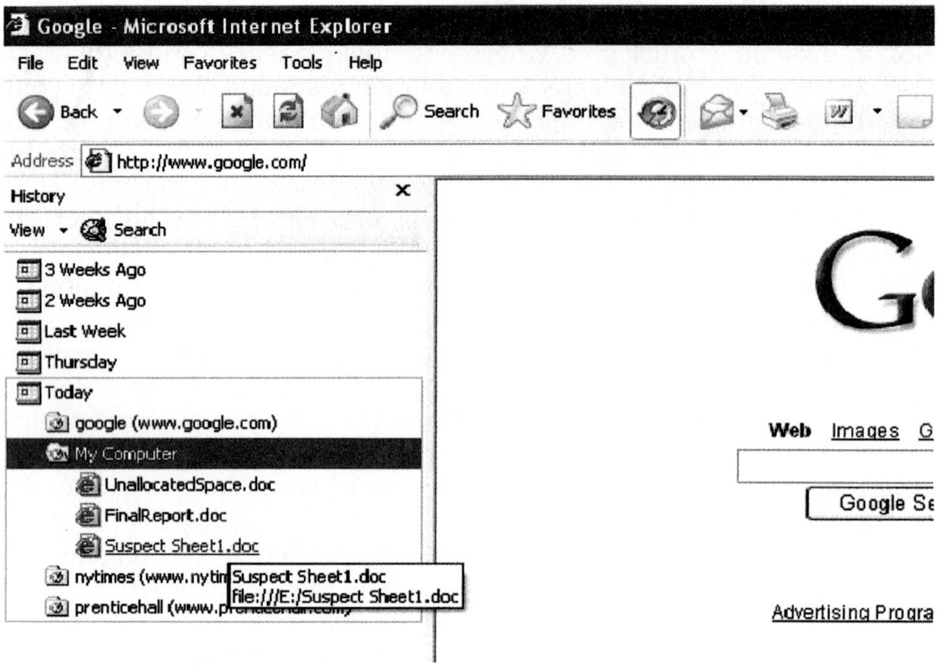

Figure 18–4 The Internet history displays more than just web browsing activity. Here we see Microsoft Word documents and a picture accessed on the current day.

Bookmarks and Favorite Places

Bookmark

A feature that enables the user to designate favorite sites for fast and easy access.

Another way users can access websites quickly is to store them in their bookmarks or "Favorite Places." Like a preset radio station, web browsers allow users to bookmark websites for future visits. A lot can be learned from a user's bookmarked sites. You might learn what online news a person is interested in or what type of hobbies he or she has. You may also see that person's favorite child pornography or computer hacking sites bookmarked.

In Internet Explorer the favorite places are kept in a folder with link (shortcut) files to a particular URL. They can be organized in subfolders or grouped by type. The same is true for the Firefox web browser, except that Firefox bookmarks are stored in a document done in HyperText Markup Language (HTML), the same language interpreted by web browsers themselves.

Forensic Investigation of Internet Communications

Computer investigations often begin with or are centered on Internet communication. Whether it is a chat conversation among many people, an instant message conversation between two individuals, or the back-and-forth of an e-mail exchange, human communication has long been a source of evidentiary material. *Regardless of the type, investigators are typically interested in communication.*

Recall that in order to communicate on the Internet, a device needs to be assigned an Internet protocol (IP) address. The IP address is provided by the Internet service provider from which the device accesses the Internet. Thus the IP address may lead to the identity of a real person. If an IP address is the link to the identity of a real person, then it is quite obviously valuable for identifying someone on the Internet. To illustrate, let's assume that a user of the Internet, fictitiously named John Smith, connects to the Internet from his home by way of a Verizon DSL connection. Verizon in this case would be responsible for providing Smith with his IP address. Verizon was issued a bank of IP addresses to service its customers from a regulatory body designed to track the usage of IP addresses (obviously so no two were used at the same time). Smith, while connected to the Internet, decides to threaten an ex-girlfriend by sending her an e-mail telling her he is going to kill her. That e-mail must first pass through Smith's Internet service provider's computers—in this case Verizon—on its way to its destination—Smith's girlfriend. The e-mail would be stamped by the servers that it passes through, and this stamp would include the IP address given to Smith by Verizon for his session on the Internet. An investigator responsible for tracking that e-mail would locate the originating IP address stamped in the e-mail header. That IP address could be researched using one of many Internet sites (*www.samspade.org, www.arin.net*) to determine which Internet service provider was given this IP as part of a block to service its customers (see Figure 18–5). The investigator then files a subpoena with the Internet service provider (Verizon) asking which of its customers was using that IP address on that date and time.

IP addresses are located in different places for different methods of Internet communications. E-mail has the IP address in the header portion of the mail. This may not be readily apparent and may require a bit of configuration to reveal. Each e-mail client is different and needs to be evaluated on a case-by-case basis. For an instant message or chat session, the particular provider (the one providing the chat mechanism—AOL, Yahoo, and so on) would be contacted to provide the user's IP address.

E-mail can be read by a number of *clients* or software programs. Two of the most popular ways to access, read, and store e-mail in today's Internet environment, however, are Microsoft Outlook and through an Internet browser. Some people even use a combination of the two. If an e-mail account is linked through Microsoft Outlook, then the e-mail is stored in a compound file (a file with several layers). Typically, a compound file exists for received (inbox), sent, and deleted e-mail. Users can also create new categories (shown as folders in Outlook) and categorize saved e-mail there. Most computer forensic software applications can view (mount) these compound files so that the e-mail can be seen, including any file attachments. These files can also be imported into a clean copy (one not attached to an account) of Microsoft Outlook and the e-mail viewed there. Investigators must also be aware that in a computer network environment, the user's outlook files may not reside on their workstation computer, but rather on a central mail or file server.

Most accounts offer the ability to access e-mail through a web-based interface as well. This way, users can access their e-mail remotely from other computers. For e-mail accessed through a web browser, the information presented earlier on Internet-based evidence applies. The web interface converts the e-mail into a document suitable for reading in a web browser. Consequently, web-based e-mail is often found in the Internet cache. This is particularly true of free Internet e-mail accounts such as Hotmail and Yahoo.

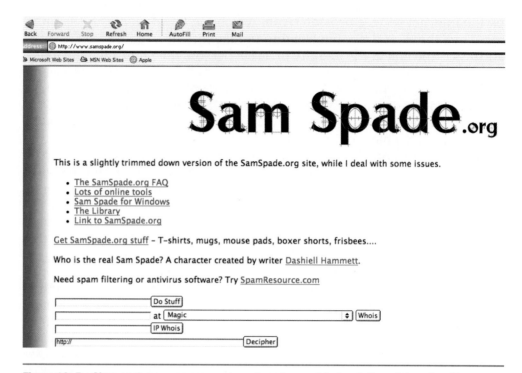

Figure 18–5 Sites such as www.samspade.org can be used to track the origins of an IP address. *Courtesy Word to the Wise*

Much of the evidence from Internet communication is also derived from chat and instant message technology. This is particularly true in the world of child sexual exploitation over the Internet. Various technologies provide chat and instant message services. Most chat and instant message conversations are not saved by the parties involved. Although most of the software does allow for conversation archiving, it is typically turned off by default. Therefore, conversations of this nature typically exist in the volatile memory space of random-access memory (RAM). Recall from Chapter 17 that RAM is termed volatile because it holds data only if it has power. Unplugging the computer will cause the data located in RAM to be lost. If, however, chat or instant message conversations are relevant as evidence and the computer was turned off, thus erasing the data in RAM, all might not be lost. Remember that there is an interaction between the computer system's RAM and the hard disk drive. RAM is a commodity and as such the computer's operating system makes an effort to conserve it as best as possible. This is done by swapping/paging that information back and forth into the swap space/paging file. Therefore remnants of chat conversations are often found in the swap space/paging file during a forensic examination of the hard disk drive. These remnants, however, are typically fragmented, disconnected, and incomplete. Therefore if the chat or instant message is still present on the screen (and thus probably still in RAM) the investigator needs a method by which to preserve and collect it.

A detailed discussion of capturing volatile data from RAM is beyond the scope of this chapter. Suffice it to say that many commercial forensic software packages can capture this data. Similarly, Linux-based tools can accomplish this as well. The examiner may even be able to export the data remotely to another device. Regardless of the method, the data needs to be acquired.

Furthermore, many programs such as America Online Instant Messenger, Yahoo Messenger, and mIRC (Internet Relay Chat) create files regarding the rooms or channels a user chatted in or the screen names with which a user sent instant messages. Each application needs to be researched and the computer forensic examination guided by an understanding of how it functions.

Hacking

Unauthorized computer intrusion, more commonly referred to as hacking, is the concern of every computer administrator. Hackers penetrate computer systems for a number of reasons. Sometimes the motive is corporate espionage; other times it is merely for bragging rights within the hacker community. Most commonly, though, a rogue or disgruntled employee with some knowledge of the computer network is looking to cause damage. Whatever the motivation, corporate America frequently turns to law enforcement to investigate and prosecute these cases.

Generally speaking, when investigating an unauthorized computer intrusion, investigators concentrate their efforts in three locations: *log files, volatile memory,* and *network traffic.* Logs and anomalons typically document the IP address of the computer that made the connection. Logs can be located in several locations on computer network. Most servers on the Internet track connections made to them through the use of logs. Additionally the router (the device responsible for directing data) may contain log files detailing connections. Similarly, devices known as firewalls may contain log files listing computers that were allowed access to the network or an individual system. Firewalls are devices (taking the form of either hardware or software) that permit only requested traffic to enter a computer system (or, more appropriately, a network). In other words, if a user didn't send out a request for Internet traffic from a specific system, the firewall should blocks its entry. If the log files captured the IP address of the intruder, then revealing the user behind the IP is the same process as for e-mail. Investigating a computer intrusion, however, does get a bit more complicated than this.

Frequently, in cases of unlawful access to a computer network, the perpetrator attempts to cover the tracks of his or her IP address. In these instances, advanced investigative techniques might be necessary to discover the hacker's true identity. When an intrusion is in progress, the investigator may have to capture volatile data (data in RAM). The data in RAM at the time of an intrusion may provide valuable clues into the identity of the intruder, or at the very least his or her method of attack. As in the case of the instant message or chat conversation, the data in RAM needs to be acquired. Another standard tactic for investigating intrusion cases is to document all programs installed and running on a system, in order to discover malicious software installed by the perpetrator to facilitate entry. The investigator uses specialized software to document running processes, registry entries, open ports, and any installed files.

Additionally, the investigator may want to capture live network traffic as part of the evidence collection and investigation process. Traffic that travels the network does so in the form of data packets. In addition to data, these packets also contain source and destination IP addresses. If the attack requires two-way communication, as in the case of a hacker stealing

WebExtra 18.9

Follow the trail of an e-mail as it travels through the Internet
www.prenhall.com/Saferstein

Hacking
Has various meanings, but is frequently used as a slang term for an unauthorized computer or network intrusion.

Firewall
Hardware or software designed to protect intrusions into an Internet network.

data, then data needs to be transmitted back to the hacker's computer using the destination IP address. Once this is learned, the investigation can focus on that system. Moreover, the type of data that is being transmitted on the network may be a clue as to what type of attack is being launched, whether any important data is being stolen, or what types of malicious software, if any, are involved in the attack.

Chapter Summary

The Internet, often referred to as the "information superhighway," is a medium for people to communicate and to access millions of pieces of information from computers located anywhere on the globe. No subject or profession remains untouched by the Internet, including forensic science. The Internet brings together forensic scientists from all parts of the world, linking them into one common electronic community.

The Internet can be defined as a "network of networks." A single network consists of two or more computers that are connected to share information; the Internet connects thousands of these networks so all of the information can be exchanged worldwide. Connections can be made through a modem, a device that allows computers to exchange and transmit information through telephone lines. Higher-speed broadband connections are available through cable lines or through DSL telephone lines. Computers can be linked or networked through wired or wireless (Wi-Fi) connections. Computers on the Internet have a unique numerical Internet protocol (IP) address and usually a name. Commercial Internet service providers connect computers to the Internet while offering the user an array of options. The most popular area of the Internet is the World Wide Web, a collection of pages stored in computers connected to the Internet throughout the world. Web browsers allow users to explore information stored on the web and to retrieve webpages they wish to read. Several directories and indexes on the Internet, known as search engines, help users locate information on a particular topic from the hundreds of thousands of websites on the Internet. A keyword or phrase entered into a search engine will locate websites that are relevant to that subject.

The service that is most commonly used in conjunction with the Internet is electronic mail (e-mail). This communication system can transport messages across the world in a matter of seconds. Extensive information relating to forensic science is available on the Internet. The types of webpages range from simple explanations of the different fields of forensics to intricate details of forensic science specialties.

Investigators seeking a history of an Internet user's destinations can take advantage of the fact that computers store or cache portions of webpages visited, and websites often create cookies to track certain information about website visitors. An investigator tracking the origin of an e-mail will seek out the sender's IP address in the e-mail's header. Chat and instant messages can typically be located in a computer's random-access memory (RAM). Finding the origin of unauthorized computer intrusions (hacking) requires investigation of a computer's log file, RAM, and network traffic, among other things.

Review Questions

1. A(n) _____ consists of two or more computers that are connected to share information.

2. The device that allows computers to exchange and transmit information through telephone lines is a(n) _____.

3. The most popular area of the Internet from which information can be searched and retrieved is known as _____.

4. The (URL, domain abbreviation) is a unique electronic address that indicates where a document is actually located.

5. True or False: The advantage of using hypertext is to be able to quickly switch back and forth between related webpages without having to retype the URL or to start over at the beginning of the search. _____

6. Typically, a user enters a keyword or phrase into a(n) _____ to locate sites on the Internet that are relevant to a particular subject.

7. (E-mail, Usenet) is a communication system that transports messages across the world in a matter of seconds.

8. A device known as a(n) _____ allows a network of computers to share a common connection to the Internet.

9. A(n) _____ takes the form of a series of numbers to route data to an appropriate location on the Internet.

10. A user's hard disk drive _____ portions of webpages that have been visited.

11. A(n) _____ is placed on a hard disk drive by a website to track certain information about its visitors.

12. E-mails have the _____ address of the sender in the header portion of the mail.

13. Chat and instant messages conducted over the Internet are typically stored in (RAM, ROM).

14. When investigating a hacking incident, investigators concentrate their efforts on three locations: _____, _____, and _____.

15. Devices that permit only requested traffic to enter a computer system are known as (caches, firewalls).

Further References

Carrier, Brian, *File System Forensic* Analysis. Upper Saddle River, N.J.: Addison-Wesley, 2005.

Casad, J., *Sams Teach Yourself TCP/IP in 24 Hours,* 3rd ed. Indianapolis, Ind.: SAMS, 2004.

Chamakura, R. P., "Forensic Science and the Internet—Current Utilization and Future Potential," *Forensic Science Review* 9 (1997):97.

Leshin, C. B., *Internet Investigations in Criminal Justice.* Upper Saddle River, N.J.: Prentice Hall, 1997.

Prosise, C., K. Mandia, and B. Pepe, *Incident Response and Computer Forensics,* 2nd ed. New York: McGraw-Hill, 2003.

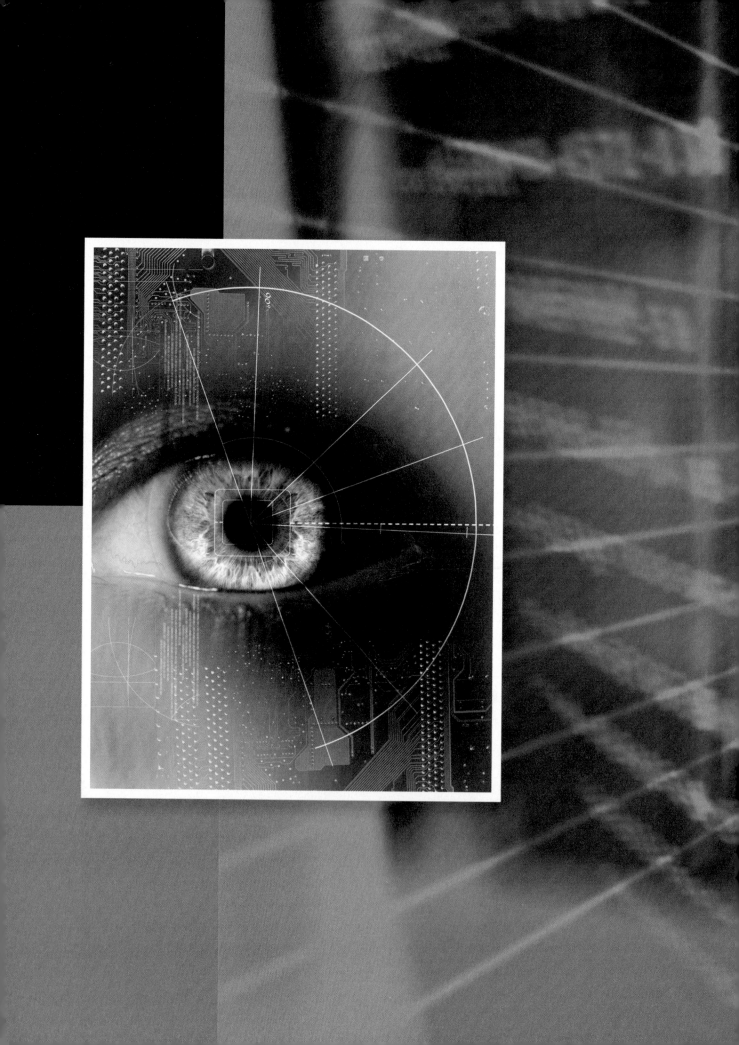

chapter 19

The
Future

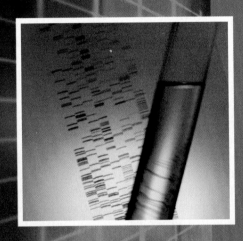

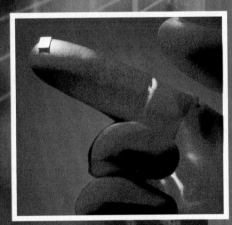

In 1949, Charles O'Hara and James Osterburg, noted criminalistics authors, wrote: "The present position of criminalistics among the sciences may properly be compared with that of chemistry in the nineteenth century." Certainly, in this new millennium, the changes that have taken place since this observation was made have been nothing short of revolutionary. Forensic science may still have many shortcomings, but it has successfully shed the distinction of being a nineteenth-century science.

Crime laboratories have now become the major benefactors of enormous advancements in scientific technology. Chromatography and spectrophotometry have already had a tremendous impact on forensic methodology. In a very short span of time, DNA typing has developed into a routine forensic science technique. The future promises even more progress. Mass spectrometry, capillary electrophoresis, and high-performance liquid chromatography, among other developments, are rapidly gaining recognition as essential forensic tools. The scanning electron microscope is already enhancing the application of microscopy to the examination of trace physical evidence. An even more impressive tool is the scanning electron microscope linked to an X-ray microanalyzer. This combination gives forensic scientists the ability to examine very small samples nondestructively while plotting the elemental composition of the specimen in view.

Not only will practitioners of forensic science continue to see the development of new instruments and techniques suitable for solving their unique problems, but the old workhorses of the crime laboratory—that is, the gas chromatograph and the spectrophotometer—have undergone a major facelift thanks to a revolutionary development in electronics called the *microprocessor*. The microprocessor contains thousands of microscopic transistors, diodes, capacitors, and the like—all hooked together on a microchip. The electronic components of a computer that once filled a room are now reduced to the size of a few microprocessor chips. Instrument manufactures are taking advantage of this development to link personal computers to many types of analytical instrumentation. This will help further automate and speed the collection of data in the crime laboratory.

However, the unabated progress of analytical technology must not obscure the fact that the profession of forensic science has reached a critical junction in its history. The preoccupation with equipping a crime laboratory with elaborate and sophisticated hardware has left a wide gap between the skill of the scientist and the ability of the criminal investigator to recognize and preserve physical evidence at the crime scene. The crime scene is the critical first step in the process of using scientific services in a criminal investigation. All the expertise and instrumentation that any crime laboratory can muster will be rendered totally impotent if evidence has been left lying unrecognized or ignored on the ground, or if the evidence has been inadvertently destroyed by careless investigators or curiosity seekers.

The theme that there is a need for trained and knowledgeable evidence collectors at crime scenes has been a recurring one throughout this text. Once again, this requirement must be reiterated. How is the evidence collector or investigator to gain the skill and appreciation for recognizing the value of physical evidence? The trend of events seems to be one of conceding past failings and acknowledging the need for creating specialists to perform evidence-collection functions. In growing numbers, police agencies are training and equipping "evidence-collection technicians" to help criminal investigators retrieve evidence at the crime scene.

If this program is to have any significant impact on investigative procedures, immediate steps will have to be taken that go beyond mere designation of an evidence-collection unit on a police agency's organizational chart. The effectiveness of such a program should not be measured by the number of oversized and overequipped mobile vans at the unit's disposal; instead, a staff of dedicated operators and administrators trained and experienced in evidence collection has to be assembled. This unit must be recognized as the essential first step in forensic analysis and must become an integral part, both administratively and functionally, of the total forensic service offered by a law enforcement agency.

The education of evidence collectors and investigators is a critical factor in improving the quality of crime-scene investigation. Although continued in-depth training of investigators by forensic scientists is an essential ingredient for the success of such a program, many agencies, for lack of space, time, or desire, have not implemented this training. It is therefore gratifying that colleges and universities are emerging as centers of education for law enforcement personnel. Criminal justice or law enforcement programs provide viable forums for teaching the philosophy and theory of criminal investigation and forensic science. However, academia must strive to supplement, not supplant, police in-service training. Police administrators now have the responsibility for selecting the personnel to perform investigative functions. These administrators cannot abdicate their responsibility to create and foster training programs to ensure competent performance of the investigator's mission.

Whether a college degree will someday be required by all police departments is still a subject of debate, but the trend is certainly in that direction. More than a thousand higher-education institutions in the United States offer some kind of law enforcement program. Future generations of criminal investigators and police administrators will be recruited from the ranks of these students. For the forensic scientist, participation in these programs offers a unique opportunity to teach, develop, and put into practice the philosophy that science is an integral part of criminal investigation.

Of course, education alone will not guarantee the success of the criminal investigator or evidence collector. Experience, perceptive skill, persistence, and precise judgment are all essential ingredients to the makeup of the successful investigator and evidence collector. Combine all of these characteristics with a careful selection process designed to choose only those who qualify for this role, and the result will be substantial enhancement of the quality of criminal investigative services.

I don't want to leave the reader with the impression that crime laboratories are not being used or that forensic scientists have difficulty justifying a full day's work. On the contrary, these facilities are overworked and understaffed. The demand imposed on them just to complete the examination of drug and blood-alcohol evidence is enough to inundate and preoccupy all but the larger crime laboratories. Most facilities can barely keep their heads above water and are drowning in a "sea" of drugs. Furthermore, the disproportionate burden placed on the skills, time, and equipment of the laboratory by drug and blood-alcohol evidence has had a detrimental effect on the capacity of the law enforcement system to process physical evidence generated by more serious or violent crimes.

The solution to the problem may seem obvious: more people, larger facilities, and, of course, more money. But crime laboratories must stand in line with other components of the criminal justice system, because skyrocketing crime rates have overburdened our police, courts, and correctional institutions. In light of public and political outcries, criminal justice administrators have sought programs geared to producing quick and dramatic reductions in crime rates. In this kind of atmosphere, hiring more scientists or buying a mass spectrometer or a gas chromatograph may hardly seem the best way to reduce crime.

I am not advocating a crash program for building crime laboratories or, for that matter, a crash program aimed at improving one segment of the criminal justice community at the expense of the others. Reduction of crime will come about only with a balanced approach to criminal justice, as well as alleviation of social injustices. We must keep the future role of the crime laboratory in its proper perspective while examining the goals and performance that we expect from all components of our criminal justice system.

The size and effectiveness of a crime laboratory directly mirror the capability of the investigative agencies that it services. If all or even most of the burglaries, homicides, assaults, rapes, and other types of major offenses were investigated with the thoroughness expected of a proper criminal investigation, the quantity of physical evidence collected would require the existence of better staffed and better equipped crime laboratories.

An important impetus behind the expansion of crime laboratory services in the United States has been the large influx of drug specimens. A required chemical analysis of these confiscated materials has made the laboratory's participation in prosecution proceedings mandatory. The criminal justice system, faced with the prospect of unreasonable delays due to understaffed laboratories, quickly moved to expand these facilities in order to keep pace with the ever-increasing number of drug seizures. Currently, the advent of DNA profiling has placed tremendous pressures on crime laboratory services. Laws passed to mandate entry into a DNA database for many convicted offenders has imposed tremendous workloads on crime laboratories that must also cope with an overwhelming variety of evidence retrieved from crime scenes collected for DNA analysis.

Although the commitment of police to improve the quality of crime-scene investigation is essential, it must be accompanied by a simultaneous effort to improve the caliber of crime laboratory services. Certainly, thorough collection of crime-scene evidence will require more forensic scientists to handle the increasing caseloads. However, forensic scientists should not be lulled into a false sense of security by believing that the tremendous strides made in the development of analytical instruments and techniques are sufficient to meet the needs and goals of their profession. Progress can be expected only if crime laboratories are staffed with trained and knowledgeable scientists.

Fortunately, more colleges and universities are offering courses and degree programs in forensic science or criminalistics. These institutions are beginning to serve as fertile training grounds for new forensic scientists. Although many of these individuals have textbook knowledge of the techniques used in forensic analysis, few arrive at the crime laboratory possessing an understanding of the practical aspects of criminal investigation. This deficiency necessitates a prolonged and time-consuming period of intensive training under the direction of trained criminalists. Not only must the new criminalist learn to apply specialized skills to the responsibilities and objectives of a working crime laboratory, he or she must also acquire a familiarity with all phases of crime laboratory operation.

The extent and depth of versatility expected of the forensic scientist are usually determined by the size of the crime laboratory's staff. Scientists in smaller laboratories are often expected to be generalists, performing a wide variety of tasks in order to fulfill the varied objectives of the laboratory. Their counterparts in larger facilities enjoy the luxury of working in specialized areas, relying on a teamwork approach to provide the spectrum of scientific skills needed for the comparison or identification of physical evidence.

In addition to his or her technical responsibilities, the newly trained criminalist must discover and master the role of the expert witness. A good courtroom demeanor and the ability to communicate thoughts and ideas in clear, concise terms are absolutely essential if the scientist's examination and conclusions are to be properly and effectively presented at a hearing or in court.

The present momentum of forensic research could very well falter unless individuals who possess relevant knowledge and skills are attracted to careers in forensic science. The recognition by a sufficient number of colleges and universities of the need to foster undergraduate and graduate programs in this field is essential for ensuring an ample supply of scientists to meet the anticipated personnel needs of the profession. Furthermore, the establishment of forensic education programs, especially at the graduate level, should be accompanied by the formulation of new academic research programs dedicated to investigating fertile areas of research that are pertinent to the expanding role of forensic science in criminal justice. In a university environment, these research programs can be pursued in an atmosphere unaffected by the pressures of everyday casework, a burden that presently weighs heavily on the shoulders of the working forensic scientist.

The prospects for significant technological advances in forensic science in the near future are great. In fact, the computer-aided search of single latent fingerprints is already a reality in most jurisdictions. The ability to search, in a matter of minutes, files composed of millions of prints in order to ascertain a probable match to a latent fingerprint represents the most significant contribution that forensic science has made to criminal investigation since the introduction of the fingerprint itself. Jurisdictions using this approach have reported startling increases in arrests.

Computerized technology is also helping investigators link multiple unrelated shooting cases to a single firearm. The automated search system NIBIN (see pp. 468–471) allows the surface characteristics of a bullet or cartridge case to be scanned and stored in a computerized database. This database is networked throughout various regions of the United States. An investigator can search the database for entries bearing similar characteristics to the evidential bullet or cartridge case. If a match is made, multiple crimes may be linked and associated with a single firearm.

Practically every week we read in our newspapers that researchers are developing new products with their ability to manipulate genes. The ability of scientists to penetrate DNA, the basic building block of genes, provides investigators with a powerful forensic tool to individualize blood, semen, and hair. The FBI has initiated an aggressive forensic research program to develop this technology along with an ambitious technical training program to instruct personnel of state and local crime laboratories throughout the United States in the use of this technology. DNA typing has already progressed to the stage at which all states are routinely DNA typing offenders involved in sex-related and other crimes. The technology of DNA profiling has progressed so rapidly that today blood and semen stains recovered from crime scenes are as revealing of human identity as a fingerprint. CODIS is a computer software program developed and maintained by the FBI that links local, state, and national databases of DNA profiles from convicted offenders, unsolved crime-scene evidence, and missing people. CODIS software has enabled local, state, and national crime laboratories to compare DNA profiles electronically. Thousands of matches have linked criminal perpetrators to DNA profiles in CODIS databases.

One unexpected dividend from DNA testing has been the reinvigorating of the investigation of "minor crimes." For decades, police have given the investigation of house burglary scenes and other property crimes low priority. Evidence now suggests that DNA evidence collected at property crime scenes may help law enforcement solve those crimes and identify perpetrators of more serious offenses. According to one state study, more than 50 percent of the DNA database hits against murder and sexual assault cases matched individuals who had prior convictions for burglary.

Apprehending perpetrators of property crimes can certainly discourage criminals from moving on to the commission of more serious violent crimes, and thus can have a dramatic long-term impact on decreasing the overall crime rate. In this respect, it is apparent that DNA collected at burglary scenes is a powerful investigative tool. In one major jurisdiction, DNA evidence from 201 burglaries yielded 86 DNA profiles for entry in CODIS. Most of the profiles resulted in links to multiple unsolved cases. One profile uncovered a five-burglary serial offender. A few were linked to more serious violent crimes such as sexual assault and robbery. Significantly, more than 30 of the burglaries were matched though CODIS to convicted offenders. In Florida jurisdictions, individuals associated with two hundred DNA samples collected from various burglary investigations were identified by CODIS.

Unfortunately, in spite of the fact that crime laboratories are equipped with expensive and sophisticated instruments, often a forensic scientist cannot report to a police officer or a jury that a scientific examination of the evidence has in itself solved a case. More often than not, a conclusive comparison of evidential and control material cannot exclude other possible sources. To further complicate matters, the statistical data available to support such conclusions are usually sketchy or nonexistent. In such situations, heavy reliance must necessarily be placed on the experience and opinion of the expert in interpreting the significance of the forensic examination.

Even though class physical evidence for corroborating investigative findings is an important contribution to any criminal case, its nonexclusive character does not always motivate investigators to go all out in their search for class physical evidence. The items most sought at the crime site are those that possess potential individual characteristics—that is, DNA, fingerprints, firearms, bullets, tool marks, and track impressions—because these are more likely to have the greatest impact on an investigation. Once these avenues have been exhausted, there seems to be little desire to progress any further. Clearly, future research will have to concentrate on defining the value of class evidence so that these items can become statistically more meaningful and attractive to scientists and investigators alike. However, a salient point of this book is that all physical evidence, whether class or individualistic in nature, is critical to a properly conducted criminal investigation. Criminalists have become extremely proficient in conducting tests that will narrow the origin of class evidence to a small number of possibilities. Yet some insist that if a scientist cannot define the significance of a comparison in statistical terms, the evidence should be excluded from consideration. To succumb to this reasoning is tantamount to eviscerating a core principle of criminalistics—the collection and presentation of impartial and objective information for evaluation by a trier of fact. The criminalistic community must aggressively communicate its capabilities and objectives to both the police and legal communities.

A major thrust of forensic research must concentrate on defining the most distinctive properties of evidence and relating these properties to statistics that measure their frequency of occurrence. The creation of data banks to collect, store, and disseminate this kind of information will facilitate the task. Because the responsibility for providing forensic services is spread among more than 350 independent government laboratories in the United States, the task of accumulating meaningful statistical data applicable to the entire country or to large regions is exceedingly difficult. Future progress will depend on the willingness of all crime laboratories to enter into cooperative programs that will ensure uniform standards of analysis as well as provide for the collection and dissemination of analytical and statistical data.

The FBI's Forensic Science Research and Training Center is a key ingredient in the development of criminalistics in the United States. The FBI has made a substantial commitment to the center in terms of personnel and equipment. This facility has established a research program concentrated in the areas of biochemistry, immunology, chemistry, and physics. This program is directed toward the development of new methods for forensic science. The research staff interacts with researchers from academia, industry, and other government and forensic science laboratories. Furthermore, the staff also participates in specialized scientific courses offered by the FBI to state and local crime laboratory personnel. These courses not only have improved the quality of forensic science practices in the United States but have encouraged standardization of many of the scientific procedures used by forensic laboratories throughout the United States.

A foundation of cooperation has been laid; much now remains to be accomplished. How successful our profession will be in fulfilling its present and future obligations to justice depends on the skill, dedication, and ingenuity of its practitioners.

Further References

Houck, M. M., "Statistics and Trace Evidence: The Tyranny of Numbers," *Forensic Science Communications* 1, no. 3 (1999), http://www.fbi.gov/programs/lab/fsc/current/backissu.htm.

Kind, S. S., "Forensic Science in the United Kingdom," *Journal of the Forensic Science Society* 19 (1979), 117.

"Status and Needs of Forensic Science Service Providers: A Report to Congress," www.aafs.org/pdf/180%20day%20study.pdf.

Zedlewski, E., and M.B. Murphy, *DNA Analysis for "Minor" Crimes: A Major Benefit to Law Enforcement*, http://www.ojp.usdoj.gov/nij/journals/253/dna_analysis.html.

Case
Readings

The "Bobby Joe" Long Serial Murder Case
A Study in Cooperation

Capt. Gary Terry
Hillsborough County Sheriff's
Office, Tampa, Florida

SA Michael P. Malone, M. S.
Hairs and Fiber Unit, Laboratory
Division, Federal Bureau of
Investigation, Washington, DC

On May 13, 1984, the Hillsborough County Sheriff's Office (HCSO) responded to the scene of a homicide in southern Hillsborough County, where the body of a nude female had been discovered. This was the beginning of an intensive, 8-month investigation into the abduction, rape, and murder of at least 10 women in 3 jurisdictions in the Tampa Bay area. This investigation would ultimately involve personnel from the HCSO, the Federal Bureau of Investigation (FBI), the Tampa Police Department (TPD), the Pasco County Sheriff's Office (PCSO), and the Florida Department of Law Enforcement (FDLE).

Never before had the HCSO been involved in a serial murder case of this magnitude. During one period of time in the 8 months, the killer was averaging a murder every other week. This series of grisly killings would eventually end due to the efforts of the homicide detectives who pored over each crime scene striving to find any and all physical evidence, the expertise and skill of the examiners in the FBI Laboratory who analyzed this evidence, the close cooperation and continuous exchange of information between the law enforcement agencies involved, and the fact that the killer released one of his victims alive, yielding physical evidence that would ultimately tie all of the cases together.

The first body, nude and bound, of a young Oriental female was discovered by young boys late in the afternoon, in a remote area of southern Hillsborough County. This

victim was identified as Lana Long, a 20-year-old Laotian female. She was employed as an exotic dancer at a lounge located on Nebraska Avenue in the city of Tampa. She normally worked the evening shift and was known to use alcohol and drugs. Long was last seen in the apartment complex where she lived. This was in an area near the University of South Florida, where many of the residents were transient. She had been missing for approximately 3 days.

Long had been dead for approximately 48 to 72 hours. She was lying face down with her hands tied behind her back with rope and fabric. A rope was also observed around her neck which had a "leash-like" extension approximately 14 inches in length. It was noted that the ropes around the wrists and neck were different in nature.[1] Under the victim's face was a piece of fabric which may have been used as a gag. The victim's feet were spread apart to a distance of over 5 feet, and it appeared as if the body had been deliberately "displayed" in this manner. The victim's clothing and personal belongings were never found. During the autopsy a large open wound was discovered on the victim's face. Decomposition was extensive in this area, but the cause of death was determined to be strangulation. Tire impressions were found on the roadway leading to the body. It appeared that three of the tires were of different brands and all were worn.

Reprinted in part from *FBI Law Enforcement Bulletin*, November/December, 1987.

[1] Ropes and cordages were found in 7 of the 10 homicide cases. All of these were compared with one another. Even though cordages found in one case were sometimes found to be of the same type, there were no instances in which cordages from two or more different cases were found to be similar. However, these cordages and knots did provide a "link" in the patterns which would associate these cases together.

Hillsborough County had been averaging about 30 to 35 homicides per year, and while some prior victims had been bound, none had been bound in this manner. Prior to the death of Long, the HCSO had completed a difficult homicide investigation in which the forensic work had been done by the FBI Laboratory. The close cooperation between the HCSO and the FBI Laboratory resulted in the successful conclusion of the case and the conviction of the individual who had committed the murder. Thus, the decision was made to fly the evidence in the Long murder to the FBI Laboratory in Washington, D.C., accompanied by an HCSO homicide detective.

The hairs that were removed from the evidence were examined and found to be either the victim's hairs or unsuitable for comparison. The serology examinations were also negative due to the decomposition of the body. The knots in the ropes were examined and were identified; however, these knots were extremely common and not unique to any particular profession or occupation. The tire casts of the tire tread impressions were examined and photographs of these impressions were kept for future reference.

The fibers which were removed from the items in this case were also examined, and this evidence would provide the first important lead in the case. Eventually, it would prove to be the most critical evidence of the entire case. The equipment used for the fiber examinations consisted of a stereoscopic microscope, a comparison microscope, a polarized light microscope, a microspectrophotometer, a melting point apparatus, and eventually, an infrared spectrophotometer. A single lustrous red trilobal nylon fiber was found on a piece of fabric found near the victim. Because of the size, type, and cross-sectional shape of this fiber, it was determined that this fiber was probably a carpet fiber. Because the body had been exposed to the elements for a substantial period of time, and fibers which have been transferred are very transient in nature,[2] it was surmised that most of the carpet fibers which had originally been transferred to the victim's body had been lost. Since the victim's body was found in a remote area, she had probably been transported in a vehicle, and the carpeting of this vehicle was probably the last item she had been in contact with. Furthermore, since there is normally a transference of trace materials (i.e., fibers) when two objects come into close contact, it was also surmised that the killer was probably driving a vehicle with a red carpet. Vehicular carpets readily shed their fibers, and these types of fibers are commonly found on the bodies of victims at crime scenes. These fibers could then provide a critical "link" in determining whether a serial murderer was operating in the Tampa Bay area.

The above information was provided to the HCSO, with the caution that the fiber information should be kept confidential. Experience has shown that if the existence of fiber evidence is publicized, serial killers might change their pattern and start disposing of the bodies in such a manner that this fiber evidence is either lost or destroyed. The most famous example of this is the Wayne Williams case. [See pp. 87–97.] The possibility also existed that if the killer knew of the existence of the red carpet fibers, he would probably get rid of the vehicle that was the source of this evidence.

Two weeks later, on May 27, 1984, at approximately 11:30 A.M., the body of a young white female was discovered in an isolated area of eastern Hillsborough County. The victim was found nude, with

---

[2] C. A. Pounds and K. W. Smalldon, "The Transfer of Fibers between Clothing Materials during Simulated Contacts and Their Persistence during Wear," *Journal of the Forensic Science Society,* 15 (1975), 29.

clothing near the body. The victim was on her back, with her hands bound at the waist and a ligature around the neck. Her throat had been cut, and she had sustained multiple blunt trauma injuries to the head. The victim had been at the scene for approximately 8 to 10 hours. The victim's hands were bound to her sides with a clothesline type of rope. The ligature at the neck was made of the same type of rope and was tied in a type of hangman's noose. There was a 3- to 4-foot length of rope extending from the noose. The victim also had what appeared to be a man's green T-shirt binding her upper arms. Hair and fiber evidence were collected from the victim's body.

Several tire tread impressions were located in a dirt roadway that passed approximately 8 feet from the victim's body. These impressions appeared to have been caused by a vehicle turning around in the area next to the victim's location.

The responding homicide detectives believed this homicide was related to the Long case. Since the victim was unidentified, a composite drawing of the victim was made and released to the media. It was through this effort that the victim was identified as Michelle Denise Simms, 22 years old and a native of California. She was last seen the previous night talking with two white males near Kennedy Boulevard in an area that is popular for working prostitutes. Simms had previously worked as a prostitute.

The evidence collected from where Simms was found was immediately flown to the FBI Laboratory. Since this had been a "fresh" site, the chances of recovering significant evidence would be tremendously improved. The tire casts were examined and one of the impressions from the right rear area was identified as being from a Goodyear Viva tire, with the white wall facing inward. The tire impression from the left rear area could not be immediately identified, as it was not in the FBI Laboratory reference files.

However, the HCSO was provided with the name of an individual in Akron, Ohio, who was a tire expert, and the tire casts were flown to Akron, where the tire impression was identified as being made by a Vogue tire, an expensive tire that comes only on Cadillacs. A Vogue tire was obtained and photographed in detail.

The fibers removed from the evidence revealed red lustrous trilobal nylon fibers, which matched the Long fiber. In addition, a second type of fiber, a red trilobal delustered fiber, was found, indicating that the killer was driving a vehicle containing two different types of carpet fibers.

Grouping tests conducted on semen stains identified on the clothing of Michelle Simms disclosed the presence of the "B" and "H" blood group substances.

The hairs from the body and clothing of Michelle Simms were examined. Brown, medium-length Caucasian head hairs were found that could have originated from the killer. Human hair is valuable evidence, and in addition to providing information on race, body area, artificial treatment, or other unusual characteristics, it can be strongly associated with a particular individual when matched with a known hair sample from the individual. With this information, the HCSO was able to build a "physical evidence" profile of the killer, which was distributed to other law enforcement agencies; however, the information on the carpet fibers and cordage was kept confidential.

On June 24, 1984, the body of another young white female was found, the third victim in this series of homicides, although this would not be known for a few months. The victim was found in an orange grove in southeastern Hillsborough County. The victim was found fully clothed, and the body was in an advanced stage of decomposition. The total body weight of the victim, including her clothes, was only 25 pounds. There were no ligatures present, and the victim was not found near an interstate as the first two victims had been. During the initial stages of the investigation, the victim's boyfriend failed a polygraph examination and appeared to be an excellent suspect. Evidence from the case was sent to the FBI Laboratory; however, no request was made for this evidence to be compared to the evidence from the previous two homicides until much later.

The victim was identified as Elizabeth B. Loudenback, 22, of Tampa. Loudenback was employed as an assembly line worker and was last seen at approximately 7:00 P.M. on June 8, 1984. She was known to frequent the area of Nebraska Avenue and Skipper Road in northern Hillsborough County, but had no criminal history.

The hairs from the Loudenback case were examined with negative results. Serology examinations were also negative due to the extensive decomposition of the body. The fibers, examined later, were determined to be both types of the red carpet fibers evidenced in the two previous cases. If this examination had been done initially, it would have been immediately known that Loudenback was, in fact, the third victim. When the evidence arrived at the FBI Laboratory, it was not assigned to the examiner who had worked the first two homicides. One of the most important aspects of handling a serial murder investigation is to have the same crime scene technician at all crime scenes and the same forensic examiners at the laboratory, so that one individual can become totally familiar with the forensic portion of the investigation, in order to recognize patterns and associations which might be present.

On October 7, 1984, the nude body of a young black female was discovered near the Pasco/Hillsborough County line, lying next to the dirt entrance road of a cattle ranch. The victim's clothing, except for her bra, was found next to the body. The bra had been tied in a knot and was found hanging from the entrance gate. The head area was in an advanced state of

decomposition, much more so than the remainder of the body. The autopsy revealed a puncture wound to the back of the neck, but a gunshot wound to the neck was the cause of death.

The victim was identified as Chanel Devon Williams, an 18-year-old black female. The victim had been previously arrested for prostitution. She was known to frequent a gay bar on Kennedy Boulevard in Tampa. She had been last seen on the night of September 30, 1984, by another prostitute with whom she had been working. The pair were working the area of Nebraska Avenue when Williams' companion was solicited by a "john." They were approximately two-tenths of a mile from the motel where they were conducting their "business." Williams' companion rode back to the motel in the "john's" car, and Williams was instructed to slowly walk back to the motel in order to check on her companion. Williams never made it back to the motel.

The homicide detectives who responded to the place Williams was found began looking for similarities to the previous homicides. Other than the fact that the victim was found nude in a rural area and that Williams was a prostitute, there were no other apparent similarities.

At this point in the investigation, the HCSO requested a criminal personality profile be done by the FBI on the Long, Simms, and Williams cases, and one other homicide in which another female had been shot. A profile was returned (see Figure R1–1) indicating strong similarities between the Long case and the Simms case. However, due to various differences (race, lack of ligatures, and cause of death), it was believed that the Williams case and the other above-mentioned cases were not related.

The evidence from the Williams case was sent to the FBI Laboratory a second time, and both types of the red nylon carpet fibers were found on various articles of her clothing. A brown Caucasian pubic hair,

Figure R1–1 FBI criminal personality profile.

Race	Caucasian
Age	Mid 20s
Personality	"Macho" Image Assaultive
Employment	Difficulty in Holding Job
Marriage	Probably Divorced
Vehicle	"Flashy Car"
Weapons	Likely to Carry Weapons
Personality	Inclined to Mentally and Physically Taunt and Torture
Victims	Randomly Selected Susceptible to Approach
Geographics	Confine Activity to Given Geographic Region

which would ultimately be associated with Robert Long, was also discovered on the victim's sweater. Grouping tests conducted on semen stains identified on Williams' clothing disclosed the presence of the "A" and "H" blood group substances. This was inconsistent with the grouping results found in the Simms case; however, this could be due to their working as prostitutes.

On the morning of October 14, 1984, the body of a white female, nude from the waist down, was discovered in an unpopulated area of northeastern Hillsborough County. The body was found in an orange grove approximately 30 feet from a dirt road, apparently dragged from the roadway. The body had been placed on a gold-colored bedspread, and a blue jogging suit was tied outside the blanket. The bedspread had been tied at both ends with common white string. The victim's hands were bound in front with a red and white handkerchief. Her right wrist and legs were bound with another white string. The victim's feet were bound with a drawstring, and there were ligature marks on the victim's throat. She had been struck on the forehead and strangled.

The victim was identified as Karen Beth Dinsfriend, a 28-year-old cocaine user and prostitute. Dinsfriend had been working the area of Nebraska and Hillsborough Avenues and was last seen during the early morning hours of October 14, 1984.

Upon arriving at the scene, the detectives strongly suspected that Dinsfriend's death was related to the previous homicides. The ligatures were almost a "signature" of the offender. Red fibers were found when the body was examined at the medical examiner's office.

By this time, all homicide detectives of the HCSO were assigned to the case. Other assaults, suicides, and unrelated homicides were assigned to property detectives. Six tactical deputies were assigned to do night surveillance in the suspect's "hunting grounds," the area of Nebraska Avenue and West Kennedy Boulevard in North Tampa. The patrol divisions were again given alerts and were continually sending in field interrogation reports (FIR), which were checked. A personal computer was purchased specifically for this investigation and was used to record information on vehicles, vehicular tags, information gathered from talking to prostitutes, and information derived from the FIRs. At this point, the HCSO again went "public" to warn the community about these related homicides. However, the fiber information was kept confidential.

The evidence from the Dinsfriend disposal site was sent directly to the FBI Laboratory, and it yielded valuable evidence. The knots in the ligatures were similar to the knots from the previous cases; a brown Caucasian pubic hair, eventually associated with Robert Long, was found on the bedspread; and semen was found on the bedspread and sweatshirt and tests again disclosed the "A" and "H" blood group substances. The bedspread was tested and found to be composed of gold delustered acrylic fibers. These fibers would also provide a link to Long's vehicle.

Both types of red nylon carpet fibers were again found on most of the items and were microscopically compared to the previous carpet fibers. The color produced by the dyes from the red carpet fibers was also compared using the microspectrophotometer. The microspectrophotometer is one of the most discriminating techniques which can be used in the comparison of fibers. Since these carpet fibers both microscopically and optically matched the red carpet fibers from the previous five cases, it was strongly believed that all of these fibers were consistent with having originated from the same source, and therefore, all of the cases were related.

On October 30, 1984, the nude mummified remains of a white female were discovered near Highway 301 in northern Hillsborough County just south of the Pasco County line. No clothing, ligatures, or any other type of physical evidence were found at the scene. Due to the amount of time the body was exposed to the elements and the fact that the victim was nude, no foreign hairs, fibers, semen, or any other type of evidence were

discovered. This victim would not be identified until after the arrest of the suspect, Robert Long, who referred to the victim by her street name, "Sugar." Using this information, the HCSO was able to identify the victim as Kimberly Kyle Hopps, a 22-year-old white female, last seen by her boyfriend getting into a 1977–78 maroon Chrysler Cordoba. Hopps would eventually be associated with Long's vehicle through a comparison of her head hairs with hairs found in his vehicle.

On November 6, 1984, the remains of a female were discovered near Morris Bridge Road in Pasco County just north of the Hillsborough County line. The bones of the victim were scattered about a large area; however, a ligature was found. Another ligature was discovered on an arm bone. A shirt, a pair of panties, and some jewelry were also found. Human head hairs, presumed to be from the victim, were also recovered.

On learning of the discovery of this body, the Hillsborough homicide detectives met with the Pasco County detectives, and because of the ligatures, believed that this case was related to their homicides. The two agencies worked together to identify the victim, Virginia Lee Johnson, an 18-year-old white female originally from Connecticut. It was learned that she split her time between Connecticut and the North Tampa area, working as a prostitute in the North Nebraska Avenue area in Hillsborough County.

The evidence from the Johnson site was sent by the PCSO to the FBI Laboratory. Again, due to the extensive decomposition, the body yielded very little physical evidence; however, in the victim's head hair from the crime scene a single red lustrous carpet fiber was found, relating this case to the others. Eventually, Virginia Johnson would also be associated with Robert Long's vehicle through a transfer of her head hairs.

On November 24, 1984, the nude body of a young white female was found on an incline off of North Orient Road in the City of Tampa, involving yet a third jurisdiction in the homicides. The victim had been at the scene less than 24 hours. A wadded pair of blue jeans and a blue flowered top were near the body. The victim was wearing knee high nylons; the body was face down with the head at the lower portion of the incline. Faint tire impressions were observed in the grass next to the roadway, and a piece of wood with possible tire impressions was found. It appeared that the killer had pulled off the road and had thrown the body over the edge and onto the incline. Examination of the body revealed that fecal matter was present on the inside of the victim's legs and on the exterior of the clothing. The body had a pronounced ligature mark on the front portion of the neck. There were also ligature marks on both wrists and on both arms; however, no ligatures were found.

This victim was identified as Kim Marie Swann, a 21-year-old female narcotics user, who worked as a nude dancer. She was last seen walking out of a convenience store near her parents' home at approximately 3:00 P.M. on November 11, 1984.

When the Tampa Police Department responded and noted the ligature marks on the victim, they immediately called the HCSO and requested that they also respond. This homicide was also believed to be related to the previous seven homicides.

The evidence from the Swann disposal site was sent to the FBI Laboratory. The tire tread impressions on the board bore limited design similarities to the tire impressions from the Lana Long and Michelle Simms homicides. Again, red nylon carpet fibers were found on the victim's clothing. The head hair of the victim was examined and would eventually be associated with the suspect's vehicle.

Even though the three jurisdictions now directly involved in the eight homicides continued to work separately on their own cases, there was continual exchange of information among these agencies, which enabled the HCSO to learn that the Tampa Police Department sex crimes detectives were working on an abduction and rape of a 17-year-old white female. This exchange of information would ultimately lead to the big "break" in the case, a case which had completely captivated the attention of the Tampa Bay area and one which was beginning to attract national attention as well.

On November 3, 1984, a young girl, Lisa McVey, was leaving a doughnut shop in northern Tampa when she was abducted. The offender took her to an unknown apartment and sexually assaulted her for 26 hours before releasing her. The HCSO urged the Tampa Police Department to send their rape evidence to the FBI Laboratory, and on November 13, 1984, the FBI Laboratory called with the biggest break yet in the serial murder case; they found the same red fibers on McVey's clothes as had been found on the homicide victims.

After the rape case had been linked to the murders, a task force was formed the next day, consisting of the Hillsborough County Sheriff's Office, the Tampa Police Department, the Florida Department of Law Enforcement, the Pasco County Sheriff's Office, and the Federal Bureau of Investigation. The rape victim, McVey, was extensively interviewed and recalled that after leaving the apartment where she was held, the suspect stopped at a "24-hour teller machine" to withdraw some money at approximately 3:00 A.M. She described the suspect's vehicle as being red with a red interior and red carpet, with the word "Magnum" on the dash. En route to the release site, the victim recalled peeking out from under the blindfold and seeing a Howard Johnson's motel as they drove up on the interstate.

At this time, there were approximately 30 officers assigned to the task force.

They immediately flooded the North Tampa area searching for the apartment and vehicle (only a 1978 Dodge Magnum has the word "Magnum" on the dash). A task force member was flown to the State capital and returned with a list of every Dodge Magnum registered in Hillsborough County. An examination of the computer printout of these registrations revealed Robert Joe Long's name as a listed owner of a Dodge Magnum.

Each team of detectives was assigned certain areas to search, and as one team drove to their area, they noticed a red Dodge Magnum driving down Nebraska Avenue in North Tampa. The vehicle was stopped, and the driver was told that they were looking for a robbery suspect. The driver, identified as Robert Joe Long, was photographed and a field interrogation report was written.

During the same time period, bank records for all bank machines in North Tampa were being subpoenaed. These bank records revealed that Robert Long had used the 24-hour teller machine close to his apartment at approximately 3:00 A.M. on the morning the rape victim was released. The rape victim identified Long as her assailant from a photo selection. Based on McVey's statements, both an arrest warrant and a search warrant were drawn up and approved by a circuit court judge.

Robert Long was located at his apartment approximately 2 hours after being stopped by the task force members. They began a 24-hour surveillance of Long, also using aircraft to minimize the chances that Long would spot the surveillance teams.

The task force then consulted the Behavioral Science Unit at the FBI Academy for guidelines to use when interviewing the suspect. A Special Agent from the FBI Laboratory in Washington was flown to Tampa for an immediate comparison of fibers from the suspect's apartment and vehicle and to assist in the crime scene searches. An aircraft was standing by so that after the arrest this

Agent could be flown immediately to the closest FDLE laboratory which had the special microscope required for comparison of the fiber samples.

The following teams were organized from the task force:

1. Arrest team selected to physically arrest Long. Two of these officers were selected to interview Long at the office after the arrest.
2. Search and seizure team for the vehicle.
3. Search team for the residence.
4. Neighborhood survey team to interview Long's neighbors in his apartment complex after the arrest and before any information was released to the media.

After all task force teams were at their assigned locations, the signal to effect the arrest was given. By this time, Long was in a movie theater; as Long walked out of the theater, he was arrested. This arrest occurred only 36 hours after the task force was formed.

Long was returned to his apartment where approximately 10 to 15 detectives were waiting. In this jurisdiction (Hillsborough County), it is preferred to serve a search warrant while the owner of the property is there to witness the search. In this case, an embarrassed Long refused to exit the police vehicle and witness the search. Long was then taken to the HCSO operations center for interrogation. The interview was begun after the interviewing officers had consulted with the FBI Agent present who had prepared the criminal personality profile. The Agent advised that this suspect would most likely cooperate if the officers displayed both their authority and a thorough knowledge of the case.

The officers opened the interview by carefully talking only about the McVey rape and abduction until the suspect confessed to the McVey case. Then, the detectives began going into the other homicide cases. Long denied any involvement in the homicides initially.

Meanwhile, the suspect's vehicle had been brought to the Sheriff's office where it was being searched. The vehicle was found to have the Vogue tire and the Goodyear Viva tire, all with the white wall inverted and in the exact location on the vehicle as had been suspected. A sample of the carpet was removed from the vehicle, and the FBI fiber expert was immediately flown with this sample and previous fiber samples to the FDLE lab in Sanford, Florida, which had a comparison microscope. A short time later, the Agent telephoned the HCSO confirming that the fibers from Long's vehicle matched the red carpet fibers found previously on the victims. Long continued to deny committing the murders until the fibers were matched. The interviewing detectives then explained the physical evidence to the suspect. They also explained the significance of the matched fibers and what other comparisons would be done, i.e., hair, blood, etc. At this time, the suspect confessed.

The suspect gave a brief description of each homicide. He admitted killing Loudenback (victim #3) and using her money card. In each case, Long had talked the victims into his vehicle, immediately gaining control of them with a knife and gun. He then bound them and took them to various areas where he sexually assaulted and then murdered them. The suspect also drew a map showing where he had placed victim number nine. This victim had been abducted from the City of Tampa during an earlier part of the investigation, and the Tampa Police Department had informed the HCSO of this fact. They believed she fit the "victim profile" but she remained missing until Long told them where to find the body.

Eventually, a total of 10 homicides which had occurred in and around the Tampa Bay area over a period of approximately 8 months were attributed to Long (see Table R1–1). The victims ranged from 18 to 28 years in age, and the majority of the victims were prostitutes. Most victims were strangled and/or asphyxiated; however, one was shot and one died of a cut throat. . . .

As a result of laboratory examinations, numerous associations were made between the various crime scenes, the suspect, the victims, and the suspect's vehicle. (See Table R1–2.) The probative value of these associations was explained to the prosecutors from the Hillsborough County State Attorney's Office and the Pasco County State Attorney's Office. The importance of the fiber evidence was apparent from the beginning, as 8 of the 10 victims were associated with Long's vehicle through fiber comparisons. The importance of the hair evidence also began to emerge as all of the forensic examinations were completed. Six of the victims were associated to Long's vehicle through hair transfers, even though Long had thoroughly vacuumed his Dodge Magnum the day before he was arrested. Two of the 10 victims were associated directly to Long by transfer of his hairs to these victims. The significance of the ligatures and knots should not be overlooked as these provided a valuable link between cases. The tire tread evidence provided many leads and would associate Long's vehicle directly to the crime scene in two of the cases. The importance of the criminal personality profile should also be noted (see Figure R1–2). In addition to providing valuable leads, it can also "guide" a case. It cannot, however, take the place of a thorough and competent investigation.

The first trial of Robert Long was held in Dade City, Florida (Pasco County), on April 22, 1985. This was the trial for the murder of Virginia Johnson. The strongest evidence presented at this trial was the hair and fiber associations, as well as the confession of Long. The trial lasted a week and received a great deal of media coverage. Long was found guilty of the murder of Virginia Johnson and was sentenced to die in the electric chair.

Table R1–1

Victim's Name	Date Victim Found	Date Victim Missing	Body Recovery Area	Cause of Death	Age	Occupation
Lana Long	5/13/84	5/10/84	Isolated Area Southern Hillsborough Co.	Asphyxiation	20	Exotic Dancer
Michelle Simms	5/27/84	5/25/84	Isolated Area Eastern Hillsborough Co.	Blunt Force, Cut Throat	22	Prostitute
Elizabeth Loudenback	6/24/84	6/8/84	Orange Grove Southeast Hillsborough Co.	Unknown	22	Factory Worker
Chanel Williams	10/7/84	10/1/84	Isolated Area Northern Hillsborough Co.	Gunshot Wound to Head	18	Prostitute
Karen Dinsfriend	10/14/84	10/13/84	Isolated Area Northeast Hillsborough Co.	Asphyxiation	28	Prostitute
Kimberly Hopps	10/30/84	9/31/84	Isolated Area Northern Hillsborough Co.	Unknown	20s	Prostitute
Juvenile Female	11/4/84	11/3/84	—	—	17	Doughnut Shop Worker
Virginia Johnson	11/6/84	10/15/84	Isolated Area Pasco Co. near County Line	Strangulation	18	Waitress (Prostitute)
Kim Swann	11/24/84	11/11/84	Tampa Near Rt. 60	Strangulation	21	Student (Part-Time Exotic Dancer)
Vicky Elliot	11/16/84	9/7/84	Isolated Area Northern Hillsborough Co.	Strangulation	21	Waitress
Artis Wick	11/22/84	3/28/84	Isolated Area Southern Hillsborough Co.	Unknown	18	

It was decided that the first case that would be tried in Hillsborough County would be the Michelle Simms case. This case was picked due to the brutal nature in which she had been killed and the fact that it contained the strongest forensic evidence. The second case to be tried would be the Karen Dinsfriend case. As a result of discussions between the Hillsborough County State Attorney's Office and the Public Defender's Office of Hillsborough County, a plea bargain was agreed upon for 8 of the homicides and the abduction and rape of Lisa McVey.

Long pled guilty on September 24, 1985, to all of these crimes, receiving 26 life sentences (24 concurrent and 2 to run consecutively to the first 24) and 7 life sentences (no parole for 25 years). In addition, the State retained the option to seek the death penalty for the murder of Michelle Simms. In July of 1986, the penalty phase of the Michelle Simms trial was held in Tampa. It lasted 1 week and again received great media attention. Long was found guilty and was again sentenced to die in Florida's electric chair.

Table R1-2

Name of Victim	Red Delustered Trilobal Nylon Fibers	Red Lustrous Trilobal Nylon Fibers	Yellow Delustered Acrylic Fibers	Hair Transfer Long→Victim	Hair Transfer Victim→Long's Car	Semen	Tire Tread	Cordage/Knots	Misc.
Lana Long	Neg.	Yes	—	Neg.	Head Hair	Neg.	Similar Design and Size	Yes	Partially Decomposed—3 Days
Michelle Simms	Yes	Yes	—	Neg.	Head Hair	"B" & "H"	Similar Design and Size	Yes	Intact Body—2 Days
Elizabeth Loudenback	Yes	Yes	—	Neg.	Neg.	—	—	No	Badly Decomposed—16 Days
Chanel Williams	Yes	Yes	—	Pubic Hair—Sweater	Neg.	"A" & "H"	—	Yes	Badly Decomposed—6 Days
Karen Dinsfriend	Yes	Yes	Blanket to Trunk	Pubic Hair—Blanket	Head Hair	"A" & "H"	Neg.	Yes	Intact Body—1 Day
Kimberly Hopps	Neg.	Neg.	—	Neg.	Head Hair	Neg.	—	No	Skeletonized—1 mo.
Juvenile Female	Yes	Yes	—	Head Hair—Shirt	Neg.	Neg.	—	Yes	Head Hairs Like Victim in Long's Apartment
Virginia Johnson	Neg.	Yes	—	Neg.	Head Hair	—	—	Yes	Skeletonized—3 wks.
Kim Swann	Yes	Yes	—	Neg.	Head Hair	Neg.	Limited Design	No	Intact Body—3 Days
Vicky Elliot	Yes	Yes	—	Neg.	Neg.	Neg.	—	Yes	Skeletonized—60 Days
Artis Wick	Neg.	Neg.	—	Neg.	Neg.	Neg.	—	Yes	Skeletonized—6 mos.

Race	Caucasian	Caucasian
Age	Mid 20s	31
Personality	"Macho" Image Assaultive with Weaker Individuals	On Probation for Assault/ Lifted Weights/Transferred from S.O. to State Penn.
Employment	Difficulty in Holding Job	Fired from Prev. Job Currently Unemployed
Marriage	Probably Divorced	Divorced
Vehicle	"Flashy Car"	Red Dodge Magnum
Weapons	Likely to Carry Weapons	Carried Gun and Knife
Personality	Inclined to Mentally and Physically Taunt and Torture	Tied "Leash" to Some Victims
Victims	Randomly Selected Susceptible to Approach	
Geographics	Confine Activity to Given Geographic Region	Tampa Bay Area

Figure R1–2 FBI criminal personality profile compared against Robert Long.

The Attempted Assassination of Archbishop Makarios
A Forensic Science Case Study

At about 7:05 a.m. on the morning of Sunday, March 8, 1970, the President of the Republic of Cyprus, Archbishop Makarios, boarded his personal helicopter in the courtyard of the archbishop's palace in Nicosia, in order to fly to Macheras Monastery to officiate at a memorial service. He sat on the left of the pilot, Major Zacharias Papadoyiannis. The helicopter took off, and when it had attained the height of the Archbishopric, it made a turn of 150 degrees, still climbing. At a point about 10 metres above the roof of the Archbishopric (Figure R2–1), a shot was heard from the left and rear, and a burst of machine-gun fire came from the same direction. The Archbishop was not hit, but his pilot sustained a severe wound in the abdomen. With great difficulty in view of his wound, the damage caused to the helicopter and the proximity of buildings and electric cables, the pilot managed to land on an open space on the corner of two neighbouring streets, out of range of the firing (Figure R2–2). The Archbishop and pilot dismounted from the helicopter and ran away from it, having in mind the

Julius Grant, MSc, Ph.D., FRIC

Reprinted by permission from the *Medico-Legal Journal*, Vol. 40, Part 2, 1972.

Figure R2–1

Figure R2–2

possibility of an explosion. However, the pilot collapsed and was taken to a hospital where, after a critical illness, he eventually recovered.

The Presidential Guard at the Archbishopric was conscious that the firing came from the roof of the Pancyprian Gymnasium opposite the Archbishop's palace, and they fired in that direction (see Figure R2–1). Shortly after the firing occurred, early risers in Thysseos and Othellos Streets, which adjoin the high side wall of the Pancyprian Gymnasium, saw four men climbing over the wall of the school into Thysseos Street. One spectator asked what was happening, but received no reply; he called out to the men to stop or he would shoot them. One then held his hands to his face, and turned back and said to one of the others who was coming up behind him and was holding a pistol, "They are shooting at us." All four then

(a)   (b)

(c)   (d)

Figure R2–3

turned into Othellos Street. The spectator and other onlookers then saw the four men board a car waiting nearby and drive off. The first spectator telephoned the police and subsequently identified the car by appearance, although he was unable to note the number. Other spectators were able to provide confirmatory evidence regarding the car, although the evidence of identification of the four persons was weak. However, eventually it seems to have been established that the car was of a light blue colour with a white line and was a Fiat, Model 850, registration number ZDR 320. In the meantime the police had been informed of the incident. They entered the Pancyprian Gymnasium, and took possession of the firearms and other exhibits found on the roof.

In another part of Nicosia, at a distance of about a mile from the scene of the attempt, a merchant opening his shop at about 8:30 in the morning noticed a self-drive car having the above description. As this had not been moved by 11:30 a.m. he telephoned the police. On Sunday, March

8, the day of the attempt, at 8:30 in the morning, one G. A. Taliadoros went to the Larnaca Road police station and reported that the car which he had hired on February 12 had been stolen from a parking place. His agitated condition and confused replies to questions aroused suspicion, and he was questioned about the circumstances of the theft of his car as well as about his own movements. In due course two associates of Taliadoros were also detained. They were questioned as to their whereabouts at the relevant time, and as their answers were deemed to be unsatisfactory, they were held in custody. Further arrests were made subsequently, and six persons, as follows, were ultimately detained, namely (Figure R2–3):

Adamos Haritonos, 23, student; and associate of Taliadoros
Georghios Alexandrou Taliadoros, 33, estate agent
Antonakis Prokopi Solomonodos, 32, former inspector of police
Antonakis Petrou Yenagritis, 28, police constable

Costas Polykarpou Ioannides, 32, newspaper editor
Polikarpos Antoni Polykarpou, 32, police constable

Monday, March 9, was a holiday and when on Tuesday, the 10th, Maria Constantinou, a cleaner of the Pancyprian school unlocked the toilets, she found below an aperture in the wall two dirty blankets in a heap. One was light grey in colour and the other a darker colour, rather brownish. These also were taken by the police for examination.

The police force acted with great promptitude and efficiency under the direction of Chief Supt. G. Hadjiloizou of the C.I.D. They took possession of the weapons found on the roof of the Pancyprian school and a number of other articles from the school roof, and also the blankets referred to above. At about the same time a shepherd found a cache of arms, also wrapped in two blankets, hidden in a ditch near Nicosia; and these were taken by the Police. They were similar to the arms found on the roof of the Gymnasium and fingerprints were obtainable from them.

Shortly after the above events, I received a telephone call from the High Commissioner for Cyprus in London asking me if I could fly to Cyprus at once; he hinted at the reason. A few days later I attended a Cabinet meeting at the Presidential Palace, where I met the President, and I was formally invited to be responsible for the forensic investigation of the assassination attempt. The resources of the police force and Government Analyst were placed at my disposal, and I take pleasure in paying tribute to the assistance and hospitality I received.

The activities of the police had resulted in the following list of articles of potential importance to be investigated:

From the school: weapons; two blankets; cigarette ends; button; fecal matter.
From the arms cache: weapons; two blankets.

From the car: dust from the floor; dust from boot; fingerprints; cigarette ends. From the persons detained: all outer clothing; also some 50 articles of other miscellaneous clothing; dust from a car and blankets from the homes of the persons detained. Miscellaneous: revolver holster; newspapers; car cover; etc.

The forensic examination of the above is now dealt with in order of importance. The jacket worn by Taliadoros, when he was arrested, bore a smear of white dust on the right shoulder approximately 3×2 cm in dimensions, and similar in colour to that of the whitewashed walls of the school. Taliadoros said that he picked it up while sitting on a bench and leaning against the wall of the police station where he was originally detained. The police had assiduously taken samples of plaster from the walls of the school along the escape route of the gunmen from the roof to the wall of Thysseos Street, but it was apparent that the mark on the jacket was a surface rubbing, and was a top coat of whitewash and not plaster. In view of the importance of this smear and the lack of wholly positive other forensic evidence concerning Taliadoros, I thought it advisable to make a fresh examination of the scene. Surface rubbings were, therefore, first taken from the areas from which the plaster had been removed. An attempt was then made to reconstruct the early stages of the escape after the shots had been fired.

It will be seen from Figure R2–1 that the gunmen must have climbed down from the flat roof where they had fired at the President on to an open air passage flanked on the right by the high whitewashed wall shown in Figure R2–4. Free passage down the area was prevented on the left by the pitched skylights (four in number) which serve the classroom below and which are apparent in the photograph. It was found that the most convenient way of travelling along this passage in a hurry was to pass between the wall and the skylight, a

Figure R2–4

distance of only 40 cm. This is too small to accommodate a man facing the direction in which he was running. Indeed there was a natural instinct, I found, to half-turn to the left, i.e., away from the wall, on passing between the narrow gaps. If this was done, the right shoulder did not necessarily touch the wall but, as a runner emerged from the gap, there was a distinct probability that his right shoulder would rub against the square-section vertical drainpipes from the roof, which project from the wall to the extent of about 10 cm. When this happened, a smear could be produced on the shoulder of the same size and type and in the same location as that found on Taliadoros's jacket.

A surface rubbing was, therefore, taken from one of the drainpipes at shoulder level, and it was found that the superficial coating was apparently unlike ordinary whitewash but was consistent with a mixture of whitewash and a white emulsion paint. A likely explanation of this is that it had been found that the whitewash would not cover the metal drainpipe, as well as on the actual wall, and a topcoating of emulsion paint had, therefore, been applied over it. The claim that the smear had come from the police station was

easily disposed of, because the bench on which Taliadoros had sat had a wooden back separating the sitter from the wall; and moreover, the whitewash on the wall was not pure white but a pale yellow colour. Table R2–1 shows the spectroscopic analysis of all the powders collected, from which it will be seen that the powder from the coat and that from the drainpipe matched perfectly; moreover they have no counterpart in any of the other samples, which are characteristic of an ordinary lime wash. The presence of both calcium and titanium is consistent with the use of a paint of good covering power, with the limewash on the pipe; and this occurs also on the coat.

In the course of the hearing the defense pointed out that in Nicosia all the drainpipes of the houses are of this rectangular type, so that the rubbing could have come from one of hundreds in the town. Having foreseen this argument I had spent nearly two hours roaming the streets of the town and rubbing my jacket against drainpipes—often to the mystification of passersby! Out of many in various parts of the town I found that about 60% were whitewashed; with the whitewash often partly rubbed off, and the remainder were

Table R2–1

Sample	J	1	2	3	4	5
Aluminum	Minor	Absent	Trace	Minor	Trace	Minor
Barium	Minor	Major	Trace	Minor	Trace	Major
Calcium	Major	Major	Major	Major	Major	Major
Chromium	Trace	Trace	Trace	Trace	Trace	Trace
Iron	Trace	Minor	Trace	Trace	Trace	Trace
Magnesium	Minor	Major	Major	Minor	Major	Major
Silicon	Major	Minor	Trace	Major	Trace	Minor
Titanium	Major	Absent	Absent	Major	Absent	Absent
Zinc	Absent	Minor	Absent	Absent	Trace	Trace

Key
J—Taliadoros's jacket.
1—Landing outside classroom door.
2—Lavatory outside wall.
3—Drainpipe on roof.
4—Lavatory wall where blankets were found.
5—Column at foot of staircase near classroom.

painted with a gloss paint which could not be rubbed off. I did not find one which had the appearance or effect of the drainpipes in the roof corridor at the school. The Court regarded this as significant, according to the Presiding Judge in his summing-up.

Coming now to the two blankets found by the lavatories, these consisted of a grey blanket, torn, with bloodstains and dark stains resembling grease. There was also a brown blanket with several holes, also with dark stains resembling grease. The majority of the fibres comprising it were of wool, and were of a rather unusual shade of brown. The grease stains were extracted, and it was possible to show that the substance present was similar to a type of greasy lubricant in the stores of the Police Department; and that both were similar to the grease on the weapons, which doubtless was used to prevent them from rusting. Infrared spectroscopy was used for this purpose. There was nothing characteristic about this grease, and this evidence, though contributory, was not in itself conclusive. However, an interesting fact noted was that the grease stains on the blanket and the grease on the weapons, while alike, were completely

dissimilar from four other types of oil or grease also kept in the police store. Thus, although the weapons were not police weapons, the grease on them could have come from the police store.

It has been mentioned that bloodstains were found on the grey blanket. These were of human blood. It was thought at first that they were associated with the observation that one of the fugitives seen climbing over the wall had his hand against his face. However, none of the men arrested had any wounds, and examination of the bloodstains showed that they were of the drop rather than of the smear type to be expected from a wound. Medical examination showed no evidence of recent nose-bleeding from any of the men detained. As the stains were old, it was not possible to carry out a grouping test. It was felt that they could have been produced before the relevant date, and this aspect of the evidence was not pursued further.

So far as the weapons found on the scene were concerned, these are shown in Figure R2–1. They comprised a Bren gun, a Lee Enfield rifle, and an M6 rifle; 39 spent cartridges were found, and there were about the same number unused. The only features of importance were the grease referred to above, and fingerprints in the grease. On the weapons were found two prints each having 13 points of diagnostic identity with the right forefinger of Haritonos; one was on the magazine of the Bren gun. On some ammunition was found a print which had 16 points of diagnostic identity with the print from the right forefinger of Yenagritis. On other ammunition was found a print which had 16 points of identity with a print from the left thumb of Solomonodos. On further items of ammunition was found a print which had 16 points of diagnostic identity with a print from the left thumb of Yenagritis. Other prints were found, but were not produced in evidence. On the loaded Bren gun magazine and ammunition found on the roof of the Gymnasium were two prints having 16 points of diagnostic identity with a print from the right thumb of Solomonodos. Other fingerprint evidence attributable to Taliadoros, Haritonos, and Yenagritis was found on the car. Some of these were found near the top edge and on the outside of one of the windows, indicating that the door had been pulled shut, using the partly opened window, by the owner of the print who was sitting inside.

In England 16 points of identity are taken as conclusive evidence of the identity of origin of two fingerprints. In Cyprus, in general the courts accept the same standards as in this country. It will be seen that except in one case the requisite 16 points were obtained. In the case of Haritonos only 13 such points per print were obtained, but points from different parts of more than one print from the same finger can be added together to make the necessary 16. It could be claimed that the lack of further points of identity was due to the poor character of the prints found on the scene in this instance and that there were no dissimilarities between the two prints which could not be accounted for in the same way. Solomonodos, who had been a police officer, accepted that the prints found could have been his. Both he and Yenagritis were in the National Guard in 1963–67, and they stated that they had been in the habit of handling arms and ammunition. In mid-1969 the police authorized the collection of arms surrounded by civilians. Yenagritis and Solomonodos claimed to have been involved in this operation; no Bren guns were among the arms then collected. Haritonos was in the National Guard in 1968 and said that he had handled Bren guns within nine months of the assassination attempt.

This gave rise to a lively controversy as to the age of the fingerprints, which is always difficult to determine with certainty. Supt. Dekatris, the capable fingerprint expert of the Cyprus C.I.D., held the view that the sharpness of the prints indicated recent origin. This was contested by the defence, but I felt that I could support the prosecution's argument because the prints were made in grease, which in the hot climate of Cyprus tends to run; and under these conditions fingerprints become blurred rapidly. An experiment in which prints made in grease on metal were kept at 20°C and 30°C (the summer temperature in Cyprus) for a few days showed a distinct difference in sharpness when developed.

The defence called an expert, formerly of the Greek police force, but he was unable to convince the Court that the fingerprints were old or that the blurring on aging theory was untenable, especially bearing in mind that at least nine months had elapsed since the alleged handling of the weapons and the discovery of the arms. In any case this referred only to the presence of the fingerprints of Solomonodos and Yenagritis, and not to those of their associates.

Fingerprint evidence was also sought from the cigarette ends. These were found on the scene, in the car, and in the police station after detention. Practically all were of the same make and had been smoked in the same way, i.e., to the extent of two-thirds of their length. They were then stubbed out in a similar way by being bent almost at right-angles. It was hoped that the stubbing-out operation would have left a fingerprint on the cigarette paper, but unfortunately nothing that could be satisfactorily used as evidence was found when we used the ninhydrin test. On the other hand, experiments in which we produced similar stubs did leave fingerprints. The reason for this difference may have been the greater heat of burning in the case of the cigarette ends believed to have been associated with the accused; or because the smoker was one of the few people whose fingerprints do not respond to the ninhydrin test. It would have been interesting to have tested the fingerprints of the six men on paper to check this. A saliva grouping test on the cigarette ends might also have been helpful, but facilities were not available.

Much of the forensic work concerned fibres. The objective was to link the fibres from one or more blankets with one or more of the accused. This applied both to the fibres of which the blankets were made and to adventitious fibres found on the blankets. To this end a large collection from the wardrobes of the six men was seized and thoroughly examined, including the pocket linings—since the latest style in trousers can apparently contain as many as seven pockets! In all some 60 outer garments, including shoes, were tested; also included were contents of cars and blankets from the homes of the accused, which the defence alleged were the source of certain of the fibres found. This was extremely laborious work but was fully justified. The connecting links in the evidence were small in number but important. In my evidence on this aspect I thought it advisable to make clear the significance and limitation of evidence based on fibres. This disarmed some anticipated cross-examination.

In making a comparison between fibres found on a suspect and fibres found at the scene of a crime or on an article associated with it, there are three principal criteria to be taken into account, namely:

a. the material of which the fibre is made;
b. the colour of the fibre;
c. its dimensions, i.e., shape and size.

1. Now, if one has two single fibres, one from the scene and one from the suspect, and they are alike in all the three above respects, then one can say that the fibres could have come from the same source, but that there is no certainty that they did so.

2. On the other hand if the fibres being compared are unusual in some respect as well as being alike, then the chance that they come from the same source is greater.

3. Finally, if one is examining groups of fibres, i.e., tufts of fibres of different kinds and different colours, then if the two groups contain the same fibres in the same proportions, then the possibility that they come from the same source is very high indeed; but one still cannot say with absolute certainty that they did so.

On the jacket belonging to Taliadoros, which had the white smear referred to above, I found a number of fibres which were not part of the composition of the jacket, i.e., extraneous fibres. On the left shoulder of the jacket was such a brown fibre, which matched closely the principal fibres of the brown blanket found at the scene of the assassination attempt. Since this was an unusual fibre, I placed it in category 2 above. This could not be regarded as conclusive evidence because the brown fibre could have come from some other source. However, as stated, the shade of the colour was unusual and it is interesting to note that although some hundreds of fibres from various items of clothing, car dust, etc. were examined, in no case did a brown fibre similar to that from the blanket occur except on the left shoulder of Taliadoros's jacket. It should be added that the police took a multicoloured blanket from the home of Taliadoros. It contained brown fibres, which were said to have accounted for the fibre on his jacket; there was a superficial resemblance, but microscopical methods showed the fibres to be quite different.

In the right-hand pocket of the trousers of Taliadoros I found a tuft of fibres which was similar to the fibres comprising one of the blankets used to wrap the weapons. Since this consisted of no less than four fibres of different colours and types in each case, I placed this in the third category, representing the strongest possibility of identity.

On a pullover belonging to Yenagritis I found a human hair which was similar to a human hair which I found on one of the blankets from the school lavatory. It is impossible to say with complete certainty that two human hairs are or are not identical. However, these were alike in colour; they were both relatively long, too long for a male hair, even in these days; and I felt that the possibility that they came from the same source was strong. This was another link between Yenagritis and the blanket.

On the left arm of the jacket of Polykarpou I also found a tuft of fibres similar to those of one of the blankets, and the nature of these was such as to put them in the third category, of the strongest possibility. I also examined debris I collected from the body and boot of the car of Solomonodos and here I found a tuft of fibres similar to those of one of the blankets presumably used to wrap the guns. Here again the nature and the proportions of the fibres placed them in the category of maximum possibility.

The forensic evidence established links as follows:

Linking:
Arms to blankets—grease.
Arms to accused—fingerprints.
Blanket to accused—fibres.
Scene to accused—white smears (Taliadoros).
Car to accused—fingerprints and fibres.

The preliminary enquiry was heard in Nicosia starting April 15, 1970, with Mr. A. Frangos, Senior Counsel of the Republic, for the prosecution. Ninety-five witnesses were called by the prosecution; cross-examination was reserved.

The subsequent trial was held in the assize court room of Nicosia in October 1970. The prosecution was conducted by Mr. Talarides, Senior Counsel, and Mr. Frangos. In Cyprus legal procedure resembles that of England except that there is no jury, the verdict resting with the three presiding Judges. In a small country such as Cyprus this is regarded as a more desirable procedure. Apart from the prosecution's forensic evidence, testimony was largely concerned with the actions, behaviour, and alleged alibis of the accused. The Defence sought to establish alibis and to prove reasonable doubt as to the forensic evidence, but the combined effect of the latter apparently convinced the Judges. The charge against Polykarpou was withdrawn at the first hearing due to lack of evidence; only that from the fibres being available. Ioannides was acquitted owing to insufficient evidence; he was expelled from Cyprus. The remaining four were sentenced to 14 years imprisonment in Nicosia and, according to the press, they subsequently confessed that theirs was one of several plots which were due to take place at the time of the attempted assassination and which undoubtedly would have done so had it not been for the prompt action of the authorities. The accused instructed their respective Counsel not to place any factors in mitigation before the Court; Haritonos stated that he did not pray for leniency.

The author is indebted to the Government of Cyprus for permission to reproduce the illustrations; and to Chief Supt. Hadjiloizou for his cooperation in the preparation of this paper.

Teamwork in the Forensic Sciences
Report of a Case

L. W. Bradford and A. A. Biasotti

Director and Supervising Criminalist, respectively, Laboratory of Criminalistics, San José, California

The scene in which the following events occurred is a single story dwelling in a quiet residential neighborhood where the victim lived. The victim was a 45-year-old woman who lived in the second house on a particular cul-de-sac street next to a red house on the corner (which is of later significance). A streetlight is situated here.

The investigative events began with the discovery of the victim lying face up over the foot of her bed with the top of her head completely blown off. Tissue debris covered both walls and the ceiling surrounding the victim. The gruesome discovery was made and reported immediately at 2:30 a.m. by an elderly male boarder who rented one bedroom in the victim's house. The boarder had entered the house, using his key, at about 1:15 a.m. after working as a bartender since 4 p.m. the previous day. He went directly to his bedroom and read for about an hour. When ready to retire, he noticed lights in the victim's bedroom and kitchen. Investigating, he discovered the victim. The first patrol unit arrived at the scene within minutes. The patrol officer found no weapon and, after a quick search for a possible intruder on the premises, called for assistance.

The detective team arrived at the scene within ten minutes and was followed within the hour by a team of four investigators who were immediately deployed to interview neighbors for possible leads. A more detailed search of the scene revealed that:

1. All doors were locked and there were no signs of forced entry.

2. The victim's clothing was neatly arranged on a chair next to her bed.

3. There was no indication of a struggle prior to the fatal shot.

4. Valuables appeared to be intact and undisturbed.

After photographing the victim and the scene, the body was removed; and a search was made for the projectile which caused the extensive trauma to the victim. A high-velocity weapon was assumed to be the cause of death.

The major portion of a 150 grain, military type, jacketed bullet was recovered in the wall space in back of the headboard of the victim's bed. A projection of the bullet path through the mattress, headboard, and wall, in conjunction with the position of the body, an apparent "defense" type wound on the lower right wrist of the victim, and the lack of powder residues indicated that the victim was shot while sitting on the end of the bed, leaning back at about a 30-degree angle, and holding her right arm in defensive fashion over her face. Class characteristics of the rifle impressed on the .30 caliber bullet indicated the possibility of Remington Rifles, Model numbers 721 to 760.

This fatal bullet was destined to be the vital link in connecting the suspect with the victim, but in a very unusual manner. The second vital link, discovered later in the investigation, was a cancelled check, which will be discussed separately.

Canvassing of the immediate neighbors developed several witnesses who on the evening before:

1. Heard a loud "bang" or "back fire" between 10:15 p.m. and 10:30 p.m.

2. Saw a red station wagon with white top, round taillights, and loud muffler start

Reprinted by permission of the American Society for Testing and Materials from *Journal of Forensic Sciences.*

up and drive out of cul-de-sac within a few minutes after hearing the "loud bang." The license number was not obtained.

3. Described the driver of the vehicle as a male—without further details.

It was also learned from persons in the neighborhood that a vehicle similar to the described station wagon had been parked near the scene on several occasions.

Careful and methodical interrogation of all the neighbors, known friends, and former husband (amicably separated) of the victim continued until such time that a conference was called by the detective-in-charge to summarize and evaluate the information assembled. Logical suspects, including the boarder, the former husband, and several known acquaintances, were quickly eliminated because alibis were confirmed by investigation. One lead, however, needed to be followed. It was learned from friends that the victim frequented a local commercial dance studio. Questioning of persons present during Wednesday afternoon at the dance studio indicated that most of the victim's dancing lessons had been with a part-time instructor who would be in a position to give more information about the victim's acquaintances and habits than anyone else.

Through further leads and contacts, the address of this man was found to be an apartment in an adjacent city. The instructor was 23 years old and married with two children. Two detectives, upon arriving at the suspect's apartment, noted a red and white 1955 Ford station wagon parked in the stall of the apartment. Upon knocking and identifying themselves they were invited into the living room by the instructor. While questioning him about the victim, her acquaintances, and his actions the night of the murder, the detectives noted a marble-topped coffee table, end table, and lamp which fitted the description of furniture taken in a burglary of the victim's residence several months prior. When asked about this furniture, the instructor said that he had purchased it

somewhere at a department store. He later changed his story indicating that it was given to him by a friend. The suspect further stated that he had visited the victim the previous week to borrow $50; but instead he sold her a painting for $140. He denied any knowledge of the murder or of owning a .30 caliber rifle.

He had a good alibi for the night of the murder. He had taken his wife (a waitress) to work early Wednesday evening, taking their children (girl, age 5; boy, age 3) with them and returned home to baby-sit, clean house, and watch TV until about 12:30 a.m. when he departed, leaving the children at home alone, to pick up his wife at work.

As the result of this initial questioning, during which the suspect had changed some of his story, and considering the presence of the stolen furniture, the investigators asked the suspect to go to police headquarters for further questioning, which he did willingly. Further interrogation of the suspect at headquarters, and interrogation of his wife, separately, strengthened the investigators' suspicions that the suspect was not telling the truth and knew more about the murder than he had admitted. At the conclusion of these interviews, the man and wife accepted the police opinion that the furniture was stolen property and allowed it to be taken from their apartment. The man was released at this time after agreeing to a polygraph examination the following day.

Shortly after midnight when the investigators arrived at the suspect's apartment to recover the furniture, they learned from a neighbor adjacent to the suspect's apartment that their apartment had been burglarized about three weeks earlier while she and her husband were away for that weekend. This burglary had been investigated and revealed a forced entry by cutting a screen over the bathroom window and entry through an unlocked window. Reported stolen were a Remington .30-'06 Model 760 Gamemaster rifle and

$10 in cash. With this information in hand, a warrant to search the suspect's apartment and station wagon was obtained and executed on Friday afternoon, the second day following the murder.

The search of the suspect's apartment brought forth the following:

1. A paper target with bullet holes which appeared to be about .30 caliber.

2. One fired caliber .30-'06 cartridge case (established by laboratory examination to be not connected with the stolen rifle).

3. A caliber .22 rifle, a .410 gauge shotgun, and a caliber .25 pistol.

4. An electric shaver identified as belonging to the boarder living in the victim's house and reported stolen in a burglary.

5. A pair of stained trousers (lab examination revealed no blood or human tissue on these trousers).

The search of the suspect's station wagon developed the following:

1. Cuff links identified as taken with the electric shaver found in the apartment.

2. A large "gunshot" penetration from interior to exterior at about a 45 degree angle in the right side with the entry in line with the top of the rear-seat cushion.

The "gunshot" hole in the suspect's vehicle was an unexplained event which later developed into yet another interesting speculative aspect of this case. From an examination of the penetration, powder, pattern, and lead pellets found in the vehicle, it was determined that this hole was consistent with the firing of a .410 gauge shotgun. It was found that this single shot, bolt action Mossberg, Model 173 A, .410 gauge shotgun found in the suspect's apartment would fire when dropped on its butt with the thumb safety in the "fire" position. This information at the time did little more than add mystery to the investigation. About 19 days after the murder, however, this event assumed new significance when one of the investigators in checking out the neighborhood near the scene observed what appeared to be a pellet pattern on the sidewalk next to the curb in front of the house on the corner next to the victim's residence. This was the area in which the red and white station wagon had been observed parked on previous occasions. Examination of the pattern in conjunction with the hole in the vehicle indicated that the pattern, size, shape, shot imprints, and angle were all consistent with the hypothesis that the suspect's .410 shotgun discharged through the right side while parked at the curb. No statements had been given by the suspect to the point of this evidence.

When again questioned about the items recovered in the search and his alibis, the suspect refused to answer most questions without his attorney. He did, however, attempt to explain the target with the caliber .30 bullet holes by saying that he had recently been to a local outdoor shooting ranch where he was shooting a "large caliber rifle" which he described as "more than a .22 and smaller than a cannon." This statement, which must have been an inadvertent "slip" by the suspect, provided a useful clue.

All information thus far obtained pointed to a connection between the suspect and the victim, the burglaries, and possibly the murder; but a direct link with the crime was not a matter of established fact. Based upon these tenuous developments and on the advice of the District Attorney of Santa Clara County, the suspect was arrested and charged with Burglary, Receiving Stolen Property, and Murder. After the arrest the chief detective found a key in the personal property taken from the suspect at the time of booking which appeared to be identical with the house key to the victim's residence. The suspect when questioned about the key said that it was for a prior residence in the area and gave an address. A check of this alibi address revealed that the suspect and his wife had lived at that address. The locks had not been changed after they had moved, and the key taken from the suspect and matching the victim's key did not open any of the locks at the alibi address; but it did open the entrance door to the victim's house. How or when the suspect obtained this key has never been determined, but it was known that the victim stored her wraps and purse in the cloak room at dancing periods when the suspect was present. Consequently, he had an opportunity to make a duplicate.

At this point, a service station attendant was located who tentatively identified the suspect as one who had stopped at his gas station in the vicinity of the death scene on the night of the murder.

The suspect, when faced with all of the apparent contradictions to his alibis, accused the police of lying and attempting to falsely implicate him and refused to answer further questions. When the time for an agreed polygraph examination arrived, he refused to undergo the examination. From this point on no further information was obtained directly from the suspect which would aid in the solution of the case.

Two days after the murder, the police were faced with an array of alibis, contradictions, and facts which appeared to be pieces of a puzzle, but which defied fitting together in any logical way. It was again time for reflection and contemplation before planning the next move. A review of the progress to date indicated that the next two main lines of investigation should be:

1. To contact the neighbors of the suspect who resided in the apartment adjacent to the suspect to determine whether any fired components from the caliber .30-'06 Remington Model 760 rifle were available from the period prior to the time of the burglary in which the rifle was taken.

2. To investigate the shooting range for spent bullets where the suspect indicated that he may have fired a rifle.

The neighbors were contacted first, and three fired .30-'06 cartridge cases were obtained which had been fired from the rifle before it was stolen. When asked when and where the rifle had last been fired, the neighbor replied that it had been at a pine tree during the recent fall deer hunting season in the Sierra Nevada mountains located about 150 miles from his apartment. This occurred while he was hunting with a friend and a nephew. The neighbor had his .30-'06 Remington Model 760 rifle; the friend had a .30-'06 Springfield Model 1903 rifle; and his nephew had a .30-30 Winchester Model 94 rifle. He said that he and his nephew had sighted in their rifles with targets placed against a large pine tree at a distance of about 150 feet from a clearing near a road. Several shots were fired. He thought that he could locate the tree. Four days after the murder, the neighbor guided investigators to a pine tree approximately 100 feet tall and about 30-in. in diameter. A small section surrounding one apparent bullet hole was cut out, and a jacketed bullet was recovered and returned to the laboratory in San Jose for examination. This bullet was found to be from a caliber .30 weapon of six right-hand riflings with a land width consistent with the Model 94 Winchester used by the neighbor's nephew. A second trip to the pine tree was made; and with permission and assistance of the U.S. Forest Service, the tree was felled. A five-foot section of the trunk was returned to Santa Clara County where it was split and dissected. With the aid of X-ray equipment, a second bullet was recovered. The bullet was fully mushroomed, leading to a cover over the rifling marks which had preserved the class and individual characteristics on the base portion of the metal jacket. The bullet proved to be a soft point fired from a caliber .30 weapon with class characteristics consistent with a Remington Model 760 rifle. These class characteristics were the same as those of the fatal bullet. Further study revealed a

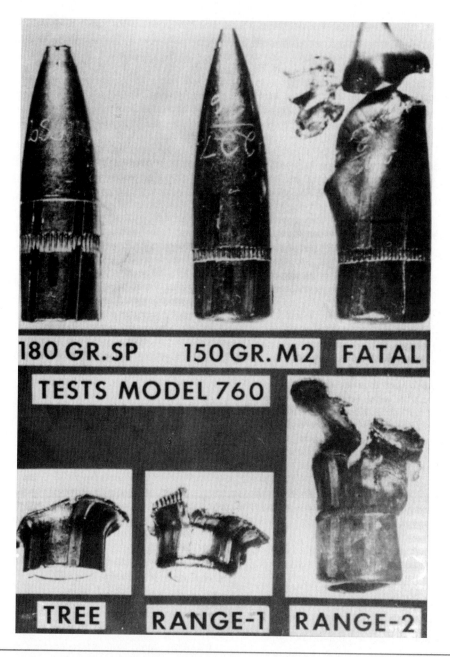

Figure R3–1 Bullets used to link the fatal bullet with the missing murder rifle. The fatal bullet and the two range bullets are metal-jacketed, spitzer, 150 grain M2 ball (U.S. Army) military type. The bullet from the tree is a 180 grain soft point corresponding to ammunition possessed by the owner of the stolen rifle. The two tests were not fired by the murder weapon and are included solely for the purpose of illustrating bullet type and class characteristics of rifling marks.

significant similarity of individual characteristics between the fatal bullet and the bullet from the tree indicating that both had been fired by the neighbor's stolen rifle (Figures R3–1 and R3–2).

The next phase of the investigation proceeded to the shooting range where it was believed that the suspect may have fired a rifle prior to the murder. Nine days after the murder the range master of the Sunnyvale Rod and Gun Club was contacted, and it was determined that the range had opened about a month prior to the murder after renovating the sandstone-shale embankment which served as a backstop at 100 yards from the firing

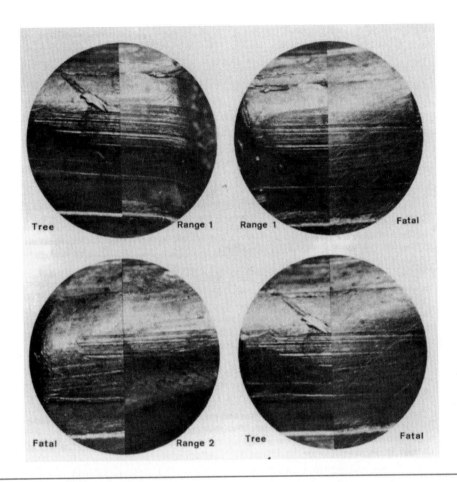

Figure R3–2 Comparison photomicrographs demonstrating the identification between the bullets shown in Figure R3–1.

point. The range had been closed for about three months while the embankment was scraped and cleared. When shown a photo of the suspect and asked if he recognized the person, the range master stated that the photo resembled a person using the range during the past month who was shooting a .30-'06 Remington Model Gamemaster "pump-action" rifle. Entries on the sign-in register required for all persons using the range were hastily searched for the name and address of the suspect. None being found, the list was submitted to the Laboratory of Criminalistics for a handwriting examination to determine whether or not the suspect could have signed the register using an assumed name.

When the register was examined at the Laboratory, the only immediately available authentic specimen of handwriting of the suspect was his endorsement of a $140 check which he had earlier mentioned in connection with the purported sale of a painting to the victim. An examination of the complete range record revealed the name of the suspect one week later than the date first indicated by the range master. This name was identified with the writing on the check endorsement. There was further examination of the check which will be discussed separately. The signature on the range record was dated three days prior to the murder. The register indicated that he was assigned to firing Point #29. Point #30 was the last firing position. A man and his son assigned lanes 27 and 28 and another person assigned lane 30 were immediately contacted and questioned. Lanes 29 and 30 were customarily the only targets used for high velocity weapons.

The man and his son from shooting lanes 27 and 28 identified the suspect from a photograph and said he was firing a .30-'06 Remington Model 742 or 760 in lane 29. Also that he was firing military type ammunition and when asked if they could have his brass, the suspect replied that he was saving it for a friend. They further noted that a girl, about 5, and a boy, about 3, accompanied the suspect at the range. Based upon this information the embankment covering targets #28, 29, and 30 was searched with the aid of a screen. Several buckets of metal jacket fragments were recovered. The buckets of projectiles were taken to the laboratory where rapid sorting based on gross class characteristics eliminated all but a few jackets and jacket fragments with class characteristics similar to the fatal bullet (see Figure R3–1).

A detailed comparison microscope examination was now begun which revealed that two bullet jackets from the range had class and individual characteristics that established an identity between the .30 caliber bullet from the tree and the fatal bullet (see Figures R3–1 and R3–2). Thus, about three weeks after the murder, the two bullets from the range

provided the needed missing link between the stolen rifle and the fatal bullet. Without this evidence a connection between the stolen rifle and the fatal bullet would never have been established because the rifle had not been found. The physical evidence had now provided a link between the murder weapon and the suspect and the fatal bullet. To strengthen this link further, a third trip was made to the area from which the neighbor had fired at the pine tree. With the aid of a metal detector, three fired .30-'06 cartridge cases were found. Microscopic comparisons of breech bolt marks on these cases led to an identification with the three fired cases previously obtained from the neighbor (Figure R3–3).

Returning to the subject of the $140 check, the endorsement was of interest as an exemplar of the defendant's signature for the purpose of comparison with the range record. Much to the surprise of the investigators during the preliminary examination of this document at the laboratory, it was discovered that the entire face of the check was traced. It was further determined that the payer signature was traced from an authentic victim's signature and the remainder of the check was traced

(a)

(b)

Figure R3–3 **Comparison photomicrographs demonstrating the identification between cartridge cases recovered near tree to cases from the owner of stolen rifle.**

from authentic writing of the suspect, including his own name as payee.

The document examiner, upon this finding, asked the detectives to obtain the victim's check stubs for the period involved with the $140 check.

It was found that the traced check was numbered in a sequence different from those covering the period of her stubs. The traced check was number 330. A new group of five personalized checkbooks had recently been received from the bank by mail. Four of these were found by the detectives in an opened bank envelope on the victim's desk. The fifth book containing checks No. 325 through 349 was missing. Speculate now as to the reason that check No. 330 was cashed by the defendant rather than Nos. 325, 326, 327, 328, and 329.

The prosecutor charged first degree murder. The defendant was found guilty and was sentenced to life. The prosecutor used the following lines of argument following the presentation of all the evidence:

1.   The victim was a lonely woman who had spent several thousand dollars for dancing lessons over a period of years as a form of recreation.

2.   The defendant gained a knowledge of the victim's habits, address, and situation through frequent association as a dance instructor.

3.   Through access to the defendant's wraps and purse while at dancing sessions, the defendant gained possession of a key by either replication or theft.

4.   Using this illicit key, the defendant had made visits to the victim's home while she was attending dance sessions in other areas. He had taken property from this home on several occasions. This included the furniture, boarder's cuff links, and checkbook.

5.   The defendant had burglarized his neighbor's apartment and had taken the .30-'06 rifle. When entering the victim's home, he was armed, first with the .410

gauge shotgun, later with the .30-'06 rifle. The long-barreled weapons were concealed by placing them on the floor behind the driver's seat of the vehicle. On one of these occasions, while the vehicle was parked near the victim's home, the shotgun was accidentally discharged while in the act of placing or removing it from this position.

6.   The defendant traced the victim's signature on check No. 325, using the technique of carbon paper; however, when he covered the tracing with ink, it was a different color than his freehand writing on the remainder of the check face. He continued practicing the forgery until he learned that tracing the entire check face was the only method of avoiding a difference in appearance of the ink color between the payer line and remaining entries. In this way he used up checks Nos. 325, 326, 327, 328, and 329, and finally perfected the forgery on check No. 330.

7.   After cashing the check, the defendant waited until the day that he thought cancelled checks through the mail would arrive at the victim's house, at which time he again entered the home armed with the rifle intending to remove the cancelled check No. 330 and destroy it in order to conceal the forgery; he unexpectedly encountered the victim and killed her.

The case is bizarre for several reasons:

1.   The connection of the fatal bullet with the suspect without the rifle is exceptionally uncommon.

2.   The fact of a defendant tracing his own name is very peculiar.

3.   The good fortune of finding exemplar bullets in examinable condition from the tree and range under the circumstances described is unlikely.

It is to the credit of the investigators, examiners, and prosecutors that they recognized the value and significance of all the facets of the evidence and were able to communicate with each other in a manner which made the most effective use of all of it.

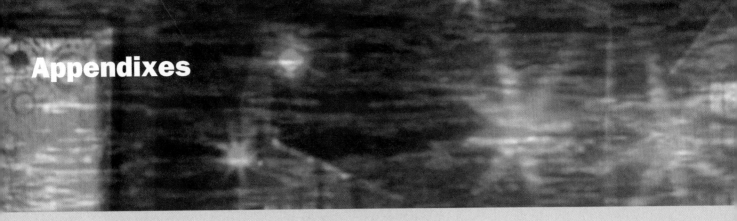

Appendixes

Appendix I
Guides to the Collection of Physical Evidence—FBI

| | Amount Desired | | |
Specimen	Standard	Evidence	Send By
Abrasives	Not less than one ounce.	All	Registered mail or equivalent
Ammunition (Live Cartridges)			Live ammunition must be shipped via Federal Express. The following guidelines must be followed to comply with U.S. Department of Transportation regulations. Pack ammunition in a cardboard container. Label invoices FEDERAL EXPRESS. The shipper's certification for restricted articles must be included. The outside of the container must be labeled ORMD AIR, CARTRIDGES SMALL ARMS. The shipping papers must also include the weight in grams
Anonymous tion Letters, and Bank Robbery Notes		Documentary evidence condition in which it was found. It should not be folded, torn, marked, soiled, stamped, written on, or handled unnecessarily. Protect the evidence from inadvertent indented writing. Mark documents unobtrusively by writing the collector's initials, date, and other information with a pencil. Whenever possible, submit the original evidence to the Laboratory. The lack of detail in photocopies makes examinations difficult. Copies are sufficient for reference file searches.	Registered mail or equivalent
Bullets (projector without cartridge) (Live Cartridges)		All found.	Same as Ammunition
Cartridge Cases (shells only)		All	Same as Ammunition

Source: Courtesy of the Federal Bureau of Investigation, Washington, D.C.

Identification	Wrapping and Packing	Remarks
Outside container: type of material, date obtained, investigator's name or initials.	Submit abrasives in heat-sealed or resealable plastic bags or paint cans. Avoid using paper or glass containers.	Abrasives settle in oil and fuel. Submit the oil and fuel from the engine sump and/or filters. Abrasives embed in bearings and other parts. Submit the bearings and other parts.
Same as above.	Ammunition components such as bullets, cartridge cases and shotshell casings can be sent via registered mail through the U.S. Postal Service. Evidence should be packaged separately and identified by date, time, location, collector's name, case number, and evidence number.	Unless specific examination of the cartridge is essential, do not submit.
Initial and date each document, if advisable.	Use proper enclosure. Place in envelope and seal with "Evidence" tape or transparent cellophane tape. Flap side of envelope should show: (1) wording "Enclosure(s) to FBI from (name of submitting office)," (2) title of case, (3) brief description of contents, (4) file number, if known. Staple to original letter of transmittal.	Do not handle with bare hands. Advise if evidence should be treated for latent fingerprints. Whenever possible, submit the original evidence to the laboratory. The lack of detail in photocopies makes examinations difficult. Copies are sufficient for reference file searches.
Do not mark bullets, cartridges and cartridge cases, and shotshells and shotshell casings. The date, time, location, collector's name, case number, and evidence number should be on the container.	Pack tightly in cotton or soft paper in pill, match, or powder box. Place in box. Label outside of box as to contents.	Unnecessary handling obliterates marks.
Same as above.	Same as above.	Spent cartridge cases.

Specimen	Amount Desired		Send By
	Standard	**Evidence**	
Casts (Dental or Die Stone Casts of Tire Treads and Shoe Prints)	Send in suspect's shoes and tires. Photographs and sample impressions are usually not suitable for comparison.	All shoe prints and entire circumference of tires.	Registered mail or equivalent
Checks (fraudulent)		See Anonymous Letter (p. 612)	Registered mail or equivalent
Check Protector, Rubber Stamp, and/or Date Stamp Known Standards (if possible, send actual device)	Obtain several copies in full word-for-word order of each questioned check-writer impression. If unable to forward rubber stamps, prepare numerous samples with different degrees of pressure.		Registered mail or equivalent
Clothing		All	Registered mail or equivalent
DNA Examinations (see pp. 624–626)			
Documents (charred or burned)		All	Registered mail or equivalent
Drugs: 1. Liquids		All	Registered mail or equivalent
2. Powders, Pills, and Solids		All to 30 g.	Registered mail or equivalent
EXPLOSIVES: Detonators, Blasting Caps, Detonating Cord, Black Powder, Smokeless Powder, Explosives, and Accessories, call FBI Laboratory, for shipping instructions.			
Fibers	Entire garment or other cloth item.	All	Registered mail or equivalent
Firearms (unloaded weapons)		Firearms must be packaged and shipped separately from live ammunition. All firearms must be unloaded.	Firearms and ammunition components such as bullets, cartridge cases, and shotshell casings can be sent via registered mail through the U.S. Postal Service. Evidence must be packaged separately and identified by date, time, location, collector's name, case number, and evidence number.

Identification	Wrapping and Packing	Remarks
On back of cast before it hardens, write location and date taken, and investigator's name or initials.	Wrap in paper and cover with suitable packing material to prevent breakage Label "Fragile." Plaster of Paris is no longer recommended.	For shoeprint and tire tread file searches, submit quality photographs of the impressions. If photographs are not available, submit casts, lifts, or the original evidence. Detailed sketches or photocopies are acceptable.
See Anonymous Letters on p. 612.	See Anonymous Letters on p. 612.	Advise what parts are questioned or known. Furnish physical description of subject.
Place name or initials, date, name of make and model, etc., on sample impressions.	See Anonymous Letters on p. 612.	Do not disturb inking mechanisms on printing devices.
Mark directly on garment or use string tag indicating type of evidence, date obtained, investigator's name or initials.	Wrap each article individually. Place in strong container with identification written on outside of package.	Do not cut out stains, leave clothing whole. If wet, hang in room to dry before packing.
Outside container: indicate if fragile, date obtained, investigator's name or initials.	Pack in rigid container between layers of cotton.	If moisture is added use atomizer, otherwise, not recommended.
Affix label to bottle in which found, including date it was found and investigator's name or initials.	Make sure container does not leak. Seal with tape to prevent any loss.	Mark "Fragile." If possible, use heat-seal plastic bags.
Outside of pillbox: affix label with date found and investigator's name or initials.	Seal with tape to prevent any loss.	If powder, pills, or solids are found in paper bags, place them in plastic bags to prevent any loss. Do not submit used drug field test kits with evidence.
Outside container or on the object fibers are adhering, include date and investigator's name or initials.	Use folder paper or pillbox. Seal edges and openings with tape.	Do not place loose in an envelope.
Do not mark the firearm. Firearms should be identified with a tag containing the caliber, make, model, and serial number. The date, time, owner(s)' name(s), location, collector's name, case number, and evidence number should be on the container.	Wrap in paper and identify contents of packages. Place in cardboard box or wooden box.	The firearm should be handled minimally to avoid loss or destruction of evidence. Do not allow objects to enter or contact the firearm's barrel, chamber, or other operating surface.

Specimen	Amount Desired		Send By
	Standard	**Evidence**	
Flash Paper	One sheet	All to 5 sheets.	Call FBI Laboratory.
Gasoline	10 ml	All to 10 ml	Call Chemistry-Toxicology Unit for instructions.
General Unknown: **1.** Solids (nonhazardous)	10 gm	All to 10 gm	Registered mail or equivalent
2. Liquids (non-hazardous)	10 ml	All to 10 ml	Registered mail or equivalent
Glass Fractures		All	Registered mail or equivalent
Glass Particles	Submit the victim(s)'and suspect's air-dried clothing. each item must be packaged separately in a paper bag. Search for particles in the victim(s)' and Suspect(s)' hair, skin, and wounds. Submit particles in leakproof containers such as film canisters or plastic pill bottles. Do not use paper or glass containers Search for particles in vehicles by vacuuming each section of the vehicle separately. Do not use tape for covering glass particles. Submit vacuum sweepings in leakproof containers. Do not use paper or glass containers.	All	Registered mail or equivalent

Identification	Wrapping and Packing	Remarks
Outside container: label indicating date and investigator's name or initials.	Flash paper is a hazardous material. Do not store flash paper near combustible materials. Seal flash paper in polyethylene envelopes and refrigerate.	
Outside container: label indicating type of material, date, and investigator's name or initials.	Use an all-metal container packed in wooden box.	An all-metal container should be used for its fireproof qualities.
Outside container: label indicating date and investigator's name or initials.	Same as Drugs (see p. 614).	Call Chemistry-Toxicology Unit for instructions.
Same as Liquid Drugs (see p. 614).	Same as Liquid Drugs (see p. 614).	Same as above.
Label the sides of the glass in the frame INSIDE and OUTSIDE. Label the glass where it was removed in the frame such as TOP, BOTTOM, LEFT, and RIGHT.	Wrap each piece separately in cotton. Pack in sturdy container to prevent shifting and breakage. Identify contents.	Submit all glass pieces so that the pieces can be fitted together to identify the radial cracks near and at the point(s) of impact and to increase the probability of matching edges. Pack all glass separately and securely to avoid shifting and breaking during transport.
Outside container: label indicating date and investigator's name or initials.	Place in film canister or plastic vial. Seal and protect against breakage.	Submit samples of glass from each broken window or source in leakproof containers such as film canisters or plastic pill bottles. Avoid using paper or glass containers.

Specimen	Amount Desired		Send By
	Standard	**Evidence**	
Gunshot Residues The Laboratory provides gunshot residue examinations to assist FBI field office investigations only.		Usually gunshot residue examinations will only be performed when samples are collected from living person's hands. Gunshot residue evidence must be collected within five hours of exposure to the discharge of a firearm.	
On cloth only to determine weapon to target distance.		All	Clothing submitted for gunshot residue examination should be handled carefully, air dried, and wrapped separately in paper. Clothing with blood must be air dried and labeled BIOHAZARD on the inner and outer containers. The date, time, location, collector's name, case number, and evidence number should be on the container.
Hair	Twenty-five full-length hairs from different parts of head and/ or pubic region.	All	Registered mail or equivalent
Handwriting and Hand Printing Known Standards			Registered mail or equivalent
Insulation **1.** Glass Wool	1″ mass from each suspect area.	All	Registered mail or equivalent
2. Safe	Sample all damaged areas.	All	Registered mail or equivalent
Matches	One to two books of paper. One full box of wood.	All	Federal Express, UPS, or equivalent
Obliterated, Eradicated, or Indented Writing		Same as Anonymous Letters (see p. 612).	Registered mail or equivalent

Identification	Wrapping and Packing	Remarks
		Collecting gunshot residue samples requires five adhesive lifts suitable for scanning electron microscopic analysis. Dab the adhesive side of the stub against the surface (right palm, back of right hand, left palm, back of left hand). Use one stub per sampling surface. The remaining stub will be used as a control. Label each sampling surface stub (e.g., RIGHT PALM, BACK OF RIGHT HAND). Cap and seal the stubs in separate, resealable plastic bags.
Outside container: Indicate date, obtained from whom, description, name or initials.	Dry and package individually in **unused** brown wrapping paper or brown grocery bag.	The deposition of gunshot residue on evidence such as clothing varies with the distance from the muzzle of the firearm to the target. Patterns of gunshot residue can be duplicated using a questioned firearm and ammunition combination fired into test materials at known distances. These patterns serve as a basis for estimating muzzle-to-garment distances.
Outside container: Type of material, date, and investigator's name or initials.	Folded paper or pillbox. Seal edges and openings with tape.	Do not place loose in envelope.
Indicate from whom obtained, voluntary statement included in appropriate place, date obtained, and investigator's name or initials.	Same as Anonymous Letters (see p. 612).	Same as Anonymous Letters (see p. 612).
Outside container: type of material, date, name or initials.	Use pillbox or plastic vial. Seal to prevent any loss.	Submit known and questioned debris in leakproof containers such as film canisters or plastic pill bottles. Avoid using paper or glass containers. Pack to keep lumps intact.
Same as above.	Safe insulation can adhere to persons, clothing, tools, bags, and loot and can transfer to vehicles. If possible, submit the evidence to the Laboratory for examiners to remove the debris. Package each item of evidence in a separate paper bag. Do not process tools for latent prints.	
Outside container: label indicating type of material, date, and investigator's name or initials.	Pack in metal container and in larger package to prevent shifting. Pack matches in box or metal container to prevent friction between matches.	Keep and label: "Keep away from fire."
Same as Anonymous Letters (see p. 612).	Same as Anonymous Letters (see p. 612).	Advise whether bleaching or staining methods may be used. Avoid folding.

	Amount Desired		
Specimen	**Standard**	**Evidence**	**Send By**
Organs of the Body		200 g of each organ.	Call Chemistry-Toxicology Unit for instructions.
Paint:			
1. Liquid	Original unopened container up to 1/4 pint, if possible.	All to 1/4 pint.	Registered mail or equivalent
2. Solid (paint chips or scrapings)	At least 1/2 sq. in. of solid, with all layers represented.	Standard: Control paint chips must be collected from the suspected source of the evidentiary paint. Controls must be taken from an area close to, but not in, any damaged area. If no damage is obvious, controls should be taken from several areas of the suspect substrate. Each layer can be a point of comparison. Controls must have all of the layers of paint to the substrate.	Registered mail or equivalent
Rope, Twine, and Cordage	One yard or amount available.	Submit the entire rope or cord. If the rope or cord must be cut, specify which end was cut during evidence collection. Label the known and questioned samples. Handle the sections of rope or cord carefully to prevent loss of trace material or contamination.	Registered mail or equivalent
Saliva Samples	1.5″ diameter stain in center of filter paper.	All	Registered mail or equivalent
Shoe Print Lifts (impressions on hard surfaces)	Photograph before making lift of dust impression.	For shoeprint and tire tread comparisons, submit original evidence whenever possible (shoes, tires, photographic negatives, casts, lifts).	Registered mail or equivalent
Soils and Minerals	Samples from areas near pertinent spot.	Collect soil samples from the immediate crime scene area and from the logical access and/or escape route(s). Collect soil samples at a depth that is consistent with the depth from which the questioned soil may have originated. If possile, collect soil samples from alibi areas such as the yard or work area of the suspect(s).	Registered mail

Identification	Wrapping and Packing	Remarks
Each biological specimen must be placed in a separate, labeled, sealed glass tube, plastic cup, or heat-sealed or resealable plastic bag. Affix BIOHAZARD labels to the inside and outside containers.	To avoid deterioration, biological specimens must be refrigerated or frozen during storage and shipping. Pack so that no breakage, leakage, or contamination occurs.	Submit a copy of the autopsy or incident report. Describe the symptoms of the suspect(s) or victim(s) at the time of the crime or prior to the death. List any known or questioned drugs consumed by or prescribed for the suspect(s) or victim(s). Describe any known or questioned environmental exposure to toxic substances by the suspect(s) or victim(s).
Outside container: Type of material, origin if known, date, investigator's name or initials.	Use friction-top paint can or large-mouth, screw-top jar. If glass, pack to prevent breakage. Use heavy corrugated paper or wooden box.	Protect spray can nozzles to keep them from going off. Avoid contact w/adhesive materials. Wrap to protect paint smears. Do not use envelopes, paper/plastic bags, or glass vials.
Same as above.	Package paint specimens in leakproof containers such as vials or pillboxes. Do not stick paint particles on adhesive tape. Do not use plastic bags, cotton, or envelopes to package paint specimens.	Avoid contact with adhesive materials. Wrap so as to protect smear. If *small amount:* seal round pillbox, film cannister, or plastic vial to protect against leakage/breakage.
On tag or container: Type of material, date, investigator's name or initials.	Submit in heat-sealed or resealable plastic or paper bags.	
Outside envelope and on filter paper: Type of sample, name of donor, date of collection, and collector's initials or name.	Seal in envelope.	Stain should be circled in pencil for identification. Filter paper available from hospitals and drugstores. Allow to dry.
On lifting tape or paper attached to tape: date, investigator's name or initials.	Prints in dust are easily damaged. Fasten print or lift to bottom of box so that nothing will rub against it.	Always secure crime-scene area until shoe prints or tire treads are located and preserved.
Outside container: Type of material, date, investigator's name or initials.	Do not remove soil adhering to shoes, clothing, and tools. Do not process tools for latent prints. Air-dry the soil and the clothing and package separately in paper bags. Carefully remove soil adhering to vehicles. Air-dry the soil and package separately in paper bags.	Ship known and questioned debris separately to avoid contamination. Submit known and questioned soil in leakproof containers such as film canisters or plastic pill bottles. Do not use paper envelopes or glass containers. Pack to keep lumps intact.

Specimen	Amount Desired		Send By
	Standard	**Evidence**	
Tape (Adhesive Tape)	Recovered roll.	All	Registered mail or equivalent
Tools/Toolmarks	Send in the tool. If impractical, make several impressions on similar materials as evidence using entire marking area of tool.	If it is not possible to submit the tool-marked evidence, submit a cast of the toolmark.	Registered mail or equivalent
Typewriting, known standards	See Anonymous Letters (p. 612).		Registered mail or equivalent
Wire	3 ft. (Do not kink.)	All (Do not kink.)	Registered mail or equivalent
Wood	One foot or amount available.	All	Registered mail or equivalent

Identification	Wrapping and Packing	Remarks
Same as above.	Place on waxed paper, cellophane, or plastic.	Do not cut, wad, distort, or separate tapes that are stuck together.
On object or on tag attached to an opposite end from where toolmarks appear: date recovered and investigator's name or initials.	After marks have been protected with soft paper, wrap in strong wrapping paper, place in strong box, and pack to prevent shifting.	Photographs locate tool-marks but are of no value for identification purposes. Obtain samples of any material deposited on the tools. To avoid contamination, do not place the tool against the toolmarked evidence. Submit the tool rather than making test cuts or impressions. Mark the ends of the evidence and specify which end was cut during evidence collection.
On specimens: serial number, brand, model, etc., date recovered, and investigator's name or initials.	Same as Anonymous Letters (p. 612).	Examine ribbon for evidence of questioned message.
On label or tab: describe type of material, date, investigator's name or initials.	Wrap securely.	Do not kink wire.
Same as above.	Submit wood in heat-sealed or resealable plastic of paper bags.	

DNA Examinations

Deoxyribonucleic acid (DNA) is analyzed in body fluids, stains, and other biological tissues recovered from evidence. The results of DNA analysis of questioned biological samples are compared with the results of DNA analysis of known samples. This analysis can associate victim(s) and/or suspect(s) with each other or with a crime scene.

There are two sources of DNA used in forensic analyses. Nuclear DNA (nDNA) is typically analyzed in evidence containing blood, semen, saliva, body tissues, and hairs that have tissue at their root ends. Mithochondrial DNA (mtDNA) is typically analyzed in evidence containing naturally shed hairs, hair fragments, bones, and teeth.

If DNA evidence is not properly documented, collected, packaged, and preserved, it will not meet the legal and scientific requirements for admissibility in a court of law.

- If it is not properly documented, its origin can be questioned.
- If it is not properly collected, biological activity can be lost.
- If it is not properly packaged, contamination can occur.
- If it is not properly preserved, decomposition and deterioration can occur.

When DNA evidence is transferred by direct or secondary (indirect) means, it remains on surfaces by absorption or adherence. In general, liquid biological evidence is absorbed into surfaces, and solid biological evidence adheres to surfaces. Collecting, packaging, and preserving DNA evidence depends on the liquid or solid state and the condition of the evidence.

The more that evidence retains its original integrity until it reaches the Laboratory, the greater the possibility of conducting useful examinations. It may be necessary to use a variety of techniques to collect suspected body fluid evidence.

Blood Examinations

Examinations can determine the presence or absence of blood in stains. Examinations can also determine whether blood is human or not. Blood examinations cannot determine the age or the race of a person. Conventional serological techniques are not adequately informative to positively identify a person as the source of a stain.

Collecting Known Samples

Blood
- Only qualified medical personnel should collect blood samples from a person.
- Collect at least two 5-ml tubes of blood in purple-top tubes with EDTA as an anticoagulant for DNA analysis. Collect drug- or alcohol-testing samples in gray-top tubes with NaF (sodium fluoride).
- Identify each tube with the date, time, subject's name, location, collector's name, case number, and evidence number.
- Refrigerate, do not freeze blood samples. Use cold packs, not dry ice, during shipping.
- Pack liquid blood tubes individually in Styrofoam or cylindrical tubes with absorbent material surrounding the tubes.
- Label the outer container KEEP IN A COOL DRY PLACE, REFRIGERATE ON ARRIVAL, and BIOHAZARD.
- Submit to the Laboratory as soon as possible.

Blood on a Person
- Absorb suspected **liquid blood** onto a clean cotton cloth or swab. Leave a portion of the cloth or swab unstained as a control. Air-dry the cloth or swab and pack in clean paper or an envelope with sealed corners. Do not use plastic containers.
- Absorb suspected **dried blood** onto a clean cotton cloth or swab moistened with distilled water. Leave a portion of the cloth or swab unstained as a control. Air-dry the cloth or swab and pack in clean paper or an envelope with sealed corners. Do not use plastic containers.

Blood on Surfaces or in Snow or Water
- Absorb suspected **liquid blood or blood clots** onto a clean cotton cloth or swab. Leave a portion of the cloth or swab unstained as a control. Air-dry the cloth or swab and pack in clean paper or an envelope with sealed corners. Do not use plastic containers.

- Collect suspected **blood in snow or water** immediately to avoid further dilution. Eliminate as much snow as possible. Place in a clean airtight container. Freeze the evidence and submit as soon as possible to the Laboratory.

Bloodstains

- Air-dry **wet bloodstained garments.** Wrap **dried bloodstained garments** in clean paper. Do not place wet or dried garments in plastic or airtight containers. Place all debris or residue from the garments in clean paper or an envelope with sealed corners.

- Air-dry small suspected **wet bloodstained objects** and submit the objects to the Laboratory. Preserve bloodstain patterns. Avoid creating additional stain patterns during drying and packaging. Pack to prevent stain removal by abrasive action during shipping. Pack in clean paper. Do not use plastic containers.

- When possible, cut a large sample of suspected **bloodstains from immovable objects** with a clean, sharp instrument. Collect an unstained control sample. Pack to prevent strain removal by abrasive action during shipping. Pack in clean paper. Do not use plastic containers.

- Absorb suspected **dried bloodstains on immovable objects** onto a clean cotton cloth or swab moistened with distilled water. Leave a portion of the cloth or swab unstained as a control. Air-dry the cloth or swab and pack in clean paper or an envelope with sealed corners. Do not use plastic containers.

Blood Examination Request Letter

A blood examination request letter must contain the following information:

- A brief statement of facts relating to the case.
- Claims made by the suspect(s) regarding the source of the blood.
- Whether animal blood is present.
- Whether the stains were laundered or diluted with other body fluids.
- Information regarding the victim(s)' and suspect(s)' health such as AIDS, hepatitis, or tuberculosis.

Semen and Semen Stains

- Absorb suspected **liquid semen** onto a clean cotton cloth or swab. Leave a portion of the cloth or swab unstained as a control. Air-dry the cloth or swab and pack in clean paper or an envelope with sealed corners. Do not use plastic containers.

- Submit small suspected **dry semen-stained objects** to the Laboratory. Pack to prevent stain removal by abrasive action during shipping. Pack in clean paper. Do not use plastic containers.

- When possible, cut a large sample of suspected **seman stains from immovable objects** with a clean, sharp instrument. Collect an unstained control sample. Pack to prevent stain removal by abrasive action during shipping. Pack in clean paper. Do not use plastic containers.

- Absorb suspected **dried semen stains on immovable objects** onto a clean cotton cloth or swab moistened with distilled water. Leave a portion of the cloth or swab unstained as a control. Air-dry the swab or cloth and place in clean paper or an envelope with sealed corners. Do not use plastic containers.

Seminal Evidence From Sexual Assault Victim(s)

- Sexual assault victim(s) must be medically examined in a hospital or a physician's office using a standard sexual assault evidence kit to collect vaginal, oral, and anal evidence.
- Refrigerate and submit the evidence as soon as possible to the Laboratory.

Buccal (Oral) Swabs

- Use clean cotton swabs to collect buccal (oral) samples. Rub the inside surfaces of the cheeks thoroughly.
- Air-dry the swabs and place in clean paper or an envelope with sealed corners. Do not use plastic containers.
- Identify each sample with the date, time subject's name, location, collector's name, case number, and evidence number.
- Buccal samples do not need to be refrigerated.

Saliva and Urine

- Absorb suspected **liquid saliva or urine** onto a clean cotton cloth or swab. Leave a portion of the cloth unstained as a control. Air-dry the cloth or swab and pack in clean paper or an envelope with sealed corners. Do not use plastic containers.

- Submit suspected small, **dry saliva- or urine-stained objects** to the Laboratory. Pack to prevent stain removal by abrasive action during shipping. Pack in clean paper or an envelope with sealed corners. Do not use plastic containers.

- When possible, cut a large sample of suspected **saliva or urine stains from immovable objects** with a clean, sharp instrument. Collect an unstained control sample. Pack to prevent stain removal by abrasive action during shipping. Pack in clean paper. Do not use plastic containers.

- Pick up **cigarette butts** with gloved hands or clean forceps. Do not submit ashes. Air-dry and place the cigarette butts from the same location (e.g., ashtray) in clean paper or an envelope with sealed corners. Do not submit the ashtray unless a latent print examination is requested. Package the ashtray separately. Do not use plastic containers.

- Pick up **chewing gum** with gloved hands or clean forceps. Air-dry and place in clean paper or an envelope with sealed corners. Do not use plastic containers.

- Pick up **envelops and stamps** with gloved hands or clean forceps and place in a clean envelope. Do not use plastic containers.

Hair

- Pick up hair carefully with clean forceps to prevent damaging the root tissue.
- Air-dry hair mixed with suspected body fluids.
- Package each group of hair separately in clean paper or an envelope with sealed corners. Do not use plastic containers.
- Refrigerate and submit as soon as possible to the Laboratory.

Tissues, Bones, and Teeth

- Pick up suspected tissues, bones, and teeth with gloved hands or clean forceps.
- Collect 1–2 cubic inches of red skeletal muscle.
- Collect 3–5 inches of long bone such as the fibula or femur.
- Collect teeth in the following order:
  1. nonrestored molar.
  2. nonrestored premolar.
  3. nonrestored canine.
  4. nonrestored front tooth.
  5. restored molar.
  6. restored premolar.
  7. restored canine.
  8. restored front tooth.
- Place tissue samples in a clean, airtight plastic container without formalin or formaldehyde. Place teeth and bone samples in clean paper or an envelope with sealed corners.
- Freeze the evidence, place in Styrofoam containers, and ship overnight on dry ice.

Appendix II

INSTRUCTIONS FOR COLLECTING GUNSHOT RESIDUE (GSR)
for Scanning Electron Microscopy and Atomic Absorption Analysis

---

NOTE

In control test firings, it has been shown that the concentration of gunshot residue significantly declines on living subjects after approximately 4 hours. In view of these findings, if more than 4 hours have passed since the shooting, it is recommended that you check with your crime laboratory before submitting samples for analysis.

S.E.M. COLLECTION PROCEDURE

(A) When the covering is removed from the metal stubs, the adhesive collecting surface is exposed and care must be used to not drop the stub or contaminate the collecting surface by allowing this exposed surface to come in contact with an object other than the area that is to be sampled. (See Figure 1.)

(B) *Do not* return paper stub cover to stubs after collection. (*Discard stub covers.*)

(C) Heavily soiled or bloody areas should be avoided if possible.

(D) When pressing the stubs on the questioned areas, use enough pressure to cause a mild indentation on the surface of the subject's hand.

STEP 1   Fill out all information requested on the enclosed Gunshot Residue Analysis Information Form.

STEP 2   Put on the disposable plastic gloves provided in this kit. *Do not substitute with other gloves!*

> NOTE: If there is blood on the subject's hands or clothing, the investigating officer should put on latex or other approved barrier gloves to protect him/her from bloodborne pathogens, then put on the plastic gloves provided in this kit.

STEP 3   <u>RIGHT BACK:</u>

(A) Carefully remove the cap from the vial labeled RIGHT BACK, then remove the paper covering from the metal sample stub.

(B) While holding the vial cap, press the collecting surface of the stub onto the back of the subject's right hand until the area shown below in Figure 2 has been covered.

(C) After sampling the back of the subject's right hand, return the cap, with metal stub, to the RIGHT BACK vial. *Do not return paper covering to metal stub!*

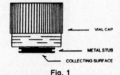

VIAL CAP

METAL STUB

COLLECTING SURFACE

Fig. 1

STEP 4   <u>RIGHT PALM:</u>

Repeat the procedure described in Step 3, using the metal stub in the vial marked RIGHT PALM. Make sure to sample the area shown below in Figure 3.

STEP 5   <u>LEFT BACK and LEFT PALM:</u>

For collection from the left hand, repeat Steps 3 and 4 using the vials labeled LEFT BACK and LEFT PALM.

STEP 6   After sampling all four areas, return capped vials to kit envelope.

Fig. 2 (BACK)

Fig. 3 (PALM)

Source: Tri-Tech, Inc., Southport, N.C., www.tritechusa.com

A.A. COLLECTION PROCEDURE

NOTE: (A) This second part of the GSR collection is *ONLY* to be performed *AFTER* sampling with the SEM stubs.

(B) If you feel that during the SEM collection procedure you have contaminated the gloves, discard contaminated gloves, then thoroughly wash your hands with soap and water and dry with a clean towel. At no time during the collection process should your hands (with or without gloves) come into contact with the cotton tip of the swab.

(C) When dispensing nitric acid, use 2 - 3 drops of 5% nitric acid solution to moisten each swab (do not over-moisten). In order to dispense an appropriate amount of the nitric acid solution, hold the acid dispenser in a horizontal position above and *almost* touching the top of the swab, and squeeze gently.

(D) To swab the subject's hands, the investigator should grasp the subject's arm above the wrist with one hand and swab with the other. The subject's hand should be in a "spread" position. Thorough swabbing of the hands is carried out by using moderate pressure while swabbing. The swab should be rotated during this procedure to insure that all of the surface of the cotton tip is utilized. At least 30 seconds per swab is required.

(E) When placing swabs in tubes, always place cotton tips *FACE DOWN*.

STEP 7 <u>CONTROL SWABS:</u> Remove *two* of the swabs from the unmarked ziplock bag. Moisten both swabs with 2 - 3 drops of the 5% nitric acid solution supplied in kit (do not substitute). Place both swabs in the tube labeled CONTROL. Then recap tube and set it aside.

STEP 8 <u>RIGHT BACK</u>:

(A) Moisten the tip of *ONE* swab with 2 - 3 drops of nitric acid solution, then thoroughly swab the back of the subject's right hand including the back of the fingers and all of the web area which would be exposed while holding a weapon. Fig. 4 illustrates the area of hand for swabbing. Place swab used in the tube labeled RIGHT BACK.

(B) Repeat the above procedure using a *SECOND* swab. Place the second swab used in the RIGHT BACK tube, then recap tube and set it aside.

Fig. 4 (BACK)

STEP 9 <u>RIGHT PALM</u>:

(A) Moisten the tip of *ONE* swab with 2 - 3 drops of nitric acid solution, then thoroughly swab the palm of the subject's right hand as shown in Fig. 5. Place swab used in the tube labeled RIGHT PALM.

(B) Repeat the above procedure using a *SECOND* swab. Place the second swab used in the RIGHT PALM tube, then recap tube and set it aside.

Fig. 5 (PALM)

STEP 10 <u>LEFT BACK/LEFT PALM:</u> Follow the same procedures described in Steps 8 and 9, but swabbing the subject's left hand.

STEP 11 <u>CARTRIDGE CASE:</u>

NOTE: For .22 cal and foreign manufactured ammunition, it is necessary that either Steps A and B described below be completed <u>OR</u> the casings be submitted to the laboratory. If latent prints are required on the expended casing(s), Steps A and B should be omitted and the casings should be submitted for latent print processing. If for any reason the CARTRIDGE CASE swabs are not used, mark the tube "*NOT USED*".

(A) Moisten the tip of *ONE* swab with 2 - 3 drops of nitric acid solution, then thoroughly swab the inside of the cartridge case. Place swab used in the tube labeled CARTRIDGE CASE.

(B) Repeat the above procedure using a *SECOND* swab. Place second swab used in the CARTRIDGE CASE tube, and then recap tube and set it aside.

FINAL INSTRUCTIONS

(A) Fill out all information requested on the front of the kit envelope.

(B) With the exception of the 5% nitric acid dispenser and the disposable gloves, return all other kit components, used or unused, to kit envelope.

(C) Moisten kit envelope flap, then seal envelope. Affix Police Evidence Seal where indicated, then initial seal.

(D) Mail or hand deliver sealed kit to the crime laboratory for analysis. (If mailed, package kit in a cardboard box to prevent damage in transit.)

Appendix III
Chromatographic and Spectrophotometric Parameters for Figures Contained in the Text

1. *Figures 5–6(a) and (b)*
   3' × 1/4" glass column; 3% OV-17 on Varaport 30, 80/100 mesh.
   T(injection port) = 280°C, T(defector) = 280°C, T(column) = 200°C
   Carrier Gas: Nitrogen at 50 ml/min

2. *Figure 5–7*
   8' × 1/8" stainless steel, 15% carbowax 20M, AW-DMCS treated 80/100
     mesh chromosorb W plus 3' × 1/8" stainless steel, 10% silicone D.C.
     200 in series.
   Temperature unknown
   Carrier Gas: Nitrogen

3. *Figure 5–10*
   Absorbent: Silica Gel G
   Development Solvent: Benzene
   Visualizer: Fast Blue B Salt

4. *Figure 5–11*
   Absorbent: Silica Gel G
   Developing Solvent: Chloroform-Diethylamine (9:1)
   Visualizer: Iodoplatinate

5. *Figure 5–18*
   Solvent: 0.1N HCL

6. *Figure 5–19(a)*
   Heroin hydrochloride in KBr

7. *Figure 5–19(b)*
   Secobartibal (free acid) in KBr

8. *Figure 8–21(a) and (b)*
   Same as Figure 5–7

9. *Figure 9–11*
   Solvent: 0.1 N HCL

10. *Figure 10–9*
    Ethanol in whole blood analyzed by "head space" technique.
    A porous polymer column was used.
    T(injection port) = 132°C, T(detector) = 132°C, T(column) = 132°C
    Carrier Gas: Helium (thermal conductivity detector was used).

11. *Figure 11–8*
    30 m × 0.75 mm I.D. glass capillary column, SPB-1, bonded phase with a
      1.0 μm film thickness.
    Column over temperature program: 40°C for 3 min., 12°C/min. up to 250°C.
    FID temperature 280°C.
    Injection port temperature 250°C. Helium carrier and make-up gas.

12. *Figure 11–16*
    RDX in KBr

13. *Figure 16–12*
    Absorbent: Silica Gel
    Developing Solvent: Ethyl acetate, absolute ethanol, water (70:35:30)

Appendix IV
Chemical Formulas for Latent Fingerprint Development

Iodine Spray Reagent

1. Prepare the following stock solutions:

Solution A	*Solution B*
Dissolve gram of Iodine in 1 liter of Cyclohexane	Dissolve 5 grams of a-Naphthoflavone in 40 ml of Methylene Chloride (Dichloramethane)

2. Add 2 ml of Solution B to 100 ml of Solution A. Using a magnetic stirrer, mix thoroughly for 5 minutes.
3. Filter the solution through a facial tissue, paper towel, filter paper, etc., into a beaker. The solution should be lightly sprayed on the specimen using an aerosol spray unit or a mini spray gun powered with compressed air.
4. Lightly spray the suspect area with several applications until latent prints sufficiently develop.

Remarks

- Solution A may be stored at room temperature. Shelf life is in excess of 30 days.
- Solution B must be refrigerated. Shelf life is in excess of 30 days.
- The combined working solution (A and B) should be used within 24 hours after mixing.
- The Iodine Spray solution is effective on most surfaces (porous and nonporous).
- A fine spray mist is the most effective form of application.
- The Cyanocrylate (Super Glue) process cannot be used prior to the Iodine Spray Reagent Process. Cyanoacrylate may be used, however, after the Iodine Spray Reagent.
- On porous surfaces, DFO and/or Ninhydrin may be used after the Iodine Spray.
- Propanol may be used to remove the staining of the Iodine Spray Reagent.
- 1,1,2 Trichlorotrifluoroethane may be substituted for Cyclohexane.

1,8-Diazafluoren-9-one (DFO)

Step 1: Stock solution: Dissolve 1 gram DFO in 200 ml Methanol, 200 ml Ethyl Acetate, and 40 ml Acetic Acid.

Source: In part from *Processing Guide for Developing Latent Prints,* Revised 2000. Washington, D.C.: FBI. http://njiai.org/fbi_2000_lp_guide.pdf

Step 2: Working solution (make as needed): Start with stock solution and dilute to 2 liters with Petroleum Ether (40° to 60° boiling point fraction). Pentane can also be used. Solution should be clear.

Dip the paper document into the working solution and allow to dry. Dip again and allow to dry. When completely dry, apply heat (200° for 10 to 20 minutes). An oven, hair dryer, or dry iron can be used.

Visualize with an alternate light source at 450, 485, 525, and 530 nm and observe through orange goggles. If the surface paper is yellow, such as legal paper, it may be necessary to visualize the paper at 570 nm and view it through red goggles.

1,2-indanedione
2.0 g 1,2-indanedione
70 ml ethyl acetate
930 ml HFE 7100 (3M Company)

Ninhydrin

20 grams Ninhydrin
3,300 ml Acetone
Shelf life is approximately one month

or

5 grams Ninhydrin
30 ml Methanol
40 ml 2-Propanol
930 ml Petroleum Ether
Shelf life is approximately one year

Dip the paper document in the working solution and allow to dry. Dip again and allow to dry. When completely dry, heat may be applied. A steam iron should be used on the steam setting. Do not touch the iron directly to the paper. Rather, hold the iron above the paper and allow the steam to heat it.

Zinc Chloride Solution (Post-Ninhydrin Treatment)

5 grams of Zinc Chloride crystals
2 ml of Glacial Acetic Acid
100 ml of Methyl Alcohol
Add 400 ml of 1,1,2 Trichlorotrifluoroethane to the mixture and stir.
Add 2 ml of 5 percent Sodium Hypochlorite solution (commercially available liquid bleach such as Clorox, Purex, and others).

Lightly spray the paper with the Zinc solution. Repeat the spraying as needed. Do not overdo the spraying.

The ninhydrin-developed prints treated with this solution may fluoresce at room temperature with an alternate light source. For maximum fluorescence, place the paper in a bath of liquid nitrogen and examine again with an alternate light source.

Physical Developer

When mixing and using these solutions, make sure the glassware, processing trays, stirring rods, and stirring magnets are absolutely clean. Do not use metal trays or tweezer.

Stock Detergent Solution: 3 grams of *N*-Dodecylamine Acetate are combined with 4 grams of Synperonic-*N* mixed in 1 liter of distilled water.

Silver Nitrate Solution: 20 grams of Silver Nitrate crystals are mixed in 100 milliliters of distilled water.

Redox Solution: 60 grams of Ferric Nitrate are mixed in 1,800 milliliters of distilled water. After this solution is thoroughly mixed, add 160 grams of Ferrous Ammonium Sulfate, mix thoroughly and add 40 grams of Citric Acid, mix thoroughly.

Maleic Acid Solution: Put 50 grams of Maleic Acid into 2 liters of distilled water.

Physical Developer Working Solution: Begin with 2,125 milliliters of the Redox Solution and add 80 milliliters of the Stock Detergent Solution, mix well, then add 100 milliliters of the Silver Nitrate Solution and mix well. Appropriate divisions can be used if smaller amounts of the working solution are desired.

Immerse specimen in Maleic Acid Solution for 10 minutes
Incubate item in PD working solution for 15–20 minutes
Thoroughly rinse specimen in tap water for 20 minutes
Air-dry and photograph

Cyanoacrylate Fluorescent Enhancement Reagents

Rhodamine 6G

Stock Solution	Working Solution

100 mg Rhodamine 6G
100 ml Methanol
(Stir until thoroughly
    dissolved.)
	3 ml Rhodamine 6G Stock
	    Solution
	15 ml Acetone
	10 ml Acetonitrile
	15 ml Methanol
	32 ml 2-Propanol
	925 ml Petroleum Ether
	(Combine in order listed.)

Ardrox

2 ml Ardrox P-133D
10 ml Acetone
25 ml Methanol
10 ml 2-Propanol
8 ml Acetonitrile
945 ml Petroleum Ether

MBD

7-(p-methoxybenzylaminol)-4-nitrobenz-2-oxa-1,3-diazole

Stock Solution	Working Solution
100 mg MBD 100 ml Acetone	10 ml MBD Stock Solution 30 ml Methanol 10 ml 2-Propanol 950 ml Petroleum Ether (Combine in order listed.)

Basic Yellow 40

2 grams Basic Yellow 40
1 liter Methanol

RAM Combination Enhancer

3 ml Rhodamine 6G Stock Solution
2 ml Ardrox P-133D
7 ml MBD Stock Solution
20 ml Methanol
10 ml 2-Propanol
8 ml Acetonitrile
950 ml Petroleum Ether
(Combine in order listed.)

RAY Combination Enhancer*

To 940 ml of either isopropyl alcohol or denatured ethyl alcohol add:

1.0 gram of Basic Yellow 40
0.1 gram of Rhodamine 6G
8 ml of Arodrox P-133D
50 ml of Acetonitrile (optional, but dye stain of prints will appear more
  brilliant)

MRM 10 Combination Enhancer

3 ml Rhodamine 6G Stock Solution
3 ml Basic Yellow 40 Stock Solution
7 ml MBD Stock Solution
20 ml Methanol
10 ml 2-Propanol
8 ml Acetonitrile
950 ml Petroleum Ether
(Combine in order listed.)

---

* *Source:* John H. Olenik, Freemont, Ohio.

The above solutions are used on evidence that has been treated with cyanoacrylate (Super Glue) fumes. These solutions dye the cyanoacrylate residue adhering to the latent print residue. Wash the dye over the evidence. It may be necessary to rinse the surface with a solvent, such as Petroleum Ether, to remove the excess stain.

CAUTION: These solutions contain solvents that may be respiratory irritants, so they should be mixed and used in a fume hood or while wearing a full-face breathing apparatus. Also, these solvents may damage some plastics, cloth, wood, and painted surfaces.

Because of the respiratory irritation possible and the general inefficiency of spraying, it is *not* recommended to spray these solutions. To obtain the maximum benefit and coverage, it is recommended that evidence be soaked, submerged, or washed with these types of solutions.

Source of Chemicals

Ardrox P-133D, Basic Yellow 40, and Rhodamine 6G may be obtained from:

Lightning Powder Company, Inc.
Jacksonville, FL 32218
Telephone Number: 1-800-428-0586

MBD may be obtained from:

Sigma Chemical Company
P.O. Box 14508
St. Louis, MO 63178
Telephone Number: 1-800-325-3010

Appendix V
Chemical Formulas for Development of Footwear Impressions in Blood

Amido Black

Staining Solution:
0.2 g Napthalene 12B or Napthol Blue Black
10 ml Glacial Acetic Acid
90 ml Methanol

Rinsing Solution:
90 ml Methanol
10 ml Glacial Acetic Acid

Stain the impression by spraying or immersing the item in the staining solution for approximately one minute. Next, treat with the rinsing solution to remove stain from nonimpression area. Then rinse well with distilled water.

Coomassie Blue

Staining Solution: (Add in this order)
0.44 g Coomassie Brilliant Blue
200 ml Methanol
40 ml Glacial Acetic Acid
200 ml Distilled Water

Rinsing Solution:
40 ml Glacial Acetic Acid
200 ml Methanol
200 ml Distilled Water

Spray object with the staining solution, completely covering the area of interest. Then spray the object with rinsing solution, clearing the background. Then rinse with distilled water.

Crowle's Double Stain

Developer:
2.5 grams Crocein Scarlet 7B
150 mg Coomassie Brilliant Blue R
50 ml Glacial Acetic Acid
30 ml Trichloroacetic Acid

Combine the above ingredients, then dilute into one liter. Place the solution on a stirring device until all the Crocein Scarlet 7B and Coomassie Brillant Blue R are dissolved.

Rinse:
30 ml Glacial Acetic Acid
970 ml Distilled Water

Apply the developer to the item(s) by dipping. Completely cover the target area, leaving the developer on for approximately 30 to 90 seconds, then rinse. Finally, rinse well with distilled water.

Diaminobenzidine (DAB)

Solution A (Fixer solution):
20 g 5-Sulphosalicylic Acid
Dissolved in 1L Distilled Water

Solution B:
100 ml 1M Phosphate Buffer (pH 7.4)
800 ml Distilled Water

Solution C:
1 g Diaminobenzidine
Dissolved in 100 ml Distilled Water

Working Solution (Mix just prior to use):
900 ml solution B
100 ml solution C
5 ml 30% Hydrogen Peroxide

Immerse impression area in fixer solution A for approximately 4 minutes. Remove and rinse in distilled water. Immerse impression area for approximately 4 minutes in the working solution or until print is fully developed. Remove and rinse in distilled water.

Fuchsin Acid

20 g Sulfosalicylic Acid
2 g Fuchsin Acid
Dissolved in 1L Distilled Water

Stain the impression by spraying or immersing the item in the dye solution for approximately one minute. Rinse well with distilled water.

Hungarian Red

This product is available from:

ODV, Inc.
P.O. Box 180
S. Paris, ME 04281

Leucocrystal Violet

10 g 5-Sulfosalicylic Acid
500 ml 3% Hydrogen Peroxide
3.7 g Sodium Acetate
1 g Leucocrystal Violet

If Leucocrystal Violet crystals are yellow instead of white, do not use. This indicates crystals are old and solution will not work.

Spray the object until completely covered. Then allow object to air dry. Development of impressions will occur within 30 seconds. Store the solution in amber glassware and refrigerate.

Leucocrystal Violet Field Kit*

When the reagents are separated in the listed manner below, a "field kit" can be prepared. The field kit separation will allow for an extended shelf life.

Bottle A:

10 grams 5-Sulfosalicylic Acid
500 ml Hydrogen Peroxide 3%

Bottle B:

1.1 grams Leucocrystal Violet
Weigh out reagent and place in an amber 60 ml (2 ounce) bottle.

Bottle C:

4.4 grams Sodium Acetate
Weigh out reagent and place in an amber 60 ml (2 ounce) bottle.

Add approximately 30 ml of Bottle A reagent to Bottle B. Secure cap and shake Bottle B for two (2) to three (3) minutes. Pour contents of Bottle B back into Bottle A.

Add approximately 30 ml of Bottle A reagent to Bottle C. Secure cap and shake Bottle C for approximately two (2) to three (3) minutes. Pour contents of Bottle C into Bottle A. Secure Bottle A's cap and shake thoroughly.

Spray the target area; development will occur within thirty (30) seconds. After spraying, blot the area with a tissue or paper towel. Then allow object to air-dry.

Patent Blue

20 g Sulfosalicylic Acid
2 g Patent Blue V (VF)
Dissolved in 1L Distilled Water

Stain object by spraying or immersing the item in the dye solution for approximately one minute. Rinse well with distilled water.

Tartrazine

20 g Sulfosalicylic Acid
2 g Tartrazine
Dissolved in 1L Distilled Water

Stain object by spraying or immersing the item in the dye solution for approximately one minute. Rinse well with distilled water.

*Source: John Fisher, Forensic Research & Supply Corp., Gotha, Fla.

Answers to Odd-Numbered Review Questions

Chapter 1

1. forensic science
3. Alphonse Bertillon
5. Leone Lattes
7. Albert Osborn
9. Edmond Locard
11. Los Angeles
13. regional
15. The Federal Bureau of Investigation; the Drug Enforcement Administration; the Bureau of Alcohol, Tobacco, Firearms and Explosives; the U.S. Postal Service
17. trace evidence
19. Firearms
21. crime-scene investigation
23. *Daubert* v. *Merrell Dow Pharmaceuticals, Inc.*
25. *Coppolino* v. *State*
27. True
29. training
31. True

Chapter 2

1. physical evidence
3. False
5. photography; sketching; notes
7. close-ups
9. systematic
11. clothing; fingernail scrapings; head and pubic hairs; blood; vaginal, anal, and oral swabs; bullets; hand swabs
13. separate
15. is not
17. False
19. standard/reference
21. arson or fire

Chapter 3

1. identification
3. comparative
5. individual
7. True
9. weight
11. False
13. False
15. False

Chapter 4

1. physical
3. metric
5. 1/100
7. 200
9. True
11. True
13. 180
15. mass
17. density
19. refraction
21. True
23. birefringence
25. glass
27. density; refractive index
29. Becke line
31. radial
33. False
35. will
37. minerals
39. True

Chapter 5

1. matter
3. 118
5. atom
7. molecule
9. has no
11. less
13. organic
15. qualitative; quantitative
17. chromatography
19. higher
21. gas chromatography
23. pyrolyzed
25. thin-layer chromatography
27. R_f
29. electrophoresis
31. wavelength
33. electromagnetic
35. laser
37. True
39. can
41. spectrophotometer
43. infrared
45. True

Chapter 6

1. oxygen; silicon
3. trace
5. emission spectrum
7. line
9. False
11. carbon
13. does
15. proton; neutron; electron
17. positive
19. protons
21. True
23. light
25. isotopes
27. alpha rays; beta rays; gamma rays
29. gamma rays
31. neutron activation analysis
33. crystalline

Chapter 7

1. lenses
3. compound
5. eyepiece or ocular lens
7. True
9. vertical or reflected
11. parfocal
13. magnifying power
15. numerical aperture
17. decreases
19. decreases
21. True
23. False
25. plane-polarized
27. polarizing
29. microspectrophotometer
31. X-rays

Chapter 8

1. hair follicle
3. True
5. medulla
7. 1/3; 1/2
9. animal
11. cannot
13. pubic
15. False
17. DNA
19. anagen
21. 24
23. Cotton
25. synthetic
27. Polymers
29. Proteins
31. visible
33. birefringence
35. class
37. layer structure
39. electrocoat primer
41. binder
43. True

Chapter 9

1. True
3. physical
5. False
7. analgesics; depress
9. morphine
11. OxyContin
13. hallucinogens
15. tetrahydrocannabinol (THC)
17. liquid hashish
19. clandestine
21. Barbiturates
23. Methaqualone (Quaalude)
25. False
27. intravenous
29. Cocaine
31. False
33. Anabolic
35. five
37. IV
39. Marquis
41. marijuana
43. Microcrystalline
45. infrared
47. cystolithic

Chapter 10

1. ethyl alcohol
3. is
5. faster
7. watery
9. oxidized
11. breath
13. stomach; small intestine
15. pulmonary
17. 2100
19. deep lung
21. fifteen to twenty
23. fuel cell
25. 45
27. decline
29. *Schmerber* v. *California*
31. blood, urine
33. greater
35. pH
37. screening, confirmation
39. percent saturation
41. synergistic
43. corroborate

Chapter 11

1. False
3. False
5. chemical, mechanical
7. absorb, liberate
9. exothermic
11. endothermic
13. ignition
15. flash point
17. Glowing combustion or smoldering
19. Spontaneous combustion
21. potassium nitrate; charcoal, sulfur
23. Origin
25. porous
27. gas chromatograph
29. True
31. cannot
33. low
35. black powder; smokeless powder
37. False
39. is not
41. RDX
43. initiating
45. collection
47. acetone
49. infrared spectroscopy

Chapter 12

1. type
3. Plasma
5. Red blood cells
7. A
9. A; B
11. antibodies
13. True
15. neither
17. serology
19. A
21. radioimmunoassay (RIA) or enzyme-multiplied immunoassay technique (EMIT)
23. 3
25. benzidine
27. precipitin
29. monoclonal
31. Enzymes
33. electrophoresis
35. gene
37. 23
39. alleles
41. phenotype
43. will
45. AA; BB; AB
47. acid phosphatase
49. oligospermia
51. True

Chapter 13

1. gene
3. polymer
5. nucleotides
7. double helix
9. A–C–G–T
11. Proteins
13. True
15. restriction enzymes
17. repeating
19. electrophoresis
21. True
23. two
25. STRs
27. PCR
29. capillary electrophoresis
31. male
33. True
35. False
37. False
39. False
41. two

Chapter 14

1. Alphonse Bertillon
3. Sir Edward Richard Henry
5. is not
7. Fingerprints
9. dermal papillae
11. loops; whorls; arches
13. arch
15. type lines
17. one
19. plain whorl
21. do not have
23. 1/1
25. True
27. Plastic
29. powder
31. Iodine
33. Physical Developer
35. Super Glue fuming
37. alternate light sources
39. pixels

Chapter 15

1. land
3. class
5. comparison microscope
7. sometimes
9. gauge
11. can
13. True
15. 12; 18
17. True
19. primer
21. False
23. is not
25. False
27. tool mark
29. individual

Chapter 16

1. questioned document
3. known, questioned
5. False
7. *Gilbert* v. *California*
9. individual
11. infrared
13. Indented
15. sound spectrograph
17. False

Chapter 17

1. preservation; acquisition; extraction; interpretation
3. Software
5. system unit
7. False
9. CPU
11. network interface card (NIC)
13. sectors; clusters; tracks; cylinders
15. byte
17. forensic image
19. swap
21. latent
23. RAM, file
25. unallocated space
27. True

Chapter 18

1. network
3. World Wide Web
5. True
7. E-mail
9. Internet protocol address
11. cookie
13. RAM
15. firewalls

Index

Photo Credits

Chapter 16
Pages 496–497, background: PhotoEdit Inc.
Page 496, left: AP Wide World Photos
Page 497, top: AP Wide World Photos; middle: Getty Images, Inc.; bottom: AP Wide World Photos

Chapter 17
Pages 522–523, background: EyeWire Collection, Getty Images—Photodisc
Page 522, left: AP Wide World Photos
Page 523, top: EyeWire Collection, Getty Images—Photodisc; middle: NewsCom; bottom: © Orjan F. Ellingvag/CORBIS. All Rights Reserved

Chapter 18
Pages 550–551, background: AP Wide World Photos
Page 550, left: AP Wide World Photos
Page 551, middle: Ted Benson—Pool, Getty Images, Inc—Liaison; bottom: Al Golub, AP Wide World Photos

Chapter 19
Pages 572–573, background: Photodisc/Getty Images
Page 572, top: Tek Image; middle: Tom Tracy, The Stock Connection; bottom: Eye Wire Collection, Getty Images–Photodisc
Page 573, left: Photodisc/Getty Images

Pearson Education, Inc.

YOU SHOULD CAREFULLY READ THE TERMS AND CONDITIONS BEFORE USING THE CD-ROM PACKAGE. USING THIS CD-ROM PACKAGE INDICATES YOUR ACCEPTANCE OF THESE TERMS AND CONDITIONS.

Pearson Education, Inc. provides this program and licenses its use. You assume responsibility for the selection of the program to achieve your intended results, and for the installation, use, and results obtained from the program. This license extends only to use of the program in the United States or countries in which the program is marketed by authorized distributors.

LICENSE GRANT
You hereby accept a nonexclusive, nontransferable, permanent license to install and use the program ON A SINGLE COMPUTER at any given time. You may copy the program solely for backup or archival purposes in support of your use of the program on the single computer. You may not modify, translate, disassemble, decompile, or reverse engineer the program, in whole or in part.

TERM
The License is effective until terminated. Pearson Education, Inc. reserves the right to terminate this License automatically if any provision of the License is violated. You may terminate the License at any time. To terminate this License, you must return the program, including documentation, along with a written warranty stating that all copies in your possession have been returned or destroyed.

LIMITED WARRANTY
THE PROGRAM IS PROVIDED "AS IS" WITHOUT WARRANTY OF ANY KIND, EITHER EXPRESSED OR IMPLIED, INCLUDING, BUT NOT LIMITED TO, THE IMPLIED WARRANTIES OR MERCHANTABILITY AND FITNESS FOR A PARTICULAR PURPOSE. THE ENTIRE RISK AS TO THE QUALITYAND PERFORMANCE OF THE PROGRAM IS WITH YOU. SHOULD THE PROGRAM PROVE DEFECTIVE, YOU (AND NOT PRENTICE-HALL, INC. OR ANY AUTHORIZED DEALER) ASSUME THE ENTIRE COST OF ALL NECESSARY SERVICING, REPAIR, OR CORRECTION. NO ORAL OR WRITTEN INFORMATION OR ADVICE GIVEN BY PRENTICE-HALL, INC., ITS DEALERS, DISTRIBUTORS, OR AGENTS SHALL CREATE A WARRANTY OR INCREASE THE SCOPE OF THIS WARRANTY.

SOME STATES DO NOT ALLOW THE EXCLUSION OF IMPLIED WARRANTIES, SO THE ABOVE EXCLUSION MAY NOT APPLY TO YOU. THIS WARRANTY GIVES YOU SPECIFIC LEGAL RIGHTS AND YOU MAY ALSO HAVE OTHER LEGAL RIGHTS THAT VARY FROM STATE TO STATE.

Pearson Education, Inc. does not warrant that the functions contained in the program will meet your requirements or that the operation of the program will be uninterrupted or error-free.

However, Pearson Education, Inc. warrants the diskette(s) or CD-ROM(s) on which the program is furnished to be free from defects in material and workmanship under normal use for a period of ninety (90) days from the date of delivery to you as evidenced by a copy of your receipt.

The program should not be relied on as the sole basis to solve a problem whose incorrect solution could result in injury to person or property. If the program is employed in such a manner, it is at the user's own risk and Pearson Education, Inc. explicitly disclaims all liability for such misuse.

LIMITATION OF REMEDIES
Pearson Education, Inc.'s entire liability and your exclusive remedy shall be:

1. the replacement of any diskette(s) or CD-ROM(s) not meeting Pearson Education, Inc.'s "LIMITED WARRANTY" and that is returned to Pearson Education, or
2. if Pearson Education is unable to deliver a replacement diskette(s) or CD-ROM(s) that is free of defects in materials or workmanship, you may terminate this agreement by returning the program.

IN NO EVENT WILL PRENTICE-HALL, INC. BE LIABLE TO YOU FOR ANY DAMAGES, INCLUDING ANY LOST PROFITS, LOST SAVINGS, OR OTHER INCIDENTAL OR CONSEQUENTIAL DAMAGES ARISING OUT OF THE USE OR INABILITY TO USE SUCH PROGRAM EVEN IF PRENTICE-HALL, INC. OR AN AUTHORIZED DISTRIBUTOR HAS BEEN ADVISED OF THE POSSIBILITY OF SUCH DAMAGES, OR FOR ANY CLAIM BY ANY OTHER PARTY.

SOME STATES DO NOT ALLOW FOR THE LIMITATION OR EXCLUSION OF LIABILITY FOR INCIDENTAL OR CONSEQUENTIAL DAMAGES, SO THE ABOVE LIMITATION OR EXCLUSION MAY NOT APPLY TO YOU.

GENERAL
You may not sublicense, assign, or transfer the license of the program. Any attempt to sublicense, assign or transfer any of the rights, duties, or obligations hereunder is void.

This Agreement will be governed by the laws of the State of New York.

Should you have any questions concerning this Agreement, you may contact Pearson Education, Inc. by writing to:

Director of New Media
Higher Education Division
Pearson Education, Inc.
One Lake Street
Upper Saddle River, NJ 07458

Should you have any questions concerning technical support, you may contact:

Product Support Department: Monday–Friday 8:00 A.M.–8:00 P.M. and Sunday 5:00 P.M.-12:00 A.M. (All times listed are Eastern). 1-800-677-6337

You can also get support by filling out the web form located at http://247.prenhall.com

YOU ACKNOWLEDGE THAT YOU HAVE READ THIS AGREEMENT, UNDERSTAND IT, AND AGREE TO BE BOUND BY ITS TERMS AND CONDITIONS. YOU FURTHER AGREE THAT IT IS THE COMPLETE AND EXCLUSIVE STATEMENT OF THE AGREEMENT BETWEEN US THAT SUPERSEDES ANY PROPOSAL OR PRIOR AGREEMENT, ORAL OR WRITTEN, AND ANY OTHER COMMUNICATIONS BETWEEN US RELATING TO THE SUBJECT MATTER OF THIS AGREEMENT.